MW00379967

MARTIN LUTHER'S THEOLOGY

Its Historical and Systematic Development

BERNHARD LOHSE

TRANSLATED AND EDITED
BY ROY A. HARRISVILLE

FORTRESS PRESS
MINNEAPOLIS

MARTIN LUTHER'S THEOLOGY
Its Historical and Systematic Development

Fortress Press edition copyright © 1999 Augsburg Fortress. All rights reserved.

Translated by Roy A. Harrisville from *Luthers Theologie in ihrer historischen Entwicklung und in ihrem systematischen Zusammenhang* by Bernhard Lohse, copyright © 1995 Vandenhoeck & Ruprecht, Göttingen, Germany.

Cover design by Craig Claeys and Derek Herzog
Book design by Michelle L. Norstad

Library of Congress Cataloging-in-Publication Data
Lohse, Bernhard, 1928–
    [Luthers Theologie in ihrer historischen Entwicklung und in ihrem systematischen Zusammenhang. English]
    Martin Luther's theology : its historical and systematic development / Bernhard Lohse; translated by Roy A. Harrisville.—Fortress Press ed.
        p. cm.
    Includes bibliographical references and index.
    ISBN 0-8066-3091-2 (alk. paper)
    1. Luther, Martin, 1483–1546. 2. Theology, Doctrinal—History—16th century. I. Title.
BR333.2.L6413 1999
230'.41'092—dc21   99-22239
                                                                              CIP

Manufactured in the U.S.A.   AF 1-3091
09   08   07   06   5   6   7   8   9   10

SUMMARY OF CONTENTS

CONTENTS

FOREWORD

For some time I intended to write a description of Martin Luther's theology. In October 1955, while at work on my study of reason and faith in Luther,[1] Paul Althaus suggested that I should later write a volume purely from the standpoint of a church historian. After the late sixties I often lectured on Luther's theology, always keeping at center the description of the origin and further shaping of his Reformation theology. Demands due to developments in German universities after 1968, and especially the fact that since 1969 I have had no assistants and have had to forego assistance even in proofreading, continually delayed the realization of my plan. Only after my retirement in the spring of 1992 was I finally able to devote all my energies to working out this description.

In contrast to previous descriptions of Luther's theology on the part of systematicians, particularly in the sixties, this description is of a special type. It is the first to evaluate Luther's theology in its historical development as well as within its systematic context. In tracing its historical development, the study takes up Luther's debates with traditions important to him along with the development of his theology in the context of the various controversies leading up to his dispute with the Antinomians. In its systematic treatment, the study has a relatively conservative structure. In this twofold discussion, I have followed an impulse pursued by Julius Köstlin as early as 1863.[2]

This description has another special quality. For the first time it depicts Luther's attitude toward the Jews within the scope of a total evaluation of his theology. After the terrible persecutions of Jews during the Third Reich, and due to the intense discussion of Luther's attitude toward them in the last decades, the task of dealing with this theme seemed unavoidable. The reason why it appears at the close of the book is to suggest that Luther's attitude toward the Jews is a marginal theological issue, not at all part of the central themes.

During the final examination of the manuscript, some important literature appeared that I could not mention. At least two works may be referred to here: first, *Cajetan et Luther en 1518: Edition, traduction et commentaire d'Augsbourg de Cajetan* by Charles Morerod, OP, in Cahiers oecumeniques 26, 2 vols. (Fribourg: Éditions Universitaires, 1994). Next, Leif Grane, *Martinus Noster: Luther in the German Reform*

---

[1] *Ratio und Fides: Eine Untersuchung über die Ratio in der Theologie Luthers,* FJDG 8 (Göttingen: Vandenhoeck & Ruprecht, 1958).

[2] Julius Köstlin, *The Theology of Luther in Its Historical Development and Inner Harmony,* trans. Charles E. Hay (Philadelphia: Lutheran Publication Society, 1897).

Movement 1518-1521, VIEG 155 (Mainz: P. von Zabern, 1994). I am happy to be in essential agreement with Morerod in the interpretation of Luther's hearing before Cajetan. As to Grane's important investigations, they have given a new evaluation of Luther within the circle of his friends and coworkers.

The volume by Schwertner furnishes the basis for abbreviations: Siegfried Schwertner, *Internationales Abkürzungsverzeichnis für Theologie und Grenzgebiete* (Berlin/New York: de Gruyter, 1974). It may be added that the abbreviation *HdB-DThD* denotes *Handbuch der Dogmen- und Theologiegeschichte,* ed. Carl Andresen, 3 vols. (Göttingen: Vandenhoeck & Ruprecht, 1980-84).

—BERNHARD LOHSE

TRANSLATOR-EDITOR'S NOTE

Due to the nature of the work, which opens with the genetic followed by the systematic treatment of Luther's theology, the reader may begin at either point without harm to the author's purpose. The newcomer to Luther's thought, however, will profit greatly from commencing with the historical treatment. Indeed, this portion of the work may initially be of more profit to both learner and scholar than the systematic portion. On the other hand, despite Lohse's modest appraisal of the systematic portion ("the study has a relatively conservative structure"), its content includes more than a mere examination of themes respecting their internal coherence. Like the genetic portion, it examines those themes in connection with the teachings of Luther's predecessors and contemporaries.

First of all, preparation of the text required matching the references in the Weimar edition of Luther's works to their English counterparts in the so-called American edition—an onerous task necessitated by omission of references to the Weimar in the greater part of the American edition. The matching reference in the American edition is denoted simply by *LW,* followed by its counterpart in the *Weimar Ausgabe* (*WA*), hence, for example, *LW,* vol. 10, pp. 332-33. *WA* 3, 397, 9-11, 15-16.

Second, since the English edition is not comparable in scope to the Weimar, translations were made directly from Middle High German or Latin works, with their titles retained in the original. Where translations of these references appear in the body of the text, the original quotation and its source appear in the footnotes. Where translations of these references appear in the footnotes, they follow the original quotation and its source in parenthesis, hence, for example, *WA* 10 III, 259, 3-8: "Babst du hast das beschlossen oder die Concilien . . ." ("Pope, you or the councils have decided . . ."). The purpose of including the original and its translation is to allow the critical reader to assess the accuracy of the translation and where necessary to substitute his or her own.

Third, due to Lohse's own habit of repeatedly employing the same adverbs, of repeating subjects within the same sentences, or of alternating tenses within the same sentence or paragraph, the attempt at a faithful translation may have resulted in a stilted text. Many thanks are due Professor Todd Nichol, Assistant Professor of Church History at Luther Seminary, St. Paul, for carefully examining the English translation and suggesting improvements.

Readers will find some works referenced only by author and short title; fuller publication data are given in prior notes in the chapter or in the chapter-specific Bibliography at the end of the volume. Aside from its enormous bibliography of secondary literature, reflecting years of reading, the volume's persistent reference to Luther's own works, on virtually every page, renders it a mine that only wading through the innumerable volumes of the *Weimar Ausgabe* could equal. With respect to its interpretation of the Luther "text" itself, the book is neither ideological nor bereft of stance, but measured in face of the decades of Luther research. Together with the author's introduction to Luther's life and work (*Martin Luther: An Introduction to His Life and Work*), this volume should serve for years as a text till the next scholar has spent an equal number of decades traversing the same field.

Finally, the translation of this work was first assigned to Professor James A. Schaaf of the theological faculty of Trinity Lutheran Seminary in Columbus, Ohio, historian and translator of various Luther studies (see, for example, his translation of the three-volume study by Martin Brecht: *Martin Luther: His Road to Reformation; Shaping and Defining the Reformation; The Preservation of the Church*). Due to his sudden death, the task was given to me, and I hope that my work may in some fashion approximate that of my predecessor.

—ROY A. HARRISVILLE

PART ONE

*Introduction: Preliminary Considerations
and Presuppositions Relative to a
Description of Luther's Theology*

Chapter 1

CRITERIA FOR DESCRIBING LUTHER'S THEOLOGY

SURVEY OF PREVIOUS DESCRIPTIONS

The attempt to describe the theology of an important person of the past requires a few preliminary remarks about the possibilities and difficulties of such an undertaking. The attempt is easily in danger of assigning to the thought of the theologian to be described a systematic tendency more suitable to that of the interpreter than to the one to be interpreted. That such danger in fact exists can be shown merely by observing that reproductions of the theology of a person of the past are often so varied that we might well ask whether the same theologian has actually been described. We need only compare a few descriptions of the theology, say, of Origen or Augustine or Thomas Aquinas to realize the difficulties and dangers of such an undertaking. As for Luther, descriptions of his theology are at times so diverse that the question arises whether the interpreter is in particular danger of laying a basis in a systematic inappropriate to the reformer and of assigning it to him uncritically and without reflection.

At bottom, none is immune from such danger. It is necessary, of course, that whoever intends to reproduce the theology of another should be aware of these problems, be clear about the presuppositions underlying what is to be described, and be conscious of one's own presuppositions in the reproduction. A brief survey of the presuppositions and impulses of a few well-known readings of Luther's theology can document the difficulty of distorting his theology.

Extensive, overall descriptions of Luther's theology have been submitted since the early second half of the nineteenth century. Theodosius Harnack was the first to undertake such an attempt. He wanted especially to elaborate the doctrine of atonement and redemption, and in doing so no doubt correctly accented a major point in Luther's thought. On the other hand, in the conservative tradition of the Lutheranism of his Baltic home, he indirectly aimed at opposing certain tendencies toward dissolution in the dogmatics of his time, in any event as he diagnosed them. In the foreword of the second volume of his presentation he disputed in detail Albrecht Ritschl's appeal to Luther and pointed to the essential difference that in his opinion, at any rate, existed between Luther and Ritschl. This first attempt at an overall description indicates that the reproduction of Luther's theology can scarcely be undertaken independently of theological movements and debates in which the interpreter is set.

The critical attitude toward an age that is superimposed on such a description is not always as clear as with Harnack. Yet there can be no doubt that every description of Luther's theology is at least linked to a given author's often very personal intent to make a statement, so that some descriptions are plainly the author's personal confession.[1] This also illustrates the way in which many evangelical theologians have arrived at their own points of view by dealing with Luther's Reformation theology. As a result, for many of them, the distinction between their own point of view and the picture of Luther's theology can be drawn only with difficulty.

Reinhold Seeberg, like Harnack, emerged from Baltic Lutheranism and was in essence stamped by an antirationalistic, "positive" attitude toward the Reformation heritage. His view of the Reformation is lodged in the overall picture that he drew of the history of dogma. Seeberg gave an account of the Reformation position from the viewpoint of the history of dogma and religion, indicating that in the struggle between Luther and Rome what was ultimately at issue was the conflict between the Germanic spirit and Catholic Romanism. To this extent, only the Reformation fixed the center of gravity over against the ancient Greek and Latin church, a process already begun in the Germanic Middle Ages. In Seeberg's reading of Luther's theology this position continually comes to the fore. On the other hand, he has submitted a presentation closely oriented to the sources, which is why it is still of value today.

Commencement of the newer Luther research generally dates from Karl Holl's important investigations early in the twentieth century. The significance of Holl's research and interpretation consists primarily in the fact that he was first to refer in comprehensive fashion to Luther's early lectures from the years after 1513, lectures coming gradually to light after the late nineteenth century. Luther's early theology could now be more intensely researched than was possible previously. With the

---

[1] See Ernst Bizer, "Neue Darstellungen der Theologie Luthers," *ThR* NF 31 (1965/1966), 316-49; see also Bernhard Lohse, "Zur Struktur von Luthers Theologie: Kriterien einer Darstellung der Theologie Luthers" (1985), in Lohse, *Evangelium in der Geschichte: Studien zu Luther und der Reformation,* ed. Leif Grane, Bernd Moeller, and Otto Hermann Pesch (Göttingen: Vandenhoeck & Ruprecht, 1988), 237-49.

choice of themes attaching to his various essays, however, Holl quite consciously and continuously took a position toward the debates of his day, especially during the First World War and the years after 1918.[2]

The connection between the portrait of Luther and one's own theological position is especially clear in descriptions submitted by systematicians such as Paul Althaus, Friedrich Gogarten, Rudolf Herrmann, or Hans Joachim Iwand. Althaus and Gogarten could publish their presentations on their own, while editors were needed to revise the manuscripts left behind by Herrmann and Iwand. In each attempt at Luther interpretation, particularly in connection with such topics as law and gospel, the two-kingdoms doctrine, political ethics, and the assessment of the importance of the dogmatic tradition for Luther, lines of convergence with the theological and political history of the time can easily be drawn. With Gogarten the link to the rise of early dialectical theology is unmistakable; with Althaus the proximity to his idea of "primal revelation"; with Herrmann the concern to clarify basic systematic concepts; and with Iwand the association with Barth's theological starting point despite their differences over law and gospel. Yet each systematician has in his own way sought to distance his view of Luther from his own theological position.

Among church historians, as already noted with Holl, proximity to one's own theological position in the respective interpretations of Luther is unmistakable. This is especially true of Emanuel Hirsch and Ernst Wolf, both of whom began their Luther research as church historians, in order later, influenced particularly by their encounter with Luther's Reformation theology, to move to the discipline of systematic theology. What is astonishing in all this is that both Hirsch, who finally came to accent religious experience in view of the impenetrable riddle of fate, and Wolf, whose reading of Luther's theology set the preaching of Christ at the center, could appeal to Luther. We might ask how it is possible that two so extraordinarily different theological positions can be indebted to the reformer. Still, one must admit that both Hirsch and Wolf enjoy certain distinction not only as systematicians but also as Luther scholars. This fact should caution us against too quickly assigning the reformer a systematic impulse without giving support for it.

Reinhold Weier's attempt to set forth Luther's understanding of theology deserves attention. Weier took up his theme not in systematic but in historical fashion, and by doing so intended to show that Luther shared important aspects with the tradition, but gave themes such as inner conflict *(Anfechtung)* or the *theologia crucis* new treatment and rendered them fruitful for the entire understanding of theology. However welcome such an attempt at discussing Luther's understanding of theology may be, it must still be said that a comparison with older as well as with contemporary positions, difficult to draw in the individual instance, would require more

---

[2] See Bernhard Lohse, *Martin Luther: An Introduction to His Life and Work,* trans. Robert C. Schultz (Philadelphia: Fortress Press, 1986), 225-27.

detailed research than Weier made.[3] On the one hand, it appears that Luther's association with the tradition was considerable. On the other, the significance of his critical stance toward many older and contemporary positions can scarcely be overestimated.

THE ALTERNATIVE: HISTORICAL-GENETIC
OR SYSTEMATIC DESCRIPTION

Previously published descriptions have provided either a systematic or a historical-genetic reading of Luther's theology. The majority of scholars have opted for the first method, the second being only sporadically pursued.

There is systematic description in the work of Theodosius Harnack, Reinhold Seeberg, Erich Seeberg, Philip S. Watson, Paul Althaus, Gerhard Ebeling in his book *Luther: An Introduction to His Thought,* in the work of Lennart Pinomaa, Friedrich Gogarten, Rudolf Herrmann, Hans Joachim Iwand, Ulrich Asendorf, and Karl-Heinz zur Mühlen. What is strange in all this is that none of these authors has attempted to give reasons for the systematic assigned to Luther, or critically to distance it from other readings of his theology. With amazing aplomb each systematic attributed to Luther is set down as the only one adequate, without any reason given for the decision. On the other hand, rapid perusal of the variously structured systematic of these representations indicates that scarcely two readings agree even on basic questions. The differences in the evaluation of Luther's theology not only have to do with the various starting points but also with the position and arrangement of important complexes of theological teaching.

A few questions arise here. That in describing Luther's theology as a whole his Reformation breakthrough and thus the Reformation doctrine of justification must assume central place should not be up for debate. Should we, however, take this as our starting point and on that basis crowd all the other questions into a systematic? Or are we dealing with an important doctrine but ultimately with the theme of salvation as aim and goal and that must always be at the center in the discussion of every other theological theme? Or what position does the trinitarian and christological dogma of the ancient church have for Luther?

Clearly, Luther held fast to the conciliar decisions of the ancient church. He affirmed them not only in a formal sense but also with respect to their content. It is likewise beyond dispute that in the various controversies, chiefly with Rome, questions touching trinitarian doctrine and Christology were in the background. On the other hand, Luther could designate the article of the Trinity and Christol-

[3] See Lohse's review of Weier's book, *ThLZ* 103 (1978), 125-27.

ogy as basic or central. What weight do such statements have in the attempt to assign him a specific systematic? It is beyond dispute that Luther almost always composed his numerous writings, critiques, opinions, and even his treatises in specific controversies. Yet, must the attempt at a systematic reading of his theology as a whole pursue the theme of these controversies, or need we bear in mind that behind the questions of the day certain fundamental decisions are not always discussed but are in fact always presupposed? Or more basically put: What weight does doctrine have alongside preaching?

It is certain that for Luther the question of the assurance of salvation and thus of preaching stood at the center. Still, may we ignore the doctrinal element in his theology that he accented in specific situations?[4]

By contrast, there are very few historical-genetic representations of Luther's theology. Julius Köstlin's comprehensive reading of Luther's theology still deserves attention. In the first section he deals with Luther's theology "in its historical development," and in the second with his theology "in its inner harmony." The first section accents Luther's dispute with Rome, the second describes in brief survey the further development in Luther's doctrine following his Wartburg sojourn, thus the intra-evangelical controversies. In his article in *Die Religion in Geschichte und Gegenwart,* Gerhard Ebeling describes Luther's theology in historical-genetic fashion, without attempting a full systematic interpretation.

There are weighty arguments for both ways of describing Luther's theology. Where Luther himself gave no comprehensive view, as was done, say, by Melanchthon in the later editions of his *Loci Praecipui Theologici,* or by Calvin in his *Institutes of the Christian Religion,* a systematic overall view can indicate the link between the various doctrines and the inner dynamic of Luther's theology. Of course, we must be on our guard against too quickly constructing a systematic that is then simply assigned to Luther.

On the other side, the historical-genetic description has the advantage of viewing Luther much more strictly within the context of his time and his debates. In particular, such a reading may be better suited for giving precise definition to the starting point of Luther's theology. In this case, of course, it would not be enough to trace the development of the various controversies and the sequence of topics in dispute. Here too the question of the systematic overall view must be raised. For these reasons a linking of the two methods would be recommended.

---

[4] On this topic see esp. Karl Gerhard Steck, *Lehre und Kirche bei Luther,* FGLP 10/26 (Munich: Chr. Kaiser, 1963).

THE ATTEMPT AT A CONNECTION OF THE HISTORICAL-GENETIC AND SYSTEMATIC PRESENTATION

If we link the historical-genetic to the systematic method, then the first should deal especially with Luther's early period, so that his early theology as well as the beginning of his dispute with Rome may be traced as accurately as possible. This must include a description of further controversies in the dispute, chiefly from 1517 to 1521, since the gulf between Luther and Rome was widened in these controversies, and since he further clarified and elaborated important aspects of his ecclesiology and his understanding of law and gospel.

Before Luther's early theology can be described, one thing needs to be said concerning the ecclesiastical-theological situation in the period around 1500. Not only traditions important to Luther must be outlined, but also the change in the ecclesiastical and theological climate around 1500. Not least in importance is that Luther became a theologian in a period characterized by the radical change from scholasticism to humanism. Finally, Luther's personal development must also be sketched in order to make clear his theological starting point.

Next to Luther's conflict with Rome, the most important intra-Reformation disputes must also be described, since these also led to further clarification and development, in part also to certain shifts in accent in his theology. Among other things, these clarifications and developments concern the concept of law and gospel; determination of the relation between letter and Spirit, as well as the so-called Reformation principle of Scripture; further, the view of temporal authority; finally, and above all, the doctrine of the sacraments in general and the view of the Lord's Supper in particular. Certainly, according to the present state of research, in none of these instances may we speak of a division caused by these debates. Earlier and frequent attempts at sharply differentiating the "young" and the "old" Luther,[5] at precisely dating the difference between them, a problem in and of itself, have in general been abandoned. On the whole, there is considerable consistency and continuity of views where Luther is concerned.

Still, further development, precising, clarifying, and defining can often be clearly observed in Luther's work. In the controversies he at times broached new themes that he had not expressly treated before. For example, it was only in his conflict with Erasmus that he explicitly distinguished or dealt in detail with the difference between the "hidden" and "revealed" God. In the Lord's Supper controversy with Zwingli, he further developed his Christology in discussing the so-called doctrine of ubiquity, that is, the concept of Christ's exalted human nature as omnipresent. Or, toward the end of the sixteenth century, in his debates with the so-called Antinomians, he treated in greater detail or more precisely developed certain

[5] On this topic see Lohse, *Martin Luther*, 152-54.

aspects of the distinction between law and gospel. To a great extent, then, Luther set forth his theology within specific disputes. He was scarcely ever able to outline or compose a treatise apart from conflicts of the day. He regarded the critical testing of preaching and doctrine as a decisive task of his own theological labors. In describing Luther's theology as a whole, one can scarcely overestimate the significance of this fact. Never before had a theologian dealt so critically with other positions as did Luther in the sixteenth century. The Reformation first made clear that theology exercises a critical function for the church's teaching and preaching. And, in its own way, traditional theology was forced to adopt a position toward this altered situation and take its place in the daily battle of opinions.

It is not enough, however, to describe Luther's theology within the context of the various controversies. We need to be aware that he always developed his view from a standpoint that he had thoroughly thought through and systematically reflected upon. Although he submitted no dogmatics, he did publish a kind of dogmatics in outline, for example, in his Large Catechism of 1529. In writings such as *On the Councils and the Church* (1539), or in the strictly polemical treatise *Against Hanswurst* (1541), he more or less exhaustively treated specific points of doctrine. For a reading of Luther's theology, one must thus attempt a systematic overall view.

Still, the significance of doctrine for Luther can scarcely be overestimated. In *The Sacrament of the Body and Blood of Christ against the Fanatics* (1526), he set forth in an exemplary way the doctrine's significance. Here he states that at the Lord's Supper two things should be known and preached: first, what one should believe, that is, the *objectum fidei,* the work or thing believed or to which one should cling; second, faith itself or its use, that is, how what is believed should be rightly used. The first is outside the heart and held externally before our eyes, namely, the sacrament, about which we believe that Christ's body and blood are truly in the bread and wine. The other is within, in the heart. It cannot show itself and consists in how the heart should behave toward the outward sacrament. Luther then continues: "Up to now I have not preached very much about the first part, but have treated only the second, which is also the best part. But because the first part is now being assailed by many, and the preachers, even those who are considered the best, are splitting up into factions over the matter . . . the times demand that I say something on this subject also."[6]

In this text Luther first confirms that he always developed his theology in relation to and in debate with the various questions of his day. Clearly, we must always note what is unexpressed but in fact assumed, and as a result is of considerable weight as a basis for theological argument.

In the attempt at a systematic reading of Luther's theology his assumptions must be considered and appropriately weighted. Such determination, it appears, is

---

[6] *LW,* vol. 36, p. 335. *WA* 19, 482, 25-483, 19.

of special significance in assigning importance to dogmas of the ancient church, such as the doctrine of the Trinity and Christology. On the whole, ancient church dogma was never a matter of dispute with Luther and Rome, though here and there the accents varied. Thus, where circumstances permit, a systematic presentation concerned to make clear the structure of Luther's theology must set forth the themes and aspects more graphically than would appear to suit Luther's writings at first glance. To put it more pointedly: If Luther had composed a dogmatics as did Melanchthon or Calvin, would he not have proceeded in a manner similar to theirs in composing and arranging his material? Or are there reasons for supposing he would have given an entirely different structure to such a dogmatics?

It seems that if there had been a dogmatics from Luther's hand, it would not have differed from others in structure and composition, but indeed in its treatment of individual doctrines. It might thus be appropriate first to discuss the problems pertaining to Luther's understanding of Scripture and the relation between reason and faith, and then in a rather "conservative" arrangement to discuss the main dogmatic topics.

Chapter 2

THE SITUATION IN THE CHURCH AROUND 1500

Decline and Reform

The situation of the church around 1500 was in many respects quite different than, say, around 1450 or 1400. Since for everyone who became a theologian in the early sixteenth century, the ecclesiastical and spiritual climate was no doubt of greater weight than in the High or late Middle Ages, and since many theologians in one way or another dealt with questions of the day, the historical background must be briefly sketched here. In doing so we can first of all ignore the question as to whether Luther himself was informed about all the tendencies and configurations to be mentioned here. In some instances it can be shown that he did have some knowledge.[1] In others he may at least have heard something, so as to be somewhat informed.

When we compare the period around 1500 with that around 1400 respecting the general ecclesiastical situation, we are struck by serious changes that sixteenth-century theology could not ignore. The papal schism after the end of the Avignon exile (1378) was finally overcome (1415) at the Council of Constance (1414-1418). This healed the worst injury to Western Christianity. Of course, after as well as before, there was an abundance of grievances, identifiable in varying degrees of intensity within the individual lands and that were felt greatly to impair the Christianity of that time. The complaints relating to these grievances were first set forth at Constance in

---

[1] See principally the index volume of *WA*: *WA* 62 (index of places); *WA* 63 (index of persons and quotations). On the whole, the indexes indicate to what an astonishing degree Luther was in the picture regarding earlier and contemporary currents.

1417, then again at the Basel Council (1431-1449).[2] In the years following they were
further lodged by individual theologians and church leaders but also by humanists. On
the other hand, they had been dealt with again and again at German diets since the
mid-fifteenth century. Corresponding to the structure of the German Empire, the
complaints of the German nation concerned ecclesiastical as well as secular questions.
The chief accent, however, lay on complaints regarding grievances in the church. The
most comprehensive collection of such charges was assembled at the Diet of Worms in
1521 and taken up at its dismissal. The "Luther affair," appended to the diet in the inter-
val, would not have directly influenced this collection of attacks and demands for
reform. In the years following the Diet of Worms the charges as previously formulated
lost significance since the diets were occupied with the newly arisen reform movement. In these activities the earlier charges still had weight only insofar as they were
taken up by the Reformation movement.

The attack on grievances in the church and the temporal sphere was widespread
in the early sixteenth century, and in part was also made at the universities. No less
important were the various impulses or tendencies toward reform that cried for help.

Conciliarism was still alive, its beginnings reaching far back to the High Middle
Ages.[3] For a long time the theological center of conciliarism was at the University
of Paris. This decisively contributed to healing the papal schism but in turn also
evoked papal reserve toward reform councils as instruments of change. In the early
sixteenth century no impulses toward church reform worth naming could be
expected from conciliarism, though it still had potential for criticism and a desire
for reform.[4] Otherwise, impulses toward reform existed chiefly in humanism,
which not only shared in criticism but also engaged on behalf of a Christianity
renewed and made inward. Still, humanistic circles were limited in their capacity to
influence. At best, secular rulers could carry out specific political and churchly
reforms, as often occurred since the mid-fifteenth century. With all their zeal for
reform, however, secular rulers were as a rule merely intent on extending their
influence over the church. In fact, they were most concerned with occupying important posts and receiving income from bishoprics, foundations, and cloisters.

In sum we must say that the indisputable decay of essential parts of the church
was generally known and that impulses toward reform were not lacking. It was
never clear, however, which of these impulses would be capable of succeeding.

[2] Bruno Gebhardt, *Die Gravamina der deutschen Nation gegen den römischen Hof,* 2d ed. (Breslau:
Koebner, 1895); Heinz Scheible, *Die Gravamina, Luther und der Wormser Reichstag 1521,* Ebernburg-Hefte
5 (1971), 58-74, as well as in *BPfKG* 39 (1972), 167-83.

[3] On this topic see Brian Tierney, *Foundations of the Conciliar Theory* (Cambridge: Cambridge University Press, 1955). See also the work of John B. Morrall, *Gerson and the Great Schism* (Manchester:
Manchester University Press, 1960), important for the history of theology.

[4] Remigius Bäumer, *Nachwirkungen des konziliaren Gedankens in der Theologie und Kanonistik des frühen
16. Jahrhunderts,* RGST 100 (Münster: Aschendorffsche Buchhandlung, 1971).

SCHOLASTICISM AND HUMANISM

Intellectual life around 1500 was marked by a greater variety than had ever existed. For centuries scholasticism dominated the universities. The thirteenth century saw the formation of the two great philosophical-theological schools of the Dominicans and Franciscans, schools still represented in the sixteenth century. Both schools, however, had in the meanwhile undergone many changes. In Thomism certain positions once formulated by Thomas Aquinas were no longer represented, either because they appeared no longer philosophically tenable or seemed liable to misunderstanding in view of certain developments emerging in more radical circles such as that of Wyclif. On the whole, in the period around 1500, Thomism was represented at only a few universities, and only a minority of theologians followed Thomas.

Franciscan theology, developed further chiefly by William of Occam (ca. 1285-1349), was all the more important. Since the late fourteenth century it held the field. It is no exaggeration to state that the questions occupying philosophy and theology toward the end of the Middle Ages, and to a great extent their answers, were determined by Occam. No one could avoid the problems concerning the doctrine of God and the order of salvation resulting from Occam's distinction between God's *potentia absoluta* (absolute omnipotence) and his *potentia ordinata* (ordered omnipotence, i.e., limited by creation and redemption), even if one attempted to follow another lead than his. Thus it is no surprise that even Thomists and Augustine himself followed Occam or at least dealt with Occam's formulations of the question in certain areas of philosophy and theology.

With regard to Augustine's influence, at the close, just as in the early and High Middle Ages, the great African father was by far the most significant and influential theologian. Among theologians of all persuasions there are more quotations from Augustine in disputed cases than from any other authority. In addition, where the late Middle Ages are concerned, we may speak in some sense of an Augustine renaissance relating to certain aspects of the doctrine of sin and grace. On topics pertaining to this doctrine, theologians such as Gregory of Rimini (ca. 1300-1358) were adherents of Augustine, though in his philosophy Gregory largely followed Occam. The resulting tensions remained unresolved; perhaps they were not even noted. Toward the close of the Middle Ages there was no pure Augustinianism but only a connection between certain Augustinian lines of thought and other predominantly Occamist views. Even in the doctrine of sin and grace Occam's doctrine of God led to conclusions ultimately irreconcilable with Augustine's theology. The theology of Johannes Paltz (ca. 1445-1511), who till 1505 worked in the Augustine eremite cloister at Erfurt and also instructed Luther, betrays some Augustinian influence, though it is entirely determined by other ideas and interests.

The result is that in the late Middle Ages there was greater variety in theology than ever before. Of course, there were shared traditions that were important to all the schools. Still, there were considerable differences in the individual instance, though the towering influence of Occam could always be traced.

In the late Middle Ages the emergence of humanism led to an even greater variety of philosophical and theological schools. During the fifteenth century, humanistic tendencies strode beyond the Alps toward middle and northern Europe. These tendencies existed partly in the small circles of friends and sympathizers typical of humanism, but partly also in the universities. What is important is that to a great extent early-fifteenth-century humanistic tendencies did not yet appear in conflict with the reigning scholasticism. To begin with, there was a separate but peaceful coexistence of scholastics and humanists, succeeded by confrontations and rivalries only at the opening of the sixteenth century. Only then did humanists strive for university reform. By this means the hitherto dominant scholasticism would be replaced and attempts made to revive classical Latin. In theology scholastic texts were to be replaced by readings from the church fathers and the Bible.

WYCLIF AND HUS

The picture of the later Middle Ages becomes even more diffuse when we recall that two important theologians were condemned by the church, whose resistance to certain abuses and teachings was still vivid in the sixteenth century: John Wyclif (ca. 1320-1384) and John Hus (ca. 1369-1415). Hus had actually been executed as a heretic at the Council of Constance. Luther, of course, dealt with Hus in greater detail when he came into conflict with Rome. But he might have known something of him even earlier. At Luther's Augustinian eremite cloister in Erfurt, Johannes Zachariae, celebrated as victor over Hus at Constance, was buried in front of the altar in the choir. To this day, a large tablet refers to his "victory." This fact alone, together with remembrance of the Hussite wars, still fresh in the Middle Germany of Luther's time, might have kept the memory of Hus and his questions alive.

We underestimate the importance of Wyclif and Hus when we see them merely as representing their nations, thus as an Englishman and a Bohemian.[5] It is correct, of course, that both represented national interests. At the core, however, both are to be regarded as theologians of reform or as reformers who from a fresh scriptural understanding attacked specific abuses and questionable doctrines, and were no longer prepared against their better judgment to subject themselves to church authority. Worth noting in all this is that neither rhetoric nor force could once more render subject to Rome the movements to which these men gave impetus. In the West the Hussites were the first example of a church independent of Rome that finally came to enjoy a certain tolerance.

[5] So Karl August Fink, in *Handbuch der Kirchengeschichte,* ed. Hubert Jedin, III/2 (Freiburg: Herder, 1968), 539-45, who refers to the "national heresies" of both men.

Like Hus, Wyclif attacked numerous abuses in the church of his day: from indulgences and the externalizing of piety to Rome's financial draining of his land, to the papacy's striving for temporal power. Earlier there had been lively debate over many of these questions. In the German Empire the so-called poverty dispute between Emperor Ludwig of Bavaria (1314-1347) and Pope John XXII (1316-1334) had been particularly violent. In this dispute Marsilius of Padua (ca. 1275-1342 or 1343) and William of Occam were the chief participants. Their criticism of the popes could scarcely be exceeded in harshness. Their concept of the church was forward looking; according to them the church comprises the totality of believers. Even their anticlerical view of the state was future directed. Naturally, Occam advocated such radical views only in polemical pamphlets dealing with church politics, not in his philosophical and theological works. Consequently, late medieval Occamism scarcely dealt with ideas critical of pope and church.

First of all, both Wyclif and Hus emphasized Holy Scripture more strongly than scholastic theology. They held Scripture to be the "divine law" which the church must follow and by which to be critically measured where needed. This, in essence, already set up the Reformation principle of *sola scriptura* and critically applied it to the church of that period. Of course, the difference between Wyclif and Hus on the one hand, and Luther on the other, is that for them Scripture was predominantly law, not also the liberating gospel.

As to their idea of the church, Wyclif and Hus had set out on new paths. From their Augustinian perspective, they saw the church as comprising those elected by God to salvation. They did not, however, understand the church on the basis of its function as mediator of salvation. This ecclesiology led to quite different results than were to be observed till then in Western Christianity. In the early sixteenth century Hussitism was still an unsettled, critical question put to Western Christianity.

New Formulations of the Question and Impulses

In addition to the narrower and theological developments, for everyone living in the early sixteenth century and working in theology there were many other important schools, figures, and events more or less directly influencing theology.

First, together with scholasticism's establishment of schools toward the end of the Middle Ages, and alongside humanist undercurrents and tendencies critical of the church, numerous efforts on behalf of piety in the broadest sense must be kept in mind. Among these around 1500 was, for example, the great influence of Bernard of Clairvaux (1090-1153), with his Christ-piety and emphasis on discipleship. Bernard's influence derived not only from his sermons and other writings but more indirectly from his spirit, leading to depictions of the suffering Christ in numerous altar paintings. In piety, however, quite diverse figures had influence, such as Johannes Paltz, who in the main advocated a massive Marian piety in conjunction with the propagation of monasticism and indulgences, the precise opposite of Bernardian spirituality with its concentration on Christ. In the piety of the cloister, but also in that of the lay brotherhoods and congregations, one could just as easily find concentration on the Christ crucified as downright superstitious striving for good works. Theologically, the one or the other was advocated and established. Even Augustine's perennial influence scarcely led to criticism of superstitious notions or practices. Clearly, such attitudes could just as easily be linked to ideas of the Augustinian as of the Thomistic or Franciscan school, without any sort of tension noted. However extensive the criticism of abuse in church and piety, it nonetheless dealt as it were only with the outward, not with the heart, of late medieval piety.

In addition to such tendencies and influences in piety, the period around 1500 reflected an increasing distinction between everyday life and intellectual pursuits. In the fifteenth and sixteenth centuries quite disparate figures lived and worked. There was, for example, Nicholas of Cusa (1401-1464), a bishop and cardinal engaged in church reform but occupied chiefly in the philosophical-theological sphere with his *coincidentia oppositorum,* and defying classification under any of the schools of that period; Niccolo Machiavelli (1469-1527), who in *The Prince* (1513) researched the conditions of power, and in his theory of the state distanced himself from the Christian-metaphysical ethic for the sake of an ethic oriented to antiquity; a scholar such as Johannes Reuchlin (1455-1522), one of the most significant humanists, who was chiefly engaged in preserving Hebrew literature and through his *De rudientis hebraicis libri tres* (1506) decisively furthered scientific occupation with the Old Testament; a humanist such as Agrippa of Nettesheim (1486-1535), who attacked scholasticism and the intolerance and tyranny of church officials but also propagated natural-philosophical and occult views; the polyhistorian Theophrastus Paracelsus (1493-1541), influential because of his view of the human being as a copy of the macrocosm, and through his mystical-natural philosophical writings attracting more than one member of the "left wing" of the Reformation or of later German pietism.[6] The picture of the period around 1500 becomes even more diffuse when we recall that the epoch is marked by discoveries that were widely noted, but the importance of which was for a long time scarcely appreciated. Nicolas Copernicus (1473-1543) challenged the Ptolemaic, geocentric view of the world. The discovery of America in 1492 took quick effect economically, though its significance was scarcely grasped.[7]

Finally, it must also be mentioned that assumptions held by the church hierarchy around 1500 were subject to a process of persistent change, due to a change in the laity's position in the world. If in the High Middle Ages nobility and clergy occu-

---

[6] On this topic see particularly Hans Schneider, "Johann Arndts Studienzeit," *JGNKG* 89 (1991), 133-75.

[7] On occasion Luther stated that "of late, many islands and lands have been discovered." See *WA* 10 I, 1, 21, 16; 10 III, 139, 20; 53, 169.

pied the strategic posts, in the waning Middle Ages learned, highly educated burghers functioning as jurists often exercised authoritative influence among secular and clerical princes and thus determined the politics of their masters. For the Reformation, the emergence of the laity, particularly in the fifteenth century, was an essential presupposition. Still, this had not been theologically reflected on or even taken into account. As to the subject itself, we may speak in some respect of a practical universal priesthood of the baptized in the late Middle Ages.

Chapter 3

THE THEOLOGICAL SITUATION AROUND 1500, ESPECIALLY IN ERFURT AND WITTENBERG

OCCAMISM AT ERFURT

When Luther became a monk and soon thereafter studied theology, he was faced not only with a multilayered situation in the church, but in a philosophical-theological respect was subject to the influence of more than one school of thought. The weight that these various persuasions had for Luther was quite varied.

At the University of Erfurt and also at the Augustinian eremite cloister that Luther entered in 1505, Occamism was predominant in philosophy and theology. Erfurt Occamism had special peculiarities that must be carefully noted.

First, a quite varied picture of Occam is still emerging. He is regarded as the founder of the *via moderna*. On the important question of the relation between philosophy and theology, he sharply distinguished the various spheres of knowledge. Meanwhile, Duns Scotus (ca. 1265-1308) subjected to sharp criticism the balanced synthesis for which Thomas Aquinas (1225-1274) had labored. As early as at the close of the Middle Ages, but in part also in modern research, Occam has been charged with advocating a "double truth": what is regarded as true in philosophy need not be true in theology, and vice versa. In addition, Occam has often been charged with epistemological skepticism. But he merely applied the Aristotelian scientific principle more critically than earlier thinkers, distinguishing a philosophy that can arrive at objective knowledge on the basis of axioms and proofs from a theology that appeals to revelation and insofar can arrive at assertions only through the authority of Scripture and church. Still, his rejection of realism and preference for nominalism led to the view that universal concepts are merely *termini* and do not exist outside the human mind. For Occam it is impossible for reason to recognize what is beyond sense. The result of this view was that philosophical effort came to be occupied more and more with the particular. Since for Occam theological statements cannot be proved, church decisions may be described as "arbitrary." On the whole, however, Occam's decided turning toward Scripture did not lead to critical opposition between Scripture and church doctrine. Naturally, for Luther, intense regard for Scripture in contrast to high scholasticism was of great import. No less significant is the fact that due to epistemological skepticism experience also gained in importance. For that reason, toward the close of the Middle Ages the speculative features of high scholasticism retreated.

Occam's doctrine of God gained significance chiefly through its distinguishing God's "absolute power" from his "ordered power."[1] This distinction was not at all intended to serve a division in the divine omnipotence. Rather, within the undivided power of God, Occam wanted to distinguish what God can and does do in an absolute sense from what God can and does do within his self-limitation in creation and redemption.[2] Naturally, this distinction could result in a kind of "dual tracking," with theological problems being reflected on in the framework of the "potentia Dei absoluta," then in the framework of the "potentia Dei ordinata." The results were often enough in considerable tension.

The situation is no different with Occam's doctrine of sin and grace. Here too one can observe a kind of dual tracking, tracing to certain aspects of his doctrine of God. In this doctrine, and in Occam's view of sin and grace, the concept of the *acceptatio divina*, the divine acceptance or permission, plays a special role. Occam regarded original sin less from the viewpoint of the gravity of the sin of the first human, as Anselm of Canterbury (1033-1109) had done, than from the idea that God imputed the sin of the first human to all subsequent generations equally: by virtue of that first offense God willed that humans should not be accepted by him. To that extent the nature of original sin could be described as the *non-acceptatio divina*. If older scholasticism had construed original sin as a "lack of original righteousness" (*carentia iustitiae originalis*), Occam did not actually reject this view but at bottom did not share it. As for individual sins, Occam understood them as acts of will that render sinners guilty according to divine decree and thus sets them under the coming punishment. On this view, however, sin has no reality. It is rather a concept. The advantage of Occam's concept of sin over earlier views is that original sin is not construed in biological terms as inherited. Rather, a divine decision of will

---

[1] See Klaus Banach, *Die Lehre von der doppelten Macht Gottes bei Wilhelm von Ockham: Problemgeschichtliche Voraussetzungen und Bedeutung*, VIEG 75 (Wiesbaden: Steiner, 1975).

[2] See Junghans, *Ockham im Lichte*, cf. p. 348, 233-43.

that is not to be puzzled out lies behind humanity's fate of sin and guilt. For that reason Occam had to be content with the fact that no decision was made respecting the content of the nature of sin.

The signal result of this view of original sin or of sin as such is that Occam assumed that humans can fulfill God's commands on the basis of their natural powers. When humans do not perform the required obedience, the cause lies in God's refusal to accept their work. The further result is that grace in essence consists in the divine acceptance of the human. What is decisive, then, is not a particular *habitus* (quality), such as Thomas and other high scholastics had taught, but the divine decision of will on behalf of humanity. The danger, of course, was that this decision could appear arbitrary.

Occam's view was partially moderated in the late Middle Ages. Gabriel Biel (ca. 1410-1495), the noted Tübingen professor of theology, adopted Occam's interpretations but linked them to traditional views. Regarding the doctrine of original sin or sin as such, Biel attached to Occam's ideas the ancient interpretation of the significance of desire in the transmission of original sin. What was taught at Erfurt on this question as well as on other important dogmas was not the "real" Occam but an Occam adjusted to the tradition through Biel's interpretation. Yet even at Erfurt with its Occamism there were sufficient points at which the perilous explosive force of Occamist theology could do its work.

Accordingly, if in theology as narrowly defined only a moderated Occamism was taught at Erfurt, something of the sort applies to Occam's views on church politics: at Erfurt they might not even have been known.[3] Occam was not only the most significant systematic theologian of the late Middle Ages but also a high-ranking author on the topic of church politics.[4] His most important treatise on this subject is *Dialogus inter magistrum et discipulum de imperatorum et pontificum potestate*. In it Occam gave his opinion on the poverty dispute in favor of Emperor Ludwig of Bavaria and against Pope John XXII. Here, as in other writings, Occam most sharply attacked the pope's abuse of office, declared the pope a heretic, but especially defended the independence of imperial over against papal authority. In the early sixteenth century, Erfurt apparently had not adopted Occam's views on church politics. Neither in his early period nor in his dispute with Rome did Luther refer to Occam's attack on the pope.[5] Had he known of Occam's criticism, he would scarcely have avoided reference to it. This does not exclude the fact that for the young Luther Occam's theology was of considerable importance at a series of strategic points.

---

[3] On this subject see E. Kleineidam, *Universitas Studii Erffordensis,* vol. 2, passim, cf. p. 348.

[4] On this topic see Wilhelm Kölmel, *Wilhelm Ockham und seine kirchenpolitischen Schriften* (Essen: Ludgerus-Verlag, 1962); Junghans, *Ockham im Lichte,* 256-79, is occupied with the question whether we may infer a basically antipapal position from Occam's critical attacks on the pope.

[5] See *WA* 63 (index of persons and quotations), 456.

HUMANISM AT ERFURT AND WITTENBERG

In Luther research until about 1970, the view prevailed that humanism was without real significance for Luther's spiritual development. Luther (it was said) differs from other reformers such as Zwingli or Bucer precisely because he was not influenced by humanism in any way worth noting. This view can no longer be held, since there is evidence of an indigenous humanist movement prior to Luther at Erfurt and Wittenberg universities.[6] This lends importance to the fact that till around 1500 there was no real opposition between late scholasticism and humanism.

Humanist tendencies existed at Erfurt since the mid-fifteenth century, transmitted not only by wandering poets but also by university instructors. Peaceful coexistence between late scholasticism and early humanism came to an end at Erfurt, when in 1500 Nicholas Marschalk attacked scholasticism with his edition of Martian Minius Felix Capella's treatise *De Arte Grammatica Liber.*[7] In 1502 Marshalk went to the newly founded University of Wittenberg and subsequently entered the lists on behalf of humanism against scholasticism. In Erfurt others continued his labors. What is of interest in all this is that the advocates of humanism not only defended the study of ancient authors but attacked abuses such as the unspiritual life of monks and the cult of relics.

Humanist efforts can also be documented among some of Luther's philosophical and theological professors such as Jodokus Trutfetter and Bartholomew Arnoldi of Usingen. Trutfetter advocated peaceful coexistence between scholasticism and humanism, while Usingen for a time went over entirely to humanism, in order to observe greater caution following the onset of Luther's dispute with Rome. Early in the sixteenth century, Konrad Mutianus Rufus had considerable influence on Erfurt humanism, which really began to flower after 1511. At this point Erasmus became the model of humanist endeavor. Then, of course, Luther was already at home in Wittenberg.

Compared to Erfurt, humanist tendencies at Wittenberg were of lesser range and intensity.[8] Among the Wittenberg university instructors who advocated humanism, Marschalk was at first the most significant. He, however, left Wittenberg as early as 1505. Martin Pollich of Mellerstedt, first rector of the University of Wittenberg, was also influential, as was John Staupitz (ca. 1465-1524). Staupitz, of course, did something to further humanist efforts, though he did not stand out from any literary perspective. The ordinances of the university of October 1, 1508, authored by Christoph Scheurl, reflect certain humanist language. The patron of the

---

[6] See in addition E. Kleineidam, *Universitas Studii Erffordensis,* and esp. the researches of Junghans.

[7] See H. Junghans, *Der junge Luther und die Humanisten* (Weimar/Göttingen: Vandenhoeck & Ruprecht, 1984), 31-49.

[8] See ibid., 56-62.

theological faculty was the *divus Paulus*. In the ordinances of the faculty Augustine was the *gymnasii nostri tutelaris deus*. Of course, this appeal to Paul and Augustine may not mislead us about the fact that it gave absolutely no hint of Reformation tendencies soon to emerge, beginning with Luther's activity in 1513. Wittenberg humanism did not lack criticism of certain forms of piety.

What is the significance of these humanist tendencies in relation to Luther's Reformation theology? They are important first of all in that in Erfurt as in Wittenberg scholasticism no longer went unchallenged. The then new movement of humanism was growing apace, and after 1500 went on the attack. Second, the humanist circle fostered ancient language studies, creating the bases for greater effort to arrive at the meaning of the biblical text. Finally, humanism established Paul and Augustine as special authorities, though there were yet no Reformation viewpoints of significance. That Luther encountered humanist influences at Erfurt contributed significantly to the loosening of the intellectual situation.

THE TRADITIONS OF SIGNIFICANCE FOR LUTHER

Today, the question as to which traditions influenced Luther in his Erfurt years and in his earliest Wittenberg period can for the most part be answered quite precisely. Naturally, in the individual instance, the importance of these traditions for Luther is contested.

Erfurt Occamism is no doubt to be named first. Trutfetter described Occam as the most significant newer philosopher.[9] Luther adopted his teacher's view and even defended it during his dispute with Rome.[10] Occamism was surely important for Luther in matters pertaining to epistemological theory, to the Aristotelian worldview, to the relation between philosophy and theology, but also in theological areas such as Christology in its relation to the doctrine of the Lord's Supper,[11] and not least in the doctrine of sin and grace. Some scholars reproach Occam for having led to a demoralizing of theology with his sharp distinctions.[12] The majority rejects this interpretation today. It can scarcely be disputed that from Occam Luther retained a keen and critical intellectual training.

[9] Gustav Plitt, *Jodokus Trutfetter von Eisenach der Lehrer Luthers* (Erlangen: A. Deichert, 1876), 29.

[10] WA 6, 183, 3-4: "Nonne Vuilhelmus Occam, Scholasticorum doctorum sine dubio princeps et ingeniosissimus?" ("Is there any doubt that William of Occam was the chief and most ingenious of the scholastic teachers?")

[11] Occam's significance for Luther's Christology and doctrine of the Supper can be seen from his recourse to Occamistic arguments in the Lord's Supper debate with Zwingli. See *LW*, vol. 37, pp. 222-26; WA 26, 335-38. See below, p. 227.

[12] So in particular Joseph Lortz, *Die Reformation in Deutschland* (Freiburg: Herder, 1939/40; 6th ed. 1982). See, e.g., 1:172-74. P. 173: The "Occamist system is at root uncatholic"; p. 174: "From the perspective of the late medieval school, this Occamism was not a 'system,' but its denial." Similarly Iserloh, *Gnade und Eucharistie*.

It was not so much Occam himself, however, as later Occamist theologians who influenced Luther. Peter d'Ailly (1350-1420), noted Parisian theologian of reform and strongly influenced by Occam, together with Gabriel Biel, were important to him. Luther studied their writings with relish and actually took from them critical questions touching specific church doctrines such as transubstantiation.[13]

Augustine is second in line. Very early on, he was of extraordinary significance for Luther. It is not certain when and in what way Luther became acquainted with Augustine; the importance to Luther of so-called medieval Augustinianism is likewise disputed. Some scholars refer to an Augustine renaissance in the late Middle Ages,[14] alleged to have led to a renewal in the doctrine of sin and grace. Others refer to the fact that at important points in the doctrine of God and of sin and grace, none of the late medieval theologians claiming to be Augustinian could have avoided the influence of Occamist formulations of the question.[15] Encouragement to busy himself with Augustine may have kept Luther at his Erfurt cloister and perhaps even at his studies. Still, the fairly comprehensive marginal notes on numerous writings of Augustine from around 1509 indicate that his own interest may have furnished the essential impulse for his intensive study of Augustine as early as at Erfurt.[16] For the preparation of lectures in those first years at Wittenberg, Luther's occupation with Augustine was intense, as indicated by extensive reference to Augustine, especially in the first Psalms lecture (1513-1515) and in the lecture on Romans (1515/1516).

While Luther received important stimuli from Occamism on many of the basic issues of philosophy and theology, Augustine gained significance precisely through his radical doctrine of sin and grace. For Luther Augustine became all but the antipode to Occam. The theology of the church father, adopted in connection with Paul, was arrayed against scholasticism.

---

[13] At that time Luther was inspired by Biel's interpretation of the canon of the Mass; see *LW*, vol. 54, p. 264; *WA TR* 3 Nr. 3146, 23-25. According to Melanchthon, Luther all but memorized Biel and d'Ailly; see *CR* 6, 1ff. = *Dokumente zu Luthers Entwicklung,* ed. Otto Scheel, SQS N.F. 2 (2d ed., Tübingen: Mohr, 1929), 199, 37-200, 2. On his criticism of transubstantiation see *LW*, vol. 36, pp. 28-29; *WA* 6, 508, 7-11.

[14] See esp. Heiko A. Oberman, "Tuus sum, salvum me fac. Augustinreveil zwischen Renaissance und Reformation," in *Scientia Augustiniana: Studien über Augustin, den Augustinismus und den Augustinerorden. FS Adolar Zumkeller OSA,* ed. Cornelius Petrus Mayer and Willigis Eckermann (Würzburg: Augustinus Verlag, 1975), 349-94.

[15] See Lohse, *Die Bedeutung Augustins für den jungen Luther,* 11-30.

[16] *WA* 9, 2-27. See Melanchthon, *CR* 6, 159 (in Scheel, 199, 33-200, 2): "Tunc [scil. in the Erfurt period] et Augustini libros legere coepit. . . . Nec tamen prorsus relinquit Sententiarios. . . . Sed omnia Augustini monumenta et saepe legerat et optime meminerat. Hoc acerrimum studium inchoavit Erphordiae." ("Then too he began to read the works of Augustine. . . . Still, he did not totally abandon the sententiarists. . . . But he often read and zealously retained in memory all of Augustine's literary remains. This most intense study began at Erfurt.")

Staupitz is to be named third. Luther may already have met him at Erfurt as a young monk.[17] In any event, through his high office in the order as vicar general of the German wing of the Augustinian eremites, and through his role as father confessor as well as through his theology, Staupitz was significant to Luther. Theologically, Staupitz can no longer be regarded as an adherent of late medieval Thomism or as a representative of nominalism. He cannot be assigned to any particular theological school.[18] He was eclectic, adopting much from Augustine but here and there pursuing one or the other late medieval line. On the whole, Staupitz was intent on a Bible-oriented theology centered on the themes of discipleship and salvation. In his encounter with Staupitz, Luther could thus come to know a theology that was not oriented to scholasticism or simply to humanism. Chiefly in this fashion Augustine's influence on Luther increased. An authentically Reformation theology cannot be noted in Staupitz, however, though at times Luther stressed that he owed the rediscovery of the gospel to him.[19]

Humanism is fourth to be named. Here again the question is moot as to precisely when humanistic tendencies or ideas influenced Luther. Here too the question of date is difficult to answer. Melanchthon reports that Luther read the literary remains of Cicero, Virgil, Livy, and others *ut humanae vitae doctrinam aut imagines*, thus as instruction and model for living.[20] Luther's later frequent quotations, especially from Virgil and Ovid, support Melanchthon's statement. The basis for Luther's solid grounding in classical antiquity might have been laid in his Erfurt student years. Further, Luther was versed in ancient rhetoric. In later years he often enough observed the rules of ancient rhetoric. Not least he gratefully used editions of the texts of ancient authors and church fathers prepared by humanist scholars. Most important to him by far was Erasmus's edition of the Greek New Testament, the first of which appeared in 1516, and a second, revised edition in 1519. When it became accessible, Luther immediately cited this edition during his Romans lecture.[21]

---

[17] M. Brecht supposes that Luther met Staupitz for the first time at Erfurt in April 1506. Cf. *Martin Luther,* vol. 1: *His Road to Reformation,* trans. James L. Schaaf (Philadelphia: Fortress Press, 1985), 70-71.

[18] See M. Wriedt, *Gnade und Erwählung* (Mainz: P. Von Zabern, 1991).

[19] See, e.g., *LW,* vol. 49, p. 48: "It would not be right for me to forget you or to be ungrateful to you, for it was through you that the light of the gospel first began to shine out of the darkness into my heart." *WA Br* 3 Nr. 659, 5-8: "Sed nos certe etiamsi desivimus tibi grati ac placiti esse, tamen tui non decet esse immemores et ingratos, per quem primum coepit evangelii lux de tenebris splendescere in cordibus nostris." *WA TR* 1 Nr. 173: "Ich hab all mein ding von Doctor Staupiz; der hatt mir occasionem geben." ("I have everything from Doctor Staupitz; he furnished me occasion.") *WA Br* 11 Nr. 4088, 5-8 (Luther to Kurfürst Johann Friedrich on 27.3.1545): "Doctor Staupitz, welchen ich rhümen mus, wo ich nicht ein verdampter, undanckbar Bepstlicher Esel sein will, das er erstlich mein Vater ynn dieser lere gewest ist und ynn Christo geborn hat." ("Doctor Staupitz whom I must praise—if I do not want to be a damned, ungrateful, papal ass—that he was first my father in this teaching and bore me in Christ.")

[20] *CR* 6, 157.

[21] From his exposition of Rom. 9:10 onward Luther cited the edition of Erasmus.

In his Erfurt and early Wittenberg years, however, Luther cannot be regarded as a genuine advocate of humanism, though he adopted certain humanist styles and forms of expression. Concerned with the proper sense of the divine Word and the question of salvation, he was too much a theologian.

Fifth, for Luther mysticism was influential. Here too, of course, the real questions are open. Careful distinction is needed among the various authors of mystical literature such as Dionysus the Areopagite, Augustine, Bernard of Clairvaux, Bonaventure, and above all the German mystics of the fourteenth century, among them especially John Tauler (ca. 1300-1361), and the unknown author of the *Theologia Deutsch,* appearing in the later fourteenth or early fifteenth century.

Mystical traditions were generally known to Luther early on. For a time he was deeply impressed with the possibility of mystical experiences. When he read in Bonaventure of the union of God with the soul, it "made [him] absolutely wild," because he wanted to experience such a union. Later he viewed the desire as fanatical.[22] More important to him than the *unio mystica,* which held a certain temporary fascination, was the more measured tradition concerned with inwardness, the deepening of piety, and absorption in the suffering Lord. In the early Wittenberg period, acquaintance with Tauler's sermons[23] as well as the *Theologia Deutsch* gained in importance. In 1516 Luther edited the *Theologia Deutsch* in an incomplete text, and in 1518 in a complete text. As he stressed in his foreword of 1518, after the Bible and Augustine he learned more from this piece than from any other, since the anonymous author was concerned with "what God, Christ, man and everything are."[24]

Discretion is required in noting the influence of mystical literature on Luther. Of importance in the formation of his Reformation theology was that through his acquaintance with mystical writings he became aware not only of scholasticism but of other types of theology. No opposition should be assumed between mysticism and scholasticism. Even more important than Areopagitic or late medieval mysticism was the German mysticism with which Luther first became acquainted as a professor of theology.

Sixth, Bernard of Clairvaux deserves special mention. Some scholars have recently spoken of his great significance for the development of Luther's Reformation theology. It is not so much Bernard's mysticism that they have in mind as his concentration on Christ, particularly on Christ crucified, together with his emphasis on faith.

In 1977, on the basis of his investigation of quotations from Bernard in Luther's lecture on Romans, Erich Kleineidam proposed the thesis that with his emphasis on personal faith Bernard was "the starting point for Luther's doctrine of faith and the

---

[22] *WA TR* 1 Nr. 644, 30-33.

[23] See Luther's marginal notes in *WA* 9, 95-104. According to *WA* 9, 95 Luther began to study Tauler in 1516.

[24] *LW,* vol. 31, p. 75. *WA* 1, 378, 21-23.

assurance of faith." The principal evidence for this is an extended quotation from Bernard in the exposition of Romans 8:16.[25] Elsewhere as well, Bernard furnished the model for Luther's theology, with its concentration on the question of salvation. Kleineidam's thesis has been enlarged upon by Theo Bell and Franz Posset, who refer to the particular reverence that Luther felt throughout his life for Bernard on essential questions.

Without disputing Bernard's influence, discretion is also required respecting the significance of Augustine and Bernard. While very early on Luther extensively studied Augustine's writings and furnished them with notes, there is no evidence for stating that he also studied Bernard's writings in depth or actually commented on them. There are comparatively few texts from Bernard to which Luther refers. It may be that he owed knowledge of these passages to mealtime oral recitation in his cloister years. Next, it must be emphasized that in later years Luther attacked certain aspects of Bernard's theology, particularly his persistent advocacy of monasticism but also his subservience to the papacy and veneration of the Virgin Mary.[26] Neither in his early period nor later on did Luther undertake a like criticism of Augustine. In any case, Bernard's significance for Luther is far less than that of Augustine.

If one attempts to relate the various traditions significant to Luther and weigh them, one must say that late scholasticism, thus Erfurt Occamism, was most important. Still, it is worth noting that Luther's teachers referred to scriptural authority and in that connection appealed especially to Augustine, as well as principally to Paul and John. Luther later reported that the ordaining bishop at Erfurt, John von Bonemilch von Lasphe, who probably ordained him as priest in 1507, impressed on his young candidate that without Aristotle no one could be a theologian, but that "we" young theologians would have had Hilary, Jerome, Augustine, or Bernard in mind.[27] Luther later states that he first learned from his teacher Trutfetter that "faith" (fidem) is owed Holy Scripture alone, that all others are due merely an opinion (iudicium), just as Augustine and especially Paul and John teach.[28] In his later emphasis on scriptural authority Luther could thus refer to stimuli received from his Occamist teachers, though they in no way advocated anything resembling a scriptural principle.

In other respects, the statements of the mature Luther cited above make clear that within student circles at least there was an instinct for the disparity between the

---

[25] Kleineidam, *Universitas Studii Erffordensis*, 239. The passage under discussion is in *LW*, vol. 25, pp. 359-60. *WA* 56, 369, 27-370, 5, or 233.

[26] See Lohse, *Luther und Bernhard von Clairvaux*.

[27] *WA* 60, 125, 38-44 (1534).

[28] *WA Br* 1 Nr. 74, 70-74 (letter to Trutfetter of May 9, 1518). Whether Trutfetter made this statement in precisely these words or merely according to their sense is difficult to say. It might be attributable to an Occamist, especially to Gabriel Biel. One certainly cannot interpret it to mean that there may be opposition between utterances of Holy Scripture and those of the church. For comparison see Biel, *Defensorium obedientiae apostolicae et alia documenta*, ed. and trans. Heiko O. Oberman, Daniel E.

theology of the scholastics and that of the church fathers. Even if opposition had not yet come to mind, there was consciousness of the difference between the two. At this point humanist tendencies might already have been influential.

Nonetheless, the astonishing intensity with which Luther turned to Augustine and later to the *Theologia Deutsch* is apparently to be traced not to the stimuli of others but to his own initiative: it is a sign of the independence with which he did theology. Speaking of this initiative, what was decisive for Luther was that neither scholastics nor the other church fathers could answer his penetrating questions.

Zerfoss, and William J. Courtenay (Cambridge: Belknap Press of Harvard University Press, 1968), esp. 70-76. In the context of his *Prima veritas,* Biel explained that the truth which Holy Mother Church defines or accepts as catholic is to be believed with the same reverence as is the truth expressed in the Holy Scriptures (ibid., 74, 23-6: "Prima veritas, quam sancta mater ecclesia tamquam catholicam diffinit vel acceptat, eadem veneratione credenda est, quasi in divinis litteris sit expressa"). We need to note here that Biel's theme was not the authority of Scripture but of the church, or more exactly, of the Apostolic See. Nevertheless, the preeminence, if not also the primacy, of the truth witnessed to in Scripture was implied here; of course, it was immediately connected with the truth proclaimed by the church. In his *Octava veritas* Biel then explained that when opposed to Scripture, to divine law, or to natural law, doctrinal decisions and papal instructions oblige none to obey (ibid., 114, 1-3: "Summi pontificis diffinitiones et praecepta, si contra scripturam canonicam, legem divinam, aut naturalem emanarent, neminem ad sui observantiam obligarent"). The assertion, however, was purely theoretical. See also W. Ernst, *Gott und Mensch am Vorabend der Reformation: Eine Untersuchung zur Moralphilosophie und-theologie bei Gabriel Biel,* EthSt 28 (Leipzig: St. Benno, 1972), 89-102, esp. 96-97. Still, from the perspective of this last word, the statement could have been made by Trutfetter. Opposition or simply tension between Scripture and church authority is naturally out of the question. For further details see Hermann Schüssler, *Der Primat der Heiligen Schrift als theologisches und kanonistisches Problem im Spätmittelalter,* VIEG 86 (Wiesbaden: Steiner, 1977).

Chapter 4

LUTHER'S PERSONAL DEVELOPMENT

THE PARENTAL HOME

In the main, very little can be said of Luther's parental home or of the relations between Luther and his parents, since the relevant sources are sparse, and occasional statements later made by Luther on the subject are quite casual. In sum, Luther's parental home and the education he received there might not have differed in any real sense from conditions existing then in other comparable families. The modern observer must guard against judging the educational practice of that time on the basis of twentieth-century pedagogical presuppositions. Measured by modern views, Luther's education, as certain allusions of the mature reformer make clear, appears to have been very harsh. In this respect, however, his education was clearly no different from practice widespread at the time; it was thus not felt by him to be uncommon. In view of the few sources at our disposal, perennial attempts to interpret Luther's journey from childhood to his entry into the cloister by means of modern psychoanalysis are freighted with enormous difficulties. In particular, there is not sufficient material to advocate the thesis of a severe conflict between Luther and his father.[1] In view of the limited sources restraint is needed here.

It is, of course, correct that Luther's father opposed his sons' entry into the cloister, and that this caused a strain in their relationship. Despite their differences in this area, there can be no talk of an enduring strain in the relations between

---

[1] See the brief survey in Lohse, *Martin Luther: An Introduction to His Life and Work,* 21; cf. also the bibliography in the German edition: *Martin Luther: Eine Einführung in sein Leben und sein Werk* (Munich: Beck, 1981), 50-51.

father and son. On the contrary, till their deaths, Luther was heartfelt in his affection for his father and mother. The thesis of psychoanalysis that Luther suffered under his father's domination, and that his own image of God was determined by his father figure, cannot be documented from the sources. On the whole, Luther's relations to his parents were entirely trusting and good. To the extent his own statements allow us to infer, he suffered no permanent harm from his strict education. His later inner conflicts (*Anfechtungen*) cannot be interpreted on the basis of his relation to his father. The image of the wrathful God, soon to give him such trouble, was determined by the church's practice of piety and theology at the time, rather than by his father. With all their strictness, Luther's parents cared for their son and shared his journey. What is remarkable in any case is that due to his parents' concern Luther received a good education that furnished him a solid foundation for later life.

In the matter of religion, there is likewise little to distinguish Luther's parental home from other families of the period. Close connection with the church, worship services, the sacraments, and a piety massive to our way of thought were absolutely natural and in no way reflect anything strange. Similarly in accord with the time was an equally massive and concrete view of the devil in Luther's parental home. The harshness of Luther's later view of the devil has its basis here.[2] Still, it should perhaps be stressed that unlike among certain humanists, Luther's university education did not lead to a refining of his view. For Luther's parents as well, there is evidence of the idea that witches ruinously interfere in the course of events.[3] Despite this, neither for his parents nor for Luther was the devil a kind of anti-God. They were certain that in spite of the devil God ultimately ruled. Moreover, with its sacraments the church offered sufficient aid so that in general people could confidently go their way. Luther's view of the devil must be seen against its contemporary background, not on the basis of modern ideas.

SCHOOLING AT MAGDEBURG AND EISENACH

Luther's father, evidently never having gone to school himself, was concerned that his gifted son receive a good education and later took interest in his university studies. As for Luther's later career and theology only a few aspects connected with his school years deserve special mention.[4] That such instruction as Luther received was handed on with a severity conditioned by the time, as well as his later criticism of certain aspects of school life in that period, can be passed over here.

---

[2] This aspect has been outlined in the biography of Heiko A. Oberman, *Luther: Man between God and the Devil,* trans. Eileen Walliser-Schwarzbart (New Haven: Yale University Press, 1989).

[3] On this subject see also the brief summary in Brecht, *Martin Luther: His Road to Reformation, (1483-1521),* translated by James L. Schaaf (Minneapolis: Fortress Press, 1985), 11-12.

[4] On this subject see ibid., 12-21.

As to Luther's later career, his first years in the school at Mansfeld (probably from March 1491 to the spring of 1497, or of 1496) were not as important as his time at Magdeburg (probably from the spring of 1497 to 1498, perhaps from 1496 to 1497), or at Eisenach (probably from 1498 to 1501, perhaps as early as from 1497). Luther's parents may have sent him to Magdeburg because a friend was studying there. In any case, it might have been clear to them that Mansfeld could furnish only a limited education. The relatively brief time that Luther spent in the noted cathedral city of Magdeburg was important to him since there, according to his later testimony, he went to the "Noughtbrothers," or Brothers of the Common Life.[5] Since at that time the Brothers had no school at Magdeburg, the sense of Luther's later remark is probably that he lived with them and visited the cathedral school there. Contact with the Brothers brought Luther into closer acquaintance with a refined and profound movement of piety. To this extent, from his own observation and experience, Luther was acquainted not only with the normal churchly, everyday life of Mansfeld in his developing years, but also with life in a half-monastic fellowship oriented to inwardness.

We can scarcely overestimate that in this way Luther not only came to know the church's practice of piety with its excesses and problems, but over a longer period daily experienced the simple spirituality of the Brothers of the Common Life attuned to discipleship and humility. If our survey of the philosophical, theological, and general intellectual trends indicates that Luther was to a great extent acquainted with the late medieval intellectual life, the same is true also of the various trends in piety. From his own experience Luther was aware of most of the trends of that period, from the everyday practice of the church with its cult of relics, preaching of indulgence, and pilgrimages, up to and including the internalized piety of discipleship. The experience of life in the cloister was to be added a bit later.

What induced Luther's parents to take their son out of the school at Magdeburg after only one year and to send him to Eisenach is not known. That various relatives lived there may have played a role. In any case, the three or perhaps four years of his time at Eisenach were of considerable significance for Luther. In his parental home Luther had come to know truly impoverished conditions. As a pupil at Eisenach he had to sing outside homes as a "colt for scraps" (*Partekenhengst*), begging for his bread. The simple way of life, as he later witnessed, did him no harm. On the other hand, at Eisenach Luther encountered affluent and intellectually open-minded families, that is, the Schalbes and the Cottas, who introduced him to a new world. The Schalbes belonged to generations of city counselors. In 1495 and 1499 Heinrich Schalbe was mayor of Eisenach. His son Caspar, somewhat younger than Luther, later attached himself to humanism.

---

[5] See Regnerus Richardus Post, *The Modern Devotion: Confrontation with Reformation and Humanism,* SMRT 3 (Leiden: Brill, 1968).

The Schalbes were also the center of an intellectually and theologically open-minded group intimately connected with the Eisenach Franciscan cloister. All in all, Luther clearly received a good education at Eisenach. What was especially important was that he developed a friendship there that would outlast all the later changes in his career. With Johannes Braun, a priest many years his senior, Luther came to know a joyful piety. In the group gathered about Braun, songs and motets for various voices were sung, giving Luther access to the world of music. When Luther later valued music so extraordinarily highly and himself emerged as hymn writer, he owed the decisive impulses and stimuli to Braun and the circle around him. Finally, in his Eisenach period Luther became acquainted with the then widespread veneration of Saint Anne,[6] devotion to whom played an important role in his later resolve to become a monk.

In his Eisenach period Luther also learned of an incident that then clearly affected him but in later years was to take on even greater weight. The incident had to do with the fate of Johann Hilten (ca. 1425-1500), a Franciscan preacher of repentance who attacked worldly Christianity and reported apocalyptic visions.[7] To Hilten Rome was the great whore whose activity would soon come to an end. In about 1516 he prophesied that "another man," an opponent of monasticism, would come and reform the church. In a political respect as well, especially due to his activity in Livonia, Hilten came into conflict with the authorities of the day. When Luther was at Eisenach, Hilten had long since been indicted. After 1477 he was first imprisoned in the cloister at Weimar, then died in the Eisenach cloister as a Catholic, but without having recanted his prophecies. Luther later recalled these events and referred repeatedly to Hilten.[8] This was clearly the first time Luther learned first-hand of steadfast opposition to the church based on a comprehensive criticism.

LUTHER AS STUDENT

With respect to Luther's later career and his theology a few aspects of his course of study at Erfurt (1501-1505) deserve mention.[9]

[6] WA 47, 383, 23-28.
[7] On Hilten see Paul Wolff, "Johann Hilten," RE, 8:78-80; Ernst Barnikol, "Hilten," RGG, 3:327; O. Scheel, CR 6, 1ff. = Dokumente zu Luthers Entwicklung, ed. Otto Scheel, SQS N.F. 2 (2d ed., Tübingen: Mohr, 1929), 1:114-16; Hans-Ulrich Hofmann, Luther und die Johannes-Apokalypse: Dargestellt im Rahmen der Auslegungsgeschichte des letzten Buches der Bibel und im Zusammenhang der theologischen Entwicklung des Reformators, BGBE 24 (Tübingen: Mohr, 1982), 662-72, excursus II: "Hiltens Leben und Schriften."
[8] See WA Br Nr. 1480, 3-12; LW, vol. 41, p. 176; WA 50, 601, 5-6. See the Apology of the Augsburg Confession, 27, 3, in The Book of Concord: The Confessions of the Evangelical Lutheran Church, trans. and ed. Theodore G. Tappert (Philadelphia: Fortress Press, 1959), 269. See also Die Bekenntnisschriften der evangelisch-lutherischen Kirche (Göttingen: Vandenhoeck & Ruprecht, 1952), 378, n. 1.
[9] The most detailed description of the state of Luther's studies at Erfurt as well as of the details of his course of study is still in Scheel, Dokumente zu Luthers Entwicklung, 1:121-234. See further Brecht, Martin Luther: His Road to Reformation, 23-44.

No less important than the philosophical orientation of the School of Arts in late medieval Occamism is that Luther had to attend lectures on grammar, logic, and rhetoric, based chiefly on the writings of Aristotle. The subject of rhetoric was the labyrinth of Eberhard of Bethune. By this means Luther was introduced to a few basic ideas of Aristotelian philosophy as then understood. He nevertheless owed his study in the arts to an excellent schooling in logic. In addition, regularly staged disputations gave students a facility for apt expression and encounter quick at repartee, likewise later to benefit Luther at every turn. In this period Luther developed the art of precise formulation, of a logical progression in thought carefully reflected and supported by argument, as well as the art of arriving at conclusions, though he himself contributed particularly good presuppositions. In structure as well as in solid argumentation, Luther's later writings indicate what the late medieval university was able to give a gifted student. Though Luther may later have attacked certain aspects of university life, and together with his friends in founding the University of Wittenberg may to some extent have taken a different route than he was once required to take at Erfurt, the simple fact that even at Wittenberg, ultimately a school of the Reformation, the art of disputation was cultivated, indicates the efficiency of the late medieval university.

Life in the bursa (it is not known precisely in what bursa Luther lived at the time)[10] was regimented down to the smallest detail. The university also regulated its students' personal behavior. In a sense the bursa may be likened to a cloister, so that following his Magdeburg period Luther learned to know a strictly regulated *vita communis* while studying at Erfurt. In the bursa spiritual life was cultivated as well. Apart from the fact that its members had to devote themselves to study, the difference between a bursa and a cloister consisted merely in the fact that in the cloister worship and spiritual life were more intensely cultivated. If we add Luther's time at Magdeburg and his student years at Erfurt to his later years as monk, when the indulgence controversy began in 1517, he had spent half his life in cloisters or similar communities. This alone witnesses to the importance of the shape of communal life for Luther.

ENTRY INTO THE CLOISTER

Luther's father had planned that his son should study law. Luther himself evidently agreed with his father's decision. When he ended his study at the School of Arts in 1505, the study of law would automatically have had to begin. As is well known, the plan was thwarted by Luther's vow to Saint Anne to become a monk. The origin of this event, so decisive for Luther, cannot be described here.[11] Still, with respect to his later career as a theologian, various points relevant to it must be pointed out.

[10] See Brecht, *Martin Luther: His Road to Reformation*, 30-32.
[11] On this subject see ibid., 46-50.

First, prior to his decision to enter the monastery, Luther underwent severe inner conflicts that were to afflict him later in the cloister and in a sense throughout his life. These were of course conditioned by various events, by the experience of narrow escapes or the sudden death of a friend. Their chief cause, however, lay in the anxious question as to how he could appear before God at the last judgment.

On the one hand, the question was conditioned by the time and its apocalyptic expectation, but on the other by Luther's personality. As for the time, toward the end of the Middle Ages death variously came to be the theme of literature and the visual arts, as in the *ars-moriendi* literature or in representations of the dance of death. At the same time the end of the world and eternal judgment were more eagerly awaited than earlier. The degree of the intensity of this expectation was scarcely present in other periods, not even in such times as witnessed the wholesale, untimely death of human beings. In this period apocalyptic expectation was clearly more intense than in others. At no other was the last judgment so frequently and graphically depicted.

In Luther's quest for a gracious God, however, a very personal note was struck. Quite clearly, he put the question of God's gracious condescension more radically and sharply than any other. He took seriously the doctrine of sin and grace as well as sacramental teaching in the preaching influenced by Occamism. What Occamist theology had to say on the subject, that is, that humans on the basis of their natural powers are automatically able to keep the commandments and thus to love God above all things, had to intensify his inner conflicts. When Luther concluded that he was unable to produce such pure love for God, then, according to Occamist theology, he had to seek for the cause of it in himself.

Further, the significance for Occamism of the divine *non-acceptatio* and *acceptatio* in turn intensified Luther's inner conflicts. Was not the activity of a God who apparently summoned humans to do the impossible necessarily arbitrary? What kind of God would it be who summons humans by their own powers to love him above all things but clearly has not given them the capacity for it, and in the end elects the one and rejects the other?

Further yet, Luther's inner conflicts were intensified by the doctrine of predestination that he might have come to know in outline as early as a student of the Faculty of Arts, though he first came to know it in its full range only as theologian. Luther felt forced into a situation with no way out. In this state he looked for a gracious God. Later, the conflicts reached their crisis in the question: How can this God be just? Perhaps as a young student Luther felt occasionally that it was this question that lay back of his conflicts. He could, however, render his question thematic only when he had studied theology and made use of special biblical knowledge.

Theologically, the consequence of Luther's inner conflicts as well as his resolve to become a monk was that theology's first concern is the question of salvation or damnation. Such knowledge need not stand in unconditional opposition to the one or other theological orientation as existed in Luther's circle around 1500. The question, of course, could clash with other views if it could not be sufficiently put and explained. In any event, with this question Luther possessed a criterion against which traditions then extant could be measured.

Chapter 5

THE UNIQUENESS
OF LUTHER'S THEOLOGY

"A Theology That Gets at the Meat of the Nut"

Early on, Luther displayed an appreciation for the theological task markedly different from views otherwise held around 1500.[1] Naturally, what is new in Luther's
position cannot be defined in such fashion that it is simply seen in opposition to particular scholastic tendencies or even to humanism. As noted, Luther could read
some scholastic works with great relish, those of Biel, for example.[2] The distinction
between the lines of monastic and scholastic theology recently drawn was also
known to him.[3] His new understanding of theology did not spell a total break with
the tradition. Likewise, one cannot say that the themes with which theology must be
occupied according to Luther would be entirely different than was the case in the
tradition.

What is new is that of all the questions with which theology must deal, the aim
and goal in any given instance is the question of salvation. Questions about the doctrine of God, about the sacraments, about ecclesiology, can be dealt with only
when this aspect is seen from the outset. This does not mean that Luther would
subordinate each complex of topics to, say, a subjectivistic narrowing. There can be

---

[1] On this subject see Weier, *Das Theologieverständnis Martin Luthers.* KKTS 36 (Paderborn: Bonifacius, 1976), who refers to numerous views on theology from the period of the ancient church and
the Middle Ages but scarcely takes note of their links to the actual horizon of questions.

[2] See p. 23, n. 13.

[3] On this subject Jean Leclercq OSB, *Wissenschaft und Gottverlangen: Zur Mönchstheologie des Mittelalters*
(Düsseldorf: Patmos, 1963). See p. 26, n. 27.

no talk of such in view of his uncommonly rich and differentiated theological work. In fact, however, the question of salvation and with it also the question of a truth that yields certainty are at the center in all the topics of theology. Otherwise theology would fail at its task.

It is clear that very early in his career Luther carried on his theological work in his own way. In a letter of March 17, 1509, to his friend, the Eisenach priest Johannes Braun, he said: "From the outset I would most rather have exchanged philosophy for theology. I mean, for a theology that gets at the meat of the nut, at the kernel of the corn, or the marrow of the bones. But God is God: man is often, in fact is always, fallible in judgment. This is our God, he will always lead us in kindness."[4] When Luther emphasizes that "from the outset" he would rather have exchanged philosophy for theology, he has an earlier period in mind, perhaps near the beginning of his theological study (1507), or the time of his entry into the cloister (1505). Shortly before composing this letter, on March 9, 1509, Luther received the *Baccalaureus Biblicus* degree. In this capacity he had to give a cursory interpretation of the biblical books. This may have led to an acute encounter with the problem of philosophy and theology. Still, this statement makes clear that "from the outset" Luther studied theology under a new, sharpened formulation of the question, in the course of which he felt deserted by scholastic theology in a way that was still unclear to him.

THEOLOGIA CRUCIS

Luther's concept of the *theologia crucis* is perhaps his best-known description of the Reformation theology that in the meantime had assumed its essential features. He coined the term in 1518 and used it in various contexts. The prehistory of its formation can more sharply illumine its precise sense. Luther's correspondence in 1517 and in the spring of 1518 is especially instructive. It concerns the direction of the University of Wittenberg reform and Luther's role in it. At the same time, the phrase *theologia crucis* is directed not merely against scholasticism but also against the humanism of Erasmus.

In a letter to Luther from the Nuremberg humanist Christoph Scheurl of January 2, 1517, it is clear that not only at Wittenberg but at Nuremberg as well Luther was regarded as one of the leaders of the University of Wittenberg reform. Scheurl

---

[4] *WA Br* 1 Nr. 5, 40-46 (letter of February 17, 1509: "studium . . . philosophiae, quam ego ab initio libertissime mutarim theologia, ea inquam theologia, quae nucleum nucis et medullam tritici et medullam ossium scrutatur. Sed Deus est Deus; homo saepe, imo semper fallitur in suo iudicio. Hic est Deus noster, ipse reget nos in suavitate et in saecula." On this subject see Ebeling, *Luther: An Introduction to His Thought*, (Philadelphia: Fortress Press, 1970), 77-78; Weier, *Das Theologieverständnis Martin Luthers*, 141-43.

directed his letter "Ad Martinum Luder, theologum scholae Augustinensis apud Witt."[5] At the same time, Staupitz was regarded as the "common father."[6] Luther was hailed first for his concern for a theology renewed and oriented to Augustine, next for combating scholasticism and furthering the study of Holy Scripture. In his reply to Scheurl on January 27, 1517, Luther accepted praise for Staupitz but rejected it for himself. In his May 18, 1517, letter to Johannes Lang, he said of the University of Wittenberg reform: "Our theology and St. Augustine are progressing well, and with God's help rule at our University. Aristotle is gradually tumbling from his throne."[7] The term "our theology" is still rather imprecise and as to content cannot suitably describe the uniqueness of the Wittenberg theology.

In the fall of 1517 events turned a somersault. Referring to Luther's *Disputation against Scholastic Theology* of September 4, 1517,[8] but still ignorant of the Ninety-five Theses of October 31, 1517, Scheurl wrote to him on November 3, 1517, praising him for holding the "fortress of right doctrine." Of particular interest are Scheurl's opening words in which he summarizes the efforts of Luther and the Wittenbergers, as viewed from Nuremberg: the task is "to restore the theology of Christ and to walk in his law."[9] According to Scheurl, then, the University of Wittenberg reform could be summed up in the concept of the "theology of Christ and Christ's law." The Nuremberg humanist had clearly coined this phrase in connection with Erasmus's *philosophia Christi*.[10] By adding the concept of "Christ's law," reference was to the ethics as well as the teaching of Christ.

In response to this letter, composed on December 11, 1517, Luther did not take a position on the concept Scheurl proposed,[11] thus neither accepting nor rejecting it. A few weeks later, however, he formed the concept *theologia crucis*, with the express intent of distancing Wittenberg's effort at renewing theology from the humanistic attempts of Erasmus, and by the "cross of Christ" of accenting what was central in Christian faith as seen at Wittenberg.

The *theologia crucis* took on precise formulation in Luther's theses for the *Heidelberg Disputation*.[12] Here the *theologia crucis* has an uneqivocally antischolastic sense. The nineteenth to the twenty-second conclusions read:

[5] WA *Br* 1 Nr. 32, 1-2.

[6] Ibid., line 6.

[7] "Letters," *LW*, vol. 48, p. 42. WA *Br* 1 Nr. 41, 8-9.

[8] *LW*, vol. 31, pp. 9-16. WA 1, 224-28.

[9] WA *Br* 1 Nr. 49: 1 f. "Ad Martinum Luder. Christi theologiam restavrare et in illius lege ambulare."

[10] On this subject see Cornelis Augustijn, *Erasmus von Rotterdam: Leben—Werk—Wirkung* (Munich: Beck, 1986), 66-81.

[11] *WA Br* 1, Nr. 54.

[12] The best edition has been produced by Helmar Junghans, in *Martin Luther: Studienausgabe*, ed. Hans-Ulrich Delius (Berlin: Evangelische Verlagsanstalt, 1979), 1:186-218. Literature: W. von Loewenich, *Luther's Theology of the Cross*, translated by Herbert J. A. Bouman (Minneapolis: Augsburg Publishing House, 1976); Karl Bauer, "Die Heidelberger Disputation Luthers," *ZKG* 21 (1901), 233-68, 299-329; Heinrich Bornkamm, "Die theologischen Thesen Luthers bei der Heidelberger Disputation 1518 und seine theologia

> That person does not deserve to be called a theologian
> who looks upon the invisible things of God as though
> they were clearly perceptible in those things which
> have actually happened [Rom. 1:20]. . . . He deserves to be
> called a theologian, however, who comprehends the
> visible and manifest things of God seen through
> suffering and the cross. . . . A theology of glory calls
> evil good and good evil. A theology of the cross calls
> the thing what it actually is. . . . That wisdom which sees
> the invisible things of God in works as perceived by
> man is completely puffed up, blinded, and hardened.[13]

The sharp contrast between the "theologian of glory" and the "theologian of the cross" is not fair to scholasticism as a whole nor even to the scholastic orientation Luther had come to know at Erfurt. It is a battle cry that in the dispute with Rome already underway was to give heightened expression to the disparate views on the knowledge of God and on the doctrine of sin and grace. At the same time, by putting the question concerning the knowledge of God, Luther singled out the problem of the connection between philosophy and theology. The "theology of glory" desires to know God on the basis of his creation. In such an attempt the *theologia crucis* sees the effort to arrive at God apart from sin and the divine judgment. For its part it holds solely to the cross, where God both hides and reveals himself. Use of the concepts *theologia gloriae* and *theologia crucis* thus helps to make the question of salvation the theme of theology. The statements concerning God's invisible and visible nature may well have been formed in remembrance of the Occamist distinction between the *potentia pactum Dei absoluta* and *potentia Dei ordinata,* but raise the distinction to a new level by allowing for the question of salvation. From this perspective the attempt at

---

crucis" (1969), in Bornkamm, *Luther: Gestalt und Wirkungen,* SVRG 188 (Gütersloh: Gerd Mohn, 1975), 130-46; Karl-Heinz zur Mühlen, "Die Heidelberger Disputation" (seminar report), in *Luther und die Theologie der Gegenwart: Referate und Berichte des Fünften Internationalen Kongresses für Lutherforschung Lund, Schweden,* 14-20. August 1977, ed. Leif Grane and Bernhard Lohse (Göttingen: Vandenhoeck & Ruprecht, 1980), 164-69; J. E. Vercruysse, "Gesetz und Liebe: Die Struktur der 'Heidelberger Disputation' Luthers (1518)" (1974), *LuJ* 48 (1981), 7-43; idem, "Luther's Theology of the Cross at the Time of the Heidelberg Disputation," *Gr.* 57 (1976), 523-48. In the last essay Vercruysse discusses all the passages in which the concept *theologia crucis* occurs. *Theologia crucis* and *theologus crucis* appear together in apparently only five passages coming mainly from the period around 1518. There are a few passages where Luther speaks in similar fashion of the "cross" as regards content; these appear mainly in the *Operationes in Psalmos* (Vercruysse, "Gesetz und Liebe," 524-26). On the *Heidelberg Disputation* see further Jared Wicks, *Luther's Reform: Studies on Conversion and the Church,* VIEG Beih. 35 (Mainz: P. von Zabern, 1992), passim.

[13] *LW,* vol. 1, pp. 52-53. The Latin text edited by Junghans, 207, 26-209, 8; *WA* 1, 361, 32-362, 36 Concl. 19-22: "Non ille digne Theologus dicitur, qui inuisibilia Dei, per ea, quae facta sunt, intellecta conspicit . . . Sed quo uisibilia et posteriora Dei per passiones (et) crucem conspecta intelligit. . . . Theologus gloriae dicit, Malum bonum, (et) bonum malum, Theologus crucis dicit, id quod res est. . . Sapientia illa, quae inuisibilia Dei, operibus intellecta conspicit, omnino inflat, excaecat (et) indurat."

a philosophical knowledge of God is subjected to biting criticism. Even in its treatment of such central questions as the law, however, Luther's *theologia crucis* had to lead to totally new statements.

In his *Operationes in Psalmos* Luther summarized in trenchant formulas the significance of the cross for the Wittenberg theology he represented. There we read: "CRUX sola est nostra theologia,"[14] or "CRUX probat omnia,"[15] which means that "the cross puts everything to the test," "preserves everything," or, "only the cross is judge and witness to the truth."[16]

As noted, these exaggerated statements sprang from a situation of conflict and are to be understood on that basis. Neither in the period when Luther formulated them nor in later years could they reduce the complexity of questions with which theology must deal.

Despite all this, the "theology of the cross" may not be seen, say, in opposition to a theology of the resurrection. When Luther sets forth the cross so sharply, he does so in contrast to scholasticism, which he reproaches for ignoring it. For him, however, the resurrection is inseparably bound with the cross.[17]

Of late the opinion has to some extent been held that the exaggerated theses of the *Heidelberg Disputation* ultimately represent a "theology of conversion," or, that where Luther is concerned, we must finally speak of a "theology of piety."[18] Such a concept is justified insofar as for Luther the relation to piety was obviously present in all his theological work. On the other hand, use of this concept runs the risk of inadmissibly narrowing Luther's new theological beginnings to a renewal of piety, and thus of suppressing his profoundly penetrating criticism of scholastic theology, at least as he and the Reformation viewed it. Luther's aim in the *Heidelberg Disputation* was not to supplement scholastic theology but to attack it and accent the genuine theological task.

"KNOWLEDGE OF GOD AND MAN"

In his 1532 lecture on Psalm 51:2, Luther gives a definition of theology linked to the older theology but that sharply expresses the new Reformation aim: "Knowledge of

---

[14] *AWA* 2, 319, 3. On this topic see *AWA* 1, 146.

[15] *AWA* 2, 325, 1.

[16] *AWA* 2, 341, 15: "crux ipsa sola iudex est testisque veritatis."

[17] See J. Vercruysse, "Gesetz und Liebe," 543-44: "For Luther a theology of resurrection is the intrinsic complement of a theology of the cross."

[18] The concept of a "theology of piety" was coined by Berndt Hamm, and in fact with reference to Johann Paltz: Hamm, *Frömmigkeitstheologie am Anfang des 16. Jahrhunderts: Studien zu Johannes von Paltz und seinem Umkreis,* BHTh 65 (Tübingen: Mohr, 1982); see also idem, "Frömmigkeit als Gegenstand theologiesgeschichtlicher Forschung: Methodisch-historische Überlegungen am Beispiel von Spätmittelalter und Reformation," *ZThK* 74 (1977), 464-97. Jared Wicks has adopted this concept in relation to Luther and often refers to his "theology-for-piety" or theology oriented to conversion; see Wicks, *Luther's Reform,* e.g., 146-47, 154.

God and man is divine wisdom, and in the real sense theological. It is such knowledge of God and man as is related to the justifying God and to sinful man, so that in the real sense the subject of theology is guilty and lost man and the justifying and redeeming God. What is inquired into apart from this question and subject is error and vanity in theology."[19]

Augustine first made clear that at issue in theology is the knowledge of God and humanity. In his *Soliloquies* we read: "Deum et animam scire cupio. Nihilne plus? nihil omnino" ("I want to know God and the soul. Nothing else? No, nothing else").[20] Although the Middle Ages often ignored this definition of the task and substituted other reflections, the essence of the Augustinian view was retained particularly by Bernard and the German mystics.[21] In addition, Augustine and a number of medieval theologians had the substance of the question of salvation in view. When dealing with the late Middle Ages, special note should be taken of Gerson, who, when all is said and done, advocated a pastoral theology.[22]

It is also a fact that scholasticism had developed a view of theology that, or so it at least appears, is to a great extent abstracted from the question of salvation and discussed the problem of the knowledge of God without taking up the themes of sin and guilt. Thomas could say: "The highest desire (*iucundissimum*) is to be able to behold something of the loftiest things in tiny and weak reflection."[23] This does not at all make clear whether, as Luther says, God can be known only on the cross, though he veils himself there also. On the whole, in late scholasticism such concentration on the cross and the question of salvation had no support.

With his definition of theology, Luther joined hands not with scholasticism but with Augustine and theologians in the Augustinian tradition. In doing so he put his

[19] WA 40 II, 327, 11-328, 3: "Cognitio dei et hominis est sapientia divina et proprie theologica, Et ita cognitio dei et hominis, ut referatur tandem ad deum iustificantem et hominem peccatorem, ut proprie sit subiectum Theologiae homo reus et perditus et deus iustificans vel salvator. Quicquid extra istud argumentum vel subjectum quaeritur, hoc plane est error et vanitas in Theologia." Cf. *LW*, vol. 12, p. 311. In the printed edition of 1538 furnished by Veit Dietrich—see WA 40 II, 327, 17-328, 20—this terse definition of theology has been altered by adding ideas from *The Disputation Concerning Man*, in *LW*, vol. 34, pp. 137-44; WA 39, I, 175-80, as well as by adopting a few specifically Melanchthonian ideas. On Dietrich's editorial activity see Matthias U. Schlicht, *Luthers Vorlesung über Psalm 90: Überlieferung und Theologie*, FKDG 55 (Göttingen: Vandenhoeck & Ruprecht, 1994).

[20] *Solil.* 1.2.7; in both books of the *Soliloquies,* this theme appears in ever-new variations.

[21] On this subject see the terse remarks by R. Weier, *Das Theologieverständnis Martin Luthers*, concerning various medieval theologians. For a comparison between Thomas and Luther see Otto H. Pesch, "Existentielle und sapientale Theologie: Hermeneutische Erwägungen zur systematisch-theologischen Konfrontation zwischen Luther und Thomas von Aquin," *ThLZ* 92 (1967), 731-42.

[22] See Christoph Burger, *Aedificatio, Fructus, Utilitas: Johannes Gerson als Professor der Theologie und Kanzler der Universität Paris*, BHTh 70 (Tübingen: Mohr, 1986); Mark S. Burrows, *Jean Gerson and 'De Consolatione Theologiae' (1418): The Consolation of a Biblical and Reforming Theology for a Disordered Age*, BHTh 78 (Tübingen: Mohr, 1991).

[23] *Summa contra Gentiles* I 8 (n. 49). On this subject see Otto Hermann Pesch, *Thomas von Aquin: Grenze und Grösse mittelalterlicher Theologie. Eine Einführung* (Mainz: Matthias-Grünewald Verlag, 1988), 46.

own mark on the definition very early on. In his first lecture on the Psalms he writes: "No one arrives at a knowledge of the Godhead if he is not first brought low and has descended to a knowledge of himself. For there he also arrives at a knowledge of God."[24] Here the existential character of the knowledge of God is clearly expressed. In this fashion, Luther distances himself from attempts at broaching the question of the knowledge of God on the basis of reason alone.

Luther's 1532 definition of the subject of theology takes up his earlier definitions. It also takes up the tradition in likewise totally independent fashion. For him too, knowledge of God and the self is the task of theology. According to him, such knowledge can be dealt with only in connection with the doctrine of justification. At the same time, the doctrine of justification is not something added to the question of the knowledge of God and the self. It must be taken up at the outset in thematizing such knowledge, if it is to be at all appropriately discussed. The doctrine of justification is ultimately the criterion respecting the propriety of dealing with the knowledge of God and the self.[25] Knowledge of God and the self are to be gained only in mutual relation. It is not true that for Luther knowledge of self, say, would first be necessary in order from it to arrive at knowledge of God.[26] Rather, knowledge of self is attained together with knowledge of God, just as true knowledge of self is at the same time knowledge of God.

---

[24] WA 55 II 1, 2, 137, 8-11. See G. Ebeling, *Lutherstudien*, 1:221.

[25] See Ebeling, *Lutherstudien*, 1:265.

[26] Veit Dietrich reshaped Luther's statements in this form: WA 40 II, 328, 30-33: "Ergo necessaria haec Theologica cognitio est, ut homo se cognoscat, hoc est, ut sciat, sentiat et experiatur, quod sit reus peccati et addictus mori, Deinde etiam, ut contrarium sciat et experiatur, quod Deus sit iustificator et redemptor talis hominis, qui sic se cognoscit." ("Therefore, this theological knowledge is necessary, that a man is aware of himself, that is, that he knows, feels, and experiences that he is enslaved to sin and given up to death, and second, that he knows and experiences the contrary, that God is the justifier and redeemer of such a man who is thus aware of himself.") The "deinde" ("second") involves a systematizing here that Luther himself specifically avoided.

PART TWO

*Luther's Theology
in Its Historical Development*

Chapter 6

BASIC THEOLOGICAL IDEAS IN LUTHER'S MARGINAL NOTES ON AUGUSTINE AND PETER LOMBARD (1509/1510)

THE TRADITIONAL AND THE NEW: THE VIEW OF SIN

Apart from a few letters from Luther's early years after 1501, his first coherent written efforts date from 1509/1510. They involve marginal notes on the numerous writings of Augustine as well as on Peter Lombard's (ca. 1100-1160) great dogmatic work: *The Four Books of the Sentences*. Soon after its composition this work had already caught on as a foundational text, and in Luther's time served as "textbook." Many of the great scholastics of the High and late Middle Ages wrote commentaries on Lombard's *Sentences*. For centuries the fact that Lombard largely followed Augustinian tradition but also cautiously attempted to systematize the dogmatic material secured to his dogmatics a preeminence in all the theological schools. Only the disputes of the sixteenth century gradually pushed this work aside and replaced it with textbooks oriented to theological controversy.

After his stay in the Erfurt cloister following his entry into the monastery, Luther was transferred to the cloister at Wittenberg in 1508. He was to finish his theological studies there, but was also to lecture on Aristotle's *Nicomachean Ethics*. On March 9, 1509, he received the degree of *Baccalaureus Biblicus* at Wittenberg. As early as in the fall of 1509 he became a *Baccalaureus Sententiarius*. When he was returned to the Erfurt cloister that fall, he had to lecture on Lombard's *Sentences*, in preparation for which he made marginal notes. His notes on the voluminous writings of Augustine, however, resulted more from intense occupation with that church father, and most probably on his own initiative.

These various notes require careful evaluation. In each instance the occasion is a specific statement in the text to be commented on, thus without coherent exposition. Completeness is also clearly lacking in the smaller contexts. Nevertheless, these marginal notes allow us to trace those first new impulses in Luther, obviously intimately linked to traditional views. In the research of the last decades, earlier attempts at finding allusions in these notes to essential Reformation views have been quite rightly abandoned. On the other hand, there is no doubt that in some passages new views are set forth that can no longer be integrated into one of the various late medieval school trends. In this period Luther evidently began to turn away from scholasticism.

Taken together, these marginal notes indicate that Luther was still a theologian shaped by Occamism. For example, he held fast to the freedom of the will.[1] Or in a longer statement on the topic of original sin, he wrote: "Original sin is the tinder of actual sin (*fomes peccati scilicet actualis*), it is the law of the flesh, the law of the members, it is desire (*concupiscentia*), the tyrant, the weakness of nature, that is, the absence of original righteousness (*carentia iustitiae originalis*)."[2] Luther thus adopted current definitions.[3]

Precisely in the midst of traditional definitions new impulses appear. First, Luther saw the difference between the definition of *concupiscentia* that he initially adopted and the view of Augustine. He conceded that by "desire" Augustine clearly understood guilt, but when Luther construed "tinder" as the remainder of original sin, he was able to ignore the aspect of guilt. Next, Luther expressed his first misgivings over the propriety of Lombard's definition that original sin is the "tinder, the weakness of nature, the tyrant." Finally, he compared these scholastic definitions with Paul's habit of referring to the "flesh" that lusts against the Spirit, and regarded this language as truly appropriate, while scholastic definitions merely paraphrase the condition tersely summarized by Paul.[4]

At this point, Luther's reflections had still not reached their conclusion. On the one hand, he sought to retain the traditional scholastic definitions of sin and to harmonize them with Augustine. On the other, he began to see that Augustine obviously differed from scholasticism in his teaching concerning the will and sin. Above all, Paul's view of sin was gaining in significance. It appears that his study of Augustine

---

[1] *WA* 9, 31, 9-10: "voluntas potest aliquid velle absolute i.e. quia est libera" ("The will is able to will something absolutely, that is, because it is free").

[2] *WA* 9, 73, 21-27.

[3] See also *WA* 9, 75, 11-13, where Luther said that original sin is of course removed in baptism, but that a tinder (*fomes*) remains.

[4] *WA* 9, 75, 11-76, 17.

led him to the study of Paul. The utterances of Paul, Augustine, and Lombard read after the fashion of an Occamist could no longer be harmonized. At the same time, Luther arrived at impulses toward a more radical view of sin. From this perspective he attacked the scholastic notion of a *habitus*, of a "quality" or "condition" that perfects the capacity for doing good.[5] Here too Luther was beginning to distance himself from traditional notions. Finally, in his idea of the human *ratio* a fresh new impulse was emerging: now the *ratio* was being viewed existentially within the context of a total anthropology, not merely as a purely intellectual capacity.

Faith and Discipleship

In Luther's view of faith what is traditional and what is new appear side by side without any balance being achieved between the two. For example, along with Gabriel Biel, Luther could speak of the three basic truths to which the laity must unconditionally hold: that God exists, that he is the "Requiter" (*remunerator*), and that he is "Redeemer" (*redemptor*).[6] Elsewhere he could name the truths of faith alongside each other as if they had to do with dogmas, thus without any ascertainable breakthrough.

Still, there were many new accents. For example, Luther pointed to the fact that Jesus' word, "I am the resurrection and the life" (John 11:25), was usually understood in terms of his divine nature, but that we must finally see it as referring to his humanity. Then he said: "Faith means to believe in Jesus' humanity, given us in this life as our life and salvation. For he himself, through faith in his incarnation, is our life, our righteousness and our resurrection."[7] Here Luther was clearly overcoming the then current idea of faith as holding something to be true. Contrariwise, as he said, faith effects life and salvation here and now. It is the Incarnate One who is our salvation and who has redeemed us by his suffering and death. Since at this point Luther was clearly connecting the incarnation and faith, what is emerging is the substance of an idea that cannot as yet be found in the marginal notes, that is, the category of hiddenness: in the hiddenness of the incarnate Christ God is present; in the hiddenness of the cross our salvation is effected, and to this hiddenness of the divine saving activity corresponds the hiddenness or nondemonstrability of faith.[8]

Luther's marginal note on Augustine's *De trinitate* 4.3 is of particular significance. Here Augustine had described Christ as *sacramentum et exemplum* (mystery or "sacrament" and example). In rather loose fashion he had explained that Christ's death and resurrection have meaning for our twofold death and resurrection: We

[5] See R. Schwarz, *Fides, Spes und Caritas beim jungen Luther under besonderer Berücksichtigung der mittelalterlichen Tradition,* AKG 34 (Berlin: de Gruyter, 1962), 35-40. On this subject see Martin Anton Schmidt, *HdBDThG,* 1:666, and elsewhere.

[6] *WA* 9, 92, 38-93, 7.

[7] *WA* 9, 17, 1-19, quotation in 12-15.

[8] On this subject see W. Jetter, *Die Taufe beim jungen Luther,* BHTh 18 (Tübingen: Mohr, 1954), 136-42.

must die to sin and rise to new life. Until our bodily resurrection we must undergo suffering and death as punishment for sin. When Paul says (Rom. 6:6) that the old man in us was crucified together [with him], he has in mind the sufferings of repentance and the pains of continence.

Luther tersely summarized and sharpened the longer exposition: "The crucifixion is a '*sacramentum*' because it thus signifies the cross of repentance in which the soul dies to sin; it is '*exemplum*,' because it summons [us] to offer our body to death or to the cross on behalf of the truth."[9] Iserloh's comment at this juncture is correct: "The crucifixion of Christ is a sacrament. It is an event that does not have its termination in itself but is a sign, that is, it points toward an event in the person affected by it."[10] The pair of concepts, "sacramentum et exemplum," most closely connect faith and discipleship.

Luther did not merely employ this Augustinian pair in his early years, say, in terms of a pre-Reformation theology.[11] The pair was present throughout his life, even in his late great lectures. Only later, in a few table talks, was there something of a criticism of the pair.[12] What is important here is that discipleship consists precisely in "offering oneself to the cross," not in supplementing the sacramental appropriation of salvation through one's own works. At this important point, Luther not only had adopted central ideas from Augustine, but very early had given them precision in his own way.

Criticism of Theology and Church

In these early marginal notes Luther displayed a comprehensive and remarkable criticism of certain shapes and trends in theology and church. The criticism is no less important than the new impulses in his theology. It makes clear that he was not prepared simply to continue in the current mode. Scarcely one area of the then contemporary theology and church was free from attack.

For example, Luther repeatedly attacked the *philosophi,* evidently having in mind the extensive significance of Aristotelian philosophy for scholastic theology.[13] Aristotle was a "chatterbox." As for statements about "happiness," Augustine

---

[9] *WA* 9, 18, 19-22: "Crucifixio Christi est sacramentum, quia significat sic crucem poenitentiae in qua moritur anima peccato; est Exemplum, quia hortatur pro veritate corpus morti offerre vel cruci." On this see Jetter, *Die Taufe beim jungen Luther,* 142-59; R. Schwarz, *Fides, Spes und Caritas,* 69-72; Erwin Iserloh, "Sacramentum et Exemplum: Ein augustinisches Thema lutherischer Theologie" (1965), in Iserloh, *Kirche—Ereignis und Institution: Aufsätze und Vorträge,* vol. 2: *Geschichte und Theologie der Reformation, RGST* Suppl. 3/1-2 (Münster: Aschendorff, 1985), 107-24.

[10] Erwin Iserloh, *Gnade und Eucharistie in der philosophischen Theologie des Wilhelm von Ockham: Ihre Bedeutung für die Ursachen der Reformation,* VIEG 8 (Wiesbaden: Steiner, 1956), 110.

[11] Ernst Bizer interprets the passage in this way: "Die Entdeckung des Sakraments durch Luther," *EvTh* 17 (1957), 64-90, esp. 66-69.

[12] Iserloh has furnished the evidence for this, *Gnade und Eucharistie,* 123-24.

[13] See also the first marginal note on Augustine: *WA* 9, 5, 2-3.

was preferable by far. Aristotle's defenders tried in vain to bring their master in agreement with the true faith.[14] Luther's criticism was not of Aristotelian philosophy as such but of its influence on theology. On his view, philosophy had birthed many monstrosities and thus created insoluble problems.[15]

Luther's criticism was also turned toward the approved heads of the schools of Franciscan theology, and in which he himself had been trained. Thus he attacked Duns Scotus, whom he all but charged with heresy,[16] or Gabriel Biel,[17] or the *moderni* in general, that is, the Occamists.[18] Attack may also be directed toward almost all the commentators on the master of the *Sentences*.[19] Augustine's statement that Stoics rejoice over nothing so much as new ideas induced Luther to fulminate against the "philosophers" of his time, among whom the Stoics appear to be most numerous, contending over mere concepts.[20] Nothing seems incomprehensible to the "philosophers."[21] For Luther, however, theology is heaven, humanity is earth, and human speculations are smoke.[22] He insisted that theological tenets, such as the doctrine of the Trinity,[23] cannot be proved through rational deduction. Because the Holy Spirit says it is so, it must be accepted as true.[24] As such it has pleased God through foolishness to save those who believe, so as to render foolish the wisdom of the world.[25]

To some extent, these statements betray Luther's origin in Occamist tradition, which had already contained considerable criticism of Aristotle and his influence on theology, as well as of the mingling of philosophy and theology.[26] Yet Luther's criticism differs not only through its greater radicality,[27] but also and chiefly through its return to biblical language and thought.

Luther engaged in comprehensive criticism not only of the theology of his day but also of the church and of particular aspects of church life. He reproached his contemporaries for holding the truth down in superstition, that is, in foolish and idle

---

[14] *WA* 9, 23, 6-11.

[15] *WA* 9, 57, 4-16.

[16] *WA* 9, 43, 21-27; see 16, 7. See Lohse, *Ratio und Fides*, 25, n. 11.

[17] *WA* 9, 74, 8-11.

[18] *WA* 9, 7, 32.

[19] *WA* 9, 52, 12-13.

[20] *De civitate Dei* 9.4.1. *WA* 9, 24, 24-26. See 16, 2-3; 25, 21-23.

[21] *WA* 9, 47, 25-28.

[22] *WA* 9, 65, 14-16.

[23] *WA* 9, 17, 1-19.

[24] *WA* 9, 34, 35-35, 5.

[25] *WA* 9, 56, 31-33.

[26] See Bengt Hägglund, *Theologie und Philosophie bei Luther und in der occamistischen Tradition: Luthers Stellung zur Theorie von der doppelten Wahrheit,* Lunds Universitets Årsskrift N.F. 1, 51/4 (Lund: Gleerup, 1955).

[27] Wicks, *Luther's Reform,* 21, and elsewhere, states that Luther often expressed himself "in terms of opposed totalities." This is correct as such, but it must be noted that in so doing Luther was adopting essential aspects of biblical thought as appear especially in Paul.

observatio, or in a superfluous, indeed, false, *religio,* like stupid old wives. While they wanted to be ever so "religious," they were superstitious, as is evident in the sacrament of extreme unction.[28] At this point as well as at many others in his marginal notes, Luther's criticism could be interpreted of the *Observantes,* that is, of those in his own order who adhered to strict observance of the rules, thus not in any general terms.[29] He did not at all intend to question the type of observance to which he pledged himself. He did object, however, that the effort on behalf of strict obedience to the order, important though it may be, could easily lead to self-righteousness, or at least to an externalizing of the discipline of the order. Those who were serious about their monasticism were thus in particular danger.

In general, it should be said of Luther's theological position in this early period that the texts, when read by themselves, do not yet allow us to detect a later Reformation theology. Most importantly, they contain no Reformation doctrine of justification. Yet it is clear that at several important points Luther was abandoning the framework of late medieval Occamist theology, above all its concept of sin. It is particularly against the Occamist definition of the relation between philosophy and theology that Luther was striking out on his own, and in doing so gleaned support from Augustine but also from the biblical statements. Equally significant is his comprehensive criticism of certain aspects in the church, including his own monastic form of existence. Deeper theological foundation for this criticism was of course still lacking.

[28] *WA* 9, 30, 23-32.
[29] On this subject see Lohse, *Mönchtum und Reformation,* 221-24.

Chapter 7

EARLY REFORMATION THEOLOGY IN THE FIRST PSALMS LECTURE (1513-1515)

THE NEW HERMENEUTIC

Compared with the marginal notes of 1509/1510, the first Psalms lecture reflects a totally different theological climate. The reason for this is first of all that we are dealing here with Luther's first exegetical lecture, no longer with mere criticisms or comments on the texts of others. In addition, the first Psalms lecture makes clear that while his interpretation to a great extent leaned on earlier expositions, of which Augustine's *Ennarationes in Psalmos* have the lion's share, in a hermeneutical respect Luther was going his own way. It would be an exaggeration to speak of a Scripture principle in those first Psalms lectures, but what is striking is the extraordinary earnestness with which he aimed at the christological sense of the psalm texts.

Luther still followed the traditional style of commentary, retained till 1518, thus the subdivision of glosses between the lines and in the margins, as well as the more detailed scholia. In many passages he also referred to the fourfold sense of Scripture, to the distinction between the *sensus literalis, allegoricus, tropologicus* or *moralis*, and the *sensus anagogicus*.[1] More significant than this retention of traditional methods is the concern for the christological sense of the text as well as for the distinction between Spirit and letter. To be sure, traditional methods of exposition were used here, but they were given new content.

---

[1] In the example of "Jerusalem" the fourfold meaning of Scripture involves literally the city, allegorically the church, tropologically the believers, and anagogically the heavenly Jerusalem.

More important than Luther's accenting of the fourfold sense is his christological exposition. Here he proceeded with more consistency than the tradition by interpreting christologically not only the statements in the Psalter dealing with majesty but also with humility.[2] In addition, the distinction between "spiritual" and "literal" is paving the way toward a differentiation between *coram Deo* and *coram mundo,* a differentiation that was later so central. One and the same word can be "letter," thus divine judgment. Spiritually interpreted, it can also be a word of grace for "the spirit is concealed in the letter."[3]

The significance of Scripture for Luther is particularly evident in this word: "The strength of Scripture is this, that it is not changed into him who studies it, but that it transforms its lover into itself and its strengths. . . . Because you will not change me into what you are . . . but you will be changed into what I am."[4]

Here Luther seized on an old Augustinian idea that in the meantime had undergone reinterpretation. In *Confessions* 7.10.16, Augustine had written that with the eye of the soul he saw the unchangeable light of truth and, returned to the alien land of the disfigured image, heard God's voice from a distant height: "I am the bread of the strong: grow, and you will eat me. And you will not change me into you as food for your flesh, but you will be changed into me." In the Middle Ages this word had been referred to the Eucharist.[5]

Luther interpreted the passage of the scriptural Word, thus indicating the significance of the biblical Word for him. It may be that he received some impulse toward this primacy of the Word from humanism.[6] More probably, he owed the impulse to Augustine's understanding.[7] Nevertheless, what is decisive is that this conception of the Word was independently developed by Luther in his first lecture.

The new hermeneutic appears in its essential features as early as in Luther's preface. If earlier commentators had dealt with questions of introduction and hermeneutics in their forewords, Luther's superscription reads: "Foreword of Jesus Christ." A few quotations from Scripture intend to show that Christ is the sole key

[2] This has been indicated chiefly by Vogelsang, *Die Anfänge Luthers Christologie,* esp. on pp. 88-98.

[3] *LW,* vol. 10, p. 212. *WA* 3, 256, 28-29 (scholia on Ps. 44:2): "Spiritus enim latet in litera, que est verbum non bonum, quia lex ire. Sed spiritus est verbum bonum, quia verbum gratie." Here and in what follows the Vulgate numbering furnishes the basis, a numbering also retained in the *WA.*

[4] *LW,* vol. 10, pp. 332-33. *WA* 3, 397, 9-11, 15-16 (scholia on Ps. 67:14) "Scripture virtus esthec, quod non mutatur in eum, qui eam studet, sed transmutat suum amatorem in sese ac suas virtutes. . . . Quia non tu me mutabis in te . . . , sed tu mutaberis in me."

[5] On the history of the exposition of this passage see Schwarz, *Vorgeschichte der reformatorischen Busstheologie,* AKG 41 (Berlin: de Gruyter, 1968), 221; Ebeling, *Die Anfänge von Luthers Hermeneutik,* 3.

[6] So Junghans, *Der junge Luther und die Humanisten,* 274-87.

[7] On Augustine's understanding of the Word see Othmar Perler, *Der Nus bei Plotin und das Verbum bei Augustinus als vorbildliche Ursache: Vergleichende Untersuchung* (diss., University of Freiburg, 1931); Joachim Ritter, *Mundus intelligibilis: Eine Untersuchung zur Aufnahme und Umwandlung der neuplatonischen Ontologie bei Augustinus* (Frankfurt: Vittorio Klostermann, 1937); Alfred Schindler, *Wort und Analogie in Augustins Trinitätslehre,* HUTh 4 (Tübingen: Mohr, 1965).

to understanding the Psalter.[8] Luther then set up this principle: "Whatever is said literally of the Lord Jesus Christ in his person must be understood allegorically of the help that is like him, and of the church conformed to him in everything. It must also be understood tropologically of every spiritual and inner person: in opposition to the flesh and outer person."[9]

This christological exposition of the Psalms is not at all new. Luther was following the entire tradition. What is new, however, is the way in which he carried it through. The thought that God acts "hiddenly beneath his opposite," so that judgment and righteousness are two aspects of God's activity, led to a new understanding of the cross of Christ. By means of the tropological method Luther could transfer statements about Christ crucified to the Christian under attack.[10] He thus approximated an existential interpretation.[11] Despite this, he always maintained the distinction between Christ and the Christian.[12] Such statements may, of course, not be systematized. However much Luther used existential language in his preface as well as in other passages, other, more markedly traditional statements that appear alongside that inhibit any attempt to draw a finished christological portrait for the Luther of the first Psalms lecture. Though actually quite seldom, Luther could nonetheless hark back to dogmatic statements on the doctrine of the two natures or the Trinity. He could also make great headway with the tropological method. What is unique in the first Psalms lecture is this open-ended, unfinished juxtaposition of various impulses, all pointing to a "process of fermentation" in Luther's theology during this period.

THE CONCEPT OF SIN

In the first Psalms lecture, Luther's statements about sin are clearly more and more radical than in the marginal notes of 1509/1510. This may be due in part to the fact that he had to interpret texts that often contain confessions of sin. Indeed, Lombard's *Sentences* gave ample occasion to comment on the systematic treatment of the concept of sin. But in his first Psalms lecture, chiefly through understanding gleaned from Paul and Augustine, Luther quite clearly went beyond 1509/1510.

In his exposition of Psalm 51 Luther set up four theses:

First. All men are in sin before God and commit sin, that is, they are sinners in fact.
Second. To this God Himself bore witness through the prophets and established the

---

[8] WA 55, I, 6-10; on this subject see Ebeling, "Luthers Psalterdruck vom Jahre 1513," 109-31, esp. 111.

[9] WA 55, I, 8, 8-11.

[10] LW, vol. 10, p. 139. WA 3, 167, 20-28; 171, 19-24; see Vogelsang, *Die Anfänge von Luthers Christologie*, 91-92.

[11] On this subject see A. Brandenburg, *Gericht und Evangelium: Zur Worttheologie in Luthers erster Psalmenvorlesung*, KKTS 4 (Paderborn: Bonifacius Druckerei, 1960).

[12] See Lohse, "Luthers Christologie im Ablasstreit" (1960), in *Evangelium in der Geschichte*, 287-99.

same at last by the suffering of Christ, for it is on account of the sin of men that He made Him suffer and die. Third. God is not justified in Himself, but in His words and in us. Fourth. We become sinners then when we acknowledge ourselves to be such, for such we are before God.[13]

The sin "before God" (*coram Deo*) is the authentic, spiritual sin, and cannot be merely identified with transgression of the Mosaic law. Luther identified this genuine, hidden sin in Psalm 51 with original sin. He was aware that to an extent his exposition was opposed to traditional interpretation, but for his part appealed to Paul in Romans 3:4: "But God is true, and every man is a liar, as it is written, 'That Thou mayest be justified in Thy words, and mayest overcome when Thou art judged.'"[14] Here, then, the intensification of the concept of sin in opposition to the tradition was based on an appeal to Paul. This statement of course implies that in the period between the marginal notes and the first Psalms lecture Luther must have intensively studied Paul and particularly Romans.

Now the knowledge of sin necessarily leads to its confession before God. A merely theoretical knowledge of sin would have no value, would be no real knowledge of sin. Rather, knowledge and confession of sin are merely two sides of one and the same event. In addition, the knowledge and confession of sin are directly expressed in the "righteousness of God," by which Luther meant that the sinner justifies God and his judgment. In the exposition of Psalm 51, therefore, Luther set up this basic principle: "Hence these things conflict with each other: Denying that one has sin, or not confessing it—and justifying God. Justifying oneself before God—and glorifying God. Therefore God is not justified by anyone except the one who accuses and condemns and judges himself."[15]

However deepened the concept of sin here, Luther's exposition of Psalm 51 still betrayed his origins in the Occamist Erfurt school:

"Behold, I was conceived in iniquity" (v. 6): Therefore it is true that before Thee I am a sinner and have sinned, so that Thou only mayest be glorious in righteousness and Thou alone mayest be justified, when all of us are sinners." It is indeed true. For we are still unrighteous and unworthy before God, so that whatever we can do is nothing before him. Yes, even faith and grace, through which we are today justified, would not of themselves justify us if God's covenant (*pactum Dei*) did not do it. It is precisely for this reason that we are saved: He made a testament (*Testamentum*) and covenant (*Pactum*) with us that whoever believes and is baptized shall be saved.[16]

---

[13] *LW,* vol. 10, p. 235. *WA* 3, 287, 32-288, 7 (scholia on Ps. 50:6). On this subject see Schwarz, *Vorgeschichte der reformatorischen Busstheologie,* 230-54.

[14] *LW,* vol. 10, p. 235. *WA* 3, 287, 20-27.

[15] *LW,* vol. 10, p. 236. *WA* 3, 288, 27-31.

[16] *LW,* vol. 10, pp. 236-37. *WA* 3, 288, 38-289, 4.

The concepts *testamentum* and *pactum* are typical of Occamist theology. They are linked to the distinction between God's *potentia absoluta* and *potentia ordinata*,[17] and intend to express God's covenant freely entered into. Luther adopted these concepts so important in Occamism but without recourse to the two *potentiae*. His deepened concept of sin would necessarily have inhibited the uncritical retention of such terms, since he could no longer have said that Adam's sin affects generations to follow due solely to the divine *acceptatio*. Later Luther adopted and supplied with new content concepts appropriated from Occamism, chiefly in his teaching on the sacraments.

Next, the concept of desire (*concupiscentia*) is keener in Luther's first Psalms lecture than in his marginal notes. The concept, much used in monasticism, may still denote fleshly lusts, as in Augustine above all. In harmony with Lombard, Luther could also state that the term denotes the "sickness of nature" that "severely imprisons and binds" the soul just coming to life, and he appealed expressly to Paul in Romans 7:23.[18] As a rule, however, when he speaks of *concupiscentia*, he has in mind sin in a quite radical sense, the "sin against the Holy Spirit" or unbelief.[19] In general, *concupiscentia* denotes "confusion of the will," or the "I will," by which humans oppose God. Accordingly, persons by their own powers cannot wage war against *concupiscentia*. They are in need of grace.[20] Luther thus distanced himself from the Occamist understanding of sin and *concupiscentia*, though in the first Psalms lecture he did not explicitly attack Occamism on this point.

THE CONCEPT OF GRACE

Luther's understanding of grace differs more markedly from scholastic theology than does his concept of sin. What is striking is that he made little use of the terminology developed to such an extraordinary degree in scholasticism, with its numerous distinctions regarding the doctrine of grace. Luther rather kept to the utterances of the Psalter without systematizing them in any way, or he developed a concept of grace totally coherent with his understanding of sin and repentance. That is, statements of the knowledge and confession of sin, or of the acceptance of divine judgment, determine the ideas about grace. What is characteristic in all this is, for example, Luther's statement that "grace and the righteousness of God are all the more rich in us (just as there is much transgression), when we judge that we have

---

[17] See above, pp. 18-22. On a few aspects of the concept of testamentum in Biel see Heiko A. Oberman, *Spätscholastik und Reformation*, vol. 1: *Der Herbst der mittelalterlichen Theologie* (Zurich: Evverlag, 1965), 253-56; Berndt Hamm, *Promissio, Pactum, Ordinatio: Freiheit und Selbstbindung Gottes in der scholastischen Gotteslehre*, BHTh 54 (Tübingen: Mohr, 1977).

[18] *WA* 55 I, 718-19.

[19] *WA* 55 II 1, 4, 2-5, 1; 3, 423, 19-25. See Bernhard Lohse, *Mönchtum und Reformation: Luthers Auseinandersetzung mit dem Mönchsideal des Mittelalters*, FKDG 12 (Göttingen: Vandenhoeck & Ruprecht, 1963), 235-38.

[20] *WA* 55 II 1, 7, 1-6.

less of righteousness. The more we condemn, confound, and curse ourselves, the more richly the grace of God flows into us (*influit*)."[21] The concept *influit* might suggest sacramental grace, but that is quite improbable given the context. The term is clearly to be understood in a merely general sense.

There are many similar statements in the first Psalms lecture, where the extent of Luther's reference to Pauline concepts is surprising. For example, he said that by faith in Christ sins are forgiven.[22] The statement in Psalm 32:2: "Blessed is the man to whom the Lord does not impute (*imputat*) sin," gave him occasion to remark: "This means that whoever is righteous, to whom God reckons righteousness (*reputat*) as He did to Abraham, according to the apostle (cf. Rom. 4:3), to such a one He does not impute sin, because he reckons righteousness to him."[23] What is of interest here first is the use of the concepts *imputare* and *reputare*, then again the interpretation of the Psalms with the aid of Paul (cf. Rom. 4:3-8). The concepts were known to Luther from his Occamist training. Here, however, he no longer used them in terms of the Occamist idea of *acceptatio* or *non-acceptatio*, but in the Pauline sense.

Extraordinarily informative for the theology of the first Psalms lecture are statements that have the doctrine of grace for their content but which in form refer to the *solus Christus*. For example, Luther could say: "The heretics, however, do the same thing the Pharisees did: For though they believe that sins are removed through Christ alone, and though they believe in Him, yet because they do not have Him truly, in that they uphold His plan, they remain in sins."[24] The phrase *solus Christus* is not yet being used here in a sense critical of the church, of certain aspects of current sacramental doctrine and practice, or of certain forms of piety. What is striking is the naturalness with which Luther urged the *solus Christus* as cause and ground of the forgiveness of sins.

At times, Luther gave special emphasis to the effect of Christ's saving work as liberating the conscience. On one occasion he wrote: "Therefore Christ's coming is our goodness, for He has taken away, first from our conscience, the punishments which are our evils, and then He will also remove them from the body, and so our goodness will be perfect."[25] Or he accented "justifying grace." Thus in the exposition of Psalm 110:4 ("He is a merciful and gracious Lord") he stated: "'Merciful' because of justifying grace, 'gracious' because of guilt forgiven." For this interpretation he again appealed to Paul in Romans 4:25 ("He died for our sins and rose again for our justification").[26]

[21] *WA* 55 II 1, 36, 26-30 (scholia on Ps. 1:5).

[22] *LW,* vol. 10, p. 146. *WA* 3, 175, 8: "in fide Christi remittuntur peccata."

[23] *LW,* vol. 10, p. 146. *WA* 3, 175, 9-11.

[24] *LW,* vol. 10, p. 145. *WA* 3, 174, 21-23 (scholia on Ps. 31:1): "Faciunt autem Heretici idem, quod illi pharisei: quia licet credant, quod per solum Christum peccata auferantur, et in eum credant: tamen quia non habent eum vere, eo quod sustineant consilium eius, ideo manent in peccatis."

[25] *LW,* vol. 10, p. 458. *WA* 4, 336, 29-31 (scholia on Ps. 118:65): "Igitur Christi adventus est bonitas nostra: quia penas, que sunt mala nostra, abstulit a conscientia primum, deinde etiam auferet a corpore, et sic perfecte erit bonitas nostra." See WA 3, 478, 4-6 (scholia on Ps. 72:1).

[26] *LW,* vol. 10, p. 378. *WA* 4, 243, 25, 29-32.

Scholasticism was in dispute over whether forgiveness precedes justification, and over how the two relate to each other. Luther did not discuss this question in the first Psalms lecture. In material agreement with Paul, he assumed an indissoluble connection between forgiveness and justification. In the exposition of Psalm 25:11 he wrote: "'Remove the evil and give the good, remove sins and give grace,'" which means, "'accept me, I who need the good.'"[27] Or, on Psalm 31:1 he wrote that it is "the prophet's" (i.e., David's) meaning, that all shall learn from his fall and so arrive at a true understanding as to how one is justified and how sin is forgiven.[28]

If we compare these ideas with the Occamist concept of the powers of the human as such, of grace and justification, what is striking is that Luther is far removed from what had been taught him at Erfurt. Paul and Augustine but also the Psalter as a mirror of confession effected this departure from Occamism. In his concept of sin and grace Luther was already urging his own, new position.

THE SACRAMENTS

What is striking about Luther's first Psalms lecture compared with older commentaries is that he seldom mentioned the sacraments. W. Jetter has counted a total of 101 references to the sacraments. What is particularly surprising is that Luther mentioned the Mass only 30 times. On the other hand, the 34 instances in which he discusses baptism are numerous by comparison.[29] In contrast to such themes as repentance, confession of sins, judgment, righteousness, faith, or humility, reference to aspects of sacramental doctrine clearly retreats. Since Luther obviously participated in the daily celebration of the Mass while at the cloister, and since the sacraments as a whole played a signal role in cloister life, his infrequent reference to the sacraments deserves special attention.

This state of affairs can be explained only by Luther's reserve toward sacramental doctrine as it was taught him during his study. This reserve could scarcely have involved reflection on the sacraments as such, since it was only a few years later that he dealt with the doctrine of the sacraments in his sermons, naturally, with a new theological impulse. Certain aspects of the doctrine of the sacrifice of the Mass might not have pleased him theologically, without his having been able precisely to formulate his discomfort. As for baptism, noticeable impulses begin to show themselves, leading to tacit correction of many a late medieval idea.

---

[27] *WA* 55 I, 234, 25-27.

[28] *WA* 55 I, 290.

[29] Jetter, *Die Taufe beim jungen Luther,* BHTh 18 (Tübingen: Mohr, 1954),175-76. See also Albert Brandenburg, *Gericht und Evangelium: Zur Worttheologie in Luthers erster Psalmenvorlesung,* KKTS 4 (Paderborn: Bonifacius Druckerei, 1960), 131-32.

First, there is nothing new in Luther's adoption of the distinction between Word and Sacrament current since Augustine. It is worth noting, however, that in doing so he gives priority to the Word.[30] Nowhere does he state that the sacraments exercise a special effect on believers in contrast to the Word. Clearly, for Luther the activity of the Word is not to be understood as different from that of the Sacrament. Further, compared with late medieval sacramental doctrine, it is striking that particular theologoumena that were current then as later were either not taken up at all or were only seldom dealt with. In only one passage did Luther take up the distinction between *ex opere operantis* (from the one performing the deed = on the basis of the action of God) and *ex opere operato* (from the deed done = on the basis of the action itself). As a theologian schooled in Occamism he preferred the idea that the sacraments work *ex opere operantis* but at the same time argued independently of Occamism. The issue for him was not how the sacrament is made valid but its proper celebration "by us," thus its spiritual benefit.[31] At the same time he could actually take up the concept of *sacrificium* in the context of statements on the Lord's Supper. Here, however, he immediately entered on the *sacrificium confessionis* (sacrifice of confession) or the *sacrificium laudis* (sacrifice of praise), once again accenting the spiritual aspect. He was not interested in statements about the sacrificial character of the Lord's Supper, loosed as it were from the factor of the celebrating congregation. Of course, he did not yet dispute certain statements of the then current theology respecting the Supper as sacrifice.

Luther's statements regarding baptism were likewise oriented to the spiritual. In this connection he referred to the Augustinian distinction between spirit and letter but then gave most attention to the problem of sin and forgiveness and discussed the character of baptism as promise. These aspects were not at all in opposition to current teaching on baptism but nevertheless set new accents. Of special significance was Luther's concept of sign (*signum*) derived from Augustine, and which gave sacramental interpretation to the baptismal event and thus to the effect of baptism throughout all of life. That even with respect to baptism Luther was already going his own way becomes especially clear in his discussion of the problem of monasticism as well as of the relation between the baptismal and monastic vows. In the late Middle Ages it was customary to compare the monastic vow with a second vow at baptism, or even with a second baptism. The comparison derived ultimately from Jerome, in fact from Pachomian monasticism.[32] Popular sermons and publications often stated that when the saving effect of baptism had been lost through mortal sin, it could be renewed by the monastic vow as a second baptism. Johannes Paltz, theological instructor in Luther's Erfurt cloister, clearly expressed himself in this vein.[33]

---

[30] Evidence in Jetter, *Die Taufe beim jungen Luther*, 176-211.

[31] *WA* 55 I, 394. On this subject see Jetter, *Die Taufe beim jungen Luther*, 202-4.

[32] For more material see Lohse, *Mönchtum und Reformation*, 37-38, 58-61. See also Lohse, *Askese und Mönchtum in der Antike und in der alten Kirche* (Munich: Oldenbourg, 1969).

[33] See Lohse, *Mönchtum und Reformation*, 167-69. See also Hamm, *Frömmigkeitstheologie am Anfang des 16. Jahrhunderts*, 294-95.

In his first Psalms lecture Luther not only did not adopt the comparison but quite the contrary construed the monastic vow entirely from the perspective of the baptismal vow.[34] Passages in the Psalter traditionally cited as a biblical basis for the monastic vow, above all Psalm 76:12, "Make vows to the Lord your God, and perform them," were referred to the baptismal vow. Luther commented on Psalm 76:12: "'Declare an oath' in baptism and bind yourselves to God in repentance through an oath, 'and fulfill your oaths to the Lord, your God,' to Jesus Christ: You, that is, 'all' his faithful in the church 'round about him,' since He is in their midst."[35] Here and in other passages of his first Psalms lecture where he dealt with the baptismal vow, Luther did not exclude the monastic vow but in the given instance included it with the baptismal vow. What deserves notice here is that Luther did not allude to the comparison of the monastic vow with a second baptism. The monastic vows are not a renewal but at best a confirmation of the baptismal vow. Thus for Luther monasticism is a particular path under the aegis of baptism, not a renewal of baptism requiring repetition. The baptismal vow is foundational; if need be it encompasses the monastic vow. With these reflections, Luther avoided the danger of challenging the significance of baptism through an exaggerated view of monasticism. He interpreted baptism in a new way, in terms of its comprehensive effect. In his theology of monasticism, therefore, Luther found his way to a profoundly new impulse over against the High and late Middle Ages. In his reflection on the nature and benefit of the sacraments, Luther made more progress respecting baptism than respecting the Supper.

FAITH

We must first single out a few aspects that mark Luther's understanding of faith in this early period. He still made use of scholastic distinctions and arguments that can no longer simply be made to harmonize with new impulses.

For example, Luther could still defend the idea of the *fides informis* (unformed faith). R. Schwarz states correctly: "The *fides informis* [unformed faith] or *fides mortua* [dead faith] remains in the person when *gratia* is lost, when the believer sins, insofar as in spite of sin the truth known in faith is retained and not denied in deliberate pride."[36] At base, however, Luther avoided the concept *forma*,[37] since it conflicts with a concept of faith to a great extent determined by biblical usage. In general, Luther was reserved toward understanding grace as *habitus,* and the idea of the theological virtues was already in retreat.

---

[34] See Lohse, *Mönchtum und Reformation,* 249-54.

[35] *WA* 55 I, 538.

[36] Schwarz, *Fides, Spes und Caritas,* 127.

[37] Ibid., 128.

It is particularly important that we understand Luther's view of the substance of faith as originating in the basic theme of his first Psalms lecture, a theme best described in the terms of judgment and gospel. In faith the Christian accepts the judgment of God in order thus to share the righteousness of God. Broadly, but not at all completely, humility and faith can be viewed synonymously. In the light of Christ's suffering, we become aware of our sinfulness. With the Christian's acceptance of the divine judgment on sin comes recognition of sinfulness before God and thus agreement with the divine sentence of judgment. In precisely this manner the Christian is at the same time justified.[38] Whoever denies being a sinner before God, or whoever does not make confession of sin or justifies oneself before God, denies God the justification and the honor due him.[39] "Therefore God is not justified by anyone except the one who accuses and condemns and judges himself."[40] In the first Psalms lecture the theme of judgment is so dominant that statements on righteousness or even on justification retreat before it.

In addition to these statements others in the first Psalms lecture give entirely new expression to the old, ultimately Pauline idea of becoming conformed to Christ (Rom. 8:29). What was particularly important to Luther in this connection was the tropological sense of Scripture, calculated to facilitate application of the text to the individual, and best suited to link his ideas, centered on salvation, with specific biblical texts. In part, Luther arrived at bold assertions on the subject, as for example when he said that

no one can "magnify" God and His gifts unless he himself is first made great by the gifts of God. For the more he is enlightened, that much greater he esteems the gifts of God and His works, and conversely, the less he is enlightened, the less he regards them. Therefore it is characteristic of the magnified and enlightened soul to magnify God in His individual works.

[In what follows Luther discusses confession and praise]:

Tropologically [scil. the statement in Ps. 103:1: "*O Lord my God, Thou hast been made very great*" must so be understood] when we honor Him with acknowledgment of this kind and with praise and honor. For then He is already such a one in us as He is in person. And faith in Him is then acknowldgement and beauty, which He puts on spiritually. For through faith we confess Him and honor and adorn (*decoramus*) Him.[41]

This signal passage makes clear once more that the justifying of self and the justifying of God are mutually exclusive. Only those who humble themselves honor God, while those who would exalt themselves deny God honor. Faith, however, is

[38] *LW,* vol. 10, p. 236. *WA* 3, 289, 20 (scholia on Ps. 50:7).
[39] *LW,* vol. 10, p. 236. *WA* 3, 288, 27-29 (scholia on Ps. 50:6).
[40] *LW,* vol. 10, p. 236. *WA* 3, 288, 30-31.
[41] *LW,* vol. 11, p. 317. *WA* 4, 172, 20-173, 1.

assigned authoritative significance. It is faith that ultimately gives God the honor. Faith is thus always and at the same time confession and "honor" done to God. Faith is also decisive in one's relation to God. Especially to be accented is the idea that when we honor him the Lord becomes in us such as he is in his person alone.[42] This transformation or change occurs by faith.

Right at this point, Luther had gotten crucial help from Augustine. We referred above to the statement that Luther formulated in adopting the Augustinian idea that Scripture has power, not to change into the one who studies it, but rather to change the one who loves it into itself and its power.[43] In other places as well Luther deliberately and appropriately traced to Augustine the idea of such change. For example, in the exposition of Psalm 113 [115]:4 ("their idols are silver and gold"; see v. 8: "Those who make them are like them"): he says: "Love, wondrous in its effects, does all these things; it changes the lover into the beloved, as blessed Augustine says: 'Love the earth, and you are earth; love gold, and you are gold; love God and you are God.'"[44]

Throughout all his life Luther reiterated what he said here with reference to Augustine. That well-known passage in his Galatians lecture of 1531, where he wrote that faith creates the Godhead not in the person but in us,[45] derived ultimately from a train of thought that he adopted from Augustine. As early as in his first Psalms lecture, and in the second passage cited above,[46] Luther gave new shape to Augustine's idea with his distinction between the person as such and the person's significance for us. This formulation he retained even into his mature years. Just such an example indicates the great significance that Augustine had early on for the formation of Reformation theology, but it also shows Luther's independent use of Augustinian ideas.

---

[42] *LW*, vol. 11, p. 217: "Second, it applies tropologically, when we honor Him with acknowledgment of this kind and with praise and honor. For then He is already such a one in us as He is in person." *WA* 4, 172, 35-37: "Secundo tropologice, quando nos confessionem huiusmodi et laudem et honorem ei exhibemus: tunc enim iam in nobis etiam talis est, qualis in persona est."

[43] See pp. 52-53.

[44] *WA* 4, 263, 37-39: "Hec autem omnia facit amor mirabilis in viribus suis, qui transmutat amantem in amatum, sicut b. Augustinus dicit: 'terram diligis, terra es: aurum diligis, aurum es: deum diligis, deus es.'" (Cf. *LW*, vol. 11, p. 399.) The passage in Augustine not documented here appears in the *In epistolam Ioannis ad Parthos tractatus*, 2 (MPL 35, 1997): "Talis est quisque, qualis eius dilectio est. Terram diligis? terra eris. Deum diligis? quid dicam? deus eris?" ("Everyone is as his love. Do you love the earth? You will be earth. Do you love God? What should I say? You will be God?") In his Romans lecture also Luther referred to this passage in Augustine; see *LW*, vol. 25, pp. 226-27; *WA* 56, 241, 4 (scholia on Rom. 3:11). One can well imagine that in either instance Luther was quoting from memory. One can hardly assume that in commenting on the Psalms or in his exposition of Romans he always had Augustine's commentary on 1 John at hand. Further, Luther considerably altered the last words of the quotation.

[45] *LW*, vol. 26, p. 227: "Faith . . . is the creator of the Deity, not in the substance of God but in us." *WA* 40 I, 360, 5-6: "Fides est creatrix divinitatis, non in persona, sed in nobis."

[46] See n. 41.

HOLY AND BLESSED *IN SPE*/*IN RE*

A further, more important aspect of Luther's concept of grace and salvation consists in his distinction between the present as marked by hope, and the future with its complete realization. Luther most often described the former as *in spe* and the latter as *in re*. Other concepts or combinations of terms also express the same idea. A few of these need to be briefly noted.

First, with reference to "salvation" or "holiness," Luther distinguished present hope from future fulfillment.[47] In his exposition of Psalm 53:5, he wrote: "Sancti autem in silentio et patientia et in spe, non in re, sicut illi, quia in nomine Domini salvantur" ("The saints, however, live in silence and patience and in hope [*spes*], not in physical activity [*res*], like those people, for they are saved by the name of the Lord").[48] Other statements read in similar fashion: "per spem salvi sumus . . . perfecte satiabuntur in futuro" ("we are saved in hope . . . they will be perfectly satisfied [only] in the future").[49] Next, with reference to the concept of "blessedness" as well, Luther could distinguish present hope from future fulfillment. For example, he wrote that now we are saved "in hope,"[50] or are saved in this life *per spem*.[51]

Finally, Luther could use quite general terms to formulate the distinction between *in spe* and *in re,* for example, when he described God as our help *per spem*,[52] or when he said: "tota vita fidelium est tantummodo in spe et nondum in re" (the entire life of believers consists only of hope, not yet of reality).[53] The promise is God's certain aid already present and bearing along whoever trusts in him: "In the promise, through the word of promise, 'you, God, have given me hope,' not yet the realization. 'This hope has given me comfort; for it is certain. For God is faithful in his promises.'"[54]

What is significant here is that Luther adopted from Augustine the distinction between *in spe* and *in re*, soon to take on even greater significance for him. In his commentary on the Psalms Augustine drew this distinction at a place where Luther did not, that is, on Psalm 49:2. Here Augustine said: "'See,' the apostle says [1 John 3:1, 2], what

---

[47] Schwarz, *Fides, Spes und Caritas,* 229-31, has gathered some of the pertinent passages but has overlooked the passage in *WA* 3, 301, 11-12, about to be cited. He has made no reference to Augustine's Psalm commentary that furnished Luther the decided impulse.

[48] *LW,* vol. 10, p. 249. *WA* 3, 301, 11-12 (scholia on Ps. 53:3).

[49] *WA* 55 I, 314 (line gloss on Ps. 35:8, 9). See *LW,* vol. 10, p. 396. *WA* 3, 453, 32-33; 55 I, 568.

[50] *WA* 55 I, 346 (line gloss on Ps. 40:2): "'Beatus' . . . in spe."

[51] *WA* 55 I, 588 (line gloss on Ps. 83:13). See *WA* 55 I, 766, 828.

[52] *LW,* vol. 11, p. 212: "So [our] refuge consists of hope, not yet of reality." *WA* 4, 67, 2 (scholia on Ps. 90:2): "Ergo per spem est refugium, nondum in re."

[53] *WA* 55 I, 752 (line gloss on Ps. 113:11). See also *LW,* vol. 11, p. 551. *WA* 4, 412, 32-33.

[54] *WA* 55 I, 776. Further passages that distinguish *in spe* and *in re* or similar concepts: *LW,* vol. 11, p. 212; *WA* 4, 67, 1-2; 55 I, 642; 4, 98, 20-21; 55 I, 782-83; *LW,* vol. 11, p. 443; *WA* 4, 326, 2-3; 4, 380, 35.

love the Father has given us, that we should be called children of God; and that is what we are.' And in another passage: 'Beloved, we are God's children now; what we will be has not yet been revealed.' Therefore we are such in hope, but not yet in reality."[55]

The distinction between *in spe* and *in re* appears more often in Luther and with more force as regards the subject at hand. Luther linked the distinction to every central aspect of the gift of salvation. His emphasis on the divine promise in this context likewise went beyond Augustine's statements. Nonetheless, the distinction itself was taken from Augustine.

THE CHURCH

As to ecclesiology,[56] the first Psalms lectures contain traditional ideas as well as new impulses that clearly point toward the later Reformation doctrine of the church. It will not do merely to emphasize the one or other series of statements and thus to ignore the complexity attaching to an area which proved so sensitive for Luther's later development. One must also note that the text of the Psalter on which Luther commented offered no occasion for a systematically structured ecclesiology. His ecclesiological statements appeared in the margin.

First, there are the traditional figures of speech, according to which the church is "God's temple," the "new Jerusalem," or the "mother of believers." Luther was able to use such ideas and concepts later, following his break with Rome. The first Psalms lecture contains nothing of a criticism of the church's hierarchical structure or even of the papacy. Luther stated, for example, that the bishops are the disciples of the apostles.[57] As for the papacy, he referred to it only once along with an attack on the "Bohemians."[58] This is meager indeed, considering the wide range of his lectures. In

---

[55] Augustine, *En. in Ps.* 49:2; *CCSL* 38, 576, 27-31. The final words read: "Ergo sumus in spe, nondum in re."

[56] On this subject see Holsten Fagerberg, "Die Kirche in Luthers Psalmenvorlesungen 1513-1515," in *Gedenkschrift für D. Werner Elert: Beiträge zur historischen und systematischen Theologie*, ed. Friedrich Hübner with Wilhelm Maurer and Ernst Kinder (Berlin: Lutherisches Verlagshaus, 1955), 109-18; Wilhelm Maurer, "Kirche und Geschichte nach Luthers Dictata super Psalterium," in *Lutherforschung Heute: Referate und Berichte des I. Internationalien Lutherforschungskongresses Aarhus, 18.-23. August 1956*, ed. Vilmos Vajta (Berlin: Lutherisches Verlagshaus, 1958), 85-101; Gerhard Müller, "Ekklesiologie und Kirchenkritik beim jungen Luther," *NZSTh* 7 (1965), 100-128; J. Vercruysse, *Fidelis Populus: Eine Untersuchung über die Ekklesiologie in Martin Luthers Dictata super Psalterium*, VIEG 48 (Wiesbaden: Steiner, 1968); Scott H. Hendrix, *Ecclesia in via: Ecclesiological Developments in the Medieval Psalms Exegesis and the Dictata super Psalterium (1513-1515) of Martin Luther*, SMRT 8 (Leiden: Brill, 1974); Kurt-Victor Selge, "Ekklesiologisch-heilsgeschichtliches Denken beim jungen Luther," in *Augustine, the Harvest, and Theology*, 259-85.

[57] *LW*, vol. 10, p. 330. *WA* 3, 395, 12 (scholia on Ps. 67:13).

[58] *LW*, vol. 11, p. 470: "Also with the Bohemians with regard to the sacraments and the primacy of the Roman Church." *WA* 4, 345, 24-25 (scholia on Ps. 118:79) "Item cum Boemis de sacramentis atque principatu Ecclesie Rhomane."

addition, he referred merely to the "preeminence" (*principatus*) of the Roman church. There is nothing to suggest the later dispute.

More noteworthy still is that concepts such as *corpus Christi* and *populus fidelis*[59] were gaining in significance. Although the use of these terms did not yet point to later disputes, they signaled a shift in accent with respect to ecclesiology: just as Luther gave special status to the "Word," and took uncommonly great pains with the meaning of the text of the Psalter, so statements about the church, faith, and the character of the church as the body of Christ took center stage. At issue here were the shift of position in ecclesiology, the new impulses, and an ecclesiology in some way developed in critical debate. Critical statements on other ecclesiological concepts were fewer than on such theological questions as penance, justification, the sacraments, or practical piety. In the first Psalms lecture polemic apparently had no important place in ecclesiology. This statement, of course, does not unqualifiedly apply.[60]

As for Luther's own ecclesiological ideas, what seems most important by far is that the contrast between "spiritual" and "worldly" or between *spiritus* and *littera* exceeds all others in significance. The result is that what is decisive for the church is not its outward but its inner nature. The true church lives in hiddenness, *coram Deo*. "Christ's work and creation, the church, does not appear to be anything outwardly, but her entire structure is inward in the presence of God, invisible. And so it is not known to physical eyes but to spiritual ones, in the understanding and faith."[61]

Luther, of course, rejected the attempt to constitute the true believers or the righteous as a separate church. The error of the heretics was that they gathered the righteous or the saints "into a corner and separate gathering," and declared them to be a separate church. On the other hand, Luther emphasized that outside the church no confession can please God,[62] and he referred explicitly to the famous sentence of Cyprian to the effect that outside the church there is no salvation.[63] There is obviously considerable difference between Cyprian's word and Luther's formulation. While Cyprian tied salvation to the church as structure, Luther emphasized that confession is pleasing to God only within the fellowship of the church. At this point Luther had in mind the proper distinction between "spiritual" and "bodily": "For indeed there is no spiritual assembly except of the truly righteous, while there can be a bodily assembly without the truly righteous."[64] Here, for the first time, Luther's later conciliar view clearly sounded through.

---

[59] On this subject see the studies of Fagerberg and Vercruysse.

[60] See pp. 65-67.

[61] *LW*, vol. 11, p. 229. *WA* 4, 81, 12-14 (scholia on Ps. 91:7) "opera et factura Christi Ecclesia non apparet aliquid esse foris, sed omnis structura eius est intus coram deo invisibilis. Et ita non oculis carnalibus, sed spiritualibus in intellectu et fide cognoscuntur."

[62] *LW*, vol. 11, p. 372. *WA* 4, 239, 17-30 (scholia on Ps. 110:1). Line 21: "Extra enim Ecclesiam nulla potest deo placere confessio."

[63] Cyprian, *Ep.* 73.21: "salus extra ecclesiam non est."

[64] *LW*, vol. 11, p. 372; *WA* 4, 239, 22-24: "Quia vero spiritualis conventus non est nisi vere iustorum, corporalis autem potest esse sine vere iustis."

CRITICISM OF THE CHURCH

Luther's first Psalms lecture contains an astonishingly sharp attack against certain aspects of the church. It does, of course, differ from the extraordinarily comprehensive criticism of the church in the later medieval period. This criticism began with specific abuses and in the course of time became more and more radical and wide-ranging; from indulgences to the externalizing of the practice of piety and the preeminence of money all the way to the papacy, scarcely one area was spared, whereas Luther's criticism began with spiritual injury and only in limited fashion with individual abuses.

In his criticism of the church Luther attacked various groups such as the *Observantes,* Jews, heretics, and the arrogant. On occasion, monks also came in for criticism. Frequently, only the one or other party was named. Most often, however, Luther attacked several of these groups, directing his criticism toward an attitude that he thought was basic to them all. What deserves particular notice is first of all his criticism of the observants, though he himself belonged to the observants of his own order. In this attack Luther not only struck at others but ultimately challenged the school to which he himself belonged. Criticism of the observants was for the purpose of calling attention to the dangers attaching to strict observance.

The chief reproach that Luther raised against the observants was that they imitated the Jews and strove to secure their own righteousness. Or he said that they followed their own counsel and wisdom and by this means wished to establish their own righteousness before God.[65] Just like the Jews or the heretics, the observants were "much too holy," trusting more in their merits than in the Word of the Lord.[66] At times Luther could warn against works in any form and emphasize that everything depends on the *imitatio Christi* through faith and hope in him. Ignoring the works of Christ results in the many deeds that people believe they must perform themselves.[67] Luther was clearly of the opinion that monasticism, especially of the observant type, though arousing little suspicion, was nevertheless in danger of ultimately serving one's own righteousness. Wherever possible, the observants preferred their own "conventicle" of fellowship, and in this way advertised their own particular holiness. Conventicle and *singularitas* in terms of isolation are precisely what miss the point of monasticism.[68]

If in all this Luther so often attacked Jews and heretics, it was because he accused both of striving for their own righteousness, or, in his later terminology, of works-righteousness. For Luther, Jews and heretics were as it were the example of

[65] See, e.g., *LW,* vol. 10, pp. 28-29; *WA* 3, 27, 11-28, 6; *LW,* vol. 11, p. 208; *WA* 4, 64, 9-12. More detail in Lohse, *Mönchtum und Reformation,* 267-72.

[66] *LW,* vol. 11, p. 492. *WA* 4, 361, 12-14.

[67] *LW,* vol. 11, pp. 45-46. *WA* 3, 565, 21-29.

[68] Evidence in Lohse, *Mönchtum und Reformation,* 269-70.

unbelief, though his somewhat "spiritual" view of the church should actually have led to more discrete language.

In many places Luther engaged in an attack scarcely to be exceeded in harshness. Yet we must reckon with the fact that back of it lies a particular historical-theological view adopted from Bernard of Clairvaux.[69] According to Bernard, the church must endure three successive periods of persecution at the hands of tyrants, heretics, and bad Christians. By means of this interpretive scheme Luther analyzed his own time, accusing it of weak faith. The church overcame the first persecution, from tyrants, through weakness; it overcame the second, from heretics, through the foolishness of faith. False peace and security mark the present third period. Here the "lukewarm" (tepidi) and the "evil" (mali) rule. This period is particularly perilous inasmuch as there are no fronts in sight and the enemy has penetrated to the heart of the church. The weakness in faith encountered at present marks the severe struggle to be endured.[70] We need to be aware that the devil himself is attacking the church through false peace and security.[71]

Luther's attack on the church thus involved a spiritual or theological judgment by which to scourge the church's inner weakness of faith. Only sporadically did he refer to specific abuses. Still, some explicit references point to later conflicts. Human rights and human traditions have gotten the upper hand, just as Aristotle's philosophy has repressed Scripture study. For this reason "the eyes of Christ are weakening in the church."[72] Unbelievers and rebellious types are corrupting Scripture. People no longer allow themselves to be taken captive in obedience to Christ (cf. 2 Cor. 10:5).[73] They think they should doubt everything and thus hope for new doctrine. This means turning against the "fathers."[74] Luther also wrote that prayer has become weak.[75] Or he stated that the incarnation and passion of Christ have been forgotten.[76] He wrote that the church has shied away from suffering, serves transitory flesh, and no longer knows that it is the body of the crucified.[77] No wonder, in view of this deep, spiritual deficit dissension, envy, luxury, and other blasphemies have penetrated the church and enjoy preeminence there.[78]

---

[69] On this subject see Maurer, "Kirche und Geschichte," 93-94. K.-V. Selge, "Ekklesiologisch-heilsgeschichtliches Denken beim jungen Luther," 270-76, makes special reference to the antichrist idea as early as in the first Psalms lecture.

[70] LW, vol. 10, pp. 352-53. WA 3, 416, 9-417, 9.

[71] LW, vol. 10, p. 361: "Thus the devil now fights the church with the greatest persecution, because he fights with no persecution, but rather with security and idleness." WA 3, 424, 12-13: "Sic enim diabolus nunc Ecclesiam impugnat maxima persecutione: quia scilicet nulla persecutione, sed securitate et ocio."

[72] LW, vol. 10, p. 359. WA 3, 423, 2-4.

[73] LW, vol. 11, p. 63. WA 3, 578, 17-20.

[74] WA 3, 578, 38-579, 1.

[75] LW, vol. 10, pp. 358-59. WA 3, 422, 16-18.

[76] LW, vol. 11, p. 46. WA 3, 565, 29-31.

[77] LW, vol. 11, pp. 50-52. WA 3, 569, 14-570, 11. See Maurer, "Kirche und Geschichte," 95.

[78] More detail chiefly in Maurer, "Kirche und Geschichte"; and in Müller, "Ekklesiologie und

These critical remarks should not be overestimated, as though Luther expected nothing more of the church of his time. Renewal, however, is to be hoped for solely by faith: "The church is daily born and always changed within the succession of believers; the church is the one and the other, yet always the same."[79] Reference to the "succession of believers" may not be construed as a systematic statement, as if it actually denoted opposition to apostolic succession. Yet it does make clear the priority of faith over everything else.

Luther's statements about the church were borne by his conviction that it is under attack in every age. His charge was not that it is attacked, but that it succumbs to the idea that it has left behind the attacks from tyrants and heretics of earlier days, and now enjoys inner and outward safety and security beyond attack. This opinion, Luther wrote, is pure illusion. Faith as well as the church remain under attack, and here on earth we can never achieve a condition free of it. In the awareness of being under attack expression is given to the fact that the church is always under the cross, that believers stretch toward the future but do not make themselves at home here on earth.

To this extent, Luther's criticism of the church must be seen in intimate connection with the fundamental theme of the first Psalms lecture, that is, with the idea of judgment and gospel. Luther's aim was a spiritual renewal of the church on the basis of intense occupation with crucial biblical statements. This renewal would then help theology to perform its real task once more.

Kirchenkritik beim jungen Luther".

[79] WA 55 I, 688 (marginal gloss on Ps. 103:21): "Ecclesia semper nascitur et semper mutatur in successione fidelium. Alia et alia est Ecclesia et tamen semper eadem."

Chapter 8

THE STRUCTURE OF REFORMATION THEOLOGY IN THE PERIOD OF PAULINE EXEGESIS (1515-1518)

SETTING THE GOAL FOR THE LECTURES ON ROMANS (1515/1516), GALATIANS (1516/1517), AND HEBREWS (1517/1518)

By itself, the choice of biblical texts interpreted by Luther in his early lectures has programmatic significance. The Psalter as prayer book, but in certain instances as a mirror to confession, could serve to develop more precisely the new understanding of sin. When, after this first great exegetical attempt Luther resolved to interpret three epistles of Paul (Hebrews then taken to be Pauline), he obviously wanted to continue the intensive study of Paul already begun and to take up in a new way the central themes of Paul's theology. The choice of Romans as the object of the second exegetical lecture thus takes on special weight: it facilitated the understanding of the entire Bible.

First, Luther reiterated the theme of his first Psalms lecture. At the very beginning of the scholia in his Romans lecture he said:

> The chief purpose of this letter is to break down, to pluck up, and to destroy all wisdom and righteousness of the flesh. This includes all works which in the eyes of people or even in our own eyes may be great works. No matter whether these

works are done with a sincere heart and mind, this letter is to affirm and state and magnify sin, no matter how much someone insists that it does not exist, or that it was believed not to exist.[1]

Admittedly, Luther did not emphasize the divine judgment in isolation. At the outset of his lecture he made clear that by "establishing sin" Scripture points us to grace, in fact, to the righteousness of God. What is new in comparison with the first Psalms lecture is that he described righteousness as coming from outside: from the outset Luther was certain of the *extra nos* of "alien righteousness."[2] The opening statements in his Romans lecture indicate the considerable progress made since the first courses of lectures.

It may be that Luther coined the *extra* formula in reminiscence of mysticism's reference to *raptus* or *exstasis,* by which one is raptured "outside the self" (*extra se*).[3] Naturally, other traditions may also have served him as model.[4] Accordingly, it seems altogether possible that Luther was induced to coin this formula through a deepened understanding of the Word that comes to us "from the outside." First, it is important to note that the formula *extra nos* does not often appear in Luther's early period. Next, as early as in his Romans lecture it can be seen linked to such concepts as the *aliena iustitia* or *extranea iustitia,* clearly not adopted from mysticism. Despite the importance of this formula in the Romans lecture, Luther's view of justification may not be extrapolated from it alone.

---

[1] *LW,* vol. 25, p. 135. *WA* 56, 157, 2-6 (scholia on Rom. 1:1).

[2] *LW,* vol. 25, p. 136: "God does not want to redeem us through our own, but through external righteousness and wisdom; not through one that comes from us and grows in us, but through one that comes to us from the outside; not through one that originates here on earth, but through one that comes from heaven. Therefore, we must be taught a righteousness that comes completely from the outside and is foreign. And therefore our own righteousness that is born in us must first be plucked up." *WA* 56, 158, 10-14 (scholia on Rom. 1:1): "Deus enim nos non per domesticam, Sed per extraneam Iustitiam et sapientiam vult salvare, Non que veniat et nascatur ex nobis, Sed que aliunde veniat in nos, Non que in terra nostra oritur, Sed que de celo venit. Igitur omnino Externa et aliena Iustitia oportet erudiri. Quare primum oportet propriam et domesticam evelli." G. Schmidt-Lauber, *Luthers Vorlesung über den Römerbrief 1515/1516: Ein Vergleich zwischen Luthers Manuskript und den studentischen Nachschriften.* AWA 6. (Cologne: Böhlau, 1994), 58-62, has shown that in the notation on Romans 1, Luther did not take up statements about the *iustitia extra nos/iustitia aliena.* Admittedly, in the course of lectures on Rom. 3:4, he was occupied with the contrast between *in nobis* and *extra nos.* See *WA* 57 I, 150, 12-13; Schmidt-Lauber, 84-86. Precise comparison of Luther's manuscript of the Romans lecture with its transcription is often extraordinarily instructive. Quite clearly, in the lecture course itself, Luther was considerably more cautious and reserved than we should have expected on the basis of his manuscript.

[3] Thus above all zur Mühlen, *Nos extra nos.*

[4] Zur Mühlen, ibid., 101, speaks of "other ways" by which Luther could have arrived at this formula. In his review of zur Mühlen's book, Ernst Koch has stated that the concept and idea of the *transitus,* widespread in the ancient and the medieval church, may have stimulated Luther to shape the *extra nos* formula; see *ThLZ* 98 (1973), 359-61, here 361.

The subjoining lectures on Galatians and Hebrews are contained only in students' notes, not in Luther's manuscript. As significant as they are, and based on Luther's notation, they do not altogether reflect what Luther might already have worked out. Nonetheless, they do document Luther's further progress. In his Galatians lecture, inspired by the first verses of Paul's letter, he opens with accenting the apostle's authority: "In no other letter does he so fervently and eloquently accent his apostleship as in this one, and which, according to his own witness, he actually wrote himself."[5] At the outset of his lecture on Hebrews, begun in the spring of 1517,[6] Luther emphasized that Paul contrasts grace with pride based on a legal and human righteousness. He further stated that in this epistle Paul makes clear that only Christ is to be taught.[7] Here too, at the commencement of his course of lectures, Luther gave sharp definition to the essential theme.

This does not militate against the fact that during his early Pauline exegesis Luther made further and in part considerable progress. With regard to the Hebrews lecture it is worth noting that he gave accent to the *solus Christus* prior to the beginning of his dispute with Rome.

THE CONCEPT OF SIN

Luther gave clear evidence of progress beyond the first Psalms lecture, particularly in his statements about sin, in which he distanced himself sharply from the scholastic view. For example, on Romans 5:14, in an excursus on the nature of original sin, Luther wrote that the scholastics with their subtleties construed it as the absence of original righteousness. In their opinion, righteousness is only subjectively present in the human will, its absence thus to be seen as merely subjective. According to Paul and its simple sense in Jesus Christ, however, original sin is not merely the absence of a quality of will, but "a total lack of uprightness and the power of all the faculties both of body and soul and of the whole inner and outer man. Besides the inclination to evil."[8] Likewise aimed at scholasticism was Luther's rejection of the idea of *forma*, by which one's natural but sinful condition is to be improved through grace. Luther polemicized most heatedly against this view as well as against the *habitus* idea, the view that grace as it were improves the human condition. He wrote to the contrary: "But this word 'formed' (*formatum*) is under a curse, for it forces us to think of the soul as being the same after as before the outpouring of love and as if the form were

---

[5] *WA* 57 II, 5, 11-13 (marginal gloss on Gal. 1:1).

[6] *WA* 57 III, III.

[7] *WA* 57 III, 5, 10-16 (marginal gloss on Heb. 1:1). These words appear in the manuscript at the head of the page and to that extent are given special emphasis. The last words read: "Omnino igitur solum Christum docendum proponit." ("Thus only Christ alone is meant to be taught.")

[8] *LW,* vol. 25, p. 299. *WA* 56, 312, 1-11 (scholia on Rom. 5:14). In the lecture course Luther did not express these ideas, especially not the polemic against scholastic distinctions; *WA* 57 I, 172-73.

merely added to it at the time of the action, although it is necessary that it be wholly put to death and be changed before putting on love and working in love."[9]

Altogether, Luther rigorously distanced himself from the Occamist concept of sin,[10] especially from the view that by their natural powers humans are able to keep the commandments of God. Luther again to the contrary: "For this reason it is plain insanity to say that man of his own powers can love God above all things and can perform the works of the Law according to the substance of the act, even if not according to the intentions of Him who gave the commandment, because he is not in a state of grace. O fools, O pig-theologians!"[11]

Luther's own ideas about sin point in an entirely different direction. It must be noted that in his exposition Luther obviously had in mind quite specific, individual sins. On the whole, however, he intended to show that persons not only commit sins but are themselves sinners. Sin is thus not only an absence or error or weakness. It has its home in the heart and from the ground up perverts the condition for which humans were created.

From this perspective Luther could speak of sin as "radical," that is, like a root (radix) affecting everything growing from it: concupiscence ultimately denotes the peccatum radicale. At the same time Luther identified this peccatum radicale with covetousness (concupiscentia ad malum), an identification medieval scholasticism could never have made.[12] In similar fashion Luther came to form other new and fresh concepts.

Most important, Luther gave more precise definition to the nature of sin in respect of content and in doing so abandoned scholastic distinctions. By its nature sin is the attempt to establish one's own righteousness before God.

Luther gave still another definition of sin, new as well as opposed to the tradition, with his reference to the "one curved in upon the self":

> The reason is that our nature has been so deeply curved in upon itself because of the viciousness of original sin that it not only turns the finest gifts of God in upon itself and enjoys them (as is evident in the case of legalists and hypocrites), indeed, it even uses God Himself to achieve these aims, but it also seems to be ignorant of this very fact, that in acting so iniquitously, so perversely, and in such a depraved way, it is even seeking God for its own sake.[13]

[9] LW, vol. 25, p. 325. WA 56, 337, 18-21 (scholia on Rom. 7:6). In his lecture course Luther in essence spoke more guardedly of the scholastics: WA 57 I, 183, 1-3.

[10] See above, p. 19-20.

[11] LW, vol. 25, p. 261. WA 56, 274, 11-14 (scholia on Rom. 4:7). The "pig theologians" do not appear again in the transcription; see WA 57 I, 163-66.

[12] LW, vol. 25, p. 264. WA 56, 277, 5-13 (scholia on Rom. 4:7).

[13] LW, vol. 25, p. 291. WA 56, 304, 25-29 (scholia on Rom. 5:4): "Ratio est, Quia Natura nostra vitio primi peccati tam profunda est in seipsam incurua, ut non solum optima dona Dei sibi inflectat ipsisque fruatur (ut patet in Iustitiariis et hipocritis), immo et ipso Deo utatur ad illa consequenda, Verum etiam hoc ipsum ignoret, Quod tam inique, curue et praue omnia, etiam, Deum, propter seipsam querat."

He gave more precise definition to this *curvitas* in his exposition of Romans 8:3:

> If we were to say that in particular cases human nature knows and wills what is good, but in general neither knows nor wills it. The reason is that it knows nothing but its own good, or what is good and honorable and useful for itself, but not what is good for God and other people. Therefore it knows and wills more what is particular, yes, only what is an individual good. And this is in agreement with Scripture which describes man as so turned in on himself that he uses not only physical but even spiritual goods for his own purposes and in all things seeks only himself.[14]

Further, Luther identified original sin with the *fomes peccati* (tinder of sin):

> This original sin is the very tinder of sin, the law of the flesh, the law of the members, the weakness of our nature, the tyrant, the original sickness, etc. For it is like a sick man whose mortal illness is not only the loss of health of one of his members, but it is, in addition to the lack of health in all his members, the weakness of all his senses and powers.[15]

From this perspective actual sins are nothing but the fruits of this "radical" sin, in other words, of one's being a sinner. When Luther described the goal of Romans as "making sin great," he had in mind awareness of self in the light of Scripture. According to Luther, the utterances of Scripture totally contradict the late scholastic doctrine of sin as he had come to know it at Erfurt. It must be added that for Luther apart from a true knowledge of sin's nature there is knowledge neither of grace nor of the righteousness of God. To this extent, a new definition of sin takes on fundamental significance for all further theological work.

The Concept of Grace

Here too Luther could make use of traditional concepts, even if they no longer corresponded to his new theology. He continued to use the idea of the "influx" of grace, an idea no longer really appropriate, given his rejection of the notion of *habitus* or *forma*. Just at this point, however, what is new shows itself, for Luther can use "influx" and "justify" synonymously, together with the idea of "reckoning": "[God is justified]

---

[14] *LW,* vol. 25, p. 345. *WA* 56, 355, 28-356, 6. The last words read: "Et hoc consonat Scripture, Que hominem describit incurvatum in se adeo, ut non tantum corporalia, Sed et spiritualia bona sibi inflectat et se in omnibus querat." See also *LW,* vol. 25, p. 244. *WA* 56, 258, 23-28.

[15] *LW,* vol. 25, p. 300. *WA* 56, 313, 4-9 (scholia on Rom. 5:14): "Peccatum illud originis Est ipse fomes, lex carnis, lex membrorum, languor nature, Tyrannus, Morbus originis etc. Est enim simile cum egroto, Cuius egritudo mortalis non tantum est unius membri privata sanitas, Sed Ultra sanitatem omnium membrorum privatam debilitatio omnium sensuum et virium."

when he justifies the ungodly and pours out His grace upon them, or when it is believed that He is righteous in His words. For through such believing He justifies, that is, He accounts people righteous."[16] This passage makes clear the radical change in Luther's thought. He was familiar with the concept of "reckoning" from Occamist theology,[17] but by construing it synonymously with "justify," it took on new meaning.

Luther's reference to "first grace" also derives from traditional usage, though here as well Luther immediately distanced himself from scholasticism:

> To the first grace as well as to the glory we always adopt a passive attitude, as a woman does toward conception . . . I call "first grace" not that which is poured into us at the beginning of conversion, as in the case of Baptism, contrition, or remorse, but rather all that grace which follows and is new, which we call a degree and increase of grace. For God first gives operative grace, which He allows to be used and worked with up to the point where He begins to pour into us a second kind of grace; and when this has been poured in, He lets it cooperate, even though when it was first infused it was operative and first grace, while with respect to the first grace it is second grace.[18]

In a fundamental way Luther's interpretation exceeds the bounds of the scholastic doctrine. The point of his exposition is that one cannot simply speak of a continuous growth of the grace one is given, as if that grace became a possession that could not be lost. At issue in the encounter of God with humanity is the totality of God's gracious condescension. Still, Luther did not get free of scholastic usage, though it no longer suited the new content.

Similarly, Luther coined the idea of various "degrees of grace":

> For whenever God gives us a new degree of grace, He gives in such a way that it conflicts with all our thinking and understanding. Thus he who then will not yield or change his thinking or wait, but repels God's grace and is impatient, never acquires this grace. Therefore the transformation of our mind is the most useful knowledge that believers in Christ can possess. And the preservation of one's own mind is the most harmful resistance to the Holy Spirit.

At this point, Abraham is the model for every Christian: just as he so also we must journey to the place of which we still know nothing. What Luther wanted to say is that "in the church God does nothing else but transform this mind."[19]

---

[16] LW, vol. 25, p. 205. WA 56, 220, 9-11 (scholia on Rom. 3:7): "Quando Impios Iustificat et gratiam infundit sive quando Iustus esse in suis Verbis creditur. Per tale enim Credi Iustificat i.e. Iustos reputat. Unde hec dicitur Iustitia fidei et Dei."

[17] See above, p. 19.

[18] LW, vol. 25, pp. 368-69. WA 56, 379, 2-16 (scholia on Rom. 8:26).

[19] LW, vol. 25, p. 438. WA 56, 446, 11-30 (scholia on Rom. 12:2, 3). The words last quoted read: "Quia in Ecclesia Nihil aliud facit Deus, Nisi ut transformet hunc sensum."

Grace must lift the person toward what is good.[20] Because of the perverted direction of human striving, humans could not do this by themselves. Naturally, only that person shares in grace who lives in fear and trembling: "We can never know whether we are justified or whether we believe. We should, therefore, consider our works as works of the Law and humbly admit that we are sinners, seeking to be justified solely by His mercy."[21]

Such passages have induced many a researcher to speak of a *humilitas* theology in the Romans lecture.[22] Without denying the importance of such passages I must note that others sound quite differently. Thus Luther emphasized that only the *satisfactio* accomplished for us by Christ frees us from our being obliged or able to perform it: so God gives grace on the basis of Christ's sole satisfaction.[23]

It is indeed striking that Luther spoke much less of "grace" than of sin or the righteousness of God or justification. In such fashion he let slip many an occasion for separating himself from scholasticism, as, for example, he could have done in connection with Romans 11:6 ("but if it is by grace, it is no longer on the basis of works"). In the scholia he said nothing about this verse; in the gloss between the lines and in the margin he offered only a bit of comment. Clearly, the themes of righteousness and justification were absolutely foremost.

God's Righteousness and Our Justification

Luther drew a sharp contrast between divine and human righteousness. In the Romans lecture he emphasized that God's righteousness is revealed only in the gospel:

> In human teaching the righteousness of man is revealed and taught, that is, who is and becomes righteous before himself and before other people and how this takes place. Only in the Gospel is the righteousness of God revealed (that is, who is and becomes righteous before God and how this takes place) by faith alone, by which the Word of God is believed, as it is written in the last chapter of Mark (16:16): "He who believes and is baptized will be saved; but he who does not believe will be condemned."[24]

Luther, however, could also describe the righteousness of God in a concept taken from scholasticism, the concept of the "cause of salvation" (*causa salutis*),

[20] *LW*, vol. 25, p. 222. *WA* 56, 237, 2-15 (scholia on Rom. 3:10).

[21] *LW*, vol. 25, p. 239. *WA* 56, 252, 20-23 (scholia on Rom. 3:22).

[22] So in particular Bizer, *Fides ex auditu,* passim.

[23] *LW*, vol. 25, pp. 31-32. *WA* 56, 37, 26-28 (marginal gloss on Rom. 3:24).

[24] *LW*, vol. 25, p. 151. *WA* 56, 171, 27-172, 3 (scholia on Rom. 1:17). In Latin the most significant words read: "in solo evangelio revelatur Iustitia Dei (i.e., quis et quomodo sit et fiat Iustus coram Deo) per solam fidem, qua Dei verbo creditur."

though admittedly he interpreted it in terms of justification. With regard to *iustitia* as well as to *salus* he had in mind not a divine attribute but God's gracious action toward humankind.[25]

First, as to their quantity, the statements on justification constitute one of the standard themes of the Romans lecture. In ever-new thrusts Luther took up the Pauline utterances on this theme, always setting forth new aspects. For his theology, *iustificare* was of central importance. At the same time, certain concepts such as *reputare* or *imputare* were from the outset used synonymously.

Luther took support from Augustine's treatise *De spiritu et littera,* which referred to God's righteousness not merely in terms of an attribute but also in terms of a divine gift. It may be that in its reference to God's righteousness and our justification, no other treatise of the ancient or medieval church comes as close to Luther's Reformation theology as this anti-Pelagian treatise. Yet in citing it Luther at important points characteristically went beyond what Augustine intended: he interpreted Augustine in line with his own new theological position. There can be no doubt that in shaping his ideas about justification Luther received essential help from Augustine, but he was conscious at times of the difference between Paul and Augustine, and began to exercise an initial, cautious criticism of the ancient church father.[26]

As for his caution, Luther's statements on Romans 2:13 are particularly instructive. He described "to justify" (*iustificare*) and "to declare" or "reckon as righteous" (*reputare*) as synonymous. In addition, he construed *declarare* or *decernere* as parallel concepts. Through such identification Luther accented God's sole authorship as well as the nature of justification as gift: it can only be received in faith.[27]

Luther developed these ideas in particularly detailed and thorough fashion in his exposition of Romans 4:7, where Paul together with the author of Psalm 32:1 says, "Blessed are those whose iniquities are forgiven, and whose sins are covered." He commented:

> The saints are always sinners in their own sight, and therefore always justified outwardly. But the hypocrites are always righteous in their own sight, and thus always sinners outwardly. I use the term "inwardly" (*intrinsice*) to show how we are in ourselves, in our own eyes, in our own estimation; and the term "outwardly" (*extrinsice*) to indicate how we are before God and in His reckoning. Therefore we are righteous outwardly when we are righteous solely by the imputation of God and not of ourselves or of our own work.[28]

---

[25] *LW,* vol. 25, p. 151-52. *WA* 56, 172, 3-8.

[26] See Lohse, "Die Bedeutung Augustins für den jungen Luther (1965)," in *Evangelium in der Geschichte,* Studien zu Luther und der Reformation ed. Leif Grane, Bernd Moeller und Otto Hermann Pesch (Göttingen, 1988) 11-30; idem, "Zum Wittenberger Augustinismus," in *Augustine, the Harvest, and Theology,* 89-109.

[27] *LW,* vol. 25, pp. 184-85. *WA* 56, 201, 10-22.

[28] *LW,* vol. 25, p. 257. *WA* 56, 268, 27-269, 2. The last words read: "Igitur extrinsece sumus Iusti, quando non ex nobis nec ex operibus, Sed ex sola Dei reputatione Iusti sumus."

In the exposition of Romans 4:7 the comparison between the sinner and a sick person is extraordinarily significant:

> It is similar to the case of a sick man who believes the doctor who promises him (*promittenti*) a sure recovery and in the meantime obeys the doctor's orders in the hope of the promised recovery and abstains from those things which have been forbidden him, so that he may in no way hinder the promised return to health or increase his sickness until the doctor can fulfill his promise to him. Now is this sick man well? The fact is that he is both sick and well at the same time. He is sick in fact, but he is well because of the sure promise of the doctor, whom he trusts and who has reckoned him as already cured (*sanum reputat*), because he is sure that he will cure him; for he has already begun to cure him and no longer reckons to him a sickness unto death. In the same way Christ, our Samaritan, has brought His half-dead man into the inn to be cared for, and He has begun to heal him, having promised him the most complete cure unto eternal life, and He does not impute his sins (*non imutans*), that is, his wicked desires, unto death, but in the meantime in the hope of the promised recovery He prohibits him from doing or omitting things by which his cure might be impeded and his sin, that is, his concupiscence, might be increased. Now, is he perfectly righteous? No, for he is at the same time both a sinner and a righteous man (*simul peccator et iustus*); a sinner in fact, but a righteous man by the sure imputation and promise of God (*peccator re vera, Sed Iustus ex reputatione ex promissione Dei certa*), that he will redeem him from sin until he heals him totally.[29]

The figure of the doctor and the sick man is an ancient topic that appears not only in scholasticism[30] but as early as in Augustine. Augustine used the figure in his commentary on the Psalms. Of course, there is considerable difference between Luther's and Augustine's comparison: at issue for Augustine was the contrite heart (*contritum cor*), aided by the Sacrament as a means to health. What restores soul and body is not the doctor's word of promise but his activity and the *contritiones* harnessed to it.[31]

In this text Luther first used the phrase *simul peccator et iustus*, one of Reformation theology's most important conceptual formulations. We should further note how in this passage Luther took up the distinction between *in spe* and *in re*. In the first Psalms lecture he adopted the contrast from Augustine, and of course broadened it.[32] In the Romans lecture he first related it to the realization of total "recovery," or, without using the figure, of *iustificatio*. Finally, comparison with corresponding passages in the first Psalms lecture indicates what importance attached to the divine promise for

[29] *LW*, vol. 25, p. 260. *WA* 56, 272, 3-19.

[30] So Johannes Ficker, *WA* 56, 272, note on line 3.

[31] See Augustine, *En. in Ps.* 146:8; *CCSL* 40, 2127, 1-19. See Adolf Hamel, *Der junge Luther und Augustin: Ihre Beziehungen in der Rechtfertigungslehre nach Luthers ersten Vorlesung 1509-1518 untersucht.* 2 vols. 1934-35; reprint (Hildesheim/New York: Georg Olms, 1980), 118-19.

[32] See above, pp. 62-63.

Luther: At this point the divine *promissio* assumes its key role in effecting salvation. Faith is not directed, as has at times been asserted,[33] toward a "future total release" from sins, but to the word of promise.

Naturally, alongside this passage, other statements do not yet reflect this Reformation sharpening. Even here Luther could write that the sick person or sinner "has the beginning of righteousness, so that he continues more and more always to seek it, yet he realizes that he is always unrighteous."[34] In any case, this much is certain, that genuine assurance of salvation is not yet to be found in the Romans lecture.[35] Luther's simile of the sick person and the doctor or the sinner and God may not be systematized or construed as a basic scheme for the doctrine of justification. Yet it might be methodologically legitimate to attach more importance to the new ideas in Luther that deviate from the tradition than to arguments still retained from late medieval theology.

We ought not to overlook other statements on the justification complex that are more intimately linked to ideas in the first Psalms lecture, such as the statement that one must be conformed to the judgment of God. Thus Luther could say that we must justify God in his words, so that we hold his Word to be true and just, and accept what occurs through faith.[36] In carrying further this train of thought Luther arrived at the pointed formulation that "through the fact that 'God is justified' we are justified. And this passive justification of God by which He is justified by us is our actual justification by God actively (*active*). For He regards that faith which justifies His words as righteousness."[37] Somewhat later he wrote: "He justifies, overcomes, in His Word when He makes us to be like His Word, that is, righteous, true, wise, etc. And He thus changes us into His Word, but not His Word into us."[38]

Luther could actually make use of mystical ideas to express his view of justification and salvation. One particularly bold word reads: "This is what it means to be blessed, to will to do the will of God and glorify Him in all things and not at all to want one's own interests, neither here nor in eternity."[39] The word is clearly reminiscent of mysticism's *resignatio ad infernum*, of the readiness to endure hell, if need be, when God wills. Elsewhere Luther employed mystical categories and without comment cited the idea of the "ascent" or mystical rapture: "For the incarnate Word

[33] So Bizer, *Fides ex auditu*, 48.

[34] *LW*, vol. 25, p. 260. *WA* 56, 272, 19-21.

[35] This statement applies chiefly to the noted essay of Karl Holl, "Die Rechtfertigungslehre in Luthers Vorlesung über den Römerbrief mit besonderer Rückblick auf die Frage der Heilsgewissheit," in *Gesammelte Aufsätze* (Tübingen: Mohr, 1948), 1:111-54.

[36] *LW*, vol. 25, p. 198. *WA* 56, 212, 26-33 (scholia on Rom. 3:4).

[37] *LW*, vol. 25, p. 211. *WA* 56, 226, 23-26: "Per hoc autem 'Iustificari Deum' Nos Iustificamur. Et Iustificatio illa Dei passiva, qua a nobis Iustificatur, Est ipsa Iustificatio nostri active a Deo. Quia illam fidem, que suos sermones Iustificat, reputat Iustitiam."

[38] *LW*, vol. 25, p. 211. *WA* 56, 227, 2-5. See above, pp. 52, 61.

[39] *LW*, vol. 25, p. 381. *WA* 56, 391, 4-6 (scholia on Rom. 9:3).

is first necessary for the purity of heart, and only when one has this purity, can he through this Word be taken up spiritually into the uncreated Word."[40]

Such statements should not be overrated. By way of comparison, in Luther's early Pauline interpretation, they seldom occur and are less characteristic of his own thought than the traditions that were of influence in his theologically developing years.

THE SACRAMENTS

Luther spoke oftener of the sacraments in his Romans lecture than in his first Psalms lecture.[41] His lecture on Hebrews contains even more references to the sacraments.[42] The reason for this lies first of all in the texts to be interpreted. In Romans it was necessary to interpret chapter 6 on baptism. Hebrews required interpreting the passages on the "testament," necessitating dealing with the Lord's Supper. Aside from these external factors, however, Luther's expositions indicate progress in his sacramental theology.

On Romans 6 and 7, and in agreement with Augustine, Luther stated that baptism remits the character of guilt attaching to sin, but that "weakness" remains as an inclination to sin.[43] Further, also in agreement with Augustine, Luther distinguished temporal and eternal death, or the death of sin and death, and the death of the damned.[44] The purpose of baptism is to assist us to the death of death, an event that in fact has just begun in the baptized.[45] Clearly, Luther was already developing fundamental ideas that would determine his later theology of baptism. Of special importance is the shift in accent over against the tradition: it is not so much the grace given at baptism as it is the promise that is at the heart of Luther's reflection.[46]

[40] *LW,* vol. 25, p. 287. *WA* 56, 300, 3-5 (scholia on Rom. 5:2).

[41] See Jetter, *Die Taufe beim jungen Luther,* 109-74, BHTh 18 (Tübingen: Mohr, 1954), 255-330, 175, n. 1; 257, n. 1.

[42] See E. Bizer, "Die Entdeckung des Sakraments durch Luther," *EvTh* 17 (1957), 64-90.

[43] *LW,* vol. 25, p. 63; *WA* 56, 70, 24-71, 5 (marginal gloss on Rom. 7:18); *LW,* vol. 25, p. 64; *WA* 72, 23-25 (marginal gloss on Rom. 7:20); *LW,* vol. 25, p. 340; *WA* 351, 3-10 (scholia on Rom. 7:17).

[44] *LW,* vol. 25, pp. 309-10. *WA* 56, 322, 11-323, 9 (scholia on Rom. 6:3).

[45] *LW,* vol. 25, p. 312: "For they are baptized 'into death,' that is, toward death, which is to say, they have begun to live in such a way that they are pursuing this kind of death and reach out toward this their goal. For although they are baptized unto eternal life and the kingdom of heaven, yet they do not all at once possess this goal fully, but they have begun to act in such a way that they may attain to it—for Baptism was established to direct us toward death and through this death to life—therefore it is necessary that we come to it in the order which has been prescribed." *WA* 56, 324, 17-23 (scholia on Rom. 6:4): "Baptisati enim sunt 'in mortem' i.e. ad mortem, hoc est inceperunt agere, ut mortem istam assequantur et hanc metam suam attingant. Sicut enim licet ad vitam eternam baptisentur et ad regnum celorum, non tamen statim habent ius summam, Sed inceperunt agere, Ut ad illud perveniant—Ordinatur enim Baptismus ad istam mortem et per eam ad vitam—Ideo necessarium est in ordine huiusmodi inveniri."

[46] The actual concept of *promissio* apparently does not occur here in Luther, but the substance of the matter does. The entire exposition of Romans 6 is borne by the dual line: first the actual deed of dying, then the realization of the new life begun at baptism.

The proper use of baptism marks realization of the divine promise. We are to be released from our "curvature" (*curvitas*). For this purpose a real dying of death is needed, a dying occurring figuratively in baptism.[47]

Luther seldom spoke of the Lord's Supper in his Romans lecture. He still kept to its character as sacrifice—it purifies from actual sins.[48] Here, too, however, there is a new accent: what is decisive in the sacrifice is the preaching of the gospel. "My [i.e., Paul's] sacrifice is to preach the Gospel and through it to offer (*sacrificare*) the Gentiles as a sacrifice to God (*Deo offere*)."[49] What is required of communicants is faith. Without polemicizing against the scholastic idea that what suffices is merely that one "places no obstacle in the way," Luther in fact already rejected it.[50]

There are also new and decisive impulses in the Romans lecture having to do with repentance. In essence, Luther held the view that the life of the Christian is under the sign of baptism and to that extent is a life of repentance: we never get beyond praying for forgiveness in the Our Father.[51] The uniqueness of baptism has as its goal the "eternal nature" of grace.[52] "Therefore sin remains in the spiritual man for the exercise of grace, for the humbling of pride, for the repression of presumptuousness."[53]

In the Galatians lecture Luther first stressed the meaning of *testamentum* and *promissio*. Inspired by Galatians 3:17 ("The law, which came four hundred and thirty years afterward, does not annul a covenant previously ratified by God, so as to make the promise void") Luther stated: "Because the apostle describes the promises of God as a 'testament' . . . he clearly shows that one day God will die so that what is meant by the promise of God as his signed testament is the incarnation and suffering of God. As it in fact reads in Hebrews 9 [v. 17]: 'A testament takes effect only at death,' so the testament of God would not be confirmed if God himself were not to die as testator."[54] Shortly thereafter, and with reference to Jerome, Luther pointed to the various significations of *pactum* and *testament*. Whoever grants a *pactum* is still alive, whereas the "testator" must die for his testament to take effect.[55] It was chiefly a theology of the Lord's Supper that Luther was developing in his lecture on Hebrews. In doing so he took up an idea he had earlier adopted,[56] that is, that Christ is *sacramentum* and *exemplum*.[57] With such terms he particularly had discipleship in mind.

[47] *LW*, vol. 25, pp. 311-12. *WA* 56, 324, 24-32 (scholia on Rom. 6:4).

[48] *LW*, vol. 25, p. 269. *WA* 56, 282, 15-18 (scholia on Rom. 4:7).

[49] *LW*, vol. 25, p. 123. *WA* 56, 142, 10-16 (marginal gloss on Rom. 15:16).

[50] *LW*, vol. 25, p. 67. *WA* 56, 74, 23-24 (marginal gloss on Rom. 8:1).

[51] *LW*, vol. 25, p. 276. *WA* 56, 289, 7-13 (scholia on Rom. 4:7).

[52] *LW*, vol. 25, p. 315. *WA* 56, 328, 8-26 (scholia on Rom. 6:10).

[53] *LW*, vol. 25, p. 339. *WA* 56, 350, 5-6 (scholia on Rom. 7:17).

[54] *WA* 57 II, 82, 2-8. On this subject see R. Schwarz, "Der hermeneutische Angelpunkt in Luthers Messereform," *ZThK* 89 (1992), 340-64, here 342-43.

[55] *WA* 57 II, 82, 10-15.

[56] See above, p. 47.

[57] *LW*, vol. 29, pp. 224-25; *WA* 57 III, 222, 12-223, 23 (scholia on Heb. 10:9).

More important, however, are references in the Hebrews lecture to the concept of *testamentum*. On Hebrews 7:22 Luther wrote: "One should note that where it is recorded in the Holy Scripture that God makes a will, there it is pointed out somewhat obscurely that at one time or other God will die and arrange the inheritance, as below in chapter 9:6: 'Where there is a testament, the death of the testator must intervene.' This has been fulfilled in Christ."[58]

On Hebrews 9:17 ("For a testament takes effect only at death") Luther next stated:

> This passage gives a clear illustration of the allegorical understanding of the Law of Moses, by which we learn that everything contained in that Law was promised and prefigured with reference to Christ and in Christ, and that for this reason . . . under the name "testament" and "promise" the death of Him who would be true God and true man was determined long ago. For since He cannot die, yet promises (namely, by making a testament) that He will die, it was necessary for Him to become man and thus to fulfill what He had promised.[59]

Luther intimately linked the terms *testamentum* and *promissio* to Christ's crucifixion. Indeed, he identified them.[60] In this way he achieved a decisively new impulse for his doctrine of the sacraments that he would develop even further, particularly in 1520.

From this perspective, Luther actually gained existential access to the reception of the sacrament. He understood the Lord's Supper as an aid to conscience. On Hebrews 9:14 ("How much more shall the blood of Christ . . . purify your conscience from dead works to serve the living God") he wrote:

> By itself our conscience is distressed and troubled (*tribulatur*), no matter where it turns. Nor is it freed from these difficulties except through the blood of Christ; and if it looks at Him through faith, it believes and realizes that its sins have been washed away and taken away in Him. Thus through faith it is at the same time purified and made calm, so that out of joy over the remission of sins it no longer dreads punishments.[61]

THE CHURCH

In Luther's Pauline exegesis ecclesiology appears to have had less place than in the first Psalms lecture.[62] The principal reason might be that since that time Luther used

[58] *LW*, vol. 29, p. 194. *WA* 57 III, 193, 18-21.
[59] *LW*, vol. 29, p. 213. *WA* 57 III, 211, 16-22.
[60] On this subject see Kenneth Hagen, *A Theology of Testament in the Young Luther: The Lectures on Hebrews*, SMRT 12 (Leiden: Brill, 1974).
[61] *LW*, vol. 29, p. 209. *WA* 57 III, 207, 18-26.
[62] See Müller, "Ekklesiologie und Kirchenkritik beim jungen Luther," *NZSTh* 7 (1965) 100-128, here 113.

the allegorical method to a lesser degree and was thus more cautious in his theological statements.

In the Romans lecture there was still much of the traditional ecclesiology. On Romans 6:12 Luther could describe the church as "the immortal body," just as also its head is immortal.[63] When he used the concept of the church as the "bride of Christ,"[64] or explained that the apostles were sent out to establish it, and that they themselves are the *fundamenta Ecclesiae*,[65] he was merely stating views retained throughout his life and never doubted even during his dispute with Rome.

On the other hand, new impulses appear. In one passage the idea of the priesthood of all believers began to sound through: "Every word which proceeds from the mouth of a leader of the church or from the mouth of a good and holy man is the Word of Christ, for He has said, 'He who hears you hears Me.'"[66]

More important than these individual ideas, however, is that the preaching of the Word is the church's genuine and noblest task. Luther did not state this in programmatic or even critical fashion toward other views, but it clearly results from numerous individual statements. On Romans 10:15 ("How beautiful are the feet of those who preach the gospel of peace") Luther said: "The feet of the church as it preaches are voices and words (*voces et verba*) by which it cuts and shakes up the people and 'beats them to pieces.' And the church does this with nothing else than with words and voices. But they are 'beautiful' and desirable to those whose consciences are pressed down by sins."[67]

The view that the church must first and foremost preach the Word can also be altered to read that the Word can be heard only in the church. Positively, this means that church and Word belong together. Negatively, with this view Luther distanced himself from all heretical attempts at constituting a church of the pure. Evil and good live together in such fashion that they cannot be separated.[68]

CRITICISM OF THE CHURCH

Luther's criticism of the church in his Pauline exegesis did not differ basically from his criticism in the first Psalms lecture. In general the criticisms followed the same lines. Naturally, at certain significant points we encounter new future-directed impulses that deserve attention. In addition, a sharpening of critical statements can be detected throughout.

---

[63] *LW*, vol. 25, p. 53. *WA* 56, 60, 6-7 (line gloss on Rom. 6:12).

[64] *LW*, vol. 25, p. 368. *WA* 56, 379, 3 (scholia on Rom. 8:26).

[65] *LW*, vol. 25, p. 124. *WA* 56, 144, 2-3 (line gloss on Rom. 15:20).

[66] *LW*, vol. 25, p. 238. *WA* 56, 251, 25-26 (scholia on Rom. 3:22).

[67] *LW*, vol. 25, p. 417. *WA* 56, 426, 1-4 (scholia on Rom. 10:15).

[68] *LW*, vol. 25, p. 431. *WA* 56, 439, 6-21 (scholia on Rom. 11:27).

Luther's charge that "as is now the case everywhere" the gospel is preached only from the desire for gain or for idle fame rather than from obedience to God or for the sake of the hearers' salvation is more trenchant than earlier but does not differ in content.[69]

What is new, of course, is that at various points Luther exercised criticism of Rome: "But now Rome, having returned to her former [bad] morals, draws almost the whole world after her in keeping with her [bad] example, if the Rome of today does not even exceed ancient Rome in her outgushing of riotousness so that it would seem to demand apostles again, but with even greater urgency. Would that their coming be kindly before they come as judges!"[70] There is even criticism of the curia. Luther spoke of the "filthy corruption of the entire curia"; it is full of "all kinds of excesses, ostentation, avarice, intrigues, and religious mischief." At the same time he quoted Bernard of Clairvaux, who had already said: "It is a marvelous thing! The bishops have at hand more than enough people to whom they can entrust souls, but they cannot find people to whom to entrust their little secular affairs . . . they devote the greatest care to the least and little or none to the most important matters."[71] Further, Luther charged that worship had virtually been made a marketplace.[72] It is possible that the impressions Luther received during his trip to Rome in 1510/1511 affected his attack.[73] Then, too, the reading of Bernard might have been of influence, together with conditions in Rome that might have reached Luther by various means.

More important, perhaps, than the charges against officials of the church are the few basic reflections on Romans 13:1 about the functioning of ecclesiastical compared to temporal authority:

> For my part, I do not know, but it seems plain to me that in our day the secular powers (*potestas seculi*) are carrying on their duties more successfully and better than the ecclesiastical rulers are doing. For they are strict in their punishment of thefts and murders, except to the extent that they are corrupted by insidious privileges. But the ecclesiastical rulers, except for those who invade the liberties, privileges, and rights of the church, whom they condemn to excessive punishments, actually nourish pride, ambitions, prodigality, and contentions rather than punish

---

[69] *LW,* vol. 25, pp. 415-16. *WA* 56, 424, 2-4 (scholia on Rom. 10:15).

[70] *LW,* vol. 25, p. 482. *WA* 56, 489, 10-14 (scholia on Rom. 13:13). In his lecture course Luther did not comment on this section; see *WA* 57 I, 226.

[71] *LW,* vol. 25, pp. 472-73. *WA* 56, 480, 10-16 (scholia on Rom. 13:1). This idea too Luther did not express in his lecture course; see *WA* 57 I, 225-26. Naturally, we must keep in mind that toward the end of the course Luther was under pressure of time and clearly had to condense the material he had prepared.

[72] *LW,* vol. 25, p. 450. *WA* 56, 458, 3 (scholia on Rom. 12:8).

[73] On this subject see Heinrich Böhmer, *Luthers Romfahrt* (Leipzig: A. Deichert, 1914), 142ff.; Herbert Vossberg, *Im Heiligen Rom: Luthers Reiseeindrücke 1510/1511* (Berlin: Evangelische Verlagsanstalt, 1966), 97-104.

them so much so that perhaps it would be safer if the temporal affairs also of the clergy were placed under the secular power (*potestas secularis*); and not only do they not prevent the unlearned, the dull, and the unfit from entering holy orders, but they actually promote them to the highest positions.[74]

These statements clearly indicate that for a long time, and before any conflict with ecclesiastical authority, Luther had considerably greater confidence in secular than in churchly authority. It is fairly certain that his statements reflect concrete experiences with the gentle and steady politics of his ruler, Frederick the Wise. In this period Luther had not yet had negative experiences with ecclesiastical rulers, though he might have heard or read something. In any case, it is remarkable that he believed personal politics in the church would be better taken care of by the secular than by the ecclesiastical authority. This may furnish something of a basis for Luther's later petition to the temporal authority to carry out the reformation of the church.

Next to its criticism of the church, the Romans lecture contains harsh criticism of monasticism. Here too Luther resumed his critical remarks from the first Psalms lectures but sharpened them in some passages.[75] "Self-righteousness," according to Luther widespread in monasticism, received sharpest censure. He must have sensed that his attack on monasticism could lead to the assumption that he wanted to abolish it entirely. At any rate, in an excursus he dealt with the question as to whether it may still be good to become a monk.[76] His reply was that as such all things are free, but that for love of God one may be bound by an oath to one thing or another. An oath performed must in any case be kept. Of course, whoever thinks salvation can be achieved merely by entering a cloister should not become a monk. Despair is no motive for becoming a monk, but rather the love with which one desires to offer something great to God in light of one's own grievous sins.[77] That said, it may be better to become a monk now than in the past two hundred years. Monks are hated now, so that they can learn to bear the cross.

What we are able to glean in theological way from these statements is chiefly that for Luther monastic vows take their place on the side of the law. Luther was ambivalent here concerning his theological reasons for monasticism. In the long

---

[74] *LW*, vol. 25, p. 471. *WA* 56, 478, 26-34. These ideas also Luther did not express in his lecture course.

[75] See Lohse, *Mönchtum und Reformation,* 294-301.

[76] *LW*, vol. 25, pp. 491-92. *WA* 56, 497, 18-498, 12 (scholia on Rom. 14:1). As *WA* 57 I, 227-28, makes clear, Luther did not present these ideas in his course of lectures.

[77] *LW*, vol. 25, p. 491: "If you think you cannot have salvation in any other way except by becoming a religious, do not even begin. For the proverb is true: 'Despair makes a monk,' actually not a monk but a devil." *WA* 56, 497, 19-21: "Si aliter salutem te habere non putas, nisi religiosus fias, Ne ingrediaris. Sic enim Verum est proverbium: 'Desperatio facit Monachum,' Immo von Monachum, Sed diabolum." See also the following lines, 21-26.

run, he could scarcely hold to this view. Precisely these statements indicate that respecting his view of the state, the Romans lecture is a revolutionary document: Luther is engaging in reflections whose outcome would lead to considerable alteration of the nature of the church, as well as of the relationship between the spiritual and temporal authority.

Chapter 9

THE REFORMATION DISCOVERY

THE PROBLEM

In Luther and in Reformation research few topics have been as persistently disputed as those regarding the moment and exact content of Luther's Reformation discovery. Though important lecture manuscripts as well as some letters and other writings are extant from Luther's early period, and though the mature Luther often speaks of his breakthrough, many of the relevant texts have been variously interpreted respecting its date, as well as respecting the point of difference between scholastic and Reformation theology. In addition, at certain strategic points there is disagreement in the interpretation of the dispute with Rome, which began in the fall of 1517.

Naturally, these differing views often screen different interpretations of the central themes in Luther's theology. It is often easy to indicate the link between a particular view of the Reformation breakthrough and the interpretation of essential topics in Reformation theology as a whole. Due to the correlation between the reading of Luther's theology and a given current theological position, discussion of Luther's Reformation breakthrough is extraordinarily complex. In addition, the prospect of agreement among the various interpretations seems minute. Still, the interpretation of Luther's theology as a whole requires acquaintance with the various views and their implications.

There are in essence two main lines in the interpretation of Luther's Reformation discovery. According to one line, Luther arrived at his discovery possibly in the autumn of 1514. Some scholars extend this period until approximately the spring of 1515. According to the other, Luther made his discovery during 1518. To some extent here, too, the period is extended over a few months. On the early and late dating, some have performed a few variations, so that the date for the breakthrough fluctuates between, say, 1513 and 1520. In part the view is held that the discovery cannot be fixed at any certain date but represents as it were the basis for all Luther's theological work.[1] This view has its basis in an alleged "tower-experience tradition," commencing as early as in the later medieval period.

Statements that Luther made later on about his breakthrough point up certain important aspects that in any case need attention.[2] First, the discovery would have to be an event that according to Luther himself took place at a specific point in time. As difficult as the question of date may be, in view of what Luther says, abandoning the attempt at dating cannot be defended. Second, statements of the mature Luther that differ somewhat in detail agree that the discovery coheres with a new, Reformation interpretation of Romans 1:17: "For in it [in the gospel] the righteousness of God is revealed." Any interpretation of the content of Luther's discovery must take this into account. Third, the Reformation discovery concerns not only an exegetical but also an existential question: it decisively aided Luther in his personal inner conflicts (*Anfechtungen*).

For the rest, it might be advisable not to give excessive weight to the question of the content of Luther's discovery by linking it to aspects of his Reformation theology as a whole. Warning must be given against defining the content of this discovery so comprehensively, as if Luther had then immediately arrived at a full-blown Reformation theology. The statements of the mature Luther give no basis for such an interpretation. We must reckon with the fact that before as well as after his discovery, Luther underwent extended theological development. From 1513 up to approximately 1520, Luther developed his theology through continual recourse to signal biblical texts, and since 1516 to a greater extent in numerous controversies. Even after 1520, we can observe important further developments touching central theological questions. Aside from this, warning must be given against interpreting Luther's discovery by way of a formula about God's righteousness and our justification. We should also note that subsequent to his new interpretation of Romans 1:17, Luther made statements that cannot be harmonized with that interpretation. The Reformation breakthrough marks an especially important caesura within a development extending over several years, rather than a total change in face of theological questions.

Finally, we must consider the consequences attaching to the interpretation of Luther's breakthrough for tracking his dispute with Rome. If the early date is chosen, the consequence is that Luther arrived at a new conception of God's righteousness and our justification that all but inevitably led to the dispute with Rome. We may then construe his attack on indulgences as well as his new concept of repentance set forth in the fall of 1517 as resulting from his Reformation discovery. But if the late date is

[1] Thus Heiko A. Oberman, "'Iustitia Christi' und 'Iustitia Dei': Luther und die scholastischen Lehren von der Rechtfertigung" (1966), in *Durchbruch*, 413-44.

[2] See *Dokumente zu Luthers Entwicklung*.

chosen, then the unavoidable consequence is that respecting the core of his theology conflict with the ancient church was decisive. In this case the result would be that in his early lectures Luther already held fresh new views on particular individual questions, but that it was the sharp debate with traditionalist opponents that led him to his new conception of God's righteousness and of justification.

ON THE STATE OF RESEARCH

Research into the Reformation breakthrough began at the opening of the twentieth century with the researches of Karl Holl.[3] Holl, the first to cite Luther's early lectures extensively, was of the opinion that the turning point should be dated between the summer of 1511 and the spring of 1513, thus before the first Psalms lecture.[4] This early dating was held to for a considerable period. It was chiefly Vogelsang who fixed the date of the discovery in the autumn of 1514.[5] Till the 1950s the majority of researchers agreed with this dating. Other proposals were made only sporadically.

E. Bizer's research, *Fides ex auditu,* challenged this widespread agreement. Until this moment, no consensus has been reached on the question of date. In his volume Bizer demonstrated that older research had rashly arrived at its result. He called attention to texts from Luther's early period that in contrast to Holl's and Vogelsang's interpretation do not yet refer to the assurance of salvation. Further, he demonstrated that even regarding the concept of God's righteousness and our justification, the situation is more complex than appeared to earlier researchers. Some texts even after 1514 do not yet set forth righteousness as received only by faith. In addition, up until about 1518, Luther held the view that one can never be certain of salvation.

Bizer fixed not only the date but also the content of Luther's discovery in a way other than research till then had done. That is, he based it on the mature Luther's most significant statements. According to Bizer the discovery did not consist primarily in a new interpretation of Romans 1:17, but in the fact that "the Word . . . [is] the means by which God justifies humans, since it wakens faith."[6] Of course, this definition of the content of the discovery cannot be documented from statements of the mature Luther, who always stressed that his breakthrough had to do with rediscovering the meaning of God's righteousness. Bizer's definition may reflect some influence from Barth's theology.

The importance of a number of Bizer's arguments is that since the publication of his book debate has concentrated to a considerable degree on his criticism of the early dating. What has resulted from this to-and-fro of the debate is that Bizer interpreted

[3] In the volume that I edited I gave a brief sketch of the history of research: *Durchbruch,* IX-XXII.
[4] See esp. K. Holl, "Der Neubau der Sittlichkeit," in *Gesammelte Aufsätze zur Kirchengeschichte,* (Tübingen: Mohr, 1921; 7th ed. 1948), 1:155-287, here 193-97.
[5] Vogelsang, *Die Anfänge Luthers Christologie nach der ersten Psalmenvorlesung, insbesondere in ihren exegetischen und systematischen Zusammenhängen mit Augustin und der Scholastik dargestellt,* AKG 15 (Berlin/Leipzig: de Gruyter, 1929), 40-61.
[6] Bizer, *Fides ex auditu,* 167.

Luther's early lectures too strictly in terms of a pre-Reformation theology; that he underestimated Reformation aspects gaining in strength, but that one may nonetheless no longer hold to the early date with Holl or Vogelsang.[7] As for Luther's own late testimony, despite all the effort, no single interpretation has been able to maintain itself.

From the wealth of interpretations represented in the last decades, only a few significant ones can be mentioned here. Some see what is new and fresh in the link between the "righteousness of Christ" and the "righteousness of God," forged by Luther in a way different from the tradition. Others see the Reformation discovery in Luther's concept of the "promise" (*promissio*), to which he gave new accent over against the entire tradition. Still others draw a distinction between the discovery, which may be dated early, and the "turning point" of the Reformation, the intent being to preserve the connection between Luther's new theology and his dispute with Rome.

As worthy of note as many of these interpretations may be, the question, of course, is whether they can actually be documented from statements of the mature Luther. In the debate over the breakthrough one cannot avoid the impression that the definition given the content of this discovery is at times a personal *confessio* of the given researcher.[8] I must also say that at times the scholar's own interpretation is given without actually engaging other interpretations.

In view of this state of research it might not be advisable in the future vigorously to represent a particular interpretation in opposition to others, but first to note this difficult state of affairs, to present one's own position in cautious debate with other views, then to concentrate on the theological movement in relation to the young Luther without isolating the topics of God's righteousness and our justification. As yet this methodological principle has not caught on everywhere. To a certain extent one particular interpretation is advocated as though no other views were to be taken seriously. At present no conclusion to this rather unsatisfactory debate is in sight. We can scarcely reckon on new sources that could possibly enrich the debate over other significant points of view.

LUTHER'S INNER CONFLICTS (*ANFECHTUNGEN*)

In an extended exposition of 1518 Luther described his inner conflicts. In the fifteenth thesis on indulgences he had written: "This fear or horror [of dying] is sufficient in itself, to say nothing of other things, to constitute the penalty of purgatory, since it is very near the horror of despair."[9] In his *Explanations of the Disputation Concerning the Value of Indulgences* he wrote:

---

[7] See the detailed reviews of O. H. Pesch, reprinted in *Durchbruch*, pp. 445-505, as well as in *Der Durchbruch: Neuere Untersuchungen*, pp. 245-341.

[8] See above, p. 18.

[9] *LW*, vol. 31, p. 27. *WA* 1, 234, 5-6.

I myself "knew a man" [2 Cor. 12:2] who claimed that he had often suffered these punishments, in fact over a very brief period of time. Yet they were so great and so much like hell that no tongue could adequately express them, no pen could describe them, and one who had not himself experienced them could not believe them. And so great were they that, if they had been sustained or had lasted for half an hour, even for one tenth of an hour, he would have perished completely and all of his bones would have been reduced to ashes. At such a time God seems terribly angry, and with him the whole creation. At such a time there is no flight, no comfort, within or without, but all things accuse. At such a time as that the Psalmist mourns, "I am cut off from thy sight" [cf. Ps. 31:22], or at least he does not dare to say, "O Lord . . . do not chasten me in thy wrath" [Ps. 6:1]. In this moment strange to say the soul cannot believe that it can ever be redeemed other than that the punishment is not yet completely felt. Yet the soul [Lohse: the punishment] is eternal and is not able to think of itself as being temporal. All that remains is the stark-naked desire for help and a terrible groaning, but it does not know where to turn for help. In this instance the person is stretched out with Christ so that all his bones may be counted, and every corner of the soul is filled with the greatest bitterness, dread, trembling, and sorrow in such a manner that all these last forever. To use an example: If a ball crosses a straight line, any point of the line which is touched bears the whole weight of the ball, yet it does not embrace the whole ball. Just so the soul, at the point where it is touched by a passing eternal flood, feels and imbibes nothing except eternal punishment. Yet the punishment does not remain, for it passes over again. Therefore if that punishment of hell, that is, that unbearable and inconsolable trembling, takes hold of the living, the punishment of the souls in purgatory seems to be so much greater. Moreover, that punishment for them is constant. And in this instance the inner fire is much more terrible than the outer fire. If there is anyone who does not believe that, we do not beg him to do so, but we have merely proved that these preachers of indulgences speak with too much audacity about many things of which they know nothing or else doubt. For one ought to believe those who are experienced in these matters rather than those who are inexperienced.[10]

This autobiographical text is extraordinarily instructive in several respects. First, it makes clear what is at the heart of the conflicts. They plainly reflect concrete experiences such as the immediacy of death, often experienced by Luther prior to his entry into the cloister, or problems that he encountered in dealing with the doctrine of predestination.[11] Still, these inner conflicts did not culminate in sorrow or despair but in the experience of the divine wrath operative in concrete life experiences of

[10] LW, vol. 31, pp. 129-30. WA 1, 557, 33-558, 18.

[11] On this subject see Brecht, Martin Luther: His Road to Reformation, 76-82; Helmut Appel, Anfechtung und Trost im Spätmittelalter und bei Luther, SVRG 165 (Leipzig: M. Heinsius Nachfolger, 1938); Wolfhart Pannenberg, "Der Einfluss der Anfechtungserfahrung auf den Prädestinationsbegriff Luthers," KuD 3 (1957), 109-39.

suffering and calamity. Luther's profoundest conflict was his experience of the divine wrath. Second, his introduction to the account, reminiscent of Paul, is worth noting: there is an unmistakable echo of 2 Corinthians 12:2. Did Luther intend to set up a certain parallel between Paul and himself?[12]

Of particular importance, however, is Luther's description of the content of his experience. That "the person [the soul] is stretched out with Christ" can only mean that one experiences as it were the crucifixion of Christ in one's own person. The most extreme bitterness, the enduring of the divine wrath, and the experience of judgment with eternal punishments totally exceed one's strength, so that these sufferings must end in collapse. The figure of the ball has its point in the fact that the experience of suffering exceeds what can be endured.

In the passage cited, Luther did not state when he underwent these conflicts. The context does not give the slightest clue to a date. This much, of course, may be clear, that the conflict must have been undergone prior to the Reformation breakthrough. In any event, there is nothing to indicate that Paul's statements about God's righteousness and justification would have spelled comfort in Luther's experience of this conflict. The text helps to determine the content of the conflicts but not their date.

This said, we should note that to some extent Luther continually experienced inner conflicts, even into his later years. Such were, of course, no longer kindled by the problem of God's righteousness, but had to do with his responsibility for dividing the church, or with sickness, death, and the like.

LUTHER'S OWN TESTIMONY (1545)

The most important statement of the mature Luther concerning his breakthrough is his so-called self-witness. It appears in the preface to the first volume of Luther's collected works. The most significant portions read:

> Meanwhile, I had already during that year returned to interpret the Psalter anew. I had confidence in the fact that I was more skilful, after I had lectured in the university on St. Paul's epistles to the Romans, to the Galatians, and the one to the Hebrews. I had indeed been captivated with an extraordinary ardor for understanding Paul in the Epistle to the Romans. But up till then it was not the cold blood about the heart, but a single word in Chapter 1 [:17], "In it the righteousness of God is revealed," that had stood in my way. For I hated that word "righteousness of God," which, according to the use and custom of all the teachers, I had been taught to understand philosophically regarding the formal or active righteousness, as they called it, with which God is righteous and punishes the unrighteous sinner. Though I lived as a monk without reproach, I felt that I was a sinner before God with an extremely disturbed conscience. I could not believe that he was placated

---

[12] See Lohse, "Luthers Selbsteinschätzung," in *Evangelium in der Geschichte*, 158-75.

by my satisfaction. I did not love, yes, I hated the righteous God who punishes sinners, and secretly, if not blasphemously, certainly murmuring greatly, I was angry with God, and said, "As if, indeed, it is not enough, that miserable sinners, eternally lost through original sin, are crushed by every kind of calamity by the law of the decalogue, without having God add pain to pain by the gospel and also by the gospel threatening us with his righteousness and wrath!" Thus I raged with a fierce and troubled conscience. Nevertheless, I beat importunately upon Paul at that place, most ardently desiring to know what St. Paul wanted.

At last, by the mercy of God, meditating day and night, I gave heed to the context of the words, namely, "In it the righteousness of God is revealed, as it is written, 'He who through faith is righteous shall live.'" There I began to understand that the righteousness of God is that by which the righteous lives by a gift of God, namely by faith. And this is the meaning: The righteousness of God is revealed by the gospel, namely, the passive righteousness with which the merciful God justifies us by faith, as it is written, "He who through faith is righteous shall live." Here I felt that I was altogether born again and had entered paradise itself through open gates. There a totally other face of the entire Scripture showed itself to me. Thereupon I ran through the Scriptures from memory. I also found in other terms an analogy, as, the work of God, that is, what God does in us, the power of God, with which he makes us strong, the wisdom of God, with which he makes us wise, the strength of God, the salvation of God, the glory of God.

And I extolled my sweetest word with a love as great as the hatred with which I had before hated the word "righteousness of God." Thus that place in Paul was for me truly the gate to paradise. Later I read Augustine's *The Spirit and the Letter*, where contrary to hope I found that he, too, interpreted God's righteousness in a similar way, as the righteousness with which God clothes us when he justifies us. Although this was heretofore said imperfectly and he did not explain all things concerning imputation clearly, it nevertheless was pleasing that God's righteousness with which we are justified was taught.[13]

Toward understanding this text I suggest the following:

1. As to date, Luther is dealing in the context of the events of 1519. The beginning of the second Psalms lecture to which he refers cannot be dated with certainty. In earlier years the summer of 1518 was often the accepted date. In his new edition, Gerhard Hammer opts for the spring of 1519.[14]

2. The words "I had indeed been captivated with an extraordinary ardor" (*Miro certe ardore captus fueram*) are an old *crux interpretum*. Taken to the letter, they are a "double pluperfect" (H. Bornkamm). If one takes this grammatically imperfect form literally, then Luther is referring to events that may have occurred earlier than the events of 1519 mentioned elsewhere. If, however, one construes this form as a

---

[13] *LW,* vol. 34, pp. 336-37. *WA* 54, 185, 12-186, 20; = *Dokumente,* 191, 28-192, 27; *Durchbruch,* 513, 1-514, 15.

[14] G. Hammer, in *AWA* 1, 1991, 108-13, 221-23.

grammatical error, then Luther is keeping to the context of events in 1519. I cannot definitely decide between the two possibilities.

3. In the sentence prefaced by the *Miro certe ardore* the content is particularly important. It is difficult to conceive that after lecturing on the three epistles to the Romans, Galatians, and Hebrews, Luther wanted to say that he was eager to learn to know Paul in Romans. The content of the sentence, whatever our opinion on the second question, urges the view that at this point Luther was thinking back to the period prior to his Pauline exegesis, at the latest to the spring of 1515.

4. Finally, on dating the breakthrough we must note that in conjunction with the text cited Luther stated that following his discovery he read Augustine's treatise, *De spiritu et littera*, and to his surprise found that Augustine interpreted the righteousness of God in similar fashion.[15] There is also no doubt that in his exposition of the *iustitia Dei* Luther moved beyond Augustine and cited him in line with his Reformation view.[16]

Accordingly, what results from this text touching the question of date is that even if the "double pluperfect" suggests the year 1519, the arguments named under points 3 and 4 assume an earlier date. Aside from this, 1518, and not 1519, is regularly accepted as the time for the discovery even by advocates of the late date.

As to the content of the discovery, I assert the following on the basis of the text itself. Attempts to define it in such fashion as though only the Word were the means of grace (Bizer), or as though a new interpretation of the promise were involved (Bayer), are not at all supported by the text. On the contrary, according to Luther's unequivocal statement, at issue is the rediscovery of Paul's meaning in Romans 1:17, "The righteousness of God is revealed in the gospel." Righteousness is received solely by faith. Previously, Luther had understood this verse in terms of punitive righteousness, as if the same God who threatened sinners through the law worsened his command and threat through the gospel. At that time, Luther did not take the comfort of the gospel from this verse. Now he realized that in the gospel God reveals his righteousness as a gift and that it is received only in faith.

Documentation in the Early Lectures

If we construe the content of Luther's witness in a fairly limited sense, then it might be altogether appropriate to keep, say, to the fall of 1514 for the date of the breakthrough. As early as in the first Psalm lectures there are passages that can be construed in this sense. It appears that the observation first made by Vogelsang is in essence still valid, that is, that in his exposition of Psalm 71 (72) Luther at essential

---

[15] *LW*, vol. 34, p. 337; *WA* 54, 186, 16-20; *Dokumente*, 192, 23-27; *Durchbruch*, 514, 10-15.

[16] See B. Lohse, "Die Bedeutung Augustins für den jungen Luther"; idem, "Zum Wittenberger Augustinismus," 89-109.

points was already championing an exposition of the *iustitia Dei* as described in his self-witness.[17]

Further, what deserves particular attention is that in his exposition of Psalm 71 (72) Luther also referred to concepts that parallel the *iustitia Dei*: "Therefore whoever wants to understand the apostle and the rest of the scripture correctly (*sapide*), must interpret all of this tropologically: Truth, wisdom, power, salvation, righteousness, that is [that] by which he makes us strong, whole, righteous, wise, etc. So also the works of God, the ways of God: Christ is all of this in a literal sense. And faith in him is all of this in a moral [thus tropological] sense."[18] It is impossible to ignore the proximity of this text to statements at the end of the self-witness. In both instances the causative is used, taken over from the Hebrew.

Admittedly, alongside such statements that in essence reflect the Reformation view of the righteousness of God, there are others according to which humans, as long as they live on earth, have no assurance of salvation but must practice humility. Scholars such as E. Bizer, K. Aland, M. Brecht, and O. Bayer have correctly referred to statements and theologoumena in the years up to about 1518 that are at least in considerable tension with the breakthrough claimed for 1514. The notion of a *humilitas* theology that Bizer chose for Luther's theology up to 1518 is too subtle. There is absolutely no such consistency in Luther in this early period.

Against assigning a *humilitas* theology to the young Luther, one should also state that advocates of the late date to a considerable degree ignore that even in his later years Luther could have used expressions appearing to be of the pre-Reformation type. In his interpretation of chapter 10 in the Hebrews lecture of 1517/1518, Luther spoke of the *sacramentum imitandi Christum* (sacrament of imitating Christ).[19] When Luther wrote this exposition, to Bizer's way of thinking he may already have made the Reformation discovery.[20] For those who follow Bizer's definition of its content, such a statement might no longer have been possible then. In a 1522 sermon Luther wrote: "So in all his epistles Paul presents Christ, first, in a picture we should follow, after which he gives us the spirit and the courage that he has, and this is the proper Christian teaching."[21] This statement does not differ basically from others that

---

[17] For purposes of research the text of this exposition should not be cited according to *WA* 3, 461-71 (cf. *LW*, vol. 10, pp. 403-14), as Bizer still does (in *Durchbruch*, 15-22), since the editor Gustav Kawerau was not then aware of a substitution of pages in the manuscript and thus did not take it into account. The corrected text was first edited by Vogelsang in Clemen 5, 151-58. It was followed by its printing in *Durchbruch*, 506-12. On the interpretation of this text see Vogelsang, *Die Anfänge von Luthers Christologie*, 40-61; Lohse, *Luthers Auslegung*.

[18] Clemen 5, 156, 20-24; *Durchbruch*, 512, 12-16.

[19] *LW*, vol. 29, p. 224; *WA* 57 III, 222, 25 (scholia on Heb. 10:19); see also the entire context on pp. 222, 12-223, 4.

[20] In setting the date for Luther's discovery Bizer vacillates somewhat between a terminus in 1518 and the winter of 1517. On this subject see Matthias Kroeger, *Rechtfertigung und Gesetz*, 242, n. 2.

[21] *WA* 10 III, 77, 22-25.

advocates of the late date have described as evidence of a pre-Reformation *humilitas* theology. The statement of 1522 could of course be read to mean that discipleship is required first, whereupon the gift of the Spirit follows. The passage could almost be interpreted in terms of works-righteousness. Yet no one would want to assign the Luther of 1522 such a view.

Apart from this, it must be emphasized that throughout his life Luther held to the fundamental biblical truth of an assize at which all are to be judged according to their deeds.[22] One should always take this fact into account in interpreting and weighing Luther's statements on the complex of God's righteousness and our justification. For this reason warning must be given against too narrow a criterion for distinguishing "pre-Reformation" and "Reformation thought."

This said, dating the Reformation breakthrough in the year 1514 in no way militates against the fact that even in the following years Luther still made significant progress in his theology as a whole, as well as in his statements about God's righteousness and our justification. For the rest, we can observe progress respecting certain aspects of the doctrine of righteousness, even in the 1530s.

LUTHER'S REFORMATION UNDERSTANDING
IN LIGHT OF THE TRADITION

Was the content of Luther's Reformation understanding actually something new? In his interpretation of Romans 1:17 did he correctly transmit Paul's view of the righteousness of God and our justification?

According to the current state of research neither question can be answered in any sweeping positive or negative sense. As regards the question of the proper interpretation of Paul, researches of the last decades have introduced into the debate points of view scarcely ever considered in the older interpretation of Paul.[23] It would be improper to measure Luther's interpretation of Paul by the state of research in Pauline interpretation near the end of the twentieth century. It must be compared with Pauline interpretation in the ancient church and Middle Ages. At the same time it must be stated that Luther set what Paul had to say about righteousness and justification at the center and from that center interpreted all of Paul's theology. In doing so he made the person under spiritual attack his point of reference. The

---

[22] See the important work by Ole Modalsli, *Das Gericht nach den Werken: Ein Beitrag zu Luthers Lehre vom Gesetz,* FKDG 13 (Göttingen: Vandenhoeck & Ruprecht, 1963).

[23] In particular see Peter Stuhlmacher, *Gottesgerechtigkeit bei Paulus,* FRLANT 87 (Göttingen: Vandenhoeck & Ruprecht, 1965); Ernst Käsemann, "'The Righteousness of God' in Paul," in *New Testament Questions of Today,* trans. W. J. Montague (Philadelphia: Fortress Press, 1969), 168-82. For the comparison in method between Paul and Luther the investigations of Paul Althaus still deserve attention. See his *Paulus und Luther über den Menschen: Ein Vergleich* (1938; 4th ed., Gütersloh: Gütersloher Verlagshaus, 1963).

propriety of this interpretation would have to be tested against what was crucial in the anthropological assumptions of Paul's time and of Luther's time.

To the question whether Luther's Reformation understanding was really something new, or whether he merely rediscovered and made fruitful in a new way what was well known to many a theologian of the ancient church and medieval period, only a measured response can be given. In a sense it is true that Luther recaptured an understanding known to many before him.[24] More recent interpretations of the content of Luther's understanding may be dictated by the desire to demonstrate the uniqueness of that understanding at a given point. In contrast, however, it must be said that Luther was aware that his understanding agreed essentially with Augustine. It is also beyond dispute that some exegetes of the medieval period understood Romans 1:17 as did Luther.

Of course, one must immediately add that in the period prior to Luther the actual weight of such an interpretation of Paul was extraordinarily light. Reference has correctly been made to the fact that we should distinguish the exegetical interpretation of Romans 1:17 from its systematic-theological relevance.[25] Whether it was a matter of developing the doctrine of the so-called divine attributes or of evaluating the way of salvation, Romans 1:17 was never the theological point of departure. With respect to the doctrine of God the entire concern, in dependence on Augustine, was to establish a balance between God's righteousness and his mercy, by means of which the *iustitia Dei* was interpreted as God's judging righteousness and the *misericordia* as his gracious condescension. In soteriology Paul's theology of justification meant nothing for questions about the meritoriousness of works or statements about purgatory and indulgence. All throughout one could affirm the *sola fide* with Paul on the one hand, and on the other advocate a robust works-righteousness.

To this extent, the assertion that the content of Luther's Reformation understanding does not represent anything entirely new is of little import. What Luther rediscovered in Paul was not unknown to theologians before him. Prior to Luther, however, the material significance of this understanding for the question of salvation was ignored. To that extent it must be said that in its essential content Luther's Reformation understanding does in fact represent something new.

---

[24] This was set forth chiefly by Heinrich Denifle in his severely polemical work: *Luther und Luthertum in der ersten Entwicklung: Quellenmässig dargestellt,* 2 vols. (Gütersloh: Bertelsmann, 1904-9). The first section of the first volume appeared in an improved second edition in 1904, the second section appeared in 1906, and the second volume in 1909, edited by Albert M. Weiss.

[25] See H. Bornkamm, "Iustitia dei in der Scholastik und bei Luther."

Chapter 10

LUTHER'S ATTACK
ON INDULGENCES (1517/1518)

LUTHER'S PATH TOWARD THE PUBLIC

The dispute over indulgences commencing in the fall of 1517 may first appear to be a continuation or new phase in the course of other disputes. Only during 1518 did it become known that not only the dimensions of this new conflict but also its themes spelled a radical turning point.

The various early-sixteenth-century debates involving humanists and scholastics as well as humanists and representatives of the official church led Luther as well to take a position. Efforts on behalf of the University of Wittenberg reform, begun in 1516, brought him in close proximity to some humanists, though at that time he was considerably reserved toward Erasmus.

First, of particular importance to Luther was the dispute surrounding Reuchlin. In a 1510 opinion, Reuchlin had opposed the burning of rabbinic literature urged by the University of Cologne and the Dominicans. For this reason action was brought against Reuchlin lasting for years and finally ending in 1520 with a judgment via a papal brief. Because of his noble as well as scientifically based persistence, Reuchlin was everywhere regarded as the real victor in the conflict. With their *Epistulae obscurorum virorum* ("Letters of Obscure Men," 1515/1517) younger humanists attacked the Cologne Dominicans in biting satire. Engaged in composing these "letters" were, among others, Crotus Rubeanus (ca. 1480-1545), a leading humanist at Erfurt in the early sixteenth century, and Ulrich von Hutten (1488-1523).[1]

---

[1] On Crotus see Helmar Junghans, *Der junge Luther und die Humanisten,* (Weimar: Böhlau, 1984), 45-48. On von Hutten see Johannes Schilling und Ernst Giese, eds., *Ulrich von Hutten in seiner Zeit,*

Luther did not take a public position in the dispute but wrote a letter, led to do so by a request from Georg Spalatin for an expert opinion, made through Johann Lang. The dispute around Reuchlin was explosive not least because the patron of Luther's university, the Saxon elector Frederick the Wise, was drawn into it. Spalatin chose the route through Luther's friend Lang because he did not yet know Luther personally.

In his response of February 1514 Luther made clear that he saw nothing heretical in Reuchlin's opinion; the conflict did not involve questions of faith but only suppositions.[2] Then appear the all but prophetic words: "When such protests and opinions [as those of Reuchlin] can no longer be freely expressed, then we must fear that finally inquisitors . . . will denounce someone as a heretic on a whim."[3] Rather than dealing with such questions, inquisitors should worry about managing the widespread blasphemies in the church.[4] This conflict around Reuchlin "served as a prelude to Luther's affair."[5] A somewhat later statement indicates that Luther was not yet skeptical of papal leadership. In it he said that he was happy that Reuchlin's case was to be judged by the Apostolic See, no longer by those from Cologne, since Rome still had the most learned people.[6]

Of course, Luther's theology retained its own profile over against Reuchlin and his defenders. This became clear in his distancing himself more and more from Erasmus and his doctrine of sin and grace. In the fall of 1516 he wrote:

> What disturbs me about Erasmus, that most learned man . . . is the following: in explaining the Apostle [Paul], he understands the righteousness which originates in "works" or in "the "Law" or "our own righteousness" (the Apostle calls it that) as referring to those ceremonial and figurative observances [of the Old Testament]. Moreover he does not clearly state that in Romans, chapter 5, the Apostle is speaking of original sin, although he admits that there is such a thing. Had Erasmus studied the books Augustine wrote against the Pelagians (especially the treatises *On the Letter and the Spirit*) . . . (then he will recognize) that nothing in Augustine is of his own wisdom but is rather that of the most outstanding fathers, such as Cyprian, [Gregory of] Nazianzus, Rheticus, Irenaeus, Hilary, Olympius, Innocent, and Ambrose.[7]

From 1516 on, Luther entered the public arena with his new theology. This meant that he presented insights gained from Paul and Augustine no longer merely

Monographia Hessiae 12 (Kassel: Evangelischer Presseverband, 1988), esp. J. Schilling, "Hutten und Luther," 87-115.

[2] *WA Br* 1 Nr. 7 (Spalatin's letter and Luther's answer).

[3] *WA Br* 1 p. 23, 15-19.

[4] *WA Br* 1 p. 23, 20-30.

[5] M. Brecht, *Martin Luther: His Road to Reformation,* 162.

[6] Letter to Spalatin of August 5, 1514, *LW,* vol. 48, p. 10; *WA Br* 1 Nr. 9, 24-28.

[7] Letter to Spalatin of October 19, 1516, *LW,* vol. 48, p. 24; *WA Br* 1 Nr. 27, 4-14.

to his students in the lecture hall but to a wider academic public. The impulse did not come from Luther himself but from the circle of his pupils: they wanted to bring out into the open what they had heard in Luther's lectures. Nevertheless, Luther is no doubt to be regarded as the actual intellectual instigator of these efforts.

On September 25, 1516, for his promotion as *Sententiarius*, Bartholomew Bernhardi prepared theses on the *Quaestio de viribus et voluntate hominis sine gratia disputata* (on human powers and will apart from grace). The disputation took place with Luther presiding.[8] Bernhardi himself had wanted to deal with the theme.[9] In his theses as Luther's then most distinguished pupil,[10] Bernhardi bluntly presented the new, radical view of sin advocated by Luther in his Romans lecture. He extensively cited Augustine's anti-Pelagian writings. This appeal to Augustine must be seen in the context of efforts to reform the University of Wittenberg, which involved replacing the hitherto existing authorities of Biel and Aristotle with Augustine and Paul. Bernhardi's formulation of his theme reflected the polemic against Biel: "Whether man, created in the image of God, can through his natural powers keep the commandments of God the Creator, or can do or intend anything good, and together with grace earn or credit merits."[11] Bernhardi replied sharply in the negative and stated outright that "a man sins when he does what is in his powers, since by himself he neither can will nor devise [anything good]."[12] Postively he stated: "Since the righteousness of believers is hidden in God, their sin is evident to them,"[13] and, "Christ Jesus, our strength, righteousness, searcher of the heart and kidneys, alone knows our merits and is judge."[14]

On September 4, 1517, with his *Disputation against Scholastic Theology,* Luther directed his own attack against scholasticism. Like Bernhardi, but more comprehensively and sharply, he attacked the influence of Aristotle on theology as well as the Pelagianizing doctrine of sin and grace. While one may well ask whether Luther actually intended or planned to reform the church, I must emphatically state that he methodically labored toward and urged on a reformation of theology as well as of instructional activity, thus distinguishing his efforts from those of humanism as early as 1516.[15] It became clear that Luther was attacking scholasticism not from a

[8] *WA* 1, 142-51; Junghans, *Martin Luther Studienausgabe* (1979), 1, 153-62.

[9] *WA Br* 1 Nr. 26, 20-24 (letter of Luther to Johann Lang in mid-October 1516).

[10] See *WA TR* 5 Nr. 5346, p. 76, 10-12.

[11] *Studienausgabe* 1, 155, 5-7; *WA* 1, 145, 5-9.

[12] *Studienausgabe* 1, 159, 15-16; *WA* 1, 148, 14-15.

[13] *Studienausgabe* 1, 160, 14-15; *WA* 1, 148, 35-36.

[14] *Studienausgabe* 1, 161, 18-19; *WA* 1, 149, 33-34.

[15] See esp. K. Aland, "Die Theologische Fakultät Wittenberg und ihre Stellung im Gesamtzusammenhang der Leucorea während des 16. Jahrhunderts," in Aland, *Kirchengeschichtliche Entwürfe,* 283-394 (Gütersloh: Mohn, 1960). See also Leif Grane, "Die Anfänge von Luthers Auseinandersetzung mit dem Thomismus," *ThLZ* 95 (1970), 241-48, esp. 246: "It is of course true . . . that Luther did not intend to overturn the church. But one thing he resolutely intended: to set scholasticism aside and to carry out a thoroughgoing reform of scholarly studies." On Luther's disputation against scholastic theology see Leif Grane, *Contra Gabrielem: Luthers Auseinandersetzung mit Gabriel Biel in der Disputatio contra scholasticam theologiam* (Copenhagen: Gyldendal, 1962).

humanist standpoint but from the standpoint of a theology oriented to Paul and Augustine and supported by Holy Scripture. With this attack a totally new theological orientation made its first public appearance.

Just like Bernhardi, Luther began by attacking the late scholastic understanding of sin, and appealed to the anti-Pelagian Augustine. "It is false to state that the will can by nature conform to correct precept. This is said in opposition to Scotus and Gabriel."[16] The will is not so free that it can ever strive toward the goal set by reason. Luther thus rejected the Occamist thesis that one may love God above all things on one's own.[17] Rather, "since erring man is able to love the creature it is impossible for him to love God."[18] "Man is by nature unable to want God to be God. Indeed, he himself wants to be God, and does not want God to be God."[19]

From these propositions Luther moved to an attack on Aristotle directed not against the Aristotelian philosophy as such but against its significance, particularly for scholastic anthropology. "Virtually the entire *Ethics* of Aristotle is the worst enemy of grace. This in opposition to the Scholastics. It is an error to maintain that Aristotle's statement concerning happiness does not contradict Catholic doctrine. This in opposition to the doctrine on morals. It is an error to say that no man can become a theologian without Aristotle.[20] This in opposition to common opinion. Indeed, no one can become a theologian unless he becomes one without Aristotle."[21] Then follow statements on law and grace, likewise defined by Paul and Augustine. At this point Luther set forth the absolute necessity of grace for salvation, which alone can put the human will to rights. Here too Luther always indicated precisely which scholastic theologians his theses opposed.

At the conclusion of the ninety-seven theses this sentence appears: "In all we wanted to say, we believe we have said nothing that is not in agreement with the Catholic church and the teachers of the church."[22] Luther might have been somewhat concerned that his theses would be construed as opposing church doctrine. This sentence would not be intelligible otherwise. The disputation against scholastic theology is in some respects sharper and more significant than the Ninety-five Theses on indulgences, for which Luther did not feel the need for a like *reservatio*. Ultimately, it must be set down to accident that the conflict around Luther did not erupt over the theses against scholastic theology but over those on indulgences.

---

[16] Thesis 6, *LW,* vol. 31, p. 9; *WA* 1, 224, 17-18; *Studienausgabe* 1, 166, 3-4.

[17] Thesis 13, *LW,* vol. 31, p. 10; *WA* 1, 224, 28-29; *Studienausgabe* 1, 166, 14.

[18] Thesis 16, *LW,* vol. 31, p. 10; *WA* 1, 224, 34-35; *Studienausgabe* 1, 166, 20-21.

[19] Thesis 17, *LW,* vol. 31, p. 10; *WA* 1, 225, 1-2; *Studienausgabe* 1, 166, 22-23.

[20] On this subject see above, p. 26.

[21] Theses 41-44, *LW,* vol. 31, p. 12; *WA* 1, 226, 10-16; *Studienausgabe* 1, 169, 1-6.

[22] *LW,* vol. 31, p. 16; *WA* 1, 228, 34-36; *Studienausgabe* 1, 172, 10-11.

LUTHER'S NINETY-FIVE THESES ON INDULGENCES:
OCCASION AND PURPOSE

What lay behind Albrecht of Mainz's heaping up of offices, or the link between his acquiring the archbishopric of Mainz in contravention of church law, or the sale of indulgences with papal approval,[23] was not known to Luther in 1517. Reasons having to do with the care of souls led him to compose his Ninety-five Theses. As father-confessor he had to identify the ruinous influence of the sale of letters of indulgence on penitents' seriousness. When he came upon a copy of the *Instructio summaria,* which Albrecht of Mainz had allowed to appear in two very similar drafts for Mainz (1516) and Magdeburg (1517),[24] he saw a challenge to his responsibility as professor of theology for the proper teaching of the church.[25] He thus felt obliged to proceed against statements of the *Instructio* that were in fact rather monstrous. Since this "instruction for service" underlay the public dissemination of indulgences, for Luther too it could only be a question of a public act.

The *Instructio summaria,* published under the name of Albrecht of Mainz, highest-ranking prince of the church in the German Empire, was able to lean on older documents for much of what it said about indulgences. In the sum total of what it offered, however, it went far beyond a view that had always been problematic. Further, individual preachers of indulgence were often most generous in commending them. Statements concerning the four "chief graces" furnished sufficient occasion for it:

> The first grace is the total remission of all sins. No greater grace than this can be named, since it gives the one who lives in sins and is bereft of God's grace total forgiveness and the grace of God anew. . . . The second chief grace is a letter of penance full of the greatest, most helpful and as yet unheard of possibilities. . . . The third chief grace is a share in all the goods of the universal church. It consists in the fact that those who give money for the new construction [of the Church of St. Peter in Rome] together with their parents who died in love will from now on and to all eternity share in all the petitions, intercessions, alms, fasts, prayers, and pilgrimages of every sort . . . To acquire these two chief graces [the second and

---

[23] See the indulgence bull of Leo X, "Sacrosanctis" of March 31, 1515, for Albrecht of Mainz in *CCath* 41 (1988), 202-24.

[24] The two drafts now appear in *CCath* 41, 224-93. For the electorate of Saxony and thus for Luther the Magdeburg draft is significant. The question of authorship is moot. It is certain that for its basic statements the *Instructio summaria* rests on older documents such as an instruction of 1515 from the papal commissioner of indulgences, Giovanni Angelo Arcimboldi. John Tetzel (ca. also 1465-1519) may also have influenced the *Instructio,* especially in extending the *facultates,* begun with acquiring letters of indulgence. But perhaps the final draft of the text may simply have been produced in Albrecht's Mainz chancellory without Tetzel's cooperation. See *CCath* 41, 247.

[25] On Luther's statements concerning indulgences prior to the Ninety-five Theses, see Brecht, *Martin Luther: His Road to Reformation,* 183-90.

third] it is not necessary to make confession. . . . The fourth chief grace consists in the total remission of all sins for souls in purgatory.[26]

The document, like others on indulgences, does not make clear that indulgences as such grant not forgiveness of sins but rather the remission of punishments for sin still remaining after forgiveness. Thus, as the *Instructio* reads, and as it was no doubt in many cases understood, indulgences should actually guarantee the entire forgiveness of sins.

In Luther's letter to Albrecht of Mainz dated October 31, 1517, as well as in the appended *Ninety-Five Theses or Disputation on the Power and Efficacy of Indulgences,* the church's and especially the bishops' responsibility for the salvation of the souls entrusted to them is at the heart. Luther charged that due to the preaching of indulgences the common people believe that when they simply purchase letters of indulgence they may be certain of their salvation. This grace of indulgence is so effective that there is no sin of such magnitude that it cannot be forgiven.[27] In opposition Luther said: "No man can be assured of his salvation by any episcopal function . . . because the Apostle [Paul] orders us to work out our salvation constantly 'in fear and trembling.'"[28] He impressed on the still youthful archbishop that "the first and only duty of the bishops, however, is to see that people learn the gospel and the love of Christ."[29]

PENANCE, FORGIVENESS, CHURCH, AND OFFICE IN THE NINETY-FIVE THESES

Two observations indicate that for Luther the Ninety-five Theses represented something extraordinary, even if the theses against scholastic theology were more radical. First, in the fall of 1517 Luther altered his surname, which till then was "Luder," to the new form "Luther," and for a time to "Eleutherius," after the Greek. The first evidence of change is in his letter to Albrecht of October 31, 1517. In alluding to the Greek term *eleutheros* (free) he wished to state that he was free of the fetters of scholastic theology.[30] The name change is thus of equal significance for his biography as for his self-understanding. Next, in his foreword to the Ninety-five Theses, inviting debate, he claims to speak "in the name of our Lord Jesus Christ."[31] None of his other numerous

---

[26] *CCath* 41, 264-69.

[27] *LW,* vol. 48, p. 46. *WA Br* 1 Nr. 48, 17-23.

[28] LW, vol. 48, p. 46. *WA Br* 1 Nr. 48, 27-29.

[29] *LW,* vol. 48, p. 47. *WA Br* 1 Nr. 48, 39-41.

[30] See Bernd Moeller and Karl Stackmann, "Luder-Luther-Eleutherios: Reflections on Luther's Names," *NGWG.PH* 7 (1981), esp. 8, 31.

[31] *LW,* vol. 31, p. 25; *WA* 1, 233, 8; *Studienausgabe* 1, 176, 4-5. On this subject see Lohse, "Luthers Selbsteinschätzung," 158-75, here 162.

disputations were introduced in such fashion. However we answer the question as to whether Luther was possessed of prophetic self-understanding, in the conflict over indulgences he was certain that he represented the cause of Christ himself.

In form, the Ninety-five Theses are theses for debate, not yet fixed doctrinal positions. To this fact Luther made repeated reference in his dispute with Rome. Still, at many places the sentences exceed the limits of theses for debate, especially theses 42-51, introduced by the formula *Docendi sunt Christiani...* (Christians are to be taught . . .).

At the fore is a new and radical understanding of repentance, learned from the New Testament: "When our Lord and Master Jesus Christ said, 'repent' [Matt. 4:17], he willed the entire life of believers to be one of repentance" (thesis 1). The second thesis indicates at least some tension between this New Testament view and the church's sacrament: "This word cannot be understood as referring to the sacrament of penance, that is, confession and satisfaction, as administered by the clergy." In this way Luther pointed out the tension between the scriptural understanding of repentance and the sacrament of the church. The tension is also significant for the question of indulgences. The consequence that Luther drew from the New Testament is that repentance and faith are synonymous: a faith that does not include repentance ignores the radicality of sinful existence. A repentance that is not inseparably bound to faith becomes "performance" and leads to "works-righteousness."

In the matter of the forgiveness of guilt and of punishment there is similar tension between Luther's New Testament ideas and the church's practice. Theses 5-7 read:

> (5) The pope neither desires nor is able to remit any penalties except those imposed by his own authority or that of the canons. (6) The pope cannot remit any guilt, except by declaring and showing that it has been remitted by God; or, to be sure, by remitting guilt in cases reserved to his judgment. If his right to grant remission in these cases were disregarded, the guilt would certainly remain unforgiven. (7) God remits guilt to no one unless at the same time he humbles him in all things and makes him submissive to his vicar, the priest.

These sentences indicate that Luther was not concerned to dispute ecclesiastical institutions and regulations. At the same time, the view that the pope can remit only punishments that he himself has inflicted at least contradicted the sale of indulgences for punishments in purgatory and for the dead. Even if the doctrine of indulgences was not yet officially defined, there could be no doubt that Luther was attacking a custom in vogue for almost three hundred years and assumed by popes in numerous bulls.

In this period Luther had not yet progressed to the point where he totally rejected indulgences. He denied that they extended to the punishments of purgatory, and further challenged the legality of "indulgences from guilt and punishment" and lastly indulgences for the dead. He could recognize only indulgences for temporal punishments within the church. In fact, he stated that whoever is serious about the sacrament of penance will never seek a reduction of the punishments imposed. Conversely, "any truly repentant Christian has a right to full remission of penalty and guilt, even without indulgence letters" (thesis 36). This indirectly challenged the entire institution.

Of particular importance are two theses that shift the accents regarding the view of salvation then widespread: "(58) [The treasures of the church are not] the merits of Christ and the saints, for, even without the pope, the latter always work grace for the inner man, and the cross, death, and hell for the outer man. (62) The true treasure of the church is the most holy gospel of the glory and grace of God." In both theses Luther attacked the theological basis for papal authority in the granting of indulgences. This basis (linked, incidentally, to the further development of the doctrine of purgatory) consisted of the thirteenth-century doctrine of the *Thesaurus Ecclesiae* (treasury of the church). According to this doctrine, the surplus merits of Christ and the saints formed as it were a heavenly treasury from which the pope could grant assistance to those still doing penance for the punishments of sin, in exchange for comparable financial contributions here on earth. In the final analysis, together with the "treasury of the church" in the scholastic sense, indulgences had to be eliminated. Here too Luther set further limits on papal power.

Compared with these critical ideas whose result Luther could no more foresee than the results of his views on penance, the individual critical questions in theses 81-90 appear secondary. In these Luther pointed to the fact that in light of the outrageous preaching of indulgences it was hard even for the learned to recapture respect for the pope. (81). In thesis 82 Luther formulated a question of the laity: "Why does not the pope empty purgatory for the sake of holy love and the dire need of the souls that are there if he redeems an infinite number of souls for the sake of miserable money with which to build a church? The former reasons would be most just; the latter is most trivial."

The Ninety-five Theses, however, did not at all end the discussion of questions pertaining to indulgences. Their significance lies in their comprehensiveness. First, among the many theologians of his time only Luther felt that the *Instructio summaria,* at various points qualifiable as blasphemous, challenged him in his capacity as a teacher appointed by the church. In the Ninety-five Theses he perceived theology's task as responsibly and critically accompanying the church's teaching. What is further decisive is that Luther did not attack indulgences because of specific abuses, as had occurred till then from various quarters, but because of a new theology gained especially from Paul and Augustine. Finally, some passages make clear that scriptural and church authority, particularly papal authority, can no longer be made to agree. Of ultimate concern to Luther was the word of Christ as the sole measure of the church's teaching and activity. To this extent, one detects a rumbling behind the Ninety-five Theses whose results at that time were quite incalculable.

EXPLANATIONS OF THE NINETY-FIVE THESES (1518)

Developments soon took a course Luther had not at all expected. In the immediate reactions of traditional ecclesiasts and theologians, the topic of indulgences was scarcely treated. All the more detailed and sharp were the responses to Luther's statements concerning papal power.

As early as on December 13, 1517, Albrecht of Mainz sent the Ninety-five Theses to the pope in the hope that "his papal holiness will thus take hold of the matter and in timely fashion act to resist such error according to need and opportunity."[32] Albrecht believed that Luther was limiting the pope's power. He did not, however, urge a condemnation of Luther but only a reprimand.

Then appeared the 106 Theses of John Tetzel and Konrad Wimpina (the latter, rector of the University of Frankfurt on the Oder, was the author), debated at Frankfurt on January 20, 1518.[33] In citing the *Instructio summaria*, the practice and teaching of indulgences were sharply upheld. The charge of "error," even of blasphemy, notable in the trials of heretics,[34] was raised against Luther's numerous arguments, especially against his limiting of papal power and de facto challenge to the idea of purgatory. Tetzel and Wimpina concluded by submitting their statements to the decision of the Apostolic See, to the local bishops, and to "inquisitors of perversity."[35] In conjunction with this disputation, the Dominican chapter resolved to accuse Luther of heresy at Rome.[36] In the *Fifty Petitions* of Tetzel printed in April or May of 1518, Luther's view on indulgences was linked to those of Hus.[37]

John Eck, the learned Ingolstadt theologian, likewise contributed to intensifying the conflict. In his *Obelisci*, composed in January or February of 1518 but circulated in handwritten form, Eck not only sharply attacked Luther but actually charged him with "spreading the Bohemian virus,"[38] as well as with numerous "errors."

In his *Explanations of the Ninety-five Theses* of August 1518, but readied in manuscript form as early as February 1518, Luther made more precise or more rigorously set forth some of his ideas. The *Explanations* made clearer than the Ninety-five Theses the New Testament basis for his view of penance.[39] His statements on the limits of papal power were bolder,[40] and his explanations concerning faith more

---

[32] *WA Br* 1, p. 115. See B. Lohse, "Albrecht von Brandenburg," in *Erzbischof Albrecht* (Frankfurt am Main: J. Knecht, 1991), 76-77. The relevant sources are found in *CCath* 41, 293-309.

[33] See *CCath* 41, 310-37.

[34] Thus in thesis 105 (against Luther's 78th thesis); *CCath* 41, 334.

[35] *CCath* 41, 337.

[36] See Helmar Junghans, in *Studienausgabe*, 1, 186.

[37] See *CCath* 41, 372, thesis 14 and n. 10.

[38] *CCath* 41, 430-31.

[39] *LW,* vol. 31, pp. 83-85. *WA* 1, 530, 19-531, 18.

[40] *LW,* vol. 31, p. 95. *WA* 1, 537, 29-32.

clear: "Therefore, we are justified by faith, and by faith also we receive peace, not by works, penance, or confessions."[41] Contrary to the assertion that the sacraments of the new covenant guarantee grace to those who "place no obstacle in the way," Luther wrote: "It is not the sacrament, but faith in the sacrament that justifies."[42]

Now doubts first began to appear with regard to the doctrine of purgatory.[43] The worsened situation is reflected in Luther's twice stating that because of his assertion that the pope has no power over purgatory, in the opinion of his opponents he has deserved death as a heretic.[44] Other than in the Ninety-five Theses, Luther in citing him attacked Albrecht's statement concerning the "first chief grace," but without naming the archbishop by name. According to Luther this statement was the worst heresy ever uttered.[45]

Indeed, Luther now raised the charge that with his assertions respecting the practice of indulgences the pope was setting up new articles of faith. Luther to the contrary: "It is not for the pope alone to decide upon new articles of faith, but, according to the laws, to make judgments and decisions about questions of faith."[46] He concluded with a reference to the need for reformation:

> The church needs a reformation which is not the work of one man, namely, the pope, or of many men, namely the cardinals, both of which the most recent council has demonstrated, but it is the work of the whole world, indeed it is the work of God alone. However, only God who has created time knows the time for this reformation. In the meantime we cannot deny such manifest wrongs. The power of the keys is abused and enslaved to greed and ambition. The raging abyss has received added impetus. We cannot stop it. "Our iniquities testify against us" [Jer. 14:7], and each man's own word is a burden to him [cf. Gal. 6:5].[47]

Luther's attitude toward the pope had worsened. In contrast to the Ninety-five Theses, he was limiting the pope's authority to decisions in matters of canon law. Yet given this limitation, the letter of dedication to Leo X, prefaced to the *Explanations*, indicates that he was still prepared to follow the pope. On the one hand he said *revocare non possum*, which does not mean he could no longer "revoke" the theses but rather "I cannot recant."[48] On the other, he submitted to the pope: "Holy Father, I lay myself at the feet of your holiness with everything I am and have. Make alive, kill, call, recall, approve, reprove, as it pleases you: I will recognize your voice as the

---

[41] *LW,* vol. 31, p. 105. *WA* 1, 544, 7-8.

[42] *LW,* vol. 31, p. 107. *WA* 1, 544, 40-41.

[43] *LW,* vol. 31, p. 135. *WA* 1, 561, 28-38.

[44] *LW,* vol. 31, pp. 154 and 211. *WA* 1, 572, 27-34; 605, 17- 21.

[45] *LW,* vol. 31, p. 183. *WA* 1, 589, 16-27; see above, n. 26.

[46] *LW,* vol. 31, p. 172. *WA* 1, 582, 37-39.

[47] *LW,* vol. 31, p. 250. *WA* 1, 627, 27-34.

[48] *WA* 1, 529, 3. Thus contra among others Karl August Meissinger and Erwin Iserloh, likewise Remigious Bäumer, *Martin Luther und der Papst,* KLK, 2d ed. (Münster: Aschendorff, 1970), 21-26.

voice of Christ who rules and speaks in you. If I have deserved death, I will not refuse to die. The earth is the Lord's and its fulness. He is praised to all eternity."[49]

THE *HEIDELBERG DISPUTATION* (1518)

Alongside the sharpening debate over indulgences and papal authority, the conflict between Wittenberg theology as a whole and scholasticism gained in acidity and intensity, a conflict that had already reached its first heights with the disputation against scholastic theology.

Luther was honored by Staupitz's summons to submit a disputation for a chapter of the Order of Augustinian Eremites at Heidelberg in 1518. The disputation did not occur in the Heidelberg cloister on April 26, 1518, as earlier supposed, but in the building of the philosophical faculty. Besides professors and students the audience was made up of some citizens and even representatives of the Palatine court, so that Luther gained wide notoriety. The setting must be seen as a conscious attempt on the part of Luther and a few friends of like mind to represent the University of Wittenberg reform outside Wittenberg, a reform involving the theological and the philosophical faculty.[50] The content of the twenty-eight theological and twelve philosophical theses (there was obviously no dispute over the latter) totally and completely matched the setting.

In the *Heidelberg Disputation,* just as in the *Disputation against Scholastic Theology,* Luther attacked scholastic theology as a whole.[51] He did not deal with indulgences or the papacy, allowing the inference that he viewed these questions as secondary and supporting the contention that he was concerned with reforming doctrine. The portion entitled *Contra Scholasticorum Sententiam* was a preliminary piece in which Bartholomew Bernhardi also played a part.[52] In the *Conclusiones* (proofs of the theses) Luther's radical teaching on sin and grace reached its sharpest point. The law of God, in itself a salutary doctrine for life, cannot, however, lead to righteousness, but rather inhibits it. Much less can works by the aid of the *naturale dictamen* (natural reason) lead to righteousness. "Although the works of man always seem attractive and good, they are nevertheless likely to be mortal sins. . . . Although the works of God are always unattractive and appear evil, they are nevertheless really eternal merits."[53] "Free will after the fall, exists in name only, and as long as it does what it is able

[49] *WA* 1, 529, 23-27.

[50] See Heinz Scheible, "Die Universität Heidelberg und Luthers Disputation," *ZGO* 131 (N.F. 92) (1983), 309-29; Gottfried Seebass, "Die Heidelberger Disputation," in *Hdjb* 28 (1983), 77-88.

[51] The best text has been furnished by Helmar Junghans: *Martin Luthers Studienausgabe,* 1, 186-218; otherwise, *LW,* vol. 11, pp. 39-70; *WA* 1, 350-74; 59, 405-26.

[52] *Studienausgabe* 1, 188.Text: 190, 1-200, 3.

[53] Conclusions 3 and 4, *LW,* vol. 31, pp. 43-44; *Studienausgabe* 1, 201, 2-3, 17-18; *WA* 1, 356, 16-17, 33-34.

to do, it commits a mortal sin."[54] The contrast between the *theologus gloriae* and the *theologus crucis* likewise appears in the *Conclusiones*.[55]

In the theses *ex theologia* (theological theses) only the lead sentences are prefixed, not their proofs. In the theses *ex philosophia* (philosophical theses) Luther drew consequences particularly for philosophy: "He who wishes to philosophize by using Aristotle without danger to his soul must first become thoroughly foolish in Christ [cf. 1 Cor. 3:18]. Just as a person does not use the evil of passion well unless he is a married man, so no person philosophizes well unless he is a fool, that is, a Christian. It was easy for Aristotle to believe that the world was eternal since he believed that the human soul was mortal."[56]

The disputation made a great impression on its hearers. Martin Bucer, an ear- and eyewitness, reported that Luther agreed with Erasmus in everything but unlike him taught freely and openly.[57] Through the manner of his argumentation Luther won many new friends and adherents who cooperated in the southwest German Reformation. Theologically, however, he was sharply rebuffed by the representatives of scholasticism. His earlier Erfurt teachers in particular would hear nothing of what he had said at Heidelberg.[58] Not only in the confined ecclesiastical sphere but in the sphere of theological study as well the confrontation became more and more harsh: everything pointed to an imminent breach, which given the nature of things had to be irreparable.

THE *DIALOGUS DE POTESTATE PAPAE* OF SILVESTER PRIERIAS (1518)[59]

Silvestro Mazzolini, usually named Silvester Prierias, was a member of the Roman Commission entrusted with introducing canonical proceedings against Luther in the spring of 1518. He composed the *Dialogus* as an expert opinion for the commission in the spring of 1518, and may have submitted it as early as April or May 1518.[60] On August 7, 1518, Luther received the *Dialogus* together with the summons to defend himself in person at Rome on suspicion of heresy. The *Dialogus,* obviously, cannot be regarded as a particularly brilliant theological treatise on the papacy. Still, as evidence of the view then dominant in Rome and of the aggravation it caused in Luther's dispute, it has a significance scarcely to be overestimated. Here we see how

---

[54] Conclusion 13, *LW,* vol. 31, p. 48; *Studienausgabe* 1, 205, 12-13; *WA* 1, 359, 33-34: "Liberum arbitrium post peccatum, res est de solo titulo, (et) dum facit, quod in se est, peccat mortaliter."

[55] Conclusion 21, *LW,* vol. 31, p. 53; *Studienausgabe* 1, 208, 20-21; *WA* 1, 362, 21-22.

[56] Philosophical Theses 29-31, *LW,* vol. 31, p. 41; *Studienausgabe* 1, 216, 16-21; *WA* 1, 355, 2-7.

[57] Bucer to Beatus Rhenanus: *WA* 9, 161-69, here 162, 8-10.

[58] See Luther's letter to Spalatin of May 18, 1518, *LW,* vol. 48, pp. 62-63. *WA Br* 1 Nr. 75.

[59] This text is now available in *CCath* 41 (1988), 33-107.

[60] *CCath* 41, 38.

those who set the tone at Rome thought of the church and the papal office, above all what they had to find fault with in Luther.

Prierias opened with four basic propositions concerning the church that formed the basis of his debate with Luther:

> (1) The entire church as to its essence (*essentialiter*) is the gathering of all believers in Christ for worship. The entire church as to its power (*virtualiter*), however, is the Roman church, the head of all churches, and the pope. The Roman church as to its representation (*repraesentative*) is the college of cardinals, but as to its power (*virtualiter*) the pope, in a manner different, of course, from Christ. (2) As the entire church cannot err when it decides concerning faith or morals, so also a true council, when it does what it can to understand the truth, cannot err, at least not in the end result (*finaliter*)—and I take this to include the head [the pope]. For even a council can initially be deceived, so long as the process of searching for the truth goes on. Yes, sometimes a council has been deceived, though it has finally recognized the truth with the help of the Holy Spirit. Likewise also the Roman church and the pope cannot err when he hands down a decision in his capacity as pope, that is, when he makes use of his office and does what is in his power to know the truth. (3) Whoever does not hold to the doctrine of the Roman church and to the pope as the infallible rule of faith, from which also Holy Scripture derives its power and authority, is a heretic.

In the final proposition (no. 4), the meaning of "what is customary" is identified with decisions of the church. Then this follows as corollary: "Whoever says of indulgences that the Roman Church cannot do what it actually does, is a heretic."[61] The four propositions are the basis for Prierias's subsequent debate with each of Luther's Ninety-five Theses.

Prierias not only represented the view of infallibility to which some gave expression toward the close of the Middle Ages, but with his third proposition actually set the Roman church over Scripture.[62] Moreover, in the corollary he described as heretical all opposition, even opposition to the Roman practice of indulgences. The Roman standpoint in the matter of indulgences could not have been more one-sidedly and pointedly maintained.

---

[61] *CCath* 41, 53-56. The third proposition reads: "Quicunque non innititur doctrine Romane ecclesie, ac Romani pontificis, tanquam regule fidei infallibili, a qua etiam sacra scriptura robur trahit et auctoritatem, hereticus est." ("Whoever does not support the doctrine of the Roman church and the Roman pontiff as the infallible rule of faith, from which also Sacred Scripture draws support and authority, is a heretic.") The proposition in the corollary reads: "Qui circa indulgentias dicit, ecclesiam Romanam non posse facere id quod de facto facit, hereticus est." ("Whoever says of indulgences that the Roman church cannot do what it in fact does is a heretic.")

[62] See Lohse, "Cajetan und Luther," 44-63, here 46-47. See also Wicks, *Luther's Reform: Studies on Conversion and the Church*, (Mainz: Verlag P. von Zabern, 1992), 156-57. Of course it is doubtful whether Cajetan's ecclesiology was really so different from that of Prierias.

When Luther was made aware of the *Dialogus,* he was convinced that the pope
was the antichrist. If in the composition of the Ninety-five Theses scriptural and
papal authority had merely been in tension, now they were irreconcilably
opposed.[63] Obviously, on the basis of the *Dialogus,* Luther arrived at the conviction
that pope and councils could err.[64] Whether this drove him to conclusions that
inhered in his original starting point, or whether the escalation inhibited any possible further development of his ecclesiological views, is a question that cannot be
easily answered. In any event, it was Prierias's *Dialogus* that first evoked the irreconcilable conflict between Luther and Rome. In this connection the debate with Cajetan was also of significance.

[63] See Oberman, "Wittenbergs Zweifrontenkrieg," 335, 340.
[64] So also the editors P. Fabisch and E. Iserloh, *CCath* 41, 40-41.

Chapter 11

LUTHER'S DISPUTE
WITH CAJETAN OVER
JUSTIFICATION, FAITH,
AND CHURCH AUTHORITY

THE SHARPENING OF THE CONFLICT
BETWEEN LUTHER AND ROME

After the spring of 1518 the conflict between Luther and Rome occurred on several levels. First, the questions broached by the Ninety-five Theses and the *Explanations* on indulgences were given wider treatment in the various literary disputes, with both points of view given greater clarity and precision. Next, preparations had begun for the canonical proceeding against Luther, all of which had its affect on Luther's position as well as on the literary debate. Finally, after the summer of 1518, the temporal authorities were occupied with Luther's affair. On the one side, at the Diet of Augsburg in 1518, the aging Emperor Maximilian intervened. On August 5 he informed the pope by letter of the danger that Luther represented to the unity of faith and declared his readiness to help carry out ecclesiastical measures against him throughout the German Empire.[1] On the other side, the Saxon elector was also occupied with the affair. On August 7, 1518, Luther received the summons to appear in Rome. On August 8 he appealed to his elector to secure a transfer of the proceedings to Germany, since a fair trial could not be expected at Rome. This development led to questions touching the relation to authority, the ecclesiastical

---

[1] Maximilian's letter is now edited in *CCath* 42 (1991), 37-44.

view of office, and even of ecclesiology, all at a time when for Luther the papal office had become more and more problematic.

When, early in August 1518, Luther received Prierias's *Dialogus,* he allowed it to be printed without commentary. He thought the piece was so questionable that it condemned itself.[2] A short time later, when the reprint was sold out, he penned a response.[3] Now, for the first time, he stated bluntly that pope and councils could err.[4] Naturally, he had believed for a long time that the Roman church had not erred or deviated from the true faith.[5] His judgment of the papacy, however, was becoming harsher. At the end of 1518, he first expressed the view that the pope might possibly be the antichrist.[6] Meanwhile, the hearing before Cajetan had taken place, the result of which likewise contributed to Luther's ever-harsher judgment.

CAJETAN

On August 23, 1518, Leo X commissioned Cajetan, the papal legate then at Augsburg for the diet, to summon Luther to Augsburg as a notorious heretic. Cajetan was authorized to extend clemency should Luther recant, or to ban him should he resist.[7] Luther's elector took the side of his professor and extracted from Cajetan the promise to hear Luther "with fatherly gentleness," guaranteeing his return to Wittenberg. In view of Rome's desire at all odds to hinder the election of Karl of Hapsburg as German emperor, it approved a settlement between Cajetan and Frederick the Wise without the summons of August 23, 1518, on that account being cancelled. Cajetan thus was charged with two different tasks in view of the impending hearing.

However problematic the attendant circumstances, the curia could scarcely have entrusted Luther's hearing to a more capable person. Cajetan was then the most important theologian. As a Dominican he had intensively studied Thomas Aquinas. He had written a commentary on Thomas's *Summa Theologiae,* in the early sixteenth century the most important achievement in Thomas interpretation, of influence even into the twentieth century. In addition, Cajetan had long represented the papal versus the conciliar persuasion. He was actually an adherent of papal infallibility, though he at least conceded the possibility that even a pope could be a heretic. Nevertheless, on the basis of his theological presuppositions, he did not lack sympathy for Luther's blunt view of sin and grace. To a certain extent, he could even sympathize with Luther's attack on indulgences.

---

[2] See *WA* 1, 644-46.

[3] *WA* 1, 647-86.

[4] *WA* 1, 656, 30-33.

[5] *WA* 1, 662, 31-38.

[6] *WA Br* 1 Nr. 121, 11-14 (letter to Linck of December 18, 1518).

[7] *LW,* vol. 31, p. 286. *WA* 2, 23-25.

Interestingly enough, in approximately the same period as Luther, Cajetan was occupying himself with the topic of indulgences. His treatise on indulgence was read-ied on December 8, 1517.[8] In typically scholastic fashion, he first defined the nature of indulgence and then attempted to explain what could be said with any certainty about it. In contrast to statements by others such as Johannes Paltz, Cajetan's exposi-tions were cautious and measured. In essence he held firm to the legality of indul-gence and also to the pope's peculiar authority to guarantee satisfaction to the faithful from the treasury of the church. At Luther's hearing questions about indulgence were raised only as they involved the treasury of the church and papal authority.

In September and October 1518, Cajetan carefully prepared himself for Luther's hearing. In addition to Luther's Ninety-five Theses, he first read through the *Sermon on Repentance* (1518), then the *Explanations of the Ninety-five Theses* (1518). In the negotiations with Luther the *Explanations* were of particular importance. Caje-tan's preparations found their deposit in his fifteen *Augsburg Tractates.*[9] Significantly, in the *Tractates* as well as at the hearing, Cajetan charged Luther with advocating new doctrines but not with heresy. Clearly, the question as to whether Luther was a heretic was still being answered differently in leading Roman circles.

LUTHER'S HEARING BEFORE CAJETAN

The hearing took place at Augsburg on October 12-14, 1518.[10] Cajetan kept his promise to treat Luther in a fatherly and gentle fashion. It may be that for this reason the objective differences between them became all the more clear. That there was no rap-prochement at any significant point contributed to further escalation of the conflict.

First, Cajetan wanted to induce Luther to recant: "1. Repent of your errors and recant. 2. Promise to teach them no longer. 3. Avoid all dealings by which [the peace of the church] could be disturbed."[11] Luther was not ready to recant without further ado. He insisted on a discussion of the content of the questions in dispute, which the cardinal would happily have avoided. In the main, two points were at issue: first, the treasury of the church, with *Unigenitus,* the 1343 bull of Clement VI at center; next,

[8] On this subject see Lohse, "Cajetan und Luther," 49-50.

[9] On these Augsburg Tractates see Hennig, *Cajetan und Luther: Ein historischer Beitrag zur Begegnung von Thomismus und Reformation,* AzTh 2/7 (Stuttgart: Calwer, 1966) as well as Lohse, "Cajetan und Luther," particularly 50-60.

[10] Regarding the hearing there are in essence the following sources: (1) Luther's report in the *Acta Augustana* (1518); *LW,* vol. 31, pp. 259-92; *WA* 2, 1-26. (2) Luther's *Appellatio M. Lutheri a Caietano ad Papam* (1518); *WA* 2, 27-33. (3) Luther's *Appellatio F. Martini Luther ad Concilium* (1518); *WA* 2, 34-40. (4) Cajetan's letter to Elector Frederick on October 25, 1518; *WA Br* 1 Nr. 110, pp. 233-35. (5) Luther's letter to Elector Frederick, probably of November 21, 1518, in which he refers to Cajetan's letter; *WA Br* 1 Nr. 110, pp. 236-46. Description is given in Brecht, *Martin Luther: His Road to Reforma-tion,* 246-65.

[11] *LW,* vol. 31, pp. 259-60. *WA* 2, 7, 22-26.

Luther's statement to the effect that not the sacrament but faith in the sacrament justifies.[12] Ecclesiology ultimately lay behind the entire conversation, which was hardly conducted in strictly systematic fashion, special significance being paid to the papal office, as well as to the importance of Scripture for the church's teaching. In none of these questions was there any approximation of points of view.

First, as to the dispute over *Unigenitus,* Cajetan made appeal to the bull so as to establish the papal view of the church's treasury. Luther retorted that he was well aware of the bull, as well as of the 1476 bull of Sixtus IV concerning indulgences for the dead.[13] He nevertheless pointed to the fact that the bull of 1343 misused Holy Scripture, citing it against its sense. Consequently, the authority of that bull had to retreat before that of Scripture.[14] Cajetan apparently assumed that Luther subordinated the authority of the pope to that of the council and thus was following the conciliarists, particularly John Gerson. In reply, he began to refer to the *potestas papae,* thus actually to set the pope above councils, Scripture, and the church.[15] The actual result of the *Augsburg Tractates* was that Cajetan interpreted the pope's authority just as Prierias had done.[16] For Cajetan, too, the real point of difference lay in Luther's attitude toward papal authority. Cajetan, like Prierias, went beyond officially established church teaching, and from the outset rejected any opposition to the papalist interpretation as worthy of condemnation.

What resulted regarding the question of the church's treasury was that the pope's authority extended even to this point. The idea, of course, sparked renewed conflict. Cajetan appealed to the bull of 1343; Luther proceeded from the fact "that the merits of Christ [gained] in the Spirit cannot be entrusted to men,"[17] just as it is absolutely certain "that no person is righteous unless he believes in God."[18] Luther also made reference to the dispute between Peter and Paul at Antioch, especially to

---

[12] See above, p. 105 at n. 42 (*LW,* vol. 31, p. 107; *WA* 1, 544, 40-41).

[13] Edited by W. Köhler, *Dokumente zum Ablassstreit,* 37-39.

[14] *LW,* vol. 31, p. 262. *WA* 2, 8, 1-9.

[15] *LW,* vol. 31, p. 262; *WA* 2, 8, 10-16; *WA TR* 5 Nr. 5523, 23-25. In *Luther's Reform,* 179, and elsewhere Wicks agrees that the most important difference between Luther and Cajetan lay with the question of Rome's authority. In support he refers to *WA* 2, 32, 24-30, where, in an appeal from Cajetan to the pope following the hearing, Luther still subjects himself to the pope's judgment and uses language similar to his dedication of the *Explanations of the Ninety-five Theses* to Leo X at the end of May 1518. For Luther's Augsburg appeal to the pope the situation at that time must, of course, be kept in mind. The "fatherly" interrogation brought no satisfactory result. This gave renewed significance to the "summons to apprehend," which had never been cancelled. While still at Augsburg, Luther was in considerable danger. Characteristically, after his return to Wittenberg, he immediately appealed to a council. We cannot treat the Augsburg appeal as if it were not made under extreme external pressure or had been voluntarily decided on: such an interpretation misunderstands the papal methods of repression.

[16] See Lohse, *Evangelium in der Geschichte: Studien zu Luther und der Reformation,* (Göttingen: Vandenhoeck & Ruprecht, 1988), 57-59.

[17] *LW,* vol. 31, p. 264. *WA* 2, 9, 29-34.

[18] *LW,* vol. 31, p. 270. *WA* 2, 13, 12-13.

the reprimand to which Peter had to submit.[19] That the hearing and the mere summons to recant became more and more a matter of debate for which Cajetan was neither authorized nor prepared led to considerable irritation on both sides.

As to the second question concerning the need for saving faith in the reception of the sacrament, the debate was just as unsuccessful. To Luther's statement that not the sacrament but rather faith in the sacrament justifies,[20] Cajetan replied in his *Augsburg Tractates:* "This means building a new church," that is, supplementing the acts of confession, repentance, and satisfaction that made up the sacrament of penance with a fourth act, that is, with the "certa fides" on the part of the recipient. Luther's proposition thus required not an answer but a correction.[21] On the question regarding the sacraments, Cajetan referred to Rome's authority. It was clear that openly or tacitly the topic of the papacy dominated the entire hearing. In his *Augsburg Tractates* Cajetan wrote: "that where the sacraments are concerned, no one is permitted to deviate from what the Roman church practices and preaches: this must be believed and not doubted." From this Cajetan drew the inevitable conclusion respecting the treasury of indulgences: what the Roman church advocates is not dreamed up or invented but is based on the authority of Holy Scripture and the doctrinal opinion of the sacred teachers of the church.[22]

Due to his starting point, Cajetan lacked the requirement simply to understand Luther's position on the question of the need for saving faith. It was of no concern to him in his theology that a person should be anxious over being accepted by God. Cajetan apparently did not say that Luther wanted to build a new church, but that he represented a "new and false theology."[23] By contrast, Luther cited Paul's reference to faith and the righteousness of faith, but also various Gospel reports attesting to the efficacy of faith for salvation.[24] It is particularly interesting that he also appealed to Augustine and Bernard. Augustine had said: "Accedit verbum ad elementum, et fit sacramentum, non quia fit, sed quia creditur" (when the Word is joined to the element, it becomes a sacrament, not because it becomes a sacrament, but because it is believed).[25] Luther also cited Bernard of Clairvaux, who stressed saving faith: "You

---

[19] *LW,* vol. 31, p. 265. *WA* 2, 10, 7-17.

[20] *LW,* vol. 31, p. 107. *WA* 1, 544, 40-41. Whether Cajetan actually let pass the second summons to recant, as K.-V. Selge thinks (*ARG* 60 [1969], 273), seems questionable. In my opinion the report of Luther in *WA* 2, 16, 22-26, clearly rules it out. J. Wicks, *Cajetan und die Anfänge der Reformation,* 103, n. 90, is also reserved toward Selge's conjecture.

[21] There is detailed quotation of the Cajetan text as well as other material in O. H. Pesch, "Das heisst eine neue Kirche bauen."

[22] Cajetan, *Opuscula Omnia* (Lyon, 1581), 113a, 30-36. That indulgences are supported by Holy Scripture, is, of course, a mere assertion, which Cajetan not once attempted to support. See Lohse, *Evangelium in der Geschichte,* 57.

[23] *LW,* vol. 31, p. 270. *WA* 2, 13, 10.

[24] *LW,* vol. 31, pp. 270-71. *WA* 2, 13, 11-15, 27.

[25] *LW,* vol. 31, p. 274. *WA* 2, 15, 28-29. Here Luther cited Augustine's detailed expositions in

must above all believe that you cannot have forgiveness of sins except through the mercy of God. But add to this that you must believe and add this too, that your sins are forgiven by God. This is the testimony which the Holy Spirit brings forth in your heart, saying, 'your sins are forgiven.' For thus the Apostle concludes 'that a man is justified by faith' [Rom. 3:28] out of grace. This is what St. Paul says."[26]

By referring to these two witnesses as well as to other unnamed authorities, Luther was urging Cajetan not to insist on the summons to recant, since he could not: "As long as these Scripture passages stand, I cannot do otherwise, for I know that one must obey God rather than men [Acts 5:29]."[27] Cajetan persisted in his demand and would not be swayed by Luther's arguments from Scripture. The result was that he only met with stronger resistance from Luther. Luther then further reported: "When he saw that I rejected the comments of the opinionated Scholastics, he promised to take action against me on the basis of Holy Scripture and canon law." Luther did not know how Cajetan would do this, since he never produced anything against Luther from Scripture throughout the entire hearing.[28]

This shattered Cajetan's attempt to settle the dispute. Certainly, due to his dual task, the attempt was ill-starred. On the initiative of Frederick the Wise, Luther had hoped for a conversation dealing with the issues. The cardinal may have been prepared for a fatherly hearing but beyond this was not competent to enter on Luther's new theological inquiry. Luther's turning away from scholasticism, his theology based on Scripture and particularly on Paul as well as on a few of the most important Latin fathers, together with his attack on indulgences, on the treasury of the church, and on the papal claim to authority for granting indulgences, considerably widened the gap between both sides.

LUTHER'S APPEAL TO POPE AND COUNCIL

Luther's two appeals after the hearing at Augsburg may be evaluated jointly, since first, they make clear the failure of the church's attempts at mediation on German soil, and second, they point to further development in Luther's attitude toward the church and ecclesiastical office.

In his Augsburg appeal to the pope dated October 16/22, 1518, Luther strove to avoid the imminent, dire results of the failed hearing before Cajetan. He would scarcely have taken this step on his own but bowed to the counsel of others.[29] In the appeal Luther described the origin of the indulgence controversy from his own point

---

compressed form. See Augustine, *In Johannis Evangelium Tractatus* 80.3; *CCSL*, 36, 529, 5-11.

[26] *LW*, vol. 31, p. 274. *WA* 2, 15, 35-16, 3. See above, p. 25-26; Lohse, "Luther und Bernhard von Clairvaux," 271-301.

[27] *LW*, vol. 31, pp. 274-75. *WA* 2, 16, 11-12.

[28] *LW*, vol. 31, p. 275. *WA* 2, 16, 31-17, 6.

[29] *WA* 2, 27; Brecht, *Martin Luther: His Road to Reformation,* 262-63.

of view, appealed to the fact that the pope was not well informed of his concern, and claimed that the judges so far in place as Thomists and Dominicans had been partisan. He petitioned for the appointment of nonpartisan, learned judges. In addition, he emphasized that throughout the entire affair he merely "disputed"; further, that for a long time there had been only differing and uncertain opinions on the entire complex of indulgences. Luther's submission to the pope and the readiness to hear his judgment as "a voice of Christ" is an almost literal quotation from his letter to Leo X at the end of May.[30] Luther was presumably advised to repeat the passage here. After those rounds of debate with Prierias and Cajetan, he would no longer have been able to express submission to the pope as he once had done. Thus it is not surprising that soon after his return to Wittenberg he sent a second, quite different appeal.

Luther's appeal to a council upon his return to Wittenberg on November 28, 1518, reflects a different tenor. As early as October 10, 1518, he had informed Spalatin by letter that he would surely appeal to a future council if Cajetan proceeded with force rather than with discretion (*magis vi quam iudicio*).[31] In the electorate of Saxony, not actually at Augsburg, Luther could freely express himself, though even in the fall of 1518 his continuance was anything but settled. Without for this reason viewing the Augsburg appeal as a mere tactical device, we will find Luther's genuine opinion expressed in the Wittenberg appeal.

With respect to form, Luther repeated the March 27, 1518, appeal of the Sorbonne against the Concordat of 1516, which had declared certain freedoms of the French church null and void.[32] Luther referred to resolutions of the Council of Constance, stating that a legally assembled council representing the entire Catholic church outranks the pope.[33] As may be inferred Luther was clearly conscious that

---

[30] *WA* 2, 32, 24-27; see *WA* 1, 529, 22-25.

[31] *WA Br* 1 Nr. 97, 59-61.

[32] See Hans-Jürgen Becker, *Die Appellation vom Papst an ein allgemeines Konzil: Historische Entwicklung und kanonistische Diskussion im spät Mittelalter und in der frühen Neuzeit,* FKRG 17 (Cologne: Böhlau, 1988).

[33] See the resolution of the Council of Constance of April 6, 1415, in *Quellen zur Geschichte des Papsttums und des römischen Katholizismus,* ed. Carl Mirbt and Kurt Aland, vol. 1, no. 767, 6th ed. (Tübingen: Mohr, 1967): "Et primo declarat [sancta synodus Constantiensis], quod ipsa in Spiritu sancto legitime congregata, generale concilium faciens, et ecclesiam catholicam militantem repraesentans, potestatem a Christo immediate habit, cui quilibet cuiuscumque status vel dignitatis, etiam si papalis exsistat, obedire tenetur in his quae pertinent ad fidem et exstirpationem dicti schismatis, ac generalem reformationem dictae ecclesiae Dei in capite et in membris." ("And first of all, [the Holy Synod of Constance] declares that what is lawfully assembled in the Holy Spirit, constituting a general council and representing the militant church catholic, has power directly from Christ, which anyone and of whatever rank or standing, even if papal, is bound to obey in those things which relate to the faith and the removal of said schism, and to the general reformation of the said church of God in head and in members.") See the similar sounding resolution of the Basel Council of May 16, 1439, no. 776. Luther did not quote these resolutions literally, and in a few instances actually gave them a harsher sound: *WA* 2, 36, 22-32.

toward the end of the Middle Ages popes had often forbidden appeal to a council. Further, he defended himself against the imputation that he wished to attack the entire church or the pope's authority. Indeed, he recalled that even the pope is a man, that even Peter, as is clear from Galatians 2:14, was weak at times and needed to be corrected by Paul. He states that by this example "we believers" are taught that we not only should not obey the pope when he orders something against God's command, but with the apostle Paul must resist him "to the face."[34] In this sense Luther pilloried the "senseless, heretical, and blasphemous" preaching of indulgences that seduce the simple, emphasizing that such sermons make a mockery of the papal office. Against the *Dialogus* of Silvester Prierias he maintains that the pope's power is "non contra nec supra sed pro et infra scripturae et veritatis maiestatem" (neither against nor above but for and beneath the majesty of Scripture and the truth).[35] For this reason he appealed to a future council that might meet at some safe place, and to which he or someone representing his cause could have free access.

The question as to how this appeal should be evaluated and what results from it for a picture of Luther's ecclesiology is not easy to answer. On the one hand, Luther was no doubt leaning on essential trends of late medieval conciliarism, as is reflected in his appeal to the resolutions of Constance and Basel concerning the subordination of papal power to conciliar authority. On the other, the difference between Luther and conciliarism is unmistakable: according to Luther, even a council is "beneath the Scripture"; its resolutions must submit to testing by Scripture.[36] We are not, however, for this reason justified in setting down Luther's appeal to a mere "maneuver."[37] The past furnished no direct model for his position. At best he could identify himself with certain conciliarist ideas. This he did but also made clear where he diverged.

---

[34] *WA* 2, 37, 12-28.

[35] *WA* 2, 39, 31-32.

[36] This has been correctly demonstrated by Christa Tecklenburg Johns, *Luthers Konzilsidee in ihrer historischen Bedingtheit und ihrem reformatorischen Neuansatz*, TBT 10 (Berlin: Töpelmann, 1966), 133-43.

[37] Thus Hubert Jedin, *Geschichte des Konzils von Trient,* 2d ed. (Freiburg: Herder, 1951), 1:143. See also Bäumer, *Martin Luther und der Papst,* 2nd ed. (Münster: Aschendorff, 1970), 36-42.

Chapter 12

LUTHER'S DEBATE WITH ECK ON THE AUTHORITY OF POPE AND COUNCIL (1519)

PREPARATION FOR THE LEIPZIG DISPUTATION

No doubt, the Leipzig Disputation represents another high point in early Reformation history. More than ever, it sharply formulated the views of both sides regarding conciliar and papal authority. In addition, the charge of heresy against Luther was given greater stress. Further, Luther developed his view of the authority of Holy Scripture in greater detail. We should also note that with the intensifying of the conflict Luther was led to accent his ecclesiology in a way he did not intend. Continuing escalation of the debate forced him to conclusions he would happily have avoided. The result was that specific possibilities that previously were open were now ruled out. It is also important for our interpretation that we refrain from evaluating the dispute as merely academic-theological, but note its relation to the question of indulgences and to the attitude of the hierarchy in the indulgence controversy.

Luther's colleague, Andreas Bodenstein von Karlstadt (1486-1541), felt that Eck's *Obelisci,* dated in the spring of 1518, involved him as well.[1] In May of 1518 Karlstadt published his *Apologeticae conclusiones,* in which he attacked Eck by name and defended not only the authority of Scripture but also the inability of the human will to do the good together with its passivity toward grace. On the basis of this

---

[1] See above, p. 104. See also Ulrich Bubenheimer, "Karlstadt," *TRE* 17 (1988), 649-57.

exchange of blows a disputation was planned for which Eck proposed Leipzig as the site.[2] In the original twelve theses published by Eck for the disputation, he rounded chiefly on Luther.[3] The twelfth thesis, thirteenth in the expanded edition soon to follow, concerned the delicate topic of Rome's preeminence. Here Eck attacked Luther's position, which he described as follows: "We deny that before the time of Silvester [I, 314-335] the Roman church was subordinate to the other churches. We have always known that the one who occupies the See of Saint Peter and the faith is the successor of Peter and the universal representative of Christ."[4]

Earlier, Luther had replied to Eck's twelve theses with twelve of his own. Now he published thirteen countertheses against Eck's thirteen.[5] Counterthesis 13 reads: "The weakest decrees of the Roman pontiffs which have appeared in the last four hundred years prove that the Roman church is superior to all others. Against them stands the history of eleven hundred years, the text of divine Scripture, and the decree of the Council of Nicaea, the most sacred of all councils."[6]

At the forefront of the disputation was Luther's comprehensive comment on his thirteenth thesis: "Resolutio Lutheriana super propositione sua decima tertia de potestate papae." Following his intense study of church history, Luther allowed the treatise to appear in June 1519, so that it was already available at the commencement of the disputation. Soon after the disputation, Luther allowed it to be republished in a somewhat expanded edition. At no other time was he so occupied with questions of church history as when preparing for the disputation. Without these preparations he could scarcely have been able to counter his opponents so knowledgeably and confidently in questions of detail. The advantage of the *Resolutiones* over the disputation is that it enabled Luther to develop his view of the papacy far more systematically than was possible during the disputation.

In light of the shape that Reformation theology would assume in the future, this treatise is significant chiefly with respect to the following questions. First, in the opening

---

[2] On the prehistory of the Leipzig Disputation see Brecht, *Martin Luther: His Road to Reformation,* 299-309; Bubenheimer, "Karlstadt," 650.

[3] Eck had originally published 12 theses (*WA* 9, 208-10), to which Luther responded with 12 of his own. Then Eck inserted a new 7th thesis, in which he attacked Karlstadt, so that it would not appear as though he attacked only Luther.

[4] *WA* 9, 209-10: "Romanam ecclesiam non fuisse superiorem aliis ecclesiis ante tempora Sylvestri negamus, sed eum, qui sedem beatissimi Petri habuit et fidem, successorem Petri et vicarium Christi generalem semper agnovimus." Eck was referring to Luther's statement in his *Explanations of the Ninety-five Theses* that at the time of Gregory I (590-604) the Roman church was not yet ranked over the other churches; *LW,* vol. 31, p. 152; *WA* 1, 571, 16-20.

[5] See *LW,* vol. 31, pp. 317-18. *WA* 2, 160-61.

[6] *LW,* vol. 31, p. 318. *WA* 2, 161, 35-39: "Romanam Ecclesiam esse omnibus aliis superiorem, probatur ex frigidissimis Romanorum Pontificum decretis intra CCCC annos natis, contra quae sunt historiae approbatae MC annorum, textus scripturae divinae et decretum Niceni Concilii omnium sacratissimi."

portion of the treatise,[7] Luther gave more accent than ever to the decisive authority of Scripture in clarifying all questions of faith. As to papal authority, at the forefront in the debate raging about Luther, he would accept only Holy Scripture as judge. Testimonies of the church fathers as well as ecclesiastical decisions of all kinds must be seen in its light,[8] the implication being that the meaning of specific passages cited to establish papal power need to be scrutinized with extreme care. The *Resolutio* indicates more clearly than before the so-called Reformation principle of Scripture.

It is also important to note that Luther defended himself against the charge of opposing the papacy, or of denying that there ever was or is a papacy. He conceded that without God's will the papacy would scarcely have taken shape. This applied even if sufficient scriptural basis was lacking. At issue was the reason given for the papacy.[9] The dispute thus concerned weightier matters than external recognition of the papacy. On this topic Luther could actually state that separation from the papacy involved the surrender of spiritual unity.[10] Naturally, he based acceptance of the papacy on the command in Romans 13 to be subject to the higher powers,[11] not on Matthew 16:18-19. Luther did not regard the reasons given for the papacy thus far as untenable.[12]

The details of Luther's argument are of interest here. In his interpretation of Matthew 16:18-19, he stressed that Jesus did not actually give the keys to Peter but promised to do so. Fulfillment of the promise is reported in John 20:22-21, according to which all the apostles received the authority to forgive sins. In other words, the keys are the fellowship of the saints given to the church, which in turn may hand them over to an individual.[13] By contrast, whoever refers the text of Matthew 16:18-19 to the Roman See and thus to the pope does violence to the text. The result, then, is that neither Matthew 16:18-19 nor John 20:22-23 decides the question as to how the papacy may be supported by the New Testament.

In the second part of the treatise Luther dealt with the decrees of canon law, in order to test them by the New Testament. He emphasized that he did not reject the decrees.[14] Then, however, he stated that if Matthew 16:18-19 refers to the Roman

---

[7] The writing has the following three parts: *WA* 2, 187, 36-197, 421; 198, 1-225, 28; 225, 29-239, 35.

[8] See esp. *WA* 2, 184, 1-3.

[9] *WA* 2, 185, 13-186, 14.

[10] *WA* 2, 186, 28-30.

[11] *WA* 2, 186, 38-187, 7. As early as in his *Explanations of the Ninety-five Theses* (1518), Luther had also founded obedience to the pope and bishops on Romans 13: *WAS* 1, 618, 24-28. On this topic see Johannes Heckel, *Initia iuris ecclesiastici Protestantium,* SBAW.PPH 1949, 5 (Munich: Bayerischen Akademie der Wissenschaften, 1950), esp. 35-39, 60-70.

[12] *WA* 2, 187, 33-35.

[13] *WA* 2, 194, 5-8.

[14] *WA* 2, 199, 8.

church, one must conclude that the primitive church was not a church.[15] Moreover, Luther attacked the notion that all bishops in the Latin church were ordained by the Roman bishop.[16] With the history of the church behind him, he stated that it simply was not correct that conciliar decrees should have come into force merely by way of Roman approval.[17] Another point he accented in his examination of canon law was that despite the Roman claim, the pope had no authority to wield the temporal sword.[18]

Finally, in a third part Luther discussed the reasons usually adduced from canon law or elsewhere for authorizing the papacy. He conceded that Rome had in fact enjoyed a preeminence in relation to most churches, but claimed that this did not apply to churches in Greece, Africa, and Asia. Here, as can be proved from history, Rome never appointed or installed bishops.[19] Luther further emphasized that in the last centuries more and more laws had been issued in order to fix Rome's authority, for which reason the church had gone more and more into decline. He adduced further arguments from history: in the Alexandrian church presbyters at times chose someone from their own ranks and elevated him as bishop, just as an army appoints someone commander.[20] The argument reduces to the absurd the Roman claim to primacy.

Luther admitted that he did not know whether Christian faith allows for another head of the universal church in addition to Christ.[21] Further, he refused to describe the papacy as *iure divino* (by divine right),[22] though he was still prepared to recognize the pope as by human right. Finally, he insisted that in cases of death or necessity every priest has the authority otherwise given bishops and the pope. Thus on the basis of the undisputed practice of the church the *iure divino* character of the papacy is refuted.[23]

This treatise reflects a new quality in Luther's way of doing theology. If he first began as exegete, then participated in the University of Wittenberg reform, next entered the academic scene, and soon after took to the general public, through it all concerned with clarifying open and disputed questions, here he submitted a polemic that attacked the foundation of the late medieval church. He would gladly have avoided it but saw himself forced by Prierias, Cajetan, and Eck to carry his criticism further than he had planned. Arguing from exegesis, from church history, and in

---

[15] *WA* 2, 202, 24-28.
[16] *WA* 2, 210, 18-32.
[17] *WA* 2, 216, 16-25.
[18] *WA* 2, 222, 11-223, 18.
[19] *WA* 2, 225, 35-38.
[20] *WA* 2, 228, 22-25.
[21] *WA* 2, 239, 23-24.
[22] *WA* 2, 227, 28-31.
[23] *WA* 2, 239, 36-240, 4.

general, he refuted the pope's claim to divine right. That he still recognized the papacy as a mere human entity indicates how he was at pains to ameliorate the results of his attack where possible; but it alters nothing of the radical consequence of his theology.

THE LEIPZIG DISPUTATION

The various *Protestationes* that Karlstadt, Eck, and Luther submitted at the outset of the disputation are instructive for their views on the controverted points. Karlstadt declared that he never wished to deviate from the Catholic church. He too stressed the authority of Scripture, apart from which he would make no claim.[24] Eck confirmed that he would maintain nothing contrary to Scripture or Holy Mother Church, and was ready to be corrected by the Apostolic See.[25] Finally, Luther adopted the *Protestationes* of the other two, then added that out of reverence for the pope and the Roman church he would gladly have ignored the "unnecessary" subject of the disputation if Eck's theses had not forced him to take it up. He regretted that those who suspected him of heresy were absent.[26] This, too, indicates that Luther did not regard the debate over papal authority to be central or decisive. It was the conflict that forced him to enter it.

In the Leipzig Disputation Luther was still far from repudiating the papacy outright. Just as in the *Explanation* of the thirteen theses that preceded, here too he was at pains to limit Rome's significance. Jerusalem is to be seen as the mother of all churches; even the Roman church originated in Jerusalem. Rome cannot be called "the head and mistress of all churches." Such a claim could rather be made for Jerusalem.[27] Luther next repeated the argument that according to Jerome the title "presbyter" is synonymous with that of "bishop."[28] The result is that Peter was first among the apostles but enjoyed no prerogative of *potestas*, rather of "honor."[29]

Interestingly enough, in his defense of papal primacy as by divine right Eck did not make final appeal to *Unam sanctam*, the famous bull of Boniface VIII in 1302, in which not only the "two-sword theory" appeared in particularly pronounced form but also the necessity of papal primacy for salvation was rigorously maintained.[30] At

---

[24] *WA* 59, 433, 18-30.

[25] *WA* 59, 433, 31-434, 38.

[26] *WA* 59, 434, 39-49.

[27] *WA* 59, 439, 194-97.

[28] *WA* 59, 439, 215-440, 218.

[29] *WA* 59, 447, 458-60: "Hoc sane fateor, apostolum Petrum fuisse primum in numero apostolorum et ei deberi honoris praerogativam, sed non potestatis." ("This I surely admit, that the apostle Peter was first in the number of apostles; that the prerogative of honor is due him, but not the prerogative of power.")

[30] See *Quellen zur Geschichte des Papsttums und des römischen Katholizismus*, vol. 1, ed. Kurt Aland, 6th

the same time, Eck referred expressly to the fact that the statements of Wyclif and Hus against this bull were condemned.[31] Eck deliberately touched on this theme in order to provoke Luther to contradict it.

Shortly thereafter Luther declared that among the articles by Hus or the Bohemians many were Christian and evangelical, articles the universal church could not condemn, such as that there is only one universal church.[32] He continued that among the most Christian affirmations of Hus was the statement that it is not necessary for salvation to believe that the Roman church is superior to the other churches. He then gruffly added that it was of no matter to him whether this sentence was from Wyclif or Hus. In support he referred to the fact that even church fathers such as Basil, Gregory of Nazianzus, Epiphanius, and many others would not have observed this article.[33]

This led to a dialogue over the consequences to be drawn from ancient church history on the subject of the primate. While Luther could rightly claim that many important church fathers would have known nothing of a Roman primate, Eck just as correctly could point to the fact that, in the christological controversy, for example, the Constantinopolitan patriarch Flavian appealed to Leo I to retain the doctrine of the two natures as per earlier decisions, and that Flavian was able to hold out thanks not least to support from Rome. In addition, the Council of Chalcedon's reinstatement of Flavian in his patriarchal office occurred with Rome's support.[34] Indeed, Eck was at pains to prove that even Athanasius appealed to Rome.[35] There is no support for such an assertion.

Luther's words have profound significance: "It is not in the power of the Roman pope or an inquisitor of heresy to create new articles of faith. Rather [it is their task] to judge according to existing articles of faith. No Christian believer can be forced [to believe an article] beyond Holy Scripture—which in the true sense is of divine right—apart from a new and confirmed revelation."[36] Just as in his *Explanation* of the

---

ed. (Tübingen: Mohr, 1967), no. 746. The bull says of the two swords: "Uterque ergo est in potestate ecclesiae, spiritualis scilicet gladius et materialis. Sed is quidem pro ecclesia, ille vero ab ecclesia exercendus." ("Both swords are thus in the church's hand, the spiritual and the temporal. The latter is to be exercised on behalf of the church, but the former by the church.") On the necessity of the papal office for salvation the bull states without restriction: "Porro subesse Romano Pontifici omnino humanae creaturae declaramus, dicimus, diffinimus et pronunciamus omnino esse de necessitate salutis" ("For the rest we declare, state, determine, and announce that it is necessary for everyone's salvation to be subject to the pope.")

[31] *WA* 59, 461, 880-91; see DS 1191.

[32] *WA* 59, 466, 1048-51.

[33] *WA* 59, 466, 1055-59.

[34] *WA Br* 1 Nr. 192, p. 482, 130-35 (letter of Eck to Frederick the Wise on 8.11.1519); see pp. 483, 142-44; 484, 212-485, 215.

[35] *WA Br* 1 Nr. 192, p. 485, 223 (Eck to Frederick the Wise on 8.11.1519).

[36] *WA* 59, 466, 1059-62.

thirteenth thesis, now too in establishing scriptural authority Luther appealed to John Gerson as well as in particular to Augustine: "I have learned to accord this honor to all those books taken to be canonical."[37] Due to his refusal to accept Rome's preeminence as necessary to salvation, Eck described him as a patron of the Bohemians.[38]

Respecting the further progress of the disputation, of particular importance in Luther's theological argument was his appeal to Panormitanus for the statement that councils can err. Nicholas of Tudeschi (1386-1445), commonly named Panormitanus, was regarded as the last great teacher of canon law in the medieval period. In his years as archbishop of Palermo (1435-1445), through written opinions and comments on canon law, he carefully pursued the course of the Council of Basel/Ferarra (1431-1449). In the sixteenth century he was revered by traditionalists and evangelicals alike, though at times for different insights.[39] For the opinion on the liability of councils for error, Luther could rightly appeal to Panormitanus,[40] further indication that on scriptural as well as on conciliar authority medieval lines of tradition could lead to Reformation as well as to anti-Reformation positions. Luther's subsequent view that the council is "a creature of the word" was obviously not pioneered by Panormitanus,[41] nor can the link between scriptural authority and conciliar liability to error be documented in Panormitanus.

In the further course of the debate Luther ameliorated his position on conciliar liability to error by conceding that in his opinion neither a council nor the church as a whole errs in questions of faith. Touching other questions it was not necessary that the church be free of error.[42]

On the question of scriptural authority, we should emphasize that it was at the Leipzig Disputation that Luther first clearly distinguished the canonical writings in the authentic sense from the Apocrypha, that is, from writings contained not in the Hebrew but in the Greek Old Testament. On the question of purgatory, 2 Maccabees 12:46 ("Therefore he [Judas Maccabeus] made atonement for the dead, so that they might be delivered from their sin") was often cited in support. Luther said: "Now it is my opinion that in all of Scripture there is not a mention of purgatory that could pass the test in case of dispute or be appealed to with conviction. As far as the book of Maccabees is concerned, since it is not in the canon, it is of course convincing to

---

[37] WA 59, 466, 1064-467, 1070; Augustine, Ep. 82.3; see above, p. 26-27, n. 28.

[38] WA 59, 472, 1230-47.

[39] Melanchthon quoted him in the Apology 11:8 (65): Book of Concord, p. 181, 8.

[40] See WA 59, 480, n. 280.

[41] WA 59, 479, 1465.

[42] WA 59, 547, 3577-79: "Et ut meo sensu loquar, credo concilium et ecclesiam nunquam errare in his quae sunt fidei; in caeteris non est necesse non errare." ("And if I may speak my mind, I believe that a council and the church never err in those things which pertain to faith; in other things it is not necessary to be free of error.")

believers but powerless against the stiff-necked."[43] Here Luther made clear that the weight of individual biblical statements must be tested throughout. Scriptural authority must be understood from the actual midpoint of Scripture.

THE EFFECT OF THE LEIPZIG DISPUTATION

As important as the results of the disputation were for the canonical proceedings against Luther,[44] it yielded important results for his own theology. First, Luther was not content with accepting as Christian and evangelical only a few of the articles of Hus condemned at Constance. On the basis of continually developing contacts with Bohemian theologians, and after reading some writings by Hus, he recognized that in all essential questions Hus had taught "evangelically" and for it suffered a martyr's death. Luther's evaluation of the Hussites thus soon came to be more positive than at Leipzig.[45] Criticism of them receded altogether. As early as in his June 1520 treatise, *To the Christian Nobility of the German Nation,* he urged serious discussions with the Bohemians with the aim of possibly overcoming division in the church. At the same time, he evaluated the separate doctrines of the Bohemians in surprisingly cautious and discrete fashion.[46]

Next, the question of scriptural authority required further clarification. Even after 1519, Luther could often insist on the letter or on particular verses of the Bible as absolute authority. From now on, however, he could reflect in a more discriminating way and in a way appropriate to the content of Scripture. Scripture may not be used as a law book or reference for answering questions that arise, but must always be interpreted with regard to its central content. Even this differentiation, however much it may be implied earlier, first occurred in the course of the indulgence controversy.

Further, the Leipzig Disputation also had important consequences for Luther's concept of the church. In his early lectures Luther had placed all the emphasis on the spiritual element and ultimately regarded the church as the number of the faithful. In the beginning, neither the papacy nor the hierarchy had been a problem for him.[47]

---

[43] *WA* 59, 527, 2936-528, 2939. On this subject see B. Lohse, "Die Entscheidung der lutherischen Reformation über den Umfang des alttestamentlichen Kanons," in *Evangelium in der Geschichte,* 211-36, here 219-20.

[44] On these aspects see first of all Brecht, *Martin Luther: His Road to Reformation,* 322-48.

[45] See Jaroslav Pelikan, *Obedient Rebels: Catholic Substance and Protestant Principle in Luther's Reformation* (New York: Harper & Row, 1964); Lohse, "Luther und Huss" (1965), in *Evangelium in der Geschichte;* 65-79; Scott H. Hendrix, "We Are All Hussites? Hus and Luther Revisited," *ARG* 65 (1974), 134-61.

[46] See esp. *To the Christian Nobility of the German Nation, LW,* vol. 44, pp. 194-200. *WA* 6, 454, 17-457, 27.

[47] See above, p. 63-64.

His ecclesiology gave particular stress to the contrast between the "spiritual" and the "bodily." In the controversies of 1519 none of these ideas was surrendered, but the disputed questions took center stage and then inevitably yielded certain new accents in Luther's own ecclesiology. The phraseology "spiritual" and "temporal" was gradually replaced by the distinction between the true and false church.

The reason for the change lies in the fact that the ecclesiastical condemnations could no longer be accepted without further ado. With the revision of Luther's evaluation of the Hussites, the identification of the Catholic church with true Christianity clearly became problematic. Luther could not avoid the perception that there were Christians outside the Catholic church. Though some outside the Western church were excommunicated, in some respects they could more properly be called Christian than members of the Catholic church. What is "Christian" could not flatly be judged by membership in a church, but rather by Holy Scripture and faith.

It is also important that Luther's identification of the pope with the antichrist, often expressed in private, led to giving greater attention to apocalyptic ideas. These ideas are less apparent in the Leipzig Disputation than in the second Psalms lecture, begun in 1519.[48] Further, it is clear that Luther's acceptance of these ideas was intimately linked to his dispute with Rome. They might have been based less on specific impulses from Luther's early period, when the idea of the antichrist was still without great significance. Luther further developed his understanding of history hand in hand with his acceptance of apocalyptic ideas.

Finally, Luther's conflict with Cajetan as well as with Eck was obviously significant for the further development of his view on the sacraments. That the need for personal faith in receiving sacramental grace was in dispute had to force Luther to reflect further on the question.

So far it may be said that the dispute with Rome from 1517 to 1519 set the switches for the further development of Luther's theology. A bit later, intra-evangelical debates also gained in significance.

---

[48] See *AWA* 1–3. On the dating of the *Operationes in Psalmos* see Gerhard Hammer, in *AWA* 1, 1991, 1:107-16. On the apocalyptic ideas and development of the antichrist idea in the young Luther see the work of Tarald Rasmussen, *Inimici Ecclesiae: Das ekklesiologische Feindbild in Luthers Dictata super Psalterium (1513-1515) im Horizont der theologischen Tradition*, SMRT 44 (Leiden: Brill, 1989).

Chapter 13

LUTHER'S DISPUTE WITH THE SACRAMENTAL TEACHING OF HIS TIME (1519/1520)

THE SERMONS ON THE SACRAMENT FROM 1519

The debate arising over Luther's Ninety-five Theses spread wider and wider. First, if the polemics of his traditionalist opponents set the topic of papal authority at center, the teaching on the sacraments soon came to be intensively discussed. In his *Explanations of the Ninety-five Theses* (1518) Luther stated that it is not the sacrament but rather faith that justifies. At the Augsburg hearing Cajetan had contested this statement.[1] It is hardly surprising that the question of the sacraments soon came to be heatedly discussed.

Soon after his hearing before Cajetan, Luther dealt with the doctrine of the sacraments in detail. In doing so he further developed an impulse observable in his early lectures.[2] He presented the result of his reflections in various "Sermons" of 1519 and 1520, a literary genre that he had used as early as 1518 for writings that were partly in Latin and partly in German. It is also clear that the sole authority of Scripture, given more and more stress as early as in the indulgence controversy, was also decisive in discussing sacramental doctrine. Just as on the question of the

---

[1] *LW,* vol. 31, p. 107; *WA* 1, 544, 40-41; *LW,* vol. 31, p. 261; *WA* 2, 7, 35-40. 13, 6-16, 12. See above, pp. 112-15.

[2] See above, pp. 57-59, 78-80.

authority of pope and council, so now on the doctrine of the sacraments, Luther was no longer prepared uncritically to follow certain church decisions. He tested these decisions by the statements of Scripture, though in this early phase of his teaching he did not yet openly attack medieval decisions.

Three of Luther's sermons on the sacraments come down to us from the year 1519: *The Sacrament of Penance*, *The Holy and Blessed Sacrament of Baptism*, and *The Blessed Sacrament of the Holy and True Body of Christ, and the Brotherhoods*. Luther gave no reason for dealing with only these three, but in a letter to Spalatin from December 18, 1519, he wrote that no one should expect sermons from him on the others, since he could not recognize them as sacraments. In this letter Luther went on to state that we may speak of a sacrament only where a divine promise is expressly given, since God never deals with his creatures apart from the Word of promise and the faith that receives it.[3] The remark indicates that Luther had already arrived at broader insights than his sermons make clear. In the early years of his dispute with Rome he was often more cautious in German than in his Latin writings or letters.[4] Despite this tension between his published position and his actual opinion given further development, these sermons have their special and to a certain extent also enduring significance.

The sermons are dedicated to the widowed Duchess Margarethe of Braunschweig-Lüneberg. Luther had been urged from various quarters to speak on the sacraments, since there were many troubled and anxious consciences "who do not know the holy and gracious sacrament, nor know how to use it," something that Luther had also experienced.[5] In the meantime he had discovered a new relation to the sacrament that was clearly not only theological but also personal. It thus took on importance for him as a means of grace and a strengthening of faith in the midst of inner conflict. Statements in his 1517/1518 lecture on Hebrews indicated a new impulse in this direction.[6] Now he had made further progress.

In all three sermons Luther gave a unique definition of the sacrament that is without precedent in all the tradition. According to Luther, what is first to be distinguished is the sacrament or sign, then its meaning, and third, faith.[7] What is

---

[3] *WA Br* 1 Nr. 231, 19-24: "De aliis sacramentis non est, quod tu vel ullus hominum ex me speret aut exspectet ullum sermonem, donec docear, quo loco queam illa probare. Non enim ullum mihi reliquum est sacramentum, quod sacramentum non sit, nisi ubi expressa detur promissio divina, que fidem exerceat, cum sine verbo promittentis & fide suscipientis nihil possuit nobis esse cum Deo negotii." ("Neither you nor anyone else should look for or expect a word from me on other sacraments, till I discover under what condition I can accept them. For no other sacrament is left to me, since there is no sacrament except where a divine promise is expressly given and evokes faith, and since apart from the word of promise and the faith that receives it there could be nothing of our dealing with God.")

[4] On this topic see Wilhelm Maurer, *Von der Freiheit eines Christenmenschen* (Göttingen: Vandenhoeck & Ruprecht, n.d.).

[5] *WA* 2, 713, 20-23.

[6] See above, pp. 79-80.

[7] *The Sacrament of Penance*, *LW*, vol. 35, p. 11; *WA* 2, 715, 21-39. *The Holy and Blessed Sacrament of*

especially striking is that faith is taken up into the definition of the sacrament. In the opinion of Luther's opponents, this endangered the objectivity of the saving gift. For Luther, however, it expressed the mutual relation between the word of promise and the faith that receives it.

According to Luther, at the heart of the sacrament of penance are God's remission of guilt as well as the faith "that the absolution and words of the priest are true, by the power of Christ's words, 'Whatever you loose . . . shall be loosed, etc.'"[8] What Luther had urged against Cajetan he now gave sharp formulation: "It follows further that the forgiveness of guilt is not within the province of any human office or authority, be it pope, bishop, priest or any other. Rather it depends exclusively upon the word of Christ and your own faith. For Christ did not intend to base our comfort, our salvation, our confidence on human words or deeds, but only upon himself, upon his words and deeds."[9] For the first time, the Reformation view of the universal priesthood of all the baptized is clearly stated: a pope or bishop does nothing more in this sacrament than a priest; "indeed, where there is no priest, each individual Christian, even a woman or child, does as much."[10]

Similarly, in the sermon on baptism Luther gave special weight to its meaning and to faith. If in the sermon on penance he had begun directly to reflect on forgiveness, it was clear that he had difficulty speaking of "sign" in connection with it; now he wrote: "Baptism is an external sign or token which so separates us from all men not baptized that we are thereby known as a people of Christ, our Leader, under whose banner of the holy cross we continually fight against sin."[11] The sign consists in being baptized in the name of the triune God, which means "a blessed dying unto sin and a resurrection in the grace of God, so that the old man, conceived and born in sin, is there drowned, and a new man, born in grace, comes forth and rises."[12] Concretely living out this blessed dying lasts till one's bodily death. Only in death is one completely "sunk in baptism, and that which baptism signifies comes to pass."[13] "Therefore the life of a Christian, from baptism to the grave, is nothing else than the beginning of a blessed death. For at the Last Day God will make him altogether new."[14] In this connection Luther spoke of the content of the divine promise shared in the baptism, or, in a favorite picture of the covenant wrote that in baptism "God allies himself with you and becomes one with you in a gracious covenant of

Baptism, *LW,* vol. 35, p. 30; *WA* 2, 727, 20-29. *The Blessed Sacrament of the Holy and True Body of Christ, and the Brotherhoods, LW,* vol. 35, p. 49; *WA* 2, 742, 5-14.

[8] *LW,* vol. 35, p. 11. *WA* 2, 715, 29-30.
[9] *LW,* vol. 35, p. 12. *WA* 2, 716, 13-18.
[10] *LW,* vol. 35, p. 12. *WA* 2, 716, 25-28.
[11] *LW,* vol. 35, p. 29. *WA* 2, 727, 20-23.
[12] *LW,* vol. 35, p. 30. *WA* 2, 727, 30-33.
[13] *LW,* vol. 35, p. 30. *WA* 2, 728, 15-16.
[14] *LW,* vol. 35, p. 31. *WA* 2, 728, 27-29.

comfort."[15] In this covenant the baptized promises ever more to put sin to death and to be exercised with many good works and various sufferings. As to the third element in baptism, "Faith means that one firmly believes all this: that the sacrament not only signifies death and the resurrection at the Last Day, by which a person is made new to live without sin eternally, but also that it assuredly begins and achieves this; that it establishes a covenant between us and God to the effect that we will fight against sin and slay it, even to our dying breath."[16]

A few aspects of the sermon on baptism deserve special emphasis. First, as early as in his Romans lecture Luther had described the Christian as *simul peccator et iustus*.[17] Here he took up the idea in a commonly understandable way, attacking the notion that sin no longer exists after baptism. In fairly unguarded language he said that "our flesh, so long as it lives here, is by nature wicked and sinful."[18] In another passage, likewise free of anxiety over misinterpretation, he referred to Augustine's word concerning the "natural and sinful appetites."[19] Admittedly, an ascetic tone was sounding through.

There is an ascetic caste to Luther's idea that there are instances when one should become a monk:

> But he who seeks more suffering, and by much exercise would speedily prepare himself for death and soon attain the goal of his baptism, let him bind himself to chastity or to the spiritual order. For the spiritual estate, if it is as it ought to be, should be full of torment and suffering in order that he who belongs to it may have more exercise in the work of his baptism than the man who is in the estate of matrimony, and through such torment quickly grow used to welcoming death with joy, and so attain the purpose of his baptism.[20]

In this context Luther was still subordinating monkhood or membership in the order to the ruling estate in spiritual government, likewise to be exercised in spiritual sufferings and works "unto death." At the same time, he emphasized that in such practices the standard should not be forgotten.

What is noteworthy here, of course, is that monasticism, as Luther already referred to it in the first Psalms lecture,[21] was recommended merely as signifying fulfillment of the baptismal covenant but was not viewed as superior to the manner of life incumbent on the average Christian.

[15] *LW*, vol. 35, p. 33. *WA* 7, 730, 21-22.
[16] *LW*, vol. 35, p. 35. *WA* 2, 732, 2-6.
[17] See above, p. 76.
[18] *LW*, vol. 35, p. 32. *WA* 2, 729, 24-25.
[19] *LW*, vol. 35, p. 33. *WA* 2, 730, 11.
[20] *LW*, vol. 35, p. 41. *WA* 2, 736, 12-18. On the subject see Lohse, *Mönchtum und Reformation: Luthers Auseinandersetzung mit dem Mönchsideal des Mittelalters*, FKDG 12 (Göttingen: Vandenhoeck & Ruprecht, 1963), 332-35.
[21] See above, pp. 58-59.

Finally, just like the sermon on baptism, *The Blessed Sacrament of the Holy and True Body of Christ* exhibits an unmistakable uniqueness over against the tradition as well as over against Luther's later teaching on the Lord's Supper. Luther called the form and appearance of the bread and wine the sign, its meaning or effect the fellowship of all the saints, to which he referred the term *communio*,[22] and lastly faith a true, personal belief in salvation.

If the "covenant" idea played a central role in the sermon on baptism, the sermon on the Lord's Supper is thoroughly interlaced with the idea of "fellowship," from and toward which all other themes were directed. Luther interpreted the *communio* with the remark:

> that Christ and all saints are one spiritual body, just as the inhabitants of a city are one community and body, each citizen being a member of the other and of the entire city. All the saints, therefore, are members of Christ and of the church, which is a spiritual and eternal city of God. And whoever is taken into this city is said to be received into the community of saints and to be incorporated into Christ's spiritual body and made a member of him.[23]

On this basis Luther described forgiveness of sins as the special gift of the Supper: "that Christ and his saints intercede for us before God, so that this sin may not be charged to our account by God's strict judgment."[24] In this sense, the Lord's Supper is the strengthening of the individual fainthearted Christian's sinful conscience: "If he would be rid of them all, let him go joyfully to the sacrament of the altar and lay down his woe in the midst of the community [of saints] and seek help from the entire company of the spiritual body—just as a citizen whose property has suffered damage or misfortune at the hands of his enemies makes complaint to his town council and fellow citizens and asks them for help."[25] Obviously, in such an action, as Luther urged against Cajetan, personal faith in salvation is indispensable.

Luther also cited the words of institution under this device of fellowship. In them Christ intended to say: "I am the Head, I will be the first to give himself for you. I will make your suffering and misfortune my own and will bear it for you, so that you in your turn may do the same for me and for one another, allowing all things to be common property, in me, and with me."[26]

In addition, the ideas concerning *sacramentum* and *exemplum*,[27] appropriated from the tradition early on, were now interpreted on the basis of the idea of fellowship: "It is Christ's will then, that we partake of it frequently, in order that we may

[22] *LW,* vol. 35, p. 50. *WA* 2, 743, 9.

[23] *LW,* vol. 35, p. 51. *WA* 2, 743, 11-17.

[24] *LW,* vol. 35, p. 53. *WA* 2, 744, 23-25.

[25] *LW,* vol. 35, pp. 53-54. *WA* 2, 745, 2-7.

[26] *LW,* vol. 35, p. 55. *WA* 2, 745, 38-746, 1.

[27] See above esp. p. 47.

remember him and exercise ourselves in this fellowship according to his example. For if his example were no longer kept before us, the fellowship also would soon be forgotten. So we at present see to our sorrow that many masses are held and yet the Christian fellowship . . . has virtually perished."[28]

Even the theme of transformation Luther dealt with purely in the context of fellowship:

> For just as the bread is made out of many grains ground and mixed together, and out of the bodies of many grains there comes the body of one bread, in which each grain loses its form and body and takes upon itself the common body of the bread . . . so it is and should be with us, if we use this sacrament properly. Christ with all saints, by his love, takes upon himself our form [Phil. 2:7], fights with us against sin, death, and all evil. . . . Again through this same love, we are to be changed and to make the infirmities of all other Christians our own; we are to take upon ourselves their form and their necessity, and all the good that is within our power we are to make theirs. . . . In this way we are changed into one another and are made into a community by love. Without love there can be no such change.[29]

Luther was not yet attacking the doctrine of transubstantiation. He actually assumed the presence of Christ's "true natural flesh," and his "natural true blood."[30] Confining the change to the idea of fellowship, however, set a new accent. If we add to this the fact that the idea of sacrifice was nowhere mentioned, that here as well Luther was not yet critical of it, then it is clear to what extent he was outlining a new theology of the Supper.

Luther adopted the essential elements of this new theology from Augustine: the idea of *communio* with Christ and the church, stout accent on the *corpus Christi* idea, and membership in the "city of God," the *civitas Dei*.[31] Of course, Luther more strongly accented these ideas than Augustine did, just as he ignored other elements in Augustine's view of the Supper.

We should note that Luther polemicized against the idea of the *opus operatum*. In doing so he did not allow for the original intent of this piece of scholastic doctrine, which is that if performed correctly, according to the intention of the church, the sacramental action is in itself salutary and not due to the priest's own state of grace. Luther believed that what was at issue here was that this *opus* "of itself is pleasing to

---

[28] *LW,* vol. 35, p. 56. *WA* 2, 747, 4-9.

[29] *LW,* vol. 35, p. 58. *WA* 2, 748, 8-26.

[30] *LW,* vol. 35, p. 59. *WA* 2, 749, 7-10.

[31] A more recent and complete description of Augustine's doctrine of the Eucharist is still lacking. The investigation by Wilhelm Gessel, *Eucharistische Gemeinschaft bei Augustinus,* Cass. 21 (Würzburg: Augustinus-Verlag, 1966), gives only limited help; see Rudolf Lorenz, *ThLZ* 95 (1970), 282. Joseph Ratzinger's *Volk und Haus Gottes in Augustins Lehre von der Kirche,* MThS 2/7 (Munich: Zink, 1954), is still important for the ecclesiological background.

God, even if whoever performs it is not."[32] To this extent his polemic was not directed at scholastic teaching. Aside from this, Luther stated that a council should restore distribution of the cup to the laity.[33]

THE TREATISE ON THE NEW TESTAMENT (1520)

In the spring of 1520 Luther composed his sermon on the New Testament. In contrast to the three 1519 sermons on the sacraments, in several respects it represents a new stage in the ongoing development of his sacramental teaching, especially his teaching on the Supper. The title itself is instructive: Luther was dealing with the "Testament," with Jesus' last will as stated in the words of institution. For this reason he no longer opened his exposition with a definition of the sacrament under which its administration would be subsumed. Rather, the words of institution and their careful interpretation were at the center. In addition, the idea of fellowship, still retained throughout, was subordinated to this new theme.

Various aspects deserve accenting. First, Luther gave preeminence to the idea that Christ intended to prepare for himself "an acceptable and beloved people."[34] The ecclesiological aspect was thus somewhat differently formulated than in the earlier idea of fellowship.

Next, Luther set up a principle that he continually stressed from this point onward, and that Reformation church orders later endeavored to follow: "Now the closer our masses are to the first mass of Christ, no doubt the better they are; and the further from Christ's mass, the more dangerous."[35] This axiom followed from the Reformation principle on Scripture. At the same time it included sharp criticism of all "additions," which at best falsify the institution of the Supper and thus Jesus' original intent.

Further, in the words of institution "lies the whole mass, its nature, work, profit and benefit. Without the words nothing is derived from the mass."[36] "These words every Christian must have before him in the mass. He must hold fast to them as the chief part of the mass, in which even the right, basis, and good preparation for the mass and sacrament is taught."[37]

---

[32] *LW*, vol. 35, p. 63. *WA* 2, 751, 18-21.

[33] *LW*, vol. 35, p. 50: "For my part, however, I would consider it a good thing if the church should again decree in a general council that all persons be given both kinds, like the priests. Not because one kind is insufficient. . . . But it would be fitting and fine that the form, or sign, of the sacrament be given not in part only, but in its entirety" (*WA* 2, 742, 24-31).

[34] *LW*, vol. 35, p. 80. *WA* 6, 354, 18-19.

[35] *WA* 6, 355, 3-4. Luther took up this idea especially in the *Babylonian Captivity: LW*, vol. 35, p. 81. *WA* 6, 523, 25-29.

[36] *LW*, vol. 35, p. 82. *WA* 6, 355, 26-28.

[37] *LW*, vol. 35, p. 82. *WA* 6, 355, 33-356, 1.

In interpreting the words of institution Luther now gave central place to the two aspects of promise and faith, accented first in a general way in the Romans lecture.[38] "If man is to deal with God and receive everything from him, it must happen in this manner, not that man begins and lays the first stone, but that God alone—without any entreaty or desire of man—must first come and give him a promise."[39] Faith is the appropriate answer to this promise "because it does God the honor." As for the promise, Luther interpreted it by way of the term "testament" in Jesus' last will. Its content is the forgiveness of sins and eternal life. In view of these gifts Jesus endured death.

Now, the so-called elements of bread and wine are subsumed under this idea: "He has affixed to the words a powerful and most precious seal and sign: his own true flesh and blood under the bread and wine."[40] With the words "under," "under which," or, the phrase "living words and signs,"[41] Luther defined the relation between the bread and wine as the body and blood of Christ. This view has been described as "consubstantiation," according to which the bread and body of Christ like the wine and the blood of Christ, and without reference to a change (transubstantiation), are present alongside each other and yet are indissolubly joined.

At this point, Luther had not yet attacked the doctrine of transubstantiation. He opposed various abuses such as that of reciting the words of institution so softly that the congregation could not hear, or opposed the lack of emphasis on faith, or sharply rejected the idea of sacrifice. In view of the falsification of Jesus' last will in the Mass, Luther declared that the pope was a "tyrant" and "antichrist."[42]

THE BABYLONIAN CAPTIVITY OF THE CHURCH (1520)

Meanwhile at Leipzig, against Luther's recommendation in his 1519 sermon that the laity be given the cup, his traditionalist opponent, Augustine of Alveld, published a tract entitled *Tractatus de communione sub utraque specie* (June 1520), in which he defended distributing only the host.[43] At first, Luther did not choose to reply. Then as early as 1519 appeared a treatise by the Italian Dominican Isidoro Isolana that attacked Luther and led him to respond.[44] Luther then conceived the plan for a

---

[38] See esp. *Lectures on Romans, LW*, vol. 25, p. 40: "Faith ratifies the promise, and the promise demands faith in him to whom it is made." *WA* 56, 46, 15-16 (marginal gloss on Rom. 4:17): "Fides ratificat promissionem. Et promissio fidem requirit in eo, cui fit."

[39] *LW*, vol. 35, p. 82. *WA* 6, 356, 3-6.

[40] *LW*, vol. 35, p. 86. *WA* 6, 359, 5-7.

[41] *LW*, vol. 35, p. 86. *WA* 6, 359, 21.

[42] *LW*, vol. 35, p. 107. *WA* 6, 374, 30.

[43] On Alveldt and this tractate see Heribert Smolinsky, *Augustin von Alveldt und Hieronymus Emser: Eine Untersuchungen zur Kontroverstheologie der frühen Reformationszeit im Herzogtum Sachsen*, RGST 122 (Münster: Aschendorffsche Verlagsbuchhandlung, 1983), esp. 107-19.

[44] Isolani, *Revocatio* [= recant] *Martini Lutherii Augustiani ad sanctam sedem*, Cremona (?), 1519.

broader treatment of sacramental doctrine.[45] The result was his treatise on *The Babylonian Captivity of the Church*. The work was composed in Latin, since it was destined primarily for scholars and assumed considerable knowledge of theology. The title was formulated in biting, polemical fashion: what Luther was offering was to be a prelude to the retraction expected of him.

In this treatise Luther for the first time publicly disputed the sevenfold number of the sacraments. He stated at the outset that he could not decide whether there are three sacraments of Baptism, repentance, and the Lord's Supper, or ultimately only one sacrament with three sacramental signs.[46] At the conclusion of the treatise he considered that only Baptism and the Supper are sacraments, penance lacking the sign that unconditionally belongs to a sacrament.[47]

Luther's detailed criticism of the church's teaching was not as harsh as his criticism of their number. His attack on the Mass and its three "captivities" is especially significant. First, he disputed the reservation of the cup. His chief argument consisted in asking when the church claimed this right arbitrarily to alter the institution of Christ. Due to the further escalation of the debate, Luther's judgment was harsher than a year earlier in his sermon on the Supper.[48] Next, he opposed the doctrine of transubstantiation, which he had not yet attacked in 1519. He incorrectly referred to Thomas as its originator, adding that as a student he learned of d'Ailly's attack on it.[49] It should be added that at bottom Luther's criticism did not strike at the true intent of the doctrine.[50] He saw in it an attempt to explain the presence of Christ's body and blood that ought not to have been made binding. The third captivity Luther described as the "abuse of the mass," expressed in the idea of sacrifice. As in his *Treatise on the New Testament*, Luther developed his teaching on the Supper on the basis of the leading concepts of testament or promise and of faith. More vigorously than in the *Treatise on the New Testament*, he gave the promise priority over the sign: "in every promise of God two things are presented to us, the Word and the sign, so that we are to understand the Word to be the testament, but the sign to be the sacrament. Thus, in the mass, the Word of Christ is the testament, and the bread and wine are the sacrament."[51] Luther added that there is greater power in the Word or testament than in the sign or sacrament, so that one may actually have the Word or

---

[45] Luther had hinted at his intention as early as in the treatise *To the Christian Nobility of the German Nation, LW*, vol. 44, p. 217; *WA* 6, 469, 1-4. For the rest see Luther's letter to Spalatin of August 5, 1520, *WA Br* 2 Nr. 324, 17-18.

[46] *Babylonian Captivity of the Church, LW*, vol. 36, p. 18. *WA* 6, 501, 33-38.

[47] *Babylonian Captivity of the Church, LW*, vol. 36, p. 124. *WA* 6, 572, 11-22.

[48] See above at n. 33.

[49] *Babylonian Captivity of the Church, LW*, vol. 36, pp. 28-29. *WA* 6, 508, 7-26. Cf. p. 23 above.

[50] On this subject see first Hans Jorissen, *Die Entfaltung der Transsubstantionslehre bis zum Beginn der Hochscholastik* (Münster: Aschendorff, 1965); Edward Schillebeeckx, *The Eucharist*, trans. N. D. Smith (New York: Sheed and Ward, 1968); Alexander Gerken, *Theologie der Eucharistie* (Munich: Kösel, 1973).

[51] *LW*, vol. 36, p. 44. *WA* 6, 518, 14-18.

testament apart from the sign or sacrament. For this he appealed to Augustine's well-known word: *Crede et manducasti* (believe, and you have eaten).[52] Obviously, Luther would not have intended to challenge the reception of the sacrament. He rather wanted to set forth the central significance of the promise and faith.

As for Baptism, Luther's criticism of the later medieval church's doctrine was in essence less harsh than his criticism of the Mass: God has allowed at least this one sacrament to be unharmed in the church. In dealing with Baptism he likewise set the divine promise and faith at the midpoint of his interpretation, no longer the granting of a new *habitus*. As the Ninety-five Theses in essence made clear, penance appears as a return to Baptism.[53] The picture frequently used of penance in the medieval period as "the second plank" to which one may cling after shipwreck Luther rejected as entirely inappropriate, since it assumes that the effect of baptism is over and done with.[54] Baptism rather spells death and resurrection; both must occur by faith throughout all of life. Luther then briefly mentioned the monastic vow, warning against taking it in addition to Baptism, since an oath endangers the freedom given in Baptism.[55]

Luther deals only briefly with the other sacraments, coming critically to terms with the question as to whether they can at all be recognized as such.

As evidenced by this great treatise, *The Babylonian Captivity of the Church,* in his doctrine of the sacraments as well Luther broke with the church of his day. He believed he was forced to it by the counterattack of his traditionalist opponents. In some respects, he had already hinted at his rejection of sacramental doctrine in the 1519 sermons. Further escalation of the debate, however, produced the sharp settling of accounts that he proposed in 1520.

---

[52] *Babylonian Captivity of the Church, LW,* vol. 36, p. 44. *WA* 6, 518, 18-19. Augustine, *In Johannis Evangelium,* tract. 25, 12; *CCSL,* no. 36, 254, 8-9. Similar statements often appear in Augustine. As early as in his 1519 sermon on the Supper Luther cited this passage, naturally without the added critical tone as in *Babylonian Captivity* (*LW,* vol. 35, p. 50; *WA* 2, 742, 27-29). Reference to this passage in his 1520 sermon on the New Testament is even more cautious: *A Treatise on the New Testament, That Is, the Holy Mass, LW,* vol. 35, p. 104. *WA* 6, 372, 15-22.

[53] *LW,* vol. 36, p. 59. *WA* 6, 528, 8-19.

[54] *LW,* vol. 36, pp. 61-62. *WA* 6, 529, 35-530, 10.

[55] *Babylonian Captivity of the Church, LW,* vol. 36, pp. 74-75. *WA* 6, 538, 26-539, 25.

Chapter 14

LUTHER'S DISPUTE
WITH THE MONASTIC IDEAL
(1520/1521)

The Urgency of the Question Concerning
Monastic Vows in 1520/1521

Until 1519, the perennial overhaul of monasticism in theology did not yet induce Luther to reject the monastic vow. On the contrary, as early as in his first Psalms lecture he construed it on the basis of the baptismal covenant, which could open the door once more to monastic life. On such terms, Luther could still recommend monasticism in *The Holy and Blessed Sacrament of Baptism* (1519). Suffering and dying fulfill the task set by Baptism of putting sin to death. "But he who seeks more suffering, and by much exercise would speedily prepare himself for death and soon attain the goal of his baptism, let him bind himself to chastity or to the spiritual order. For the spiritual estate, if it is as it ought to be, should be full of torment and suffering in order that he who belongs to it may have more exercise in the work of his baptism than the man who is in the estate of matrimony."[1]

During the initial conflicts surrounding Luther, there were also questions concerning monasticism. We should mention first the spring of 1519 debates between the Franciscans at Jüterbog and Thomas Müntzer, then still regarded as an adherent

---

[1] *LW,* vol. 35, p. 41. *WA* 2, 736, 12-16.

of Luther,[2] then the so-called Franciscan disputation at Wittenberg on October 3 and 4, 1519, involving various representatives of the Saxon Franciscans and some members of the Wittenberg theological faculty.[3] As early as during this disputation, Luther expressed ideas on the verge of attacking monasticism, such as his reference to the disparity between Jesus' attitude as recorded in the Gospels and the Franciscan requirement of poverty, or his denial of the Franciscan claim that its order was ultimately established by God.[4] Controversies surrounding the papacy and scriptural authority were also involved.

In conjunction with the dispute over the authority of Scripture in its significance for judging ecclesiastical affairs as well as for eventual reforms, the question was variously raised concerning the celibacy of priests and monks. In the debates carried on since 1517 over indulgences, the papacy, and church authority, the question of celibacy was at first more or less relegated to the periphery. In his treatise *To the Christian Nobility of the German Nation Concerning the Reform of the Christian Estate* (1520), Luther had stated in the context of his numerous proposals for reform that it should be left to the priests whether they wanted to marry or remain celibate. He advised candidates for the priesthood not to take the required oath of celibacy, and to apprise the bishop of the fact that he had no scriptural support to demand it.[5]

As for monasticism, Luther proceeded more cautiously in the treatise *To the Christian Nobility*. He intimated that many made vows, but only a few kept them. He objected that there were too many orders; their number had to be reduced. For the rest, religious institutions and cloisters should again be voluntary, just as at the time of the apostles and long after, so that anyone should be at liberty to enter an order or leave it again. The requirement of vows was an "eternal prison" to be abolished.[6] Luther did not take a position on the question as to whether a vow once performed remained binding. He simply thought: "It is my heartfelt wish for everybody to be helped. I do not want to let Christian souls get entangled in the self-contrived traditions and laws of men."[7] In the *Babylonian Captivity of the Church* (1520) Luther added that life under oaths imperils the church since oaths rest merely on human

[2] See Manfred Bensing and Winfried Trillitzsch, "Bernhard Dappens Articuli . . . contra Lutheranos: Zur Auseinandersetzung der Jüterboger Franziskaner mit Thomas Müntzer und Franz Günther 1519," *Jahrbuch für Religionsgeschichte* 2 (1967), 113-47; further Bernhard Lohse, "Thomas Müntzer in neuer Sicht: Müntzer im Licht der neueren Forschung und die Frage nach dem Ansatz seiner Theologie," Berichte aus den Sitzungen der Joachim Jungius-Gesellschaft der Wissenschaften 5 (Hamburg: Joachim Jungius-Gesellschaften der Wissenschaften in Kommission beim Verlag Vandenhoeck & Ruprecht, 9, 1991), 2, 81-89.

[3] *WA* 59, 606-97.

[4] See, respectively, *WA* 59, 684, 16-31; 59, 686, 29-30, and elsewhere.

[5] *To the Christian Nobility of the German Nation, LW,* vol. 44, pp. 175-79. *WA* 6, 440, 15-443, 24.

[6] *To the Christian Nobility of the German Nation, LW,* vol. 44, p. 174. *WA* 6, 438, 14-440, 14.

[7] *LW,* vol. 44, p. 175. *WA* 6, 440, 12-14.

tradition and are not supported by Holy Scripture.[8] In addition, monasticism, at least at present, only serves self-justification.[9]

In wake of the escalation of his dispute with Rome, Luther, in a 1521 polemic against Hieronymus Emser, and by appeal to 1 Timothy 4:3, called the prohibition against the marriage of priests a "doctrine of the devil" and summoned priests to disobey the pope in this matter.[10] Toward monasticism he was, of course, still reserved, since monks and nuns had voluntarily taken the vow of chastity. Theologically, the question of the celibacy of priests and monks could not be addressed with the same arguments.

The question of monasticism turned volatile because many monks and nuns were leaving the cloisters under the influence of Reformation criticism. These incidents grew more and more numerous, especially in 1521, when Luther was at the Wartburg and could not be personally involved in a Wittenberg ruling. In May of 1521 the first priests were married. The ecclesiastical authorities tried to return "runaway" monks, nuns, and married priests to churchly jurisdiction, and for that purpose usually sought the aid of temporal princes. In addition, among the Wittenberg theologians efforts were initiated to deal with the question of monasticism on the basis of the Reformation theology. The arguments were, of course, quite diverse.

On June 20, 1521, Karlstadt published theses on monasticism for a disputation to be held at Wittenberg on June 28. In the theses, among other things, he stated that a monk suffering from desire had the right to break the vow of chastity and marry. In doing so, of course, he sinned, but such a sin was milder than the sin of desire.[11] Melanchthon, who had already dealt with the problem somewhat earlier, found no fault with Karlstadt's argument. In his *Loci communes* of 1521 he discussed the monastic vow from the perspective of freedom relative to all human tradition.[12] Luther was considerably reserved toward Karlstadt's and Melanchthon's argument. In his opinion the fact that monks and nuns took their oaths voluntarily deserved first consideration. Next, the nonbinding character of an oath could not be inferred from the difficulty of keeping it. If so, one might dispense with obedience to the Ten Commandments.[13]

---

[8] *Babylonian Captivity of the Church, LW,* vol. 36, pp. 76-77. *WA* 6, 539, 33-540, 10.

[9] *Babylonian Captivity of the Church, LW,* vol. 36, pp. 75-76. *WA* 6, 539, 5-10.

[10] *LW,* vol. 39, p. 210. *WA* 7, 674, 3-675, 26.

[11] Karlstadt, *De Coelibatu, Monachatu et Viduitate* (Wittenberg, 1521). On this subject see Bernhard Lohse, "Die Kritik am Mönchtum bei Luther und Melanchthon (1961)," in *Evangelium in der Geschichte,* 80-96, here 92.

[12] See *Melanchthon, Studienausgabe,* 1/1, 2d ed. (Gütersloh: Gerd Mohn, 1978), 52-54; on this subject see Lohse, *Evangelium in der Geschichte,* 90-93.

[13] Letter of Luther to Melanchthon, August 1, 1521, *WA Br* 2 Nr. 424, 1-50 (this comment does not appear in the letter's translation contained in *LW,* vol. 48, pp. 277-82).

LUTHER'S *THEMATA DE VOTIS* (1521)

Forced by a situation mounting toward crisis as well as by faulty theological argument, in September of 1521 Luther composed two series of theses under the title
Themata de votis (Themes concerning vows). They contain the principal ideas that he
was to set forth somewhat later in an extended treatise entitled *Judgment of Luther on
Monastic Vows* (1521).[14]

In the first series of theses Luther opened with a sentence from Romans 14:23:
"Whatever does not proceed from faith is sin," interpreting this word of justifying
faith.[15] When a specific deed is performed to obtain righteousness before God, commandments of the first table are transgressed. Hence what is decisive is the spirit in
which vows are performed. For Luther it in no way necessarily followed that monks
and nuns should leave the cloister. If need be, the false intent (*abusus*) with which the
vows were taken must be laid aside.

In a second move Luther examined monastic vows from the legal viewpoint. Vows
are a law binding on the conscience. As a result, Paul's word about the abolition of the
law applies also to them: if they have been taken apart from faith, they must be broken.

In the second series of theses Luther opened with the idea of Christian freedom:
"Christian freedom is of divine right."[16] After a brief exposition of freedom according to
the New Testament, Luther stated that "vows must be of such sort that they do not conflict with it." They would do so, however, if they were not always voluntary.[17] According
to Luther, Paul's counsel to remain unmarried wherever possible cannot be cited to establish an eternally binding oath. What is decisive is not what is good or better, but what may
or may not occur.[18] In Baptism we have pledged ourselves to this freedom; it cannot be
annulled by a later vow.[19] God does not recognize a vow that conflicts with evangelical
freedom; we cannot surrender the freedom promised in baptism even if we would.[20]

Luther did not connect these theses with the intention of abolishing monasticism.
He stated expressly that "vows are voluntary, they are not condemned; they can be
viewed both temporally and eternally."[21] Of course, in taking them, Christian freedom
had always to be preserved if the vows were not to become a "work."

---

[14] On this subject see Lohse, *Mönchtum und Reformation,* 356-62.

[15] *WA* 8, 323-29, quotation, 323, 6.

[16] *WA* 8, 330-35; quotation, 330, 3.

[17] *WA* 8, 330, 12-20.

[18] *WA* 8, 330, 25-28.

[19] *WA* 8, 331, 6-9: "XXVII. Ad haec in baptismo universi primario voto huic libertati nos astrinx-
imus. XXVIII. Quare non est, ut alio voto illud irritare, fraudare, superordinare possimus." ("By this
first universal vow in baptism we have obligated ouselves to this freedom. For which reason we may not
provoke, defraud, or add to it by another vow.")

[20] *WA* 8, 332, 9-18.

[21] *WA* 8, 335, 18-19: "Summa: Vota libera sunt, non damnata, tum temporaliter, tum perpetuo
servabilia."

THE JUDGMENT (IUDICIUM) OF LUTHER
ON MONASTIC VOWS (1521)

In November 1521 Luther composed this treatise in a week and a half at the Wartburg.[22] The word *iudicium* in the title indicates that with this "opinion" he intended to take a position toward the possibility of leaving the cloister. Despite its partially harsh tone, Luther did not intend that the treatise, laid out in more rigorously systematic fashion than any other, should be a polemic, but an instruction for consciences. In this period, such counsel was in fact urgently needed. In early November 1521, at Luther's Wittenberg Augustinian Eremite cloister, the preacher Gabriel Zwilling summoned his companions to leave the cloister. Up to November 12, thirteen monks had already answered the summons. Because of Spalatin's misgivings concerning the radical content of Luther's treatise, it did not appear until February 1522. Luther dedicated it to his father,[23] commenting on the doubts his father had once expressed regarding his resolve to become a monk.

As in the two series of theses, Luther proceeded to argue with Karlstadt and Melanchthon not from the problem of the difficulty of keeping the vows but from the perspective of which vows are pleasing to God and which are to be viewed as godless. The conclusion respecting obedience to vows may then be easily drawn: vows pleasing to God must obviously be kept, but godless vows must be broken in obedience to God.[24]

From this perspective Luther took up various aspects in five sections:[25]

I. Vows Do Not Rest on the Word of God:
   They Run Counter to the Word of God.
II. Vows Are against Faith.
III. Vows Are against Evangelical Freedom.
IV. Vows Are Contrary to the Commandments of God.
V. Monasticism Is Contrary to Common Sense and Reason.

In these sections Luther kept strictly to each announced theme without building on previously proposed arguments. The nature of the writing as a *iudicium* was strictly preserved.

Luther opened the first section with this assertion: "There is no doubt that the monastic vow is in itself a most dangerous thing because it is without the authority

---

[22] *WA* 8, 564.

[23] *WA* 8, 573-76. Cf. the letter of Luther to his father, November 21, 1521, *LW*, vol. 48, pp. 330-36.

[24] *LW*, vol. 44, p. 252. *WA* 8, 577, 22-27.

[25] On the structure of this writing see Lohse, "Luthers Kritik am Mönchtum," 413-32; idem, *Mönchtum und Reformation,* 363-70.

and example of Scripture. Neither the early church nor the New Testament knows anything at all of the taking of this kind of vow."[26] The section indicates how Luther critically applied the authority of Holy Scripture: he did not deny in biblicistic fashion that there may be institutions in the church for which there is no direct scriptural support. Such institutions are of course "dangerous" and must submit to critical testing. Things established as obligatory without scriptural basis are not only dangerous but actually opposed to Scripture. Consequently, this word applies: "The Scriptures clearly compel us to condemn whatever is only a matter of rules, statutes, orders, schools of thought, and, in addition, whatever falls short of, is contrary to, or goes beyond Christ, even if these things had been handed over by angels from heaven or confirmed by mighty miracles."[27]

In particular Luther opposed the distinction drawn in the late second century and everywhere adopted since between commandments and evangelical counsels, as well as the reference to states of imperfection and perfection. Such denies that the gospel belongs to all, or that the so-called counsels apply to all. The monk's vow of obedience, poverty, and chastity is in the New Testament sense binding on all Christians, irrespective of any particularly holy deeds: obedience as the humility handed down in the gospel, poverty as the use of one's own possessions for the neighbor's good, and chastity as hallowing the body. No special monastic virtues can be made of these gospel requirements.

In the second section Luther specifically attacked the eternally binding nature of vows. They impose a law unsupported by Scripture. Because they are opposed to faith, they are null and void before God, and not only can but actually must be broken.

In the third section Luther took up ideas first elaborated in his Romans lecture[28] then chiefly in his principal Reformation writings of 1520. The freedom given in Baptism cannot be abrogated by any churchly institution or regulation. Again, Luther did not have in mind the abolition of monasticism but stated the condition that if need be it may be entered upon as an "exercise." A vow taken in this sense would, for example, read like this: "Look, O God, I vow to you this kind of life, not because I think it is the way to righteousness and salvation, or satisfaction for sins. From such may your mercy preserve me. . . . But I am striving for this: as long as we live in the flesh and since we should not be idle, I would like to take up this kind of life, in order to discipline my body, serve my neighbor, meditate on your Word, as another chooses farming or a trade."[29] Life as a monk or a nun is thus a calling that is ultimately no different from any other secular calling. The sacralizing of an especially sacred career has come to an end theologically on Reformation soil.

---

[26] *LW*, vol. 44, p. 252. *WA* 8, 578, 6-8.
[27] *LW*, vol. 44, p. 254. *WA* 8, 579, 1-4.
[28] See above, p. 83-84.
[29] *WA* 8, 604, 9-23. Cf. *LW*, vol. 44, p. 294.

In the fourth section Luther stated that because of its particular claim, monasticism is opposed to the First Commandment, which requires no more and no less than total faith. There is no place for a particular holiness. Monasticism is also opposed to the commandment of love for neighbor, since by entering the cloister monks often enough dispense with tasks pertaining to that love. Even with respect to obedience, the monk's vow inadmissibly narrows the obedience commanded by the New Testament.

In the fifth section Luther finally came to argue on the basis of the *ratio*. This section, alongside the late *Disputation Concerning Man* (1536),[30] belongs to Luther's most significant statements on the capacities and tasks of human reason.[31] The following sentences are of particular importance: "Even if natural reason in itself is not concerned with spiritual truth or divine activity, nevertheless, when it asserts affirmative statements (to use their jargon) its judgment is wrong, but when it asserts negative statements its judgment is right. Reason does not comprehend what God is, but it most certainly comprehends what God is not."[32] Among other things Luther referred to the fact that with every vow exception is made for the impossibility of keeping it, and asked why no exception is made in the case of celibacy, where the Bible recognizes no eternally binding oath.

Compared with the statements of Karlstadt and Melanchthon, Luther's treatise on monastic vows stands out, first through its formulation of the question pursued radically to the end; next through its elaborating the contrast between Holy Scripture and eternally binding vows; and finally through its argument by means of the *ratio*. We should also not forget that on the condition that evangelical freedom is preserved, Luther allowed for the possibility of vows and even of monasticism as a secular calling. In fact, however, the treatise contributed essentially to bringing monasticism to an end on Reformation soil.

[30] WA 39 I, 174-80; see on this subject the detailed commentary by Gerhard Ebeling, *Lutherstudien*, vol. 2: *Disputatio de homine* (Tüblingen: Mohr, 1977-89).

[31] On this subject see Lohse, *Ratio und Fides*.

[32] *LW*, vol. 44, p. 336. *WA* 8, 629, 23-27: "Quinto comparemus institutum istud etiam ad rationem naturalem, hoc est, ad crassum illud lumen naturae, quae tametsi lucem et opera dei non attingat per sese, ita ut in affirmativis (quod aiunt) fallax sit eius iudicium, in negativis tamen est certum. Non enim capit ratio, quid sit deus, certissime tamen capit, quid non sit deus."

Chapter 15

LUTHER'S DISPUTE WITH THE WITTENBERG REFORMERS

THE WITTENBERG REFORMS AND THE QUESTION OF SCRIPTURAL AUTHORITY

The circle of Wittenberg theologians involved since 1516 in reforming theology and the university, thus with linking humanistic goals to Reformation renewal, was never entirely homogeneous. In the years of their attack on scholasticism differences within the circle had been muted. The more university reform progressed and the sharper Luther's dispute with Rome grew, the more differences appeared that till then had been asleep in the deep. Even Luther and his friend Melanchthon differed at various points, as was already clear in dealing with monastic vows. More significant, of course, were the differences between Luther and Karlstadt as well as between Luther and Müntzer later on. During the hot debates with the traditionalists these differences were only gradually noted. It soon became apparent, however, that they concerned the heart of Reformation theology: the view of Holy Scripture as norm and guide for churchly life, and the view of justification and sanctification. It made clear that the Reformation movement, of which Luther was now as much as ever the initiator and representative, was not a monolithic but a pluriform movement.

Luther and Karlstadt differed in their dependence on Augustine, particularly in their evaluation of his treatise *De Spiritu et Littera*.[1] Luther saw it as supporting his

---

[1] See B. Lohse, "Zum Wittenberger Augustinismus," 89-109.

new view of God's righteousness and justification, though in part he advanced
beyond it. Karlstadt remained with the theme of "spirit" and "letter" but developed
further Augustine's understanding of Spirit. He did not share Luther's accent on the
"imputation" of alien righteousness but stressed the gift of the Spirit as enabling fulfillment of the law.

Differences and tensions arose between Luther and Karlstadt during the Leipzig
Disputation. Indeed, prior to it Eck noted differences between them over the topic of
justification and thought he could come to terms with Karlstadt.[2] Following the disputation Luther and Karlstadt were alienated. Karlstadt applied himself to the study of
Scripture and in 1521 published his important *De canonicis scripturis libellus* (a pamphlet
concerning the canonical Scriptures). In it he distanced himself from Luther's criticism of the Epistle of James. His view that the Gospels, the letters of Paul, and other
New Testament writings enjoyed graduated authority differed entirely from Luther's
understanding of the canon and his readiness for content criticism.[3] The divergence in
their evaluation of James reflected differences not only in their understanding of Scripture but also in their view of justification and sanctification.

When, after the Diet of Worms, Luther tarried longer at the Wartburg, leadership of the Wittenberg movement almost automatically fell to Karlstadt. At the
time, Melanchthon was only twenty-four years old. As early as in their treatment of
monastic vows it became clear that Karlstadt held firmly to the literal validity of Old
Testament regulations but in a peculiar way allowed the activity of the Holy Spirit to
set the standard.[4] Characteristically, Luther did not correspond with Karlstadt at all,
but rather with Melanchthon, thus ignoring the leading position Karlstadt was
enjoying at Wittenberg in 1521. Coherent with their contrary views on monasticism, the validity of vows, freedom to leave the cloister, and the marriage of priests,
Karlstadt developed his idea of Spirit and letter as well as of flesh and Spirit, and
Luther developed his view of the external Word as well as his doctrine of law and
gospel.

The reforms that Karlstadt effected at Wittenberg toward the end of 1521 and
in January of 1522, with Melanchthon uncertain of him but not opposed, served to
achieve ecclesiastical and social goals. The neuralgic point was the question of the
removal of images from the churches. According to Karlstadt the Old Testament law
was in a sense obligatory also for Christians. That Luther could later describe Moses
as the Jewish *Sachsenspiegel*[5] was highly offensive to Karlstadt. Nor did he accept

---

[2] See U. Bubenheimer, *TRE* 17 (1988), 650, 11-19.

[3] Lohse, *Evangelium in der Geschichte*, 222-23.

[4] See above, p. 139.

[5] *LW*, vol. 35, p. 167 (sermon, 1525); *WA* 16, 378, 11; *LW*, vol. 40, p. 98; *WA*, 18, 81, 14-15
(*Against the Heavenly Prophets in the Matter of Images and Sacraments*, 1525). Cf. Heinrich Bornkamm,
Luther and the Old Testament, trans. Eric W. Gritsch and Ruth C. Gritsch, ed. Victor I. Gruhn (Philadel-
phia: Fortress Press, 1969), 120-24.

Luther's view that the Old Testament law was binding on Christians only insofar as it was upheld by Christ. According to Karlstadt, the prohibition of images was also binding on the church. Not least, he pointed to the dangers that the veneration of images posed for the purity of faith, as well as to the need on this very issue for preserving simple Christians from temptation. Further, he insisted that because of grace and the activity of the Spirit Christians were in fact able to keep the law. As early as 1517 he had stated that grace makes us friends and doers of the law.[6] Christian faith had to be preserved in obedience; justification had to lead to sanctification; Christian freedom had to express itself in new forms even of social structure. Karlstadt thus represented a basically "puritan" form of Reformation Christianity.[7] The difference between him and Luther involved not only questions of strategy but basic aspects of Reformation theology.[8]

LUTHER'S ATTITUDE TOWARD THE WITTENBERG REFORMS

To begin with, Luther was in total agreement with the reforms carried out at Wittenberg under Karlstadt's leadership. When early in December 1521 he was hiding out at Wittenberg, he said: "Everything else that I hear and see pleases me very much."[9] Earlier, of course, he had voiced some misgiving about a few tumultuous scenes,[10] so that he apparently had some reservations. In January 1522 he still voiced approval of Karlstadt's marriage.[11]

For various reasons, Luther soon became more and more critical of the Wittenberg movement. Events surrounding the so-called Zwickau prophets may have been decisive.[12] Toward the end of December 1521, attracted by reports of events, these prophets arrived at Wittenberg and against Melanchthon appealed to revelations from God. Their intention was to initiate reforms there. They also expressed doubt in the legitimacy of infant baptism. Melanchthon was uncertain and anxious toward them.[13] In opposition Luther insisted that the prophets had first to prove their calling, that God

---

[6] Ernst Kähler, *Karlstadt und Augustin: Der Kommentar des Andreas Bodenstein von Karlstadt zu Augustins Schrift De spiritu et littera*, HM 19 (Halle: M. Niemeyer, 1952), 25: "Gratia facit nos legis dilectores et factores" (151 theses of April 26, 1517).

[7] See Gordon Rupp, "Andrew Karlstadt and Reformation Puritanism," *JThS* 10 (1959), 308-26.

[8] Cf. R. Sider, *Karlstadt,* 201.

[9] *LW,* vol. 48, p. 351 (letter of Luther to Spalatin ca. December 5, 1521). *WA Br* 2 Nr. 443, 18.

[10] *LW,* vol. 48, p. 327 (letter of Luther to Spalatin, November 11, 1521). *WA Br* 2 Nr. 438, 16-35.

[11] *LW,* vol. 48, p. 363 (letter of Luther to Amsdorf, January 13, 1522). *WA Br* 2 Nr. 449, 45-47.

[12] On the Zwickau prophets see first Abraham Friesen, *Thomas Muentzer, a Destroyer of the Godless: The Making of a Sixteenth-Century Religious Revolutionary* (Berkeley: University of California Press, 1990), 73-99; Susan C. Karant-Nunn, *Zwickau in Transition, 1500-1547: The Reformation as an Agent of Change* (Columbus: Ohio State University Press, 1987).

[13] Cf. *LW,* vol. 48, pp. 365-66 (letter of Luther to Melanchthon, January 13, 1522); *WA Br* 2 Nr. 450. On the question of infant Baptism see *LW,* vol. 48, pp. 369-72. *WA Br* 2 Nr. 450, 98-116.

never yet called anyone not identified either by persons or signs, not even his own Son. Should the Zwickauers maintain they were called by a *nuda revelatio*, such was without precedent in Holy Scripture. For the rest, Melanchthon should determine whether they had undergone inner conflicts (*Anfechtungen*) over their revelation. If everything was proceeding quietly and in seemingly devout fashion, the revelations were not to be accepted: God does not speak thus with humans. As for infant baptism, Luther rejected the Zwickauers' Scripture interpretation.

Alongside his opposition to the Zwickau prophets it was also important to Luther that on January 20, 1522, the imperial government, via an advertisement of Duke Georg of Saxony, issued a decree to combat "innovations against traditional Christian usage."[14] What would follow from this could still not be seen. It seemed possible that Wittenberg would lose the protection and quiet patience of the Saxon elector. Further, it was feared that the Wittenberg movement would get out of hand and risk conflict with the authorities. Luther was then already of the conviction that no reforms whatsoever should be introduced against them. In his *Invocavit* sermons he had this to say: "You say it was right according to the Scriptures. I agree, but what becomes of order? For it was done in wantonness, with no regard for proper order and with offense to your neighbor. If, beforehand, you had called upon God in earnest prayer, and had obtained the aid of the authorities, one could be certain that it had come from God."[15] Early on Luther had been positive in his opinion of the temporal powers.[16] Here for the first time he spoke explicitly of their divine commissioning, even in questions of church reform. The question as to how he arrived at this extraordinarily positive view must ultimately remain open.

Finally, Luther took a negative stance toward the development of the Wittenberg reform. What first seemed to be a natural outcome of Reformation impulses was fixed in writing with the January 24, 1522, *Order of the City of Wittenberg*: prohibition against begging, even by monks; removal of images and altars, up to three, from the churches; a new order of the Mass prescribing that the priests give the host and chalice to the communicants. For Luther these detailed regulations surrendered evangelical freedom. They merely replaced the papal imposition of order with a no less strict Reformation order. Specifically, Luther objected that by this means no care was taken for the "weak," who still clung to the old order and were offended by changes. The reformers had lacked the required patience and love. In the activity of the Wittenberg reformers Luther saw the same work of Satan, who had served the papists for so long, though he was certain Christ would crush him "under our feet."[17]

---

[14] Luther cautiously alludes to it in *LW*, vol. 36, pp. 238, 246 (*Receiving Both Kinds in the Sacrament*, 1522); *WA* 10 II, 25, 1-3.

[15] *LW*, vol. 51, p. 73. *WA* 10 III, 9, 9-13.

[16] See above, pp. 81-83.

[17] *LW*, vol. 48, pp. 371-72 (letter of Luther to Melanchthon, January 13, 1522). *WA Br* 2 Nr. 450, 117-20.

Against the elector's advice, Luther returned to Wittenberg from the Wartburg. In his *Invocavit* sermons, preached from March 9 to 16, 1522, he attacked the Wittenberg reformers and quickly silenced the ensuing agitation.

Luther's Further Development of His Doctrine of Holy Scripture, Law, and Gospel, and His View of the Temporal Authorities

Conflict with the Wittenberg reformers led Luther to make precise and in part also to modify many of his important views, thus leading to a permanent break with his opponents on the "left." No doubt, till 1521, Luther could have expressed himself as did the Wittenberg reformers, though there had long been differences between him and Karlstadt. Nevertheless, in his 1521 exposition of the Magnificat he could say: "No one can correctly understand God or His Word unless he has received such understanding immediately from the Holy Spirit. But no one can receive it from the Holy Spirit without experiencing, proving, and feeling it. In such experience the Holy Spirit instructs us as in His own school, outside of which nothing is learned but empty words and prattle."[18] After his experiences with the Wittenberg reformers Luther was more cautious on the subject. Now he accented the necessity of the external Word, as found in Scripture, and which must be preached ever anew. The Spirit does not work independently of the external Word but always in union with it. The external Word is also the criterion for judging possible inspirations. In his treatise *Against the Heavenly Prophets* (1525), Luther had this to say: "Now when God sends forth his holy gospel he deals with us in a twofold manner, first outwardly, then inwardly. Outwardly he deals with us through the oral word of the gospel and through material signs, that is, baptism and the sacrament of the altar. Inwardly he deals with us through the Holy Spirit, faith, and other gifts. But whatever their measure or order the outward factors should and must precede."[19]

Here, more clearly than before, Luther elaborated the difference and the relation between law and gospel. Karlstadt interpreted the Old Testament prohibition against images literally. Luther took a different stance: The brass serpent set up by Moses during the wilderness wandering was also an image. Hence it is not the production of images as such that is prohibited, but rather the invoking of them. For the rest, Luther maintained that Moses did not forcibly restrain from but warned of images.[20] Literal obedience to the prohibition against images thus risks making Christian freedom toward them a law and at the same time risks externalizing faith.

[18] *LW*, vol. 21, p. 299. *WA* 7, 546, 24-29.
[19] *LW*, vol. 40, p. 146. *WA* 18, 136, 9-15.
[20] *LW*, vol. 51, p. 82; *WA* 10 III, 27, 1-29, 10, and elsewhere.

Further, Luther gave greater stress to the fact that the law has a permanent punitive function that the Wittenberg reformers in fact denied. As early as in 1521 he wrote:

> But even though we are already in the New Testament and should have only the preaching of the Spirit, since we are still living in flesh and blood, it is necessary to preach the letter as well, so that people are first killed by the law and all their arrogance is destroyed. Thus they may know themselves and become hungry for the Spirit and thirsty for grace. . . . that he made the people ready for Christ through the preaching of repentance. . . . After that he led them to Christ.[21]

For the first time, in a postil for the third Sunday in Advent of 1522, Luther detailed the difference between law and gospel.[22]

Finally, Luther was also further developing his idea of the temporal authority, the earliest reference to which is in his letter to Melanchthon of July 13, 1521. Here he explained that the temporal power is necessary to maintain external order. Without it not even the church can have stability. He further appealed to Romans 13 and 1 Peter 2: "[Governmental] authority is from God, and whosoever resists [governmental] authority resists God's ordinance."[23] He went on to state: "Since it is in the gospel that Christ should have authority over divine and heavenly things, why is it surprising that he has not made use of the sword, which [moreover] men can easily arrange, and despite that treats it in such a way that if it is not against the gospel it is appointed according to his will."[24] This relatively detailed exposition makes clear that Luther had sketched out the essentials of his idea before developments at Wittenberg had become radicalized and appeared to be in tension with or in opposition to the secular authorities. Luther's view of the authorities was thus not merely a reaction to developments at Wittenberg, but conversely, his attitude toward the Wittenberg reformers not least resulted from a view of the authorities that had already been fixed in its basic features.

---

[21] *LW,* vol. 39, p. 188 (*To the Goat in Leipzig,* 1521). *WA* 7, 658, 26-33.

[22] *WA* 10 I 2, 147-70, esp. 155, 21-159, 4. On the formation of Luther's doctrine of law and gospel in this period see Gerhard Ebeling, "On the Doctrine of the *Triplex Usus Legis* in the Theology of the Reformation," in Ebeling, *Word and Faith,* trans. James W. Leitch (Philadelphia: Fortress Press, 1963), 62-78.

[23] *LW,* vol. 48, p. 260 (letter of Luther to Melanchthon, July 13, 1521); *WA Br* 2 Nr. 418, 32-107; this quotation from lines 69-70 reads: "Potestas a Deo est, et ordinationi Dei resistit, qui potestati resistit." See M. Brecht, "Luther und die Wittenberger Reformation in der Wartburgzeit," in *Luther, Leben, Werk, Wirkung,* 74-75.

[24] Ibid., lines 88-92.

With regard to church reforms effected at Wittenberg, the statement cited above[25] on the need for involving the authorities or "heads" represents what is of course a more pointed view, but ultimately one that Luther had already expressed in his letter of July 13, 1521. On the other hand, from his affirmation of the task assigned the authorities by God, he never concluded that he now had to obey all their regulations without question. His resolve to return from the Wartburg against the will and advice of the elector militates against such an assertion.[26]

[25] See n. 15.

[26] On this subject see also Luther's letter to the Saxon elector of March 5, 1522; LW, vol. 48, pp. 388-93; WA Br 2 Nr. 455. See also Luther's letter to the elector of (August?) 7, 1522, LW, vol. 48, p. 395: "Human authority is not always to be obeyed, that is, when it undertakes something against the commandments of God; yet it should never be despised but always honored." WA Br 2 Nr. 456, 17-19: Denn wiewohl nicht allzeit der menschlichen Oberkeit zu gehorchen ist, nämlich wenn sie etwas wider Gottes Gebot furnimpt, so ist sie doch nimmer zu verachten, sondern zu ehren."

Chapter 16

LUTHER'S DISPUTE
WITH RADICAL TENDENCIES
TO "RIGHT" AND "LEFT"

THE DISTINCTION BETWEEN THE TWO KINGDOMS
AND THE TWO GOVERNMENTS

THE SHIFT IN FRONTS

Certain basic ideas appearing later in Luther's distinction between the two kingdoms can be documented early on in his work. On the basis of Augustine's great
work, *De civitate Dei,* he customarily identified the church with the "City of God."[1]
In view of the various symptoms of decline in the late medieval church, he clearly
placed more confidence in political than in ecclesiastical government.[2]

When in his treatise *To the Christian Nobility* (1520) Luther turned to the temporal authorities and, due to the obvious failure of the spiritual heads, summoned
them to undertake comprehensive measures of reform in the temporal and ecclesiastical sphere, he reflected a view of the independence of the temporal authority
that had its peculiar task from God and was not subject to churchly authority. This
view is not simply identical to late medieval theory according to which emperor and

---

[1] See *WA* 55 I, 378 (marginal gloss on Ps. 47, 2); 55 I, 596 (marginal gloss on Ps. 86:3); 55 I, 814,
816 (title and marginal gloss on Ps. 121:4); *LW,* vol. 11, p. 543; 4, 402, 38 (scholia on Ps. 121:4: "Ecclesia . . . edificatur ut civitas"). On the difficulty of translating the concept *civitas Dei,* see Wilhelm Kam-
lah, *Christentum und Geschichtlichkeit: Untersuchungen zur Entstehung des Christentums und zu Augustins
"Bürgerschaft Gottes,"* 2d ed. (Stuttgart/Cologne: Kohlhammer, 1951), 155-90.

[2] See above, p. 82-83.

pope may represent each other where needed,[3] or to imperial positions adopted toward the papacy, say, in the fourteenth century. Nonetheless, Luther may have received some impulses from this quarter.

Regarding the further development of his view, we can scarcely overlook that during his sojourn at Wittenberg Luther continually received sympathetic aid from his elector and above all the promise of temporal protection. His situation in the fall of 1518 was especially critical, once the hearing before Cajetan had miscarried and the papal warrant for his arrest was again in force. The fact that Frederick wavered briefly over whether he could protect Luther, and soon thereafter resolved to promise protection, secured to Luther and the Reformation movement increased possibility for action.[4] Neither then nor later did Frederick simply follow Luther's ideas. Nor was there lack of tension between the elector and his professor. Still, Frederick always dealt sympathetically and discriminatingly with his stormy man of God. He never responded to Luther with an uncompromising no. For this reason, it is scarcely surprising that Luther's early confidence in the temporal power developed more and more into a view of its independence. By contrast, toward the end of 1521 and the beginning of 1522, Karlstadt ignored needed consideration for the elector, which, in view of the promise to protect Luther, the elector could very well have expected. In his July 13, 1521, letter to Melanchthon,[5] Luther first unfolded his principal ideas on the nature and task of the temporal power.

If Luther's concern was to establish the independence of the temporal power in opposition to Rome, now he had to accent the need for temporal order in opposition to the more radical reformers. This shift in fronts occurred during the development of the Wittenberg Reformation under Karlstadt in 1521/1522, but soon took on greater significance when revolutionary forces attempted to reshape conditions by violence and erect a supposed reign of God. For this reason, Luther's view of the spiritual and temporal power, till now stated only in first attempts, soon had to be more precisely reflected upon and given further shape. Here too biblical statements had to have decisive significance for him.

[3] See, e.g., Wilhelm Kölmel, *Wilhelm Ockham und seine kirchenpolitischen Schriften* (Essen: Ludgerus-Verlag, 1962).

[4] See Ingetraut Ludolphy, *Friedrich der Weise-Kurfürst von Sachsen 1463-1525* (Göttingen: Vandenhoeck & Ruprecht, 1984), 397-444.

[5] See above, p. 149.

LUTHER'S TREATISE ON *TEMPORAL AUTHORITY, TO WHAT EXTENT IT SHOULD BE OBEYED* (1523)

Evidently as early as the summer of 1522, Luther conceived the idea of a treatise on authority.[6] In his sermons on 1 Peter, published in the late summer of 1522, he interpreted the section on authority in 1 Peter 2:13-17.[7] In it certain basic ideas of his so-called two-kingdoms doctrine already appear, especially the concepts of "spiritual" and "temporal" rule. In addition, Luther discussed the limits of obedience toward authority.

In various sermons preached at Weimar in October 1522, Luther dealt with the questions of spiritual and temporal rule. Two sermons preached before Duke Johann at the Weimar Castle Church on October 24 and 25, 1522, are especially important.[8] Luther used the occasion to interpret Matthew 3:2, "Repent, for the kingdom of heaven is at hand." In these sermons Luther likewise used such concepts as "kingdom of Christ," "spiritual rule," "temporal authority," or "temporal government." The concepts have equal weight. At the same time, the nature and task of both kingdoms and governments were clearly outlined. Luther's so-called two-kingdoms doctrine had thus already assumed its unmistakable character. A bit later, on November 3, 1522, Luther wrote to Spalatin that he had explained the kingdom of God and temporal power in his October 25 sermon. The letter also makes clear that Duke Johann had requested its publication.[9] Luther further wrote that he had "long since" planned to expand the sermon into a treatise.[10] Somewhat later he said that he was dealing "with the two powers" (*de utraque potestate*).[11] The reason why he wanted to use this sermon as a basis for his treatise may be that he felt he had achieved new clarity on the subject.

Actually, there was another reason for composing a treatise on the authorities. In September 1522, by way of the electoral counselor Philip of Feilitzsch, Luther came into possession of a book authored by the well-known jurist and politician Johann Freiherr von Schwarzenberg, which he acknowledged with thanks on September 21, 1522.[12] Unfortunately this book has been lost. It may have been a manuscript that

---

[6] Luther spoke of *Oberkeit*, not *Obrigkeit*. The usage indicates that he was thinking less of an institution than of "heads" entrusted with power.

[7] *LW*, vol. 30, pp. 117-25, 125-30. *WA* 12, 327-35.

[8] *WA* 10 III, 371-79, 379-85.

[9] *WA Br* 2 Nr. 546, 9-12: "Vimarie semel de regno & potestae seculari dixi, quod rogatus sum edere, alioqui iam diu edendi cupidus & studiosus eiusdem. Exibit autem sub nomine principis Iohannis Senioris statim." ("I once spoke of the temporal kingdom and power at Weimar, which I was asked to publish. I have long since been anxious and eager for its publication. Naturally, it is submitted under the name of Duke John the Elder.")

[10] Ibid. Cf. *LW*, vol. 49, p. 18.

[11] *WA Br* 2 Nr. 560, 15 (letter of December 20, 1522, to Wolfgang Stein).

[12] *WA Br* 2 Nr. 538. On Schwarzenberg see Erik Wolf, *Grosse Rechtsdenker der deutschen Geistesgeschichte*, 4th ed. (Tübingen: J.C.B. Mohr, 1963), 102-37.

Schwarzenberg asked Luther to appraise. Luther promised to enter his remarks in the book.[13] In any event, here too Luther announced: "I will nearly [= soon] . . . publish a separate little book on how the temporal sword agrees with the gospel."[14] The reference was to the treatise entitled *Temporal Authority* (1523). Schwarzenberg, author of the rulings of the Bamberg criminal court, participated in an Imperial Commission that in essence led to unifying the criminal justice system. Toward Luther he was always very friendly.

Greater urgency attached to the proposed treatise due to the measures of Duke Georg of Saxony and other strict traditionalist princes against the sale of Luther's New Testament translation. Duke Georg directed the copies to be confiscated, naturally with compensation for the sale price. Similar measures were taken in other territories. The question for Luther was whether the temporal authority should intervene in spiritual matters in such fashion.[15]

It may have been in mid-December 1522 that Luther was able to compose his treatise on authority. The date of the dedicatory letter to Duke Johann is New Year's, 1523. The treatise appeared in print early in March 1523. The title alone sets a particular accent over against earlier sermons on the same subject, since it deals expressly with the limits of obedience to authority. The dedication indicates that many had asked Luther to publish the treatise, since they were moved by Christ's word that one should not resist evil but agree with the adversary (Matt. 5:39). Luther stated further: "I hope, however, that I may instruct the princes and the temporal authorities in such a way that they will remain Christians—and Christ will remain Lord—and yet Christ's commands will not for their sake have to become mere counsels."[16]

THE DISTINCTION BETWEEN THE TWO KINGDOMS AND THE TWO GOVERNMENTS

The extraordinarily extensive literature on Luther's view of authority ought not obscure our view of the historical situation behind the origin of this little treatise or of its original intent. It would be particularly inappropriate to interpret it as an outline of exceptional systematic consistency.[17] The summarizing of Luther's ideas under the concept of "the two-kingdoms doctrine" is problematic. The term was evidently first used by Karl Barth in 1922.[18] It is scarcely suitable for describing

---

[13] WA Br 2 Nr. 538, 28-33. On this subject see Sieghard Mühlmann, "Von weltlicher Obrigkeit," in *Martin Luther: Studienausgabe*, 3:27-28.

[14] WA Br 2 Nr. 538, 24-26.

[15] See LW, vol. 45, pp. 112-13. WA 11, 267, 14-29.

[16] LW, vol. 45, p. 83. WA 11, 246, 6-8.

[17] Especially J. Heckel might be prey to this danger.

[18] K. Barth, in his review of the book by Paul Althaus, *Religiöser Sozialismus: Grundfragen der*

Luther's ideas, since it assumes a system and consistency in application that simply cannot be documented. In saying this we of course do not deny that the treatise gives evidence of profound exegetical and systematic reflection. For Luther it was always a high art to apply this distinction in the given concrete situation.

The treatise is divided into three parts. In the first, Luther was concerned "to provide a sound basis for the civil law and sword so no one will doubt it is in the world by God's will and ordinance."[19] The words make clear that Luther opposed those who regard the authorities as superfluous or do not assign them a divine task. This first part contains the chief ideas. In it Luther again drew support chiefly from Romans 13 and 1 Peter 2:13-14, but also from statements in Genesis 4:14-15; 9:6; and Exodus 21:14 and 23ff. The result is that the "sword" was present "from the beginning of the world."[20] Christ's word that one should not resist evil (Matt. 5:38-39) does not denote abolition of the Mosaic law. What must be taken into account is the person whom Christ is addressing.

In this context these words appear:

> Here we must divide the children of Adam and all mankind into two classes, the first belonging to the kingdom of God, the second to the kingdom of the world. Those who belong to the kingdom of God are all the true believers who are in Christ and under Christ, for Christ is King and Lord in the kingdom of God. . . . these people need no temporal law or sword. If all the world were composed of real Christians, that is, true believers, there would be no need for or benefits from prince, king, lord, sword, or law. . . . All who are not Christians belong to the kingdom of the world and are under the law. There are few true believers, and still fewer who live a Christian life, who do not resist evil and indeed themselves do no evil. For this reason God has provided for them a different government beyond the Christian estate and kingdom of God. He has subjected them to the sword so that, even though they would like to, they are unable to practice their wickedness.[21]

From this perspective Luther warned against wanting to rule the world with the gospel.[22] Such would let loose the evil beasts; it would abuse evangelical freedom. The rule applies "that Christians, so far as they themselves are concerned, are subject neither to law nor sword, and have need of neither." The world and the mob, however, remain "un-Christian," "even if they are all baptized and Christian in name."[23]

---

christlichen Sozialethik (Gütersloh: Bertelsmann, 1921), in *Das Neue Werk* 4 (1922), 461-72, printed in *Anfänge der dialektischen Theologie,* part 1, ed. Jürgen Moltmann, TB 17 (Munich: Chr. Kaiser, 1962), 152-65, esp. 154-56.

[19] *LW,* vol. 45, p. 85. *WA* 11, 247, 21-23.

[20] *LW,* vol. 45, p. 86. *WA* 11, 247, 31.

[21] *LW,* vol. 45, pp. 88-90. *WA* 11, 249, 24-250, 1; 251, 1-7.

[22] *LW,* vol. 45, p. 91. *WA* 11, 251, 22.

[23] *LW,* vol. 45, p. 91. *WA* 11, 251, 32-37.

Next, Luther spoke of the two governments: "We must carefully distinguish between these two governments. Both must be permitted to remain; the one to produce righteousness, the other to bring about external peace and prevent evil deeds. Neither one is sufficient in the world without the other."[24] No government can be exercised without the other. If there were only the temporal, the heart would lack the Holy Spirit who makes righteous. If there were only the spiritual, the door would be open for all manner of rascality. In fact, Christ not only did not forbid the sword but confirmed it, just as he did not abolish the estate of marriage but confirmed it.[25] On this basis Luther actually stated that the power and sword are a "divine service."[26]

In the second part Luther took up the question of the extent of temporal authority. What is most important is that the temporal power "not extend too far and encroach upon God's kingdom and government."[27] "For God cannot and will not permit anyone but himself to rule over the soul."[28] Faith is a "free act" and cannot be forced. In this connection Luther censured the abuse of office on the part of many secular rulers. It may even be that God wishes to make an end of them. Their "stripping and fleecing" has become unbearable. "You must know that since the beginning of the world a wise prince is a mighty rare bird, and an upright prince even rarer."[29] Since faith is voluntary, heresy cannot be restrained by force, a principle to which Luther himself did not adhere strictly in his later years. "For even if all Jews and heretics were forcibly burned no one ever has been or will be convinced or converted thereby. . . .The bishops . . . are to turn over to the worldly princes the job of ruling souls with the sword."[30] From this perspective Luther proceeded to delineate the office of the temporal and spiritual authorities. Temporal government involves an authority or force, spiritual government "a service and an office."[31]

Finally, the third part held up a kind of mirror for princes, in which Luther gave counsel as to how the prince should understand his task. Where possible he should exercise lordship or proceed not with force but with reason and discretion. Luther had no instruction as such to give the princes but could only instruct their "heart." Above all, a prince should make it his business to protect his subjects. The impression here, as with other statements, is that Luther had in mind the model of his elector Frederick, especially when admonishing princes to avoid war and to be concerned with preserving peace.

---

[24] *LW,* vol. 45, p. 92. *WA* 11, 252, 12-14.
[25] *LW,* vol. 45, p. 101. *WA* 11, 258, 32-34.
[26] *LW,* vol. 45, p. 103. *WA* 11, 260, 32.
[27] *LW,* vol. 45, p. 104. *WA* 11, 261, 30-31.
[28] *LW,* vol. 45, p. 105. *WA* 11, 262, 9-10.
[29] *LW,* vol. 45, p. 113. *WA* 11, 267, 30-31.
[30] *LW,* vol. 45, p. 115. *WA* 11, 269, 29-35.
[31] *LW,* vol. 45, p. 117. *WA* 11, 271, 12.

If we keep the historical context in mind, then the question is moot as to whether "the sum of Luther's political ethics" can be seen in his treatise on authority.[32] It is, of course, correct that following its composition he retained and continually gave new accent to the fundamental distinction between the spiritual and temporal government, as well as between God's kingdom or Christ's kingdom and the kingdom of the world. To that extent it yields the basic features of Luther's political ethics as well as essential aspects of his ecclesiology. On the other hand, the treatise's application of these principles to concrete problems is entirely determined by questions then acute and to that extent is narrowly confined. With its emphasis on the distinction between "spiritual" and "temporal" and its setting forth of the authorities' peculiar divine task, Luther attacked Rome and the radical reformers. He later found nothing to change in it but still had to learn that not all the essential topics of Christian political responsibility could by any means be properly evaluated on the basis of these principles. Not even strict distinction between questions concerning the body and the soul could always be maintained. In this regard Luther's later opinions on political questions, especially on the politics of the estates, are extraordinarily instructive.[33] His attitude toward the most varied problems of public life as well as his expression of points of view offered as "Christian" would have to be taken into account.

LUTHER'S ATTITUDE TOWARD THE REBELLIOUS PEASANTS

In general, Luther's attitude toward the peasants and princes in the peasants' revolt[34] coheres with his basic ideas in the treatise on *Temporal Authority*. Of course, some things came to be accented more sharply than during the debates with the Wittenberg reformers in 1521/1522.[35]

If Luther and Karlstadt were divided over the question of drawing direct consequences from the gospel regarding the social and political commonwealth, they were totally in agreement in rejecting the application of force in conjunction with their reforms. For Karlstadt the establishment of a divine government was absolutely out of the question. On the other hand, for their demands the peasants not only appealed to the gospel but took to arms. That Thomas Müntzer supported the peasants' cause with his apocalyptic-revolutionary preaching merely gave the dispute between Luther and the peasants its theological edge and volatility.[36] The

---

[32] Thus H. Bornkamm, *Luther's Doctrine of the Two Kingdoms.*

[33] On this subject see E. Wolgast, *Die Wittenberger Theologie.*

[34] See Gottfried Maron, "Bauernkrief," in *TRE* 5 (1980), 319-38.

[35] On Luther's writings in connection with the Peasants' War see the detailed evaluation in Heinrich Bornkamm, *Martin Luther in der Mitte seines Lebens: Das Jahrzehnt zwischen dem Wormser und dem Augsburger Reichstag,* ed. Karin Bornkamm (Göttingen: Vandenhoeck & Ruprecht, 1979), 314-53.

[36] On Müntzer's theology see first *Der Theologie Thomas Müntzer: Untersuchungen zu seiner Entwicklung und Lehre,* ed. Siegfried Bräuer and Helmar Junghans (Göttingen: Vandenhoeck & Ruprecht, 1989); in addition, Bernhard Lohse, *Thomas Müntzer, der Prophet mit dem Schwert,* in *Luther* 61 (1990), 1-20.

peasants obviously did not appropriate many of Müntzer's ideas, though they thoroughly welcomed his support.

Luther upbraided the peasants chiefly as follows. First, they should neither call themselves a "Christian association or union," nor allege that they act "according to divine law." Next, they should not judge their own affairs. Finally, the mere fact that they were first to take up arms renders their cause unjust.[37] In so stating, Luther in no way intended to deny that the authorities had done the peasants some injustice, or that some of their demands were justified. Most of their demands he, of course, soundly rejected. He was concerned to instruct consciences as to what is and what is not legitimate for a Christian to do. On the positive side, he impressed on the authorities as well as the peasants that the preservation of peace was the first and decisive task of all involved. Even during the revolt Luther kept strictly to this view.[38] In this respect he held to his earlier view throughout. For the rest, he feared that open conflict between peasants and princes would have three dire consequences: It would lead to both kingdoms being "destroyed and there would be neither worldly government nor word of God."[39] Further, Germany would be laid waste and everything ruined. Finally, both lords as well as peasants would risk their souls' salvation.[40]

Obviously, where the authorities' task was concerned, Luther expressed himself much more sharply and pointedly in the context of the peasants' revolt. In the *Admonition to Peace* he had addressed both sides and warned the princes and lords against false security and depicted them as inciting the wrath of God.[41] Now, since the peasants had taken to arms he summoned the authorities to take severe measures. He stressed most forcibly that the peasants merited death for three reasons. First, they broke their oath of obedience to the authorities, and thus resisted the authority established by God. At this point Luther appealed to Romans 13. Next, by rebelling, robbing, and plundering they proved to be highwaymen and murderers. Finally, they cloaked their action in the gospel and thus committed the sin of blasphemy. "See what a mighty prince the devil is, how he has the world in his hands and can throw everything into confusion, when he can so quickly catch so many thousands of peasants, deceive them, blind them, harden them, and throw them into revolt, and do with them whatever his raging fury undertakes."[42]

---

[37] See *LW,* vol. 46, pp. 17-43 (*Admonition to Peace, a Reply to the Twelve Articles of the Peasants in Swabia,* 1525), esp. pp. 24-43; *WA* 18, 291-334, esp. 301, 14-304, 8; Gottfried Maron, "Niemand soll sein eigener Richter sein: Eine Bemerkung zu Luthers Haltung im Bauernkrieg," *Luther* 46 (1975), 60-75.

[38] See on this subject above all the investigation of J. Wallmann, "Ein Friedensappell."

[39] *LW,* vol. 46, p. 18. *WA* 18, 292, 16-17.

[40] *LW,* vol. 46, pp. 40-41. *WA* 18, 329, 2-12; 332, 3-17. See H. Bornkamm, *Martin Luther in der Mitte seines Lebens,* 323-24.

[41] *LW,* vol. 46, p. 19. *WA* 18, 293, 10-294, 16.

[42] *LW,* vol. 46, p. 51. *WA* 18, 357, 21-358, 32.

These concluding words make clear that for Luther the peasants' revolt had apocalyptic significance: the devil was threatening to extend his rule. In this imperiled situation the authorities should prevent the final chaos from breaking in. In view of the situation Luther concentrated more intensively on the tasks of the temporal authorities and their various duties in the temporal realm. To this the treatise *Whether Soldiers, Too, Can Be Saved,* composed while Luther was still under the impress of the peasants' revolt (1526), gives eloquent witness.[43] Some of his late disputations, however, reflect this shift in accent, particularly the *Circular Concerning the Right to Resist the Emperor* (Matt. 19:21).[44]

On the other hand, following the peasants' revolt, Luther gave much less place to subjects' rights and possibilities for action. As early as in his treatise *To the Christian Nobility,* he never strictly adhered to the principle of the universal priesthood of the baptized that he had urged against Rome in 1520, nor did he establish it as a basis for a new concept of the church.[45] Yet in 1523 he could publish the treatise *That a Christian Assembly or Congregation Has the Right and Power to Judge All Teaching and to Call, Appoint, and Dismiss Teachers, Established and Proven by Scripture.*[46] After the peasants' revolt Luther no longer advocated such ideas, and in the Lutheran Church orders this principle was not adopted. This too indicates a shift in accent following the peasants' revolt.

[43] *LW,* vol. 46, pp. 93-137. *WA* 19, 623-62.

[44] *WA* 39 II, 34-91.

[45] See Bernd Moeller, "Klerus und Antiklerikalismus in Luthers Schrift an den christlichen Adel Deutscher Nation of 1520," in *Anticlericalism in Late Medieval and Early Modern Europe,* ed. Peter Dykema and Heiko A. Oberman (Leiden: Brill, 1993), 353-65.

[46] *LW,* vol. 39, pp. 305-14. *WA* 11, 408-16.

Chapter 17

LUTHER'S DISPUTE WITH ERASMUS

ERASMUS'S *DIATRIBE DE LIBERO ARBITRIO* (1524)

While the debate about reforms was still going on and Luther was developing in greater detail his view of the temporal authority against opponents to "left" and "right," the next great dispute occurred, this time between Luther and Erasmus. The dispute had to do with the starting point of Reformation theology, with the radical view of sin and bondage of the human will in respect of grace, which, oddly enough, had till then been rather summarily treated.[1] In the debate with Erasmus, Luther further developed and honed his view of sin and the will, and in some respects also his view of God. Without the dispute between these two, the depths of Luther's Reformation position would have remained hidden. We may not, however, ignore that Luther never returned to some of the views he developed in this dispute. He would scarcely have surrendered them but would have regarded them as something to be dealt with last of all, not to be taken up unqualifiedly in preaching and teaching.

However great the debt of Luther and the Reformation to humanism as a whole, but also to Erasmus, and not least to the editions of the church fathers that Erasmus prepared, differences slumbered in the depths that for a while neither

---

[1] The question of the freedom of the will played a role in the condemnations of the Louvain and Cologne universities in 1519, with particular reference to Laurentius Valla and Pico. In 1520 Luther stated his opposition. See WA 6, 183, 19-36. Also important was the bull threatening excommunication against Luther as well as the treatise *Assertio omnium articulorum M. Lutheri per bullam Leonis X. novissimam damnatorum* (1520), WA 7, 91-151.

made public.[2] Erasmus advocated a Christianity reinvigorated by the Sermon on the Mount. It was not the abundance of ecclesiastical norms and regulations, and certainly not the subtleties of scholasticism that should determine the church's teaching and preaching, but rather humility and discipleship. Erasmus held that some questions with which philosophy and theology dealt were too complex for him to want to discuss them in public. Among them was the problem of the freedom of the will.

When, after intense pressure, Erasmus finally dealt with the freedom of the will in his *Diatribe,* he singled out that point at which he knew he was in conscious agreement with Luther's traditionalist opponents, despite all their other differences. We should note first that since Laurentius Valla and Pico della Mirandola there had been discussion of the freedom of the will, a discussion significant for Erasmus as well as for Luther.[3] We should note next that with the genre of "diatribe" Erasmus was making use of a deliberative rhetoric that avoids any decision and is oriented to prudence and temperance.[4] It should also be emphasized that in contrast to earlier discussions, Erasmus did not treat the question of the will as a philosophical problem, but cited and evaluated numerous relevant biblical utterances. In doing so he followed the method of Luther, who, as he emphasized, aside from Holy Scripture assigned authority neither to councils nor to church tradition.

What is significant is Erasmus's definition of free choice or freedom of the will: "By free choice in this place we mean a power of the human will by which a man can apply himself to the things which lead to eternal salvation, or turn away from them."[5] Erasmus argued that Scripture as well as ancient and more modern scholars hold various views regarding the freedom of the will. Against Luther he stressed that to contest the freedom of the will easily opens the door to godlessness.[6] Since the New Testament speaks often of reward, there can be no such thing as mere necessity.[7] Erasmus left open the question whether as primary cause of all occurrences God effects some things only through secondary causes, or whether he is

---

[2] See the brief survey by Lohse, *HdBDThG,* 2:33-35. Among Erasmus's numerous editions of the church fathers those of Jerome (9 volumes) and Augustine (10 volumes) are especially important.

[3] On this subject see Lohse, "Marginalien zum Streit zwischen Erasmus und Luther," 118-37.

[4] On this subject see Manfred Hofmann, "Erasmus im Streit mit Luther," in *Humanismus und Reformation: Martin Luther und Erasmus von Rotterdam in den Konflikten ihrer Zeit,* ed. Otto Hermann Pesch, Schriftenreihe der Katholischen Akademie der Erzdiözese Freiburg (Munich/Zurich: Schnell and Steiner, 1985), 91-118, here 107. See further idem, *Rhetoric and Theology: The Hermeneutic of Erasmus* (Toronto: University of Toronto Press, 1994).

[5] *Luther and Erasmus: Free Will and Salvation,* trans. E. Gordon Rupp, LCC 17 (Philadelphia: Westminster, 1969), p. 47. *De libero arbitrio* Ib 10 (p. 36): "liberum arbitrium hoc loco sentimus vim humanae voluntatis, qua se possit homo applicare ad ea, quae perducunt ad aeternam salutem, aut ab iisdem avertere."

[6] Ibid., p. 42. Ia 10 (p. 18).

[7] Ibid., p. 60. IIb 2 (p. 74/76).

omnipotent.[8] For his defense of a limited freedom of the will he also cited the scholastic distinction between *necessitas consequentis* (unconditioned necessity) and *necessitas consequentiae* (conditioned necessity).[9] Above all he opposed the idea that God would harden a person's heart.[10] For the rest, he emphasized that we owe God "all the work without which we can do nothing, and that the contribution of free choice is extremely small, and that this itself is part of the divine gift."[11] We may summarize his position to read that the grace of God is the principal cause and the human will the secondary cause in obtaining salvation.[12]

Admittedly, at certain points in his *Diatribe,* Erasmus laid himself open to attack. His statement on skepticism is highly problematic: "And, in fact, so far am I from delighting in 'assertions' that I would readily take refuge in the opinion of the Skeptics, wherever this is allowed by the inviolable authority of the Holy Scriptures and by the decrees of the church, to which I everywhere willingly submit my personal feelings, whether I grasp what it prescribes or not."[13] Luther responded in all asperity: "Spiritus sanctus non est Scepticus" (the Holy Spirit is no skeptic).[14] Of course in his *Hyperaspistes* Erasmus made clear what he meant by these unguarded statements: "It is not a matter of indifference but of reserve toward too hasty assertions, just as the ancient church reflected long before it handed down decisions, for example, in the doctrine of the Holy Spirit."[15] This very passage indicates to what great extent Erasmus and Luther misunderstood each other.

LUTHER'S RESPONSE IN *THE BONDAGE OF THE WILL* (1525)

In drafting his refutation, Luther took more time than with any other polemical piece against the traditionalists. He was naturally averse to being forced to respond to "such an uneducated book by such a learned man."[16] Nonetheless, *The Bondage of the Will* became one of Luther's most important publications. We should also note that while writing it, he was occupied with the problems of the peasants' revolt, with Müntzer's revolutionary, spiritual Christianity, and with the newly initiated

[8] Ibid., p. 67. IIIa 8 (p. 100).

[9] Ibid., p. 68. IIIa 9 (p. 102).

[10] Ibid., p. 65. IIIa 2 (p. 92).

[11] Ibid., pp. 89-90. IV 7 (p. 170).

[12] Ibid., p. 90. IV 8 (p. 172).

[13] Ibid., p. 37. Ia 4 (p. 6): "Et adeo non delector assertionibus, ut facile in Scepticorum pedibus discessurus sim, ubicumque per divinarum scripturarum inviolabilem auctoritatem et ecclesiae decreta liceat, quibus meum sensum ubique libens submitto, sive assequor, quod praescribit, sive non assequor."

[14] *LW,* vol. 33, p. 24. *WA* 18, 605, 32.

[15] Erasmus, *Hyperaspistes* I (*De libero arbitrio Diatribe sive Collatio.* Erasmus von Rotterdam: Ausgewählte Schriften, edited by Winfried Lesowsky. Vol. 4. [Darmstadt: Wissenschaftliche Buchgesellschaft, 1969], p. 252).

[16] *WA Br* 3 Nr. 789, 29-31 (letter to Spalatin on November 1, 1524).

controversy over the Lord's Supper, to say nothing of his personal career, amid all these complications considerably altered by his marriage and the founding of his own large household in June 1525. The *De servo arbitrio* was composed mainly in the autumn of 1525. By the end of December 1525, it was in print.

In order to interpret Luther's treatise we must take into account its character as polemic. If in adopting the form of deliberative rhetoric Erasmus had chosen a genre calculated to spare him any personal involvement and avoid or worsen a dispute over the question, Luther attempted to take Erasmus literally and treat his diatribe as a dogmatic tract. To this extent, the men argued on two different levels, as a result of which no authentic dialogue ever occurred. In the main, Luther followed each of Erasmus's arguments step by step. As significant as Luther's statements are, we must warn against construing his response as a systematic treatise in any strict sense. In what follows I briefly evaluate some basic questions and chains of argument in *De servo arbitrio*.

CENTRAL THEMES IN *DE SERVO ARBITRIO*

First, as to its context in the history of theology, Erasmus and Luther were aware that their dispute had to do with a problem that was repeatedly discussed and with varied results in the late Middle Ages. While Erasmus often maintained a certain distance from Laurentius Valla, Luther appealed to this Renaissance philosopher.[17] This fact is worth noting, since Valla did not exclude the freedom of the will outright, though he severely limited it.[18] More appropriately, Luther cited Wyclif in support of his position.[19] In view of his infrequent references to Valla and Wyclif,[20] the appeal to either indicates that he was clearly informed of the late medieval theological-philosophical controversy over the freedom of the will. In any event, he set his own dispute with Erasmus in this context. Finally, we should note first Luther's choice of title for the treatise, a title that he did not explain but about the background of which scholars at that time were certainly aware. Only once had Augustine spoken of the "servum arbitrium" (bound will).[21] By using this title Luther intended to make clear that he understood himself as defender of the Augustinian doctrine of sin and grace against Pelagians old and new. With the quotation from Augustine he was appealing to the tradition of the church fathers.

[17] *LW,* vol. 33, p. 72. WA 18, 640, 6-10. On this subject see B. Lohse, *Evangelium in der Geschichte,* 124. In the *Hyperaspistes* (p. 562), Erasmus stated that Luther could make unconditional appeal to Valla.

[18] See Lohse, *Evangelium in der Geschichte,* 123-24.

[19] *LW,* vol. 31, p. 72; *WA* 18, 640, 6-10.

[20] See the passages in *WA* 63 index.

[21] Augustine, *Contra Iulianum* 2.8.23; on this subject see Harry McSorley, *Luther,* 90-93.

If with his choice of deliberative rhetoric Erasmus had tried to avoid taking a decisive position on the question, at the outset Luther emphasized that *assertio,* thus a firm assertion or confession, belongs to faith: "It is not the mark of a Christian mind to take no delight in assertions; on the contrary, a man must delight in assertions or he will be no Christian. And by assertion—in order that we may not be misled by words—I mean a constant adhering, affirming, confessing, maintaining, and an invincible preserving."[22] With this statement Luther seized on Erasmus's word about skepticism,[23] in order to set up a blunt alternative between it and faith: "Let Skeptics and Academics keep well away from us Christians, but let there be among us 'assertors' twice as unyielding as the Stoics themselves."[24] It is in this context that the phrase "the Holy Spirit is no skeptic" appears.[25]

Luther further discussed the theological assumption back of his view of *assertio* as a necessary form of Christian faith, that is, in the clarity of Holy Scripture. Erasmus, of course, was also able to say that in essential questions the Holy Scripture is clear. According to him, the narrowly limited freedom of the human will belonged to such questions. He nevertheless pointed to the fact that in Scripture some questions are obscure, just as also at essential points God is inscrutable.[26] In reply Luther referred to the central content of Holy Scripture: "Take Christ out of the Scriptures, and what will you find left in them?"[27]

Luther also distinguished a double clarity (*claritas*) and a double obscurity (*obscuritas*):

> There are two kinds of clarity in Scripture, just as there are also two kinds of obscurity: one external and pertaining to the ministry of the Word, the other located in the understanding of the heart. If you speak of the internal clarity, no man perceives one iota of what is in the Scriptures unless he has the Spirit of God. . . . If, on the other hand, you speak of the external clarity, nothing at all is left obscure or ambiguous, but everything there is in the Scriptures has been brought out by the Word into the most definite light, and published to all the world.[28]

---

[22] *LW,* vol. 33, pp. 19-20. *WA* 18, 603, 10-13.

[23] See above at nn. 13-15.

[24] *LW,* vol. 33, p. 20. *WA* 18, 603, 22-23.

[25] *LW,* vol. 33, p. 24. *WA* 18, 605, 32.

[26] On this subject see Lohse, *Lutherdeutung heute,* 55-56.

[27] *LW,* vol. 33, p. 26. *WA* 18, 606, 29: "Tolle Christum e scripturis, quid amplius in illis invenies?"

[28] *LW,* vol. 33, p. 28. *WA* 18, 609, 4-14. The same thematic of the clarity and obscurity of the Scripture is also discussed by Luther on pp. 653-56. On this subject see esp. Rudolf Hermann, *Von der Klarheit der Heiligen Schrift: Untersuchungen und Erörterungen über Luthers Lehre von der Schrift* (Berlin: Evangelische Verlagsanstalt, 1958); Friedrich Beisser, *Claritas Scripturae bei Martin Luther,* FKDG 18 (Göttingen: Vandenhoeck & Ruprecht, 1966); Ernst Wolf, "Über 'Klarheit der Heiligen Schrift' nach Luthers 'De servo arbitrio,'" *ThLZ* 92 (1967), 721-30.

For "external" and "internal" clarity we may substitute "objective" and "subjective" clarity.[29] "Objective" clarity has to do with the clarity of the Christian witness, "subjective" clarity with the inner clarity of the heart in the hearer or reader of the biblical witness. As to its external clarity, the Scripture is unequivocal: "For what still sublimer thing can remain hidden in the Scriptures, now that the seals have been broken, the stone rolled from the door of the sepulcher [Matt. 27:66; 28:2], and the supreme mystery brought to light, namely, that Christ the Son of God has been made man, that God is three and one, that Christ has suffered for us and is to reign eternally?"[30]

With these statements on the dual clarity of Scripture Luther was defending the so-called Reformation principle of Scripture according to which Scripture as such is clear and requires no binding exposition by a Roman teaching office to overcome possible obscurities. The clarity of Scripture thus emerges from its "subject matter." This does not mean that it contains no tensions or even contradictions in detail.

Alongside Luther's discussion of the *assertiones* and *claritas scripturae*, special weight attaches to the section in which he distinguished the *Deus absconditus* (hidden God) and the *Deus revelatus* (revealed God).[31] The occasion for these statements was the disputed interpretation of Ezekiel 18:23: "Have I any pleasure in the death of the wicked, says the Lord God, and not rather that he should turn from his way and live?" Among the numerous passages that Erasmus cited in his favor, Ezekiel 18 was the most important; he wanted to use it to defend the limited freedom even of the sinner.[32]

Luther began by stating that it seems senseless to maintain with the *Diatribe* that God laments the death of those he himself effects. On the other hand he said: "We have to argue in one way about God or the will of God as preached, revealed, offered, and worshiped, and in another way about God as he is not preached, not revealed, not offered, not worshiped. To the extent, therefore, that God hides himself and wills to be unknown to us, it is no business of ours. For here the saying truly applies, 'Things above us are no business of ours.'"[33] In what follows he broadened this distinction: "God must therefore be left to himself in his own majesty, for in this regard we have nothing to do with him, nor has he willed that we should have anything to do with him. But we have something to do with him insofar as he is clothed and set forth in his Word, through which he offers himself to us." In what follows Luther comes close to splitting the concept of God in two:

[29] See Althaus, *The Theology of Martin Luther,* translated by Robert C. Schultz (Philadelphia: Fortress Press, 1966), 78.

[30] *LW,* vol. 33, p. 26. WA 18, 606, 24-28: "Quid enim potest in scripturis augustius latere reliquum, postquam fractis signaculis et voluto ab hostio sepulchri lapide, illud summum mysterium proditum est, Christum filium Dei factum hominem, Esse Deum trinum et unum, Christum pro nobis passum et regnaturum aeternaliter?"

[31] *LW,* vol. 33, pp. 136-49. WA 18, 683, 11-691, 39.

[32] Erasmus, *Hyperaspistes* I *(De libero arbitrio Diatribe sive Collatio,* pp. 55-57. IIa 15-16.

[33] *LW,* vol. 33, p. 139. WA 18, 685, 1-7.

In this regard we say, the good God does not deplore the death of his people which he works in them, but he deplores the death which he finds in his people and desires to remove from them. For it is this that God as he is preached is concerned with, namely, that sin and death should be taken away and we should be saved. . . . But God hidden in his majesty neither deplores nor takes away death, but works life, death, and all in all. For there he has not bound himself by his Word, but has kept himself free over all things.[34]

Scholarly interpretations of this section, which differ to an extraordinary degree, cannot be more carefully evaluated here. They extend from the view that Luther's distinction between the *Deus absconditus* and *revelatus* is reminiscent of Marcion's doctrine of the two gods,[35] to the view that he referred here to the nominalist distinction between the *potentia Dei absoluta* and *ordinata*,[36] up to various attempts to establish a unity in his concept of God.

The nominalist distinction between the two *potentiae* was obviously not identical to Luther's distinction between the *Deus absconditus* and *revelatus*. Behind the former lay the effort to link the divine omnipotence and the divine revelation. Behind Luther's distinction was the impenetrable experience of inner conflict and abandonment, counteracted by the divine mercy and grace. We should neither overemphasize nor hastily harmonize Luther's exaggerated remarks. They are extreme, occasioned by the exegetical debate with Erasmus, to which he never again returned in such form, and which he never made the starting point of his statements about God. In view of the central place of Jesus Christ in all of Luther's theology, the reproach that he split the concept of God is surely unjustified. The treatise's concluding section also militates against such a charge.[37]

Not least, the question of the freedom of the will is at the heart of this treatise. Luther continually engaged this theme. He took it to be simply intolerable that Erasmus should reckon this question among things that were at bottom superfluous and not necessary to know. Erasmus had discussed the question without reference to Christ, while he had described the nature of Christianity in such a way that one should repent with all one's might, should hope in the mercy of God without which no human will is effective, and should never despair of divine pardon.[38] Erasmus thus avoided taking a position on the question as to how far our powers reach, what we can and cannot do.[39]

---

[34] *LW,* vol. 33, pp. 139-40. *WA* 18, 685, 14-24. The peculiarly exaggerated final sentence reads: "Neque enim tum verbo suo definivit sese, sed liberum sese reservavit super omnia."

[35] Thus Otto Ritschl, *Dogmengeschichte des Protestantismus,* 3:16.

[36] Thus Reinhold Seeberg, *Lehrbuch der Dogmengeschichte,* 4/1:182. See above, pp. 13, 19.

[37] See below, p. 167.

[38] *LW,* vol. 33, p. 31. *WA* 18, 609, 15-611, 24.

[39] *LW,* vol. 33, p. 33. *WA* 18, 613, 1-14.

For his part, Luther wrote that we are free only respecting things beneath us, not respecting those above us. At one significant point he went beyond Augustine, whom he most often correctly cited against Erasmus: the bondage of the will is no longer as for Augustine and the entire tradition merely a result of the fall. It results from human creatureliness. In a few passages Luther approximated the deterministic view that even in external things of life humans have no freedom but are controlled by God. At the same time, he referred to the scholastic distinction between *necessitas consequentis* (unconditioned necessity) and *necessitas consequentiae* (conditioned necessity), which was calculated to hold to the sole activity of God as well as to humans' limited freedom to decide.[40]

On the other side, Luther limited determinism throughout. This is clear first of all in his treatment of Judas. To the question that the medieval period continually put, as to whether Judas was forced to betray Jesus, Luther answered that he of course acted with necessity, though not forced, rather voluntarily.[41] And, allowing for the difference in Vallas's position on the question of free will and determinism, Luther's appeal to him made clear that he was striving to avoid the danger of denying any freedom to the human will whatsoever.[42]

Finally, we need to note the concluding section in *De servo arbitrio,* which is probably decisive for the interpretation of the entire treatise. Earlier, Luther pursued Erasmus's argument step by step. In the brief concluding section he summarized his own view in five lead sentences.

The first reads: "If we believe it to be true that God foreknows and predestines all things, that he can neither be mistaken in his foreknowledge nor hindered in his predestination, and that nothing takes place but as he wills it (as reason itself is forced to admit), then on the testimony of reason itself there cannot be any free choice in man or angel or any creature." And the fifth reads: "If we believe that Christ has redeemed men by his blood, we are bound to confess that the whole man was lost; otherwise, we should make Christ either superfluous or the redeemer of only the lowest part of man, which would be blasphemy and sacrilege."[43]

This concluding section is significant chiefly with regard to the assumptions on the basis of which Luther was debating with Erasmus. It indicates more clearly than the individual debating points that Luther was uttering his biting remarks from the

---

[40] *LW,* vol. 33, pp. 39-41, 64-65, 192-95. On this subject see McSorley, *Luther,* 143-59; *WA* 18, 616, 13-617, 22; 634, 14-36 (on the problem of the *Necessitarismus*); 720, 28-722, 29.

[41] *LW,* vol. 33, p. 185. The most important sentence reads: "If God foreknew that Judas would be a traitor, Judas necessarily became a traitor. And it was not in the power of Judas or any creature to do differently or to change his will, though he did what he did willingly and not under compulsion." *WA* 18, 715, 17-716, 1: "Si praescivit Deus, Iudam fore proditorem, necessario Iudas fiebat proditor nec erat in manu Iudae aut ullius creaturae, aliter facere aut voluntatem mutare, licet id fecerit volendo non coactus."

[42] See above at nn. 17-18.

[43] *LW,* vol. 33, p. 293. *WA* 18, 786, 3-7, 17-20.

perspective of faith. Humanity's lostness is not an assertion that can be made solely on the basis of experience but results ultimately from the redemption in Christ.[44] In the light of this basis some of the exaggerated remarks in *De servo arbitrio* appear more intelligible and justified. Even Luther's blunt statement regarding the bondage of the will must ultimately be seen from its christological basis.

[44] See K. Schwarzwäller, *Theologia crucis,* 57-58; Lohse, *Evangelium in der Geschichte,* 131-34.

Chapter 18

LUTHER'S DISPUTE
WITH ZWINGLI

THE LORD'S SUPPER CONTROVERSY

THE EMERGENCE OF INTRA-EVANGELICAL DIFFERENCES

From approximately 1517 to 1520, when Luther's dispute with Rome reached its zenith, no attention was paid to differences among the evangelicals over sacramental doctrine. Controversy with the traditionalists relegated all other viewpoints to the periphery. Only from a later perspective did it become clear that as early as in the attack on the late medieval doctrine of the sacrifice and celebration of the Mass arguments were raised that hinted at later differences.[1] In the dispute with Rome, topics that later became controversial were not treated at all, in particular the topic of the real presence. There had been united attack against the idea of sacrifice, agreement in setting forth the once-for-allness of Christ's sacrifice on the cross, and a common accenting of the need for faith. The words of institution themselves, however, were in part variously interpreted.

Further, in the years since approximately 1517/1518, with almost all the participants in the coming dispute we can observe more or less serious developments in points of view. Luther originally began with the idea of communion,[2] then more

---

[1] On this subject see first of all Eberhard Grötzinger, *Luther und Zwingli* (Gütersloh: Gerd Mohn, 1980).

[2] See above, p. 127-28.

and more rigorously set the words of institution at the center. Conversely, Zwingli did not initially surrender the idea of the real presence but accented the Supper's spiritual character.[3]

For the Lord's Supper controversy considerable importance attaches to the fact that Karlstadt was the first publicly to state a view other than Luther's. According to Karlstadt, when Jesus spoke the words of institution, he was pointing to his own body. This interpretation of the words "this is my body" was not Karlstadt's invention, but can be documented from the thirteenth century.[4] For Karlstadt, then, the spiritual aspect was at the center: the communicant must be certain of redemption before receiving the Supper. As for the Supper itself, it serves the memory.[5] Karlstadt defended his view in various writings, particularly in his *Auslegung dieser wort Christi. Das ist meyn leyb / welcher für euch gegeben würt. Das ist mein bluth / welches für euch vergossen würt . . .* ("Exposition of this word of Christ. This is my body / which is given for you. This is my blood / which is shed for you . . .") (1524).

Prior to Karlstadt the question of the Supper had been variously broached. In a letter probably written in 1522, the Dutch humanist Cornelius Honius (Hoen), stimulated by the tract *De sacramento Eucharistiae* of Wessel Gansfort (+ 1489), but also by Erasmus, stated a view widespread elsewhere in Dutch humanist circles that the words of institution are to be taken in the significative sense: the bread and wine thus "signify" Christ's body and blood but "are" not such.[6]

Next, contacts developed between Luther and the Bohemian Brethren following the Leipzig Disputation (1519) led Luther to deal with the Bohemians' peculiar doctrine of the Supper.[7] They rejected the scholastic doctrine of transubstantiation and thus also homage to Christ in the elements of the Supper. They taught, however, that Christ's body and blood are present in the Supper, and referred to "Christ's true body," though they construed this presence "spiritually," in terms of "another existence." Luther had some objection to this doctrine, but distinguished the Bohemians' view, which held firmly to the presence of Christ in the Supper, from an interpretation of the words of institution in terms of a *significat*.

Luther dealt with the view of Honius and of the Brethren in his treatise *The Adoration of the Sacrament* (1523). Here for the first time he clearly advocated the real presence of Christ's body and blood in the elements of the Supper, proceeding from

[3] See B. Lohse, *HdBDThG*, 2:51-55; Gottfried W. Locher, *Huldrych Zwingli in neuer Sicht: Zehn Beiträge zur Theologie der Zürcher Reformation* (Zurich / Stuttgart: Zwingli Verlag, 1969), 250-65.

[4] See U. Bubenheimer, *Karlstadt*, 652, 32-36.

[5] See F. Kriechbaum, *Grundzüge der Theologie Karlstadts*, 102-4.

[6] More detail in Lohse, *HDBDThG*, 2:53-54.

[7] See Jaroslav Pelikan, *Obedient Rebels: Catholic Substance and Protestant Principle in Luther's Reformation* (New York: Harper & Row, 1964).

the words of institution, just as he had done since 1520: "Everything depends on these words,"[8] words that are "far more important than the sacrament itself,"[9] to be regarded as "a living, eternal, all-powerful Word that can make you alive, free from sin and death."[10] He further stated that this word "brings with it everything of which it speaks, namely, Christ with his flesh and blood and everything that he is and has. For it is the kind of Word that can and does do all these things, and therefore it should be so regarded."[11]

In the years of his dispute with Rome Luther had set the words "for you" at the center. Now the "is" became central. Against Honius he wrote:

> For if we permit such violence to be done in one passage, that without any basis in Scripture a person can say the word "is" means the same as the word "signifies," then it would be impossible to stop it in any other passage. The entire Scripture would be nullified, since there would be no good reason why such violence should be valid in one passage but not in all passages. In that case one should say: That Mary is a virgin and the mother of God is equivalent to saying that Mary signifies a virgin and the mother of God. Likewise: Christ is God and man; that is, Christ signifies God and man.[12]

This set the real presence at the heart of Luther's teaching on the Supper. First against Karlstadt in the treatise *Against the Heavenly Prophets* (1525), and later in other pieces, particularly against Zwingli, he defended the Supper as a means of grace.

THE FURTHER DEVELOPMENT OF LUTHER'S POSITION DURING THE LORD'S SUPPER CONTROVERSY

In the controversy between Luther and Zwingli above all, but in which many took sides, on occasion supplying their own accents, the one or the other further developed and in part modified his own point of view.[13] Naturally, in essence both sides held to their point of departure. The debate nevertheless forced the participants to develop their positions more precisely and thus to pay attention to opposing points of view. From his starting point Zwingli insisted that nothing creaturely can support faith. Jesus' word that the flesh is of no avail (John 6:63) applied also to the Supper. From Hoen, Zwingli appropriated the significative

---

[8] *LW,* vol. 36, p. 277. *WA* 11, 432, 19.

[9] *LW,* vol. 36, p. 277. *WA* 11, 432, 25-26.

[10] *LW,* vol. 36, p. 278. *WA* 11, 433, 25-27.

[11] *LW,* vol. 36, p. 278. *WA* 11, 433, 27-30.

[12] *LW,* vol. 36, p. 280. *WA* 11, 434, 30-435, 3.

[13] On the controversy see the survey in Lohse, *HdBDThG,* 2:56-60.

interpretation of the *est* in the words of institution. Without more precise differentiation, he rejected the doctrine of transubstantiation as well as the idea of the real presence, describing those who taught that Christ's body is eaten in the Lord's Supper as cannibals or carnivores.[14] He believed that the Supper represented a "*commemoratio* by which those who firmly believe they are reconciled with the Father through Christ's death and blood proclaim this life-giving death."[15]

It was chiefly in critical debate with Zwingli that Luther further developed his own position. For this reason his attack on Zwingli is of considerable importance. When Zwingli appealed to John 6:63 in support of his significative interpretation, Luther denied that it could be cited on behalf of a doctrine of the Supper, a view he had long defended prior to the controversy over the Supper.[16] Against Zwingli he defended the simple meaning of the words of institution: The word "is" could not mean "signifies." At the same time, he dealt in detail with hermeneutical questions.[17] Not only the particular problems of the Lord's Supper were at issue for Luther, but ultimately the fundamental question of God's presence in the incarnate Christ. God's revelation in Jesus Christ and the presence of Christ's body and blood in the Supper were indissolubly connected since both have to do with the paradox of God's presence in the flesh or, in terms of the traditional christological concepts, with the unity of the divine and human natures.

After the model of Antiochene Christology, Zwingli strictly divided the divine and human natures: Christ suffered according to his human, not his divine, nature. Furthermited freedom of the will he also cited the scholastic distinction between necessitas consequentis (unconditioned necessity) and necessitas consequentiae (conditioned necessity).9 Above all he opposed the idea that God would harden a person's heart.10 For the rest, he emphasized that we owe God "all the work without whicture. Only at his return will the exalted Lord be present again according to his human nature. The assertion that Christ is present in the Supper according to his human nature treads too near the majesty of God. Further, faith is not bound to anything creaturely but is spiritual.

---

[14] Zwingli, *CR* 90, 789, 3-4; 794, 23 (*De vera et false religione Commentarius,* 1525).

[15] Zwingli, *CR* 90, 807, 11-14.

[16] See *LW,* vol. 36, p. 19 (*The Babylonian Captivity of the Church,* 1520): "The sixth chapter of John must be entirely excluded from this discussion, since it does not refer to the sacrament in a single syllable." *WA* 6, 502, 7: "c. vi. Iohannis in totum est seponendum."

[17] On this subject see Jaroslav Pelikan, *Luther the Expositor, LW Companion Volume* (St. Louis: Concordia, 1959); Gerhard Ebeling, *Evangelische Evangelienauslegung: Eine Untersuchung zu Luthers Hermeneutik* (1942; 2d ed., Darmstadt: Wissenschaftliche Buchgesellschaft 1962), 311-44.

In arguing thusly, Zwingli did not give as much emphasis to the words of institution, "this is my body," "this is my blood," as to the words: "Do this in remembrance of me." By "remembrance" he did not have merely reminiscence in mind. For him, "remembrance" (*memoria*) denoted a making contemporary, a valid presence, of the Lord.[18] In the background of Zwingli's argument lay what he had already set at the center in his dispute with Rome, that Christ's death on the cross effected redemption once for all. "Remembrance" (*memoria*) was thus no mere idea but the saving significance of Christ's death rendered effective in the present.

For Zwingli, to assign the attributes of one of Christ's natures to the other (*communicatio idiomatum*) spelled an *alleiosis* (interchange). In this way he intended to hold fast to the unity of Christ's person, but against Luther to stress the difference between the two natures, whose peculiarities should in no way be confused.

After the outbreak of the dispute Luther further shaped and gave precision to his doctrine in a critical attack on all of Zwingli's chief arguments. Against the view that the flesh is of no avail, he stressed not only the incarnation but also the cross: precisely in the flesh and sufferings of the incarnate Lord, God encounters us for salvation. Whoever denies this imperils the heart of Christian faith.

Luther could not avoid addressing the question as to how we are to conceive the presence of Christ's exalted human nature in the elements of the Supper. In 1523 he could say:

> There have also been many who have been concerned about how the soul and the spirit of Christ, and thereby the Godhead, the Father and the Holy Spirit, is in the sacrament. . . . All these are the thoughts of idle souls and empty hearts, who forget the words and works of God in this sacrament and give themselves over to their own thoughts and words. The more simply you stick to the words of the sacrament the better it will be for you. . . . Eat and drink there, and nourish your faith. . . . And say to yourself: I am not commanded to investigate or to know how God, the Father, the Son and the Holy Spirit, or how the soul of Christ is in the sacrament.[19]

Luther could not keep to this reservation but had to go on to state how we should understand the presence of Christ's exalted body in the elements of the Supper.

After 1526 Luther developed his doctrine of ubiquity. In it, characteristically, he harked back to scholastic arguments, not a trace of which had shown itself till

---

[18] Thus correctly Gottfried W. Locher, *Streit unter Gästen: Die Lehre aus der Abendmahlsdebatte der Reformatoren für das Verständnis und die Feier des Abendmahls heute,* ThSt B 110 (Zurich: Theologischer Verlag, 1972), 10-11.

[19] *LW,* vol. 36, p. 297 (*The Adoration of the Sacrament,* 1523). *WA* 11, 449, 34-450, 13.

then. In his sermon of 1526, *The Sacrament of the Body and Blood of Christ—Against the Fanatics,* he stated: "We believe that Christ, according to his human nature, is put over all creatures [Eph. 1:22] and fills all things. . . . Not only according to his divine nature, but also according to his human nature, he is lord of all things, has all things in his hand, and is present everywhere."[20] The objections to which Luther replied had chiefly to do with the traditional notion that since his ascension Christ's exalted human body was present at a specific place and thus could not also be present at different places on earth.

In his student years Luther must have become acquainted with Occam's and Biel's doctrine of ubiquity, so that he now could refer to them.[21] Like Biel, Occam had distinguished a "circumscriptive esse in loco" (the spatial presence of an object) and a "definitive esse in loco" (e.g., the presence of the soul in the body). In addition, Biel had weighed the possibility of a "repletive" presence (the presence of an object apart from its objectivity), with God's omnipresence (ubiquity) in mind. The common assumption not only of Occam and Biel but of the entire dominant tradition was that "the right hand of God" at which the exalted Christ was "seated" denoted a particular place.

Luther adopted this distinction between the various forms of presence but reshaped Occamist tradition at one important point: he no longer conceived "the right hand of God" as a particular place in heaven: ". . . that Christ's body is everywhere because it is at the right hand of God which is everywhere, although we do not know how that occurs. For we also do not know how it occurs that the right hand of God is everywhere."[22] Despite this new definition, Luther still took up the Occamist distinction between the various forms of presence: "An object occupies places repletively, i.e., supernaturally, if it is simultaneously present in all places whole and entire, and fills all places. Yet without being measured or circumscribed by any place, in terms of the space which it occupies. This mode of existence belongs to God alone."[23] Luther's concern was not with proof but with a mode of thought by which to conceive ubiquity.[24]

---

[20] *LW,* vol. 36, p. 342. *WA* 19, 491, 17-20.

[21] On Occam see Erwin Iserloh, *Gnade und Eucharistie in der philosophischen Theologie des Wilhelm von Ockham,* VIEG 8 (Wiesbaden: Steiner, 1956), 197ff., 253-66; on Biel see Oberman, *Spätscholastik und Reformation,* (Tübingen: Mohr, 1965), 256-58; Seeberg, *Lehrbuch der Dogmengeschichte,* 3:789-91.

[22] *LW,* vol. 37, p. 214 (*Confession Concerning Christ's Supper,* 1528). *WA* 26, 325, 26-29.

[23] As scriptural proof Luther cites Jer. 23:23: "[God says:] I am a God at hand and not afar off. I fill heaven and earth," *LW,* vol. 37, p. 216. *WA* 26, 329, 27-32.

[24] See *LW,* vol. 37, p. 216: "All this I have related in order to show that there are more modes whereby an object may exist in a place than the one circumscribed, physical mode on which the fanatics insist." *WA* 26, 329, 34-36.

Obviously, the doctrine of ubiquity had a consequence that Luther scarcely intended. If till now he had inferred the presence of Christ's exalted body in the elements of the Supper solely from the words of institution, now the doctrine of ubiquity presupposed that since the ascension Christ's body and blood are everywhere present. If one took seriously the doctrine of ubiquity, then the meaning of the words of institution could only be to make evident the hidden presence of Christ's exalted body and blood. Luther did not yet draw this conclusion. His reflections on the ubiquity of Christ's human nature were an expedient used only in debate with Zwingli, and to which he did not return in other contexts.

Naturally, Luther often drew another consequence from the idea of the ubiquity of Christ's body and blood, that is, the consequence of unworthily eating Christ's body and blood. In his mature years Luther placed more and more accent on the "eating of the ungodly" (*manducatio impiorum*): even the "ungodly" receive Christ's body and blood in the Supper, but only for judgment. He also asserted that consequences for the body accrued from taking the Supper: "But since the mouth is the heart's member it also must ultimately live in eternity on account of the heart, which lives eternally through the Word, because here it also eats physically the same eternal food which its heart eats spiritually at the same time."[25] Here Luther embraced a view of the Supper as a "medicine of immortality" first held by Ignatius of Antioch.[26] In the total context of Luther's maturer teaching such expressions are somewhat marginal. They do not at all represent its heart, though they also should not be overlooked.

Respecting the various phases observable in Luther's doctrine of the Supper after 1518/1519, the question arises as to the internal consistency of its development. It is quite certain that after 1520 Luther held true to his doctrine of the Supper, that the words of institution always remained its basis and norm. And there is no doubt that in reflecting on the benefit of the Supper the aim and goal always lay in the words "for you." With his emphasis on the real presence over against the so-called sacramentarians, however, Luther's statements on the Supper assumed a concentration no longer coherent with his accent on *testamentum* and *promissio* in *The Babylonian Captivity* (1520).

---

[25] *LW,* vol. 37, p. 87 (*That These Words of Christ,* "*This Is My Body,*" etc. *Still Stand Firm Against the Fanatics,* 1527). *WA* 23, 181, 11-15. On this subject see A. Peters, *Realpräsenz,* 140-53; Ulrich Asendorf, "Das Wort Gottes bei Luther im sakramentalen Zusammenhang patristischer Theologie. Systematische und ökumenische Überlegungen zu Luthers Schrift 'Das diese Worte Christi' (1527)," *KuD* 39 (1993), 31-47.

[26] Ignatius, *Eph.* 20:2.

The Marburg Colloquy (1529)

Due chiefly to the efforts of Philip of Hesse, the Marburg Colloquy took place in October 1529.[27] The most noted theologians of the Reformation participated in it. Though it did not then achieve a compromise, sufficient agreement was established in the articles. This is true even of the doctrine of the Supper. As a result, the Marburg Formulation must be taken into account for Luther's doctrine of the Supper, though he later scarcely held to the text set down at Marburg that he signed.

The fifteenth Marburg Article reads:

> *Fifteenth*, we all believe and hold concerning the Supper of our dear Lord Jesus Christ that both forms should be used according to the institution [=1]; also that the mass is not a work whereby one obtains grace for another, dead or living [=2]; also that the sacrament of the altar is a sacrament of the true body and blood of Jesus Christ [=3], and that the spiritual partaking of this body and blood is especially necessary to every true Christian [=4]. In like manner, as to the use of the sacrament, that like the Word of God Almighty, it has been given and ordained, in order that weak consciences might be excited by the Holy Ghost to faith and love [=5]. And although we are not at this time agreed as to whether the true body and blood of Christ are bodily present in the bread and wine, nevertheless the one party should show to the other Christian love, sofar as conscience will permit, and both should fervently pray God Almighty that by His Spirit He would confirm us in the true understanding.[28]

Though dissent clearly persisted, if only in a subordinate clause, agreement was reached at several points. Zwingli agreed to accept the concept "sacrament" [3], which for a time he had entirely abandoned. In addition, he conceded that the Lord's Supper is a means of grace [4, 5]. Luther conceded the idea of "spiritual partaking" [4] and did not introduce views that went beyond. As to the real presence, Zwingli agreed to the formulation "sacrament of the true body and blood of Jesus Christ."

Only to a certain extent does the Marburg text furnish ideas central to Luther's mature teaching. On the other hand, the agreements that Luther identified despite the persisting dissent should not be overlooked. Agreements arrived at in Marburg can at least be described as something that Luther was still prepared to tolerate.

---

[27] For the course of events see the brief sketch: Lohse, *HdBDThG,* 2:60-64. In detail: Heinrich Bornkamm, *Martin Luther in der Mitte seines Lebens,* 558-85; Martin Brecht, *Martin Luther: Shaping and Defining the Reformation,* 325-34.

[28] The text appears in a somewhat modernized version in Nils Forsander, *The Marburg Colloquy,* (Rock Island, Ill.: Augustana Book Concern, 1919), 32-33. For the rest, see *WA* 30 III, 160-71, as well as the supplements in *WA* 30 III RN.

The case is similar with the Wittenberg Concord of 1536.[29] It did not represent a consensus, as some maintain,[30] but was a doctrinal statement of the South Germans in the shape of a provisional agreement. For Luther's doctrine, the concord may be regarded as a statement to which he could still assent but not as a position that he made his own. In his mature years Luther vigorously defended the idea of the real presence of Christ's body and blood in the elements of the Supper.

[29] On this subject see the survey in Lohse, *HdBDThG,* 1:96-97.

[30] Thus E. Bizer, *Studien zur Geschichte des Abendmahlsstreits im 16. Jahrhundert* (Darmstadt: Wissenschaftliche Bucheesellschaft, 1962), 127.

Chapter 19

LUTHER'S DISPUTE WITH THE ANTINOMIANS

THE QUESTION OF REPENTANCE IN REFORMATION THEOLOGY

Another important dispute, which led Luther more precisely to develop his view and in part also to modify it, had to do with establishing a basis for repentance as well as with the entire range of law and gospel doctrine. Fundamentally at issue was the Reformation view of justification and to that extent the heart of Luther's theology. At the same time the various contestants were united in rejecting the Roman "works-righteousness." Chiefly in dispute, however, was the question whether the preaching of repentance, an undoubted task of the church, belongs theologically to the exposition of the law or must follow the preaching of the gospel. There was the further question in what sense and to what extent the preaching of the law is the church's abiding task. This controversy indicates the multilayered character of the Reformation movement in its earliest stages. Only in the course of the years did this feature clearly emerge.

In the early years of his dispute with Rome, Luther responded to questions touching the basis for repentance that did not appear altogether unambiguous. His inner conflicts (*Anfechtungen*) had been ignited by the divine command and thus by the law, the deadly seriousness of which he set forth theologically and personally. Theologically speaking, it would appear that repentance belongs to the sphere of the legal. On the other hand, there was the danger that if assigned solely to that sphere, it would become an occasion for hopelessness. For such a view one could likewise appeal to Luther. In his inner conflicts he had painfully experienced his own insufficiency in view of the divine command. In his letter of dedication to Spalatin prefaced to his *Explanations of the Ninety-five Theses* (1518), Luther thanked the head of his order for emphasizing that "true repentance" begins "with the love of righteousness and of God." This word stuck in him like "the sharp arrow of a warrior" (Ps. 120:4). While previously there was no bitterer word in all the Bible than the word "repentance," now no other was more sweet and pleasant.[1]

These two approaches on the topic of repentance, taken at the onset of Luther's dispute with Rome and intimately connected, were variously adopted within the circle of Luther's adherents in the years following. Melanchthon, Luther's closest friend and coworker, stressed that the law first had to expose sin in order for the gospel to mediate grace.[2] He thus construed the order of salvation in successive stages consisting of the law, the gospel, and the necessary renewal by the Holy Spirit,[3] while Luther saw the person within the dialectic of judgment and grace or law and gospel. On the other hand, Johann Agricola (ca. 1499-1566), since 1515/1516 a pupil and friend of Luther and for some years among his closest intimates, emphasized that repentance is a fruit of the gospel since the law cannot lead to faith. An argument that Agricola continually made in this context read that Christ in fact fulfilled the law, for which reason it had been abolished as a way of salvation. Further, according to Paul, the law by itself works wrath; it cannot lead to the gospel.[4] Material differences were exaggerated by personal animus, poisoning the atmosphere between Melanchthon and Agricola.

After a prelude of initial differences in 1524,[5] a controversy arose in 1527 on the occasion of the Articles of Visitation authored by Melanchthon (*Articuli, de quibus egerunt per visitatores in regione Saxoniae*).[6] Melanchthon had stated that the preaching of faith cannot be understood without a prior call to repentance. The law must thus first be preached in order that one repent. Only then can the gospel be preached. For the rest, the law is necessary for daily sanctification. Agricola opposed the articles by challenging the chronological and material status of repentance prior to the gospel. He appealed to Luther's statement of 1518, that repentance must begin with the love of righteousness.[7] From Luther, Agricola also adopted the view that the law is the Jews' *Sachsenspiegel* (Saxon code of law) and no longer applies to the Christian.[8] Agricola was first to appeal to Luther's early statements by which to oppose

---

[1] *WA* 1, 525, 4-23 (May 30, 1518).

[2] Melanchthon, *Loci communes* (1521), in *Melanchthon and Bucer*, ed. Wilhelm Pauck, LCC 19 (Philadelphia: Westminster, 1969), 71.

[3] Ibid. (28, 4-29, 30), 38-39.

[4] On this subject see S. Kjeldgaard-Pedersen, *Gesetz, Evangelium und Busse*, AThD 16 (Leiden, 1983), 219-25, and elsewhere. E. Koch, *Johann Agricola*, 148-50, refers to Tauler's influence on Agricola.

[5] On this subject see Lohse, *HdBDThG*, 2:41-42.

[6] Melanchthon, *CR* 26, 9-28; 1, 919.

[7] See *CR* 1, 915-16.

[8] Luther: *LW*, vol. 35, p. 167. *WA* 16, 378, 11; 18, 81, 14-15. Agricola: *130. Gemeiner Fragestücke für die jungen Kinder* (Wittenberg, 1528).

Melanchthon and later actually cited the young against the mature Luther. Naturally, he did not take into account the context of Luther's remarks in his dispute with Rome. He further ignored the fact that since 1521/1522 Luther had set forth the permanent significance of the law against the so-called fanatics.

At a gathering in Torgau on November 26-29, 1527, Luther, Bugenhagen, Melanchthon, and Agricola deliberated over their differences. Luther distinguished a general faith (*fides generalis*) still beset with "terrors," at base to be described as "repentance" (*poenitentia*), and a justifying faith that lays hold of grace under the terror of conscience.[9] The initial disagreement was bridged by a formula that all supported and was adopted in Melanchthon's "Instruction of Visitors" (1528). The formula referred to a "common faith" to which repentance belongs, though it was emphasized that forgiveness of sins cannot be understood apart from repentance.[10] Though the formula was a compromise calculated to give either side its due, Agricola believed he had won. He held to his view that the preaching of the law should not precede the preaching of the gospel. As for Luther, the formula of 1527/1528 scarcely sufficed to express the depth of his view on repentance. It was not really clear from this text that in repentance law and gospel are linked to each other in an exemplary way and may not be separated, though they must be distinguished.

THE CONFLICT OVER LAW AND GOSPEL

Agricola, rector of the school at Eisleben from 1525 to 1536, was an opponent of Pastor Georg Witzel (1501-1573), active in the same city since 1533. Witzel, influenced by a theology of reform along the line of the church fathers, the *Devotio moderna,* and Erasmus, was for some time influenced by the Reformation movement, but then returned to the old church. Against him Agricola formulated his antinomian position. When Agricola returned from Eisleben to Wittenberg in 1536, the earlier dispute flamed up in aggravated form. From 1537 to 1540 occurred violent debates in which the disputations against the Antinomians have particular weight. During these disputes the Saxon elector gave more and more place to Luther's teaching as the norm by which Agricola had to be judged.

The process of fixing Luther's authority in doctrinal matters was then in full swing. For his part Luther did nothing to halt the process or to give others the same freedom to teach that he had once claimed for himself over against Rome.[11] These events were of considerable significance for Agricola's subsequent behavior during negotiations over the interim.

---

[9] *CR* 1, 916.
[10] Melanchthon, *Studienausgabe* 1, 221, 7-222, 27.
[11] A brief survey of these events is in G. Kawerau, *RE,* 1 (1896), 251-52.

In this new phase of the conflict Agricola not only defended his earlier views but reproached Luther with not having kept to his original position. Agricola rebutted the idea that the church must also preach the law. In his opinion, Luther's doctrine of law and gospel obscured the promise of grace. Of course, he did not deny the first, so-called political use of the law.[12] The phrase attributed to him by Luther to the effect that "the Decalogue belongs in the courthouse, not in the chancel," cannot be documented in any of his writings.[13] It may have been advocated by his adherents. As for the law, Agricola insisted that it may not be called "God's Word."[14] Naturally, the place that the doctrine of the law usually assumed had to be filled in another way: the gospel leads to a better discipline, or, in the gospel God dictates how we should live; or, Christ has issued new laws. In a sense, then, the gospel is also a law. Repentance can be ignited at the cross, that is, in the "violatio of the Son" (*violatio filii*).[15]

LUTHER'S DOCTRINE OF LAW AND GOSPEL IN THE ANTINOMIAN CONTROVERSY

The debate between Agricola with his in part more radical adherents and Luther with his various friends is one of the most important doctrinal disputes to which the mature Luther was exposed. The dissent had to do with the doctrine of justification, but also with repentance, and not least with the assurance of salvation. For Luther at issue first was a proper understanding of the law as well as the necessary dialectic between law and gospel, a dialectic that Agricola had abolished. According to Luther, then, the dispute with Agricola did not involve a particular sort of problem. "He [regarded] antinomianism . . . as a fate by which all of theology and church were under a bad omen."[16]

If in opposition to Rome Luther had accented the gospel as God's gracious condescension toward humankind, now, against the Antinomians he accented the abiding significance of the law. Like the fanatics, Agricola was in danger of making a new law of the gospel through annulling the dialectic. Luther stated it in this way: "Whoever abolishes the law abolishes the gospel also."[17] The law is, of course, not necessary for justification. It is of no use and incapable for that, but it does not at all follow that it is to be rejected. Alongside the political use of the law Luther now set its theological use. Proof of sin is necessary, in that Christians are still sinners: "The law

---

[12] See J. Rogge, *TRE* 2 (1978), 114, 40-41.

[13] *WA* 39 I, 344, 30. See J. Rogge, *Johann Agricolas Lutherverständnis,* 154-55.

[14] *WA* 39 I, 344, 25.

[15] Rogge, *Johann Agricolas Lutherverständnis,* 81.

[16] Ibid., 188.

[17] *WA TR* 3 Nr. 3650c, 30-31 (Dec. 21, 1537): "Qui tollit legem, et evangelium tollit."

shows sins; it does not justify, but shows us to be sinners; it does not make alive, but mortifies and kills."[18] To this extent it is correct that the law does not lead to justification. Still, the exhibiting of sin involves a "necessary use" (*necessarius usus*), since none can be justified without repentance.[19] As to the question of the necessity of the law for justification, there must be differentiation: in one sense the question is to be answered in the negative, but in another, in the affirmative.

Luther went even a step further. Fundamentally, not even the saving significance of the cross can be grasped apart from the law. If Agricola emphasized Christ's fulfillment of the law, concluding that the law is no longer of significance for the Christian, Luther argued that only on the basis of a knowledge and experience of the law can its fulfillment through Christ be understood. If Agricola was pointing to the divine wrath on the basis of the *violatio filii*, then what is actually involved is preaching the law, not the gospel. Clearly, Agricola assumed that the law is to be identified with the Old and the gospel with the New Testament, while for Luther such an undifferentiated identification did not do justice to the interrelationship or connection between law and gospel or between the old and new covenants.

As to the significance of the law in justification, the result for Luther was that the law is not "the efficient cause" (*causa efficiens*) of justification but *materialiter* is still its presupposition.[20]

It is true, then, that repentance is first evoked through the preaching of the law. Of course, only faith leads to repentance resulting in conversion. Only faith knows that the preaching of the law is required for a knowledge of sin. True repentance is thus effected not by the preaching of the law but only by the preaching of the gospel.[21] If only the law were preached it would lead to despair, not to conversion. Only when faith is added is the "good intention" able to emerge. Thus far the rule applies: Repentance includes both law and gospel."[22]

In Luther's debate with the Antinomians only one passage deals with the so-called threefold use of the law. The conclusion of the second disputation reads:

[18] *WA* 39 I, 382, 2-4: "Lex non est necessaria ad iustificationem, sed inutilis et impossibilis, quia non aufert peccata, sed ostendit ea, non iustificat, sed nos peccatores constituit, non vivificat, sed mortificat et occidit."

[19] *WA* 39 I, 382, 7-10.

[20] *WA* 39 I, 469, 13-19: "Lex est una de causis rerum efficientium iustitiam. Negamus hoc. Nam iustificatio non est inter res illas, quae causantur lege, sed mors, damnatio, terror et tremor, cognitio peccati, ut dixi supra de requirere materialiter." ("The law is among the causes of things that work righteousness—this we contest. For justification is not among those things caused by the law, but rather death, damnation, horror and trembling, knowledge of sin [which] as I said above are [only] materially required [for justification].")

[21] *WA* 39 I, 444, 14-446, 5.

[22] *WA* 39 I, 414, 11-12: "poenitentia includit utrumque, legem et Evangelium."

The law is to be taught for its [external] discipline according to that word of Paul in I Timothy [v. 9]: The law is given to the unrighteous, so that through this custodian men may come to Christ, as Paul says to the Galatians 3 [v. 24]: the law was our schoolmaster until Christ. Second, the law is to be taught so that it shows sin, accuses, terrorizes, and damns consciences, [as Paul says] to the Romans 3 [v. 20]: through the law [comes] knowledge of sin, as well as in the 4th chapter [v. 15]. Third, the law is to be retained so that the saints know what works God commands, in which they can exercise obedience toward God.[23]

Modern research has made clear that this passage is an interpolation on the part of a pupil of Melanchthon, who in transcribing it assigned to Luther what his teacher had said.[24] In his new edition of the *Loci* of 1535,[25] Melanchthon was the first to defend the doctrine of the threefold use. By contrast, Luther did not advocate such a use.[26] This does not mean that for Luther the law should not be preached to "saints" or "believers." For them too the law is needed continually to convict of sin. Beyond this, the law has significance in terms of its command, but it cannot claim to determine the "saints'" relation to God. "The law is abrogated as accuser and indictor before God, and thus neither justifies nor condemns. It is likewise abrogated in respect of damnation, but not of obligation."[27]

Of almost greater importance than the question of the relation between Luther and Melanchthon over the problem of a *duplex* or *triplex usus legis* is that though Luther often distinguished the law's political and theological uses, since his debate with the fanatics he absolutely avoided any schematizing. After his debate with the Wittenberg reformers in 1521/1522 he preferred to regard the law first

[23] *WA* 39 I, 485, 16-24: "Lex docenda est propter disciplinam iuxa illud Pauli I. Timoth. 1: Lex est iniustis posita, atque ut hac paedagogia homines ad Christum perveniant, quemadmodum Paulus ad Galatas ait: Lex est paedagogia in Christum. Secundo. Lex docenda est, ut ostendat peccatum, accuset, perterrefaciat et damnet conscientias, ad Romanos 3: Per legem cognitio peccati, item capite quarto: Lex iram operatur. Tertio. Lex est retinenda, ut sciant sancti, quaenam opera requirat Deus, in quibus obedientiam exercere erga Deum possint."

[24] See Werner Elert, "Eine theologische Fälschung zur Lehre vom tertius usus legis," *ZRGG* 1 (1948), 168-70; as well as above all Gerhard Ebeling, "On the Doctrine of the *Triplex Usus Legis* in the Theology of the Reformation," in *Word and Faith*, 62-78.

[25] Melanchthon, *CR* 21, 405-6; cf. *Studienausgabe* 2, 1, 321-26 (with notes). The concept *triplex usus legis* is not yet used in 1535; but the subject matter can be found. See Ebeling, "Doctrine," 65.

[26] The passage in *WA* 10 I, 1, 456, 8-457, 14 (*Kirchenpostille*), where Luther also spoke of a "threefold use" of the law, has another meaning. It excludes a *tertius usus legis* in Melanchthon's sense, since Luther (ibid., 457, 3-5) said: "das er yhe bey leyb den dritten nitt predige das gesetz, als solten sie dadurch frum werden; denn das were vorfurerey." ("So as on no account to preach the law to the third group as if they should be saved thereby; for that would be corruption.") See Ebeling, "Doctrine," 64. According to Ebeling (72-73) this passage is "very near the original source of the term *usus legis*."

[27] *WA Br* 12 Nr. 4259a supplement I, 8-10: "Lex est abrogata ut accusatrix et exactrix coram deo et sic nec iustificat nec condemnat, item abrogata est quo ad condemnationem, non quo ad obligationem."

under the aspect of preserving external order, then under the aspect of revealing sin and as "accuser." To his mind, however, the law's significance could never be reduced to these two functions. There is certainly a "pedagogical use"[28] construed as a positive use of the law or the commandments. Luther's numerous catechetical writings and statements document this. Incidentally, we should note that it is precisely when he distinguished the various *usus legis* that Luther still intended to hold fast to the unity of the law as an expression of God's will. It would be a total misunderstanding to suppose that he could view the political use of the law detached from its theological use.

Similarly, if we inquire into the actual existence of a "third use of the law" in Luther, we must note that for him the law must be preached to "believers" in an entirely different way than to "unbelievers." This raises the question as to whether and in what manner a clear distinction may be drawn between believers and unbelievers.[29] What is decisive in all this is that Luther is clearly the first in all the history of dogma and theology to view the law from the viewpoint of its *usus,* thus in its concrete function.[30] In other words, "for Luther law is an existential category."[31]

[28] B. Hägglund, "Gesetz und Evangelium," 158. On this subject see Ivar Asheim, *Glaube und Erziehung bei Luther: Ein Beitrag zur Geschichte des Verhältnisses von Theologie und Pädagogik,* PF 17 (Heidelberg: Quelle & Meyer, 1961).

[29] On these questions see above all Ebeling, "Doctrine."

[30] Evidence in ibid.

[31] Ibid., 65.

PART THREE

Luther's Theology in Its Systematic Context

Chapter 20

SOLA SCRIPTURA

THE AUTHORITY OF SCRIPTURE

The conviction that Scripture is or should be the primary authority in the church was shared by the ancient church as well as the medieval church. Luther himself said that as early as among his scholastic teachers he learned that "faith" is due the Bible alone, while only an "opinion" should be assigned all others.[1] His extraordinarily intensive occupation with the meaning of Scripture, as reflected particularly in his early lectures, does not yet represent something totally new, though it is without precursors.

What is decisively new in Luther over against medieval tradition is that though till the onset of the indulgence controversy he ranked authorities such as the church fathers, the councils, and the *ratio* alongside Scripture,[2] in the course of his dispute with Rome he was forced more and more to give Scripture critical value against specific traditions and doctrinal opinions in tension with or actually opposed to Scripture. Initially, the so-called scriptural principle, used by Luther after he began to teach exegesis at Wittenberg, did not contradict the doctrinal position of that

---

[1] See above, pp. 26, 123.

[2] So esp. in his treatise *Explanations of the Ninety-five Theses* (1518). See, e.g., *LW*, vol. 31, p. 83: "First, I testify that I desire to say or maintain absolutely nothing except, first of all, what is in the Holy Scriptures and can be maintained from them; and then what is in and from the writings of the church fathers and is accepted by the Roman Church and preserved both in the canons and the papal decrees. But if any proposition cannot be proved or disproved from them I shall simply maintain it, for the sake of debate, on the basis of the judgment of reason and experience, always, however, without violating the judgment of any of my superiors in these matters." *WA* 1, 529, 33-530, 3. See also *LW*, vol. 31, pp. 93-94. *WA* 1, 536, 37-537, 2. In this treatise are found additional utterances of like content.

period. It was his critical application of scriptural authority to church teaching after 1517/1518 that first spelled a breach, since for scholasticism and church leadership the church and the Scripture could not contradict one another.

In the course of Luther's numerous disputes, he arrived at the irrefutable certainty that there is no "prestabilized harmony" between Scripture and church,[3] that Scripture exists prior to and is ranked before and above the church. In this regard it was significant that the traditionalists scarcely ever attempted to answer Luther on the basis of Scripture. As a rule, they were content to set forth the authority of pope, councils, or the church against him, and to require his strict subordination to these authorities. At the same time, Luther continually declared that he was ready if need be to accept better instruction from Holy Scripture but uncompromisingly rejected the mere summons to recant.

The difference between Luther and Rome touching the relation between Scripture and church clearly requires careful defining. In contrast to the Roman view that Scripture is ultimately to be interpreted by the teaching office, that thus ultimately Scripture and church cannot be played off against each other, since the church has preserved the Scripture and the individual receives it from the church, Luther never advocated individualistic isolation in Scripture interpretation. He was also convinced that Scripture and church belong together. B. Hägglund has correctly stated that the "evidence" of Holy Scripture "is recognized only in the Christian community, only among believers in Christ."[4] Scripture, faith, and community thus belong together, meaning, according to Luther, that the determining factor is not the individual's teaching office but the self-authentication of Scripture in utterances of faith.

Naturally, scriptural authority also requires careful consideration. On the one hand, Luther often appealed to the wording. The *est* in the words of institution is particularly important to him. On the other hand, he was able critically to judge not only individual statements of Scripture but in fact entire books. The entire spectrum of Luther's view of scriptural authority is reflected in the following statements. First, he could say: "Neither councils, fathers, nor we, in spite of the greatest and best success possible, will do as well as the Holy Scriptures, that is, as well as God himself has done."[5] Next, he could state that "no book but Holy Scripture can comfort . . . for it contains God's word."[6] A third word reads: "Duae res sunt Deus et Scriptura Dei, non minus quam duae res sunt, Creator et creatura Dei" ("God and the Scripture of God are two things, no less than Creator and creature").[7]

---

[3] It was just this that Eck maintained versus Luther at the Leipzig Disputation; see above, p. 122.

[4] B. Hägglund, "Evidentia sacrae scripturae," 119.

[5] *LW*, vol. 34, p. 284 (*Preface to the Wittenberg Edition of Luther's German Writings,* 1539). *WA* 50, 657, 25-27.

[6] *WA* 10 I 2, 75, 3-7 (Advents postille, 1522).

[7] *LW,* vol. 33, p. 25 (*Bondage of the Will,* 1525). *WA* 18, 606, 11-12.

Thus, on the one hand, Luther could all but identify God and Scripture; on the other, he could strictly separate the two as Creator and creature. It would not be appropriate to systematize these various statements and attempt precisely to state when and where they apply in each case. The question of scriptural authority cannot be treated apart from its application in the given instance. The Lord's Supper controversy makes clear that in his exposition of the words of institution Luther was in essence more flexible toward the Moravian Brethren than toward Zwingli. With Zwingli, due to his notion of the *significat,* Luther feared a dissolution of central scriptural utterances and contents. The authority of Scripture, however certain at the outset, can be appropriately weighed only in respect of the given situation.

CHRIST AS MIDPOINT OF SCRIPTURE: WORD AND SPIRIT

In order properly to understand scriptural authority, pains must be taken in each case with the actual sense and precise content of the biblical utterance. Even in interpreting individual texts, the central theme of the whole Bible must be considered. Against Erasmus, Luther was able to say: "Tolle Christum e Scripturis, quid amplius in illis invenies?" ("Take Christ from the Scriptures, and what else will you find in them?").[8] Of course, in exegesis as well as in Bible translation, Luther painstakingly guarded against advocating a christological interpretation in any immediate sense. Still, in all Bible interpretation, next to the *scopus* of the individual text, the essential content of the entire Scripture must be in view, so as to avoid the danger of finding in the Bible merely a collection of various and sundry disconnected individual statements.

In accord with this view, Luther emphasized the priority of the oral proclamation over the written deposit. God encounters us in the Word, but this Word is an oral Word, a living proclamation.

> So it is not all in keeping with the New Testament to write books on Christian doctrine. Rather in all places there should be fine, goodly, learned, spiritual, diligent preachers without books, who extract the living Word from the old Scripture and unceasingly inculcate it into the people, just as the apostles did. For before they wrote, they first of all preached to the people by word of mouth and converted them.[9]

[8] *LW,* vol. 33, p. 26. *WA* 18, 606, 29.

[9] *LW,* vol. 52, p. 206 (*The Gospel for the Festival of the Epiphany,* Matthew 2[1-12], 1522). *WA* 10 I 1, 626, 15-20.

Gospel . . . means nothing but a sermon and a crying out of the grace and mercy of God, earned and won by the Lord Christ with his death. And it is really not what is in books and composed in letters, but is more an oral sermon or living word, a voice which sounds in all the world and is publicly cried out so that one hears it everywhere.[10]

Luther voiced this differentiated view of scriptural authority and its application in the well-known formula that the Holy Spirit interprets himself: "ut sit ipsa per sese certissima, facillima, apertissima, sui ipsius interpres, omnium omnia probans, iudicans et illuminans" (that by itself [Scripture] is most certain, most easy to understand, most clear, its own interpreter, testing, judging and illuminating everything by everything).[11]

This significant statement, coherent with the more elaborate argument in *The Bondage of the Will*, claims first that "by itself [Scripture] is most certain," requiring no support or empowerment by another institution. Here Luther was again taking issue with Pirerias's argument that Scripture takes its authority solely from the Roman church.[12] Next, he emphasized that Scripture is most easy to understand and most clear, thus does not need to be interpreted, say, by a papal teaching office. Precisely for this reason the Scripture is its own interpreter.

Luther stressed this principle with equal force against the fanatics who in one way or another conceived of the Spirit as an authority above Scripture. In this respect, Karlstadt and Müntzer were ultimately agreed. When, according to Karlstadt, the Spirit is to determine which portions of the Old Testament are binding on the Christian, and when, according to Müntzer, it is the present revelation of the Spirit that is authoritative, albeit in analogy to scriptural revelation, Luther insisted that it is the Spirit who discloses the Scriptures, and thus allows the revelation of God in the past to become living once more in its significance for the present.

The principle *sacra scriptura sui ipsius interpres* implies that Scripture is to be interpeted according to its literal sense. If in his early lectures Luther could often stress the fourfold meaning of Scripture, the literal sense soon became authoritative for him.[13] And though particularly in his sermons and even later he could at times still employ allegory, after the indulgence controversy he all but surrendered this traditional method of exposition. In controversy with Rome and the fanatics only the literal sense of Scripture was determinative.

Luther's distinction between the "outer" and the "inner Word" is also significant, and to a degree identical to his differentiation of "letter" and "spirit." The distinction

[10] *WA* 12, 259, 8-13 (*Epistel Sanct Petri gepredigt und ausgelegt,* 1523).
[11] *WA* 7, 97, 23-24 (*Assertio omnium articulorum,* 1520).
[12] See above, pp. 107-9.
[13] On this subject see first of all Ebeling, *Evangelische Evangelienauslegung.*

harks back to Augustine. In the Middle Ages it enjoyed a long history,[14] with German mysticism playing a significant role. Augustine, of course, connected the outer and inner Word, but on the basis of his Neoplatonic hermeneutic of signification intended to make clear that the relation between the Word and its "object" is similar to the relation between a symbol or sacrament and its object, namely, grace. Thus, just as the symbol is ultimately only a reference to the actual object behind it, without that object's actually being present in the symbol, so the Word is ultimately only a reference to a truth behind it that cannot be expressed or communicated. From this perspective words for Augustine were merely "given signs,"[15] not the object itself.

By contrast and particularly in his debate with the fanatics, Luther connected the outer and inner Word much more intimately. He retained the old distinction but on the basis of his new "philosophy of language"[16] actually merged Word and Spirit. There is a parallel here between Luther's understanding of the Lord's Supper and his philosophy of language: just as the body and blood of Christ are "truly present" in the bread and wine of the Lord's Supper, so the truth is totally present in the Word. It must be sought not behind but within it.[17] For Luther "the human word itself" becomes "bearer of the divine Spirit," indeed, is "actually wrapped in the swaddling cloth of the human word."[18]

OLD AND NEW TESTAMENT: LAW AND GOSPEL

A further, extraordinarily important distinction for Luther involved the relation between the Testaments and Scripture as law and gospel. Here too he distanced himself from the fanatics, particularly from Karlstadt, but also from Agricola and the Antinomians, and most of all from the medieval view.

God's Word is always encountered as law and gospel, never in any absolute form beyond law and gospel. Law and gospel cannot thus be simply parceled out among the two Testaments, as if the Old contained only law, and the New only gospel. Though the Old Testament as a whole chiefly contains law, it also contains the gospel, just as the New Testament chiefly contains the gospel but also contains the law.[19] It is important always to see the Testaments in their mutual relation. The promissory character of the Old is initially hidden and becomes clear only from the

---

[14] See the terse, instructive survey by P. Meinhold, *Luthers Sprachphilosophie* (Berlin: Lutherisches Verlagshaus, 1958), 45-57.

[15] So Meinhold, ibid., 53.

[16] Meinhold, ibid., purposely and with good reason speaks of Luther's actual philosophy of language.

[17] On this subject see esp. Erwin Metzke, *Sakrament und Metaphysik: Eine Lutherstudie über das Verhältnis des christlichen Denkens zum Leiblich-Materiellen,* Schriftenreihe Lebendige Wissenschaft 6 (Stuttgart: Kreuz, 1948).

[18] Meinhold, *Luthers Sprachphilosophie,* 56.

perspective of the New Testament: Christ first brought it to light. Through his word that God is a God of the living and not of the dead, Christ made clear the true meaning of the First Commandment. More still, the New has ultimately no other sense than to disclose the actual meaning of the Old Testament. "The New Testament is nothing but a revelation of the Old; it is as if somebody had a sealed letter and later on broke it open."[20] Of the Old Testament Luther said: "Here you will find the swaddling cloths and the manger in which Christ lies, and to which the angel points the shepherds [Luke 2:12]. Simple and lowly are these swaddling cloths, but dear is the treasure, Christ, who lies in them."[21] The New Testament as well contains the law, though naturally not as its authentic content. Not even the cross of Christ is merely gospel; it is also the harshest preaching of the law.

It would, however, be incorrect to construe law and gospel as two different words of God. God's Word is one. It merely has this dual shape and way of working by which it encounters us as law and gospel. That God's Word has these two aspects is first of all a result of the fall; such a distinction cannot apply to paradise, where law and gospel were still a unity. Further, law and gospel belong most intimately together since both are given for life.[22] The result of sin is that the law, which as such was to effect life, took on its character as accuser and judge.

For Luther's understanding of Scripture in the context of this distinction between law and gospel, we must be aware of an aspect of the Old Testament applicable only to Israelites and not to Christians. Here too Luther was at considerable remove from the fanatics. The Old Testament contains not only the Decalogue but also Israel's national law, the Jews' *Sachsenspiegel*.[23] To that extent, it has no significance for Christians. Against the fanatics Luther could say that "all such Mosaic teachers deny the gospel, banish Christ, and annul the whole New Testament. I now speak as a Christian for Christians. For Moses is given to the Jewish people alone, and does not concern us Gentiles and Christians."[24]

Luther could actually state that to an extent even the Decalogue concerns only Israel. It too has two sides: first, it is given to Israel, but it is also a summary of the natural law written in everyone's heart. In sum, this natural law reads that one should love God and the neighbor. Nature, too, teaches "as does love, that I should do as I would be done by."[25] Here too conscience plays a role, since it is the place where one senses an obligation toward God given in the natural law. In his *Third Disputation against the Antinomians* (1538), Luther replied to his opponents' argument that "the law is given to a particular people, that is, to the Jews. But we are not Jews, thus the law does not concern

---

[19] See above, pp. 181-84.

[20] *LW*, vol. 52, p. 41 (*The Gospel for the Christian Service*, John 2[:1-14]). *WA* 10 I, 1, 181, 24-182, 1.

[21] *LW*, vol. 35, p. 236 (*Preface to the Old Testament*, 1523). *WA DB* 8, 12, 5-8.

[22] *WA* 39 I, 448, 10-450, 14 (*2. Disputation gegen die Antinomer*, 1538).

[23] *LW*, vol. 35, p. 167; *WA* 16, 378, 11; *LW*, vol. 40, p. 98; *WA* 18, 81, 14-15.

[24] *LW*, vol. 40, p. 92 (*Against the Heavenly Prophets*, 1525). *WA* 18, 76, 24.

[25] *LW*, vol. 45, p. 128 (*Temporal Authority*, 1523). *WA* 11, 279, 19-20.

us."[26] "I sense in my heart that I owe God this [keeping of commandments], not because the Decalogue was handed down or written with us in view, but because we know we brought these laws into the world with us."[27] In this context Luther stated that Moses was not the originator but in a sense merely the interpreter of the laws written in the human heart: he made clear and explained the law.[28]

With these reflections Luther did not intend to deny that even in portions applicable only to Jews the Mosaic law can often be a model for the laws of others. He was concerned to clarify the question concerning the Old Testament law as binding on Christians. Here the distinction between the abiding function of the law and the Word of Christ as the end of the law (Rom. 10:4) takes on significance.

THE CLARITY OF SCRIPTURE

The view that Holy Scripture interprets itself, but also that Christ is its decisive content, is the presupposition underlying Luther's conviction that Scripture is "clear." He first publicly defended this view in his dispute with Rome, though he dealt with the subject matter in his early lectures.[29]

For what he meant by the Scripture's "clarity," Luther could use various terms. In his debate with Latomus (1521) he thematized it briefly using the terms *sinceritas* and *simplicitas*. He thus reproached scholastic theologians for ignoring the clarity of Scripture in their statements on anthropology and the doctrine of grace, thus obscuring understanding for the question at issue (*intelligentia rerum*).[30]

---

[26] *WA* 39 I, 539, 4-5.

[27] *WA* 39 I, 540, 10-12: "sentio in corde, me certe hoc debere Deo, non quia traditus et scriptus decalogus sit nobis, sed quod scimus vel leges has nobiscum in mundum attulimus."

[28] *WA* 39 I 454, 4-16 (*2. Disputation gegen die Antinomer,* 1538): "Neque tamen Moses autor fuit decalogi. Sed a condito mundo decalogus fuit inscriptus omnium hominum mentibus. . . . Nam nulla natio unquam sub sole tam crudelis aut barbara fuit ac inhumana, quin senserit Deum colendum, diligendum esse atque eius nomen laudibus ferendum. . . . Moses fuit tantum quasi interpres et illustrator legum scriptarum in mentibus omnium hominum, ubicunque terrarum sub sole sint." ("And yet Moses was not the author of the Decalogue. Rather, from the foundation of the world, the Decalogue was inscribed in the hearts of all. . . . For no race under the sun was ever so rude or barbaric and inhuman but that it sensed that God is to be worshiped, loved, and his name exalted in praise. . . . Moses was no more than an interpreter and illustrator of the law written in all human hearts, and of whatever lands may be under the sun.")

[29] In the lecture on Romans Luther often emphasized that the entire Scripture has to do with Christ. See, e.g., *LW,* vol. 25, p. 405; *WA* 56, 414, 15-18 (scholia on Rom. 10:6): "Quod universa Scriptura de solo Christo est ubique . . . omnia in Christum sonant." ("Because all Scripture is everywhere about Christ alone . . . all things sing of Christ.") As early as in the first Psalms lecture, but with special clarity in the course of Luther's lectures on Romans, interpretation toward and from Christ was superimposed on the medieval exegetical methods that he still retained.

[30] *LW,* vol. 32, pp. 236-37 (Against Latomus, 1521). *WA* 8, 112, 21-31.

In *The Bondage of the Will,* Luther dealt in much greater detail with the question of Scripture's clarity. He expressly opposed the view of Erasmus that it is unclear in important matters and thus requires exposition by the tradition. At the outset of his *Diatribe Concerning Free Choice,* Erasmus discussed the problem and claimed that God had willed that some things reported in Scripture should be inaccessible to us. According to Erasmus there was profound significance in the obscurity of such passages. They were to lead us to recognize the unsearchable sublimity of the divine wisdom as well as the weakness of the human spirit. One day, Erasmus said, we will no longer know only as through a mirror or in an enigmatic word, but will see the glory of the Lord with unveiled eye.[31] With these reflections Erasmus did not at all intend to assert that the "clarity" of Scripture meant "the logical-systematical agreement of individual utterances and passages."[32] He was rather holding up the idea of the divine *eruditio,* threading through all his theology, an *eruditio* that requires from us discipleship and humility.

At this point, Luther and Erasmus were not so far removed from each other. At the conclusion of *The Bondage of the Will,* Luther distinguished "three lights" (*tria lumina*). He wrote that in view of the *lumen naturae* the problem of how a good person should suffer and a bad person prosper is insoluble; further, that in view of the *lumen gratiae* the problem of how God can damn a person who is unable by his or her own strength to do anything but sin is insoluble; finally, that the *lumen gloriae* will some day bring the solution: in the *lumen gloriae* we will see that God always acts "with the most righteous and manifest righteousness," that even in view of the *lumen naturae* and *lumen gratiae* God is not unjust.[33] Luther recognized that even the inability to master important questions that appear insoluble in Scripture and life is harnessed to a divine plan. Nevertheless, the actual agreement between Erasmus and Luther cannot screen the significant disagreement between them. For Luther God's righteousness is revealed in the gospel and seized by faith alone. This core statement of the Bible is "clear." For Erasmus divine pedagogy and human discipleship are at the center of the Bible and faith.

The essential difference between Erasmus and Luther consists in the fact that despite some obscure passages[34] Luther insisted that in its decisive utterances Holy Scripture is clear and unequivocal.

---

[31] Erasmus, *Diatribe,* Ia 7: "Sunt enim in divinis literis adyta quaedam, in quae deus noluit nos altius penetrare, et si penetrare conemur, quo fuerimus altius ingressi, hoc magis ac magis caligamus, quo vel sic agnosceremus et divinae sapientiae maiestatem impervestigabilem et humanae mentis imbecillitatem." *Luther and Erasmus: Free Will and Salvation,* p. 38: "For there are some secret places in the Holy Scriptures into which God has not wished us to penetrate more deeply and, if we try to do so, then the deeper we go, the darker and darker it becomes, by which means we are led to acknowledge the unsearchable majesty of the divine wisdom, and the weakness of the human mind."

[32] Thus Hans-Joachim Iwand, *Martin Luther—Ausgewählte Werke, Erg. Reihe,* 3d ed. (Munich: Chr. Kaiser, 1954), 3:271 (commentary on *De servo arbitrio*).

[33] *LW,* vol. 33, p. 292. *WA* 18, 785, 26-38.

[34] See Luther's statements at the beginning of *Bondage of the Will, LW,* vol. 33, p. 25, and elsewhere. *WA* 19, 606, 37-39.

For what still sublimer thing can remain hidden in the Scriptures, now that the seals have been broken, the stone rolled from the door of the sepulcher [Matt. 27:66; 28:2], and the supreme mystery brought to light, namely, that Christ the Son of God has been made man, that God is three and one, that Christ has suffered for us and is to reign eternally? Are not these things known and sung even in the highways and byways? Take Christ out of the Scriptures, and what will you find left in them? The subject matter of the Scriptures, therefore, is all quite accessible, even though some texts are still obscure owing to our ignorance of their terms.[35]

Finally, then, all Scripture must be read and interpreted from and toward Jesus Christ. This in no way implies a christological interpretation of Scripture in the narrow sense, but an interpretation of the entire Bible in relation to the revelation of Christ. Scripture interpretation that does not produce such theological interpretation in the real sense fails its task, though it may yield considerable information in detail.

For Luther this clarity of Scripture is an "outer clarity" (claritas externa), distinguishable from an "inner clarity" (claritas interna), just as an outer is distinguishable from an inner obscurity (obscuritas). Inner clarity is furnished solely by the Holy Spirit, who in his activity makes use of Scripture by disclosing its true meaning. Correspondingly, inner obscurity is inner resistance to the revelation of God witnessed in Scripture, while outer obscurity denotes the unintelligibility or inaccessibility of individual scriptural utterances. "If you speak of the internal clarity, no man perceives one iota of what is in the Scripture unless he has the Spirit of God. All men have a darkened heart, so that even if they can recite everything in Scripture, and know how to quote it, yet they apprehend and truly understand nothing of it. They neither believe in God, nor that they themselves are creatures of God."[36]

---

[35] LW, vol. 33, pp. 25-26. WA 18, 606, 24-31.
[36] LW, vol. 33, p. 28. WA 18, 609, 5-9.

Chapter 21

REASON AND FAITH

REASON

Luther did not develop a theory of cognition comparable to the various views of high or late scholasticism, nor, as at times has been maintained,[1] did he dismiss reason from theology. No doubt, he could speak very harshly of the arbitrariness of human reason over against revelation. He often spoke in "opposed totalities."[2] Nevertheless, all his theological work reflects an established as well as extensively developed view of reason and its application, so that it will not do simply to emphasize the contrast between reason and revelation. Further, on the basis of Luther's statements it is necessary to distinguish reason's tasks within the scientific sphere and the sphere of temporal authority, and reason in view of the relation to God.

Of all the gifts God has given human beings, the *ratio* is the greatest and most important.[3] It constitutes the uniqueness of humans within the created world,

---

[1] Thus, e.g., Arnold Lunn, *The Revolt against Reason* (London: Eyre and Spottiswoode, 1950). On this subject see Lohse, *Ratio und Fides,* 2 n. 8.

[2] Thus Wicks, *Luther's Reform: Studies on Conversion and the Church* (Mainz: Verlag P. von Zabern, 1992), 21.

[3] On this subject see first Luther's *Disputation Concerning Man* (1536), e.g., *LW,* vol. 34, p. 137: "4. And it is certainly true that reason is the most important and the highest in rank among all things and, in comparison with other things of this life, the best and something divine. 5. It is the inventor and mentor of all the arts, medicines, laws, and of whatever wisdom, power, virtue, and glory men possess in this life. 6. By virtue of this fact it ought to be named the essential difference by which man is distinguished from the animals and other things." *WA* 39 I, 175, 9-15: "4. Et sane verum est, quod ratio omnium rerum res et caput et prae ceteris rebus huius vitae optimum et divinum quiddam sit. 5. Quae est inventrix et gubernatrix omnium Artium, Medicinarum, Iurium, et quidquid in hac vita sapientiae, potentiae, virtutis et gloriae ab hominibus possidetur. 6. Ut hinc merito ipsa vocari debeat differentia essentialis, qua constituatur homo, differre ab animalibus et rebus aliis." On this disputation see the detailed commentary by G. Ebeling, *Luther Studien,* Vol. 2, part 1, 1-45.

enabling them to count days and years, thus allowing them a relation to time.[4] The *ratio*, further, is the inventor of all the sciences. The gift of *ratio* gives humans their peculiar position between angels and beasts. In common with angels, humans have the capacity to reflect and understand,[5] by virtue of which they can exist consciously and thus historically. Their *anima* is distinguished from the beasts by the fact that it is *rationalis*.

Moreover, it is the gift of *ratio* that in Adam constituted the image of God prior to the fall. Luther is clearly speaking here of an "enlightened reason" that was "in the right," and thus was linked to "good will."[6] To that extent, according to Luther, humans could "know" God by means of reason. Further, they could fulfill the task of creation and subordinate the other creatures. *Ratio,* for Luther, always denoted the capacity to understand and judge.[7]

Obviously, some statements in Luther suggest that even prior to the fall reason could not know God. In *The Bondage of the Will,* he once wrote: "If his righteousness were such that it could be judged to be righteous by human standards, it would clearly not be divine and would in no way differ from human righteousness. But since he is the one true God, and is wholly incomprehensible and inaccessible to human reason, it is proper and indeed necessary that his righteousness also should be incomprehensible."[8] Here, of course, Luther was speaking of God's saving and judging righteousness, so that the statement relates to the human situation after the fall. In what follows, however, he expanded the remark so as to distinguish God and humanity in relation to creation and nature. In the last analysis, even for humans before the fall, God is absolutely incomprehensible in omnipotence and righteousness.

Luther dealt in various ways with the question of the knowledge of God after the fall. On the one hand, he shared with the entire tradition the view that by virtue of reason humans know that there is one God, that all good comes from God, in fact,

---

[4] *LW,* vol. I, p. 44 (*Lectures on Genesis,* 1535-1545); *WA* 42, 33, 8-13.

[5] *LW,* vol. I, p. 112: "What is worthy of wonderment is God's plan in creating man, that although He had created him for physical life and bodily activity, He nevertheless added intellectual power, which is also in the angels, with the result that man is a living being compounded of the natures of the brute and of the angels." *WA* 42, 85, 10-13: "Dignum autem admiratione est consilium Dei in creando homine, quem cum condidisset ad animalem vitam et actiones corporales, addidit tamen potentiam intellectivam, quae in Angelis quoque est, ut sit homo mixtum animal ex brutali et angelica natura."

[6] *LW,* vol. I, p. 63: "Therefore when we speak about that image, we are speaking about something unknown. Not only have we had no experience of it, but we continually experience the opposite; and so we hear nothing except bare words. In Adam there was an enlightened reason, a true knowledge of God, and a most sincere desire to love God and his neighbor." *WA* 42, 47, 31-34: "Ergo cum de imagine illa loquimur, loquimur de re incognita, quam non solum non sumus experti, sed perpetuo contraria experimur, et nihil praeter nuda vocabula audimus. Fuit enim in Adam ratio illuminata, veranoticia Dei et voluntas rectissima ad diligendum Deum et proximum."

[7] *WA* 42, 93, 37: "vim intelligendi et iudicandi" (cf. *LW,* vol. I, p. 124).

[8] *LW,* vol. 33, p. 290. *WA* 18, 784, 9-13.

that they know something of the so-called divine attributes such as goodness, grace, and mercy, as well as something of God's power.[9] He could also state that by nature humans know that God has created the world, that God is just and punishes the godless.[10] In addition, he often states that reason has some information respecting the divine commandments, and thus knows what is just and what is not.[11]

Admittedly, such statements are almost regularly followed by critical remarks challenging reason's knowledge of God. For example, Luther emphasized that reason "wants to use its preference and judgment to determine what are God's work and word."[12] In *The Bondage of the Will,* he often stated that the *ratio* knows something of God. For example, he wrote that reason must admit that God works all in all.[13] Even the knowledge that God predestines everything is, after all, written in everyone's heart.[14] Against Erasmus, Luther emphasized that reason is actually aware that there is no freedom of the will.[15] Still, at a particularly important place in *The Bondage of the Will,* he stated that reason can arrive at the conclusion that there is no God or, if there should be such, that this God must be unjust.[16] In the course of the

[9] See, e.g., the more extended context in *WA* 19, 206, 7-30; also the following section on pp. 206, 31-207, 13 (*Der Prophet Jona ausgelegt,* 1526).

[10] *WA* 40 I, 607, 5-10 (*Galaterbriefvorlesung,* 1531): "'Nescire deum' et 'colere deum,' quomodo simul sunt etc.? Divinitas est naturaliter cognita. Deum esse per se notum, Sophistae. Cultus satis testantur, omnes homines habere noticiam dei per manus traditam. Quare ergo dicit Paulus, quod non cognoverint deum?" ("'Not to know God' and 'to worship God,' how are they the same, etc.? The deity is known by nature. On their own the Sophists know that there is a God. Forms of worship give ample testimony that all men have a knowledge of God by way of tradition. So why does Paul say that they did not know God?" Cf. *LW,* vol. I, p. 399.) In the revision for printing that appeared in 1535 on the basis of Rörer's lecture notes, assisted by Kaspar Cruciger, this train of thought was considerably enlarged and systematized: *LW,* vol. I, p. 399: "There is a twofold knowledge of God: the general and the particular. All men have the general knowledge, namely, that God is, that He has created heaven and earth, that He is great, that He punishes the wicked, etc. But what God thinks of us, what He wants to give and to do to deliver us from sin and death and to save us—which is the particular and the true knowledge of God—this men do not know." *WA* 40 I, 607, 28-32: "Duplex est cognitio Dei, Generalis et propria. Generalem habent omnes homines, scilicet, quod Deus sit, quod creaverit coelum et terram, quod sit iustus, quod puniat impios etc. Sed quod Deus de nobis cogitet, quid dare et facere velit, ut a peccatis et morte liberemur et salvi fiamus (quae propria et vera est cognitio Dei), homines non noverunt." On the question of the transmission of the Galatians lecture see the brief summary in M. Brecht, *Martin Luther: Shaping and Defining the Reformation,* 451-55. The differences between the notes and revisions for printing are in part so great that the latter should never be cited without the former.

[11] See, e.g., *LW,* vol. 52, p. 84 (*The Gospel for the Main Christmas Service,* 1521-1522); *WA* 10 I 1, 240, 7-21.

[12] Thus in the last-cited text: *LW,* vol. 52, p. 84. *WA* 10 I 1, 240, 8-10.

[13] *LW,* vol. 33, pp. 175, 189. *WA* 18, 709, 10-11; 718, 19-20.

[14] *LW,* vol. 33, pp. 190-91. *WA* 18, 719, 20-26.

[15] *LW,* vol. 33, p. 191: "We find it written in the hearts of all alike, that there is no such thing as free choice." *WA* 18, 719, 30-31: "in omnium cordibus scriptum invenitur, liberum arbitrium nihil esse."

[16] *LW,* vol. 33, p. 29: "As you can see, God so orders this corporal world in its external affairs that if you respect and follow the judgment of human reason, you are bound to say either that there is no God or that God is unjust." *WA* 18, 18, 784, 36-39: "Ecce sic Deus administrat mundum istum corporalem in

years Luther expressed himself more and more critically regarding a natural knowledge of God or regarding humans' knowledge of God. In the Promotion Disputation of Petrus Hegemon of 1545, he rejected the view that the Gentiles know of God's creation of the world. He only admitted that they know something of the world's being ruled, but not of its creation.[17]

In only one passage of his numerous writings did Luther speak in any fundamental way of reason's knowledge of God. In his *Judgment on Monastic Vows* (1521), constructed more systematically than any other,[18] he penned a few basic remarks on the *ratio* in view of the problem of the knowledge of God:

> Fifth, let us go one step further and compare the monastic system with natural reason; that is, let us look at it in the plain light of nature. Even if natural reason in itself is not concerned with spiritual truth or divine activity, nevertheless, when it asserts affirmative statements (to use their jargon) its judgment is wrong, but when it asserts negative statements its judgment is right. Reason does not comprehend what God is, but it most certainly comprehends what God is not. Granted, reason cannot see what is right and good in God's sight (faith, for instance), but it sees quite clearly that infidelity, murder, and disobedience are wrong. Christ also applies reason in the same way when he declares that every kingdom divided against itself is brought to desolation [Luke 11:17]. Paul, too, when he said it was contrary to nature for a woman to prophesy with her head uncovered [1 Cor. 11:5]. If anything is really contrary to reason, it is certainly very much more against God also. For how can anything not be in conflict with heavenly truth when it is in conflict with earthly truth?[19]

Here Luther denies that God may be reached by way of the *ratio in affirmativis*, that is, that the *ratio* can make positive statements about God. Yet he conceded a

rebus externis, ut si rationis humanae iudicium spectes et sequaris, cogaris dicere, aut nullum esse Deum, aut iniquum esse Deum."

[17] *WA* 39 II, 345, 4-346, 23. See Lohse, *Ratio und Fides*, 61-64.

[18] Here Luther argues against the monks' oath under five motifs: First, "Vows Do Not Rest on the Word of God: They Run Counter to the Word of God" (*LW*, vol. 44, pp. 252-53; *WA* 8, 578, 4-5); second, "Vows Are against Faith" (*LW*, vol. 44, 273; *WA* 8, 591, 4-5); third, "Vows Are against Evangelical Freedom" (*LW*, vol. 44, pp. 295-96; *WA* 8, 605, 1); fourth, "Vows Are Contrary to the Commandments of God" (*LW*, vol. 44, pp. 317-18; *WA* 8, 617, 16); fifth, "Monasticism Is Contrary to Common Sense and Reason" (*LW*, vol. 44, pp. 336-37; *WA* 8, 629, 22).

[19] *LW*, vol. 44, p. 336; *WA* 8, 629, 23-33: "Quinto comparemus insitutum istud [monasticism] etiam ad rationem naturalem, hoc est ad crassum illud lumen naturae, quae tametsi lucem et opera dei non attingat per sese, ita ut in affirmativis (quod aiunt) fallax sit eius iudicium, in negativis tamen est certum. Non enim capit ratio, quid sit deus, certissime tamen capit, quid non sit deus. Ita licet non videat, quid rectum et bonum sit coram deo (nempe fidem), scit tamen evidenter infidelitatem, homicidia, inobedientiam esse mala. Qua et Christus utitur, dum disserit, omne regnum in seipsum divisum desolari . . . Quomodo enim coelesti veritati non pugnabit, quod terrenae veritati pugnat?" On this passage and similar passages from the same period see Lohse, *Ratio und Fides*, 65-68.

judgment of the *ratio in negativis*. In stating this, Luther did not allow for the possibility of arriving at positive statements about God through denial (*via negationis*), such as occurred in mysticism.

It is also worth noting that in his speech before the Diet at Worms, for which he evidently prepared most carefully, Luther appealed to the *ratio evidens:*

> Since then your serene majesty and your lordships seek a simple answer, I will give it in this manner, neither horned nor toothed: Unless I am convinced by the testimony of the Scriptures or by clear reason (for I do not trust either in the pope or in councils alone, since it is well known that they have often erred and contradicted themselves), I am bound by the Scriptures I have quoted and my conscience is captive to the Word of God. I cannot and I will not retract anything, since it is neither safe nor right to go against conscience.[20]

Naturally, Luther would not have assigned to conscience or the *ratio evidens* an authority independent of Holy Scripture. To that extent the formula at Worms may not be interpreted, say, in Enlightenment terms. On the other hand, he no doubt saw more in reason and conscience than merely the subjective side of the preached Word. At issue was an independent reception and appropriation of the divine revelation. From the principles enunciated in *The Judgment on Monastic Vows* it is probable that even in the Worms formula Luther intended to say that what clearly contradicts the *ratio evidens* is also against God's Word.[21]

At the same time, we should not overlook the fact that for Luther reason continually inclines toward arbitrariness and autocracy. If the sinful act occurs primarily through a decision of the will, the *ratio* is always affected in that decision. This inhibits any appeal to reason in a totally unequivocal sense.

FAITH

Just as Luther developed no actual theory of cognition, so he did not treat faith in theoretical fashion. In his references to biblical statements, and chiefly of course to the Gospels and Paul,[22] he always set forth exegetically the essential aspects of faith.

---

[20] *LW,* vol. 32, p. 112. *WA* 7, 838, 2-8: "Quando ergo S. Maiestas vestra dominationesque vestrae simplex responsum petunt, dabo illud neque cornutum neque dentatum in hunc modum: Nisi convictus fuero testimoniis scripturarum aut ratione evidente (nam neque Papae neque conciliis solis credo, cum constet eos et errasse sepius et sibiipsis contradixisse), victus sum scripturis a me adductis et capta conscientia in verbis dei, revocare neque possum nec volo quicquam, cum contra conscientiam agere neque tutum neque integrum sit."

[21] See p. 199.

[22] See, respectively, Walther von Loewenich, *Luther als Ausleger der Synoptiker,* FGLP 10/5 (Munich: Chr. Kaiser, 1954), esp. 143-200; Walter Grundmann, *Der Römerbrief des Apostels Paulus und seine Auslegung durch Martin Luther* (Weimar: Hermann Böhlau, 1964).

This close tie to biblical texts explains the absence of any comprehensive exposition of "reason and faith," as well as the absence of any systematic discussion of "reason and revelation." Instead, we find an abundance of statements on important aspects of these themes, variously accented in the given instance. Here we can lift out only a few viewpoints of particular importance for the contrast with reason and for reason's task in arriving at theological statements.

To some extent, reason and faith exist in humans at different levels. Reason denotes the capacity for knowledge, thus critical understanding, insight, mental activities in the broadest sense, the weighing of arguments, the capacity for drawing conclusions, as well as, finally, the philosophical effort at a comprehensive view of the world and humankind. Faith, on the other hand, is a matter of the "heart." It concerns chiefly one's relation to God under the perspective of judgment and grace. This is why the areas to which faith is directly assigned always concern human existence as a whole. For example, conscience is described as that organ by which one is conscious of actual duty and failure, or as the ranking of values in life, or as trust in the divine promise in view of human sin.

Naturally, faith contains specific ingredients that pertain to the sphere of knowledge. These spheres are of a special kind when compared with other tasks and capacities of reason. They always include elements such as the knowledge of one's own sinfulness that affect deeper levels than the purely rational or intellectual. To that extent, the spheres of reason and faith in part intersect. The larger areas belonging to each of these spheres are nevertheless quite different.

Faith is directed to the Word of God, in fact, is itself worked by God or Christ and is ultimately not a human "work," although in faith the person is present and totally participates. In the Word that God directs toward human beings, he encounters them as summoning and pardoning, as Judge and Reconciler. In the midst of the inner conflict caused by the threat of divine judgment, faith means to trust in God's promise of grace. In this trust one gives God the honor refused him by one's sin. "When the soul firmly believes God's word, then it holds him to be just, good, and true, so that it does him the greatest honor of all it can do him, since it gives him his due."[23] Or, as Luther states in the Large Catechism, "For these two belong together, faith and God."[24] In faith trusting in God alone, we let God be God.

Faith is also a personal "affair" in terms of a conscious decision and a making sure. In his *Invocavit* sermons of March 1522, following his return to Wittenberg from the Wartburg, Luther opened with these words: "The summons of death comes to us all, and no one can die for another. Every one must fight his own battle with death by himself, alone. We can shout into another's ears, but every one must be prepared for the time of death, for I will not be with you then, nor you with me. Therefore every one

[23] *WA* 7, 25, 9-12 (*Von der Freiheit eines Christenmenschen*, 1520). Cf. *LW,* vol. 31, p. 350.
[24] *Book of Concord*, p. 365.

must himself know and be armed with the chief things which concern a Christian."[25] Where faith is at issue, none can stand in for the other. Luther thus rejected the scholastic differentiation between *fides informis* (unformed faith) and *fides caritate formata* (faith formed by love). We need to realize, however, that this scholastic distinction had once been drawn in order by means of the Aristotelian philosophy to express the causative effect of grace respecting the believer's renewal,[26] while Luther had in mind the situation at the last judgment.

Under this aspect Luther also stressed that in the matter of faith none can help the other. "So my faith cannot help you other than to be useful and helpful to you for your own."[27] In saying this Luther by no means intended to surrender the Christian to isolation or to represent the fellowship of believers as ultimately unimportant. Still, the help that one may give another consists finally in the intercession by which one may pray for the strengthening of a fellow Christian's faith.[28] "The faith of others can only help me to believe for myself."[29] One's own faith cannot be removed by any churchly authority[30] or by anyone else. For Luther the situation at death is an example of this nonrepresentable character of faith.

Just as faith does nothing but to allow God to be God and to cling totally to the Word, so also it is faith that allows the truth of God to become alive in us. In an uncommonly bold and at times misunderstood phrase, Luther wrote: "Faith is the creator of the Deity, not in the substance of God, but in us. For without faith God loses His glory, wisdom, righteousness, truthfulness, mercy, etc., in us; in short, God has none of His majesty or divinity where faith is absent."[31] Ludwig Feuerbach thought he could appeal to this word and similar statements for his view that the idea of God is a projection of the human onto the cosmic scale, that thus the mystery of

---

[25] *LW,* vol. 51, p. 70. *WA* 10 III, 1, 15-20 (print).

[26] On this subject see, e.g., Marie-Dominique Chenu, O.P., *Das Werk des Hl. Thomas von Aquin,* Die Deutsche Thomas-Ausgabe, Erg. vol. 2, 2d ed. (Graz/Vienna/Cologne: Verlag Styria, 1982), 111.

[27] *WA* 10 III, 310, 23-24 (sermon, 1522).

[28] *WA* 10 III, 308, 26-309, 4 (ibid.)

[29] Althaus, *The Theology of Martin Luther,* translated by Robert C. Schultz (Philadelphia: Fortress Press, 1966), 54.

[30] *WA* 10 III, 259, 3-8 (sermon, 1522): "Babst du hast das beschlossen oder die Concilien, nun hab ich noch ein urteyl, das ichs an nemen mag oder nit, dann du wirst nit fur mich streitten noch antworten, wen ich sterben sol, Sonder ich muss sehen, wie ich daran sey, das es gottes wort sey als gewiss als du lebst und noch gewiser, darauff du dein gewissen stellen kanst." ("Pope, you or the councils have decreed. Now I have a verdict which I may accept or not, since you will not fight for me nor answer when I shall die. But I must see how it matters to me that God's Word is as sure as you live and even surer, [a word] on which you can fix your conscience.")

[31] *LW,* vol. 26, p. 227 (*Lectures on Galatians, Chapters One to Four,* 1531); *WA* 40 I, 360, 5-7: "Fidex est creatrix divinitatis, non in persona, sed in nobis. Extra fidem amittit deus suam iustitiam, gloriam, opes etc., et nihil maiestatis, divinitatis, ubi non fides." In readying it for print the point of this idea was blunted: ibid., p. 360, 20-35.

theology is anthropology.[32] Karl Barth stated that Feuerbach's statement was not altogether wrong.[33] The interpretation is, however, incorrect. With Luther the priority of the Word of God, thus of the truth of faith, remains intact prior to faith. Obviously, despite his exaggerations, Luther intended to say that in clinging to something by faith it is not enough to hold the truth of faith to be true; that what is needed is a truly saving faith, that the divine truth also applies *pro me*.

THE TASK OF THEOLOGICAL KNOWLEDGE

In the context of his discussion of the *ratio,* Luther never spoke of its significance for theological understanding.[34] Nevertheless, his reflections on human reason prior to the revelation, on reason and revelation, and not least his use of reason in theology, yield sufficiently clear contours to enable us to determine the role of *ratio* in his theology.

According to Luther, not only in the person prior to the revelation but in the Christian as well the *ratio* is continually in danger of becoming autocratic and of wanting to judge God's activity according to its own criteria. This made it impossible for him to describe the spheres of *ratio* and *revelatio* as merely supplementing each other. His ambivalence concerning a possible natural knowledge of God or its impossibility ruled out the notion that the *ratio* can as it were develop ideas regarding the doctrine of God that could serve as basis for ideas derived from revelation. Nor can the spheres of *ratio* and *revelatio* be set in mere opposition to each other. The danger of the *ratio's* autocracy exists prior to as well as following revelation.

The "enlightenment" required by the *ratio* in its service to theology[35] cannot be assumed as a fact fixed for all time but must always be tested anew in the acquisition of knowledge. As much as Luther believed that the *ratio* required enlightenment for performing service, so little did he advocate a program of the enlightened *ratio* separable from the activity of the unenlightened *ratio*.

---

[32] L. Feuerbach, *The Essence of Faith According to Luther,* trans. Melvin Cherno (New York: Harper & Row, 1967).

[33] K. Barth, *Protestant Theology in the Nineteenth Century: Its Background and History* (Valley Forge, Pa.: Judson, 1973), 537-38. On this subject see G. Ebeling, *Lutherstudien,* 3:450-51; also idem, *Luther: An Introduction to His Thought,* trans. R. A. Wilson (Philadelphia: Fortress Press, 1970), 250-51.

[34] On this subject see Lohse, *Ratio und Fides,* 113-19.

[35] See, e.g., *LW,* vol. 26, p. 294 (*Lectures on Galatians, Chapters One to Four,* 1531): "[They are forced to grant . . . that every good work proceeds from choice. If this is true in philosophy] it is much more necessary in theology that a good will and a right reason based on faith should precede a work." *WA* 40 I, 457, 6-7: "Voluntas bona, recta ratio procedat omne opus, plus in theologia oportet esse rectam rationem per fidem, ergo ante opera oportet." In the preparation of the ms. for printing there was reference in particular to Aristotle: ibid., 457, 21-27.

A *ratio* that is conscious of its limits in this sense and that does not arbitrarily judge in matters of salvation is, of course, extraordinarily significant for service to theology. Such a *ratio* aids in understanding Scripture.[36] It helps to form "new vocables" in theology, and not simply to adopt philosophical concepts.[37] However much the *ratio* and faith are at first opposed,[38] in the believer the *ratio* is not extinguished by the Holy Spirit but freed of its autocracy and pressed into service. In this sense Luther could speak of a "supernatural theology."[39] The use of such terms, however, does not denote a program. They were intended to refer to the change occurring in the *ratio* through faith.

In every instance, the danger of the *ratio's* arbitrariness is as great as ever. Reason can easily deal autocratically with God's Word. According to Luther, this may lead, for example, to the false distinction between law and gospel or between the temporal and spiritual estate.[40] Reason cannot grasp trinitarian doctrine, the doctrine of the two natures, or the presence of Christ in the Supper.[41] These as well as other doctrines can only be grasped by faith; reason can merely "think after" them.[42]

For Luther, then, the service of *ratio* in theology is marked by an unresolvable dialectic. The service of the *ratio* is indispensable and necessary, but the danger of

[36] *LW*, vol. 54, p. 71: "Reason that is under the devil's control is harmful, and the more clever and successful it is, the more harm it does. We see this in the case of learned men who on the basis of their reason disagree with the Word. On the other hand, when illuminated by the Holy Spirit, reason helps to interpret the Holy Scripture"; *WA TR* 1 Nr. 439 (p. 191, 23-26): "Ratio obsessa a Diabolo obest, et quo est beatior et felicior, eo plus nocet sicut videmus in sapientibus viris, qui a verbo ratione dissentiunt; sed illustrata a Spiritu hilfft judicirn die heylig schrifft."

[37] *LW*, vol. 26, p. 267 (*Lectures on Galatians, Chapters One to Four*, 1531); *WA* 40 I, 418, 3-6, 15-20.

[38] On this subject see G. Ebeling, "Fides occidit rationem," in *Lutherstudien*, 3:181-222.

[39] *WA* 40 II, 342, 7-9 (*Vorlesung über Psalm 51*, 1532): "Das ist non theologia rationis, sed supernaturalis, quod peccator nihil videat quam misericordiam, et tamen ibi sentit iram dei." ("This is not a theology of reason but a supernatural theology, because the sinner sees nothing but mercy and yet here he feels the wrath of God.") In *LW*, vol. 34, p. 144 (*The Disputation Concerning Man*, 1536); *WA* 39 I, 180, 19-25, Luther distinguishes between *ratio theologica* and *ratio humana*. On this subject see G. Ebeling, *Lutherstudien*, vol. 2: *Disputatio de homine*, part 2, 187-202, 211-332; part 3, 208-29, and elsewhere.

[40] On the first see *LW*, vol. 26, p. 113 (*Lectures on Galatians, Chapters One to Four*, 1531/1535); *WA* 40 I, 204, 1-2, 11-15. On the second, *LW*, vol. 14, p. 23 (*Commentary on Psalm 117*, 1530); *WA* 31 I, 241, 25-32.

[41] See, respectively, *WA* 39 II, 253, 9-14 (*Promotionsdisputation von Erasmus Alber*, 1543); *LW*, vol. 36, p. 35 (*The Babylonian Captivity*, 1520); *WA* 26, 334, 20-25; *LW*, vol. 37, p. 221 (*Confession Concerning Christ's Supper*, 1528); *WA* 6, 511, 37-39.

[42] *WA TR* 3 Nr. 2938b (p. 105, 12-27): "Doctor interrogatus, cum in articulis fidei rationem nobis claudendam esse oportet, an etiam illa in christianis aliquid valeat? respondit rationem anti fidem et cognitionem Dei esse tenebras, sed in credentibus optimum instrumentum. Nam sicut omnia dona et naturalia instrumenta in impiis sunt impia, ita et in piis sunt salutaria. . . . Erleuchte vernunfft vom glauben eingenumen entpfehet leben vom glauben, ist mortificata et iterum vivificata. . . . Ratio subiecta est vanitati, sicut et omnes Dei creaturae vanitati . . ., sed fides substantiam a vanitate separat." ("The doctor [Luther] is asked, When in articles of faith should reason be closed to us, or may it still have some value for Christians? He answers: Before faith and the knowledge of God reason is dark, but

overstepping its bounds is always present. Whoever disputes the enlightenment of the *ratio* by the Spirit, or the perpetual opposition of *ratio* and *revelatio,* stresses only one of the two views that for Luther belong most intimately together.

---

in believers it is the greatest aid. For just as all gifts and natural means are evil in the ungodly, so in the godly they are salutary. . . . Enlightened reason taken captive by faith commends a life by faith. It has been put to death and made alive again. . . . Reason has been subjected to vanity, just as all the creatures of God . . . but faith separates the substance [of the thing] from vanity.")

Chapter 22

THE VIEW OF GOD

LUTHER'S ATTITUDE TOWARD TRADITIONAL DOGMA

Generally, trinitarian dogma was not in dispute, either between Luther and Rome or between Luther and the other great reform movements. Specific questions, of course, were at times the object of controversy. For Luther, debates with anti-Trinitarians were of relatively little concern.[1] Nevertheless, in his last years he regularly allowed for the discussion of trinitarian doctrine in conjunction with promotion disputations.[2] The danger of anti-Trinitarianism formed the background. All in all, statements on trinitarian doctrine seldom appear in Luther.

There are, however, enough passages in which Luther stated that the "great articles of the divine majesty," as he called them in his Smalcald Articles,[3] are the foundation for Christian faith and theology. After a brief evaluation of the doctrine's content, he said: "There is no quarrel or dispute over these articles, since we both share the same (faith and) confession. So there is no need to deal further with them now."[4] There are also passages in which Luther referred emphatically to trinitarian doctrine. In *The Bondage of the Will,* he stated against Erasmus:

---

[1] But see especially his preface to Bugenhagen's text of *Athanasii libri contra idolatriam,* 1532, *WA* 30 III, 528-32. In addition, see Bernhard Lohse, "Luther und Athanasius," in *Auctoritas Patrum: Zur Rezeption der Kirchenväter im 15. und 16. Jahrhundert,* ed. Leif Grane, Alfred Schindler, and Markus Wriedt, VIEG 37 (Mainz: Philipp von Zabern, 1993), 97-115.

[2] See J. Koopmans, *Das altkirchliche Dogma in der Reformation,* 60.

[3] *WA* 50, 197, 1-3; Hans Volz, ed., *Urkunden und Aktenstücke zur Geschichte von Martin Luthers Schmalkaldischen Artikeln (1536-1574),* KIT 179 (Berlin: de Gruyter, 1957), 37, 4.

[4] Ed. Volz, 37, 23-25; *WA* 50, 198, 13-16. Luther first of all wrote the words "*(gleuben und)*" but then struck them in preparation for printing. The omission reflects Luther's view that the traditionalists did not have authentic faith in the Trinity.

For what still sublimer thing can remain hidden from the Scriptures, now that the seals have been broken, the stone rolled from the door of the sepulcher [Matt. 27:66; 28:2], and the supreme mystery brought to light, namely, that Christ the Son of God has been made man, that God is three and one, that Christ has suffered for us and is to reign eternally? Are not these things known and sung even in the highways and byways? Take Christ out of the Scriptures, and what will you find left in them?[5]

We should also note that the "doctrine" as such had considerable weight with Luther.[6] In his debate with the fanatics he once wrote that at the Lord's Supper one should know and preach two things:

First, what one should believe, that is, the *objectum fidei,* that is, the work or thing in which one believes or to which one is to adhere. Secondly, the faith itself, or the use which one should properly make of that in which he believes. The first lies outside the heart and is presented to our eyes externally, namely, the sacrament itself, concerning which we believe that Christ's body and blood are truly present in the bread and wine. The second is internal, within the heart, and cannot be externalized. It consists in the attitude which the heart should have toward the external sacrament.

Then he said:

Up to now I have not preached very much about the first part, but have treated only the second, which is also the best part. But because the first part is now being assailed by many, and the preachers, even those who are considered the best, are splitting up into factions over the matter . . . the times demand that I say something on this subject also.[7]

This statement forces us to the conclusion that some of Luther's assumptions in his polemical writings have particular weight precisely because they were not in dispute and thus were scarcely mentioned by him, to say nothing of being discussed. The doctrine of the Trinity as well as the doctrine of the two natures are among these. We thus need to take note that for Luther the trinitarian and christological dogmas of the ancient church always formed the basis for his arguments. These dogmas he took to be fundamental. It was his firm conviction that they appropriately reflected the witness of Scripture.

---

[5] *LW,* vol. 33, pp. 25-26. *WA* 18, 606, 24-29.

[6] On this subject see first Karl Gerhard Steck, *Lehre und Kirche bei Luther,* FGLP 10/26 (Munich: Chr. Kaiser, 1963).

[7] *LW,* vol. 36, p. 335 (*The Sacrament of the Body and Blood of Christ against the Fanatics,* 1526). *WA* 19, 482, 25-483, 19.

For example, Luther said: "The article of the Trinity is grounded in Holy Scripture," or that "there are many places in Scripture that clearly witness to the Trinity."[8] Or as Georg Major expressed in Luther's terms: "In the New Testament there are entirely clear witnesses to the plurality of persons in the unity of the divine nature."[9] In reference to conciliar decisions Luther wrote: "In some councils there are articles whose belief is explained by Scripture, such as the Nicene Creed; and some things are set down which are drawn from and based on Scripture, and are held to just as much as God's Word."[10]

On occasion Luther was critical of certain aspects of traditional doctrine. For example, he had doubts concerning the term *Dreifältigkeit* (threefoldness), widely used in German, since it did not sufficiently express the unity of the persons. The concept was "risky." Luther actually said: "Call it a third (*gedritts*); I cannot give it a name." Each of the three persons is the true God.[11] The terms "Trinity" and "person" are merely attempts to conceptualize the matter.[12] These critical statements should not be overemphasized. They alter nothing of Luther's basic affirmation of the material content of the doctrine of the Trinity.

Luther may have been totally in accord with ancient and medieval trinitarian dogma; research has nonetheless always appropriately lifted out the particular feature that is characteristic of his view or image of God. Emanuel Hirsch has described Luther's image of God in an especially sympathetic way, referring to the depth of his experience of God, or to the seriousness with which he sees himself and others in their status before God (*coram Deo*).[13] Further, Hirsch has accented the idea of the sole efficacy of the divine, for Luther an absolute certainty. At the same time, what Hirsch has referred to as Luther's view of God belongs mainly within the framework of a so-called natural view.

No doubt, Luther was not only able to speak of God in uncommonly lively fashion but quite clearly had his own, deep experience of God. What is unique about his speaking of God is that it is never theoretical. It is always clear that where God is concerned we have to do with the Lord of world and history, thus of our own life. There is thus an incomparable concreteness and directness about Luther's speaking of God. There is no mere doctrine of God, but a statement of faith in ever-new variations to the effect that God calls to life, that he judges and pardons his creatures, and takes them again to himself.[14] This fact has extraordinary significance for the way in which Luther adopted trinitarian dogma.

[8] *WA* 39 II, 304, 16 (*Promotionsdisputation Georg Major und Johannes Faber*, 1544): "Articulus trinitatis . . . est fundatus in sacris literis"; *WA* 39 II, 382, 6-7 (*Promotionsdisputation Petrus Hegemon*, 1545): "Multi sunt in scriptura loci, qui clare testantur esse trinitatem."

[9] *WA* 39, II, 323, 20-21 (*Promotionsdisputation Georg Major*, 1544).

[10] *WA* 8, 149, 34-150, 4 (*Von der Beicht*, 1521).

[11] *WA* 46, 436, 7-12; see also *WA* 49, 237-38.

[12] *WA* 41, 270, 2-23; 272, 1-13; 52, 338, 1-10.

[13] E. Hirsch, *Luthers Gottesanschauung*.

[14] The following section contains more detail on this subject.

In passages where Luther explicitly took up trinitarian dogma, particularly in the independently formulated confession of faith at the end of the *Confession Concerning Christ's Supper* (1528),[15] in the two Catechisms,[16] and in the *Smalcald Articles* (1537),[17] he set his own accents throughout, without on that account deviating from the doctrine. On the one hand, what he said about the terminology betrays a certain expansiveness or abandon that is nonetheless intentional: Concepts such as "essence," "nature," "manner," were not strictly distinguished but in part deliberately used against the tradition. At this point he did not distinguish precisely between terms. On the other hand, he emphasized the unity of God and the persons more strongly than the tradition had ever done,[18] referring in particular to what Augustine had to say. For example, Luther's emphasis on the unity of God is reflected in his interpretation of the Credo: the world's creation is by no means limited to God the Father. At just the point in the Credo that deals with the creation he enunciated the Augustinian principle that the activities of the Trinity toward creation are not divided:[19] the world was created by the entire Trinity in the Unity, not only by God the Father.[20] Correspondingly, respecting other activities assigned the second or third person, Luther speaks of the cooperation and participation of all the persons.

Luther scarcely said anything of the relations among the three persons in the Trinity. Such questions as were discussed in the later ancient church of East and West as well as in the late Middle Ages were not in dispute in the sixteenth century. For Luther, quite clearly, there was no time for turning to these questions. Here too, however, there is little doubt that in essence he held to the traditional doctrine.

THE GODHEAD OF GOD

A peculiar accent attaches to Luther's language about God. The traditional doctrine of the divine attributes, recognizable partly through natural reason and partly

---

[15] *LW*, vol. 37, pp. 360-72. *WA* 26, 499-509.

[16] *The Book of Concord*, 337-56, 357-461; *WA* 30 I, 125-238; *WA* 30 I, 243-425.

[17] *WA* 50, 197-98; but see also, e.g., *LW*, vol. 34, pp. 201-29 (*The Three Symbols or Creeds of the Christian Faith*, 1538); *WA* 50, 262-83.

[18] On this subject see Johannes Meyer, *Historischer Kommentar zu Luthers Kleinem Katechismus* (Gütersloh: Gerd Mohn, 1929); Albrecht Peters, *Kommentar zu Luthers Katechismen*, vol. 2: *Der Glaube—Das Apostolicum* (Göttingen: Vandenhoeck & Ruprecht, 1990-94).

[19] See Ekkehard Mühlenberg, *HdBDThG*, 1:428-29.

[20] *LW*, vol. 37, p. 361: "First, I believe with my whole heart the sublime article of the majesty of God, that the Father, Son, and Holy Spirit, [in?] three distinct persons, are by nature one true and genuine God, the Maker of heaven and earth." *WA* 26, 500, 27-29: "Erstlich gleube ich von hertzen den hohen artickel der göttlichen maiestet, das Vater, son, heiliger geist drey unterschiedliche personen, ein rechter, einiger, natürlicher, warhafftiger Gott ist, schepffer hymels und der erden."

through revelation,[21] did not appear in him in such form. At times he could state that reason has a proximate, murky knowledge of God. The following passage is especially clear:

> Let us here also learn from nature and from reason what can be known of God. These people regard God as a being who is able to deliver from every evil. It follows from this that natural reason must concede that all that is good comes from God; for He who can save from every need and misfortune is also able to grant all that is good and that makes for happiness. That is as far as the natural light of reason sheds its rays—it regards God as kind, gracious, merciful, and benevolent. And that is indeed a bright light. However, it manifests two big defects: first, reason does admittedly believe that God is able and competent to help and to bestow; but reason does not know whether He is willing to do this also for us. That renders the position of reason unstable. Reason believes in God's might and is aware of it, but it is uncertain whether God is willing to employ this in our behalf, because in adversity it so often experiences the opposite to be true . . . Free will cannot go beyond that. . . . The second defect is this: Reason is unable to identify God properly; it cannot ascribe the Godhead to the One who is entitled to it exclusively. It knows that there is a God, but it does not know who or which is the true God. It shares the experience of the Jews during Christ's sojourn on earth . . . they were aware that Christ was among them and that He was moving about among them; but they did not know which person it was. . . . Thus reason also plays blindman's bluff with God; it consistently gropes in the dark and misses the mark. It calls that God which is not God and fails to call Him God who really is God. Reason would do neither the one nor the other if it were not conscious of the existence of God or if it really knew who and what God is.[22]

This statement does not denote outright renunciation of the traditional doctrine of the divine attributes, but it is indeed a considerable correction. The knowledge of God through reason as well as through revelation cannot be linked in merely supplementary fashion. Between the two there is the question of the true God. In Luther's terms, we must say that reason knows something of God as well as that it knows nothing of God. It possesses no "neutral" knowledge of God.[23]

Consequently, though Luther did not treat the question in any thematic way, he did not give priority to the so-called divine attributes, but first of all to the divine omnipotence or all-sufficiency, and second to the will of God and freedom. Clearly, the intent of the traditional distinction between the various attributes was to speak of the Godhead of God. From Luther's perspective, the question is whether the

[21] On the treatment of this theme in Thomas Aquinas see Martin Anton Schmidt, *HdBDThG*, 1, esp. 659-64.

[22] *LW*, vol. 19, pp. 54-55 (*Lectures on Jonah,* 1526). *WA* 19, 206, 7-207, 7.

[23] See Lohse, *Ratio und Fides,* (Göttingen: Vandenhoeck & Ruprecht, 1958), 59-76.

attempt at a mere distinction between natural and revealed knowledge is inevitably doomed to fail.

The paraphrases that Luther used of God always express the divine all or sole sufficiency. The great variety of his statements derives from the fact that he was continually roused to reflection by particular biblical texts. In the exposition of the Magnificat he said first that God is "an energetic power, a continuous activity, that works and operates without ceasing. For God does not rest, but works without ceasing."[24] Here Luther was translating the word "he who is mighty" in Luke 1:49. The passage reads: "For he who is mighty has done great things for me, and holy is his name." Reason imagines a sleeping God, but God is always active, continually at work. In other words: God is Creator. According to Luther this does not mean that God is in addition the Creator. To be God and to be Creator are ultimately one and the same. God is God. He thus works hiddenly in history and yet solely according to his will.

In the exposition of the Magnificat Luther explained these features in his view of God. On Luke 1:52 ("he has put down the mighty from their thrones, and exalted those of low degree") he wrote:

> He destroys and puts down the mighty and the great with their strength and authority, on which they depend, venting their pride on their inferiors, the godly and weak, who must suffer injury, pain, death, and all manner of evil at their hands. And just as He comforts those who must suffer wrong and shame for the right, truth, and word, so He comforts those who must suffer injury and evil. And as much as He comforts the latter so much He terrifies the former. But this, too, must all be known and waited for in faith.[25]

Against all the attempts of the fanatics to derive the right to revolt from a single such word of the Bible, he added: "Observe, however, that Mary does not say He breaks the seats, but He casts the mighty from their seats."[26]

What Luther said here of God's hidden activity in history he sharpened in reference to the individual. Particularly impressive are the admonitions in his treatise, *A Sermon on Preparing to Die* (1519):

> Twelfth, you must not regard hell and eternal pain in relation to predestination, not in yourself, or in itself, as in those who are damned, nor must you be worried by the many people in the world who are not chosen. . . . You must force yourself to keep your eyes closed tightly to such a view, for it can never help you, even

[24] *LW*, vol. 21, p. 328. *WA* 7, 574, 29-32 (1521).
[25] *LW*, vol. 21, p. 343. *WA* 7, 589, 20-27.
[26] *LW*, vol. 21, p. 344. *WA* 7, 590, 3-4.

though you were to occupy yourself with it for a thousand years and fret yourself to death. After all, you will have to let God be God and grant that he knows more about you than you do yourself. So then, gaze at the heavenly picture of Christ.[27]

In referring to the doctrine of God, Luther could occasionally use the traditional concept of the *prima causa*. For example, in a lengthier disquisition contained in his interpretation of Psalm 127:1 ("unless the LORD builds the house, those who build it labor in vain") he distinguished a *principalis causa,* an *instrumentalis causa,* and a *finalis causa.* The manuscript does not actually contain the statement that God is first cause. What is said is, "assign to God *principalem causam.*"[28] The accent in interpretation lies clearly on "our" understanding ourselves as the means through which God directs and preserves this world. In readying the manuscript for printing, presumably by Veit Dietrich,[29] this train of thought was systematized, though even here God was not yet described as *prima causa.*[30] Thus, despite the scholastic terminology, Luther did not adopt the argument that the first cause can be arrived at by way of inference from the second, and from this can establish God's existence. For the rest, it is clear that Luther seldom referred to the idea of the *prima causa*.

Those few statements that approximate the idea of God's using human beings and things as "instruments" are far more important and are made by Luther in a unique way: the creatures are as it were God's masks behind which he hides himself, or, they are God's larvae that he assumes in order to do his work. "All creatures are God's larvae and mummery that he will let work with him and help in all sorts of creating, but that he otherwise can and does do without their help, so that we cling only to his word."[31] In the doctrine of justification Luther rejected the "cooperation" of humans with God. In the secular sphere, which involves absolutely every kind of activity, and not merely that of the temporal authority, he saw a cooperation between God and humanity throughout. This is not to deny that in this sphere as well it is finally God alone who acts, but nevertheless makes use of his creatures in order to remain hidden. God's activity is thus not limited to extraordinary events or "miracles," but is behind all occurrences in nature and history, as well as in individual life.

This omnipotence and omnipresence of God was a basic conviction of Luther's own faith as well as of all his theology. In the *Operationes in Psalmos* he wrote:

---

[27] *LW*, vol. 42, p. 105. *WA* 2, 690, 10-18.

[28] *WA* 40 III, 210, 11-211, 11; the quotation on p. 211, 4.

[29] See *WA* 40 III, 2-3.

[30] *WA* 40 III, 210, 26-211, 33; see esp. 211, 22-12: "Nisi enim adsit prima causa, secunda causa per se nihil agit. Sic docet Psalmus de causa efficiente." ("For unless there is a first cause, a second cause does nothing automatically. This is what the Psalm teaches about the efficient cause.")

[31] *WA* 17 II, 192, 28-31 (Fastenpostille, 1525).

What does the one who hopes in God come to, if not to his own nothingness? And where does the one go who goes to nothing, if not to where he comes from? Now, he comes from God and his own nothingness, so that whoever returns to nothing returns to God. For whoever falls from himself and every creature which God holds in his hand, cannot fall from his hand. . . . Run through the world, then, where will you run? Forever into the hand and lap of God.[32]

For Luther this divine omnipresence is not a general truth to be left to itself. For us mortals, it always spells salvation or ruin.[33] It is a saving or terrifying presence. Here, then, there is no distinction between God's presence and God's activity: God's presence always involves his activity, just as conversely his activity rests on his omnipresence. "[God] is present everywhere, in death, in hell, in the midst of our foes, yes, also in their hearts. For He has created all things, and He also governs them, and they must all do as He wills."[34]

The mystical background of such statements is unmistakable. The same is true of others such as the following, which reflects the enormous dynamic in Luther's idea of God: "Nothing is so small but God is still smaller, nothing is so large but God is still larger, nothing is so short but God is still shorter, nothing so long but God is still longer, nothing is so broad, but God is still broader, nothing so narrow but God is still narrower and so on. He is an inexpressible being, above and beyond all that can be described or imagined."[35] Here too, of course, the context must be taken into account: Luther was attacking Zwingli's denial of the real presence of Christ's body and blood "in, with, and under" the elements of the Supper. He was at pains to hold fast to this real presence and to set forth its possibility in thought. The purpose of the statement is to make clear that God has several possibilities for being present in one place, not only the corporeal-real or "comprehensible." By contrast Luther emphasized that "God is no such extended, long, broad, thick, high, deep being. He is a supernatural, inscrutable being who exists at the same time in every little seed, whole and entire, and yet also in all and above all and outside all created things."[36]

Other motifs in Luther's picture of God cohere most intimately with his leading idea of the "Godhead of God," such as especially the idea of the freedom of God. Here too the discussion is not of God's freedom as one attribute alongside others.

---

[32] *AWA* 2, 305, 20-306, 1; *WA* 5, 168, 1-7: "Quo enim perveniat, qui sperat in deum, nisi in sui nihilum? Quo autem abeat, qui abit in nihilum, nisi eo, unde venit? Venit autem ex deo et suo nihilo; quare in deum redit, qui redit in nihilum. Neque enim extra manum dei quoque cadere potest, qui extra seipsum omnemque creaturam cadit, quam dei manus complectitur. . . . Per mundum ergo rue, quo rues? Utique in manum et sinum dei!"

[33] There is more on this subject, particularly in the statements on law and gospel.

[34] *LW*, vol. 19, p. 68 (*Lectures on Jonah*, 1526). *WA* 19, 219, 28-33.

[35] *LW*, vol. 37, p. 228 (*Confession Concerning Christ's Supper*, 1528). *WA* 26, 339, 39-340, 2.

[36] *LW*, vol. 19, p. 228. *WA* 26, 339, 33-36.

God is, as it were, by definition free. This too implies, however, that God alone is free, whereas humans are unfree. It may be that Luther's emphasis on the freedom of God was conditioned by Occamist influence. Still, his idea of the freedom of God differed from that of Occam. He did not set the freedom of God in the context of a distinction between the *potentia Dei absoluta* and the *potentia Dei ordinata*,[37] but always under the aspect of the question of salvation.

Nonetheless, some of Luther's statements on divine freedom recall the Occamist view of the *potentia Dei absoluta*. This is especially true of the following sentence in *The Bondage of the Will:* "Free choice is plainly a divine term, and can be properly applied to none but the Divine Majesty alone."[38] Here Luther was in danger of wanting to prove more than was advisable in his debate with Erasmus. For if freedom of the will is exclusively a predicate of God, the question arises as to how one can maintain human responsibility for acting and thinking.[39] Naturally, in the absolute sense Luther's view is irrefutable. On the other hand, when theology takes seriously the statement about humanity's creation by God and its personal relation to God, a limited human freedom must be maintained over against the unlimited freedom of God. Luther did in fact indirectly maintain such limited freedom, even in *The Bondage of the Will*.[40]

DEUS ABSCONDITUS AND DEUS REVELATUS

Luther distinguished the "hidden" and "revealed God" with such rigor only in his dispute with Erasmus.[41] In the context of his doctrine and idea of God, however, the distinction has extraordinarily great significance, far beyond his exaggerated statements in the dispute with Erasmus. Here, too, as with his statements about the freedom of God, Luther at times came near to exceeding the limits of what we are allowed to think or say, though at their core they cohere most closely with the heart of his theology. The theme of the hidden and revealed God threads through all of Luther's writings, from the first Psalms lecture onward.

In his early period, Luther stressed that God acts hiddenly under his opposite. In the first Psalms lecture he wrote this on Psalm 111:4: "These are wonderful works: not only the miracles which He did, but much more the fact that He killed death by death, punishment by punishment, sufferings by suffering, disgrace by disgrace, so

---

[37] See above, pp. 18-19.

[38] *LW*, vol. 33, p. 68. *WA* 18, 636, 27-29: "Sequitur nunc, liberum arbitrium esse plane divinum nomen, nec ulli posse competere quam soli divinae maiestati."

[39] Thus correctly H. McSorley, *Luther: Right or Wrong? An Ecumenical-Theological Study of Luther's Major Work, The Bondage of the Will,* (New York: Newman Press, 1968), 321-53.

[40] See particularly the distinction that Judas in fact betrayed *necessario* (necessarily) but *non coactus* (not forced); *LW*, vol. 33, pp. 185-86; *WA* 18, 715, 15-716, 10.

that in Christ death is so precious in the sight of the Lord (Ps. 116:15) that it is eternal life, punishment is joy, suffering is pleasure, disgrace is glory; and, on the contrary, life is death. . . . these wonderful works as to their root and cause were done in Christ's suffering."[42] This makes clear that Luther's view of the hiddenness of God was not identical to the traditional view of God's invisibility, just as being revealed and being visible are not simply to be equated. The cross is visible to all, but that God is "revealed" in it as the one who acts hiddenly under his opposite and creates life in death is recognizable only to faith. Respecting the doctrine of God, Luther's distinction between "hidden" and "revealed" is new, and for him fundamental.

In the Romans lecture Luther sharply summarized his ideas: "For the work of God must be hidden and never understood, even when it happens. But it is never hidden in any other way than under that which appears contrary to our conceptions and ideas."[43] Faith is therefore "understanding in concealment."[44]

In the *Heidelberg Disputation* Luther not only contrasted wisdom and foolishness or the *theologia gloriae* and the *theologia crucis,* but also God's hiddenness and being revealed: "That person does not deserve to be called a theologian who looks upon the invisible things of God as though they were clearly perceptible in those things which have actually happened [Rom. 1:20]. He deserves to be called a theologian, however, who comprehends the visible and manifest things of God seen through suffering and the cross."[45] In this disputation the term *absconditus* also appears: "Because men misused the knowledge of God through works, God wished again to be recognized in suffering, and to condemn wisdom concerning invisible things by means of wisdom concerning visible things, so that those who did not honor God as manifested in his works should honor him as he is hidden in his sufferings."[46] Here, then, the knowledge of God *in gloria et maiestate* (in his glory and majesty) is contrasted with a knowledge *in humilitate et ignominia crucis* (in the humility and shame of the cross).[47] At this point in the *Heidelberg Disputation* the

---

[41] See above, p. 165-66.

[42] *LW*, vol. 11, pp. 377-78. *WA* 4, 243, 7-15.

[43] *LW*, vol. 25, p. 366. *WA* 56, 376, 31-377, 1 (scholia on Rom. 8:26) "Necesse est enim opus Dei abscondi et non intelligi tunc, quando fit. Non autem absconditur aliter quam sub contraria specie nostri conceptus seu cogitationis."

[44] *LW*, vol. 25, p. 224: "This understanding of which he speaks is faith itself, or the knowledge of the invisible things and the things which must be believed. Therefore it is an understanding in concealment because it deals with those things which a man cannot know of himself." *WA* 56, 238, 28-239, 2 (scholia on Rom. 3:11): "Intellectus iste, de quo hic loquitur, Est Ipsa fides seu notitia Invisibilium et credibilium. Ideo est intellectus in abscondito, quia eorum, que homo ex seipso nosse non potest."

[45] *LW*, vol. 31, p. 40. *WA* 1, 354, 17-20: "19. Non ille digne Theologus dicitur, qui invisibilia Dei per ea, quae facta sunt, intellecta conspicit, 20. Sed qui visibilia et posteriora Dei per passiones et crucem conspecta intelligit."

[46] *LW*, vol. 31, p. 52. *WA* 1, 362, 5-9. The last words read: ". . . ut sic, qui Deum non coluerunt manifestum ex operibus, colerent absconditum in passionibus."

two concepts *absconditus* and *Deus in . . . maiestate* are first linked, concepts that, of course, were used against Erasmus in a somewhat different way. Against Erasmus, Luther no longer distinguished the attempt to know God on the basis of his works or on the basis of his suffering, the former an impossibility after the fall and only the latter willed by God, but transferred the category of hiddenness to God himself. He no longer stated that God is hidden in suffering yet wills to be known there, but that the "hidden God" or *Deus absconditus in maiestate sua* must be distinguished from "the revealed God" or *Deus revelatus*.[48]

In his mature years Luther attempted to forge a link between the doctrine of the Trinity and his distinction between the hidden and revealed God. In the *First Disputation against the Antinomians* (1537) he wrote:

> So we distinguish the Holy Spirit as God in his divine nature and essence from the Holy Spirit as he is given to us. God in his nature and majesty is our enemy; he requires the fulfilling of the Law. . . . So also the Holy Spirit: When he writes the Law with his finger on Moses' stone tablets, then he is in his majesty and assuredly accuses sins and terrifies the hearts. But when he is "swaddled" in tongues and spiritual gifts, then he is called "gift," then he sanctifies and makes alive. Without this Holy Spirit who is "gift," the Law points to sin, because the Law is not a "gift," but the word of the eternal and almighty God.[49]

Elsewhere Luther did not take up or continue this attempt at linking the Trinity and the *Deus absconditus/revelatus*. For this reason we can scarcely say anything about the relevance of this passage. Just this much is clear: Luther at least saw the task of mediating between the two themes; thus he would not allow them simply to stand side by side, though he did not take up the task.

The distinction between the *Deus absconditus* and the *Deus revelatus* may be Luther's most important contribution to the tradition of the Christian doctrine of God. It is, of course, correct that since Neoplatonism the theme of God's hiddenness or unknowability continually occupied Christian theology, and that it was Nicolas of Cusa in particular who was of some importance to Luther.[50] Luther, however, gave further point to these statements about the hidden God. At the same time, what he wrote in *The Bondage of the Will* may neither be relativized through harmonization with his early statements on this theme nor isolated: they represent a final critical point at which he saw himself forced to oppose Erasmus for exegetical and general theological reasons. Is the depth of Luther's own experience of God reflected

[47] *LW*, vol. 31, p. 52. *WA* 1, 362, 12-13.
[48] *LW*, vol. 33, pp. 138-40. *WA* 18, 684, 14-658, 24.
[49] *WA* 39 I, 370, 12-371, 1. See Lohse, *Evangelium in der Geschichte*, 261.
[50] Thus Reinhold Weier, *Das Thema vom verborgenen Gott von Nikolaus von Kues zu Martin Luther*, BCG 2 (Münster: Aschendorff, 1967). Weier might have considerably overestimated this significance; see the

here,[51] experience that he then took up into his theology? Or, in light of such state-ments about the hidden God must Christian theology avoid the danger of taking the revelation for granted? Luther's distinction between the *Deus absconditus* and *Deus revelatus* keeps these questions open.

review by Lohse, *ZKG* 79 (1968), 414-17.

Chapter 23

CHRISTOLOGY

LUTHER'S ATTITUDE TOWARD TRADITIONAL DOGMA

In all essential points christological dogma was not a matter of dispute between Luther and Rome. Within the various Reformation groups there were certain differences, as especially between Luther and Zwingli over the doctrine of the Lord's Supper. Nevertheless, the doctrine of the two natures was not in dispute. There were differences regarding the consequences to be drawn from Christology for the Lord's Supper. Even the differences from some of the fanatics on christological questions remained totally within bounds.

Nevertheless, with reference to Christology, it is somewhat more difficult to trace Luther's position from a systematic point of view than is the case with his adherence to trinitarian doctrine. He obviously affirmed the christological dogma of the ancient church and adopted it in his own formulations of the Credo.[1] When we search his writings in the order of their origin for central christological motifs,[2] however, a variety of accents appears. In his early period "Christ is the *simul* who unites all contradictions: God and humanity, judgment and grace, etc. And he is that, not only as an image or figure of an ultimate unity that lies beyond him. But he is in truth that place where all these things and contradictions have found their unity!"[3]

In the indulgence controversy it is chiefly the idea that Christ is Lord, over the church as well as over every Christian, that Luther emphasized in attacking the indulgence doctrine of the late medieval church and the arbitrariness of the papacy

[1] See the passages cited above, p. 209.
[2] M. Lienhard, *Luther: Witness to Jesus Christ*, has pioneered in this respect.
[3] Ibid., 43.

and hierarchy.[4] In this attack Luther first gave preeminence to this theme. The theme can also be documented from his early lectures, so that they may not merely be claimed for the view that God always acts hiddenly under his opposite. At the same time, in the dispute with Rome, the *theologia crucis* took on sharp profile, particularly in the *Heidelberg Disputation*[5] but also in the *Explanations of the Ninety-five Theses.*[6] This means that the *theologia crucis* cannot at all be viewed as an early form of Luther's theology, where possible to be dubbed "pre-Reformation."[7]

In the Lord's Supper controversy Luther more precisely developed his view of the presence of Christ's body and blood "in, with, and under" the bread and wine, and in this context set forth his "doctrine of ubiquity," a further development of the traditional two-natures doctrine.

Alongside these motifs we need to consider the numerous christological statements and aspects contained in Luther's lectures, in his sermons, in the postils, in his translation of the Bible, and not least in his letters of pastoral care. Here he adopted essential features of the Christology of Augustine and of Bernard of Clairvaux, not to speak of late medieval passion piety.[8] Above all, he appropriated the various christological statements of the New Testament.[9]

In view of this variety of motifs, which can scarcely be outbid, it would be arbitrary to declare this or that idea as original, from which then all further ideas developed or derived. Luther's devotion to Christ was so central and at the same time so closely linked to the entire christological tradition that a wealth of features had been integrated from the outset, and from which one or the other for various reasons assumed center stage.

If we mention first Luther's acceptance of ancient church dogma, it is not to support the view that he assumed the ancient church's "theology of mysteries," in order then to insinuate his own christological ideas.[10] Similarly, we should not adopt

---

[4] See Lohse, *Luthers Christologie im Ablassstreit,* 287-99.

[5] *LW,* vol. 31, pp. 39-70; *WA* 1, 353-74; *Studienausgabe* 1, 186-218.

[6] *LW,* vol. 31, pp. 83-252. *WA* 1, 525-628.

[7] It was the abiding service of the work of Walther von Loewenich, *Luther's Theology of the Cross,* trans. J. A. Bouman (Minneapolis: Augsburg, 1976), to have pointed this out.

[8] More detail in Martin Elze, "Züge spätmittelalterlicher Frömmigkeit in Luthers Theologie," *ZThK* 62 (1965), 381-402; idem, "Das Verständnis der Passion Jesu im ausgehenden Mittelalter und bei Luther," in *Geist und Geschichte der Reformation: Festgabe für Hanns Rückert zum 65. Geburtstag* (Berlin: de Gruyter, 1966), 127-51.

[9] See particularly von Loewenich, *Luther und das johanneische Christentum;* idem, *Johanneisches Denken: Ein Beitrag zur Erkenntnis der johanneischen Eigenart* (Leipzig: Hinrichs, 1936); idem, *Luther als Ausleger der Synoptiker,* FGLP 10/5 (Munich: Chr. Kaiser, 1954); idem, *Die Eigenart von Luthers Auslegung des Johannes-Prologs,* SBAW.PPH 8 (Munich: Bayerischen Akademie der Wissenschaften, 1960); Walter Grundmann, *Der Römerbrief des Apostels Paulus und seine Auslegung durch Martin Luther* (Weimar: Hermann Böhlau, 1964). In terse and summary form in Lienhard, *Luther: Witness to Jesus Christ,* 383-85.

[10] Thus Wilhelm Maurer, *Von der Freiheit eines Christenmenschen,* 51-55. Ernst Wolf takes a critical stance toward it in *Die Christusverkündigung bei Luther,* 54-57.

the thesis recently defended by a few Finnish Luther scholars that Luther gave great weight to the ancient church's idea of "deification."[11] Though we cannot dispute a deification motif alongside others, we must be cautioned against overestimating this line of the tradition. In the sense of Luther's well-known word in the preface to his Galatians commentary (1535), a few central ideas respecting the *fides Christi* should be pointed out here: "In my heart this one article holds sway, that is, faith in Christ, from, through, and in which all my theological reflections flow to and fro, day and night. Still and all, I do not believe I have grasped the wisdom of such great height, breadth, and depth, except for a few weak and poor rudiments and fragments."[12]

Luther thus affirmed the christological dogma of the ancient church because he regarded it as a materially correct summary of the Scripture's witness to Christ. At the same time he always gave it a particular interpretation. His explanation to the Second Article of the Creed in the Small Catechism is instructive here. In the sentence, "I believe that Jesus Christ, true God, begotten of the Father from eternity, and also true man, born of the virgin Mary, is my Lord,"[13] the words concerning Christ as God and man are in grammatical apposition to Jesus Christ. As to its content, the two-natures doctrine is interpreted as a presupposition for Jesus' status as Lord, and in words that "I" confess. What is remarkable first of all is that Luther took up the two-natures doctrine, which is absent from the Apostles' Creed, and second, that he cited the doctrine in support of his statement about Jesus Christ as Lord. The following relative clause, "who has redeemed me, a lost and condemned creature, delivered me and freed me from all sins, from death, and from the power of the devil,"[14] interprets the statement about Jesus as Lord through reference to the redemption.

The explanation thus affirms in most tightly concentrated form the ancient church's two-natures doctrine, the new Reformation emphasis on Jesus as Lord, and the doctrine of redemption. The three themes are fused here into a unity, without giving priority to one or the other.

---

[11] Of the numerous publications on this theme only the following are named here: Tuomo Mannermaa, *Der im Glauben gegenwärtigen Christus: Rechtfertigung und Vergottung. Zum ökumenischen Dialog,* AGTL N.F. 8 (Hanover: Lutherisches Verlagshaus, 1989); Simo Peura, *Mehr als ein Mensch? Die Vergöttlichung als Thema der Theologie Martin Luthers von 1513 bis 1519* (Mainz: Philipp von Zabern, 1994). Among others Friedrich Beisser occupies himself with the Finnish interpretation of Luther, "Zur Frage der Vergöttlichung (theosis) bei Martin Luther," *KuD* 39 (1993), 266-81; Steffen Kjeldgaard-Pedersen, "Der finnische Beitrag zur heutigen Lutherforschung," in *Nordisk Forum för Studiet av Luther och Lutherisk Teologi* I, ed. Tuomo Mannermaa, SLAG 28 (Helsinki: Luther-Agricola-Gesellschaft, 1993), 7-23.

[12] *WA* 40 I, 33, 7-11: "Nam in corde meo iste unus regnat articulus, scilicet Fides Christi, ex quo, per quem et in quem omnes meae diu noctuque fluunt et refluunt theologicae cogitationes, nec tamen comprehendisse me experior de tantae altitudinis, latitudinis, profunditatis sapientia nisi infirmas et pauperes quasdam primitias et veluti fragmenta."

[13] *Book of Concord,* p. 345. *WA* 30 I, 365, 15-366, 1.

[14] *Book of Concord,* p. 345. *WA* 30 I, 366, 1-3.

With respect to this linkage of the various christological themes, Luther's hermeneutic, particularly in his early period, is of extraordinary importance, as is his tropological method of exposition. In the "Preface of Jesus Christ" to his first Psalms lecture (1513-1515) Luther set up this axiom:"Whatever is said literally concerning the Lord Jesus Christ as to His person must be understood allegorically of a help that is like Him, and of the church conformed to Him in all things. At the same time this must be understood tropologically of any spiritual and inner man against his flesh and the outer man."[15] In his application of this interpretation Luther went to great lengths with respect to Christology as well as tropology. As regards Christology, he interpreted christologically what the Psalter had to say not only about majesty but also about suffering and humiliation. Here he went beyond Augustine, who had reservations about interpreting the psalmist's utterances concerning humiliation and anxiety over suffering with reference to Christ.[16] In this way the severity of Jesus' forsakenness on the cross first became the object of theological reflection.[17] By means of the tropological method Luther could express in a newer and profounder way than before the significance of the anguished Christ for the Christian. Through the bold axiom that all statements about Christ also apply to the Christian in a figurative sense, reflection on discipleship was also broadened and deepened. In addition, "works-righteousness" was avoided at the outset.

At the same time, Luther seized upon the theme of Christ as *sacramentum et exemplum,* first enunciated by Augustine and continually reflected on in the medieval period.[18] Of course, he altered somewhat Augustine's treatment of the formula. Augustine had distinguished a twofold resurrection, the one from sin to new life, and the other from bodily death. In doing so he stated that by his once-for-all resurrection Christ became the *sacramentum et exemplum* for our twofold resurrection.[19] Luther tightened and sharpened this train of thought: Christ can be a model for us only when he is first a sacrament; "that means that his death is to be realized in me and I am to die with him before I can imitate him."[20]

---

[15] *LW,* vol. 10, p. 7; *WA* 3, 13, 14-17; *WA* 55 I, 8, 8-11. Cf. above, p. 53.

[16] Evidences in Vogelsang, *Die Anfänge von Luthers Christologie,* 18-19; Lienhard, *Martin Luthers christologisches Zeugnis,* 20-21.

[17] On this subject see Vogelsang, *Der angefochtene Christus bei Luther.*

[18] The earliest passage is in *WA* 9, 18, 18-23. On this theme in Luther see Erwin Iserloh, "Sakramentum et exemplum: Ein augustinisches Thema lutherischer Theologie" (1965), in *Kirche- Ereignis und Institution: Aufsätze und Vorträge,* vol. 2: *Geschichte und Theologie der Reformation* (Münster: Aschendorff, 1985), 107-24.

[19] Augustin, *De trinitate* 4.3; see Iserloh, "Sakramentum et exemplum," 109.

[20] Lienhard, *Luther: Witness to Jesus Christ,* 25.

The Work of Christ

Luther could not conceive a separation or strict differentiation between Christ's person and work. For him Christology and soteriology belong indissolubly together. We advise separate treatment of his statements concerning Christ's person and work for purely practical reasons. In doing so, however, we should also heed his warning:

> Through the Gospel we are told who Christ is, in order that we may learn to know that He is our Savior, that He delivers us from sin and death, helps us out of all misfortune, reconciles us to the Father, and makes us pious and saves us without our works. He who does not learn to know Christ in this way must go wrong. For even though you know that He is God's Son, that He died and rose again, and that He sits at the right hand of the Father, you have not yet learned to know Christ aright, and this knowledge still does not help you. You must also know and believe that He did all this for your sake, in order to help you.[21]

Even in his reference to Christ's work Luther took up and linked very different traditions and motifs, without giving priority to one or the other. At the same time, it is always clear that he adopted the various impulses in an extraordinarily independent way. It is chiefly his doctrine of justification that effects the reshaping of these traditions, at least in part.

Luther's hymn, "Dear Christians, One and All, Rejoice,"[22] makes particularly clear the way in which he linked the various traditions. In stanza 1 we want to sing with "holy rapture" what God has done for us. In stanza 2, sin is described in the first person:

> Fast bound in Satan's chains I lay,
> Death brooded darkly o'er me,
> Sin was my torment night and day;
> In sin my mother bore me.

Stanza 3 deals with the conflict befalling us in view of our insufficiency before God, after which the mercy of God is described in stanza 4:

> But God had seen my wretched state
> Before the world's foundation,
> And, mindful of his mercies great,
> He planned for my salvation.
> He turned to me a father's heart.

[21] *LW*, vol. 30, pp. 29-30 (*The Catholic Epistles,* 1523). *WA* 12, 285, 9-17.
[22] The English translation by Richard Massie appears in the *Lutheran Book of Worship* (Minneapolis: Augsburg Publishing House, 1978), no. 299. *WA* 35, 422-25; *AWA* 4, 154-57.

In the stanzas that follow the redemption once occurred on the cross is interpreted entirely in the present tense as given "to me." Stanza 7 reads:

> To me he [the Son] said: "Stay close to me,
> I am your rock and castle.
> Your ransom I myself will be;
> For you I strive and wrestle;
> For I am yours, and you are mine,
> And where I am you may remain;
> The foe shall not divide us."

What is unique about this hymn is not so much the graphic description intimately linking trinitarian, christological, and soteriological motifs, but the idea of the simultaneity of "then" and "now": "my" misery and "my" sin are the occasion for God the Father's sending his Son. Jesus' redemptive work applies "to me"; it overcomes "my" conflict. In view of God's work of salvation there is no "loathsome historical ditch" (Lessing). Human sin, but also God's work of salvation, are ever-present powers. The goal of Christology is soteriology, as conversely soteriology has its basis in Christology.

In this context a few other aspects deserve particular notice. First, as few theologians before him, Luther set the earthly, historical Jesus at midpoint, thus emphasizing Christ's humanity. As early as in his 1509/1510 marginal notes on Augustine he wrote that "faith means to believe in his [Jesus'] humanity, given to us in this life for life and salvation."[23] In a letter of 1519 he wrote: "Whoever wants to reflect or speculate in a salutary way about God, let him set everything aside for the humanity of Christ."[24] In the Large Catechism (1529) he called Christ "a mirror of the Father's heart."[25] More than half of Luther's extant sermons are devoted to texts from the Synoptic Gospels.

This impulse may not, of course, be interpreted to mean that Luther ascended from the earthly, human Jesus to the Father in heaven, that he intended to arrive at divinity from the true humanity, and in this way to sketch a theology "from the bottom up." Affirmation of ancient church dogma always underlies Luther's emphasis on Jesus' humanity. It is always assumed. Those features in the earthly Jesus that appear to be divine are not to be emphasized, so that we ascend from his humanity to his Godhead and to the Father in heaven. Rather, in the earthly Jesus the believing observer should clearly see how God acts. Only in Jesus is this manner of the

[23] WA 9, 17, 12-13: "Sed hoc credere est in humanitatem ejus credere quae nobis data est in hac vita pro vita et salute."
[24] WA Br 1 Nr. 145, 50-52 (letter to Spalatin, February 12, 1519): "quicunque velit salubriter de Deo cogitare aut speculari, prosus omnia postponat praeter humanitatem Christi." See Walther Köhler, Wie Luther den Deutschen das Leben Jesu erzählt hat, SVRG 127-28 (Leipzig: Heinsius, 1917).
[25] Book of Concord, p. 419. WA 30 I, 192, 5.

divine activity knowable. In him, in his person and work, God reveals his whole fatherly heart.

Next, the question as to how Luther interpreted Jesus' redemptive work deserves attention. Throughout the history of dogma and theology soteriology has been represented under various accents.[26] While the ancient Greek church predominantly interpreted Christ's redemptive work as liberation from the might of sin and death, the Latin West more strongly accented the character of sin as guilt and the divine grace as help and salvation. Toward the end of the ancient church period, the theory was propounded that since Adam's fall the devil had a claim to lordship over humanity, then lost this right through Christ. This led to the development of rather massive ideas such as the devil's being outwitted by Christ.

By contrast, the theory of satisfaction developed by Anselm (1033-1109) marked a considerable deepening. Anselm overcame the older "ransom theories," first by giving greater stress to the weight of sin, and second by placing at the center of redemption a reparation that had to redound to the divine "honor." This reparation had to consist either in punishment of the human race or in a deed of satisfaction. Since punishment would have destroyed God's plan of creation, what remained was the way of satisfaction. Yet, since the weight of sin was greater than the whole world, the satisfaction could only be performed by God himself. Still, humans also had to make satisfaction: accordingly, only a God-Man could perform the deed.

Peter Abelard (1079-1142) advocated a soteriology of an entirely different stripe, which was also to be of considerable influence, especially in the modern period. According to Abelard, the issue in redemption is not that God is reconciled but that humanity overcomes its hatred of God. This can only occur through God's encountering humanity with love and assuring them that he will forgive their sin. The work of redemption thus consists in Christ's revealing God's love. To this humanity responds in love for God.

Toward the close of the medieval period, the various types of soteriology were seldom consistently represented. On the whole, one took the route of compromise between Anselm and Abelard, without adopting all the details of the various theories. Just for this reason it is improbable that Luther may be associated with one or the other form of medieval soteriology, as has at times been attempted.

In his statements about Christ's redemptive work, Luther often pursued the motif of the "happy exchange." The motif originated in the ancient church and was variously interpreted in the medieval period, in the course of which a link was often

---

[26] See Raymund Schwager, *Der Wunderbarer Tausch: Zur Geschichte und Deutung der Erlösungslehre* (Munich: Kösel, 1986).

forged with the idea of satisfaction.[27] Luther took up this motif again and again throughout his life. In his treatise *The Freedom of the Christian* (1520), he wrote that Christ and the soul become as it were one body. Then he stated:

> So Christ has all the blessings and the salvation which are the soul's. And so the soul has upon it all the vice and sin which become Christ's own. Here now begins the happy exchange and conflict. Because Christ is God and man who never yet sinned, and his piety is inconquerable, eternal and almighty. So, then, as he makes his own the believing soul's sin through the wedding ring of its faith, and does nothing else than as if he had committed it, just so must sin be swallowed up and drowned.[28]

Although Luther had elements from Anselmian and Abelardian soteriology, we cannot on that account speak of a tension or lack of balance in his statements about Christ's redemptive work. Luther often used words such as "reparation" or *satisfactio,* to that extent no doubt referring to Anselm of Canterbury. For example, he emphasized that through Christ we do not receive salvation "for nothing or without satisfying his righteousness; . . . for mercy and grace are not a space above us, to be made in us, or to help us to eternal benefits and bliss. Righteousness must have occurred long before, in the most perfect way of all. . . . So none may come to God's rich grace unless he has satisfied God's commandments to the fullest."[29] Or, with respect to Christ's priestly office, he said: "But if he was to be priest and reconcile us with God through his priestly office, he had to satisfy God's righteousness for us. But no other satisfaction was possible than that he offered himself and died and in his own person conquered sin together with death. Thus in dying he became priest and through his priesthood he received the kingdom."[30]

---

[27] For the tradition as well as for Luther see Walter Allgaier, *"Der fröhliche Wechsel" bei Martin Luther: Eine Untersuchung zu Christologie und Soteriologie bei Luther unter besondere Berücksichtigung der Schriften bis 1521* (diss., Erlangen-Nürnberg, 1966); Theobald Beer, *Der fröhliche Wechsel und Streit: Grundzüge der Theologie Martin Luthers,* 2 vols. (1974; 2d ed., Einsiedeln: Johannes, 1980). Erwin Iserloh is critical toward Beer's book in "Der fröhliche Wechsel und Streit: Zu Theobald Beers Werk über Grundzüge der Theologie Martin Luthers," *Cath (M)* 37 (1982), 101-14; cf. Otto Hermann Pesch, "Neuere Beiträge zur Frage nach Luthers 'reformatorische Wende,'" *Catholica* 37 (1983), 259-87; 38 (1984), 66-133.

[28] *WA* 7, 25, 28-26, 1. Cf. *LW,* vol. 31, pp. 351-52.

[29] *WA* 10 I 1, 121, 16-122, 9.

[30] *LW,* vol. 52, pp. 280-81 (*Kirchenpostille* Epiphany, 1521/1522); *WA* 10I 1, 720, 18-721, 2. Similar statements also in the following passages: *WA* 10 I 1, 470, 18-471,6 (*Kirchenpostille,* 1522); *LW,* vol. 51, p. 92 (*Eight Sermons at Wittenberg,* 1535); *WA* 10 III, 49, 8-13. *WA* 17 II, 291, 6-18 (Fest Postille, 1527). WA 29, 578, 2-5; 579, 3-5 (sermon, 1529). *LW,* vol. 34, p. 111 (*Thesis Concerning Faith and Law,* 1535): "For these two propositions battle each other: Christ was delivered to make satisfaction for our sins; and, we ourselves are justified from our sins through the law"; *WA* 39 I 46, 11-12: "Pugnant enim ista duo, Christum pro nostris peccatis traditum satisfacere, Et nos ipsos per legem a peccatis iustificari." Ibid., p. 119: "So that instead of all of us or for the sake of all of us the Son was made obedient to

Naturally, now and again Luther was able to distance himself from implications linked to the concept of satisfaction:

> And even if we should just keep the word satisfaction and interpret it to mean that Christ has made satisfaction for our sin, still it is too weak, and too little is said of the grace of Christ, and not enough honor paid the suffering of Christ, to whom we must give higher honor, that he not only made satisfaction for sin but also redeemed us from the power of death, the devil and hell, and establishes an eternal kingdom of grace and a daily forgiveness even of the remainder of sin that is in us.[31]

Christ's satisfaction consists in fulfilling God's will as reflected in the law, in vicariously taking upon himself punishment for sin and thus bearing the wrath of God "for us." The central passages of the New Testament to which Luther appealed are Galatians 3:13 ("Christ redeemed us from the curse of the law, having become a curse for us") and Philippians 2:8 ("He humbled himself and became obedient unto death, even death on a cross").

At the same time, Luther did not adopt some of the ideas essential to Anselm's satisfaction theory: first, the significance of the honor of God; next, the argument that after the fall the sole alternative was *satisfactio aut poena;*[32] and finally the view that Anselm actually did not hold, that satisfaction pertained exclusively to Jesus' sacrifice on the cross, not also to his preaching.

As for Abelard, Luther seems never to have mentioned his name.[33] His soteriology was occasionally taken up by Luther, but never to the exclusion of the Anselmian type. Marc Lienhard states correctly: "It is striking, in fact, to note that the terminology and characteristic themes of those various tendencies can be found in Luther, but that he cannot be attached to any one of these systems."[34]

It is an oft-discussed question whether the motif of Christ's battling the powers of chaos, thus death, devil, and hell, has more importance for Luther than the motif of vicarious suffering. Albrecht Ritschl (1822-1889) held to this "victory motif" and disputed Luther's adoption of Anselmian ideas.[35] Against Ritschl, Theodosius Harnack (1817-1889) in particular pointed to the significance of the wrath of God in

---

God; WA 39 I, 53, 2-3: "ut loco nostrorum omnium, seu pro nobis omnibus Dei filius oboediens fieret." On the other hand, a comparison of Rörer's lecture notes with Luther's lecture on Psalm 51 (1532) and the editing for printing by Veit Dietrich (40 II, 405, 5-10, 21-34) shows how strongly Luther's statements were systematized in the theology stamped by Melanchthon.

[31] *Crucigers Sommerpostille,* 1544, WA 21, 264, 27-33.

[32] Anselm, *Cur Deus Homo* I, 15.

[33] See the index in WA 63; WA Br 16; and WA TR 6.

[34] Lienhard, *Luther: Witness to Jesus Christ,* 178-79.

[35] Ritschl, *The Christian Doctrine of Justification and Reconciliation,* ed. and trans. H. R. Mackintosh and A. B. Macaulay (Edinburgh: T. & T. Clark, 1900).

Luther's theology and thus also in Anselm's line of thought.[36] In a different way, Gustaf Aulen (1879-1977) took up the victory motif: Christ waged the battle against the powers of chaos and ruin and conquered them for us. Reconciliation is thus strictly interpreted as God's deed: God's love breaks through the legal relationship between himself and the creature.[37] In dependence on Aulen, though in altered shape, Swedish systematicians and Luther scholars in particular have elaborated the "victory motif."

With regard to Luther, rejection of the Anselmian tradition might be too subtle.[38] On the other hand, the importance of the victory motif should not be ignored. Not only in the context of atonement doctrine but also in ethics and in general observation of the world, the idea of victory has considerable significance.

LUTHER'S FURTHER FORMATION
OF ANCIENT CHURCH CHRISTOLOGY

Luther adopted christological dogma in its entirety. Despite the deepening and interiorizing observable in his devotion to Christ, in a particular sense he more precisely interpreted or gave further shape to the ancient church's christological dogma. His understanding of the unity of the divine and human natures comes to mind, with its particularly important consequences for the doctrine of the Supper.

Decisions of the ecumenical councils of the fifth to the eighth centuries pertaining to Christology stressed in part the totality of Christ's divine and human natures, and in part the unity of the person of the God-Man.[39] To that extent these decisions reflected the christological schools of the Alexandrian and Antiochene persuasions: the former followed the "Word became flesh" motif, the latter "the Word became man."

In his theological reflection, Luther was altogether of the Alexandrian persuasion, putting most stress on the unity of the person of the God-Man. At the same time, there were points at which he went beyond Alexandrian tradition. Though his statements must be interpreted with caution since Christology in the sixteenth

[36] Th. Harnack, in the detailed foreword to the second volume of his description of *Luthers Theologie mit besonderer Beziehung auf seine Versöhnungs- und Erlösungslehre* (Erlangen: T. Blaesing, 1886), 1-19.

[37] G. Aulen, *Christus Victor: An Historical Study of the Three Main Types of the Idea of Atonement*, trans. A. G. Hebert (New York: Macmillan, 1951).

[38] For the debate with Aulen see Paul Althaus, "Das Kreuz und das Böse," *ZSTh* 15 (1938), 165-93; as well as above all Osmo A. Tililä, *Das Strafleiden Christi: Beitrag zur Diskussion über die Typeneinteilung der Versöhnungsmotive*, AASF 48/1 (Helsinki, 1941).

[39] See the description by Adolf Martin Ritter and Klaus Wessel, in *HdBDThG*, 1:222-318, as well as the terse sketch by Lohse, *Epochen der Dogmengeschichte*, 8th ed. (Hamburg/Münster, 1994), 77-104.

century was generally never in dispute, we can observe a tendency in Luther to give a fresh interpretation to the "emptying" (*kenosis*) at the incarnation.[40] Philippians 2:7 furnished the background: Jesus Christ "emptied himself, taking the form of a servant, being born in the likeness of men. And being found in human form. . . ." Luther often went so far as to say that at his incarnation Christ did not leave his Godhead in heaven, but in his earthly life continually renounced it. For example, in 1519 he wrote: "The 'form of God' is wisdom, power, righteousness, goodness and freedom too; for Christ was a free, powerful, wise man, subject to none of the vices or sins to which all other men are subject. . . . He relinquished that form to God the Father and emptied himself, unwilling to use his rank against us, unwilling to be different from us. Moreover, for our sakes he became as one of us and took the form of a servant, that is, he subjected himself to all evils."[41] At this juncture Luther departed from ancient church Christology.

Another statement in the Fasten Postille of 1525 reads:

> [The form of a servant] means that Christ divested or emptied himself, that is, acted as though he laid his Godhead aside, and would not use it. . . . Not that he removed it or could put it off or remove it, but that he put off the form of the divine majesty, and did not behave as God, which he truly was. Just as he did not put off the form of God so that one would not feel or see it, for then there would be no form of God there, but did not make use of it, did not make a display of it against us, but much rather served us with it.[42]

From this position Luther used extraordinarily charged speech. He attacked the formula according to which the divine assumed a human person, which would result in a Christ with two persons. One must rather say that the divine person assumed human nature.[43] At this point Luther even went beyond Augustine, or concluded from the unity of the person of Christ that we may say, "God has suffered, the Man has created heaven and earth . . . that the Servant [Christ] . . . is Creator of all things."[44]

With such remarks Luther might have been in danger of abbreviating Christ's human nature. He thus adopted and sharpened the doctrine of the *enhypostasis* to read that the human nature of Jesus Christ has no *hypostasis* (separate existence) of its own but possesses it in the divine nature.

Luther came into some theological difficulty with this view of the emptying when treating the problem of Jesus' abandonment at the cross. He often stated that

[40] On this subject see first of all Althaus, *Theology of Martin Luther,* 193-98.

[41] *LW,* vol. 31, p. 301 (*Two Kinds of Righteousness,* 1519). WA 2, 148, 2-16.

[42] WA 17 II, 243, 2-11. The thought is similar in *LW,* vol. 45, p. 120 (*Temporal Authority,* 1523); WA 11, 273, 21-24.

[43] WA 39 II, 93-96; 116, 27-118, 4 (*Disputatio de divinitate et humanitate Christi,* 1540).

[44] WA 39 II, 280, 16-22 (*Promotionsdisputation Theodor Fabricius und Stanislaus Rapagelanus*).

at his crucifixion and death Jesus' Godhead so to speak "withdrew." A sermon of 1525 reads: "Christus in cruce pendens non sentit divinitatem, sed ut purus homo [when Christ hung on the cross, he did not sense the deity, but (suffered) as a mere man]."[45] Luther also wrote that Jesus' human nature was "subject" to death and hell, but that in his humiliation he "devoured" the devil and hell.[46] In a sermon on Psalm 8 in 1537, he went so far as to state that on the cross the deity was indeed not separated from the humanity, but it "withdrew" and "hid." The humanity was "left alone," so that the devil had free access to Christ, leaving his humanity to fight alone.[47] Luther was taking up questions that occupied many theologians in the ancient church.[48] His statements make clear that he avoided speaking of the death of God. On the other hand, those statements exist in tension: it is inconsistent with the accent on the unity of the deity and humanity to speak of a "withdrawal" on the part of the deity.

Luther's idea of the total person is also basic to the further development of his Christology that is best known to us, that is, his doctrine of ubiquity, the idea of Christ's exalted human nature as everywhere present. He was led to develop this view in his dispute with Zwingli. What concerned him was the literal, unequivocal sense of the words of institution, of which, after 1523, the *est* ("this *is* my body . . . this *is* my blood") became more and more important to him. In his 1526 sermon *The Sacrament of the Body and Blood of Christ against the Fanatics,* he said: "We believe that Christ, according to his human nature, is put over all creatures [Eph. 1:22] and fills all things . . . Not only according to his divine nature, but also according to his human nature, he is a lord of all things, has all things in his hand, and is present everywhere."[49]

If Luther first expressed his view of the omnipresence of Jesus' exalted human nature without giving a reason for it, he saw himself forced to do so by Zwingli's criticism. He referred to reflections in Occam and Biel, who had already distinguished a *circumscriptive esse in loco* (the spatial presence of an object) from a *definitive esse in loco* (e.g., the presence of the soul in the body).[50] Biel had gone beyond to reckon with the possibility of a "repletive" presence (the presence of an object outside itself). The divine ubiquity involved such a presence.

---

[45] *WA* 17 I, 72, 12-13 (Rörer's lecture notes; Roth's lecture notes are almost identical).

[46] *LW,* vol. 5, p. 219 (*Lectures on Genesis, Chapters 26 to 30,* 1524ff.): "Such humanity has been made liable and subject to death and hell yet in that humiliation has devoured the devil, hell, and all things in itself." *WA* 43, 579, 42-580, 2: "talis humanitas morti, inferno obnoxia facta et subiecta: et tamen in ea humiliatione devoraverit Diabolum, infernum et omnia in semetipso."

[47] *LW,* vol. 12, pp. 126-27. *WA* 45, 239, 32-40.

[48] Aloys Grillmeier, S.J., *Der Logos am Kreuz: Zur christologischen Symbolik der älteren Kreuzigungsdarstellung* (Munich: Herder, 1956).

[49] *LW,* vol. 36, p. 342. *WA* 19, 491, 17-20.

[50] See, respectively, Iserloh, *Gnade und Eucharistie in der philosophischen Theologie des Wilhelm von Ockham: Ihre Bedeutung für die Ursachen der Reformation,* VIEG 8 (Wiesbaden: Steiner, 1956), 174, 197ff., 253-66; Heiko A. Oberman, *Spätscholastik und Reformation,* vol. 1: *Der Herbst der mittelalterlichen Theologie,* 256-58.

Luther took up these reflections but distanced himself from the entire tradition at one very crucial point: he no longer conceived the "right hand of God" as a particular place in heaven where the Credo describes Christ as "seated" after his ascension: "Christ's body is everywhere because it is at the right hand of God which is everywhere, although we do not know how that occurs . . . that the right hand of God is everywhere."[51] Then, however, in order to render omnipresence intelligible, Luther appealed to the nominalist distinction between various forms of an object's presence in space: "An object occupies places repletively, i.e. supernaturally, if it is simultaneously present in all places whole and entire, and fills all places, yet without being measured or circumscribed by any place, in terms of the space which it occupies. This mode of existence belongs to God alone."[52] In so stating, Luther did not intend to prove the ubiquity of Christ's exalted human nature. Rather: "All this I have related in order to show that there are more modes whereby an object may exist in a place than the one circumscribed, physical mode on which the fanatics insist."[53]

The doctrine of ubiquity corresponds far better to the thrust of Luther's Christology than do his statements on Jesus' self-emptying at his incarnation, or on his abandonment by God at the cross. Since Luther regarded this doctrine as an aid to construction, neither the doctrine itself nor his dependence on nominalist trains of thought should be overestimated. The fundamental position that God's presence is salutary only where connected with the humanity of Jesus Christ is central to Luther's theology.

---

[51] *LW*, vol. 37, p. 214 (*Confession Concerning Christ's Supper*, 1528). *WA* 26, 325, 26-29.
[52] *LW*, vol. 37, p. 216. *WA* 26, 329, 27-30.
[53] *LW*, vol. 37, p. 216. *WA* 26, 329, 34-36.

Chapter 24

SPIRITUS CREATOR

LUTHER'S ATTITUDE TOWARD TRADITIONAL DOGMA

With respect to the doctrine of the Holy Spirit, Luther adopted the same attitude toward the doctrinal decisions of the ancient church and the tradition of Western theology as he had advocated toward the doctrine of the Trinity generally and toward statements about God and Christ. His pneumatology nonetheless reflects some singularities that need to be carefully noted.

Older research supposed that the Holy Spirit had no further significance in Luther's theology: He merely adopted the traditional statements without apportioning to them any particular weight. Above all, he did not strictly conceive the Holy Spirit as a third person of the Trinity.[1] Erich Seeberg's contribution marked a change in the evaluation of Luther's pneumatology, indicating that it was christologically oriented. This is particularly true of Luther during the controversy over the Lord's Supper.[2]

In what is still a foundational investigation, Regin Prenter described Luther's pneumatology first in his confrontation with Rome, then with the so-called fanatics. Yet, however significant Luther's distance from either side may have been, and allowing for all the differences between him and particular strands of the tradition, what they shared may no more be overlooked than the proprium of his position.[3] By contrast, Albrecht Peters, with Luther's catechetical publications as a basis,

---

[1] Thus Rudolf Otto in his dissertation of 1898.

[2] E. Seeberg, in *FS Reinhold Seeberg*, 43-80.

[3] In this respect H. Gerdes, *LuJ* 25 (1958), 42-60, has subjected Prenter's book to a full, sharp, critical review.

offered a comprehensive evaluation of Luther's penumatology that relegated polemics to the rear.[4]

On the whole, when compared with its statements about God, Jesus Christ, and the Trinity, pneumatology in the ancient church as well as in the medieval period was considerably less developed. The decisions of the first two ecumenical councils dealt only briefly with pneumatology. At the second ecumenical council of Constantinople in 381, the Godhead of the Holy Spirit as well as his *homoousia* with the God-Father and Son was made a dogma. At that time, the pneumatology of the West was strongly influenced by Augustine, who emphasized the total equality of the Spirit with the God-Father and Son, but also deepened the distinction between the Spirit as *persona* and *donum* (person and gift), and sought to connect it with his view of the Spirit's procession from the Father and the Son.[5] In the medieval period it was chiefly Lombard who adopted Augustine's pneumatology and provided for its wide dissemination in the West. Though the later pneumatology did not follow him in everything, his identification of the Spirit with the divine *caritas* had the great advantage of directly connecting the doctrine of grace with the doctrine of God. Of course, difficulties arose when it came to a more precise development of the doctrine of the Spirit.

Luther knew of and at times also adopted the distinction between the Spirit as person and as gift but on the whole accented more vigorously than Lombard the Spirit's Godhead and personhood, without on that account attacking the tradition. In a late disputation he cited the distinction between the Holy Spirit as person and gift: "So we distinguish the Holy Spirit as God in his divine nature and essence from the Holy Spirit as he is given to us."[6] This passage makes clear that Luther linked his distinction between law and gospel to Lombard's distinction respecting the Spirit, for he went on to say that "God in his nature and majesty is our enemy; he inculcates the law in us and threatens transgressors with death. But when he unites himself with our weakness, takes on himself our nature, our sins, and evil, then he is not our enemy."[7] Similarly, Luther elsewhere linked the medieval distinction to his Reformation theology, especially to his own distinction between the hidden and revealed God: "We are not speaking here of the office and service of the Spirit, nor of his

---

[4] A. Peters, *Kommentar zum Luthers Katechismen*, vol. 2.

[5] See Michael Schmaus, *Die psychologische Trinitätslehre des hl. Augustinus* (Münster: Aschendorff, 1927, 2d ed. 1967, with supplements); Ekkehard Mühlenberg, "Dogma und Lehre im Abendland," *HdBDThG*, 1:428-32. A brief sketch of the dogmatic-historical development is given in Martin Anton Schmidt, "Heiliger Geist, dogmengeschichtlich," *RGG* 2 (1958), 1279-83. On the problematic of the Augustinian pneumatology see Wolfhart Pannenberg, *Systematic Theology*, trans. G. W. Bromiley, vol. 3 (Grand Rapids: Eerdmans, 1998), 8-9.

[6] *WA* 39 I, 370, 12-13 (*1. Disputation gegen die Antinomer*, 1537): "Distinguimus igitur de Spiritu sancto ut de Deo in sua divina natura et substantia et nobis dato."

[7] *WA* 39 I, 370, 13-16.

essence, as it exists of itself and in its nature. I am inquiring [rather] whether the Holy Spirit is present in us according to his essence or according to his effect."[8] Here again Luther was rather carefree about using terms precisely in his doctrine of God.

When Luther took up statements about the Spirit purely from the perspective of Christology, he intended no opposition to the traditional pneumatology. What led him to link Christology with pneumatology were the various controversies, especially the controversy over the Lord's Supper: the bodily gift of the Supper is also "spiritual." The Spirit, as the Supper and naturally also the incarnate Word of God make clear, is not to be viewed in opposition to the body. Of course, in Luther the connection between pneumatology and Christology had a significance far beyond the complexities of theological dispute. It ultimately cohered with the *solus Christus*, which he continually stressed from the beginning.

The consequence of this *solus Christus* principle is that for Luther the task of the Holy Spirit is to point to Christ. "If Christ is not God, then neither the Father nor the Holy Spirit is God, because our article reads that Christ is God. When I therefore hear Christ speak, then I believe the undivided Godhead is speaking."[9]

For the rest, Luther scarcely ever spoke of the relations within the Trinity. Yet he did allude to the subject now and again. What is worth noting is that even in sermons he could at times broach such topics. In a Christmas sermon of 1514, he preached at considerable length on the subject,[10] though still strongly influenced by Augustinian reflection. In his later sermons, he seldom dealt with questions of the relation between Christ and the Spirit, but if he thought the text required it, he did so in thorough fashion.[11] In general, Luther's reflection or his remarks regarding the relations within the Trinity receded behind statements concerning the effects of the Spirit in which it is precisely the relation to Christ that is central.

---

[8] *WA* 39 I, 243, 6-12 (*Promotionsdisputation von Palladius und Tilemann*, 1537). "Nos loquimur hic de officio et ministerio Spiritus, non de essentia, ut est per se et in sua natura. Quaero, an Spiritus sanctus adsit in nobis essentialiter, an vero virtualiter."

[9] *WA TR* 2 Nr. 1265, p. 16, 27-29: "Si Christus non est Deus, tunc nec Pater nec Spiritus Sanctus Deus est, quia noster articulus sic sonat Christum esse Deum. Quando ergo ego audio loqui Christum, tunc credo indivisam divinitatem loqui."

[10] *WA* 1, 20-29 (Dec. 25, 1514). See, e.g., the informative passage on the Holy Spirit, on p. 28, 14-18: "ubi semper Deus movetur et quiescit . . . , movendo filius, quiescendo Spiritus Sanctus procedit. Quia Spiritus Sanctus finis est emanationis Dei, imo dum semper ex Patre profluit motus, i.e. filius, semper ex utroque provenit quies, in qua et mobile et motus finitur." ("Whereas God is always in motion and at rest . . . the Son proceeds from the One who is in motion, the Holy Spirit from the One who is at rest. Because the Holy Spirit is the end of the emanations of God; indeed, while the One who is moved, i.e., the Son, always flows from the Father, the One who is at rest [the Spirit] always proceeds from both, so that he is bounded both as moving and as moved.")

[11] Sermons on John 14:23ff. are chiefly involved, in which vv. 25-26 furnished Luther the occasion for such statements. See Gerhard Heintze, "Luthers Pfingstpredigten," 139-40. But see also the instructive passage in Luther's 1519 commentary on Galatians, *LW*, vol. 27, p. 290: "We have our being because of the Father, who is the 'Substance' of the Godhead. We are moved by the image of the Son,

The Work of the Holy Spirit

With this constant reference to Christ the Holy Spirit assumed an extraordinarily important place in Luther's theology. This statement applies equally to his theological statements and to his giving shape to church life.

It was Luther's wish that each service of worship should end with his paraphrase of Psalm 67, as expressed in the hymn, "May God Bestow on Us His Grace." The last lines of the hymn read:

> May God the Father and the Son
> And Holy Spirit bless us;
> Let all the world praise him alone,
> Let solemn awe possess us.
> Now let our hearts say, "Amen."[12]

Each service was to conclude with the warning about the sin against the Holy Spirit, indicative of the actual importance of the Spirit in Luther's theology.

For Luther, there was not a single doctrine in all of theology where the activity of the Spirit would not be fundamental. The Spirit's activity may thus not be limited to the sphere of faith and the church.[13] The Spirit is present and at work in all creation as well as in every human deed, even in every natural occurrence. According to Luther, all activity in which God engages with reference to the world and humankind is mediated through the Spirit. It is entirely in Luther's sense, though not without a certain systematizing, that a late disputation should read: "the Holy Spirit is among humans in a twofold way. First through a universal activity, by which he preserves them as well as God's other creatures. Second, the Holy Spirit is given from Christ to believers."[14] Where Luther is concerned, we may actually establish

---

who, moved by a divine and eternal motion, so to speak, is born of the Father. We live according to the Spirit, in whom the Father and the Son rest and live, as it were." *WA* 2, 536, 28-31: "sumus propter patrem qui substantia divinitatis est, movemur imagine filii qui ex patre nascitur divino et aeterno velut motu motus, vivimus secundum spiritum in quo pater et filius quiescunt et velut vivunt."

[12] See Otto Schlisske, *Handbuch der Lutherlieder* (Göttingen: Vandenhoeck & Ruprecht, 1948), 144-51; *AWA* 4, 66-68, 184-87; Kurt Dietrich Schmidt, "Luthers Lehre vom Heiligen Geist," 111; *Lutheran Book of Worship*, no. 335.

[13] Not only the researches of R. Prenter but also those of A. Peters and incidentally most of the descriptions of Luther's theology discuss the work of the Holy Spirit almost exclusively with reference to salvation, faith, and the church.

[14] *WA* 39 II, 239, 29-31: "Spiritus sanctus duplici modo est in hominibus. Primo generali quadam actione, qua conservat eos et caeteras creaturas Dei. Deinde datur etiam piis Spiritus sanctus a Christo." This statement would contradict the following thesis: "If the Holy Spirit is [also] given to those who are without faith, then he is also given to the godless. But it is absurd to say that the Holy Spirit is given to the godless. Therefore the Holy Spirit is not present apart from faith" (ibid., lines 24-26). Incidentally, this thesis would also contradict Luther's understanding of the Supper, especially his view of the "eating of the ungodly."

the principle that a relationship with God is possible only through the Spirit. The Spirit is thus understood in the strict sense as a person of the Trinity.

Not even the so-called natural gifts and activities are to be understood apart from this activity of the Spirit. In his 1531 lecture on Galatians, Luther said: "So all these things are services and fruits of the Spirit. Raising one's children, loving one's wife, and obeying the magistrate are fruits of the Spirit. According to the papists they are fleshly things, because they do not understand creaturely things."[15] Naturally, Luther did not intend to claim that so-called natural things could be done only by Christians. What he intended to say is that even what is termed natural can ultimately be understood only on the basis of its creatureliness, that only those who understand themselves as creatures of God and accept their creatureliness use natural things in the right way. This is what it means to understand and use the natural from the perspective of the Holy Spirit.

Luther's view that finally not even sin in its actual essence can be known by the so-called natural human, but can be recognized only through revelation, points in the same direction.[16] Here too the Spirit is at work.

Aside from this, Luther made clear that the Spirit is of fundamental significance for the Christian's entire journey. First, it is the Spirit who brings one to Christ. Without the Spirit it is entirely impossible to come to him. When in interpreting Christ's crucifixion and his own inner conflict Luther proceeded continually from the fact that his hearer/reader is ultimately contemporaneous with Christ or that the troubled and crucified Christ has saving significance in a present that is ever new, we need to add that it is the Spirit who bridges that "loathsome ditch" between past and present and creates such contemporaneity. In the Large Catechism Luther wrote:

> Neither you nor I could ever know anything of Christ, or believe in him and take him as our Lord, unless these were first offered to us and bestowed on our hearts through the preaching of the gospel by the Holy Spirit. The work is finished and completed, Christ has acquired and won the treasure for us by his sufferings, death, and resurrection, etc. But if the work remained hidden and no one knew of it, it would have been all in vain, all lost. In order that this treasure might not be buried but put to use and enjoyed, God has caused the Word to be published and proclaimed, in which he has given the Holy Spirit to offer and apply to us this treasure of salvation. Therefore to sanctify is nothing else than to bring us to the Lord Christ, to receive this blessing, which we could not obtain by ourselves.[17]

---

[15] WA 40 I, 348, 2-5: "Ergo omnia officia et fructus spiritus sancti: alere prolem, diligere uxorem, obedire magistratui sunt fructus spiritus. Apud Papistas sunt carnalia, quia non intelligunt, quid creatura." Cf. LW, vol. 26, p. 217.

[16] In the Smalcald Articles Luther stated: "This hereditary sin is so deep a corruption of nature that reason cannot understand it. It must be believed because of the revelation in the Scriptures" (*Book of Concord*, p. 312).

[17] *Book of Concord*, pp. 415-16.

Here the Spirit appears as author of the preaching of the gospel. At the same time he is also the gift enclosed in the Word. Here too Luther is taking up Lombard's distinction so as to use it in line with his own Reformation theology. His well-known exposition of the Third Article of the Creed in the Small Catechism yields the same thought, though more tersely: "I believe that by my own reason or strength I cannot believe in Jesus Christ, my Lord, or come to him, But the Holy Spirit has called me through the Gospel, enlightened me with his gifts, and sanctified and preserved me in the true faith."[18]

Luther often spoke of the *solus Christus,* and we must add a corresponding *solo Spiritu Sancto* (through the Holy Spirit alone), though he never coined such a formula. That such a formula does indeed appropriately paraphrase Luther's position is clear from his doctrine of justification. Neither our coming to faith nor faith itself is our "work." God himself must open our eyes "through the Holy Spirit alone."

At the same time, Luther often accented the freedom of the Spirit. In the *Disputation Concerning Justification* (1536), he wrote: "The Holy Spirit breathes where he wills [John 3:8] and God justifies whom he wishes. He takes hold of the contrite and justifies him through faith in Christ which he pours into him through the preaching of the gospel."[19]

Next, it is important to note that for Luther the Spirit always makes use of the means of Word and Sacrament. The Spirit encounters persons not directly but always mediately. In his early period Luther could speak differently on this point. As late as in his 1521 exposition of the Magnificat, he could say: "No one can correctly understand God or His Word unless he has received such understanding immediately from the Holy Spirit. But no one can receive it from the Holy Spirit without experiencing, proving, and feeling it. In such experience the Holy Spirit instructs us as in His own school, outside of which nothing is learned but empty words and prattle."[20] Still, even in this early period, Luther never conceived the activity of the Spirit as independent of external means. After his debate with the so-called fanatics, however, he spoke more cautiously on the subject, always accenting the Spirit's relation to the external means of Word and Sacrament.

If we were to seek the Spirit apart from Word and Sacrament, then the Spirit would be encountered as a "hidden God." Indeed, in the task of inculcating the law in us, the Holy Spirit is a *Deus absconditus.*

---

[18] *Book of Concord,* p. 345.

[19] *LW,* vol. 34, p. 173. *WA* 39 I, 103, 16-21: "spiritus sanctus ubi vult spirat, et Deus quos vult iustificat, apprehendit contritum et iustificat eum per fidem in Christum, quam infundit ei per praedicationem Evangelii."

[20] *LW,* vol. 21, p. 299. *WA* 7, 546, 24-29.

When the Holy Spirit writes the law with his finger on Moses' stone tablets, then he is in his majesty and assuredly accuses sins and terrifies the hearts. But when he is "swaddled" in tongues and spiritual gifts, then he is called "gift," then he sanctifies and makes alive. Without this Holy Spirit who is "gift," the law points to sin, because the law is not a "gift," but the word of the eternal and almighty God, to consciences a consuming fire.[21]

For this very reason Luther warns against being occupied with the Spirit apart from the Word: "Of God's right hand let this be said once for all: God makes us alive, gives us birth, nourishes us, educates, protects, preserves, and leads us to eternal life through nothing else than through his Word."[22]

In his debate with the fanatics Luther held to the same idea by taking up the distinction between "outward" and "inward": "Now when God sends forth his holy gospel, he deals with us in a twofold manner, first outwardly, then inwardly. Outwardly he deals with us through the oral word of the gospel and through material signs, that is, baptism and the sacrament of the altar. Inwardly he deals with us through the Holy Spirit, faith, and other gifts. But whatever their measure or order the outward factors should and must precede."[23]

Luther thus does not deny the inner working of the Spirit but binds the Spirit to the external means of Word and Sacrament. The intention is not to limit the freedom of the divine activity. Luther emphasized that God himself has established this "order" in this way. Due to his teaching concerning God, his distinction between the *Deus absconditus* and the *Deus revelatus*, as well as his Reformation distinction between law and gospel, Luther disputed the fanatics' right to appeal to special inspirations apart from revelation or Word and Sacrament. In Luther's eyes such a claim spells hubris.

To Luther's way of thinking, there is a further, important consequence: there is no special guidance of the Spirit in the life of the Christian. Exception is made only in the case of prayer. "Characteristically, Luther first instructs the one praying to hold to something firm, to a word of God, to the Our Father, etc." He was nonetheless able to report that in his prayer the Holy Spirit himself sometimes "preaches."[24] Luther was still far removed from the so-called fanatics, but also from the later pietists.

---

[21] *WA* 39 I, 370, 18-371, 1 (*1. Disputatio gegen die Antinomer*): "Sic Spiritus sanctus, quando scribit digito suo legem in tabulas Moysi lapideas, est in maiestate sua ac certe arguit peccata et terret corda. Quando vero involvitur linguis et donis spiritualibus, tum vocatur donum, sanctificat, vivificat. Sine isto Spiritu sancto, qui donum est, arguit lex peccatum, quia lex non est donum, sed Dei aeterni et omnipotentis verbum, qui est ignis conscientiis."

[22] *WA* 5, 477, 40-478, 3 (*Operationes in Psalmos,* 1519-1521): "Hoc semel pro omnibus de dextera dei dictum sit, nec enim alio quopiam quam verbo suo vivificat, gignit, alit, educat, exercet, protegit, servat et triumphat in aeternam vitam."

[23] *LW,* vol. 40, p. 146 (*Against the Heavenly Prophets,* 1525). *WA* 18, 136, 9-15.

[24] See K. D. Schmidt, "Luthers Lehre vom Heiligen Geist," 123-24, with reference to *WA* 38, 363 (*LW,* vol. 43, p. 198).

Finally, it is the peculiar office of the Spirit to comfort believers, make them alive, and sanctify them. Of course, toward them as well the Spirit exercises a punitive office; but this is his "alien" work. The Spirit's proper work is precisely a strengthening in faith, as Luther put it in his explanation to the Third Article.

> But the Holy Spirit has called me through the Gospel, enlightened me with his gifts, and sanctified and preserved me in true faith, just as he calls, gathers, enlightens, and sanctifies the whole Christian church on earth. . . . In this Christian church he daily and abundantly forgives all my sins, and the sins of all believers, and on the last day he will raise me and all the dead and will grant eternal life to me and to all who believe in Christ.[25]

Here too Luther shunned any pietistic narrowness: "Therefore to sanctify is nothing else than to bring us to the Lord."[26]

In this fashion Luther held fast to the Spirit as altogether person and altogether gift: person in the manner in which he comes to us and thus always remains the Lord; gift in the manner in which he brings us to Christ and preserves us in faith.

---

[25] *Book of Concord,* p. 345.
[26] *Book of Concord,* p. 415.

Chapter 25

HUMANITY AS
CREATURE OF GOD

THE CREATION OF THE WORLD

As often as particular aspects of Luther's view have been researched, until now
only David Löfgren has attempted a comprehensive description of Luther's theology of creation. Löfgren's intent was to pursue Luther's ideas throughout almost
all the important dogmatic themes, with a salvation-historical sketch as the basis.
In this way ideas customarily treated in a doctrine of creation are in the background.[1]

No doubt, Luther could develop the idea of the creation in areas for the most
part not dealt with under the rubric of creation, just as he elsewhere breached the
wall of specific doctrines.[2] Nevertheless, it is advisable, and not merely for reasons
of conceptual clarity, to give preference to his statements about the creation of the
world and humanity. In his catechisms but also in various lectures,[3] Luther dealt
chiefly with questions of the creation and preservation of the world and humanity,

---

[1] In this respect Löfgren's book, *Die Theologie der Schöpfung,* has been criticized in reviews.

[2] See also Hägglund, "Luthers Anthropologie," 63: "Theological anthropology does not consist of
isolated remarks on humans' conditions and qualities, which then are used as building blocks in theology, but it is integrated into the entire doctrine of creation and redemption."

[3] Naturally, Luther refers most often and in greater detail to questions of creation in his Genesis
lecture of 1535-1545. Still, the problems having to do with the transmission of the lecture are so com-
plicated that a description of Luther's idea of creation can only secondarily be supported by its statements. In his description, Hägglund has collected the most important text complexes where Luther
speaks of creation.

though here too he gave greater breadth to the idea of creation.[4] Particularly for this reason we may treat the creation and preservation of the world and humanity here.

In a host of places Luther spoke of the creation and of the preservation of the world, in the course of which he united the two activities respecting their content, though he distinguished them respecting the idea and the concept. For example, in the *Disputation Concerning Justification* (1536), he said: "That whatever God creates, he also preserves is simply true and must be granted, but still it does not follow that human nature is unspoiled, which is corrupted daily. For God has made creatures changeable. . . . For as he creates, so he preserves. Thus we have been created so that we can be changed."[5] Similarly, the Small Catechism distinguishes creation and preservation: "I believe that God has created me and all that exists; that he has given me and still sustains my body and soul, all my limbs and senses, my reason and all the faculties of my mind, together with food and clothing, house and home, family and property."[6] The uniqueness of Luther's exposition of the article on creation consists first in its existential reference, then in its inclusion of justification: "all this he does out of his pure, fatherly, and divine goodness and mercy, without any merit or worthiness on my part."[7]

Despite the emphasis on the existential, however, we may not overlook that this article has as its content the creation of the entire world as well as of all other living creatures. The statement on creation contains a series of important aspects that Luther emphasized continually in the most diffuse contexts.[8] First, it was directed against the Aristotelian idea of the eternity of the world. For this reason, the traditional formula *creatio ex nihilo* was especially important to Luther. It expresses God's absolute sovereignty, but also the world's finitude. In support of his statement regarding the *creatio ex nihilo* Luther appealed first to Psalm 33:9: "For he spoke, and it came to be; he commanded, and it stood forth"; next, to 2 Maccabees 7:28: "Look at the heaven and the earth and see everything that is in them, and recognize that God did not make them out of things that existed. Thus also mankind comes into being"; then to Romans 4:17: "[God] who gives life to the dead and calls into existence the things that do not exist."[9]

---

[4] See A. Peters, *Kommentar zu Luthers Katechismen,* edited by Gottfried Seebass. 3 vols. (Göttingen: Vandenhoeck & Ruprecht, 1990-94), 2:56-91.

[5] *LW,* vol. 34, pp. 176-77. *WA* 39 I, 107, 17-22: "Quicquid Deus creat, hoc conservat etiam, est simpliciter verum et concedendum, sed tamen non sequitur, naturam esse integram, quae quotidie corrumpitur. Deus enim creavit creaturas mutabiles. . . . Qualiter enim creat, taliter conservat; sic sumus creati, ut possimus mutari."

[6] *Book of Concord,* p. 345.

[7] Ibid.

[8] On this subject see Löfgren, *Die Theologie der Schöpfung bei Luther,* FKDG 10 (Göttingen: Vandenhoeck & Ruprecht, 1960), 21-37; Peters, *Kommentar,* 71-77.

[9] See *WA* 40 III, 154, 11-13 (*Vorlesung über die Stufenpsalmen,* 1532/1533): ". . . eus natura, ex nihilo omnia creare. Et propriissime eius natura: vocat, quae non, ut sint." (". . . his nature, to create everything from nothing. And it is most proper to his nature to call into being things that are not.")

Against dualistic notions of the world as created by an evil god, the significance of the statement on creation is that this world is ordered by and oriented to God. Time was also created with the world—for the creatures an insurmountable arrangement. It is not possible for humankind to entertain ideas about what is outside time and space. All attempts to get beyond the origin of the world are idle.[10]

Though Luther always emphasized that God created the world in freedom, he often said that God created the world and the creatures so that each might share in the struggle against the devil and on behalf of life. In the Genesis lecture he wrote: "God has created all these creatures to be in active military service, to fight for us continually against the devil."[11] For this interpretation Luther referred to the creation account in which the stars are called "the host" (*exercitus*) or the "militia" (*milicia*).[12]

The inference is that the entire created world has the task of cooperating with God. The creature's *cooperatio*, rejected with reference to justification, is now affirmed for the activity of all creation, thus also of humankind. Here too, of course, the boundaries should not be removed: "In all their working together there is one thing the creatures cannot do, they cannot produce or give life on their own; this the Creator has reserved to himself alone. He will have his creatures as 'coworkers,' not 'cocreators.'"[13]

This *cooperatio* occurs in the world at various levels: at the lowest level of the nonhuman, in the temporal as well as in the spiritual realm. Even the angels are set within this all-embracing struggle.[14] Everything belonging to creation in one way or another participates in this comprehensive task. Even when persons at all three levels persist in acting contrary to the divine commission by misusing the nonhuman creatures, or perverting the temporal or spiritual order, not only their task but also their capacity for *cooperatio* with God ultimately remains in force.

Luther expresses himself similarly with reference to Christ, *WA* 40 III, 90, 10: "Et eius officium proprium, quia est deus: ex nihilo omnia etc." ("And because he is God, his proper work is that everything [comes] from nothing, etc."). *WA* 39 I, 470, 1-4 (2. Antinomer disputation): "nihil et omnia sunt unsers herrgots materia. Nam ipse ex omnibus facit nihil et ex nihil facit omnia. Haec opera sunt creatoris, non nostra." ("Nothing and everything are the materials of our Lord God. For he makes nothing from everything and everything from nothing. These are the Creator's works, not ours.") See *WA TR* 6 Nr. 6515. See also Althaus, *Theology of Martin Luther*, 119-20.

[10] *WA* 12, 445, 1-5 (sermon, 1523): "vor Got ist der anfang der welt ya so nahet als das ende, tausent jar als eyn tag, und Adam, der am ersten geschaffen ist, als der letzt mensch, der da geborn wird werden; dann er sicht dy zeit also an, wie des menschen auge zway dinge, die weyt von eynander synd, yn eym augenplick zusamen bringt." ("Before God the beginning of the world is in fact as near as the end, a thousand years are as a day, and Adam, first to be created, is last to be born. For he sees time just as the eye in a single moment brings together two things that are far apart.")

[11] *LW*, vol. 1, p. 74. *WA* 42, 56, 30-31: "Deus creavit istas creaturas omnes, ut stent in milicia et sine fine pugnent contra Diabolum pro nobis."

[12] *LW*, vol. 1, p. 74. *WA* 42, 56, 22-27.

[13] Peters, *Kommentar*, 74 by way of reference to *WA* 47, 857, 35 (sermon, 1539): "as coworkers, not cocreators."

[14] On this subject see Peters, *Kommentar*, 73.

HUMANITY IN THE WORLD

Luther's statements about human creation must be seen first in connection with his view of the world's creation, and second within the context of the history of salvation. What theology has to say about creation is a prius compared to statements about the fall, sin, and the sending of Jesus Christ. Hence, from the outset, a theological anthropology is structured differently than a philosophical anthropology: It is oriented in much more unified fashion.[15] Sin and justification thus stand at the midpoint of Luther's anthropology. Of course, the temporal and material prius is and remains the fact that God created humankind good and assigned it specific tasks in the world.

A few aspects of Luther's statements concerning humanity deserve special emphasis. In his anthropology he took up in detail the lower and higher powers of the soul as well as human corporeality,[16] but on the basis of the creation narrative as well as of numerous other biblical statements he put greatest stress on humanity's peculiar position within the creation, due to its likeness to God. The significance of the image of God is that humanity was not only created for earthly life as were the beasts, but was destined for something higher. In *The Disputation on Justification* (1536) we read: "Man was created in the image of God, in the image of righteousness, of course, of divine holiness and truth, but in such a way that he could lose it."[17] The advantage of humans over the beasts was their capacity or possibility for immortality: Following his earthly life, Adam was to lead an eternal, spiritual life with God.[18] He was

---

[15] Chiefly Gerhard Ebeling worked this out in his detailed commentary on *Disputatio de homine* (1536): *Lutherstudien,* vol. 2, part 3.

[16] See Wilfried Joest, *Ontologie der Person bei Luther* (Göttingen: Vandenhoeck & Ruprecht, 1967); G. Ebeling, *Lutherstudien,* vol. 2, part 2 (1982).

[17] *LW,* vol. 34, p. 177. *WA* 39 I, 108, 5-8: "Homo conditus est ad imaginem Dei. Ergo imago Dei fuit. Hoc sequitur, nam homo erat conditus ad imaginem Dei, ad imaginem scilicet iustitiae, sanctitatis et veritatis divinae, sed ita, ut eam amittere posset." On Luther's view of the *imago Dei* see Ivar Asheim, *Glaube und Erziehung bei Luther: Ein Beitrag zur Geschichte des Verhältnisses von Theologie und Pädagogik,* PF 17 (Heidelberg: Quelle & Meyer, 1961), 202-25.

[18] See, e.g., *LW,* vol. 1, p. 56 (*Lectures on Genesis, Chapters One to Five,* 1535-1536): "Adam was not to live without food, drink, and procreation. But at a predetermined time, after the number of saints had become full, these physical activities would have come to an end; and Adam, together with his descendants, would have been translated to the eternal and spiritual life"; *WA* 42, 41, 36-43, 11, esp. p. 42, 25-28: "Nam Adam non erat sine cibo, potu et generatione victurus. Cessassent autem ista corporalia praefinito tempore post impletum numerum Sanctorum, et Adam cum posteritate sua esset translatur ad aeternam et spiritualem vitam." *LW,* vol. 1, p. 57: "Thus Adam had a twofold life: a physical one and an immortal one, though this was not yet clearly revealed, but only in hope. Meanwhile he would have eaten, he would have drunk, he would have labored, he would have procreated, etc. In brief words I want to call attention to these facts concerning the difference which God makes through His counsel, by which He sets us apart from the rest of the animals with whom He lets us live"; *WA* 42, 43, 7-11: "Habuit igitur Adam duplicem vitam: animalem et immortalem, sed nondum revelatam plane sed in spe. Interim edisset, bibisset, laborasset, generasset etc. Haec paucis admonere volui de dif-

"capable of immortality" (*capax immortalitatis*).[19]

In making this statement Luther was aware that all statements about the condition of the first man prior to the fall are inappropriate insofar as the object referred to is no longer known. For this reason he may not be understood as intending to historicize the Genesis narratives of humanity's creation. On the other hand, he guarded against construing the narrative in purely symbolic fashion. What concerned him here is "that we, who are alive now, who hear the Word, are drawn into what is said of Adam."[20] If in late scholasticism the image of God was interpreted in primarily psychological categories, and thus was viewed chiefly in terms of the rational capacity, Luther interpreted the image within the context of the history of salvation, thus viewing the person as a unity.[21]

Obviously, the gift of *ratio* is of particular significance.[22] By *ratio* Luther meant the human faculty for knowing. It thus can denote "understanding" as well as "reason." It is the greatest and most important gift God has given to humankind. Because of this gift, humankind is God's peculiar creation.[23] In his *Gospel for the Main Christmas Service*, Luther wrote: "No man exists in whom there is not the natural light of reason; this is the sole ground for calling him human and for his having human worth."[24]

It is the particular task of the *ratio* to establish humanity's lordship over the earth.

> It is certainly true that reason is the most important and the highest rank among all things and, in comparison with other things of this life, the best and something divine. It is the inventor and mentor of all the arts, medicines, laws, and of whatever wisdom, power, virtue, and glory men possess in this life. By virtue of this fact it ought to be named the essential difference by which man is distinguished from the animals and other things. Holy Scripture also makes it lord over the earth.[25]

---

ferentia ista, quam Deus facit per suum consilium, quo discernit nos ab aliis animalibus, cum quibus nos sinit vivere." In these statements Augustinian ideas about predestination and the predestined number of the saints are clearly in the air. On Luther's idea of immortality see Ebeling, *Lutherstudien,* vol. 2, part 2, 60-183.

[19] *LW,* vol. 1, p. 84. *WA* 42, 63, 37.

[20] Hägglund, "Luthers Anthropologie," 71.

[21] See ibid., 73-74.

[22] On what follows see Lohse, *Ratio und Fides*, 55-58.

[23] *LW,* vol. 1, p. 44: "Man is an extraordinary creature of God." *WA* 42, 33, 17-18: "hominem esse singularem creaturam Dei."

[24] *LW,* vol. 52, p. 60. *WA* 10 I, 1, 207, 5-7.

[25] *LW,* vol. 34, p. 137 (*The Disputation Concerning Man*, 1536); *WA* 39 I, 175, 9-16: "4. Et sane verum est, quod ratio omnium rerum res et caput et prae ceteris rebus huius vitae optimum et divinum quiddam sit. 5. Quae est inventrix et gubernatrix omnium Artium, Medicinarum, Iurium, et quidquid in hac vita sapientiae, potentiae, virtutis et gloriae ab hominibus possidetur. 6. Ut hinc merito ipsa vocari debeat differentia essentialis, qua constituatur homo, differre ab animalibus et rebus aliis. 7. Quam et scriptura sancta constituit talem dominam super terram."

On the basis of the *ratio* human beings take their place between angels and beasts. Their capacity for reflection and understanding links them to the angels. Their *anima,* which is *rationalis* (gifted with reason),[26] distinguishes them from the beasts. Luther's extraordinarily high view of reason is no mere inconsequential theologoumenon. It is an essential presupposition for his view of the authorities and temporal rule: due basically to the gift of reason, constituted authority is in position to perceive its tasks responsibly and competently, requiring no tutelage on the part of the hierarchy. Reason's independence toward spiritual rule is one of the essential consequences of this new portrait of humanity. What is also reflected here is the dovetailing of various doctrines.

The so-called orders of creation pose a special problem.[27] The doctrine of the orders arose in nineteenth-century neo-Lutheran theology. Its purpose was to single out particular life arrangements that none can escape since they have been established at creation, and among which are marriage, family, nation, state, economy, and temporal authority. Human life, so it was emphasized, is lived in the context of these orders, which must thus be respected as such. Connected with the question of orders were questions as to how they are to be recognized, whether they can be recognized only from the perspective of faith, or by, say, the married person independently of faith; further, how these orders relate to natural law; further yet, what changes such orders have undergone throughout history, and whether these changes have had any effect on their nature; and finally, how to conceive the relation between these orders of creation and the doctrine of the two kingdoms in particular. In all this, we should note that the question of the orders of creation has been heavily freighted with disputes over natural theology, particularly during the Third Reich.

We can only refer to the profusion of topics here without discussing them. As for Luther, there should be no doubt that he believed that at creation God established specific structures or orders indispensable to life, that not only Christians but even non-Christians can recognize and respect them, though their real meaning is disclosed only on the basis of faith. With regard to terminology, various concepts appear in Luther. At times, he spoke of estates, orders, institutions, offices, or hierarchies. We should note that he apparently never used the term *Ordnungen* (ranks). His term, *Orden* (orders), allows the idea of "putting in order" or of "arranging" to sound through. The concept "estate" or "station" differs fundamentally from the same term as used in the social sciences. That is, estates are not marked off from each other. According to Luther, a person may belong to several.

---

[26] *LW,* vol. 4, p. 208; *WA* 43, 285, 25-30; *LW,* vol. 1, p. 46; 42, 34, 37-35, 7; *LW,* vol. 2, p. 135; 42, 357, 14-22.

[27] See Franz Lau, "Schöpfungsordnung," *RGG* 5 (1961), 1492-94.

For Luther, moreover, three "estates" or "hierarchies" have greatest weight: the priestly office, the estate of marriage, and the temporal authority, and not necessarily in that order.[28] To the priestly estate belong not only pastors but also those responsible for the "community chest," including sextons, messengers, and servants active on behalf of the spiritual estate. To the marriage estate belong not only married persons but also children, servants, and even widows and virgins. Finally, to civil government belong city counselors, judges or officials, chancellors, and scribes, in addition to princes; likewise servants and maids who work for the government.

It is significant that among these three hierarchies or estates none is ranked above or over the others. Luther broke with the medieval idea that the spiritual estate is above the temporal, that the latter must serve the former. To the contrary, all three estates are equally foundational, though in the given instance each has a different task in the preservation of life. And, respecting their honor, they are equal.[29] To oppose them means to open the door to unrighteousness. Therefore: "God declares concerning these stations that they must remain if the world is to stand, even though many oppose and rage against them. Therefore the Psalmist says that His righteousness endures forever. All sects and man-made righteousness will finally perish, but these estates remain and preserve righteousness in the world."[30] Even after the fall these estates, hierarchies, or orders of creation are altogether in force. Naturally, they too are affected by sin, so that there is continual danger of perversion. At this point the concept of the orders encounters the greatest obstacle, since the term suggests that the order it denotes has been preserved intact since the fall. According to Luther, this is not at all the case. Surely, the offices or hierarchies remain intact, but the persons who exercise them are sinners just like all others. There is no unimpaired order of creation, though God's commission for preserving the world continues unaltered.

---

[28] *LW,* vol. 37, p. 364 (*Confession Concerning Christ's Supper,* 1528): "The office of priest, the estate of marriage, the civil government"; *WA* 26, 504, 30-31. See *LW,* vol. 41, p. 177 (*Of the Councils and Church,* 1539): hierarchies or "these three high divine governments"; *WA* 50, 652, 18-35. *LW,* vol. 3, p. 217 (*Lectures on Genesis, Chapters 18 to 20,* 1535-1545): "This life is profitably divided into three orders: (1) life in the home; (2) life in the state; (3) life in the church. To whatever order you belong—whether you are a husband, an officer of the state, or a teacher of the church—look about you, and see whether you have done full justice to your calling and there is no need of asking to be pardoned for negligence, dissatisfaction, or impotence"; *WA* 43, 30, 13-17. See Wilhelm Maurer, *Luthers Lehre von den drei Hierarchien und ihr mittelalterlicher Hintergrund,* SBAW.PPH 4 (Munich: Bayerischen Akademie der Wissenschaften, 1970); Reinhard Schwarz, "Luthers Lehre von den drei Ständen und die drei Dimensionen der Ethik," *LuJ* 45 (1978), 15-34 (both particularly on medieval preliminary forms of Luther's differentiation); Althaus, *Ethics of Martin Luther,* 36-42.

[29] *LW,* vol. 14, pp. 14-15 (*Commentary on Psalm 117,* 1530); *WA* 31, I, 233, 17-234, 34; *LW,* vol. 13, pp. 368-71 (*Commentary on Psalm 111,* 1530); *WA* 31 I, 408, 35-411, 34.

[30] *LW,* vol. 13, p. 358. *WA* 31 I, 400, 1-6.

Humans as creatures of God are under the divine command to exercise lordship over the world as God's representatives, so to speak, as well as to serve God. In *The Disputation Concerning Man* Luther first wrote: "Man is a creature of God consisting of body and a living soul, made in the beginning after the image of God, without sin, so that he should procreate and rule over the created things, and never die."[31] The human being is thus under a divine *mandatum* (commandment, task), not under a "law" in the actual sense, though for the first humans the divine word was at the same time law and gospel.[32] This *mandatum* takes on concretion precisely in the midst of one's station and calling.[33]

[31] *LW,* vol. 34, p. 138. *WA* 39 I, 176, 7-9: "21 . . . homo est creatura Dei, carne et anima spirante constans, ab initio ad imaginem Dei facta, sine peccato, ut generaret et rebus dominaretur nec unquam moreretur."

[32] See Löfgren, *Die Theologie,* 79-89.

[33] See Althaus, *Ethics of Martin Luther,* 38-39; Gustaf Wingren, *Luther on Vocation,* trans. Carl C. Rasmussen (Philadelphia: Muhlenberg, 1957).

Chapter 26

SIN

The Knowledge of Sin

In Luther's own biography as well as in the structuring of his new theology a radical view of sin had been given preeminence. It is not an exaggeration to state that in his Reformation theology this new view of sin comprises the actual motif for practically all other themes. Luther arrived at his new interpretation partly through critical self-examination and partly through intensive study of Paul. He began his lecture on Romans in 1515/1516 with these words: "The whole purpose and intention of the apostle in this epistle is to break down all righteousness and wisdom of our own . . . to blow (sins) up and to magnify them (that is, to cause them to be recognized as still in existence and as numerous and serious), and thus to show that for breaking them down Christ and His righteousness are needed for us."[1] This indicates the extraordinary importance of the awareness of one's sinfulness for Christian faith and all of theology.

For Luther it would be too easy a matter if theology were to furnish a definition by which the nature of sin could be comprehensively described. Certainly, all have a knowledge of sin or of individual sins, since the law is written in everyone's heart and the voice of conscience is continually heard. Yet it is true that "absolutely no man can ever discover or comprehend his wickedness, since it is infinite and eternal."[2]

---

[1] *WA* 56, 3, 6-11 (marginal gloss on Rom. 1:1); see *LW,* vol. 25, p. 3; *WA*, 157, 2-158, 14 (scholia on Rom. 1:1). See above, pp. 70-72. On the significance of the view of sin for all of Luther's theology, see E. Seeberg, *Luthers Theologie in ihren Grundzügen.* (Stuttgart: Kohlhammer, 1940); reprint 1950, 103-13, 103ff. Seeberg is clearly elaborating the difference between Luther and mysticism.

[2] *LW,* vol. 32, p. 240 (*Against Latomus,* 1521); *WA* 8, 115, 4-6: "Neque enim malum eius ullus hominum unquam investigare aut comprehendere penitus potuit, cum sit infinitum et aeternum."

This is true also of Christians. "Root sin, deadly and truly mortal, is unknown to men in the whole wide world."[3] The person as such has a most inaccurate clue to the nature and power of sin.[4] Knowledge of sin comes only through the Word of God.

From this point Luther arrives at the statement that sin must actually be believed. He had already defended this view in the Romans lecture of 1515/1516.[5] Similar statements can be elicited from his numerous other writings.[6] Particularly well known is the sentence in the Smalcald Articles (1537): "This hereditary sin is so deep a corruption of nature that reason cannot understand it. It must be believed because of the revelation in the Scriptures."[7]

THE NATURE OF SIN

However much Luther's self-examination is reflected in what he has to say about sin, what is unique about his understanding can be gleaned not from particular definitions but from the fact that he joined his interpretation to central biblical utterances appearing chiefly in the Psalter, in the Prophets, and quite especially in Paul. Of particular importance are statements such as that sin is "pride" or "self-will" (*superbia*), or, that the human is "flesh" or "self-righteous," and thus will not receive "righteousness" from God alone.

Some definitions that Luther gave to sin were, of course, not new as such, but they did in fact have a new meaning. The definition *peccatum radicale,* used as early as in the Romans lecture of 1515/1516, appears to be without a model in scholasticism.[8] It denotes the "root sin," thus the sin of Adam or "hereditary sin." The concept

[3] *LW,* vol. 34, p. 154 (*The Disputation Concerning Justification,* 1536); WA 39 I, 84, 10-11: "Peccatum radicale, capitale et vere mortale est incognitum hominibus in universo mundo." See *WA* 39 II, 365, 25-26 (*Promotionsdisputation von Petrus Hegemon,* 1545): "Homo sua natura non solum nescit, unde peccatum sit, sed ipsum peccatum nescit. Manet autem cognitio peccati in homine per verbum Dei." ("Man by nature not only does not know where sin comes from, but does not know his own sin. On the other hand, the knowledge of sin abides in man through the Word of God.")

[4] *WA* 39 II, 210, 25-26 (*Promotionsdisputation von Johannes Marbach,* 1543): "Ex quo patet, et nos non intelligere veram peccati definitionem, sed tantum simulacra et ambigua" ("From which it is clear that we do not understand the true definition of sin, but everything is shadows and uncertainties.") See the previous statement in ibid., 210, 20-22: "Si homo sentiret magnitudinem peccati, non viveret uno momento, tantam vim habet peccatum." ("Sin has such force that if a man were to know the magnitude of his sin he would not live one second.")

[5] *LW,* vol. 25, p. 215: "By faith alone we must believe that we are sinners, for it is not manifest to us." WA 56, 231, 6-11 (scholia on Rom. 3:5), lines 9-10: "sola fide credendum est nos esse peccatores, Quia non est nobis manifestum."

[6] See, e.g., *LW,* vol. 33, p. 225 (*Bondage of the Will,* 1526); WA 18, 742, 12-14; *LW,* vol. 12, p. 340 (*Commentary on Psalm 51,* 1532); WA 40 II, 370, 3-4.

[7] *Book of Concord,* p. 302.

[8] *LW,* vol. 25, p. 264; WA 56, 277, 12-13: identified here with *concupiscentia ad malum*; similarly in *LW,* vol. 25, p. 272; WA 56, 285, 15-16. See G. Ebeling, "Der Mensch," 3:77-78.

is intended to point to sin's continually begetting new sin. Hereditary sin is thus the *peccatum radicale*. This definition reflects a new point of departure over against the scholastic understanding. Luther saw an indissoluble connection between "hereditary sin" and individual sinful deeds, while for scholasticism humanity's entire condition worsened through hereditary sin, though individual sinful deeds occurred more or less independently of it.

The concepts *peccatum personale* and *peccatum naturale*, which also appear in Luther, were already in use in scholasticism.[9] Despite the identical terminology, one detects a different understanding: for scholasticism hereditary or original sin was *peccatum naturae* in terms of a weakening of human nature, while actual sin was the sin of the individual. For Luther hereditary or original sin, sin of nature or of person, described one's existence as sinner. "When scholasticism describes sin by means of the concept of person, it intends to accent human activity in contrast to the universal conditions of human nature. But when Luther describes sin by means of the same concept, he intends to distinguish the person as such from the person's deeds, thus not from an underlying nature, but in a certain sense from the culture which the person creates."[10]

Luther paraphrased this nature of sin in ever-new variations. "Sin, in the Scripture, means not only the outward works of the body but also all the activities that move men to do these works, namely, the inmost heart, with all its powers."[11] Sin is lodged in the inmost part, in the "heart." To a great extent it can enlist in its service works that are outwardly honorable. No work as such is immune to serving the self-willed person. In other words, the nature of sin is ultimately unbelief, the lack of trust in God, the absence of love for God. Of ingratitude Luther could say that it is the most disgraceful blasphemy and greatest dishonor toward God.[12]

Thus sin is the desire to set oneself in place of God, not allowing God to be one's God. Luther had this hubris in mind when he construed sin as self-will (*Ichwill*).

> But just as the adherents of the flesh feign love in tranquil times, so it is with joy too. They praise God and the gifts of God in men, but only till they are offended. Then the works of the flesh come rushing forth. They disparage the gifts of God which they had formerly praised. They are saddened if their disparagement meets with no success and if the reputation of their neighbor is not diminished. For no one believes how deep the malice of the flesh is, so many does it send smugly to destruction until they are tried and approved.[13]

[9] See Ebeling, "Der Mensch," 82-88, who cites specific evidence from Thomas.

[10] Ibid., 85.

[11] *LW,* vol. 35, p. 369 (*Preface of the Epistle of St. Paul to the Romans,* 1546); *WA DB* 7, 7, 27-29; the same text with a different orthography occurs as early as 1522).

[12] 3. *Antinomerdisputation, WA* 39 I, 580, 13-14: "Quod enim peccatum ingratitudine praesertim erga Deum maius?" ("For what sin is greater than ingratitude, especially toward God?")

[13] *LW,* vol. 27, p. 374 (*Lectures on Galatians,* 1519). *WA* 2, 593, 28-34.

Conversely, the chief thing is to praise God and the divine mercy day and night, even in the midst of the world's storms, even in the fiery furnace; to refrain from envying the neighbor's gifts; to rejoice over them as though they were one's own; and to praise God's gifts to the neighbor.[14]

Sin is consequently self-love (*amor sui*). In the last analysis, people will take pleasure in themselves and allow themselves to be adored.[15] Precisely those "good works" that are performed in this sense are an occasion for pride and self-presumption. This is what Luther meant when, as early as in his Romans lecture, he spoke of the *homo incurvatus in se* (the person turned in upon the self).[16] Luther interpreted the concept of "flesh" in this comprehensive way. Persons are "flesh" not merely in the sense that lower forces influence them in their willing and acting.[17] "Hereditary sin or natural sin or personal sin is the truly chief sin. If this sin did not exist, there would also be no actual sin. This sin is not committed, as are all other sins; rather it *is*. It lives and commits all sins and is the real essential sin which does not sin for an hour or for a while; rather no matter where or how long a person lives, this sin is there also."[18]

INHERITED SIN

Despite his new definition of the relation between inherited and actual sin, Luther's view of inherited sin did not differ from the tradition to any great degree. He also took literally the narrative of the fall: before the fall Adam was righteous, pious, and holy. What is significant, of course, is the assertion that even before the fall Adam did not really have a free will, since free will is ultimately a predicate of God.[19] Naturally, there is danger here of making God responsible for sin. Nevertheless, Luther could say that the devil sins by the will and permission of God,[20] though he often

---

[14] *LW,* vol. 27, p. 374. *WA* 2, 593, 25-28.

[15] *LW,* vol. 31, p. 46 (*Heidelberg Disputation,* 1518): "But this is completely wrong, namely to please oneself, to enjoy oneself in one's works, and to adore oneself as an idol"; *WA* 1, 358, 5-7: "Haec autem tota est perversitas, scilicet sibi placere fruique seipso in operibus suis seque idolum adorare."

[16] *LW,* vol. 25, p. 345. *WA* 56, 356, 5-6.

[17] See Erdmann Schott, *Fleisch und Geist nach Luthers Lehre: Unter besonderer Berücksichtigung des Begriffs "totus homo"* (Darmstadt: Wissenschaftliche Buchgesellschaft, 1928).

[18] *LW,* vol. 52, p. 152 (*Gospel for New Year's Day,* 1521/1522); *WA* 10 I, 1, 508, 20-509, 4.

[19] See above, p. 166-67.

[20] *LW,* vol. 33, p. 178 (*Bondage of the Will,* 1525): "In this way he finds the will of Satan evil, not because he creates it so, but because it has become evil through God's deserting it and Satan's sinning; and taking hold of it in the course of his working he moves it in whatever directions he pleases. Yet that will does not cease to be evil even under this movement of God"; *WA* 18, 711, 7-10: "Sic Satanae voluntatem malam inveniens, non autem creans, sed deserente Deo et peccante Satana malam factam arripit operando et movet quorsum vult, licet illa voluntas mala esse non desinat hoc ipso motu Dei." This significant statement raises the question as to whether Satan's evil will or God's permission takes precedence; the ablative absolute allows for either interpretation.

said that wanting to know more of this was prying. As for the devil's apostasy and influence on humans, Luther likewise intended to hold to the conviction that God is not the author of sin, but that the devil's sin did not occur in opposition to God's will. Apart from this, he cautioned against further curiosity, stating that we should hold solely to God's revealed will,[21] and with this took up the ancient church's motif of the *felix culpa* (happy guilt).

As to the transmission of sin to subsequent generations, Luther at times attempted to avoid a historicizing view. On the other hand, he could state with the traditional view that hereditary sin is transmitted through procreation. For example, he wrote in the Fasten Postille of 1527: "So it . . . is with inherited sin that we did not commit, but rather our parents, that we also must help to bear and pay for."[22] Luther explained the situation in this fashion: Originally, Adam and Eve had an "inherited righteousness," "but then as soon as they ate from the forbidden tree and sinned, just as soon this hereditary righteousness failed and was ruined. Then evil desires began to be roused and grow in them, then they were inclined to haughtiness, unchastity, lust of the flesh and all sins such as we find now."[23] It is interesting that wherever Luther discussed hereditary sin in greater detail, he unhesitatingly adopted two traditional views: first, he defined it as "a ruination of hereditary righteousness," in scholastic terms as a *carentia iustitiae originalis* (lack of original righteousness). Next, he stated that "in paradise we were punished through the first Adam's sin. And so it is called a hereditary sin that we did not commit, but carry with us from our parents, and it is no less reckoned to us than if we had done it ourselves."[24] Here Luther adopted the view of Duns Scotus and Occam that God "reckons" Adam's sin to subsequent generations. Here too it is clear that despite essentially new impulses, Luther could adopt scholastic views quite without scruple, provided they cohered with his Reformation theology.

In the lecture on Psalm 51 (1532) Luther spoke in similar fashion. Verse 5 in particular ("Behold, I was brought forth in iniquity, and in sin did my mother conceive me") led to more detailed reflection. At the same time Luther stated that *conceptio, augmentatio, nutritio in matris utero* (conception, growth, nutrition in the mother's womb) were all corrupted (*corrupta*) by hereditary sin. Everything

---

[21] See, e.g., *LW*, vol. 54, pp. 385-86: "If God should be asked at the last judgment, 'Why did you permit Adam to fall?' And he answered, 'In order that my goodness toward the human race might be understood when I gave my Son for man's salvation.'" *WA TR* 4 Nr. 5071, p. 643, 28-31: "Wenn Gott am jüngsten Tage und Gerichte gefragt wird: worum hat er Adam fallen lassen? wird er antworten und sagen: auf dass meine Güte gegen dem menschlichen Geschlechte könnte gesehen und erkannt werden in dem, dass ich meinen Sohn gebe zum Heiland der Welt."

[22] *WA* 17 II, 282, 26-28.

[23] Ibid., 283, 3, 13-17.

[24] Ibid., 282, 14-21.

occurred in the state of sin. "I" thus belong to the *massa perditionis*.[25] Naturally, Luther emphasized that marriage should not at all be spurned on this account. It has its own unquestioned value irrespective of the sinfulness attaching to it.

THE DEVIL

There is much of the traditional in Luther's idea of the devil.[26] The triad of sin, the world, and the devil, or flesh, world, and devil, was often combined as early as in medieval catechetics, from which Luther appropriated it for his own explanations to the catechism.[27] In Luther's own life the idea of the devil played a signal role: his struggle with the papacy and against the falsifying of the gospel, for which he reproached the popes, was also a struggle against the devil and his attack on the Christian church.[28] From this perspective, Heiko Oberman has attempted to interpret Luther's self-understanding and Reformation as a final, apocalyptic struggle.[29]

In his reference to the devil Luther primarily followed Scripture but also church tradition. We cannot, however, ignore a certain influence from the side of then current thought. When H.-M. Barth maintains that "Luther's idea of the devil emerges directly from his understanding of Christ or from his image of God, and must unconditionally be seen along with it,"[30] this is in essence the case but cannot account for all the aspects of Luther's idea.

---

[25] *WA* 40 II, 380, 11-381, 4 (cf. *LW,* vol. 12, pp. 347-48); see the entire context, *WA* 40 II, 380, 1-385, 3. There is a similar statement in *WA* 37, 55, 38-56, 2 (sermon, 1533): "For this is what Scripture says about our conception and birth . . . [in Psalm 51]: 'Behold, I was begotten of sinful seed, and in sin my mother conceived me.' That is, my mother contributed nothing but sinful flesh and blood. And my father, and what he did there, was also not pure. So both did the same thing through evil desire and impure nature. I am thus conceived of such flesh and blood. For this reason there can be nothing pure in me." Or, in *WA* 12, 403, 29-32 (sermon, 1523) Luther says of the virgin birth: "So the Holy Spirit has seen to it that a child should be born without sin, by a woman conceiving alone, not by the man. And if it still could happen that a woman could conceive without male seed, that birth would also be pure."

[26] See Harmannus Obendiek, *Der Teufel bei Martin Luther: Eine theologische Untersuchung* (Berlin: Furche Verlag, 1931); H.-M. Barth, *Der Teufel und Jesus in der Theologie Martin Luthers,* FKDG 1 (Göttingen: Vandenhoeck & Ruprecht, 1967), Ebeling, *Lutherstudien,* vol. 2, part 3, 246-71: "Luthers Reden vom Teufel"; Hans Christian Knuth, "Zwischen Gott und Teufel: Martin Luther über den Menschen," *Luther* 64 (1993), 10-23.

[27] See Johannes Meyer, *Historischer Kommentar zu Luthers Kleinem Katechismus* (Gütersloh: Gerd Mohn, 1929), 100-101; the triad of the powers of temptation, the devil, the world, and the flesh, is already present in Augustine.

[28] See, e.g., Luther's sentence in the Smalcald Articles, *Book of Concord,* p. 292: "On this article (of Jesus Christ) rests all that we teach and practice against the pope, the devil, and the world. Therefore we must be quite certain and have no doubts about it. Otherwise all is lost, and the pope, the devil, and all our adversaries will gain the victory." *BSLK,* no. 416, 3-6.

[29] Oberman, *Luther: Man between God and the Devil,* trans. Eileen Walliser-Schwarzbart (New Haven: Yale University Press, 1989). I have expressed certain reservations over the apocalyptic interpretation of Luther; see Lohse, *Luthers Selbsteinschätzung, in Evangelium in der Geschichte,* 158-75.

[30] H.-M. Barth, *Der Teufel und Jesus,* 13.

According to Luther, humans are positioned as it were between God and the devil. It is not true, as they suppose, that they are like observers in the battle between God and the devil. They must themselves do battle in the arena: one is "ridden"[31] either by God or by the devil. Humanity thus stands in the midst of a struggle between God and the powers hostile to God. We may thus speak of the devil only as those who are involved, who experience ever anew our own incapacity for coming to terms with those powers.

Compared with the tradition, Luther more strongly accented the power of the devil but also held to the idea that ultimately God alone has the power, even to the point of drawing the devil into the divine plan. Luther thus avoided an actual dualism, though some of his statements have a dualistic tone.

With respect to the devil as God's antagonist, Luther wrote that the devil is ultimately involved in everything opposed to God's will, doing injury to the world and humankind. He is the one at work behind the scenes, bringing misfortune, sickness, and death. For this view Luther took biblical support from Hebrews 2:14: "that he [Jesus] might destroy him who has the power of death, that is, the devil." Death and sin are thus the *regnum diaboli*.[32] Further, the devil not only misled the first humans to fall into sin but continually leads their descendants into temptation. It is he who is at work behind all false doctrine and heretics. Consequently not merely fanatics but the Roman church as well are ultimately instruments of the devil.[33] Indeed, the devil is at work in the church itself to falsify the pure Word.[34] Precisely for this reason it is necessary to be entirely certain in matters of doctrine.[35] The doctrine of justification

---

[31] *LW*, vol. 33, pp. 65-66 (*Bondage of the Will*, 1525). *WA* 18, 635, 17-22.

[32] *WA* 40 III, 68, 9-12 (*Vorlesung über die Stufenpsalmen,* 1532/1533): "Nos scimus, quod custodia divina sit omnipotens super nos, quia ex scriptura habemus hoc principium: Regnum diaboli est mortis, peccati. Stanti hoc principio sequitur, quod diabolus omni momento noceat." ("We know that God's custody over us is almighty, because we have this principle from Scripture: The devil's reign is one of death, of sin. This principle is always followed, that the devil does injury in every moment.")

[33] On this subject see Luther's incomparably harsh treatise *Against Hanswurst* (1541), *LW*, vol. 41, pp. 185-256; *WA* 51, 469-572. Not only Duke Heinrich von Braunschweig-Wolfenbüttel is apostrophized as "Lucifer's companion" (*LW*, vol. 41, p. 256; *WA* 51, 570, 31, and elsewhere), but "the devil and his Hanswurst" are continually named in one breath (e.g., *LW*, vol. 41, p. 188; *WA* 51, 472, 24). The Roman church also appears as the church of the devil (e.g., *LW*, vol. 41, pp. 191-94; *WA* 51, 475-77). In this connection Luther deliberately referred to Augustine's distinction between the two *civitates* in *LW*, vol. 41, p. 194: "For there are two kinds of churches stretching from the beginning of history to the end, which St. Augustine calls Cain and Abel. The Lord Christ commands us not to embrace the false church"; *WA* 51, 477, 13-15.

[34] *LW*, vol. 33, p. 258 (*Bondage of the Will*, 1525). *WA* 18, 764, 14-22.

[35] *WA* 39 II, 266, 9-13 (*Promotionsdisputation von Fabricius und Rapagelanus,* 1544): "Est ergo nobis quoque concessum, docere de nostro liberatore, quia compertum est, diabolum non dormire, sed semper rugire contra nos. Ideo non solum necesse est, ut nos simus certi de vera Euangelii doctrina sed etiam ut nostri posteri habeant aliquid veri et certi de religione." ("So we are also allowed to teach concerning our Liberator, because we know that the devil does not sleep but is always roaring against us.

is in particular peril.[36] The devil engages in continual attack on all other articles of doctrine, or calls them into question, and in doing so happily makes use of human reason. The devil's human agents stereotyped by Luther are the pope, the Turks, and the Jews: all of them are wiseacres.[37]

In conjunction with Paul's word in 2 Corinthians 4:4, Luther could go on to describe the devil as the god of this world: "The world and its god cannot and will not endure the Word of the true God, and the true God neither will nor can keep silence, so when these two Gods are at war with one another, what can there be but tumult in all the whole world?"[38] Luther's dualism extended to the idea that wherever God's kingdom is not present, there is necessarily the kingdom of the devil.[39]

Despite these rather far-reaching assertions Luther always maintained the Godhead of God. Though the devil is God's enemy and the power of good is locked in combat with the power of evil throughout history, even the devil must ultimately serve God, just as do the law and even death. It would be a sign of unbelief merely to trace the good to God and not also to receive what is difficult and evil from his hand. To be sure, God hides himself behind the dark powers in order to humble us. Yet in the midst of suffering we should flee to God's mercy and thus escape the divine wrath.[40] Death is a tool in God's hand, as Luther stated in his lecture on Psalm 90:3 (1534/1535): "Thou turnest man back to the dust." Through accepting this word we can conquer death by God's power.[41]

So it is not only necessary for us to be certain of the true doctrine of the gospel, but that our descendants may have something of the truth and certainty of religion.")

[36] *WA* 39 I, 420, 15-421, 4 (*2. Antinomerdisputation,* 1538).

[37] *WA* 37, 58,11-38 (sermon, 1533).

[38] *LW,* vol. 33, p. 52 (*Bondage of the Will,* 1535); *WA* 18, 626, 22-24: "Mundus et Deus eius verbum Dei veri ferre non potest nec vult, Deus verus tacere nec vult nec potest; quid iam illis duobus Diis bellantibus nisi tumultus fieret in toto mundo?"

[39] *LW,* vol. 33, p. 98 (*Bondage of the Will,* 1535): "For what is the whole human race without the Spirit but (as I have said) the kingdom of the devil . . . a confused chaos of darkness"; *WA* 18, 659, 6-7: "Quid enim est universum genus humanum, extra spiritum nisi regnum Diaboli . . . confusum cahos tenebrarum." *LW,* vol. 33, p. 227: "And if it is a stranger to the Kingdom and Spirit of God, it necessarily follows that it is under the kingdom and spirit of Satan, since there is no middle kingdom between the Kingdom of God and the kingdom of Satan, which are mutually and perpetually in conflict with each other"; *WA* 18, 743, 32-35: "Quodsi a regno et spiritu Dei alienum est, necessario sequi, quod sub regno et spiritu Satanae sit, cum non sit medium regnum inter regnum Dei et regnum Satanae, mutuo sibi et perpetuo pugnantia."

[40] *WA* 40 II, 417, 5-6 (*Vorlesung über Psalm 51,* 1532): "Deus dissimulat, donec per instrumenta humana nos humiliet, donec discamus sola misericordia confidere." ("God disguises himself, while he humbles us through human means, until we learn to trust his mercy alone." Cf. *LW,* vol. 12, p. 374.) *WA* 40 III, 517, 4-5 (*Vorlesung über Psalm 90,* 1534/1535): "Sic non cogitandum de Deo, ut tantum reservemus misericordiam etc.; hoc est declinare et velle effugere, effugere iram divinam." ("We should not think of God in such a way that we keep aloof from such great mercy; this means to turn aside and wish to escape, to escape the divine wrath." Cf. *LW,* vol. 13, p. 96.)

[41] *WA* 40 III, 517, 13-518, 11.

Next, Luther maintained the Godhead of God by continually emphasizing that redemption through Christ abolishes enslavement under the devil's power. Just as we grasp the nature of sin ultimately only by faith, so by faith we are set free through Christ. Through Christ the devil's power has already come to an end. Yet throughout history the battle is still being waged between God and the devil, and in this battle humans, as all other creatures, are engaged.

THE BOUND WILL

If Adam prior to the fall was free to accept the divine grace and thus keep the commandments of God,[42] with the fall this limited freedom was altogether lost. Since the 1515/1516 Romans lecture, and for the rest of his life, Luther polemicized in the harshest manner against assigning fallen humanity a free will. Whether in the *Heidelberg Disputation*,[43] the *Defense and Explanation of All the Articles* (1521),[44] the debate with Latomus (1521),[45] or *The Bondage of the Will* (1525),[46] to name only these signally important writings, Luther always held that his position on the human will's bondage to sin was the chief question in dispute between him and Rome.

For Luther the following viewpoints were decisive. First, he referred to the witness of Scripture, particularly to Paul's Epistle to the Romans, in which chapters 1-4, as well as 7, set forth humans' total incapacity for achieving salvation on their own. The decision as to the correctness or narrowness of Luther's view rests on his exposition of the relevant scriptural statements. In his debate with Erasmus, he referred mainly to the fact that any other view would ultimately render the redemption through Christ superfluous.[47] Next, if after the fall humans were in possession of some freedom of will enabling them to accept the grace of God on their own, then the certainty of God's promise of grace would also depend on them, and as a result never really yield assurance of salvation.

Luther, however, avoided the danger of denying to humans a passive capacity for receiving divine grace. Leaning on the scholastic habit of referring to an *aptitudo passiva* (passive capacity or aptitude), he wrote in *The Bondage of the Will*: "If the power of free choice were said to mean that by which a man is capable of being taken hold of by the Spirit and embued with the grace of God, as a being created for eternal life or death, no objection could be taken. For this power or aptitude, or as the Sophists

---

[42] See above, pp. 239-41.

[43] See thesis 13 in *LW*, vol. 31, p. 40. *WA* 1, 354, 5-6.

[44] *WA* 7, 94-151.

[45] *LW*, vol. 31, pp. 137-260. *WA* 8, 43-128.

[46] *LW*, vol. 33, pp. 3-295. *WA* 18, 600-787.

[47] On this subject see particularly Althaus, *Paulus und Luther über den Menschen* (Gütersloh: Mohn, 1951); Lohse, *Lutherdeutung heute* (Göttingen: Vandenhoeck & Ruprecht, 1968). On Luther's position in the debate with Erasmus, see above, p. 167.

say, this disposing quality or passive aptitude, we also admit."[48] At the same time, Luther expressly emphasized that this *aptitudo passiva* distinguishes humans from trees and beasts. Here the agreement between Luther and scholasticism as well as between Luther and Erasmus might have been much greater than was clear in their dispute over the question of the freedom of the will.

---

[48] *LW,* vol. 33, p. 67. *WA* 18, 636, 16-20: "si vim liberi arbitrii eam diceremus, qua homo aptus est rapi spiritu et imbui gratia Dei, ut qui sit creatus ad vitam vel mortem aeternam, recte diceretur; hanc enim vim, hoc est, aptitudinem, seu ut Sophistae loquuntur dispositivam qualitatem et passivam apti-tudinem et nos confitemur." By "sophists" Luther might well have had Bonaventure in mind: Sent. 2 dist. 29 art. 1 qu. 1 concl.; *Bonaventura, Opera Omnia,* Quaracchi, 2:695-96. See *Martin Luther—Studi-enausgabe,* 3, 208, n. 234.

Chapter 27

JUSTIFICATION

The Theological Function of the Doctrine of Justification

There is no doubt that the heart and soul of Luther's Reformation theology is the article on justification. If his theology has its peculiarity not least in the fact that all its topics are intimately linked, so that ultimately none may be treated in isolation, then in a quite special way the doctrine of justification is decisive for all theological questions, for opening as well as carrying on their discussion. It is with this doctrine that "the church stands or falls," as the well-known formula of Reformation theology reads.[1] Or, Luther said of this article that it is "the central article of our teaching," "the sun, the day, the light of the church."[2] In a disputation of 1537, he stated: "The article of justification is master and

---

[1] In his lecture on the *Stufenpsalmen* of 1532/1533, *WA* 40 III, 352, 1-3, Luther already stated: "Sic audivistis . . . quod iste versus [scil. Ps. 130:4] sit Summa doctrinae Christianae et ille sol, qui illuminat Sanctam ecclesiam dei, quia isto articulo stante stat Ecclesia, ruente ruit Ecclesia." ("So you have heard . . . that this verse [Ps. 130:4] is the sum of Christian doctrine and that sun which shines on the Holy Church of God; for when this article stands, also the church stands; when this article falls, the church falls also.") See Friedrich Loofs, "Der articulus stantis et cadentis ecclesiae," *ThStKr* 90 (1917), 323-420.

[2] *WA* 40 III, 335, 5-10: "Iste Psalmus [scil. Psalm 130] est de electissimis et principalibus psalmis, qui tractat illum principalem locum doctrinae nostrae, nempe iustificationem. Sic enim audistis et sepe predicatur, quod ille unicus locus conservat Ecclesiam Christi; hoc amisso amittitur Christus et Ecclesia nec relinquitur ulla cognotio doctrinarum et spiritus. Ipse sol, dies, lux Ecclesiae et omnis fiduciae iste articulus." ("This psalm is among the choicest and chief psalms, which deals with that central article of our teaching, that is, justification. For so you have heard, and it is always preached, that this one article preserves the church of Christ; when it is lost, Christ and the church are lost, nor is there any knowledge of doctrine or of the Spirit left. This article is itself the sun, the day, the light of the church and of all believers.")

prince, lord, leader and judge of all kinds of teachings, which preserves and guides all churchly teaching and establishes our consciences before God."[3]

It was the first time in all the history of theology and dogma that the decisive truth of Christian faith was concentrated in such fashion on one specific article. Not in Augustine or Peter Lombard or Thomas Aquinas or Bonaventure, to name but a few, is the entirety of theological reflection determined from such a center, however defined. Prior to the sixteenth century, the doctrine of justification never assumed a significance even remotely comparable to that in Luther. Since Augustine and his dispute with Pelagius, the doctrine of sin and grace had been the continual object of reflection, particularly in scholasticism. The doctrine had been variously developed and particular aspects obviously discussed that Luther treated in a new way. Yet such concentration on one particular article as we find in Luther is without precedent.

This concentration must be evaluated from two aspects. First, the article of justification is not a teaching to be treated relatively loosely alongside others. It is ultimately "the formal expression of the new preaching of Christ."[4] The article is thus intended to develop the Second Article concerning Jesus Christ toward the question of sin and grace, damnation and salvation. In his own life, but likewise also in his Scripture study, Luther set the question of salvation under this point of view. Next, during the indulgence controversy, Luther came to the conclusion that in the church and theology of his time the Second Article was in fact neglected. As a result, the doctrine of justification took on primary significance in theological controversy. That the tradition had given relatively little thought to it, but that Luther supported himself totally on Holy Scripture, gave enormous weight to this article as the genuine shibboleth.

We must note further that Luther's statements on justification are to be seen against the horizon of the last judgment. He had no interest in reflecting on a psychological event within the person being justified, and none in the question as to how, if the will is bound, the person participates in it. What concerned him is how one may appear before God in the judgment. "The article of justification is nothing else than faith in Christ, when this is properly understood."[5] This also means that the article for its part may not be loosed from statements about Christ. Only as unfolding the comprehensive significance of Christ's saving work can it be appropriately treated.

One significant conclusion to be drawn is that for Luther the doctrine of justification did not involve some sort of definition or formula.[6] He could totally dispense

---

[3] WA 39 I, 205, 2-5 (*Vorrede zur Promotionsdisputation von Palladius und Tilemann,* 1537): "Articulus iustificationis est magister et princeps, dominus, rector et iudex super omnia genera doctrinarum, qui conservat et gubernat omnen doctrinam ecclesiasticam et erigit conscientiam nostram coram Deo."

[4] E. Wolf, *Peregrinatio,* [1:] 30, n. 2; similarly *Peregrinatio,* 2:19.

[5] Althaus, *Theology of Martin Luther,* trans. Robert C. Schultz (Philadelphia: Fortress Press, 1966), 225. It was chiefly A. Peters who in his various investigations made clear that the article on justification is always to be seen against the horizon of the judgment.

[6] This fact might furnish one of the reasons why there is as yet no agreement as to the time of the Reformation breakthrough; see above, pp. 85-88.

with concepts relevant to the theological discipline and still develop the Reformation view, as he did in his Small Catechism. Even the terminology of the discipline can be varied. For example, the word *iustificare* has various meanings. Luther defined it as a being declared righteous by God.[7] On the other hand, he could define it as the event by which one is "acquitted," changed, and renewed by virtue of the divine promise and grace. In the latter instance, justification is understood as a "process" extending over all of life, reaching its goal only in the resurrection.[8] Any description of Luther's doctrine must guard against abbreviating this variety, or against summarizing it in mere formulas, however carefully defined.[9] Characteristic of this breadth of interpretation is Luther's statement that what is at issue in justification is that "by faith we get a new and clean heart and that God will and does account us altogether righteous and holy for the sake of Christ, our mediator."[10]

Only by a strict orientation to the subject matter does the oft-asserted principle apply that a link to the doctrine of justification must always be forged when evaluating separate questions of doctrine in Luther. When this does not occur, Luther's position is caricatured. Thus, coherent with the enormous concentration of all his theological work is its great breadth, with the result that all the variety and abundance of the various themes and tasks of theology are retained and in each instance intensively discussed.

THE IMPUTATION OF "ALIEN RIGHTEOUSNESS"

With reference to Paul,[11] Luther stressed first that we cannot be righteous through our own works, but that only faith in the God who justifies the godless "is

[7] So, e.g., in the 1515/1516 Romans lecture, *LW,* vol. 25, p. 33; *WA* 56, 39, 8-9 (line gloss on Rom. 3:28). Here *iustificare* is equated with *Iustum apud Deum reputari.* On this subject see the exposition in the scholia, p. 264, 21-267, 7. Similar statements appear in Luther in great number.

[8] Also in this sense in the Romans lecture: *LW,* vol. 25, p. 260; *WA* 56, 272, 3-273, 2 (scholia on Rom. 4:7). From a later period *The Disputation Concerning Justification,* 1536, may perhaps be cited, *LW,* vol. 34, p. 152: "For we perceive that a man who is justified is not yet a righteous man, but is in the very movement or journey toward righteousness"; *WA* 39 I, 83, 16-17: "Iustificari enim hominem sentimus, hominem nondum esse iustum, sed esse in ipso motu seu cursu ad iustitiam." *LW,* vol. 34, p. 167: "and then at last we shall be made perfectly righteous"; *WA* 39 I, 98, 10-11: "et tunc demum perfecte iustificabimur."

[9] What little value Luther gave to mere formulas is clearest from what he says in the Smalcald Articles. On the one hand he said of the "first and chief article" concerning Jesus Christ: "On this article rests all that we teach and practice against the pope, the devil, and the world" (*Book of Concord,* p. 292). On the other, among articles that can be discussed with learned and reasonable people of the opposite side, he included the question: *How Man Is Justified before God, and His Good Works* (*Book of Concord,* p. 315). Accordingly, Luther was thoroughly prepared to deal with individual formulations when defining justification.

[10] *Book of Concord,* p. 315.

[11] See particularly Rom. 3:28–4:25. Rom. 4:5: "And to one who does not work but trusts him who justifies the ungodly, his faith is reckoned as righteousness."

reckoned as righteousness." In this connection the concepts *reputare* and *imputare* play a signal role.

The question from where Luther appropriated these concepts has been discussed often.[12] On occasion, Augustine could use them. Since Luther later made repeated reference to Augustine's significance for the origin and formation of his theology, and especially of his doctrine of justification,[13] Augustinian influence is altogether probable. In Occamism as well the concept *reputare* was used, though as a rule the term *acceptare* was employed.[14] This suggests that it was chiefly the biblical text itself that furnished Luther his stimulus. The Vulgate version of Romans 4:5 uses the term *reputare*: "To the one . . . who trusts in him [God] who justifies the ungodly, his faith is counted as righteousness." Luther thus interpreted the Greek term *logizetai* in terms of the Latin *reputatur*, reflecting the influence of the tradition of Augustine's and Occam's ideas on the subject. What is new is that Luther furnished the term *reputare/imputare* with its content. At issue is the "acquittal" of the guilty one, or the promise of the grace of God.

When Luther described faith in this way as the reception of this promise, this may not be understood to mean that he substituted faith for works. Faith would then be construed as a "work" needing to be performed on one's own in order to receive divine grace. Rather, faith here denotes disavowal of one's own performance or will-to-be-in-the-right as well as trust in grace alone. This faith is possible only as a response to the divine word of forgiveness. Word and faith are thus in a mutual relation, in which the Word always has preeminence. Paul Althaus has correctly stated: "It is . . . not enough to say that faith receives justification, or, that one receives justification by faith. We must state it more precisely, in Luther's terms: Justification is received by faith, that is, in the shape of faith."[15] This way of speaking of the "alien" righteousness of Christ as received by faith is intended to retain the difference from the scholastic idea of grace as *habitus*,[16] and also to express the freedom of the divine gift of grace. In this sense Luther could hark back to the old idea of the "happy exchange," or even to Anselm's doctrine of satisfaction, or, absent any reference to older imprecise attempts, could state again and again that faith seizes hold of Christ. "Therefore faith justifies because it takes hold of and possesses this treasure, the present Christ."[17] In other words, in faith Christ is present. This is the decisive content of justification and at the same time the basis for one's renewal.

---

[12] See, among others, Matthias Kroeger, *Rechtfertigung und Gesetz: Studien zur Entwicklung der Rechtfertigungslehre beim jungen Luther*, FKDG 20 (Göttingen: Vandenhoeck & Ruprecht, 1968), 72-85; Theobald Beer; Otto Hermann Pesch, *Hinführung zu Luther* (1982; 2d ed., Mainz: Matthias-Grünewald, 1983), 314-15.

[13] See above, p. 75.

[14] See above, p. 22.

[15] Althaus, *The Theology of Martin Luther*, 230-31.

[16] See above, pp. 18-21, as well as pp. 59-61.

[17] *LW*, vol. 26, p. 130 (*Lectures on Galatians, Chapters One to Four*, 1535); *WA* 40 I, 229, 4-5: "Ideo iustificat fides, dicimus, quia habet illum thesaurum, quia Christus adest."

JUSTIFICATION AND THE NEW EXISTENCE

For a long time, the fact that for Luther justification involved not merely forgiveness of sins or acquittal but also renewal has not been sufficiently appreciated. Melanchthon restricted the doctrine entirely to the imputation of Christ's righteousness.[18] Following him, Lutheran theology long advocated merely the "forensic" view of justification. It was Karl Holl who first insisted that for Luther justification ultimately embraces the person's total renewal up to the consummation.[19] Actually, as Holl had indicated, Luther developed this comprehensive idea as early as in his 1515/1516 Romans lecture.[20]

Luther expressed this indissoluble connection between justification as acquittal and renewal in several variations. In the Galatians commentary of 1519, for example, he wrote: "Therefore just as the name of the Lord is pure, holy, righteous, true, good, etc., so, if it touches, or is touched by, the heart (which happens through faith), it makes the heart entirely like itself."[21] Somewhat later he wrote: "Every one who believes in Christ is righteous, not yet fully in point of fact, but in hope. For he has begun to be justified and healed."[22] Or, in connection with Galatians 2:20, Luther emphasized that Christ lives in the believer, makes his dwelling in him through faith.[23] Or, in the 1522 preface to Romans he wrote:

> Faith, however, is a divine work in us which changes us, makes us to be born anew of God, John 1 [:12-13]. It kills the old Adam and makes us altogether different men, in heart and spirit and mind and powers; and it brings with it the Holy Spirit.

[18] See, e.g., *Book of Concord*, p. 30: "It is also taught among us that we cannot obtain forgiveness of sin and righteousness before God by our own merits, works, or satisfactions, but that we receive forgiveness of sin and become righteous before God by grace, for Christ's sake, through faith when we believe that Christ suffers for us and that for his sake our sin is forgiven." *CA* 4: "Item docent, quod homines non possunt iustificari coram Deo propriis viribus, meritis aut operibus, sed gratis iustificentur propter Christum per fidem, cum credunt se in gratiam recipi et peccata remitti propter Christum." See *Loci praecipui theologici* (1559), ed. Hans Engelland, *Melanchthons Werke*, 2/2 (Gütersloh: Gütersloher Verlagshaus Mohn, 1952), 359, 10-12: "Iustificatio significat remissionem peccatorum et reconciliationem seu acceptationem personae ad vitam aeternam" ("Justification signifies the forgiveness of sins and reconciliation or acceptance of the person unto eternal life"). At times Melanchthon also held to a broader understanding. See the Apology, IV, 72, *Book of Concord*: "And 'to be justified' means to make unrighteous men righteous or to regenerate them, as well as to be pronounced or accounted righteous." "Et quia iustificari significat ex iustis iustos effici seu regenerari, significat et iustos pronuntiari seu reputari."

[19] See Karl Holl, *Gesammelte Aufsätze zur Kirchengeschichte* (Tübingen: Mohr, 1921; 7th ed. 1948), 1:111-54, esp. 117-26.

[20] See pp. 74-78 above.

[21] *LW*, vol. 27, p. 221. *WA* 2, 490, 23-25: "Sicut ergo nomen domini est purum, sanctum, iustum, verax, bonum etc., ita si tangat tangaturque corde (quod fit per fidem) omnino facit cor simile sibi."

[22] *LW*, vol. 27, p. 227. *WA* 2, 4495, 1-2: "Omnis qui credit in Christum iustus est, nondum plene in re, sed in spe. Caeptus est enim iustificari et sanari."

[23] *LW*, vol. 27, p. 238: "Besides, the righteous man himself does not live; but Christ lives in him,

O, it is a living, busy, active, mighty thing, this faith. It is impossible for it not to be doing good works incessantly. It does not ask whether good works are to be done, but before the question is asked, it has already done them.[24]

In the large commentary on Galatians Luther wrote: "Therefore Christian faith is not an idle quality or an empty husk in the heart . . . it is a sure trust and firm acceptance in the heart. It takes hold of Christ."[25] Again, in the *Disputation Concerning Justification* (1536) he stated: "We perceive that a man who is justified is not yet a righteous man, but is in the very movement or journey toward righteousness."[26] Or again, "Sin remains, then, perpetually in this life, until the hour of the last judgment comes and then at last we shall be made perfectly righteous."[27] Other concepts that express the same idea refer to "putting Christ on." The Galatians commentary of 1519 stated that "to put Christ on is to put on righteousness, truth, and every grace, and the fulfillment of the whole law."[28] Or it reads that "you are righteous . . . because by believing in Christ you have put on Christ."[29] Still other concepts may be cited that simply register the profusion of the various biblical terms but always denote an all-embracing renewal beginning with faith in Christ and embracing the Christian's entire life.

Still and all, what Luther had elaborated in his Romans lecture remained in force,[30] that is, that the justified "is at the same time righteous and a sinner": righteous insofar as God imputes the alien righteousness of Christ but in oneself as such a sinner. Both apply in the total sense: "For this is true, that according to the divine reckoning we are in fact and totally righteous, even though sin is still present. . . . So we are in fact [at the same time] and altogether sinners."[31]

---

because through faith Christ dwells in him and pours His grace into him, through which it comes about that a man is governed, not by his own spirit but by Christ's." *WA* 2, 502, 12-14: "Tum vivit iustus non ipse, sed Christus in eo, quia per fidem Christus inhabitat et influit gratiam, per quam fit, ut homo non suo sed Christi regatur."

[24] *LW,* vol. 35, p. 370. *WA DB* 7, 10, 6-12.

[25] *LW,* vol. 26, p. 129. *WA* 40 I, 228, 12-15: "Fides non est aliqua otiosa qualitas in corde . . . sed . . . est quaedam fiducia cordis et firmitas assensus quo apprehendo Christum."

[26] *LW,* vol. 34, p. 152. *WA* 39 I, 83, 16-17: "Iustificari enim hominem sentimus, hominem nondum esse iustus, sed esse in ipso motu seu cursu ad iustitiam."

[27] *LW,* vol. 34, p. 167. *WA* 39 I, 98, 9-11: "Igitur perpetuo in hac vita manet peccatum, donec venerit hora extremi iudicii, et tunc demum perfecte iustificabimur."

[28] *LW,* vol. 27, p. 279. *WA* 2, 529, 30-31: "Christum autem induere est iusticiam, veritatem omnemque gratiam totiusque legis plenitudinem induere."

[29] *LW,* vol. 27, p. 280. *WA* 2, 530, 3-4: "Iustus es . . . quia in Christum credens Christum induisti."

[30] *LW,* vol. 25, p. 260. *WA* 56, 272, 3-273, 2.

[31] *WA* 39 I, 563, 13-564, 4 (*3. Antinomerdisputation*): "Nam hoc verum est, quod reputatione divina sumus revera et totaliter iusti, etiamsi adhuc adsit peccatum. . . . Sic etiam revere sumus et totaliter peccatores."

It was chiefly Wilfried Joest who made clear that these various statements must always be seen unabbreviated, though indissolubly connected: the "total" and the "partial aspect," that is, that the Christian in a total sense is both sinner and righteous, but likewise through the divine justifying and making righteous is in a "partial" sense still sinner and in a "partial" sense already righteous.[32]

Faith and Works

Compared with the tradition, but also with some New Testament writings, Luther seldom spoke of "works." Characteristically, he preached only once on the pericope of the world judgment in Matthew 25:31-46,[33] dealing, of course, with the point of the text regarding the inquiry into deeds of love for the neighbor at the last judgment, and for his part stressing that works should never be isolated from faith. For this reason Walther von Loewenich gives the following opinion: "We might suppose that at this point Luther would have to come radically to terms with the idea of judgment according to works, but are really disappointed after reading this sermon."[34]

In fact, Luther always claimed that where one's status before God is involved, works are not decisive: here, only justification *sola fide* applies.[35] Only in a very limited sense did he hold to the "necessity" of works. In the *Disputation Concerning Justification* (1536) he wrote:

> I reply to the argument, then, that our obedience is necessary for salvation. It is, therefore, a partial cause of our justification. Many things are necessary which are not a cause and do not justify, as for instance the earth is necessary, and yet it does not justify. If man the sinner wants to be saved, he must necessarily be present, just

[32] Joest, *Gesetz und Freiheit: Das Problem des tertius usus legis bei Luther und die neutestamentliche Parainese.* 1951. 4th ed (Göttingen: Vandenhoeck & Ruprecht, 1968).

[33] *WA* 45, 324, 19-329, 22. Of course, Luther also dealt with this text in *Crucigers Sommerpostille* (1544): *WA* 22, 410, 7, 423, 28. Here Luther did more justice to the text when he said (*WA* 22, 411, 16-20): "Und wie die meisten Evangelien fast allein den Glauben leren und treiben, Also lautet dis Evangelium von eitel wercken, die Christus am Jüngsten tage anziehen wird, Damit man sehe, das er der selben wil auch nicht vergessen, sondern getrieben und gethan haben von denen, die da wollen Christen sein, und in seinem Reich erfunden werden." ("And just as most of the Gospels almost exclusively teach and commend faith, so this Gospel speaks just of works that Christ will tally up on the last day, so that we see that he will not ignore them, but will have urged and have them done by those who want to be Christians and be found in his kingdom.") There is, of course, no thorough discussion of the problem of faith and works here. Instead, Luther quickly resumed his usual polemic.

[34] Walther Von Loewenich, *Luther als Ausleger der Synoptiker* (Munich: Chr. Kaiser, 1954), 199. See also A. Peters, *Glaube und Werk*, 113-14; Modalsli, *Das Gericht nach den Werken* (Göttingen: Vandenhoeck & Ruprecht, 1963), 10.

[35] Modalsli, *Das Gericht nach den Werken,* 15, makes the following distinction: "I. The integral aspect of the Christian as believing and doing in view of the judgment. II. The sole validity of faith in *loco iustificationis.* III. The judgment according to works *extra locum iustificationis.*"

as he asserts that I must also be present. What Augustine says is true, "He who has created you without you will not save you without you." Works are necessary to salvation, but they do not cause salvation, because faith alone gives life. On account of the hypocrites we must say that good works are necessary to salvation.[36]

For Luther, then, everything depended on holding fast to justification by faith alone against "works-righteousness." When justification is at issue, "works" should not be emphasized.

Naturally, at times Luther stated that where works are absent one may conclude that faith is dead. In the *Thesis Concerning Faith and Law* (1535), he said: "If good works do not follow, it is certain that this faith in Christ does not dwell in our heart, but that dead faith."[37] On occasion he expressed the same idea in an inversion: where good works are present, they may have significance for the assurance of salvation, since they indicate that the divine grace is not at work in us in vain. Thus he stated in *The Disputation Concerning Justification:* "True faith is not idle. We can, therefore, ascertain and recognize those who have true faith from the effect or from what follows."[38]

Luther often went so far as to say that "love" witnesses to the fact that we set our confidence in the mercy of God. For example, in the Promotion Disputation of Hieronymus Nopp and Friedrich Bachofen (1539) he wrote: "Love is a witness to faith, gives us confidence, and makes us stand securely on the mercy of God. And we are commanded to make our calling sure through good works. And when works follow, then it is clear that we have faith. If no works are present, faith is simply lost, as also the fruits bear witness to the tree."[39] For such statements Luther took his principal support from a word in 2 Peter 1:10: "Therefore, brethren, be the more zealous to confirm your call and election, for if you do this you will never fall."

---

[36] *LW,* vol. 34, p. 165. *WA* 39 I, 96, 1-9: "Respondeo igitur ad argumentum: Nostra obedientia est necessaria ad salutem. Ergo est partialis causa iustificationis. Multa sunt necessaria, quae non causant et iustificant, ut terra est necessaria, et tamen non iustificat. Homo peccator si volet iustificari, necesse est ut adsit. . . . Verum est quod dicit Augustinus: Qui creavit te sine te, non salvabit te sine te. Opera sunt necessaria ad salutem, sed non causant salutem, quia fides sola dat vitam. Propter hypocritas dicendum est, quod bona opera sint etiam necessaria ad salutem." The quotation from Augustine is in his *Sermo* 169, 11, 13; *MPL* 38, 923: "Qui ergo fecit te sine te, non te iustificat sine te." See *Martin Luther Studienausgabe,* 5, ed. Hans-Ulrich Delius (Berlin: Evangelische Verlagsanstalt, 1991), 172, n. 622; Hans-Ulrich Delius, *Augustin als Quelle Luthers—Eine Materialsammlung* (Berlin: Evangelische Verlagsanstalt, 1984), 121-22. In this disputation Luther was evidently quoting from memory.

[37] *LW,* vol. 34, p. 111. *WA* 39 I, 46, 20-21: "Quod si opera non sequuntur, certum est, fidem hanc Christi in corde nostro non habitare, Sed mortuam illam."

[38] *LW,* vol. 34, p. 183. *WA* 39 I, 114, 28-30: "Vera fides non est otiosa. Ergo ex effectu aut posteriori concludere et cognoscere eos, qui veram fidem habent." See Paul Althaus, "Sola fide numquam sola: Glaube und Werke in ihrer Bedeutung für das Heil bei Martin Luther," *US* 16 (1961), 227-35; Modalsli, *Das Gericht nach den Werken,* 44-51.

[39] *WA* 39 II, 248, 11-15: "Charitas est testimonium fidei et facit, nos fiduciam habere et certo statuere de misericordia Dei, et nos iubemur, nostram vocationem firmam facere bonis operibus. Et tunc apparet, nos habere fidem, cum opera sequuntur, wenn kein werck da sein, so ist fides gar verlhorenn, sicut et fructus sunt testimonia arboris."

Luther, however, did not speak of a judgment according to works in connection with justification but rather apart from it.[40] At times he could actually distinguish a double justification. Thus in the Promotion Disputation of Palladius and Tilemann (1537): "Scripture teaches a double justification, one of faith before God, the other of works before the world." In this connection he referred to Luke 7:47, where Jesus says of the sinner, "Her sins, which are many, are forgiven, for she loved much."[41]

Naturally, such occasional utterances may not be too heavily weighted. It would be totally inappropriate to use them as a basis for a complex structure in which works somehow have independent weight. Rather, here again we have evidence of Luther's habit of developing his own ideas in connection with a variety of biblical statements, thus of adopting a variety of biblical motifs. As a rule, Luther did not distinguish a dual justi-fication as was advocated by a few sixteenth-century theologians such as Martin Bucer or Johannes Gropper, persons particularly eager for compromise. Their differentiation was vastly different from that proposed by Luther here.[42] Luther held himself aloof from such attempts.

In summary, therefore, one must say that in general, through appeal to Paul and to texts of the Gospels interpreted in the Pauline sense, Luther set forth justification *sola gratia* and *sola fide,* and in doing so deferred judgment according to works. Yet the works that will be of significance at the last judgment are interpreted as signs of faith or unbelief. In this way faith's preeminence is preserved. The goal of Luther's doctrine of justification is liberation from all busyness and a turning solely to Christ. "This is the reason why our theology is certain: it snatches us away from ourselves and places us outside ourselves, so that we do not depend on our own strength, con-science . . . but . . . on the promise and truth of God, which cannot deceive."[43]

---

[40] Modalsli, *Das Gericht nach den Werken,* has produced the evidence for this.

[41] *WA* 39 I, 208, 9-11: "Duplex in scripturis traditur iustificatio, altera fidei coram Deo, altera operum coram mundo." In what follows Luther cites Luke 7.

[42] See Reinhard Braunisch, *Die Theologie der Rechtfertigung im 'Enchiridion' (1538) des Johannes Grop-per: Sein kritischer Dialog mit Philipp Melanchthon,* RGST 109 (Münster: Aschendorff, 1974); B. Lohse, *HdBDThG,* 2:102-8.

[43] *LW,* vol. 26, p. 387 (*Lectures on Galatians, Chapters One to Four,* 1531); *WA* 40 I, 589, 8-10: "Ideo nostra theologia est certa, quia ponit nos extra nos: non debeo niti in conscientia mea . . . , sed in promissione divina, veritate, quae non potest fallere." See Karl-Heinz zur Mühlen, *Nos extra nos.*

Chapter 28

LAW AND GOSPEL

THE DISTINCTION BETWEEN LAW AND GOSPEL

For Luther the distinction between law and gospel coheres most intimately with his doctrine of justification, since that doctrine can be developed only on the basis of that distinction. For this reason one might ask whether a systematic treatment should not first deal with the doctrine of law and gospel and only then with the doctrine of justification. The answer is that we dealt first with justification, and now will deal with law and gospel, since Luther developed his new doctrine of justification prior to his distinction between law and gospel, though some initial forms of that distinction appear as early as in the lectures after 1513.

What is of first importance is that Luther assigned highest relevance to the distinction. In 1521 he wrote: "Almost all Scripture and the understanding of all theology hangs on the proper understanding of law and gospel."[1] In a sermon from 1532 he stated that the proper distinction "between law and faith, commandment and gospel . . . is the highest art in Christendom."[2] In the commentary on Galatians (1531), we read: "Whoever knows well how to distinguish the Gospel from the Law should give thanks to God and know that he is a real theologian."[3] In the first disputation against the Antinomians (1537), he wrote: "But now you have often heard that there is no better art of handing on and preserving the pure doctrine than to follow

---

[1] *WA* 7, 502, 34-35: "pene universa scriptura totiusque Theologiae cognitio pendet in recta cognitione legis et Euangelii."

[2] *WA* 36, 9, 26-29 (printed version); see 10, 2-4.

[3] *LW,* vol. 26, p. 115. *WA* 40 I, 207, 3-4: "qui istas 2 distinctiones bene novit, gratias agat deo et sciat se Theologum."

267

this method, that is, to divide Christian doctrine into two parts, law and gospel. And so there are two things set before us in God's Word, that is, the wrath or the grace of God, sin or righteousness, death or life, hell or heaven."[4] In a somewhat different formula Luther reproached Erasmus for omitting to distinguish the Old from the New Testament.[5]

The doctrine of law and gospel is the new Reformation formulation of the distinction between law and grace first proposed by Augustine. In *De Spiritu et Littera* Augustine had written: "The law is given that grace might be sought; grace is given that the law might be fulfilled."[6] Naturally, Augustine's distinction was primarily oriented to the history of salvation. According to Luther, it is not true that the law is merely superseded by the gospel. Rather, in the old as well as the new covenant law and gospel remain in a dialectic relation.

Of central importance to Luther in his early period were other pairs of contrasts similar to the later contrast between law and gospel. In his first Psalms lecture (1513-1515) he could say: "In the Holy Scriptures it is best to distinguish the Spirit from the letter, for this makes one truly a theologian."[7] According to Gerhard Ebeling, the same intent lay behind this distinction as behind the later law-gospel distinction.[8] The first Psalms lecture already contains an early form of the later distinction. In it Luther said: "The Law is the Word of Moses to us, while the Gospel is the Word of God into us." Here he intended to make clear that in contrast to the law the gospel is actually at work within us.[9] Others, with equal right, have claimed that the distinction between judgment and gospel in this lecture is almost as important as the later distinction between law and gospel.[10]

---

[4] WA 39 I, 361, 1-6: "Audistis autem iam saepe, meliorem rationem tradendi et conservandi puram doctrinam non esse, quam ut istam methodum sequamur, nempe ut dividamus doctrinam christianam in duas partes, scilicet in legem et evangelium. Sicut etiam duae res sunt, quae in verbo Dei nobis proponuntur, scilicet aut ira aut gratia Dei, peccatum aut iustitia, mors aut vita, infernus aut coelum."

[5] LW, vol. 33, p. 150 (Bondage of the Will, 1525); WA 18, 693, 5-8. But in LW, vol. 33, p. 132; WA 18, 680, 28-30, Luther stated again that Erasmus did not know what law or gospel is.

[6] De Spiritu et Littera 19. 34: "Lex ergo data est, ut gratia quaereretur, gratia data est, ut lex impleretur."

[7] WA 55 I, 4, 25-26: "In Scripturis Sanctis optimum est Spiritum a litera discernere, hoc enim facit vero theologum."

[8] Ebeling, Luther: An Introduction to His Thought, 1964, 110-11.

[9] LW, vol. 11, p. 160: "This touches the difference between Law and Gospel. For the Law is the Word of Moses [that comes up] to us (ad nos), while the Gospel is the Word of God [that comes] into us (in nos). The former remains outside and speaks of figures and visible shadows of things to come, but the latter comes inside and speaks of internal, spiritual, and true things"; WA 4, 9, 28-31 (scholia on Ps. 84:9): "In hoc tangitur differentia euangelii et legis. Quia lex est verbum Mosi ad nos, Euangelium autem verbum dei in nos. Quia illud foris manet, de figuris loquitur et umbris futurorum visibilibus: istud autem intus accedit et de internis, spiritualibus et veris loquitur."

[10] Albert Brandenburg, Gericht und Evangelium: Zur Worttheologie in Luthers erster Psalmenvorlesung (Paderborn: Bonifacius Druckerei, 1960). O. Pesch follows him in his Theologie der Rechtfertigung, 32.

Luther's distinction not only differs from the tradition insofar as it is no longer structured in salvation-historical but in dialectical fashion. What is also new is that the distinction between law and gospel cannot be made once for all, but must be drawn ever anew. What concerned Luther was not that law and gospel are merely separated in a proper manner, then combined. There is no alternative here, as if the law could be played off against the gospel, or the gospel against the law. Luther passionately protested against the antinomian thesis[11] that the church must preach the gospel whereas the Decalogue belongs to city hall: the law too must be preached. At the same time, Luther knew right well that there is not only a difference but an actual hostility between the two: the law kills, whereas the gospel makes alive.

What is further unique about Luther's distinction is that law and gospel cannot be assigned to the Old or New Testament, nor to particular biblical passages, so as to establish for all time that one text is only law and the other only gospel. Most texts assigned to the law have also a gospel side, just as most texts assigned to the gospel have also a law side. In the Decalogue, in the summary of the law, Luther could also find the gospel, insofar as God promises to be present with the words, "I am the Lord, thy God." The cross, the heart of the Christian message of reconciliation and salvation, is at the same time the harshest judgment on human sin.

According to Luther, the distinction between law and gospel could be properly drawn only when drawn afresh, when the situation that it addresses is carefully noted. Where the "law" is in fact already encountered, in suffering, temptation, or other severe experiences, the preaching of the gospel is to be given priority. On the other hand, where the law is denied through self-confidence or hubris, a too hasty preaching of the gospel would only lead to one's feeling supported in self-righteousness. Luther's distinction is clearly related to the context of proclamation.

Above all, then, theology has the task of maintaining the distinction between law and gospel.[12] The law can only fulfill its God-intended function when seen in constant contrast with the gospel, just as the gospel is properly preached only in constant contrast to the law. Both must be preserved in their true nature and authentic function through being continually related to each other. There is always the danger that both can be falsified, that a new law can be made of the gospel. Law and gospel may neither be mixed nor separated. As Luther put it in his first Antinomian Disputation, they are "bound together."[13]

---

[11] See above, p.180.

[12] Gerhard Ebeling especially has repeatedly pointed to this. See, e.g., his essay: "Das rechte Unterscheiden Luthers Anleitung zu theologischer Urteilskraft," *ZThK* 85 (1988), 219-58.

[13] *WA* 39 I, 416, 8-14: "Lex et Evangelium non possunt nec debent separari, sicut nec poenitentia et remissio peccatorum. Ita enim sunt inter se colligata et implicita. Nam praedicare remissionem peccatorum nihil aliud est, quam indicare et ostendere adesse peccatum. Ipsa remissio indicat adesse peccata, nec impletio quid sit potest intelligi, nisi intelligatur, quid sit lex, ut nec remissio peccatorum

DUPLEX USUS LEGIS (THE TWOFOLD USE OF THE LAW)

In the course of developing his view of law and gospel Luther distinguished various functions of the law and in this context spoke of a double *usus* (use). In doing so he made clear terminologically that the distinction is to be related to preaching.[14] The distinction between various uses of the law first appears in 1522. If early in his career Luther could speak of a threefold use, without anticipating the doctrine of the *triplex usus legis* later proposed by Melanchthon,[15] in February of 1523 he could open his sermons on the Decalogue with the remark that the commandments are given *ad duplicem usum.*[16] After 1519 Luther put the question of "profit or use" relative to other important themes such as the teaching on the sacraments in particular.[17] Under this methodological viewpoint, first formulated with respect to the sacraments,[18] he discussed the doctrine of the law in dispute with the Wittenberg reformers.

Luther's treatment of the law under the concept of *usus* was clearly a decision made without precursors in all the tradition.[19] The term *usus* refers to the proper distinction between the law's various functions and effects. The question who then "uses" or applies it can be variously answered. In the second Antinomian Disputation Luther had this to say: "Both the devil and Christ use the law to terrify, but the goals are quite different, entirely opposed."[20]

In accord with his intention to view the law as continually at work, Luther's reference to a *duplex usus legis* or twofold use of the law is never rigid. Everything of a formal nature is lacking. The reference apparently reaches its zenith in the 1531 lecture on Galatians. Remarkably, however, this formula appears only once in the Antinomian Disputations, though we would expect to see it there.[21] Luther seldom

---

potest intelligi, nisi prius sciatur, quid sit peccatum, nec fieri etiam potest impletio, nisi constituatur aliqua lex." ("Just as repentance and forgiveness of sins, so law and gospel neither can nor should be separated. They are so linked and entwined. For to preach the forgiveness of sins is nothing but to show and point out the presence of sin. Forgiveness itself indicates that sin is present; and fulfillment [of the law] cannot be understood unless the law is understood; and forgiveness of sins cannot be understood unless sin is first recognized; and fulfillment cannot occur, unless some law is established.")

[14] See first of all G. Ebeling, "On the Doctrine of the *Triplex Usus Legis* in the Theology of the Reformation," in *Word and Faith,* 62-78, esp. 69-76.

[15] *WA* 10 I 1, 449-63, esp. 456, 8-9; 457, 14 (*Kirchenpostille,* 1522).

[16] *WA* 11, 31, 6-7; see the context, p. 31, 2-33, 13.

[17] *LW,* vol. 42, p. 10 (*Meditation on Christ's Passion,* 1519). *WA* 2, 138, 15-19. Additional material in sermons on the sacraments: *LW,* vol. 42, p. 108; *WA* 2, 692, 22-24; *LW,* vol. 42, p. 111; *WA* 2, 695, 3-12; *LW,* vol. 35, p. 49; 742, 10-14; *LW,* vol. 35, pp. 63-64; *WA* 2, 751,29-752, 11.

[18] See Ebeling, "Doctrine," 72-73.

[19] See Ebeling, "Doctrine."

[20] *WA* 39 I, 426, 31-427, 21: "tam diabolus, quam Christus utitur lege in terrendis hominibus, sed fines sunt dissimillimi et prorsus contrarii."

[21] See Ebeling, "Doctrine," 69-72. The passage in the Antinomian disputations is *WA* 39 I, 441, 2-3.

summarized the distinction between the two uses of the law in a formula, though he continually dealt with the subject. The distinction as formally defined appears only in Melanchthon, who later on distinguished a threefold use.[22]

The two functions of the law are the "political" or "civic" and the "theological." Here too there is a profusion of formulas and terms. By means of the political use, external order on earth is to be maintained, and peace and the securing of justice preserved. The law has also the task of inculcating the divine commandments and of instructing consciences. It also is to furnish the needed means by which to punish evildoers. The order established by the political use of the law is effected through the offices of the temporal authorities, of parents, of teachers, and of judges, instituted by God for that purpose. If the law in its political sense is obeyed, then an "external," "civic" righteousness is achieved, to which Luther assigned highest value. In the second Antinomian Disputation, he wrote: "Political righteousness is good and worthy of praise, though it cannot stand in the sight of God."[23] Another word from the same disputation reads: "Among men, temporal righteousness has its own honor and its own reward in this life, but not with God."[24]

The "theological" use comprises the authentic task of the law. It is, so to speak, the law in its spiritual sense. This use serves to show persons their sin, to "convict" them of sin. In this connection, Luther often spoke of the "convicting use of the law." The law "accuses," "horrifies," indicating that owing to their guilt humans are not what they should be before God. Ultimately, no one can avoid this law. "Even if you wanted to wipe out these letters—*LEX*—which can [in fact] be easily erased, the word 'unrighteous' is still written in our hearts, still condemns and torments us."[25] Spiritually construed, this law in no way assists us to achieve righteousness. On the contrary, it only reveals our sinfulness and increases it. In such fashion, the law spiritually construed delivers up to the divine wrath.

Luther did not describe this effect of the law as a *causa efficiens* (efficient cause) but rather as a *causa ostensiva* (ostensive cause).[26] The law is to lead to sin's becoming "great." It is to strike at the heart, so that the wide world becomes too narrow and help is to be had nowhere but with Christ.[27] Only in such distress is there experience

---

[22] Melanchthon's addition to the two uses appears in an allusion as early as in 1528. We meet up with the subject matter of his "triplex usus legis" after the mid-1580s, and as a formula after 1540.

[23] WA 39 I, 459, 16-17: "politica iustitia bona est et laudibus digna, etsi in conspectu Dei non possit consistere."

[24] WA 39 I, 441, 5-6: "Iustitia mundi habet suam gloriam et sua praemia in hac vita inter homines, sed non apud Deum."

[25] WA 39 I, 456, 19-457, 1: "Nam etiamsi tollas has literas: LEX, quae facillime deleri possunt, tamen manet chirographum inustum cordibus nostris, quod nos damnat et exercet."

[26] WA 39 I, 529, 3-4; 554, 3-560, 12 (*3. Antinomerdisputation*).

[27] WA 39 I, 456, 7-8 (*2. Antinomerdisputation*): "Talis enim est doctrina legis, ut, si vere tangat cor, so wirt einen die weite welt zu enge, neque hic erit auxilium ullum reliquum praeterquam Christus." ("For the teaching of the law is such that if it truly strikes the heart, then the wide world becomes too narrow, and here will be no help apart from Christ.")

of the might of sin, a might so great that no punishment can make satisfaction for it. Humans are aware of their inability to love God despite their proper desire to love God. The law cannot be kept. "God prescribes nothing to a person that would be impossible [for one], but through sin one sinks into an impossible situation."[28]

Of course, no one can withstand the awareness to which the law in its theological use leads, a use that leads either to despair or to self-righteousness. The one who takes seriously the law's requirement and strives to keep the commandments arrives inevitably at the view that salvation is attained through the law, which means to tempt God and increase sin. It is also possible that the attempt to keep the law results in despair despite honorable self-examination. In despair one surrenders self-righteousness, and no longer attempts to justify oneself before God. Despair of itself leads finally to hell and to the gates of death. One is then in a state in which one can neither live nor die. One would gladly die but cannot, since one is unreservedly delivered up to God's holy wrath.[29] It is also possible to despair of God himself. Then one sins against the First Commandment. In this instance the law leads to hatred toward God and to blasphemy.[30]

The church must preach the law in its dual function. As for the "usus politicus," the church should never instruct the temporal authorities about what they must do in the concrete. According to Luther, the church has no commission to do so, but through its preaching should remind the temporal authorities of the task assigned them by God to care for external peace and order in this transitory world. It should also warn against encroachment upon the spiritual realm.

The *usus theologicus* is of particular importance. The gospel assumes the law and its preaching. Faith assumes the consciousness of sin, or better, includes it. Whoever knew nothing of sin could not believe in the God who justifies the godless (Rom. 4:5). That works do not justify before God does not mean that for believers the law is annulled. It is done away with as a way to salvation, but as God's Word it retains its validity, insofar as the Christian remains a sinner.

Thus, as long as we live, we can never reach a state "beyond law and gospel." The law accuses, the gospel acquits. When the message of forgiveness is heard, then, looking to oneself and one's sinfulness results in fresh anxiety, so that refuge is

---

[28] *WA* 39 I, 515, 16-17 (*3. Antinomerdisputation*): "Deus non praecipit homini impossibilia. Sed ipse homo per peccatum incidit in impossibilia."

[29] *WA* 39 I, 508, 24-509, 24 (*3. Antinomerdisputation*, text B): "Impii vellent mori, sed non possunt mori, optabunt sibi mortem anxie, sed vivent et cruciabuntur in aeternum." ("The godless wish to die, but they cannot. Full of anxiety they will long for death, but will live and be tortured forever.")

[30] *WA* 39 I, 559, 12-14: "lex iubet amare ac diligere Deum et fidere Deo, hic cum animadvertit, se non posse huic legi satisfacere, incipit desperare, odisse Deum, blasphemare Deum. Natura enim tota corrupta est." ("The law commands that we love and trust God. When a man observes that he cannot satisfy this law, he begins to despair, to hate God, to blaspheme. For all nature has been corrupted.")

sought once more in the forgiveness of God. Law and gospel relate to each other as the *Deus nudus* and *Deus revelatus*.[31] "God in his nature and majesty is our enemy; he demands (that we keep) the law and threatens transgressors with death. But when he unites himself with our weakness, then he is not our enemy."[32] In this fashion law and gospel belong indissolubly together, as long as there are creatures on this earth.

NATURAL LAW AND MOSAIC LAW[33]

According to Luther, the law was not first given by Moses, or, more popularly put, was not given after the fall. On occasion, he can say that there is a law for the angels, or that there was a law even for Adam prior to the fall. At issue here, of course, is not a law by which angels and Adam would first have needed to be instructed about what to do. Before the fall, both angels and the first human kept the law voluntarily and with interior consent, as a matter of course, so to speak. To that extent, we cannot say that the angels are "under the law," since with them the law does not have the character of summons. "In an improper sense we say that angels are under the law, that they fulfill the law in everything, since their nature leads them to it voluntarily, not because the law demands it. So the law cannot accuse the angels."[34] Law can only "improperly" be applied to the human condition prior to the fall. In either instance Luther's use of the concept reflects that the law as God's Word has a significance not conditioned by time or era, that it is eternally valid, though its function is considerably altered in light of the given situation.

We may speak of the law of God in the proper sense only after the fall. After all, it was not the law that was altered after the fall, but rather humankind. Through disobeying God humanity's relation to God as well as to the law was altered. Now the law no longer directs its activity from within but becomes an entity interposed between God and humanity, encountering it as demanding, accusing, and judging.

Luther held to the position that even after the fall people know something of the law. He could actually say: "Indeed, all by nature have a certain knowledge of the law, though it is very weak and hazy. Hence it was and is always necessary to hand on to them that knowledge of the law so that they may recognize the magnitude of their

---

[31] See above, pp. 214-17.

[32] *WA* 39 I, 370, 13-16 (*1. Antinomerdisputation*): "Deus in natura et maiestate sua est adversarius noster, exigit legem et minatur transgressoribus mortem. Sed quando associat se infirmitati nostrae, . . . ibi non est adversarius noster."

[33] For what follows see Heinrich Bornkamm, *Luther and the Old Testament,* trans. Eric W. Gritsch and Ruth C. Gritsch, ed. Victor I. Gruhn (Philadelphia: Fortress Press, 1969).

[34] *WA* 39 I, 436, 2-4 (*2. Antinomerdisputation,* text A): "improprie dicitur, angelos esse sub lege, qui per omnia satisfaciunt legi ultro natura sua ad hoc illos ducente et non propterea, quia lex exigat, unde neque accusare angelum lex potest."

sin, the wrath of God, etc."[35] The natural law, as Luther often stated, is written in everyone's heart. People of all times and lands are aware that crime and idolatry are forbidden. Still, awareness of natural law is not sufficient, due not so much to the fact that humans would not know enough of the law as to the fact that they draw no conclusions from what they know.

For this reason God gave the Decalogue through Moses, or, as Luther characteristically put it, God renewed the knowledge of the law through Moses. Consequently, after Moses there has been an official office for teaching the law. Naturally, within the Mosaic law Luther distinguished this renewal of natural law from Jewish national law; thus he did not construe the Mosaic law as binding in all its parts. It applies to all only to the extent of its inculcating the natural law afresh. Insofar as the Mosaic law has to do with Jewish national law, it is nothing more than the Jews' *Sachsenspiegel*.[36] The judicial and ceremonial laws do not apply not only to Christians but not even to Gentiles in the old covenant period. Here Luther asserted that the Old Testament itself illustrates that the observance of certain laws was not required of Gentiles. First, prior to Abraham there was no circumcision; next, in certain instances Gentiles came to faith without anything being said of circumcision. The principle applies that one must consider to whom God's word is being addressed.[37]

Luther also applied this sharp distinction between the obligatory and nonobligatory character of the Mosaic law to such regulations of the Old Testament as seemed ideal to him in and of themselves. Such include the tithe or regulations concerning the year of jubilee, the sabbath year, or the rules for treating the poor. All of these appeared to Luther to be altogether worthy of imitation, but he refused to set them down as divine law and thus as divine requirements. They are matters of choice, requiring to be decided in one's own time at one's discretion. He charged the fanatics with claiming nonexistent divine authority for specific practical requirements for reform. "Moses is dead. . . . He is of no further service."[38] Even the Decalogue is binding only as a summary of natural law, which in essence consists of the two commandments to worship God and to care for one's fellow human beings in terms of love for neighbor. Whatever in Moses exceeds this natural law applies only to Jews, not to Christians.

---

[35] *WA* 39 I, 361, 19-22 (*1. Antinomerdisputation,* text A): "Habent quidem omnes homines naturaliter quandam cognitionem legis, sed eam valde infirmam et obscuratam. Ideo necesse fuit et semper est tradere hominibus illam legis notitiam, ut cognoscant magnitudinem peccati sunt, irae Dei etc."

[36] *LW,* vol. 40, p. 98 (*Against the Heavenly Prophets,* 1525): "So we are to let Moses be the *Sachsenspiegel* of the Jews, and not to confuse us Gentiles with it, just as the *Sachsenspiegel* is not observed in France, though the natural law there agrees with it"; *WA* 18, 81, 14-17: "Darümb las man Mose der Juden Sachssenspiegel seyn, und uns Heyden unverworren damit, gleich wie Franckreich den Sachssenspiegel nicht achtet und doch ynn dem naturlichen gesetze wol mit yhm stymmet."

[37] *LW,* vol. 35, pp. 171-72 (sermon, 1525). *WA* 16, 384, 13- 385, 16.

[38] *LW,* vol. 35, p. 165 (sermon, 1525). *WA* 16, 373, 12; 375, 14.

TERTIUS USUS LEGIS (THE THIRD USE OF THE LAW)

If we ignore the passage in the *Kirchenpostille* of 1522, with its reference to the "threefold use of the law,"[39] Luther spoke only once of such a use, namely, at the conclusion of his second Antinomian Disputation (1538).[40] It is clear, however, that the passage is not from Luther but is an interpolation based on Melanchthon's doctrine of the threefold use.

Since the 1530s, Melanchthon had been developing the doctrine of a threefold use of the law, and particularly for teaching purposes had furnished it with a certain schematic. Luther never advocated any such use, whether in terminology or subject matter. This, of course, does not mean that Luther believed the law had no meaning for the "justified." First, it retains its accusing function; it must continually remind believers that they cannot satisfy the divine requirement but are free from its judging power only by faith in Christ. Next, it has an educative function, in which case it is better to speak of a commandment rather than of a law. In any event, the function of the law in this sense is not identical with its accusing function. Particularly in his sermons, Luther continually adverted to the law in terms of paraenesis.[41]

So much is in any case important: Due to its vicarious fulfillment through Christ, the law is abrogated as a way of salvation but by no means simply eliminated. Alongside its accusing function it remains in effect as commandment, as admonition, as announcement of the divine will. Luther actually assumed a persistence of the law into eternity. Just as he would sometimes inexactly refer to a law in the angelic world, and among the first humans before the fall, so he would occasionally speak of a law in the end time. The law is and remains God's Word. Luther could even state that law and gospel will be most intimately linked in eternity.[42] The condemning character of the law will cease;[43] the *officium legis* will cease, but the law

---

[39] *WA* 10 I 1, 456, 8-9; 457, 14.

[40] See above, pp.182-83.

[41] See Joest, *Gesetz und Freiheit: Das Problem des tertius usus legis bei Luther und die neutestamentliche Parainese,* 4th ed. (Göttingen: Vandenhoeck & Ruprecht, 1968); as well as Heintze, *Luthers Predigt von Gesetz und Evangelium.* FGLP 10/11 (Munich: Chr. Kaiser, 1958).

[42] *LW,* vol. 26, p. 343 (*Lectures on Galatians, Chapters One to Four,* 1535): "Thus Paul distinguishes beautifully between the time of Law and the time of grace. Let us learn also to distinguish the times of both, not in words but in our feelings, which is the most difficult of all. For although these two are utterly distinct, yet they must be joined completely together in the same heart. Nothing is more closely joined together than fear and trust, Law and Gospel, sin and grace; they are so joined together that each is swallowed up by the other. Therefore there cannot be any mathematical conjunction that is similar to this." *WA* 40 I, 527, 21-27 (print version): "Sic pulchre distinguit Paulus tempus legis et gratiae. Discamus et nos recte distinguere utriusque tempus, non verbis sed affectu, id quod est omnium difficillimum. Quanquam enim distinctissima sunt illa duo, tamen etiam coniunctissima sunt etiam in eodem corde. Nihil magis coniunctum est quam timor et fiducia, Lex et Evangelium, peccatum et gratia; tam coniuncta enim sunt, ut alterum ab altero absorbeatur. Ideo nulla Mathematica coniunctio potest dari quae esset huic similis."

[43] *WA* 39 II, 142, 5-6 (*Promotionsdisputation von Joachim Mörlin,* 1540): "Paulus dicit de lege damnante: quando venerimus ad coelum, tunc non amplius praedicabimus legem." ("Paul speaks of the law as condemning: When we get to heaven, then we will no longer preach the law.")

still retains its significance as "fulfilled."[44] Luther stated explicitly: "Therefore the law is not annulled in eternity, but will remain—either to be fulfilled among the damned, or among the saved."[45]

For this reason we cannot state that for Luther the law is in force only at a particular stage of salvation history. As God's Word it has abiding significance. Of course, its *officium* (office) is altered by sin, but also by the renewal of the person.

[44] *WA* 39 I, 431, 5-10 (*2. Antinomerdisputation*).
[45] *WA* 439 I, 350, 3-4 (*Thesen Gegen die Antinomer,* 1537): "Quare lex nunquam in aeternum tollitur sed manebit vel implenda in damnatis, vel impleta in beatis."

Chapter 29

THE CHURCH

The Nature of the Church

In order to evaluate Luther's ecclesiology a few points require particular attention. First, in the medieval period ecclesiology was generally dealt with as a separate theme. Naturally, ecclesiological questions were discussed in other dogmatic contexts. It was only in the late Middle Ages that John Wyclif and John Hus composed their *de Ecclesia*, not least reflecting their own criticism of the church of that time.[1] In the late medieval period there was nothing in the way of a separate ecclesiology as an object of theological reflection. Still, one may say that partly papal, partly conciliar ideas dominated. Second, at the heart of Luther's ecclesiological statements in his early lectures is the idea that the chief thing in the church is the hearing of the Word.[2] Finally, all during the various controversies since 1517, questions of church and especially of papal authority as well as the idea of the universal priesthood naturally assumed center stage. Accordingly, for a complete evaluation of Luther's ecclesiology, we need to be aware that throughout his life, even in the midst of controversies, he held fast to fundamental aspects of the traditional ecclesiology.

The fact that during his dispute with Rome, especially from 1517 till, say, 1524, Luther often treated the relevant questions in polemical fashion explains why attempts to evaluate his ecclesiology have arrived at opposite results. In part, the

---

[1] See Friedrich Merzbacher, "Wandlungen des Kirchenbegriffs im Spätmittelalter," *ZSRG.K* 39 (1953), 274-361; Hubert Jedin, *Ekklesiologie um Luther,* FuH 18 (Berlin/Hamburg: Lutherisches Verlagshaus, 1968), 9-29; Bernhard Lohse, *LuJ* 52 (1985), 145-47.

[2] See above, pp.63-64 and 80-81.

spiritual character of the church as the *communio sanctorum* is given sharp emphasis.[3] In part there is considerable agreement with traditional ecclesiology, particularly on Augustine's terms. This, of course, raises the question whether we are dealing here with the retention of Catholic "vestiges," or whether these features are essential to Luther's ecclesiology. Especially noteworthy is the evidence produced by Vilmos Vajta that in his ecclesiology Luther allowed for the invocation of the saints, though he sharply attacked the cult of the saints.[4]

Important as well is that Luther's ecclesiological statements underwent considerable change. In his early lectures, he saw the church entirely from the perspective of the Word preached and believed, though he entertained no reservations worth naming toward the traditional view, which he, of course, had not yet reflected on in any dogmatic way.[5] The controversy over the papal office began with the dispute over indulgences. Obviously, then, in the dispute with Rome spiritual aspects were at the forefront.[6] Naturally, it would be one-sided to evaluate Luther's ecclesiology only on the basis of the writings he composed in this period. One should also note that as soon as the situation allowed, Luther took concrete steps toward reforming the church.[7] One should further keep in mind that he often attempted to introduce the evangelical office of bishop. The importance of this point is not reduced by the fact that these attempts were without result for various reasons, and that the episcopal functions as a whole devolved on the princes.

Any attempt to evaluate Luther's ecclesiology as a whole must thus take note of its spiritual aspects and do justice to the fact that on the basis of new orders evangelical congregations were constituted as the true and proper church.

What persists in all of this and at the same time brackets Luther's variously accented ecclesiological statements is the unconditional preeminence of the Word and the definition of the church as the fellowship of those who hear it. Statements such as that the church is the number or assembly of believers appear continually in Luther with certain variations. Materially, this means that the doctrine of justification is also at the basis of Luther's ecclesiology.[8] In the Smalcald Articles (1537) we read: "Thank God, a seven-year-old child knows what the church is, namely, holy

[3] Althaus, *The Theology of Martin Luther,* translated by Robert C. Schultz (Philadelphia: Fortress Press), 1966, 288, states that "an institutional concern is . . . missing from Luther's descriptions of the 'church.'" The reason why is that Luther was not forced to deal with the institutional aspect on the basis of the theme of his early lectures, but that since 1517 that aspect became a matter of dispute. One should not infer from this, however, that the institutional element would have been unimportant to the young Luther.

[4] Vajta, "Die Kirche als geistlich-sakramentale communio mit Christus und seine Heiligen bei Luther," *LuJ* 51 (1984), 10-62.

[5] See above, p. 64 and 81.

[6] C. A. Aurelius and K. Hammann have brought this out in their investigations.

[7] M. Beyer, "Luthers Ekklesiologie," in *Leben und Werk Martin Luthers von 1526 bis 1546,* 1:93-118; 2:755-65, 93, states correctly that Luther's ecclesiology "together with the other elements of his theological reflection was formed in constant exchange with his ever-increasing criticism of the church and the broadening of his theological horizon."

[8] Among others see ibid., 94. See also the investigation of Jürgen Lutz.

believers and sheep who hear the voice of their Shepherd [John 10:3]. So the children pray, 'I believe [in] one holy Christian church.'"[9] Naturally, Luther immediately added, "Its holiness does not consist of surplices, tonsures, albs, or other ceremonies of theirs which they have invented over and above the Holy Scriptures, but it consists of the Word of God and true faith."[10] Toward the term "church" Luther entertained considerable reserve: "This word 'church' is not German and does not convey the sense or meaning that should be taken from this article."[11] Instead he wrote that the church is "a communion of saints, that is, a crowd or assembly of people who are Christians and holy, which is called a Christian holy assembly or church."[12]

Other concepts that Luther likewise preferred are *communio*, "gathering," or even "fellowship." By "fellowship" he has in mind a common participation or sharing. The Latin *communio sanctorum* denotes either the fellowship of the saints or fellowship in the Holy One at the Supper. Luther did not defend the second view, originating in the ancient church.[13] By *communio sanctorum* he understood the "sharing of goods" among the believers,"[14] thus mutual engagement on behalf of the other in bodily and spiritual goods.

In this sense Luther understood the church, particularly in his early sermons on the Sacrament: it is the

> incorporation with Christ and all saints. It is as if a citizen were given a sign, a document, or some other token to assure him that he is a citizen of the city, a member of that particular community. . . . This fellowship consists in this, that all the spiritual possessions of Christ and his saints are shared with and become the common property of him who receives this sacrament. Again all sufferings and sins also become common property; and thus love engenders love in return and [mutual love] unites.[15]

The following motifs are thus determinative. First, it is of fundamental significance that Luther most stressed that Christ is Head of the church. He always made this clear.[16] In his dispute with Rome after 1517, the idea naturally assumed special importance.[17] Christ as Head of the church is, of course, an idea represented in the

---

[9] *Book of Concord*, p. 315.

[10] Ibid.

[11] *LW*, vol. 41, p. 143 (*On Councils and the Church*, 1539). *WA* 50, 624, 18-20.

[12] *LW*, vol. 41, p. 143. *WA* 50, 624, 15-18.

[13] See Werner Elert, *Abendmahl und Kirchengemeinschaft in der alten Kirche, hauptsächlich des Ostens* (Berlin: Lutherisches Verlagshaus, 1954).

[14] Althaus, *The Theology of Martin Luther*, 296.

[15] *LW*, vol. 35, p. 51 (*The Blessed Sacrament of the Holy and True Body of Christ*, 1519). *WA* 2, 743, 21-30.

[16] Holsten Fagerberg in particular documented this for the period of the first Psalms lecture: *Die Kirche in Luthers Psalmenvorlesung 1513-1515*, 109-18.

[17] See Lohse, "Luthers Christologie im Ablassstreit," in *Evangelium in der Geschichte: Studien zu Luther und der Reformation* (Göttingen: Vandenhoeck & Ruprecht, 1988), 287-99.

entire tradition. It first gains antipapal and anti-Roman significance with Wyclif and Hus. Luther was not intimately acquainted with their ecclesiology, though in essence he gave new force to the anti-Roman utterance that if Christ is Head of the church, then the pope cannot be. It was chiefly in his 1520 treatise, *On the Papacy in Rome against the Most Celebrated Romanist in Leipzig,*[18] that he elaborated this idea of Christ as Head: "Christ certainly is a lord of all things, of those who are godly and those who are evil, of angels and of devils, of virgins and of whores. But he is the head only of the godly, faithful Christians assembled in the Spirit. For a head must be joined to the body."[19]

These ideas would appear to approximate some views of the fanatics. Still, in the sentence just quoted Luther made clear that he did not intend to set up a program for arranging the world on the basis of the headship of Christ.

Second, just as Luther understood the church as Christ's body, so he saw it as the special work of the Spirit. In the Large Catechism he wrote: "For where Christ is not preached, there is no Holy Spirit to create, call, and gather the Christian church, and outside it no one can come to the Lord Christ."[20] Here again we see the significance of trinitarian doctrine for all of Luther's theology: the church is the work of the triune God. At this point Luther took up the famous sentence of Cyprian to the effect that outside the church there is no salvation,[21] but supplied it with his own accent: all depends on "coming to the Lord Christ."

Third, it is materially the same, though again with his own accent, when Luther described the church as the "creature of the gospel": "Ecclesia . . . creatura est Euangelii, incomparabiliter minor ipso" (the church is the creature of the gospel, incomparably less than the gospel).[22] Word and Sacrament are at the same time the only marks of the church: "Not Rome or this or that place, but baptism, the sacrament, and the Gospel are the signs by which the existence of the church in the world can be noticed externally."[23] Here Luther had the Word in mind.[24]

Fourth, God's Word and people belong inseparably together. In his treatise *On Councils and the Church* (1539), Luther coined the trenchant formula: "God's word cannot be without God's people, and conversely, God's people cannot be without

[18] *LW*, vol. 39, pp. 55-104; *WA* 6, 277-324; in particular see, e.g., *LW*, vol. 39, pp. 71-73; *WA* 6, 297, 36-299, 14. On Augustine of Alveldt attacked by Luther here, see Herbert Smolinsky, *Augustin von Alveldt und Hieronymus Emser: Eine Untersuchungen zur Kontroverstheologie der frühen Reformationszeit im Herzogtum Sachsen,* RGST 122 (Münster: Aschendorffsche Verlagsbuchhandlung, 1983).

[19] *LW,* vol. 39, p. 76. *WA* 6, 301, 30-302, 4.

[20] *Book of Concord,* p. 416.

[21] Cyprian, *Ep.* 73.21: "Salus extra ecclesiam non est."

[22] *Resolutiones Lutherianae super propositionibus suis Lipsiae disputatis,* 1519, *WA* 2, 430, 6-7.

[23] *LW,* vol. 39, p. 75 (*On the Papacy in Rome,* 1520); *WA* 6, 30-31, 3-5.

[24] See *LW,* vol. 39, p. 305 (*That the Christian Assembly or Congregation Has the Right and Power to Judge All Teaching,* 1523): "The sure mark by which the Christian congregation can be recognized is that the pure gospel is preached there." *WA* 11, 408, 8-10.

God's word."[25] How strong Luther's awareness that the church is not a human work affected him personally and strengthened him in the midst of his inner conflicts is indicated by his familiar word in the little treatise *Against the Antinomians* (1539): "For after all, we are not the ones who can preserve the church, nor were our forefathers able to do so. Nor will our successors have this power. No, it was, is, and will be he who says, 'I am with you always, to the close of the age.' As it says in Hebrews 13 [v. 8], 'Jesus Christ is the same yesterday, and today, and forever.'"[26]

Fifth, God's redeeming and justifying activity occurs in and through the church. In Luther's quest for a gracious God, the individual may be articulated in a new way, but the individualism often declared to be typically Protestant is absent. According to Luther, one may be a Christian only in the fellowship of the church. This does not mean that the church mediates salvation, but it does mean that Jesus Christ has not merely redeemed individuals but called a new people to his discipleship. The church is thus the new people of God or, in another figure, the body of Christ. The individual is set within this fellowship by the message of the gospel. It was inconceivable to Luther that one could be a Christian without being connected to the church.

THE TRUE AND FALSE CHURCH

Conditioned by his intense disputes with Rome first, then with the fanatics, Luther's question of the true or false church is of extraordinary significance not only for his ecclesiology but also for the ecclesiology of the traditionalists and other reformers. As great as the agreements among Catholics and Protestants appear to us to have been, despite their deepening division, from the Reformation perspective the differences were seen as a wall of separation between the true and false church, or between the church of Christ and the church of the pope, with the harshest judgments levied on the traditionalists. The differences spilled over into political life: civil security depended on whatever confession was binding in a territory. In practice, political and confessional boundaries were not to be separated.

We must be clear about this situation, but also about the current change of perspective, in order to understand the harshness with which the question was formulated, as well as the consistency in Luther's ecclesiology. Luther flatly disputed "Rome's" claim to be a church. When the pope excommunicated him, he in turn banned the pope and all his adherents: "And as they excommunicate me in accord with their godless heresy, so I in turn excommunicate them in accord with God's holy truth. Christ the judge will see which excommunication matters to him.

---

[25] *LW,* vol. 41, p. 150. *WA* 50, 629, 34-35.
[26] *LW,* vol. 47, p. 118. *WA* 50, 476, 31-35.

Amen."[27] We cannot imagine how serious both sides were about these excommunications. Views on indulgence, on "works," on papal authority, or on the sacraments were much too divergent. Luther's conviction that the pope is the antichrist was not intended to defame the pope personally, but was based on the charge that with his claim to full power even over the souls in purgatory the pope had set himself in Christ's place.[28]

From this perspective Luther denied Rome's existence as a church: "We do not concede to the papists that they are the church, for they are not."[29] Conversely, Luther claimed that his own church was perfectly in accord with Scripture and Christ: "By God's grace our church is closest and most like the church of the apostles. For we have the pure doctrine, the catechism, and the sacrament, as Christ taught and instituted it, as well as how we should exercise rule in the world and at home."[30] Thus, when he was thinking of a church of the Reformation, Luther did not have a confessional church in mind, certainly not a "Lutheran" church. What concerned him as well as the traditionalists or even the other Reformation persuasions was, Who can raise the claim to be the right, true, apostolic, and Christian church? For those on the side of the Reformation, the criterion for judgment was Scripture alone, which, of course, was variously interpreted.

The distinction between the true and the false church was important also for Luther's attitude toward the authority of councils.[31] Just as he in fact construed the church on the basis of the hearing of the Word, so the authority of councils depends on whether the Word of God has been acknowledged in conciliar decisions, or whether human interpretations have prevailed. The authority of councils can thus be established or demonstrated not in any formal way but only on the basis of the content of their resolutions. On the other hand, councils are the highest representative organs of universal Christianity. For this reason, it is no contradiction when Luther continually appealed to a future council following 1518 but was not prepared uncritically to accept conciliar decisions over his affair. He gave particular expression to this

---

[27] *Adversus execrabilem Antichristi bullam,* 1520, WA 6, 612, 21-23: "Et sicut ipsi me excommunicant pro sacrilega haeresi sua, ita eos rursus ego excommunico pro sancta veritate dei. Christus Iudex viderit, utra excommunicatio apud eum valeat, Amen."

[28] On this subject see Ernst Bizer, *Luther und der Papst,* TEH 69 (Munich: Chr. Kaiser, 1958); Hans-Günter Leder, *Ausgleich mit dem Papst?* AsTh 1/38 (Stuttgart: Calwer, 1969); Remigius Bäumer, *Martin Luther und der Papst* in KLK 30, 2d ed. (Münster, 1971); Gerhard Müller, "Martin Luther und das Papsttum," in *Das Papsttum in der Diskussion,* ed. Georg Denzler (Regensburg: Pustet, 1974), 73-101. For brief references see Gottfried Seebass, "Antichrist: IV. Reformations- und Neuzeit," TRE 3 (1978), 28-43, esp. 28-32; idem, "Apokalyptik: VIII. Reformation und Neuzeit," ibid., 280-89, esp. 280-81.

[29] *Book of Concord,* p. 315 (*Smalcald Articles,* 1537).

[30] *WA TR* 4, Nr. 4172, p. 179, 9-11.

[31] See particularly Christa Tecklenburg Johns, *Luthers Konzilsidee in ihrer historischen Bedingtheit und ihrem reformatorischen Neuansatz,* TBT 10 (Berlin: Töpelmann, 1966); Friedrich Wilhelm Kantzenbach, "Auftrag und Grenze eines christlichen Konzils in der Sicht Luthers," *ThZ* 23 (1967), 108-34; M. Beyer, "Luthers Ekklesiologie," 111-14.

point of view in his *Disputatio de potestate concilii* (1536?).[32] The council as such is not essentially the "church" but merely "represents" it.[33]

THE *NOTAE ECCLESIAE*

In his debate with Donatism Augustine developed the view that the true church is characterized by four marks: oneness (*unitas*); holiness (*sanctitas*); catholicity (*catholicitas*), in terms of a worldwide fellowship outlasting the times; and apostolicity (*apostolicitas*), in terms of its originating with the apostles and preserving apostolic character. In the Middle Ages these criteria were in essence maintained. If other aspects were important to Augustine, such as the distinction between the elect and the external, sacramental fellowship; or the visibility or invisibility of the church, or, not least, the church identified as the *civitas Dei*,[34] in the medieval period, to the extent ecclesiological questions were dealt with, the Augustinian *notae* were on the whole retained, though in some cases interpreted in greater detail. This was true especially of papal authority, of obvious significance for several of the *notae*.

Luther took up the distinctions among the various *notae* but characteristically gave them fresh definition. On the one hand he described the Word as the only infallible mark of the church: "For the only perpetual and infallible mark of the church was always the Word."[35] On the other, he could list a greater number of marks.

Early in his dispute with Rome, Luther at times distinguished three marks of the church. Thus in his treatise *On the Papacy in Rome* (1520): "Not Rome or this or that place, but baptism, the sacrament, and the gospel are the signs by which the existence of the church in the world can be noticed externally."[36] In this connection he also distinguished "the two churches":

[32] *WA* 39 I, 181-97.

[33] *WA* 39 I, 186, 24-32: "19. Hoc recte dicunt quod represent [scil. die Konzilien] Ecclesiam universalem, Non enim necessario sunt Ecclesia, sed saepius repraesentant Ecclesiam tantum. 20. Et si tantum representant Ecclesiam, tunc sunt Ecclesia, sicut homo pictus est homo, id est, tantum repraesentans." ("19. For this reason they correctly state that [the councils] represent the universal church. For they are not necessarily the church, but often represent the entire church. 20. And if they represent the entire church, then they are the church, just as a man whose picture is painted is a man, that is, represents the whole [man].")

[34] On Augustine's ecclesiology see esp. Fritz Hofmann, *Der Kirchenbegriff des heiligen Augustinus in seine Grundlagen und in seiner Entwicklung* (Munich: Heuber, 1933, repr. 1978) (still always basic); Joseph Ratzinger, *Volk und Haus Gottes in Augustins Lehre von der Kirche*, MThS 2/7 (Munich: Zink, 1954). On the relation between church and the "civitas Dei," see Bernhard Lohse, "Zur Eschatologie des älteren Augustins," *VigChr* 21 (1967), 221-40.

[35] *WA* 25, 97, 32-33 (*Vorlesung über Jesaja*, 1527, according to printing B; see pp. 84, 86). Further evidence in Althaus, *Theology of Martin Luther*, 288-91.

[36] *LW*, vol. 39, p. 75; *WA* 6, 301, 3-5. Similarly also in *WA* 7, 721, 9-14 (*Ad librum eximii Magistri nostri Ambrosii Catharini*, 1521). See M. Beyer, "Luthers Ekklesiologie," 97-98.

Therefore, for the sake of better understanding and brevity, we shall call the two churches by two distinct names. The first, which is natural, basic, essential, and true, we shall call 'spiritual, internal Christendom.' The second, which is man-made and external, we shall call 'physical, external Christendom.' Not that we want to separate them from each other; rather, it is just as if I were talking about a man and called him 'spiritual' according to his soul, and 'physical' according to his body.[37]

Since, despite the biting harshness of his polemic against Rome, Luther warned against separating the two churches, we should not attempt to separate them in reconstructing his ecclesiology.[38] In carrying out the Reformation as well as in structuring the churches, Luther took a path by which to give Christianity as spiritually understood an outward shape appropriate to it.

In the treatise *On Councils and the Church* (1539), Luther listed seven marks: (1) the Word of God; (2) the Sacrament of Baptism; (3) the Sacrament of the Altar; (4) the power of the keys; (5) the calling and ordaining of pastors and bishops; (6) prayer, praise, and thanks to God; (7) enduring the cross, and inner conflict (*Anfechtung*).[39] What is significant here is that "a Christian holy people is to be and to remain on earth until the end of the world. This is an article of faith that cannot be terminated until that which it believes comes, as Christ promises, 'I am with you always, to the close of the age.'"[40]

In his treatise *Against Hanswurst* (1541), Luther distinguished the following marks of the church: (1) Holy Baptism; (2) the Holy Sacrament of the Altar; (3) the keys; (4) the office of preaching and God's Word; (5) the apostolic confession of faith; (6) the Our Father; (7) honor due the temporal power; (8) praise of the marriage estate; (9) the suffering of the true church; (10) the renouncing of revenge for persecution. Fasting may constitute an additional, eleventh mark, since it can assume new shape among evangelicals:

Yet someone might say, 'You lack one thing, namely, fasting, because you heretics do not fast' (they say). Lord God, if there is one thing we have from the ancient church, it is unfortunately fasting. If there is one thing the papists have from the new church, it is that they do not fast but live riotously and on fast days even more than on feast days. Indeed, we do not just fast, but (with St. Paul [1 Cor. 4:11]) we suffer hunger. We see it daily in our poor ministers, their wives and children, and in many other poor people.[41]

[37] LW, vol. 39, p.70 (*On the Papacy in Rome*, 1520). WA 6, 296, 37-297, 5.

[38] J. Heckel, "Die zwo Kirchen: Eine juristische Betrachtung über Luthers Schrift von dem Papsttum zu Rom" (1956), in Heckel, *Das blinde, undeutliche Wort "Kirche," Gesammelte Aufsätze*, edited by Siegfried Grundmann, 111-31 (Cologne/Graz: H. Böhlau, 1964), has been occupied with an extensive systematizing of his distinction.

[39] LW, vol. 41, pp. 148-65. WA 50, 628, 16-642, 21.

[40] LW, vol. 41, p. 148. WA 50, 628, 16-19.

[41] LW, vol. 41, p. 198. WA 51, 486, 6-12. The entire list of *notae* are on pp. 479, 4-487, 2.

Among these enumerations the following deserve accenting. First, the unconditioned preeminence of the Word is as distinct in the *notae* as in the young Luther.
Next, Luther made clear that the church, however great a spiritual entity, nonetheless exists visibly and corporeally. The presence of the right, true church can be seen
in preaching according to the gospel, but also in lived faith, particularly in the
renouncing of revenge. Finally, both lists serve to deny to the Roman Catholic
Church its existence as church. "Thus we have proved that we are the true, ancient
church, one body and one communion of saints with the holy, universal, Christian
Church. Now you too, papists, prove that you are the true church or are like it."
Things such as indulgence indicate "that you are the new false church, which is in
everything apostate, separated from the true, ancient church, thus becoming Satan's
whore and synagogue."[42]

Luther was also aware that the tradition has been preserved in the Roman
church, from which evangelicals have received the true tradition.

> We on our part confess that there is much that is Christian and good under the
> papacy; indeed everything that is Christian and good is to be found there and has
> come to us from this source. For instance we confess that in the papal church
> there are the true holy Scriptures, true baptism, the true sacrament of the altar,
> the true keys to the forgiveness of sins, the true office of the ministry, the true cat-
> echism in the form of the Lord's Prayer, the Ten Commandments, and the articles
> of the creed. . . . I contend that in the papacy there is true Christianity, even the
> right kind of Christianity. The Christianity that now is under the papacy is truly
> the body of Christ and a member of it. If it is his body, then it has the true spirit,
> gospel, faith, baptism, sacrament, keys, the office of the ministry, prayer, holy
> Scripture and everything that pertains to Christendom. So we are still under the
> papacy and therefrom have received our Christian treasures.[43]

Luther was also aware that the tradition has been preserved in the Roman
church, from which evangelicals have received the true tradition. Luther
reproached Rome not for lacking the fundamental *nota Ecclesiae* but for the intrusion
of human additions. His judgment on the existence of the Roman church as church
is thus ambivalent: on the one hand, he conceded that it is altogether a church, that
it lacks nothing that constitutes a church, but on the other asserted that it has
become a church of the devil.

---

[42] *LW*, vol. 41, p. 199. *WA* 51, 487, 3-8. See also *LW*, vol. 41, p. 214; *WA* 51, 513, 28-29; *LW*, vol.
41, p. 215; *WA* 51, 515, 27 (adapted for printing), and elsewhere, in which Luther called the pope's
church the "devil's church."

[43] *LW*, vol. 40, pp. 231-32 (*Concerning Rebaptism*, 1528). *WA* 26, 147, 13-40.

Chapter 30

OFFICE AND ORDINATION

THE STARTING POINT OF LUTHER'S VIEW OF OFFICE

For more than a hundred years the interpretation of Luther's statements on the ministerial office and universal priesthood, but also on ordination and not least on the episcopal office, has been the subject of extraordinary controversy. In essence, the fronts observable as early as in the confessional theology of the nineteenth century are still intact. It was chiefly J. W. F. Höfling (1802-1853) who advocated the so-called transfer theory, deriving the spiritual office from the universal priesthood. According to Höfling, the ministerial office and the universal priesthood were to a certain extent identical.[1] In opposition, others such as Theodor Kliefoth (1810-1868), Friedrich Julius Stahl (1802-1861), and especially August Friedrich Christian Vilmar (1800-1868) vigorously stressed the independence of the ministerial office over against the congregation and universal priesthood.[2]

These two interpretations are in essence still represented today. W. Brunotte concedes that in his various disputes Luther at times exaggerated. He nevertheless stresses the "unity in Luther's view," which consists of the "independence of the spiritual office alongside the universal priesthood . . . in the early . . . as well as in the later period."[3] According to Brunotte, Luther never derived the office bearer's authority from the

---

[1] Johann Wilhelm Friedrich Höfling, *Grundsätze evangelisch-lutherischer Kirchenverfassung* (1850; 3d ed. Erlangen: T. Bläsing, 1853). See Manfred Kiessig, *Johann Wilhelm Friedrich Höfling, Leben und Werk*, Die Lutherische Kirche, Geschichte und Gestalten 14 (Gütersloh: Gerd Mohn, 1991), esp. 138-59. Kiessig is concerned with giving Höfling's view a warily discrete interpretation.

[2] See more detail in Holsten Fagerberg, *Kirche und Amt in der deutschen konfessionellen Theologie des 19. Jahrhunderts* (Uppsala/Wiesbaden: Almquist and Wiksells, 1952).

[3] Brunotte, *Das geistliche Amt bei Luther.* (Berlin: Lutherisches Verlagshaus, 1959), 112-14.

universal priesthood. By contrast, H. Lieberg speaks of a "bipolarity" in Luther's doctrine of the pastoral office.[4] This bipolarity consists in the fact that the office is founded
on the universal priesthood, as well as on the institution by Christ. To the former idea
corresponds the call of the congregation, to the latter ordination as being entrusted
with an office.[5] Evidence furnished by P. Manns yields an important supplement: in
those early stormy years of the Reformation Luther resisted all requests for house
communions among evangelical Christians in a predominantly Catholic area, and he
linked the celebration of the Lord's Supper strictly to office and congregation.[6]

Given this stage of the research, it might be less meaningful simply to emphasize
one or the other interpretation. Where it is a matter of office and ordination, it is
important to note the situation to which Luther addressed his ideas. At least to
Luther's mind, the dispute with Rome did not originally concern the ministerial
office, or even the papal office. Of course, it was unavoidable that he should collide
with the bearers of high office, and that the question of the task and nature of the
office and its various shapes should soon emerge. It would be totally unrealistic to
expect from Luther a balanced view on the question of office at the height of his early
dispute with Rome. On this question, we should note what was repeatedly stressed
above, that it was precisely in sharp debate that Luther tacitly held views that he did
not further elaborate but that are still of significance for his entire theology.

Only in later years did Luther express himself more comprehensively on the
nature and task of the office. It is also significant that in his treatise *On Councils and
the Church* (1539), as well as in *Against Hanswurst* (1541), he numbered the ministerial office among the marks of the church. In *On Councils and the Church* he wrote:

> Fifth, the church is recognized externally by the fact that it consecrates or calls
> ministers, or has offices that it is to administer. There must be bishops, pastors, or
> preachers, who publicly and privately give, administer, and use the aforemen-
> tioned four things or holy possessions [the Word of God, Baptism, the Lord's Sup-
> per, and the forgiveness of sins in penance] in behalf of and in the name of the
> church, or rather by reason of their institution by Christ.[7]

It is further worth noting that at no time did Luther basically challenge the episcopal office. He clearly distinguished between the papal office and the office of
bishop. Of course, we should emphasize that in the years of his sharp dispute with
Rome and later, he always accented the unconditional preeminence of the Word of

---

[4] Lieberg, *Amt und Ordination bei Luther und Melanchthon,* KKDG 11 (Göttingen: Vandenhoeck &
Ruprecht, 1962), 235ff.

[5] Ibid., 235.

[6] Manns, "Amt und Eucharistie in der Theologie Martin Luthers" (1973), in Manns, *Vater im
Glauben: Studien zur Theologie Martin Luthers: Festgabe zum 65. Geburtstag,* edited by Rolf Decot, VIEG 131
(Stuttgart: Steiner Verlag Wiesbaden, 1988), esp. 115-25.

[7] *LW,* vol. 41, p. 154. *WA* 50, 632, 35-633, 3. See *LW,* vol. 41, p. 196; *WA* 51, 481, 7-16. See above,
pp. 282-83.

God. Just as the chief thing in the church is its proclamation of the Word, so this proclamation is the authentic task of the spiritual office. To proclamation belongs the preaching of the Word and administration of the sacraments.

One of Luther's most significant innovations was his doctrine of the universal priesthood of the baptized. The first hint of this view, to be evaluated further below, is present early on in Luther. As early as in the Romans lecture of 1515/1516 he said: "Every word which proceeds from the mouth of a leader of the church or from the mouth of a good and holy man is the word of Christ, for He said: 'He who hears you hears me' (Luke 10:16)."[8] Only in 1520, however, did Luther hold the view of the universal priesthood of all the baptized, first of all in *A Treatise on the New Testament*: "Thus it becomes clear that it is not the priest alone who offers the sacrifice of the mass; it is this faith which each one has for himself. This is the true priestly office, through which Christ is offered as a sacrifice to God, an office which the priest, with the outward ceremonies of the mass, simply represents. Each and all are, therefore, equally spiritual priests before God."[9]

In essence, the following phases in Luther's reflections on office and ordination are to be clearly distinguished:

1. In the period from 1517 till 1520, Luther lost confidence in the churchly authorities and developed his view of the universal priesthood of all the baptized.

2. In the period from the fall of 1520, or early in 1521, till 1523, he gave the harshest formulation to his anti-Roman view, but against the radical wing of the Reformation gave new accent to the need for a structured office.

3. From 1524 to 1529, in opposition to the fanatics, Luther developed in greater detail the intimate connection between the work of the Holy Spirit and preaching on the part of the ministerial office.

4. After 1530, in the wake of the structuring of evangelical provincial churches, the ministerial office took on more and more fixed contours, and various attempts were made at installing evangelical bishops.

We also need to consider that the total insecurity in those early years of the Reformation led to adopting emergency solutions that of course could be given sufficient theological support but were nonetheless not retained under settled conditions. Since no bishop in the German Empire attached himself to the Reformation, and since, further, only at the onset of the disputes did any number of pastors go over to the Reformation, the problem of caring for congregations by ordained persons soon became acute. Some of Luther's reflections in this early period must be understood against this emergency situation. Even when evangelical provincial churches began to be formed, Luther appealed to emergency privilege. The firmer the evangelical alliance, and the more painstaking the establishment of provincial church order, the less the appeal to

[8] *LW,* vol. 25, p. 238. *WA* 56, 251, 25-26 (scholia on Rom. 3:22).
[9] *LW,* vol. 35, pp. 100-101. *WA* 6, 370, 7-11.

emergency privilege. We should note also that the formation of evangelical provincial churches did not follow according to a fixed plan but depended on local conditions and situations. To these situations Bugenhagen in particular gave attention in the drafting of church orders. It would have best corresponded with Luther's view if the churches had been led by episcopal offices synodically constituted. Such was not possible then, for many reasons. All sorts of compromises resulted that Luther regarded as defensible theologically but scarcely a solution.

THE UNIVERSAL PRIESTHOOD

As mentioned above, it was in his *Treatise on the New Testament* (1520) that Luther first submitted his view of the universal priesthood of the baptized. Shortly thereafter, in much greater detail and in harsh polemic against the Roman view, he set forth his own position in the treatise *To the Christian Nobility of the German Nation Concerning the Reform of the Christian Estate* (1520). The context must be noted here. Luther's reproach was that the "Romanists" had built three walls around themselves: "Hitherto they have protected themselves by these walls in such a way that no one has been able to reform them. As a result, the whole of Christendom has fallen abominably."[10] The first wall signifies that when pressed by the temporal power, the Romanists respond that it has no jurisdiction over them, that the spiritual power is above the temporal. The second wall signifies that when attempt is made to reprove them with the Scriptures, they object that no one is suited to interpret the Bible but the pope. Finally, the third wall signifies that when threatened with a council, they invent the idea that none may summon a council but the pope.[11]

To this Luther opposed his view of the universal priesthood: "It is pure invention that pope, bishop, priests, and monks are called the spiritual estate while princes, lords, artisans, and farmers are called the temporal estate. This is indeed a piece of deceit and hypocrisy. Yet no one need be intimidated by it, and for this reason: all Christians are truly of the spiritual estate, and there is no difference among them except that of office."[12] There is no missing the polemical tone. This is true also of the words that follow: "For whoever comes out of the water of baptism can boast that he is already a consecrated priest, bishop, and pope, although of course it is not seemly that just anybody shall exercise such office."[13]

[10] *LW*, vol. 44, p. 126. *WA* 6, 406, 21-23.
[11] *LW*, vol. 44, p. 126. *WA* 6, 406, 23-29.
[12] *LW*, vol. 44, p. 127. *WA* 6, 407, 10-15.
[13] *LW*, vol. 44, p. 129. *WA* 6, 408, 11-13. Hans-Martin Barth, *Einander Priester sein: Allgemeines Priestertum in ökumenischer Perspective,* KiKonf 29 (Göttingen: Vandenhoeck & Ruprecht, 1990), 27ff., has analyzed in greater detail the relevant texts where Luther spoke of the universal priesthood.

What Luther had in mind is clearer in Latin than in English. All throughout he used the term *sacerdos / sacerdotes* (priest) for the universal priesthood of the baptized, while as a rule he used the term *minister / ministri* (minister) of the pastor. He never used the term *ministerium* for the universal priesthood. After 1520 he seemed to use the term *sacerdotium* of pastors in only a few isolated instances. In the treatise entitled *Concerning the Ministry* (1523), he said first of all that "a priest is not identical with Presbyter or Minister—for one is born [in baptism by water and Spirit] to be priest, one becomes a minister [through the *vocatio*]."[14] A statement from 1530 is even clearer: "It is true that all Christians are priests, but not all are pastors. To be a pastor one must be not only a Christian and a priest but must have an office and a field of work committed to him. This call and command make pastors and preachers."[15]

Statements concerning the universal priesthood accordingly mean that no mediation is required between God and humanity. The Christian's salvation is not dependent on mediation through a particular priest. All the baptized are priests in the New Testament sense, thus in faith have free access to God. As priests they can promise forgiveness of sins to other Christians and thus have all the blessings of the gospel.

Naturally, we must also keep in mind the polemical context in which Luther developed these ideas: statements about the universal priesthood always serve to counter the resistance of the Catholic hierarchy and especially the papacy to demands for reform. Luther was breaking here with the medieval idea of the hierarchy of estates, according to which the spiritual is above the temporal, with the pope at the apex. By contrast, he emphasized the independence of the temporal estate, which has its own task from God, and in fulfilling it need not be obedient to the spiritual estate.

To establish his view, Luther interpreted the universal priesthood on the basis of baptism or of faith. In the so-called principal Reformation treatises of 1520, he referred to baptism by which every Christian is consecrated a priest. He could, however, establish the universal priesthood simply on the basis of faith in Christ, or could even describe faith as the proper priestly office. Thus, as early as in *A Treatise on the New Testament,* he wrote: "Faith must do everything. Faith alone is the true priestly office. It permits no one else to take its place. Therefore all Christian men are priests, all women priestesses, be they young or old, master or servant, mistress or maid, learned or unlearned. Here there is no difference, unless faith be unequal."[16] A bit later, in a sermon he wrote: "If I believe now, then I am also a priest, who will deny me that? If the platen makes us priests, then we could just as well make a goose and an ass a priest. . . . So faith carries the priesthood along with it. It

---

[14] *LW,* vol. 40, p. 18. *WA* 12, 178, 9-10: "Sacerdotem non esse quod presbyterum vel ministrum; illum nasci, hunc fieri."

[15] *LW,* vol. 13, p. 65 (*Commentary on Psalm 82,* 1530). *WA* 31 I, 211, 17-20.

[16] *LW,* vol. 35, p. 101. *WA* 6,370, 24-28.

is a great power that we can all be priests. It has nothing at all to do with bishops."[17] Indeed, Luther could say that "thus only those are the holy and spiritual priesthood who are true Christians and are built on the Stone," that is, who believe in Christ.[18] Or, he put it more brusquely: "He who does not believe is no priest."[19]

As a result, the universal priesthood cannot simply be understood as the "objective" gift of baptism. Everything depends on the relation between baptism and faith.

Clearly, even around 1520, when Luther spoke most pointedly of the universal priesthood, he always held to the particular task of the ministerial office. It is not clear what ecclesiological consequences he intended to draw from his view of the universal priesthood.[20] What is certain is that he conceded to every baptized person the authority to hear confessions and forgive sins. In any event in his early years he held the opinion *That the Christian Assembly or Congregation Has the Right and Power to Judge All Teaching and to Call, Appoint, and Dismiss Teachers.*[21] Despite this, Luther did not make this Reformation view of the universal priesthood the basis for drafting an evangelical church constitution. He limited himself to giving a theological reason for it and for the basic equality of the various callings and estates in church and world. At no time did he draw consequences for congregations from his doctrine. Nevertheless, his early statements made clear that the evangelical church could have been shaped in a vastly different way. In later years Luther spoke less often and in less pronounced fashion of the universal priesthood.[22]

THE MINISTERIAL OFFICE

In the phases that we are able to observe, Luther's statements on the ministerial office were variously accented. In his early years he could speak in a way suggesting that he intended to derive the ministerial office from the universal priesthood. In the treatise *To the Christian Nobility of the German Nation* he wrote:

[17] Sermon, 1522, *WA* 10 III, 398, 24-29.

[18] *LW,* vol. 30, p. 53 (*Sermons on the First Epistle of St. Peter,* 1522); *WA* 12, 307, 22-23.

[19] *LW,* vol. 30, p. 62. *WA* 12, 316, 26-27.

[20] On this subject see H.-M. Barth, *Einander Priester,* 37ff. Barth, 46-48, identifies a few "hazy and obscure elements" in Luther's statements on the universal priesthood and points to a certain contradiction in Reformation practice.

[21] *LW,* vol. 39, p. 305. *WA* 11, 408-15. Even in this treatise with its far-reaching proposals for limiting episcopal power, the particular conditions in Leisnig, which furnished the occasion for its composition, must be taken into account. In addition to the introduction in *LW,* vol. 39, p. 305; *WA* 11, 401-2; see also *WA* 12, 1-8.

[22] Barth, *Einander Priester,* 48.

Therefore, when a bishop consecrates it is nothing else than that in the place and stead of the whole community, all of whom have like power, he takes a person and charges him to exercise this power on behalf of the others. It is like ten brothers, all king's sons and equal heirs, choosing one of themselves to rule the inheritance in the interests of all. In one sense they are all kings and of equal power, and yet one of them is charged with the responsibility of ruling. To put it still more clearly: suppose a group of earnest Christian laymen were taken prisoner and set down in a desert without an episcopally ordained priest among them. And suppose they were to come to a common mind there and then in the desert and elect one of their number, whether he were married or not, and charge him to baptize, say mass, pronounce absolution, and preach the gospel. Such a man would be as truly a priest as though he had been ordained by all the bishops and popes in the world. That is why in cases of necessity anyone can baptize and give absolution.[23]

From this text one can plainly derive a democratic principle of delegation. Of course, the polemical context must be kept in mind. And here, after all, it is not the office as such that derives from the universal priesthood; what is recommended is merely the installation of a particular occupant on the basis of that priesthood. Finally, the question as to whether Luther had only an emergency privilege in mind must remain open.

In *The Babylonian Captivity of the Church* (1520), Luther denied that ordination is a sacrament. The idea was invented by the church of the pope.[24] In the course of his debate with the Roman view, he appealed to the universal priesthood: "But the priests, as we call them, are ministers chosen from among us. All that they do is done in our name, the priesthood is nothing but a ministry."[25] Here too Luther did not dispute the divine institution of the ministerial office but merely rejected the institution of the sacrament of consecration as divine.

In 1520 Luther expressed himself clearly on the divine institution of the office. In the treatise *To the Christian Nobility of the German Nation,* he wrote: "I want to speak only of the ministry which God has instituted, the responsibility of which is to minister word and sacrament to a congregation, among whom they reside."[26]

---

[23] *LW,* vol. 44, p. 128. *WA* 6, 407, 29-408, 2. See also *LW,* vol. 36, p. 116 (*The Babylonian Captivity,* 1520): "Let everyone, therefore, who knows himself to be a Christian, be assured of this, that we are all equally priests, that is to say, we have the same power in respect to the Word and the sacraments. However, no one may make use of this power except by the consent of the community or by the call of a superior. For what is the common property of all, no individual may arrogate to himself, unless he is called." *WA* 6, 566, 26-30: "Esto itaque certus et sese agnoscat quicunque se Christianum esse cognoverit, omnes nos aequaliter esse sacerdotes, hoc est, eandem in verbo et sacramento quocunque habere potestatem, verum non licere quenquam hac ipsa uti nisi consensu communitatis aut vocatione maioris (Quod enim omnium est communiter, nullus singulariter potest sibi arrogare, donec vocetur)."

[24] *LW,* vol. 36, pp. 106-7. *WA* 6, 560, 20-21.

[25] *LW,* vol. 36, p. 113. *WA* 6, 564, 11-13: "Sacerdotes vero quos vocamus ministri sunt ex nobis electi, qui nostro nomine omnia faciant, et sacerdotium aliud nihil est quam ministerium."

[26] *LW,* vol. 44, p. 176. *WA* 6, 441, 24-26.

This statement appears to be without connection to the argument that the office is required for the sake of order. Luther himself saw no contradiction, indeed, not even a tension, between the two arguments.

Since the mid-1520s, on the basis of his experiences with the so-called Reformation left wing and in agreement with the new church structuring, Luther more strongly stressed the need for order. In the treatise *On Councils and the Church* (1539), he stated:

> There must be bishops, pastors, or preachers. . . . The people as a whole cannot do these things, but must entrust or have them entrusted to one person. Otherwise what would happen if everyone wanted to speak or administer, and no one wanted to give way to the other? It must be entrusted to one person, and he alone should be allowed to preach, to baptize, to absolve, and to administer the sacraments. The others should be content with this arrangement and agree to it. Whenever you see this done, be assured that God's people, the holy Christian people, are present.[27]

Taking into account the various accents within the various phases as well as the basic view retained throughout, one can single out the following aspects in Luther's view of the particular task of the ministerial office:

1. The ministerial office or office of preaching has to do with public proclamation of the Word and administration of the sacraments. Although there is no basic difference between authorization in the context of the universal priesthood and in that of the ministerial office, the public character of the *ministerium* requires that the occupant exercise his functions on the basis of the consent of the church. For Luther, "public character" means first of all that the office is perceived *coram ecclesia* (in the presence of the church) and *in nomine ecclesiae* (in the name of the church), and second, that the ministerial office is always related to a specific congregation.[28]

2. The ministerial office exists for the sake of order. If all Christians, due to their authorization by the universal priesthood, were to lay claim to exercising rights that are theirs as such, the result would be chaos. The task of public proclamation is not given to the individual Christian. In this sense the ministerial office serves order in the congregation as well as in the entire church.

---

[27] *LW,* vol. 41, p. 154. *WA* 50, 632, 36-633, 1.

[28] Lieberg, *Amt und Ordination,* 69-74, has demonstrated this viewpoint of the public character of the ministerial office. See *LW,* vol. 40, p. 34 (*Concerning the Ministry,* 1523): "For since . . . all of these things are the common property of all Christians, no one individual can arise by his own authority and arrogate to himself alone what belongs to all. . . . But the community rights demand that one, or as many as the community chooses, shall be chosen or approved who, in the name of all with these rights, shall perform these functions publicly. Otherwise there might be shameful confusion among the people of God." *WA* 12, 189, 17-25: "Nam cum omnium Christianorum haec sint omnia . . . communia, nulli licet in medium prodire autoritate propria et sibi arripere soli, quod omnium est. . . . Verum haec communio iuris cogit, ut unus, aut quotquot placuerint communitati, eligantur vel acceptentur, qui vice et nomine omnium, qui idem iuris habent, exequantur officia ista publice, ne turpis sit confusio in populo dei."

3. Without prejudice to the fact that he at times could base the *ministerium* on the *sacerdotium*, and could regard its essential function as building up the community in orderly fashion, Luther always held to the divine institution of the ministerial office. Ephesians 4:11 reads: "And his gifts were that some should be apostles, some prophets, some evangelists, some pastors and teachers." In this text, but also in other New Testament passages, Luther found scriptural support for the fact that Christ instituted the offices, including the ministerial office. Such institution holds good not only for the first generation, but, since the church shall remain till the end of the world, for all times.

4. The primary tasks of the ministerial office are proclamation of the Word and administration of the sacraments. Luther also named among the pastor's tasks especially care of souls and leadership of the congregation. In his treatise *To the Christian Nobility of the German Nation,* he speaks of "the ministry which God has instituted, the responsibility of which is to minister word and sacrament to a congregation, among whom they reside."[29]

5. The ministerial office is the office absolutely, and as to its form the office of pastor. Here, like the other reformers, Luther was referring to conditions in the early church where there was no difference between bishop and pastor. Basically, the pastor is the bishop of his congregation, or the bishop is the pastor of a larger area. There is thus no difference in the power of consecration, and no special episcopal ordination. There are only differences respecting specific functions. Even in relation to other offices the ministerial office is the authentic office. The reason lies in its divine institution.

6. Since the office lends no higher quality of being, but serves the exercise of particular functions, it stands or falls with the actual performance of these functions. If this does not occur, if the office bearers do not function, if they no longer act according to the commission and institution of Christ, if they are false teachers, then the congregation has the right to dismiss them. Indeed, it is obliged to do so. In doing so, however, no arbitrary measures may be used. In such cases, the congregation must act in obedience to the commission of Christ, to whom the office bearer is also obligated. Aside from this, the pastor may also resign on his own, in which case he again becomes a member of the congregation just like the others.[30]

7. The pastor's status consists in carrying on his activity in the service of God. For this reason the office bearer must also stand far back of his task. In the treatise *Against Hanswurst* (1541), Luther stated that a pastor should not beg forgiveness for what he preaches. He should rather say: "*Haec dixit dominus,* 'God himself has said this' [1 Cor. 1:10]. And again, 'In this sermon I have been an apostle and a prophet

[29] *LW,* vol. 44, p. 176. *WA* 6, 441, 24-27.
[30] See *WA* 41, 209, 11-14 (*Der 110. Psalm gepredigt und ausgelegt,* 1539, 1535).

of Jesus Christ' [1 Thess. 4:15]. Here it is unnecessary, even bad, to pray for forgiveness of sins, as if one had not taught truly, for it is God's word and not my word."[31]

8. According to Luther, *vocatio* (calling) to a particular congregation and *ordinatio* are not synonymous. While in his restructuring program Bugenhagen wanted every ordination to take place in the congregation issuing the call, Luther's position was that ordination should be held at Wittenberg as the ecclesiastical-theological center of the Reformation. On occasion he did state that ordinations could be held in individual congregations later on. From 1525 on, ordinations were held at Wittenberg. Up to that time, enough ordained priests had gone over to the Reformation that the question of ordination did not yet arise. The first to be ordained by Luther at Wittenberg was Magister Georg Rörer. On May 14, 1525, he was ordained a deacon by prayer and the laying on of hands at a congregational worship service.[32] In the years following ordinations occurred only sporadically, since it was still an open question whether church unity could be preserved through comprehensive reform. Following the Imperial Diet at Augsburg in 1530 with its consolidation of fronts, ordination was frequently held at Wittenberg. By decree of the Saxon elector Johann Friedrich in 1535, ordination of the new generation of pastors was introduced at Wittenberg by prayer and the laying on of hands at congregational worship services.

9. For Luther, ordination denoted an actualizing of the choice and calling to ministerial office.[33] It confirmed the legitimacy of the call; it was an assignment to office in the church, not only in the congregation, as well as a blessing on the office.[34] During the prayer of the congregation the ordinand was given the Holy Spirit, "who preserves them in the pure doctrine, permits them to be true evangelists and to remain faithful and true against the devil, the world, and their own flesh."[35] Luther did not recognize a *character indelibilis,* supposedly transmitted to the priest through consecration, but was all the more convinced that the authority and power to exercise the office were transmitted to the ordinand. To this extent ordination was the effective transmission of the ministerial office.

10. For Luther, the consequence of this view is that ordination is nonrepeatable.

[31] *LW,* vol. 41, p. 216. *WA* 1, 517, 5-13.

[32] See Lieberg, *Amt und Ordination,* 182.

[33] See the detailed investigation in ibid., 168-234.

[34] See ibid., 196-97.

[35] Ibid., 200-201.

THE EPISCOPAL OFFICE

Luther's view of the office of bishop can be tersely evaluated, since he believed it merely represented a particular instance of the ministerial office.[36] It is significant that despite his attack on the papacy based on New Testament teaching as well as on development throughout church history, he never challenged the office of bishop. The reason for this is that in various places the New Testament clearly refers to the episcopal office. New Testament statements furnished the basis for Luther's view of the office as developed in the treatise *Exempel, einen rechten christlichen Bischof zu weihen* (1542).[37]

According to Luther the implication of statements in 1 Timothy 3:2 and Titus 1:7, 9, is "that a bishop should be holy, should preach, baptize, bind and loose sins, comfort and help souls to eternal life."[38] The bishop's tasks are in essence the same as those of the pastor. With this argument Luther was harking back to the practice of the early church, for which the office of bishop was related to the community and ultimately identical with the office of pastor. What is special about the office is merely that the bishop should also care for pastors. In consequence, any power of jurisdiction peculiar to the bishop is nonexistent.

Luther charged the Roman church with lacking such bishops. There, the office of bishop was disfigured to the point of unrecognizability. At the same time, he was prepared to make certain concessions. He insisted that the bishop must carry out the task of preaching but would yield if bishops entrusted other suitable persons with the task, as, for example, Bishop Valerius once left preaching to the young priest Augustine. Luther emphasized that he did not intend to abolish the cathedral foundations, but to reform them and spur them on to proper conduct of office.

In view of the Catholic bishops' resistance to reform, the evangelical prince in large measure took over the vacant episcopal see, and in the church tailored to the Reformation functioned as *summus episcopus*. Luther regarded this as a makeshift, for which he coined the term "emergency bishop" (*Notbischof*).[39]

---

[36] Besides the literature cited above, see Bernhard Lohse, "Die Stellung zum Bischofsamt in der Confessio Augustana," in *Evangelium—Sakramente—Amt und die Einheit der Kirche*, ed. Karl Lehmann and Edmund Schlink, Dialog der Kirchen 2 (Freiburg im Breisgau: Herder, 1982), 80-108.

[37] *WA* 53 (219), 231-60; on this subject see the brief evaluation in M. Brecht, "Martin Luther und das Bischofsamt," 141-43.

[38] *WA* 53, 253, 6-8.

[39] See *WA* 53, 255, 5-8: "Mussen doch unsere weltliche Herrschafften jtzt Not Bischove sein und uns Pfarherr und Prediger (Nach dem der Baptist und sein Rotte nicht dazu, sonder da wider thut) schutzen und helffen, das wir predigen, Kirchen und Schulen dienen konnen." ("Now our temporal rulers must be emergency bishops, must protect and help us pastors and preachers—since the pope and his horde will not, but are opposed to it—so that we can preach, serve churches and schools.") Ibid., 256, 1-3: "Denn sie [die Landesfürsten] haben solchs gethan und wol thun mussen als Patronen des Stiffts, die Kirchen des Stiffts bey dem heiligen Euangelio und erkandten Warheit zu erhalten, als

Attempts to install an evangelical theologian as bishop in a vacated see, such as Luther undertook in Naumburg and Merseburg,[40] indicate that he was struggling to arrive at his own structuring of the episcopal office, and to prevent the temporary assistance of princes from becoming a permanent arrangement. His attempts failed in view of the fusion of political and confessional issues.

---

rechte Not Bischove in solchem fall." ("For they [the provincial rulers] have done and indeed must do it as patrons of the foundation, in order to preserve the churches of the foundation with the holy gospel and the accepted truth, in such cases functioning as proper emergency bishops.") See Karl Holl, "Luther und das landesherrliche Kirchenregiment," in *Gesammelte Aufsätze zur Kirchengeschichte,* 3 vols. (Tübingen: Mohr, 1927-28), 1, 7 aufl. 326-80; Hans-Walter Krumwiede, *Zur Entstehung des landesherrlichen Kirchenregiments in Kursachsen und Braunschweig-Wolfenbüttel,* SKGNS 16 (Göttingen: Vandenhoeck & Ruprecht, 1967).

[40] See the researches of I. Höss and H.-U. Delius.

Chapter 31

BAPTISM

The Starting Point of Luther's Theology of Baptism

Formation of a new, Reformation theology of baptism went hand in hand with Luther's entire theological development, particularly during his first lectures on the Psalms and Romans.[1] In dealing with the sacraments, concentration on questions such as judgment and gospel, righteousness and faith, or on the divine promise and human confidence, led to a new impulse and important consequences: the criterion under which Luther dealt with baptism was baptismal usage. In other words, the relation of baptism to life from the perspective of the acceptance of the divine judgment promised in baptism took center stage.[2] Since Luther's understanding of the nature of sin was more radical than the theology of late scholasticism, he could no longer share the view that baptism purges inherited sin, of which a mere "tinder" (*fomes*) remains, and against the seductions of which the baptized can successfully resist. He understood baptism in the total sense.

> For they are baptized "into death," that is, toward death, which is to say, they have begun to live in such a way that they are pursuing this kind of death and reach out toward this their goal. For although they are baptized unto eternal life and the kingdom of heaven, yet they do not all at once possess this goal fully, but they have begun to act in such a way that they may attain to it—for Baptism was established to direct us toward death and through this death to life.[3]

---

[1] See above, pp. 57-59 and 78-80.

[2] This has been elucidated particularly by Werner Jetter, *Die Taufe beim jungen Luther*, BHTh 18 (Tübingen: Mohr, 1954), passim.

[3] *LW*, vol. 25, p. 312. *WA* 56, 324, 17-22 (scholia on Rom. 6:4).

This statement contains the quintessence of Luther's later theology of baptism. Its most important characteristic is the relation of baptism to life under the sign of faith.

Since the onset of his dispute with Rome, Luther was led to occupy himself in greater detail with baptism and the proper understanding of it. Controversy over indulgences and penance furnished him the impetus for composing various sermons on the sacraments in 1519/1520, of which the sermon on baptism contained his first treatment of it.[4] From the fall of 1521 or the spring of 1522 Wittenberg was in turmoil over the sacraments generally. Naturally, the Lord's Supper was in greater dispute than baptism.[5] The topic of baptism became central when at Zurich, around 1524/1525, the Anabaptist movement took shape with its rejection of infant baptism and its advocacy of "believer's baptism," thus of adults. From that time on, Luther strongly insisted that baptism follows not from the faith of the one to be baptized but from divine institution and disposition.

Alongside these shifts in accent that the reflection on the nature of baptism involved, we need to note other specifically terminological changes respecting sacramental doctrine in general and baptism in particular. Augustine had once coined the now famous formula: "Accedit verbum ad elementum, et fit sacramentum, etiam ipsum tamquam visibile verbum" (the word is added to the element and a sacrament occurs, a visible word, as it were).[6] In scholasticism, influenced by Aristotelian philosophy, one spoke of *materia* and *forma* rather than of "element" or "word." Very early on, Luther reverted to Augustinian usage, suggesting that he developed his doctrine of the sacraments in exegetical fashion and thus avoided terms without basis in New Testament usage.

The following points are of special importance:

1. Luther did not begin with a sacramental doctrine from which to derive the interpretation of each sacrament. He rather developed his view of each sacrament by recourse to the New Testament.

2. For a time, that is, in 1519/1520, Luther still gave his own particular definition to the "sacrament," that is, by way of the terms "sign," "meaning," and "faith."[7] After 1520, he no longer held to such a definition, though he returned to the juxtaposition and union of Word and Sacrament.

---

[4] *LW,* vol. 35, pp. 29-43 (*The Holy and Blessed Sacrament of Baptism,* 1519). *WA* 2, 727-37.

[5] See esp. Luther's treatise, *The Sacrament of the Body and Blood of Christ against the Fanatics,* 1526, *LW,* vol. 36, pp. 335-61. *WA* 19, 482-523.

[6] Augustine, *Tract. in Joh.* 80.3; *CCSL* 36, 529, 5-7. On Luther's reception of this formula see K.-H. zur Mühlen, *ZThK* 70 (1973), 50-76. Zur Mühlen indicates that through his new understanding of Word and faith Luther to some extent gives new meaning to this formula (ibid., 56-57).

[7] See above, pp.127-33.

3. After 1520, in statements on baptism and the Lord's Supper, as well as in treating other sacraments taught by the church in this period, Luther gave centrality to the duality of "promise" (*promissio*) and "faith" (*fides*).

4. Due to Anabaptist resistance to infant baptism, as well as to the various symbolical interpretations of the elements in the Supper on the part of Karlstadt, Zwingli, and others, Luther emphasized the institution or establishment of the sacraments of Baptism and the Lord's Supper. The accent on faith is preserved throughout; it does not compete with the character of Baptism and Lord's Supper as instituted.

5. We should note that Luther employed the term *sacramentum* (sacrament) in a narrower as well as in a broader sense. Particularly in his early period he could use *sacramentum* synonymously with *signum* (sign). In addition, *sacramentum* could also express the entire activity of Baptism or the Lord's Supper.[8] In such twofold usage Luther was following Augustine.[9]

6. When Luther at times used the word "sign," particularly in his doctrine of the Supper, that use may not be construed in Zwinglian terms. Luther never intended the term to be merely "symbolic."

Thus, throughout the various phases of his thought and activity, Luther consistently retained the Reformation impulse in his doctrine of the sacraments. At the same time, in his debate with fanatics and Anabaptists, he came more and more to reflect on presuppositions held early in his career and accordingly shored up his emphasis on promise and faith against possible misinterpretation.

THE INSTITUTION AND NATURE OF BAPTISM

In Luther's late phase, that is, following his debate with the Anabaptists, he put great stress on the divine institution of baptism. His opening statements in the Large Catechism emphasize that the sacraments are "instituted by Christ," that "every Christian ought to have at least some brief, elementary instruction in them, because without these no one can be a Christian, although unfortunately in the past nothing was taught about them."[10]

[8] See Schwab, *Entwicklung und Gestalt der Sakramententheologie bei Martin Luther*, 303-64. 320-21.

[9] See Ekkehard Mühlenberg, *HdBDThG*, 1:420-24.

[10] *Book of Concord*, p. 436. On Luther's criticism of an earlier lack in treating the institution of Baptism, see *BSLK*, p. 554, n. 8: "Vgl. Mathesius, *Luthers Leben in Predigten*, 129, 13-16: 'Auf der Kanzel kann ich mich nicht erinnern, dass ich in meiner Jugend, der ich doch bis in 25. Jahr meines Alters (1529) im Bapsttumb leider bin gefangen gelegen, die zehen Gebot, Symbolum, Vaterunser oder Taufe gehöret hätte. In Schulen lase man in der Fasten von der Beicht und einerlei Gestalt [des Abendmahls].'" ("I cannot remember that in my youth, when till the 25th year of my age [1529] I unfortunately lay captive to the papacy, I ever heard from the pulpit the Ten Commandments, the creed, the Our Father, or Baptism. In schools we read in Lent about confession and the one kind [of the Supper].") As a historical judgment on sacramental doctrine in scholasticism, Luther's statement is decidedly too harsh.

For Christ's institution of baptism he appealed especially to Matthew 28:19: "Go therefore and make disciples of all nations, baptizing them in the name of the Father and of the Son and of the Holy Spirit." He also took support from the word at the conclusion of Mark's Gospel (16:16): "He who believes and is baptized will be saved; but he who does not believe will be condemned." About this word Luther wrote:

> Observe, first, that these words contain God's commandment and ordinance. You should not doubt, then, that Baptism is of divine origin, not something devised or invented by men. As truly as I can say that the Ten Commandments, the Creed, and the Lord's Prayer are not spun out of any man's imagination but revealed and given by God himself, so I can also boast that Baptism is no human plaything but is instituted by God himself. Moreover, it is solemnly and strictly commanded that we must be baptized or we shall not be saved.[11]

That baptism was instituted by Christ means that the New Testament utterances regarding baptism and their significance must be carefully interpreted and observed.

Luther gave a terse definition of baptism in the Small Catechism: "Baptism is not merely water, but it is water used according to God's command and connected with God's word."[12] The Large Catechism reads in similar fashion: "[Baptism is] water comprehended in God's Word and commandment and sanctified by them. It is nothing else than a divine water, not that the water in itself is nobler than other water but that God's Word and commandment are added to it."[13] Against those who disparage baptism, Luther said that we should not regard baptism according to its external mask (*larva*), but attend to how "God's Word is enclosed" in it.[14]

As to the benefit of baptism, Luther kept close to the scriptural evidence cited for its institution but referred to other New Testament texts. As he stated in both Catechisms, as well as in many other places, the benefit of baptism consists first of all in killing the old, then in resurrecting the new man. In the Large Catechism he wrote: "These two parts, being dipped under the water and emerging from it, indicate the power and effect of Baptism, which is simply the slaying of the old Adam and the resurrection of the new man, both of which actions must continue in us our whole life long. Thus a Christian life is nothing else than a daily Baptism, once begun and ever continued."[15]

Early in his career Luther had used the covenant concept to indicate the special character of the divine promise given in baptism.[16] This concept later retreated, and

---

[11] *Book of Concord*, p. 437.

[12] *Book of Concord*, p. 348.

[13] *Book of Concord*, p. 438.

[14] *Book of Concord*, p. 439.

[15] *Book of Concord*, pp. 444-45.

[16] *LW*, vol. 35, p. 33. *WA* 2, 730, 18-22; 732, 9-16. See Stock, *Die Bedeutung der Sakramente in Luthers Sermone von 1519,* passim.

he kept more strictly to concepts appearing in the Great Commission and particularly in Paul's statement in Romans 6, without on this account giving up the substance of the covenant idea.

Thus, with all his accenting of the uniqueness and unrepeatability of baptism, Luther gave equal stress to its lifelong "use," or to the actual achievement of what takes place in it parabolically. Clearly, Luther was developing his baptismal theology in intimate connection with his doctrine of justification, as well as with his view of the Christian as *simul peccator et iustus*.

No doubt, at this point Luther was after setting his own accent over against Paul. According to Paul, as is clear from Romans 6:4, the dying and rising is an event that has already occurred: "We were buried therefore with him by baptism into death, so that as Christ was raised from the dead by the glory of the Father, we too might walk in newness of life." For Paul, then, the old man is already killed in the baptism, and the new has already arisen. Baptism is thus an event that is complete in itself and that the Christian should confess ever anew. In his reflection, however, Luther depicted baptism as something to be accomplished ever anew: the old Adam "should" be drowned. In Luther, then, the Pauline idea that through baptism one has already died the death with Christ retreated. Paul more strongly accented the "indicative," thus the happenedness of baptism, while Luther gave greater stress to the "imperative," the benefit of baptism.[17] Of course, in noting this difference, we must take into account the situation of Paul and of Luther: Paul was speaking to new Christians who had just experienced a decisive change in their life; Luther was speaking to a Christendom become sluggish.

THE BAPTISM OF INFANTS

Until the Reformation period infant baptism was practically the only form in which the sacrament was administered. Whatever the practice in the church's earliest beginnings, that is, whether infant baptism was administered in addition to adult baptism among the newly converted, church practice and theological reflection held infant baptism to be valid beyond question. The criteria for this assumption were the institution of baptism by Christ, the concept of the sacrament as "effective in itself" (*ex opere operato*), and the long and on the whole undisputed tradition of the practice of infant baptism. Postponement of baptism, at times requested by the ancient church, was due to uncertainty over the possibility of forgiveness for mortal sins committed after baptism. Aside from a few exceptions, the church was opposed to postponement.

A totally new situation arose with the Reformation. With his emphasis on the strict correlation of baptism and faith, Luther gave new accent to traditional bap-

---

[17] See Althaus, *The Theology of Martin Luther,* translated by Robert C. Schultz (Philadelphia: Fortress Press, 1966), 306-7.

tismal theology, though on the whole did not attack it. Of course, with this new accent, Luther intended to say not that faith is the presupposition for baptism, but that faith is its only proper use.[18] On occasion he also said that a child should not be baptized without faith.[19] Obviously, neither then nor later did he draw the conclusion that one may or can refuse infant baptism. On the contrary, the validity of infant baptism was unquestioned. Nevertheless, in 1523, even for Luther the problem of baptism and faith, or of faith and baptism, was hanging fire.

The Anabaptist movement, emerging in Zurich from 1523 to 1525, had its origin within the heart of Reformation groups there. It was only too soon apparent that many other questions were connected with the problem of infant or adult baptism. The most important was whether the practice of infant baptism, without direct witness in the New Testament, should be retained, thus whether only such rites should be celebrated as are witnessed to in the New Testament, or whether only those rites should be altered as contradict New Testament teaching. The former position was taken by the Baptists, the latter by Luther, but on the whole also by Zwingli and the Reformed. Linked to this problem was the further question whether the church as such should be organized as a voluntary community and intimate connection with the state surrendered.

Luther adduced various reasons for infant baptism.

1. He referred to the tradition of the entire church. Infant baptism had been practiced since the beginning. At times he conceded that it was not directly witnessed to in the New Testament, nor even commanded. Congruent with his largely conservative stance, he allowed such traditions to stand as did not directly contradict Scripture. Further, he believed that God would not have allowed something improper to be in force for so long.

2. Luther referred to the fact that many who were baptized as infants later stood the test as Christians. From this one had to conclude that they were in possession of the Spirit. On this point the Large Catechism reads: "That the Baptism of infants is pleasing to Christ is sufficiently proved from his own work. God has sanctified many who have been thus baptized and has given them the Holy Spirit. Even today there are not a few whose doctrine and life attest that they have the Holy Spirit."[20]

---

[18] W. Schwab, *Entwicklung,* 317, has correctly referred to this.

[19] See *LW,* vol. 36, p. 300 (*The Adoration of the Sacrament,* 1523): "I have said it would be better not to baptize any children anywhere at all than to baptize them without faith, since in doing such the sacrament and God's holy name are taken in vain [Exod. 20:7], and to me that is a serious matter. For without faith the sacrament should not and cannot be received, or if it is received, it works greater injury." *WA* 11, 452, 29-33: "Da hab ich gesagt, Es were besser, gar uberall keyn kind teuffen denn on glawben teuffen, Syntemal daselbs das sacrament und gottis heyliger name vergebens wirtt gebaucht, wilchs myr eyn grosses ist. Denn die sacrament sollen und kunden on glawben nicht empfangen werden odder werden tzu grosserm schaden empfangen."

[20] *Book of Concord,* p. 442.

3. Against the Anabaptists Luther stated that if they were in the right, there would have been no Christianity for over a thousand years, since there would have been no valid baptism. Such, however, would contradict the Third Article of the creed: "I believe in the holy Christian church." According to Luther the Anabaptists were breaking with all church tradition. On this subject he said: "We should not discard or alter what cannot be discarded or altered . . . God is wonderful in his works. What he does not will, he clearly witnesses to in Scripture. What is not so witnessed to there, we can accept as his work. We are guiltless and he will not mislead us."[21]

4. Though Luther conceded that infant baptism is not directly attested in the New Testament, in his opinion some passages suggest it, such as the pericope of the blessing of the children (Mark 10:13-16), the word "see that you do not despise one of these little ones" (Matt. 18:10), and especially the command to baptize (Matt. 28:19).

5. The question of the faith of children (*fides infantium*) posed a special problem, and Luther dealt with it in various ways. In his early years prior to the controversy over infant baptism he wrote that children are baptized on the vicarious faith of the godparents.[22] In 1522, however, he said that no one can be saved through the faith of another, only through one's own.[23] From this he drew the admittedly problematic conclusion that underage children believe at their baptism, or that faith is infused into them at baptism. He did not, however, establish the right to infant baptism on this questionable thesis. As to the validity of infant baptism, he ultimately always argued on the basis of its divine institution.

By arguing in this fashion, Luther distanced himself from the traditional view that children were baptized upon the faith of the church. In 1525 he wrote: "So we say here too that children are not baptized in the faith of their godparents or of the churches. But the godparent and the faith of Christendom prays and seeks that they may have their own faith, in which they are baptized and believed."[24] In later years Luther expressed himself a bit more cautiously, allowing for the possibility of faith's arising later, of its absence at the infant's baptism. In the Large Catechism (1529) we read: "We do the same in infant baptism. We bring the child with the purpose and hope that he may believe, and we pray God to grant him faith. But we do not baptize him on that account, but solely on the command of God. Why? Because we know that God does not lie. My neighbor and I—in short, all men—may err and deceive, but God's Word cannot err."[25] Luther actually set up the principle that "when the word accompanies the water, Baptism is valid, even though faith be lacking. For my

[21] *LW*, vol. 40, p. 255 (*Concerning Rebaptism*, 1528). *WA* 26, 167, 11-16.
[22] See *LW*, vol. 32, p. 14 (*Defense and Explanation of all the Articles*, 1521). *WA* 7, 321, 15-18.
[23] *WA* 10 III, 304-12 (sermon, 1522), esp. 310, 15-18.
[24] See *LW*, vol. 32, p. 14 (*Defense and Explanation of All Articles*, 1521). *WA* 7, 321, 15-18.
[25] *Book of Concord*, p. 444.

faith does not constitute Baptism but receives it. Baptism does not become invalid even if it is wrongly received or used."[26] Still, there is indication that even the mature Luther retained the idea of the *fides infantium*.

For our evaluation of Luther's position on infant baptism, his attacks on the Anabaptists are of further significance. His most important argument reads that when baptism is made dependent on faith, we will scarcely ever arrive at the assurance of having sufficient faith and thus at the validity of our baptism. Further, Luther reproached the Anabaptists for works-righteousness and even idolatry, since the one to be baptized is forced as it were to summon up faith so as to be baptized in view of the effort. Finally, and precisely on the basis of his own experiences of inner conflict, Luther warned against continual self-reflection. Baptism rather points to the fact that salvation comes only from God.

[26] Ibid.

Chapter 32

THE LORD'S SUPPER

The Words of Institution and the Real Presence

Research into the various phases in Luther's development of the doctrine of the sacraments in general, and of his doctrine of the Lord's Supper in particular, has made clear the extent of the shift in accents.[1] If in 1519 or 1520, in dependence on Augustine, Luther gave an entirely independent definition of sacrament with his distinction between sign, meaning, and faith, now, since 1520, the words of institution and the institution of Baptism by Christ are at center. After 1523 and particularly during the debate with Zwingli, Luther accepted the real presence of the body and blood of Christ in the elements of the Supper.

These changes raise the question of the continuity in Luther's view. We obviously need to caution against hasty judgment. That specific doctrines such as the Trinity or certain basic ecclesiological data were demonstrably of fundamental significance for Luther, a significance easily overlooked in superficial observation, should caution us against seeing in the real presence a view to which he gave greater accent for the simple reason that others contested it. It may rather be that with elaboration of the doctrine of the real presence specific motifs of his theology and experience of faith were given a doctrinal formulation deeply anchored in the Reformation impulse. To this extent, one may say that Luther's Reformation theology took on particularly significant shape in the debate with Zwingli over the Supper.

As to the significance of the words of institution, from his early period onward Luther was concerned with a complex but materially necessary connection between Christ's establishing or instituting the Supper, the sign of the presence of

---

[1] See above, pp. 127-36 and pp. 169-77.

the crucified and risen Lord under the bread and wine, and the meaning or promise as apprehended in faith. To begin with, he left unclear the relation between Christ's body and blood shed on the cross for the forgiveness of sins, the words of institution, and the presence of Christ's body and blood "under" the elements.[2] His later accent on the real presence succeeded in clarifying and securing a connection previously assumed. Clearly, what resulted was a new accent, though nothing new was added to the doctrine of the Lord's Supper as Luther first developed it, merely that its purpose was set forth in consistent fashion. Similarly, nothing was altered of the central position of the words of institution. They remained at center. After 1523 Luther interpreted not only the words "for you" in all their breadth, but also the words preceding, "this is my body, this is my blood."

Next to the words of institution, the word in 1 Corinthians 10:16 ("The cup of blessing which we bless, is it not a participation in the blood of Christ? The bread which we break, is it not a participation in the body of Christ?") was of special importance for Luther's doctrine of the Supper. He wrote that it was "a thunderbolt on the head of Dr. Karlstadt and his whole party."[3] He continually stressed that what is at issue in this text is the fellowship of the body of Christ.[4] It thus excludes a merely symbolic interpretation, just as do the words of institution themselves. "So this verse of Paul stands like a rock and forcefully requires the interpretation that all who break this bread, receive, and eat it, receive the body of Christ and partake of it. As we have said, it cannot be spiritual, so it must be a bodily participation."[5]

For Luther, the words of institution as well as the text of 1 Corinthians rendered the real presence absolutely certain: "I see here the clear, distinct, and powerful words of God which compel me to confess, that the body and blood of Christ are in the sacrament." To this fact all questions as to how this could be possible had to yield: "Such should be our answer, and ridicule we can meanwhile disregard. How Christ is brought into the bread or strikes up the tune we demand, I do not know. But I do know full well that the Word of God cannot lie, and it says that the body and blood of Christ are in the sacrament."[6] When they read this text, even heathen or

[2] Thus Ernst Sommerlath, *Der Sinn des Abendmahls nach Luthers Gedanken über das Abendmahl 1527/1529* (Leipzig: Dörffling und Franke, 1931), 104; Althaus, *Theology of Martin Luther,* 379-80; W. Schwab, *Entwicklung und Gestalt der Sakramententheologie bei Martin Luther,* EHS.T 79 (Frankfurt am Main/Bern: P. Lang, 1977), 233.

[3] *LW,* vol. 40, p. 177 (*Against the Heavenly Prophets,* 1525). WA 18, 166, 32-34.

[4] See, e.g., *LW,* vol. 40, p. 178: "The bread which is broken or distributed piece by piece is the participation in the body of Christ . . . wherein does the participation in the body of Christ consist? It cannot be anything else than that as each takes a part of the broken bread he takes therewith the body of Christ." WA 18, 168, 16-20.

[5] *LW,* vol. 40, p. 181. WA 18, 172, 12-15.

[6] *LW,* vol. 40, p. 176. WA 18, 166, 8-13.

unbelievers would have to admit that they assert the real presence of the body and blood of Christ.[7]

Luther had no time for counterarguments. One objection that Karlstadt and Zwingli raised against Luther was based on John 6:63, "It is the spirit that gives life, the flesh is of no avail." Early on Luther had denied that this text related to the Lord's Supper.[8] Further, the term "flesh" referred to the sinfulness of the natural human.[9] Another objection derived from the statement concerning Jesus' ascension and his "sitting at the right hand of God," a session that excluded his presence according to his exalted human nature. This argument too Luther flatly repudiated. Even if the idea were correct, which he, however, denied with his "teaching concerning ubiquity,"[10] it still could not annul the text of the biblical passages cited. Altogether, Luther saw in such counterarguments mere "human wisdom" or objections of "arbitrary reason," not to be pursued.

In addition to the scriptural witnesses, the entire tradition may have been significant for Luther. Since 1520, he expressly rejected the doctrine of transubstantiation, not because of its theological intent but because he saw in it a mere theory that should not have been made binding. In its theological content, Luther's view of the real presence was not so far removed from the doctrine of transubstantiation. It is interesting to note that he distanced himself from Berengar of Tours (+ 1088), who had advocated a symbolic-spiritualistic doctrine of the Supper; indeed, Luther expressly approved the pope's repudiation of Berengar.[11]

The *unio sacramentalis*, "Spiritual" and "Bodily" Eating

In opposition to the various symbolic and significative interpretations of the words of institution, Luther was not content with emphasizing their simple, unadulterated sense, but reflected on his position in a systematic-theological way in order to render intelligible and secure his view of the real presence. His view of the *unio sacramentalis* might thus have greater weight than the spatial idea elaborated in his doctrine of ubiquity.[12] The idea of the *unio* furnishes the link among the other questions on the doctrine of the Supper. Luther discussed it chiefly in his treatise *Confession Concerning Christ's Supper* (1528).

---

[7] WA 26, 406, 9-407, 1; 496, 34-497, 1. Cf. LW, vol. 37, p. 272 (*Confession Concerning Christ's Supper,* 1528).

[8] LW, vol. 36, p. 19 (*The Babylonian Captivity of the Church,* 1520). WA 6, 502, 7-17. With this view, Luther followed scholastic tradition; see Hilgenfeld, *Mittelalterlich-traditionelle Elemente in Luthers Abendmahlsschriften,* SDHSTh 29 (Zurich: Theologischer Verlag, 1971), 440-44.

[9] LW, vol. 37, pp. 78-101 (*That These Words of Christ 'This Is My Body,' etc. Still Stand Firm against the Fanatics,* 1527). WA 23, 167, 28-205, 31.

[10] See above, pp. 173-74.

[11] LW, vol. 37, pp. 300-301 (*Confession Concerning Christ's Supper,* 1528); WA 26, 442, 39-443, 3; 29, 195, 12-196, 1 (sermon, 1529).

[12] On the doctrine of ubiquity see above, pp. 172-75.

Opposed to interpreting the *est* in the words of institution in terms of a *significat* as first advocated by Cornelius Honius (Hoen), Luther stressed first that "two things can interpenetrate,"[13] and was content with establishing the possibility of Christ's body and blood being in, with, and under the bread and wine without treating it in more detail. From the outset he rejected speculation as to how such unity or interpenetration was possible or actually took place.

In the *Confession Concerning Christ's Supper* (1528), Luther proceeded further along this line. Against the thesis that the *praedicatio identica de diversis naturis* (a single designation for two different natures/essences) contradicts both Scripture and reason, he argued that the Bible as well as ordinary language speak of identity in this way.[14] This is especially true of Christian language about God. For example, we point to the man Christ and say, "This man is God's Son." Similarly, in the doctrine of the Trinity, we speak of Father, Son, and Holy Spirit, and yet each is the one God. The different persons are thus to be regarded as one essence. It thus cannot be contrary to Scripture to say that two different things are one or are one essence, just like the bread and the body of Christ. This unity of bread and body Luther described as a *unio sacramentalis* (sacramental unity).[15]

This concept of "sacramental unity" is better suited to describe Luther's doctrine of the Supper than that of "consubstantiation," a term that he never used. We encounter it only in the 1550s, in the description of Lutheran doctrine on the part of reformed theologians.[16]

Along with the *unio sacramentalis,* importance attaches to Luther's distinction between "spiritual" and "bodily" eating following his dispute with Zwingli. In that distinction, the spiritual may not be separated from the bodily eating—both belong together. At the same time, as a result of the debates, Luther occasionally placed extraordinarily strong accent on the bodily eating.[17]

Early in his career, Luther had emphasized the necessity of a spiritual eating, appropriating this terminology from Jesus' word concerning the bread in John 6. Though he did not relate John 6 to the Lord's Supper and did not accept John 6:63 as evidence for disparaging bodily eating, he still adopted such figurative speech as

[13] See *LW,* vol. 40, p. 196 (*Against the Heavenly Prophets*, 1525): "Since now iron is fire and fire is iron, according to the simple sense of language, and the two are in each other and as one, though each retains its own nature, they might well have exercised humility." *WA* 18, 186, 22-24. On Hoen see above, pp. 170-71.

[14] See the context in *LW,* vol. 37, pp. 296-303; *WA* 26, 440-45. What is involved in the *praedicatio identica* is that two different subjects can be identified by a single predicate, since they have some common basis. See *LW,* vol. 36, p. 29; *WA* 6, 508, 11- 22; *Studienausgabe* 4, 176, n. 2291.

[15] *LW,* vol. 37, pp. 299-301. *WA* 26, 442-43.

[16] See Hilgenfeld, *Mittelalterlich-traditionelle,* 467ff.; Schwab, *Entwicklung,* 262, n. 27.

[17] On this twofold eating see Friedrich Gogarten, *Luthers Theologie,* (Tübingen: Mohr, 1967), 114-21; Schwab, *Entwicklung,* 292-98, with justified criticism from A. Peters.

identifies spiritual eating with faith. No evidence is needed from Luther's early period to prove his emphasis on faith as spiritual eating, but it is important to note that he held fast to this spiritual eating even after his dispute with Zwingli. In a sermon on John 6:52-53, delivered on a weekday in 1531, he said: "Faith eats and believes in Christ. The soul and faith do not have a mouth, teeth, throat, and stomach, as the body has; they have a different kind of mouth, stomach, and ears. . . . It also has its mind, its will, its mood, understanding, desire, or reason."[18] Just as: "Faith, too, cannot be a mere thought of our Lord God; for thoughts are not sufficient. The pope, for instance, assumes that it is enough just to think of God; that is his faith. My heart must take hold of and apprehend Christ; I must cleave to His flesh and blood and say: 'To this I cling, to this I will remain faithful. I would rather surrender life and limb. May I fare with it as God wills.'"[19] On the basis of these statements we can understand how at the Marburg Colloquy of 1529 Luther could justifiably embrace the concept of "spiritual eating" without being untrue to his own position.[20] Emphasis on the bodily eating was not intended to relativize the need for a spiritual eating.

In the controversies after 1523, however, Luther gave more and more accent to the bodily eating. Of particular importance in this connection are his statements in the treatise *That These Words of Christ, "This Is My Body," etc. Still Stand Firm against the Fanatics* (1527). Here he wrote:

> Once again I ask: What if I eat Christ's flesh physically in the Supper in such a way that I also eat it spiritually at the same time; would you not concede then that Christ's flesh in the Supper avails very much? "But how can this be?" you say. Precisely thus: I shall eat his body with the bread physically, and yet at the same time believe in my heart that this is the body which was given for me for the forgiveness of sins, as the words read, "This is my body, which was given for you"—which you yourselves call the spiritual eating. Now if the spiritual eating is there, the physical eating cannot be harmful but must also be useful on account of the spiritual eating.[21]

Here especially, the accents were carefully and reflectively set: "for the sake of the spiritual eating" the bodily eating was necessary and profitable.

In the course of the debates bodily eating took on almost independent weight. In the same treatise, *That These Words of Christ,* he all but merged the bodily and spiritual eating:

---

[18] *LW,* vol. 23, p. 116. *WA* 33, 178, 21-28 (H).

[19] *LW,* vol. 23, p. 128. *WA* 33, 199, 7-19 (H).

[20] See above, pp. 173-77.

[21] *LW,* vol. 37, p. 85; *WA* 23, 179, 7-15 (printed version).

The mouth eats the body of Christ physically, for it cannot grasp or eat the words, nor does it know what it is eating. As far as taste is concerned the mouth surely seems to be eating something other than Christ's body. But the heart grasps the words in faith and eats spiritually precisely the same body as the mouth eats physically, for the heart sees very well what the uncomprehending mouth eats physically. But how does it see this? Not by looking at the bread or at the mouth's eating, but at the word which is there, "Eat, this is my body." Yet there is only one body of Christ, which both mouth and heart eat, each in its own mode and manner. The heart cannot eat it physically nor can the mouth eat it spiritually.[22]

The context of these remarks indicates that in distinguishing the spiritual and bodily eating Luther was not thinking of two eatings in parallel. He had in mind a spiritual use of the bodily eating, as conversely the spiritual use was not possible apart from the bodily action. Luther referred to Mary, who received the word of the angel in her heart and conceived when she accepted that word in faith. Or, he cited the example of the shepherds on the field at Bethlehem, who "saw" the child in the crib but for whom this seeing was of use only because they believed.[23]

In the same vein, Luther's occasional utterances on the particular use of the bodily eating should not be one-sidedly emphasized. No doubt, at times he could speak of the Lord's Supper as though it were a "medicine of immortality."[24] Similar statements predominate in the treatise *That These Words*. For example, he wrote: "But since the mouth is the heart's member, it also must ultimately live in eternity on account of the heart, which lives eternally through the Word, because here it also eats physically the same eternal food which its heart eats spiritually at the same time."[25] Or: "But the soul sees and clearly understands that the body will live eternally because it has partaken of an eternal food which will not leave it to decay in the grave and turn to dust."[26] Or:

So, when we eat Christ's flesh physically and spiritually, the food is so powerful that it transforms us into itself and out of fleshly, sinful, mortal men makes spiritual, holy, living men. This we are already, though in a hidden manner in faith and hope; the fact is not yet manifest, but we shall experience it on the Last Day.[27]

[22] *LW*, vol. 37, p. 93. *WA* 23, 191, 11-20.
[23] *LW*, vol. 37, p. 93. *WA* 23, 184, 30-185, 29. See W. Schwab, *Entwicklung*, 294.
[24] See Ignatius of Antioch, *Eph.* 20.2.
[25] *LW*, vol. 37, p. 87. *WA* 23, 181, 11-15.
[26] *LW*, vol. 37, pp. 93-94. *WA* 23, 191, 25-28.
[27] *LW*, vol. 37, p. 101. *WA* 23, 205, 20-25. There are similar statements in *LW*, vol. 37, pp. 124-25, 129-30, 132, 134, 136; *WA* 23, 243, 34-244, 2; 251, 20-25; 255, 24-28; 259, 4-10; 261, 33-35. Further evidence in A. Peters, *Kommentar*, vol. 4, 144-45.

From such passages Albrecht Peters would prefer to draw this conclusion: "If we may exaggerate a bit, the chief thing for Luther . . . is not the forgiveness of sins, but the *unio* with Christ."[28] By contrast, we insist that for Luther, in the language of the Small Catechism, "by these words (in the Lord's Supper) the forgiveness of sins, life, and salvation are given to us in the sacrament, for where there is forgiveness of sins, there are also life and salvation."[29] Luther's statements on bodily eating were intended merely to secure the idea of the real presence.[30] No particular accent was given to statements regarding the physical consequences of eating the Lord's Supper.

This statement should also apply to Luther's view of the so-called *manducatio indignorum* (the eating of the unworthy), or *manducatio impiorum* (the eating of the ungodly). During the Lord's Supper controversy and on the basis of 1 Corinthians 11:27 ("whoever, therefore, eats the bread or drinks the cup of the Lord in an unworthy manner will be guilty of profaning the body and blood of the Lord"), Luther accented the eating of the unworthy or even of the godless and wicked.[31] In doing so he made clear that there is no neutrality over against the gift of the Supper, that in it salvation is either accepted in faith or rejected.

Luther naturally insisted that the word in 1 Corinthians 11:27 should be accepted in respect of its subject matter, but was lax toward a more detailed formulation. He thus allowed the statement in the Wittenberg Concord of 1536 to stand: "That the body and the blood of Christ is truly given even to the unworthy, that the unworthy truly receive it in keeping with the Lord Christ's institution and command,"[32] only, that is, to their condemnation. Consequently, Luther neither positively nor negatively constructed a special topic from statements regarding the results of the bodily eating of the Supper.

THE LORD'S SUPPER AS CRYSTALLIZATION POINT OF CHRISTOLOGY AND FAITH

The development of Luther's doctrine of the sacraments in general and of his doctrine of the Lord's Supper in particular, together with his defense of the real presence against Karlstadt, Zwingli, and others, all make clear the central position of the Supper for Luther personally and for his theology. In the Supper numerous central motifs of his theology and piety intersect.

[28] Ibid., 147.
[29] *Book of Concord*, p. 352.
[30] See the debate with Peters in Schwab, *Entwicklung*, 292-98.
[31] See, e.g., *LW,* vol. 37, pp. 188, 367; vol. 51, p. 189; vol. 38, pp. 300-301; *WA* 26, 288, 13-19; 506, 21-29; 30 I, 26, 16-17; 118, 2-5, and elsewhere; *LW,* vol. 38, pp. 300-301; *WA* 54, 153, 3-9; *Book of Concord*, p. 311.
[32] *WA Br* 12 Nr. 4261, Beilage I, 21-23. On this subject see Lohse, *HdBDThG,* 2:96-97.

As for piety or lived faith, throughout the development of his views Luther held to the leitmotiv that in the reception of the Lord's Supper there occurred a "happy exchange": Christ becomes ours, and sin is no longer reckoned to us. Or, as he formulated it after 1520, the word of promise "for you" is apprehended only in faith.

The fact that after 1523 the real presence took center stage was obviously a considerable advance. Still, this new accent cohered with motifs evident in Luther's theology from the outset. We note in particular the idea that God is omnipresent, that he is at work hiddenly, that we know God only in Jesus Christ, that God is present only in Christ for our salvation, or, that it is necessary to defend the theology of the cross against the theology of glory. It is further important that Luther understood "flesh" and "spirit" in agreement with Paul, not in terms of Greek antiquity, that for this reason what is "spiritual" is opposed not to what is "bodily" but to what is "fleshly." In the Lord's Supper the "for you" is expressed with particular clarity.

Respecting the central position of the Lord's Supper in piety and theology, we need to point to still other aspects. In the various debates over the Mass and the Lord's Supper, first with the Roman church, then with Karlstadt and Zwingli, but also in conflicts within his own circle due to the decline in preparation for the Supper, what was ultimately always at issue for Luther was the Lord's Supper as God's gracious condescension that excluded all works-righteousness but could not be rejected or ignored with impunity. Despite changes in the details, his deep devotion to the Supper and his effort theologically to set it forth as God's gift of salvation persisted throughout. The Lord's Supper gives comfort and aid in midst of all tribulation. Whoever receives it can say:

> I have received the sacrament, in which my Lord Christ says comfortingly to me through his word that this body and blood of his is mine. This I believe, not merely as you do, that it is his flesh and blood, but that everything is given to me which the words contain. So I raise this faith against you [scil. the devil] and every misfortune, and stand firm on the words which will never lie to me, for they are God's word and God's sign.[33]

In addition, for Luther the Supper had significance for the Christian life. Throughout his career, he retained the old *sacramentum—exemplum* (sacrament—model for discipleship) formula originating with Augustine.[34] Even the relation to the church universal and its fellowship was viewed in the context of his doctrine of the Supper.[35]

---

[33] *WA* 12, 482, 5-11 (sermon, 1523, text B).

[34] See Ervin Iserloh, "Sakramentum und Exemplum: Ein Augustinisches Thema Lutherischer Theologie," in idem, *Kirche: Ereignis und Institution,* vol. 2 (Münster, 1985), 107-24.

[35] On this subject see Jürgen Lutz, *Unio und Communio: Zum Verhältnis von Rechtfertigungslehre und Kirchenverständnis bei Martin Luther,* KKTS 55 (Paderborn: Bonifatius, 1990); in addition, the review by Lohse, *ThRv* 87 (1991), 400-402.

Chapter 33

THE DOCTRINE
OF THE TWO KINGDOMS

On the Historical and Theological Place
of the Distinction between the Two Kingdoms
or the Two Governments

In examining Luther's early formation of the distinction between the two kingdoms
and the two governments,[1] we referred to the fact that the distinction must be seen
from the perspective of the history of tradition as well as in the wake of Luther's conflict with Rome. From the perspective of the history of tradition the distinction represents a reformulation of the ancient theme of the two *civitates,* first developed by
Augustine, that is, the distinction between the *civitas Dei* and the *civitas terrena,*
adopted in the Middle Ages and further developed in all sorts of variations. Behind
Luther's distinction, however, must be seen the numerous debates between emperor
and pope in the Middle Ages, particularly the bitter disputes toward the end of that
period together with imperial propaganda against papal claims to world rule. Not
least in importance are Luther's personal experiences as a university professor, as
well as his experiences in various debates with ecclesiastical and theological opponents. That Luther, professor at the University of Wittenberg founded by Frederick
the Wise, was in modern parlance an electoral official, thus did not lecture at a papal
university, has significance not only for his dispute with the Roman church as well as
for his legal standing, but in particular also for his two-kingdoms doctrine. Naturally,
we need to be cautious about overtaxing the concept on systematic-theological

[1] See above, pp.151-59.

grounds, or even on the ground of the history of its effects, as has at times occurred in the last decades.

This caution applies first in that the distinction between the two kingdoms and two governments was not actually a "doctrine" or even the outline of a political ethic applicable in principle to the evangelical cause. As such, the idea of the two-kingdoms doctrine is problematic. Karl Barth first coined the expression.[2] However we judge the political ethics of Lutheran theologians in the nineteenth and twentieth centuries, it absolutely will not do simply to trace to Luther the views on state and church held by Lutherans throughout the centuries, and for good or ill make him responsible for the history of Lutheran political ethics. Such a procedure would be unhistorical and do justice neither to Luther in his historical situation nor to Lutheran theologians and the problems with which they were confronted. The two-kingdoms doctrine, with all the significance no doubt due it, is not the heart of Luther's theology, however much it coheres with it. The two-kingdoms doctrine, if we retain the concept for lack of a better one, must be seen in the importance given to it. Recent attempts to recover in Luther the substance of an idea derived from Barthian theology of Christ's royal rule have a certain propriety in that they deny the thesis of "independent legitimacy" on the part of the kingdom of this world.[3] It must of course be said that neither terminologically nor in any systematic sense is this idea at the heart of Luther's two-kingdoms doctrine or of his political ethics.

The intent behind the differentiation between the two kingdoms or two governments, both of which exist side by side in Luther,[4] is to distinguish human existence "before God" (coram Deo) and "before the world" (coram mundo), and to that extent to grasp with acuity the spiritual and temporal in their relation to as well as in their difference from each other. It is important to realize that not only the temporal authorities or the state belong to the kingdom of the world, but absolutely everything necessary for preserving and continuing life in the world. The distinction between the two kingdoms or governments thus corresponds to the distinction between law and gospel, without these pairs of concepts being identical. Both the distinction between law and gospel and that between the two kingdoms or governments are calculated to help secure gospel purity and faith. They are especially to serve the purpose that the spiritual remain spiritual and the temporal temporal, lest the two be confused.

Caution must also be taken against an inadmissible overevaluation of this distinction, since it is not true that Luther first outlined his two-kingdoms doctrine in principle and then applied it to specific situations. Such an interpretation would totally misjudge the problem's continually changing shape in the various debates between Luther and others. Alongside the distinction, Luther's concrete perception

---

[2] See above, p. 154.

[3] See esp. G. Forck, *Die Königsherrschaft Jesu Christi bei Luther (1959): Mit einem Beitrag von Bernhard Lohse*, 2d ed. (Berlin: Evangelisches Verlagsanstalt, 1988).

[4] See above, pp. 153-57.

of his political responsibility as counselor and his persistent efforts at taking a theo-logically and politically responsible position must always be given their due. At any given time, Luther's political stance is always his "commentary" on the distinction between the two kingdoms or governments. Concretely put, this means that the treatise entitled *Temporal Authority: To What Extent It Should Be Obeyed* can be under-stood only in the context of the various conflicts of 1521 and 1522.

With these remarks we do not intend to deny that the distinction between the two kingdoms and the two governments has extraordinary significance, or that in various respects it introduced a new epoch in the history of political theory.

The History of the Tradition of the Two Kingdoms Doctrine

As mentioned, Augustine was the first constantly to reflect on the relations between state and church, and with his distinction between the *civitas Dei* and the *civitas ter-rena* laid the foundation for all subsequent theological efforts on behalf of relations between the church in the world and the order of the state. The significance of this fact can scarcely be exaggerated.

As early as in his *De catechizandis rudibus* (composed ca. 399/400), Augustine outlined the basic features of his *civitas* idea.[5] Because of the questions arising after Rome's fall in 410 he composed his great work *De civitate Dei* (413-426). In it he defended the church as the earthly portion of the *civitas Dei* against charges by citi-zens of the *civitas terrena* that the Christians were guilty of Rome's fall. Recent research should have made clear that with this *civitas* idea Augustine intended neither to outline a Christian theology of history nor to develop a Christian view of the state.[6] His goal was pastoral-paraenetic, intended to remind Christians that the church is ultimately part of the *civitas Dei,* thus has its home in heaven, not on earth.[7]

In the medieval reading, Augustine's *civitas* idea[8] was further developed through interpreting the dialectical relation between the two *civitates* in terms of the superi-ority of the *civitas Dei* and thus of the pope over the *civitas terrena,* that is, over the

---

[5] *De cat. rud.* 19.31. See Bernhard Lohse, "Augustins Wandlung in seiner Beurteilung des Staates," in *StPatr* 6 (= *TU* 81) (1962), 447-75.

[6] In older research Roman Catholics in particular attempted to derive a Christian view of the state from Augustine by tacitly interpreting him in terms of the scholasticism of Thomas. The Catholic theologian who moved farthest in this direction was Otto Schilling, *Die Staats- und Soziallehre des hl. Augustinus* (Freiburg: Herder, 1910), whose theme followed a suggestion of Reinhold Seeberg.

[7] Thus esp. Ernst Kinder, *Gottesreich und Weltreich,* 24-42. See Bernhard Lohse, "Zur Eschatologie des älteren Augustin," *VigChr* 21 (1967), 221-40.

[8] U. Duchrow, *Christenheit und Weltverantwortung: Traditionsgeschichte und systematische Struktur der Zweireichelehre,* 2d ed. (Stuttgart: Klett-Cotta, 1983), has provided the most important discussion of the entire subject. Obviously, it is not enough to evaluate the history of the two-kingdoms doctrine merely

emperor. At other points, significant elements of the Augustinian *civitas* idea were retained. This is true especially of the eschatological components, which were authoritative for Augustine and ultimately furnished the locus of study for medieval historiography.[9]

An extraordinarily important development of the idea itself as well as of views on church and state resulted from the various conflicts between emperor and pope but also from conflicts within the church. Equally important in this connection was the so-called theory of subsidiarity, which read that in an emergency emperor and pope, and insofar state and church, could mutually represent each other. Originally, this theory had been developed by canon lawyers for the purpose of responding to certain emergency situations.[10] In the wake of late medieval debates between emperor and pope, such ideas were further developed, particularly by William of Occam and Marsilius of Padua, into entirely new political theories and ecclesiological programs.

Though Luther scarcely had any precise knowledge of the history of medieval political and ecclesiological theory,[11] elements of views developed in the late Middle Ages had more or less penetrated the politics of the local princes and to that extent became known to a wider circle. In any case, as early as in his composition of the treatise on the nobility, Luther was aware to a considerable extent of the problems relating to the questions up for debate.

Precisely in view of this situation it is all the more significant that with his differentiation of the two kingdoms and governments Luther did not simply adopt or continue theories developed by Occam or Marsilius. In some respects, his discussion of this ancient theme reflected a new structure and setting of goals.

---

from the perspective of the history of ideas. The concrete historical situation must always be taken into account. There are a few references to the history of the tradition in H.-J. Gänssler, *Evangelium und weltliches Schwert: Hintergrund, Entstehungsgeschichte und Anlass von Luthers Scheidung zweier Reiche oder Regimente,* VIEG 109 (Wiesbaden: Steiner, 1983), though on the whole only the immediate, historical context of Luther's statements is researched. A few texts on the history of the tradition are present in *Die Vorstelling von Zwei Reichen und Regimenten bis Luther,* ed. Ulrich Duchrow and Heiner Hofmann, TKTG 17 (Gütersloh: Gerd Mohn, 1972).

[9] See Herbert Grundmann, *Religious Movements in the Middle Ages,* trans. Steven Rowan (Notre Dame: University of Notre Dame Press, 1995); Otto Bischof von Freising, *Chronik oder Die Geschichte der zwei Staaten,* trans. Adolf Schmidt, ed. Walther Lammers, FSGA 16, 4th ed. (Darmstadt: Wissenschaftliche Buchgesellgeschaft, 1980), esp. XLIV-LI (Lammers).

[10] See B. Tierney, *Foundations of the Conciliar Theory* (Cambridge: Cambridge University Press, 1955).

[11] Thus among other things he has no closer acquaintance with the medieval right of resistance. See E. Wolgast, *Die Wittenberger Theologie und die Politik der evangelischen Stände: Studien zu Luthers Gutachten in politischen Fragen,* QFRG 47 (Gütersloh: Gerd Mohn, 1977); Bernhard Lohse, "Die Bedeutung des Rechtes bi der Frage des Widerstandes in der frühen Reformation," in *FS Horst Rabe,* forthcoming.

THE NEW IMPULSE IN LUTHER'S DISTINCTION BETWEEN THE TWO KINGDOMS AND THE TWO GOVERNMENTS

The distinction between the two kingdoms and the two governments must be seen as equal in weight.[12] What results for our evaluation of Luther's position is that every attempt to describe his conception purely on the basis of the two kingdoms or purely on the basis of the two governments is one-sided and cannot actually do him justice.[13] Of course, it is correct that to some degree the two kingdoms and the two governments can be seen as more or less identical. Yet in each instance the viewpoint from which the two distinctions are drawn is different.

Heinrich Bornkamm has given an apt interpretation of the distinction between the "kingdoms" and "governments" by stating that "kingdom" denotes a "sphere of rule," whereas "government" denotes a "type of rule."[14] Bornkamm has further indicated that Luther's originality lies in his arrangement of the two types of observation. According to Bornkamm attention must be given the three-dimensional orientation of the two-kingdoms doctrine: it has to do first with the relation of church and state; then with the relation of the spiritual to the temporal, or the kingdom of Christ to the kingdom of the world; and finally it gives orientation for Christian activity on behalf of self and others.[15]

In indicating the differences between Augustine and Luther, Bornkamm also deserves agreement. For Bornkamm these differences consist first in the fact that Augustine viewed the state in more strictly ontological fashion, on the basis of its nature, whereas Luther saw it within the scope of the divine activity. Next, to a great extent Augustine thought ascetically, that is, more in terms of flight from the world, while Luther reflected more intensively on the Christian's activity and thus distinguished activity on behalf of self and others. Finally, Augustine had no compunctions about appealing to the power of the state against heretics, whereas Luther recognized the problem of the "Christian" state.[16] Nevertheless, according to Bornkamm, Augustine and Luther agree in their ultimately eschatological view of the conflict between the kingdom of the world and the kingdom of God.[17]

---

[12] See above, pp. 153-57.

[13] This means that many sketches of Luther's position are one-sided. If one intends to interpret Luther, however, then the all but exclusive reference to the two kingdoms must be seen as in error. On the other hand, it will not do merely to speak of the two governments in Luther's terms. What is unique about him consists in his linking the two types of observation.

[14] Heinrich Bornkamm, "Die Frage der Obrigkeit in Reformationzeitalter," in Bornkamm, *Das Jahrhundert der Reformation: Gestalten und Kräfte*, 2d ed. (Göttingen: Vandenhoeck & Ruprecht, 1966), 15.

[15] Ibid., 14-16.

[16] Ibid., 18-20.

[17] This viewpoint has been elaborated particularly by E. Kinder, "Gottesrecht und Weltreich." It is an aspect that usually gets short shrift in many investigations of Luther's two-kingdoms doctrine.

The particular historical contribution of Luther's distinction between the two kingdoms and the two governments consists first in the fact that in the world of the waning Middle Ages he made a decisive contribution toward unraveling the then hopelessly entangled spiritual and temporal interests. In revolutionary fashion he delivered a theological challenge to the medieval superiority of the spiritual over the temporal power. He did not, however, simply stand medieval theory or praxis on its head, but keenly elaborated the difference between the "spiritual" and the "temporal." He established and developed theologically the independence of the temporal arm. At the same time he accented and likewise theologically grounded the summons to the church to renounce temporal power: "The sword" belonged to the kingdom of the world; the business of the church was "the Word."

It is correct that in his own political behavior Luther was by no means always able to keep strictly to this principle. Particularly in his debate with the so-called fanatics, as well as in his conflict with the rebellious peasants, he appealed to the temporal arm for aid. What induced him to do so was no longer the idea that a territory had to be confessionally self-contained, but that Thomas Müntzer had called for a general uprising and for this reason the debate with him had to be carried on not merely theologically, but also politically and militarily. To exercise tolerance toward Müntzer would have spelled outright surrender on the part of the Saxon church and the elector. With his two-kingdoms doctrine Luther with full and objective right opposed Müntzer and his revolutionary spiritual Christianity with "rationality," with the legitimacy of the temporal power and its function in establishing order.

Naturally, the case was different with respect to some of the so-called fanatics such as Karlstadt, but also with respect to the Anabaptists. Here, on the basis of his own presuppositions, Luther would have had to renounce appeal to the temporal power. That he did not could be explained by his fear of the dangers to public order from the doctrine of these fanatics.[18] It may be that the practice long in use of the temporal powers' persecution of heretics was simply too widespread a tradition for Luther to break with altogether.

So then, alongside this distinction between the spiritual and temporal tasks, the distinction between the two governments has its peculiar function in that not only the church but also the world is viewed as strictly under the divine sovereignty. With this idea Luther distanced himself from Augustine, who for the most part sharply contrasted the *civitas Dei* and the *civitas terrena*. Luther's view also differs from the various medieval ideas of the *corpus christianum*. The correlation, indeed, "the unity of the two governments,"[19] is established by the fact that God has ordained both. The

---

[18] See Heinrich Bornkamm, "Die Frage der Obrigkeit," 291-315; B. Lohse, "Luther und der Radikalismus," 7-27.

[19] Thus Althaus, *Ethics of Martin Luther,* 54.

temporal government is to care for external peace and the spiritual to make Christians "godly men."[20]

On this basis Luther could never adjudge the kingdom of the world as the *civitas diaboli*. However great the difference between the two kingdoms, however much a confusion of the two is to be avoided, God is nonetheless at work in both with his goodness and mercy. Luther could also describe the kingdom of the world as a kingdom of wrath.[21] Yet over wrath always stands the divine will to preserve and love. To that extent it would be entirely inappropriate to interpret Luther's concept of the kingdom of the world purely by way of the motif of the divine wrath.

THE IMPULSE TOWARD ETHICS

From this perspective important consequences follow for Christian ethics that we may at least hint at here.[22] In essence it applies that for Luther the Christian is a citizen of both kingdoms and also has responsibility toward both. Attempts to move Luther closer to Augustine and to characterize the Christian merely as a citizen of Christ's kingdom have miscarried.[23] Indeed, one must state that the Christian is first a citizen of the kingdom of the world and only then a citizen of the kingdom of God or of Christ. Similarly, it applies that the Christian is under both governments. Since God is also at work in the temporal government, there is ultimately no conflict, since the divine will is authoritative in both kingdoms or governments.

There are, of course, problems with this attempt at an ethic, since the Christian, though the kingdoms and the governments are to be seen as from God, is nonetheless subject to different masters. Indeed, Luther persistently emphasized against the fanatics that the world cannot be governed by the gospel, but that justice and the "sword" are needed to maintain external order. In other words, the Christian as all

---

[20] *LW,* vol. 45, p. 91 (*Temporal Authority*, 1523): "For this reason God has ordained two governments: the spiritual, by which the Holy Spirit produces Christians and righteous people under Christ; and the temporal, which restrains the un-Christian and wicked so that, no thanks to them, they are obliged to keep still and to maintain an outward peace." *WA* 11, 251, 15-18.

[21] With particular sharpness in, e.g., *LW,* vol. 46, p. 70 (*An Open Letter on the Harsh Book against the Peasants*, 1525): "But the kingdom of the world, which is nothing else than the servant of God's wrath upon the wicked and is a real precursor of hell and everlasting death, should not be merciful, but strict, severe, and wrathful in fulfilling its work and duty. Its tool is not a wreath of roses or a flower of love, but a naked sword; and a sword is a symbol of wrath, severity, and punishment"; *WA* 18, 389, 31-36. At this point, of course, the historical context of the letter must be taken into account. From this perspective any systematizing of this idea, as undertaken especially by J. Heckel, *Lex charitatis,* 411-12, is ruled out.

[22] See the terse, good sketch in Althaus, *Ethics of Martin Luther,* 61-78.

[23] Heckel, *Lex charitatis,* has gone furthest in this direction. But in doing so Heckel has righly received lively opposition. See esp. Franz Lau, "Leges Caritatis: Drei Fragen an Johannes Heckel," *KuD* 2 (1956), 76-89.

others is obliged to keep the Ten Commandments, which set forth in the second table the basic order for the kingdom of the world. The Christian is also obliged to regard the Sermon on the Mount as the fundamental law, so to speak, of the new aeon with its radical, "pacifist" ethics. How can both be suited to each other? Is the Christian being tested for a durability that exceeds his or her capacities?

In keen and consistent fashion Luther thought through the problems arising here. In order to make clear the Christian's twofold duty, he spoke of the Christian as being "two persons," a Christian person and a person of the world.[24] It is worth noting that this distinction occurs mainly in the sermons, in the exposition of texts relevant to preaching, and in reflection on real life situations. At the same time, Luther emphasized that the Christian always lives *in relatione*, thus also in relation to other persons. Where Christians have duties and tasks toward the persons in their care, they are not required to offer no resistance to evil. They must protect their neighbor.[25]

This distinction between Christ-person and world-person, together with taking care for the concrete relation to others, may not be misunderstood to read that the specifically Christian ethic applies only to the internal, while the universal ethic of the early Decalogue applies to the outward sphere. What is at issue is a distinction on the basis of the particular office, commission, or estate of the Christian in relation to others. Toward the same person the Christian may be obligated first as an "official," then as a Christ-person. In other words, "a distinction must be made between acting (and suffering) in my own behalf in a private relationship with my neighbor on the one hand, and acting (and suffering) in my office, that is, in the responsibility for others inherent in my station."[26] This distinction between activity in one's own cause or in responsibility for others is at bottom a universal ethical

---

[24] *LW,* vol. 21, p. 23 (*The Sermon on the Mount,* 1532): "Here we have two different persons in one man. The one is that in which we are created and born, according to which we are all alike—man or woman or child, young or old. But once we are born, God adorns and dresses you up as another person. He makes you a child and me a father, one a master and the other a servant, one a prince and another a citizen"; WA 32, 316, 23. Respecting the Christian as world-person and Christ-person, *LW,* vol. 21, p. 108; *WA* 32, 390, 8-18; *LW,* vol. 21, p. 109: "According to your own person you are a Christian; but in relation to your servant you are a different person, and you are obliged to protect him"; *WA* 390, 30-32: "Ein Christ bistu fur deine person, aber gegen deinem knecht bistu ein ander person und schuldig jn zu schutzen." Similarly in *WA* 34 I, 121, 10-13 (sermon, 1531). For the historical background it is important that the idea of a *duplex persona* was altogether common in the Middle Ages, especially with reference to the functions of a ruler. See the monumental work of Ernst Kantorowicz, *The King's Two Bodies: A Study in Medieval Political Theology* (Princeton: Princeton University Press, 1957).

[25] See *LW,* vol. 21, pp. 109-10: "You see, now we are talking about a Christian-in-relation: not about his being a Christian, but about this life and his obligation in it to some other person, whether under him or over him or even alongside him, like a lord or a lady, a wife or children or neighbors, whom he is obliged, if possible, to defend, guard, and protect. Here it would be a mistake to teach: 'Turn the other cheek, and throw your cloak away with your coat.'" *WA* 32, 390, 33-38.

[26] Althaus, *Ethics of Martin Luther,* 68.

problem, not merely a problem peculiar to Christian ethics. In Christian ethics some questions are particularly critical due simply to the conflict of norms as Luther saw it, but which are ultimately known to any responsible ethical reflection. Thus, in any critical evaluation of Luther's two-kingdoms doctrine, it is not so much the distinction as such that should merit criticism. Rather, where Luther's concrete political statements are concerned, we must inquire whether the complexity of the situation was at times sufficiently taken into account.

The Distinction between the Three Estates

For Luther's ethics not only his distinction between the two kingdoms and the two governments is of importance, but also his distinction between the "three estates." His reference to the estates has not been given the same attention as his two-kingdoms doctrine; but it can claim to be an important supplement, since, like the distinction between the governments, it is suited to avoid possible misunderstanding.

The three estates include the priestly estate, the estate of marriage, and the temporal authority. With respect to terms, Luther can use the Latin *ordo* or *hierarchia*. In German *Stand, Hierarchie, Orden,* but also *Amt* most often appear. The usage is thus considerably broader and less precise than with the distinction between the two kingdoms and two governments. It is nonetheless customary to refer to Luther's three-estate doctrine.

The tradition-historical background for his doctrine of the three estates can be less clearly defined than for the two-kingdoms doctrine. According to Wilhelm Maurer, "Luther's three-estate doctrine . . . grew out of medieval catechetical instruction," to which popular preaching of the time also adhered.[27] At the same time, for use of the concept "hierarchy" Dionysius the Areopagite and his work *On the Heavenly Hierarchy* were influential. In addition, Reinhard Schwarz has emphasized that the social structures of Luther's own time, not least the usual division of ethics into three distinct areas, influenced his three-estate doctrine. Aristotelian moral philosophy was of particular importance in this connection.[28] It might still be an open question as to where the ultimately decisive tradition is to be sought, without on that account disputing the significance of other lines. What is important is that Luther first spoke of "estates" or "offices," and only later used the concept of "hierarchies," and then rather seldom.[29] What he had to say in essence about these estates was not affected by this terminological change.

---

[27] Maurer, *Luthers Lehre von den drei Hierarchien und ihr mittelalterlicher Hintergrund,* SBAW.PPH 4 (Munich: Bayerischen Akademie der Wissenschaften, 1970), 9.

[28] R. Schwarz, "Luthers Lehre von den drei Ständen und die drei Dimensionen der Ethik," *LwJ* 45 (1978), 15-34, esp. 19-20.

[29] Maurer, *Luthers Lehre von den drei Hierarchien und ihr mittelalterlicher Hintergrund,* 39; Schwarz, "Luthers Lehre."

There is an important word on the three estates in the *Confession Concerning Christ's Supper* (1528). In the section on cloisters and foundations, to his mind best retained as educational institutions, Luther spoke in a lengthier context of the three "orders" or "institutes" that, in contrast to monastic institutions, God himself established.[30] The reference is to the priestly state, the estate of marriage, and the temporal authority. Whoever exists in one of these lives in an "order" pleasing to God. A monk, however, is in an estate he himself has chosen, and not instituted by God. The estates are to serve the protection and preservation of the creation. They thus do not lead to salvation, which is received solely by faith.

In a few passages Luther wrote still further of the estates and their significance, giving a somewhat different definition by means of the Latin *ecclesia, oeconomia,* and *politia*. In the *Lectures on Genesis* (1535-1545), which due to their transmission need to be cited only with caution, Luther derived the establishing of the *ecclesia, oeconomia,* and *politia* from the command in Genesis 2:16-17: "And the Lord God commanded the man, saying, 'You may freely eat of every tree of the garden; but of the tree of the knowledge of good and evil you shall not eat, for in the day that you eat of it you shall die.'" The church was established first, though without any pageantry. The *oeconomia* was established with the creation of woman as man's companion. Prior to the fall *politia* was not yet necessary. It was founded as an external disciplinary means against the consequences of sin. To that extent we may appropriately describe the *politia* as a *regnum peccati* (kingdom of sin).[31]

Finally, the *Circular Disputation on the Right to Resist the Emperor* of May 9, 1539, deserves special notice. The title itself uses the concept of "hierarchies": *Septuaginta Propositiones disputandae, de tribus Hierarchiis, Ecclesiastica, Politica, Oeconomica, et quod Papa sub nulla istarum fit, sed omnium publicus hostis* (Seventy conclusions regarding the three hierarchies: the ecclesiastical, political, and economic, to the effect that the pope belongs to none of them, but is the public enemy of all).[32] As the title makes clear, here also the dispute with Rome lies back of the distinction between the hierarchies. Indeed, just as in the *Confession Concerning Christ's Supper,* polemic against monasticism and the papacy plays a decisive role. In respect of subject matter, the statements in this treatise do not lead us beyond what was said earlier. Luther's initial concern may have been with proving that the papacy has no place in any of the three hierarchies, for which reason resistance to it is commanded. The required obedience to it cannot at all be based on appeal to Romans 13. Resistance to thieves and

---

[30] *LW,* vol. 37, pp. 364-65. *WA* 26, 504-5.

[31] *LW,* vol. 1, p. 104. *WA* 42, 79, 1-19. But there is similar material in *WA* 40, III, 646, 17-21 (*Vorlesung über Jesaja 9,* 1543/1544).

[32] *WA* 39 II (34), 39-91. The title corresponds to the first printed edition. On this disputation see Rudolf Hermann, "Luthers Zirkulardisputation über Matthäus 19:21" (1941), in Hermann, *Gesammelte Studien zur Theologie Luthers und der Reformation* (Göttingen: Vandenhoeck & Ruprecht, 1960), 206-50.

robbers is likewise necessary. On the other hand, resistance by force to temporal authority is strictly forbidden. Therefore, just as the temporal authority must care to preserve the peace, so the individual may never resist it by force. What is important here is Luther's insistence that in all three hierarchies the Christian must act responsibly, particularly in the economic sphere.[33]

The language used of the three hierarchies is significant, not least because it again makes evident that for Luther not merely the temporal authority or the state is included in the kingdom of the world or the secular government, but absolutely everything needed for life in the world. At the same time, with this doctrine Luther avoided the misinterpretation that his earlier statement did not always avoid, that the Christian lives only in Christ's kingdom. That the Christian also lives life in the world is given greater emphasis in the doctrine of hierarchies than in the two-kingdoms doctrine.

---

[33] On this subject see Hans-Jürgen Prien, *Luthers Wirtschaftsethik* (Göttingen: Vandenhoeck & Ruprecht, 1992).

Chapter 34

ESCHATOLOGY

Death and the Last Judgment

In his own life as well as in all his theology, the idea of death and the last judgment was Luther's constant companion. In his biography the question as to how he might stand before God in the judgment played a decisive role. The Reformation understanding of the righteousness of God and the justification of the sinner is unintelligible apart from its eschatological context.[1] In Luther's doctrine death and the last judgment have fundamental significance: justification is of course received in the here and now, but it will be fully realized only in the hour of judgment before the eternal God. From this perspective, even for Luther's anthropology, but naturally also for his view of history, death and the last judgment must always be kept in view. That humans are creatures and must see themselves in this creaturely conditioned state if they are not to fall prey to hubris implies that they know of the end that awaits them. Thus, for both his biography and his theology, Luther's attitude toward death and judgment is the touchstone for the truth and authenticity of everything said or written. A theology that does not reflect on this horizon of the end time misses both the truth of the gospel and the reality of human existence.

Certainly, Luther's view owed much to the waning medieval period, when the universal power and presence of death was experienced and reflected on with great intensity.[2] No doubt, Luther appropriated something from views then dominant

---

[1] See above, pp. 257-65.

[2] See Hans Preuss, *Die Vorstellungen vom Antichrist im späteren Mittelalter, bei Luther und in der konfessionellen Polemik: Ein Beitrag zur Theologie Luthers und zur Geschichte der Frömmigkeit* (Leipzig: J. Hinrichs, 1906).

about death and judgment, about the antichrist and end-time expectation. Particularly in his early period influences from the later Middle Ages are detectable. Still, from the perspective of his Reformation theology, he reflected on the various problems and aspects in a new way and made contributions extending far beyond the ideas circulating then. Characteristic of Luther is his view of the intimate connection between the death of the individual and the last judgment. He could also express different ideas, just as the Bible and especially Paul are not strictly uniform in their ideas of death and the beyond. One peculiarity, however, attaches to Luther's eschatology, and it lies chiefly in its close link to the Reformation view of law and gospel.

Luther shared with the tradition the dualistic view that at death the soul is separated from the body, though on this point he entertained some doubt. In the Promotion Disputation of Petrus Hegemon of 1545 he said: "[In death] the spirit returns to the Lord. This is what the entire church teaches, as well as that in death the soul is separated from the body. But it is another question whether the body and soul are separate things."[3] Luther's view was that the soul of the deceased sleeps "between heaven and earth," and is then reawakened on the last day.[4] What he meant is that those who one day waken will have no idea at all as to how long they slept or where they were: "So also death is called sleep in Scripture. For just as one who does not know how it is that he sleeps and comes to morning unawares when he wakes, so we who suddenly arise in the Last Day will not know how we died and came through death."[5]

This leaves no doubt that Luther held to the immortality of the soul.[6] Naturally, he established it differently than scholasticism with its pursuit of the ancient worldview. Luther's argument was strictly theological. For example, he wrote: "those who believe in him, and acknowledge him from whom they have their being never die. Their natural life will be stretched out into life eternal, so that they never taste death, as he says in John 8 [v. 51]: 'If any one keeps my word, he will never see death.'"[7] Or, he could argue as follows: "When we are dead, we are not dead to [God]. For he is not a God of the dead but the God of Abraham etc., who live; as it is said in Matthew 22 [v. 32], 'they are not dead but live to me.'"[8] Again, Luther said

---

[3] WA 39 II, 354, 10-15: "Spiritus redit ad dominum. Hoc tota ecclesia dicit, et quod in morte separatur anima a corpore. Sed alia questio est, an corpus et anima sint distinctae res."

[4] Instead of the many examples that could be cited here, we refer merely to Luther's more detailed and particularly reflective exposition in his January 13, 1521, letter to Amsdorf, WA Br 2 Nr. 449, 27-44, esp. lines 29-31.

[5] WA 17 II, 235, 16-20 (Fasten Postille), 1525).

[6] Evidence for this, among other things, has finally been furnished by W. Thiede, "Nur ein ewiger Augenblick: Luthers Lehre vom Seelenschlaf zwischen Tod und Auferweckung," Luther 64 (1993), 112-25.

[7] LW, vol. 52, p. 55 (The Gospel for the Main Christmas Service, 1522). WA 10I, 1, 200, 6-8.

[8] WA 37, 149, 19-21 (sermon, 1533): "Quando sumus mortui, non sumus mortui coram eo. Quia ipse non est deus mortuorum, sed deus Abrahae etc. qui vivunt, ut Matth. 22 q.d. non sunt mortui, sed vivunt mihi."

that God creates the soul immortal in the womb,[9] and he wrote: "He speaks with man alone. Accordingly, where and with whomever God speaks, whether in anger or in grace, that person is surely immortal. The Person of God, who speaks, and the Word point out that we are the kind of creatures with whom God would want to speak eternally and in an immortal manner."[10] Luther was thus convinced that since God has created humans and speaks with them, the relation between them and God is never at an end.

Luther, of course, could speak quite differently from the idea of soul sleep. From the pericope of the rich man and Lazarus (Luke 16:19-31) he could infer that God may temporarily waken the dead from sleep, but added that "no certain rule may be set up about this."[11] In the lectures on Genesis (1535-1545) he compared our sleep at night with the sleep of the soul at death. On earth our body sleeps and our soul is awake and thus has visions or hears conversation between God and the angels. After death the soul also goes to sleep, but then God wakens and preserves it. Luther added that we do not know how this can happen.[12]

Especially significant is Luther's remark on the death of Urbanus Rhegius in the preface to his *Prophetiae veteris testamenti de Christo* (1542). It reflects an entirely different idea of the period after death:

So we know that our Urbanus, who always lived in faithful appeal to God and faith in Christ, who faithfully served the church, and adorned the gospel with the chastity and piety of his manner of life, is saved, has eternal life, and eternal joy in fellowship with Christ and the church in heaven. There now he is clearly learning, judging, and hearing what he set forth here in the church according to the Word of God.[13]

[9] *WA* 39 II, 401, 4-8 (*Promotionsdisputation von Petrus Hegemon,* 1545). On the peculiarity of Luther's view of the immortality of the soul, see Gerhard Ebeling, *Lutherstudien,* vol. 2: *Disputatio de homine,* part 2, 60-183. Ebeling in particular elaborates Luther's position toward Aristotle in contrast to late scholasticism (ibid., 136-45).

[10] *LW,* vol. 5, p. 76 (*Lectures on Genesis, Chapters 26 to 30,* 1525-1545); *WA* 43, 481, 32-35: "Cum solo homine loquitur. Ubi igitur et cum quocunque loquitur Deus, sive in ira, sive in gratia loquitur, is certo est immortalis. Persona Dei loquentis et verbum significant nos tales creaturas esse, cum quibus velit loqui Deus usque in aeternum et immortaliter."

[11] *WA* 10 III, 194, 10-21 (sermon, 1522).

[12] *LW,* vol. 4, p. 313; *WA* 43, 360, 24-33, with reference to the death of Abraham (Gen. 25:7-10).

[13] *WA* 53, 400, 14-19: "Quare et Urbanum nostrum, qui in vera invocatione Dei et fide Christi assidue vixit et fideliter servivit Ecclesiae et Euangelium castitate et pietete morum ornavit, sciamus beatum esse et habere vitam et laeticiam aeternam in societate Christi et Ecclesiae coelestis, in qua nun ea coram discit, cernit et audit, de quibus hic in Ecclesia iuxta verbum Dei disseruit." The quotation is preceded by reference to Rev. 14:13: "Blessed are the dead who die in the Lord henceforth."

This significant statement about fellowship with Christ immediately after death is in considerable tension with the assertion of soul sleep. It is fundamentally irreconcilable with it. Luther may have been thinking especially of Paul's statement in Philippians 1:23: "My desire is to depart and be with Christ, for that is far better."

This utterance renders it doubtful that the words concerning soul sleep, which are certainly more numerous, can really be promoted to the rank of a "doctrine of Luther."[14] It is just as indefensible, however, to reject the idea of soul sleep in Luther.[15] It must rather be said that like Paul, Luther could express himself in various ways. We should not attempt to regard the one or other idea as his true opinion. By means of these various ideas Luther intended to translate the biblical statements. At the heart is his view that fellowship with God and Christ does not cease with death, not because the soul is an eternal substance but because God has created and speaks with us.

Next in significance is Luther's connection of death and judgment. Luther shared with the tradition the expectation of the last judgment at the close of history. If in his inner conflicts he had once experienced anxiety and horror before the judgment,[16] later he could rejoice over the last day and pray: "Come [dear, last] day, Amen."[17] On the basis of John 3:18 ("He who believes in him is not condemned"), Luther was convinced that whoever believes in Christ is already "clear of judgment": "If our hearts could grasp the fact that we need not fear the Final Judgment, what joy they would find!"[18]

At the same time, Luther could say that at death each individual experiences the last day, emphasizing that all our ideas of time here on earth are inappropriate to our state after death:

Here we must put time out of mind and realize that in that world there are neither time nor hour, that everything is one eternal moment.[19]

Adam is as present to God as the last man. . . . When Adam and the others rise, they will think they have just died in the very same hour . . . when we have died, each will have his last day.[20]

---

[14] Thus the title of the essay by W. Thiede, "Nur ein ewiger Augenblick" (1993).

[15] Thus F. Heidler in his various works; see Heidler, *Die Biblische Lehre von der Unsterblichkeit der Seele,* 18, and often.

[16] See the "self-witness" in *LW,* vol. 34, p. 328; *WA* 54, 179, 31-33 (1545).

[17] *LW,* vol. 50, p. 220 (letter to his wife of July 16, 1540). *WA Br* 9 Nr. 3512, 17.

[18] *LW,* vol. 22, p. 380 (*Sermons on the Gospel of St. John,* 1538-1540). *WA* 47, 102, 19-33.

[19] *WA* 10 III, 194, 10-12 (sermon, 1522).

[20] *WA* 14, 70, 8-71, 5 (*Die ander Epistel S. Petri und S. Judas ausgelegt,* 1523/24): "Coram deo Adam tam praesens ut ultimus est . . . Adam et ceteri cum resurgent, putabunt se iam primum et in eadem hora mortuos esse . . . quando mortui sumus, quisque suum habebit extremum diem." Cf. *LW,* vol. 30, p. 196. Similarly in *WA* 12, 596, 26-30 (sermon, 1523): "Und wenn man auffersteen wirt, so wurde es Adam und den alten vetern werden, gleich als weren sie vor einer halben stundt noch im leben gewest.

Significantly enough, Luther spoke of an annulment of time not only with regard to our own subjective experience but also in view of God's eternity.[21] In these words he in essence stated the view that space and time are categories of our thought and world that are invalid in face of God's eternity.

The result is that the last day is an event occurring at the end of time, but for each individual occurs already at death.

DEATH IN THE LIGHT OF LAW AND GOSPEL

Luther's view of death in the light of law and gospel gives special clarity to the Reformation view of death and the last judgment. For this new interpretation, Luther's 1534/1535 lecture on Psalm 90 is particularly significant. The problem of the transmission of the text must, of course, be noted. The interpretations of Werner Elert and Paul Althaus are in essence based on Veit Dietrich's edition, in which Luther's ideas were to a great extent altered.[22] To lift out Luther's original view, one may cite only the lecture notes.[23] The picture that then emerges is considerably different from that of Elert or Althaus.

The content of Psalm 90 as well as Luther's then broken health were the occasion for dealing with the problem of death in more detail. In this lecture the distinction between law and gospel forms a second principal theme. Luther drew the distinction entirely from statements in the text relative to death and resurrection, whereas in the edition of Dietrich dogmatic shape is given to the theme. What is worth considering, however, is that the actual theme is neither death and human suffering nor the question of law and gospel, but rather life. Luther adduced various arguments in support.

The hermeneutical rule set up in Luther's exposition of the title of this psalm ("The Prayer of Moses") reads that Moses is to be regarded as a *publica persona dei,* as an *organum dei,* whose words and deeds are inspired by God himself. Moses must thus be seen in his office as a *minister legis* (a servant of the law).[24] This idea, however,

---

Dört ist kain zeyt, derhalben kan auch kain besunder ort sein und seind weder tag noch nacht." ("When we will rise, then for Adam and the old fathers it will be just as if they had still been alive a half hour earlier. There is no time there, so there can also be no special place, and there are neither day nor night.") WA 36, 349, 8-12 (sermon, 1532). WA 40 III, 525, 5-6 (*Vorlesung über Psalm 90,* 1534/1535): "quando Adam excitabitur, erit ut 1 hora" ("when Adam will be raised, it will be like one hour"). Cf. *LW,* vol. 13, p. 101.

[21] Thus correctly Althaus, *Theology of Martin Luther,* 416.

[22] See Elert, *Structure of Lutheranism,* esp. 17-28; Althaus, "Luthers Wort vom Ende und Ziel des Menschen," *Luther* 28 (1957), 97-108. Note B. Lohse's criticism of Althaus in "Gesetz, Tod und Sünde in Luthers Auslegung des 90. Psalms" (1968), in *Evangelium in der Geschichte,* 379-94.

[23] More detailed evidence is in Matthias Schlicht, *Luthers Vorlesung über Psalm 90—Überlieferung und Theologie,* FKDG 55 (Göttingen: Vandenhoeck & Ruprecht, 1994).

[24] WA 40 III, 490, 4. Cf. *LW,* vol. 13, p. 79.

is only one facet of the hermeneutical rule. The other is the supplement that is furnished on the basis of Luther's doctrine of law and gospel, but also on the basis of his exegesis of the psalm: "It is the rule and fixed canon: wherever in Scripture the First Commandment is dealt with, there it is to be applied to Christ, who says in Matthew [22:32]: 'He is not God of the dead, but of the living.'"[25]

What is especially impressive is that in interpreting the first verse of this psalm Luther departed from his earlier view and the view of Augustine according to which God is to be described in this psalm as a refuge. In the meantime he had busied himself once more not merely with the Hebrew text but also with Jerome's translation, with the result that he agreed with Jerome against Augustine. Jerome had translated the Hebrew *ma'on* here with *habitaculum*, "dwelling" or "abode." Against his own translation then, Luther rejected the interpretation employing the term "refuge." In general, he seldom departed from a position adopted from the great African church father in order to side with Jerome, whom he held in less esteem.[26] Luther drew important consequences from the altered translation: "If God is our 'dwelling place,' then it is necessary that we should 'live.'"[27] Or, "God is our house, our protector." The result is "that there is hope in eternal life, that all who should pray in this way may know that they do not die, suffer, or live in vain, but that there is a most sure dwelling place where we will live."[28] In such fashion Luther connected the problem of death with the Reformation theme of law and gospel.

In light of the law, death is under the wrath of God. Since this is so, humans cannot accept death as a natural phenomenon, but march toward death full of anxiety and fear, since judgment is linked to death. Luther shared the traditional view that death should not be, that it was imposed as punishment because of sin. As such there should be no death "but rather life. And that great fear of death in man means that his death is something quite different than the death of beasts. It means that no beast has such fear of death as man, and of course as a sign that he is created for life."[29] "Death

---

[25] WA 40 III, 492, 11-493, 1: "Regula et certus Canon: In quocunque loco scripturae agitur de l. praecepto, quod applicandus est Christus, qui dicit Matth. 22: 'Non est Deus mortuorum.'" Cf. LW, vol. 13, p. 81.

[26] See Augustine, *En. in Ps.* 89:2; CCSL, 39, 1245, 1 F. : "'Domine,' inquit, 'refugium factus es nobis in generatione et generatione" ("'Lord,' he says, 'you have been our refuge from generation to generation'"). As early as in his first Psalms lecture, Luther followed Augustine. See WA 55 I, 620, 4-5 (Marginal Gloss Ps. 89:1): "'Domine' Ihesu Christe 'refugium' extra te enim non nisi afflictio est etiam in bonis 'factus es' . . ." ("'Lord,' Jesus Christ, 'you have been a refuge,' for without you there is nothing but affliction, even in blessings").

[27] WA 40 III, 497, 6-7. Cf. LW, vol. 13, p. 88.

[28] WA 40 III, 498, 2-5: "Deus . . . Domus est nostra, tutela, . . . ut sit spes vitae aeternae, ut omnes, qui debent orare, sciant se non frustra mori, pati, vivere, sed esse certissimum habitaculum, ubi vivemus." Cf. LW, vol. 13, p. 88.

[29] WA 39 II, 367, 20-24 (*Promotionsdisputation von Petrus Hegemon,* 1545.

always appears in the company of sin and the law."[30] Death, sin, and law are the terrible triad that always attacks us. Because Christians know of law and sin, they sense more strongly than others the horror of death.

In light of the gospel, however, this horror of death retreats, and death assumes another shape. It remains God's judgment on the human become sinful. Yet hidden beneath the mask of judgment there is grace. Now the Christian can sense "that God sends him death" as "the father's rod and a child's chastisement."[31]

It is particularly in Luther's theology of Baptism that he forged a link between the two interpretations of death from the viewpoint of law and gospel. In his 1519 baptismal sermon, Luther had this to say:

> This significance of baptism—the dying or drowning of sin—is not fulfilled completely in this life. Indeed this does not happen until man passes through bodily death and completely decays to dust. As we can plainly see, the sacrament or sign of baptism is quickly over. But the spiritual baptism, the drowning of sin, which it signifies, lasts as long as we live and is completed only in death. Then it is that a person is completely sunk in baptism, and that which baptism signifies comes to pass. Therefore this whole life is nothing else than a spiritual baptism which does not cease till death.[32]

In this sense the Christian may accept death in the hope of being freed from sin.[33] In this sense also the Christian may actually long for death and with it eternal life.[34] Thus Luther could take up the old motif of the *felix culpa,* the idea of guilt as "fortunate" to the extent it is forgiven through Christ's redemptive work: "Therefore, we have no greater horror than of sin and death. Yet God can so comfort us in it that we may boast, as St. Paul [Romans 5:20-21] says, that sin has even served for this, that we should be justified, and that we also gladly would be dead and long to die."[35] So it can happen, as Luther interpreted the song of the aged Simeon (Luke 2:29: "Lord, now lettest thou thy servant depart in peace, according to thy word") that "death has become my sleep."[36]

---

[30] *LW,* vol. 14, p. 83 (*Commentary on Psalm 118,* 1529/1530). *WA* 31 I, 146, 17.

[31] *LW,* vol. 14, p. 90. *WA* 31 I, 160, 20-24.

[32] *LW,* vol. 35, p. 30. *WA* 2, 728, 10-17.

[33] *WA* 10 III, 76, 8-10 (sermon, 1522): "das wir der sünd loss werden. Aber das ist das beste des sterbens, das sich der will darein geb. Dann der leyb ist bald gestorben, so sich der gayst darein ergeben hatt" ("that we are free of sin. But this is the best part of dying, that the will surrenders to it. For the body is soon dead when the spirit has surrendered to it").

[34] *WA* 6, 14, 12-14 (*Eine kurze Form, das Paternoster zu verstehen und zu beten,* 1519): "Hilff uns auss disem sundtlichen ferlichen leben. Hilff unns jhenes leben begeren und disem feyndt werden. Hilff uns den todt nit forchten, sonder begeren." ("Help us out of this sinful, perilous life. Help us to desire that life and to be hostile to this one. Help us not to fear death but to desire it.")

[35] *WA* 12, 410, 31-34 (sermon, 1523).

[36] Hymn no. 349 in the *Lutheran Book of Worship:* "I leave, as you have promised, Lord, in peace and gladness." *WA* 35, 439, 2: "Myt frid und freud ich far do hyn"; *AWA* 4, (1985), 78, 229-31.

In a profusion of various figures Luther expressed the idea that when accepted in faith, death alters its character. In the 1519 *Sermon on Preparing to Die* he stated: "We must turn our eyes to God, to whom the path of death leads and directs us. Here we find the beginning of the narrow gate and the straight path to life [Matt. 7:14]." It is a path comparable to the narrow way to this life at birth.[37] Or, in his lecture on Psalm 90 he summarized his view of dying accepted in faith to the effect that the law says: "'In the midst of life we are ringed 'round by death,' but the gospel reverses this, saying: 'in midst of death we are ringed 'round by life, because we have the forgiveness of sins.'"[38]

THE GOAL OF HISTORY

Not only every individual but history as such is moving toward its end. Since the New Testament age, expectation of the end time has been part of Christian faith.[39] Obviously, throughout the history of the church futuristic eschatology has assumed very different characteristics. In the ancient and medieval church there were periods of distinct apocalyptic expectation, while in other epochs expectation of the end retreated for the sake of an eschatology more suited to the present. The late medieval period as well as the early Reformation years were marked partly by an extraordinarily strong apocalyptic. Within certain limits this is certainly true of Luther himself, but chiefly of Thomas Müntzer and considerable segments of the peasant movement.[40] But it is also true of wide circles of various persuasions within the "left wing of the Reformation," thus of the Anabaptists and particularly of the adherents of a certain Melchior Hoffmann.[41] Apocalyptic expectation was in part coupled with a pronounced chiliasm.

The question is moot as to how strongly Luther was influenced by apocalyptic expectations. While a few scholars assign considerable significance to apocalyptic in

---

[37] *LW*, vol. 42, p. 99. *WA* 2, 685, 20-26.

[38] *WA* 40 III, 496, 4-5: "Das ist vox legis: Mitten: Vox Euangelii: Media etc., quia remissionem peccatorum habemus." See the materially correct revision by Dietrich, ibid., 496, 16-17. Cf. *LW*, vol. 13, p. 83.

[39] See esp. Althaus, *Die letzten Dinge*.

[40] On Müntzer see Hans-Jürgen Goertz, *Thomas Müntzer: Mystiker, Apokalyptiker, Revolutionär* (Munich: Beck, 1989); Abraham Friesen, *Thomas Muentzer, a Destroyer of the Godless: The Making of a Sixteenth-Century Religious Revolutionary* (Berkeley: University of California Press, 1990); B. Lohse, *Thomas Müntzer in neuer Sicht: Müntzer im Licht der neueren Forschung und die Frage nach dem Ansatz seiner Theologie*, Berichte aus den Sitzungen der Joachim Jungius-Gesellschaft der Wissenschaften e. V., 9, H. 2 (Göttingen: Vandenhoeck & Ruprecht, 1991). On the peasant movement see, e.g., Heiko Oberman, "Tumultus rusticorum: Vom Klosterkrieg zum Fürstensieg. Der deutsche Bauernkrieg aus der Nähe betrachtet" (1974), in Oberman, *Die Reformation—Von Wittenberg nach Genf* (Göttingen: Vandenhoeck & Ruprecht, 1986), 144-61.

[41] See Klaus Deppermann, *Melchior Hoffman: Social Unrest and Apocalyptic Visions in the Age of Reformation*, trans. Malcolm Wren, ed. Benjamin Drewery (Edinburgh: T. & T. Clark, 1987).

Luther, others give it less weight.[42] However much he may have pointed to the imminent inbreaking of the end time, there is no lack of evidence that Luther reckoned on a longer historical development.[43] What allowed him to expect that the end was near was chiefly the rule of the pope, in whom he saw the antichrist. From this it followed that the sufferings of the faithful increase in the end time. These thoughts appear following Luther's early dispute with Rome, and from the emergence of the so-called fanatics as well, he drew support for his end-time expectations. The pope, he believed, did not allow Christ and his Word to hold sway. This, he was convinced, witnesses to the presence of the antichrist in the church itself, as foretold in the Bible. If as early as in late medieval polemic against Rome the pope was often described as the antichrist, with Luther a new reason was given for that description in the pope's claim to be above God's Word.[44]

On the other hand, Luther was absolutely clear about the fact that the true church is always under attack. Seemingly calm and stable periods can actually be times of severest temptation.

However we judge Luther's own apocalyptic expectation, what is most significant is that for theological reasons he always resisted the desire to predict when the world would come to an end. Though events may appear to herald the catastrophe of the end time, the Christian is forbidden to speculate about the time.[45] Luther thus neither approved nor consciously participated in efforts to predict the end, even when the attempt was made among his closest associates. Luther's calculations regarding the "thousand years" in his *Supputatio annorum mundi* (1541-1545) do not

---

[42] For the former see esp. Oberman, *Luther: Man between God and the Devil* (New Haven, Conn.: Yale University Press, 1989); idem, "Martin Luther: Vorläufer der Reformation" (1982), in *Die Reformation—Von Wittenberg nach Genf*, 162-88; for the latter see Lohse, "Luthers Selbsteinschätzung," 158-75, esp. 65-66.

[43] See Luther's letter to Duke George of Saxony, May 16, 1519, in *WA Br* 1 Nr. 177, 21-22: "ich weyss wol, das vor myr unnd nach myr die Welt an meyn disputiren bliben ist unnd bleybenn wirdt." ("I know full well that the world has been occupied with my dispute before me and will do so after me.")

[44] Thus correctly G. May, "'Je länger, je ärger'? Das Ziel der Geschichte im Denken Martin Luthers," *ZW* 60 (1989), 213.

[45] See, e.g., *WA* 10 I 2, 93, 21-28 (Advents postille, 1522): "Zum ersten ist tzu wissen, das disse tzeychen des jungsten tages, ob sie wol manchfeltig und gross sind, werden sie doch vollnbracht werdenn, das niemant odder gar wenig sie achten und fur solche tzeychen hallten wirt. Denn disse tzwey werden und mussen beyde geschehen mit eynander, sind auch beyde mit eynander von Christo und den Aposteln vorkundigt, das erst, das viel und grosse tzeychen komen sollen. Das ander, das denn och der jungst tag alsso unvorsehens kome, das sich seyn die wellt von anbegynn nie weniger vorsehen hatt, denn eben tzu der tzeyt wenn er fur der thur ist." ("First of all, we need to know that these signs of the last day, whether they are in fact great and varied, are yet to be fulfilled—which no one or only very few will note or regard as such. For these two things will and must happen together, both of which are preached by Christ and the apostles: First, that many and great signs shall appear. The other, that then too the last day will come unforeseen, a day that since the world began has never yet been seen till the very moment it is at the door.")

contradict this statement.[46] He interpreted the standard text of chiliasm in Revelation 20:3-7, with its word about the thousand years and first resurrection, not with reference to the end time but with reference to the history of the church, as the *Supputatio* indicates. This removes any biblical basis from speculation about a thousand-year reign prior to the last judgment. With this interpretation Luther followed Augustine, who also interpreted this text of the time of the church.[47]

Danger from the Turks also gave rise to end-time expectations. For the first time, in the fall of 1529, a Turkish army stood before Vienna. Defensive war against the Turks and the always difficult attempt to obtain the needed approval of taxes for that war were a chief concern of imperial politics in the first half of the sixteenth century. Luther saw in the Turkish advance a punishment of God, in fact, a horde of Satan in the struggle of the end time. He thus could lump the papacy and Turks together: "The pope is the spirit of the antichrist, and the Turk is the flesh of the antichrist. The two help each other to strangle us, the latter with body and sword, the former with doctrine and spirit."[48] On the other hand, Luther opposed the idea of a crusade against the Turks. It may be that the end of the world is coming with them. Should this be so, it would be the end of them. For now, we should not want to search out God's secret decree but keep to our tasks. If we do this in right faith, we need not fear even apocalyptic enemies, the pope or the Turks.[49]

Just as death when accepted in faith loses its horror and becomes a "sleep," so also the last day loses its threatening character: it becomes the "dear Last Day." That the day of imminent judgment becomes a day of coming salvation has its ultimate basis in justification, further evidence of that doctrine's central function for all the topics of theology.[50] Just as Luther developed his doctrine of justification within the horizon of eternal judgment, so now the judgment is transformed through the new relation to God begun with justification.

In the last times before the end the malice of the wicked and attacks on believers will be carried to extremes. As Luther believed he could infer from the New Testament, the revelation of the antichrist will be first to occur. Since he believed that the antichrist was already present in the papacy, his own struggle against it, but also the historical-theological interpretation coupled with it, took on an apocalyptic cast. Naturally, he distinguished the revelation of the antichrist and the return of

---

[46] *WA* 53, 152-54. On this subject see zur Mühlen, *Luther,* here, 560.

[47] See Augustine, *De civitate Dei* 20.9.

[48] *WA TR* 1, Nr. 330: "papa est spiritus Antichristi, et Turca est caro Antichristi. Sie helffen beyde einander wurgen, hic corpore et gladio, ille doctrina et spiritu."

[49] A brief discussion of this subject is in May, "'Je länger, je ärger'?", 214-15. Further, M. Brecht, *Martin Luther,* vol. 3: *The Preservation of the Church,* trans. James L. Schaaf (Minneapolis: Fortress Press, 1993), 353-54; Hartmut Bobzien, "Martin Luthers Beitrag zur Kenntnis und Kritik des Islam," *NZSTh* 27 (1985), 262-89.

[50] On this subject see Forell, "Rechtfertigung und Eschatologie bei Luther," in *Reformation 1517-1967,* edited by Ernst Kähler (Berlin: Evangelische Verlagsanstalt, 1968), 145-5.

Christ. Of course, he thought he could infer that the parousia would no longer be delayed. "As for me I content myself with the fact that the last day must be at hand. For almost all the signs which Christ and the apostles Peter and Paul announced, have now appeared. The trees sprout, the Scripture greens and blooms. Whether or not we can know the day in just this way does not matter; let another do it better. It is certain that everything is coming to an end."[51] These words obviously reflect reserve toward any attempt at determining more precisely the time of the end.

As for all of history, here too Luther rejected speculation regarding the manner of its fulfillment. He was led by the certainty that with the end would come a conclusion to the struggle that threads through the various periods and furnishes the real theme of historical life and development. At times he hinted at the notion that humanity in his day had in a manner of speaking arrived at its dotage. From this viewpoint it is no surprise that "the older things are the poorer they are, the longer the worse," or that the world has become "an old man."[52] Yet even such statements were made with restraint. What remains is that we can scarcely say anything about the end or about the eternity then breaking in.

---

[51] *WA DB* 11 II, 124, 15-20 (*Vorrede über den Propheten Daniel,* 1541).
[52] Thus *WA* 29, 619, 10-11 (sermon, 1529).

Chapter 35

EXCURSUS
Luther's Attitude toward the Jews

Jews in the West around 1500

Luther's statements concerning the Jews, often represented in placative and abbreviated form, can be evaluated in unbiased fashion only when we first take into account the Jewish situation in the West on the eve of the Reformation, and next, when we evaluate the context in which Luther made these statements. If these two factors are not observed, access is obstructed to historical understanding as well as to a critique, with any basis, of Luther's position. The attempt at hastily uniting Luther's position with later developments leads inevitably to misrepresentation.

Respecting the Jewish condition around 1500, one may say in general that in large sections of Europe Jews living then fared worse than in previous centuries. In addition, literary debate with the Jews was carried on more sharply and rigorously in this period than earlier. In the entire late Middle Ages, expulsion of Jews was common practice. Pogroms occurred continually, often for more or less empty reasons.

As early as in 1290, King Edward I of England (1272-1307) ordered the Jews banished from his kingdom. When many of them immigrated to France, King Philip the Good (1285-1314) ordered their expulsion from his land. These measures not only affected Jews native to England but also those who had long been inhabitants of France. Anti-Jewish politics in France were so successful that none other than Erasmus could boast in 1517 that in contrast to other European lands France was "free of Jews." France was the purest and most flourishing section of Christendom, since only France was free of infection by heretics, Bohemian schismatics, Jews,

336

and half-Jewish Maranos.[1] In 1492 the Jews were driven from Spain. Some of them settled in Portugal, but they were banished from there in 1497. On the eve of the Reformation, then, there was a sizable migration of the Jewish minority within many European countries, which naturally fed certain prejudices. In the late medieval period measures hostile to Jews in western Europe led to an aggravated anti-Jewish attitude in the German Empire. Here, at least, Jews had legal protection from the emperor and the territorial princes, who were of course well reimbursed through special taxes for guaranteeing them privileges.

In the German Empire, anti-Jewish measures in the late Middle Ages did not originate with the princes but entirely with the people. Individual pogroms were a continual occurrence and often involved a great many murders. On the whole, this real insecurity, despite a modicum of legal protection, lasted into the early period of the Reformation. During the plague in the middle of the fourteenth century, Jews who in many places were alleged to be responsible for it were murdered or forced to suicide. They were charged with having created the plague by poisoning the wells. In the early sixteenth century there were no longer any Jews in many German cities. Nonetheless, even around 1520, when the Reformation movement was reaching its zenith, measures were taken in many places to banish the Jews. Events at Regensburg in 1519 are particularly well known. Here there lived and worked the cathedral preacher Balthasar Hubmaier, at that time still a Catholic prelate, but soon after a follower of Luther, and after that again one of the noted Anabaptist theologians.[2] Hubmaier attacked the Jews chiefly for exacting interest and for usury. In fact, since other vocations were closed to them, some Jews did function as lenders and were thus in violation of the church's prohibition against usury. There was no difference between traditionalists and adherents of Luther in their hostility toward the Jews.

Various measures against the Jews were accompanied by a varied polemic shared by leading theologians of the late Middle Ages.[3] Representatives of very different persuasions, not least among them leading representatives of humanism, were participants in the dispute. It would be a major error to assume that the humanists, pioneers of a more independent attitude of mind, were on principle and in particular tolerant toward Jews. Not the humanists but, as usual, conservative

---

[1] Erasmus, *Letter to Richard Bartholinus* (March 10, 1517), *Opus Epistolarum des Erasmi Roterodami*, vol. 2, ed. P. S. Allen (Oxford: Clarendon, 1910), Nr. 549, p. 501, 9-14: "Christianus orbis aduersus Christianae ditionis purissimam ac florentissimam partem conspirabit? Sola Gallia nec haereticis est infeca nec Bohemis schismaticis nec Iudeis nec semiiudeis Maranis, nec Turcarum confinio afflata; quemadmodum aliae quas et citra nomenclaturam suo quisque animo agnoscit." ("Will the Christian world conspire against the purest and most flourishing section of the Christian dominion? France alone is not infected by heretics or Bohemian schismatics or Jews or half-Jewish Maranos, or by a border filled with Turks; as well as others anyone knows without naming names.")

[2] See Torsten Bergsten, *Balthasar Hubmaier: Seine Stellung zu Reformation und Täufertum 1521-1528*, AUU, Studia Historico-Ecclesiastica Upsaliensia 3 (Kassel: J. G. Oncken, 1961), 76-86.

[3] On this subject see Oberman, *Roots of Anti-Semitism*, 18-64.

forces such as the emperor and princes were, if any, the guarantors of legal protection for Jews. As for Erasmus, he clung to a deeply rooted, exaggerated hatred of Jews.[4] However correct it may be that he advocated "harmony" (*concordia*) and "peace" (*pax*), he nevertheless believed that such ideals could best be realized in the fellowship of Christians. There would be no place for Jews.

If this was the opinion of the leading humanist of that period, it is scarcely surprising that John Eck (1486-1543), leading traditionalist in the contest with Luther, was mired in the swamps of vulgar anti-Judaism. In 1541 appeared his treatise *Ains Judenbüechlins Verlegung* (Refutation of a Little Jewish Book), opposing Osiander's rejection of the charge against Jews of ritual murder and embracing the most primitive biases and suspicions.[5] Indeed, Eck did not hesitate to adduce evidence for the accuracy of the charge. He maintained that he could report at first-hand ritual murders that had been committed.[6]

The dire consequence of all this was that the well-known Jew Johannes Pfefferkorn (1469-1522/23), following his baptism in 1505, authored numerous anti-Jewish tracts replete with polemic and the reviling of his earlier comrades in faith. In these tracts Pfefferkorn made proposals as to how Christian authorities should deal with Jews. What was particularly grave was the proposal that with the exception of the Old Testament, all Hebrew books should be confiscated and burned. He also urged the banishment of Jews from German cities and incited to regular preaching against them. The goal of such forcible measures was to be their conversion.

In the dispute over Hebrew literature initiated by Pfefferkorn, it was Reuchlin who succeeded in having the Jewish writings retained.[7] Due to the extensive literary feud resulting with Pfefferkorn, however, long-standing prejudices were everywhere incited or revived. No doubt, Pfefferkorn is due the dubious service of aggravating the dispute with the Jews in the early sixteenth century that resulted in the pogroms.

At the same time we must always keep in mind that in that period the conflict between Jews and Christians was neither national nor racial but exclusively religious. As soon as a Jew became a Christian, prejudices and reproaches collapsed of their own weight. Jews were rejected because they were "murderers of God" and because of their loyalty to the Jewish law, which Christendom since Paul was convinced had come to its end through Jesus.

---

[4] See Guido Kisch, *Erasmus' Stellung zu Juden und Judentum* (Tübingen: Vandenhoeck & Ruprecht, 1969), 29. Cornelis Augustijn, "Erasmus und die Juden," *NAKG* 60 (1980), 22-38, represents a somewhat different view. Augustijn maintains correctly that by "Jews" Erasmus sometimes had legalistic Christians in mind. But this assertion alters nothing of Erasmus's unquestionably harsh anti-Jewish statements.

[5] On the history of the origin of this treatise, see Oberman, *Roots of Anti-Semitism,* 36.

[6] See Brigite Hägler, *Die Christen und die 'Judenfrage:' Am Beispiel der Schriften Osianders und Ecks zum Ritualmordvorwurf* (Erlangen: Palm Und Enke, 1992).

[7] See Arno Herzig and Julius H. Schoeps, eds., *Reuchlin und die Juden,* Pforzheimer Reuchlinschriften 3 (Sigmaringen: Thorbecke, 1993); in it see particularly Marianne Awerbuch, "Über Juden

LUTHER'S EARLY ATTITUDE TOWARD THE JEWS

Our statement that the opposition between Jews and Christians in the sixteenth century was exclusively religious applies without restriction to Luther's statements on Judaism, in his early career as well as in the last phase of his activity. We must immediately add that owing to the new debates and conflicts over Luther's theology certain traditional arguments were shelved and Judaism in part was put in a more friendly light, but in part was also attacked in an even harsher polemic than previously. In particular, one should note the context of the relation between Jews and other groups or persuasions in Luther's time.

As early as in his first lectures Luther frequently attacked the Jews for their legalism and self-righteousness. The reproaches had to do with the attempt to establish one's own righteousness before God, with false trust in one's own works, with "pride" that spurned the required "humility," or with the attempt to strive after one's own holiness.[8] On this subject Luther often set the Jews in a series with heretics and schismatics, naming the "Bohemians" in particular, but also with the strict *Observantes* in the late medieval orders, or with Christians who trusted in their own righteousness before God instead of hoping for their salvation from God alone. In this connection, he also raised the charge of following the antichrist.[9] It was congruent with the tradition to set the Jews within such a series. Similar statements appear occasionally as early as Augustine.[10] Hence it was not so much the status given the Jews as the harshness of the reproof of "self-righteousness" that marked the peculiarity of Luther's polemic. His picture of the Jews may thus be drawn only when his view of heretics, schismatics, and "false Christians" is also included.

With the formation of Reformation theology this polemic was necessarily intensified. In some Jewish circles, however, the emergence of Luther spelled great hopes for a change in the relations with Christians. Such hopes were after all quite unjustified, however understandable in light of Jewish distress in that period. Luther also harbored great expectations. He thought that the true gospel had not yet been preached to the Jews, that if the rediscovered gospel were heard now, wherever possible it would finally reach them.

Luther's treatise *That Jesus Christ Was Born a Jew* appeared in 1523.[11] The opinion has often been expressed that in it Luther indicates that he is entirely open toward

---

und Judentum zwischen Humanismus und Reformation: Zum Verständnis der Motivation von Reuchlins Kampf für das jüdische Schrifttum," 189-200.

[8] Evidence for this in Lohse, *Mönchtum und Reformation*, FKGD 12 (Göttingen: Vandenhoeck & Ruprecht, 1963), 267-72.

[9] Oberman contains a more detailed survey of these charges against the Jews in the first Psalms lecture in *Leben und Werk Martin Luthers*, 2:522-23.

[10] See Bernhard Blumenkranz, *Die Judenpredigt Augustins: Ein Beitrag zur Geschichte der jüdisch-christlichen Beziehungen in den ersten Jahrhunderten* (Basel: Helbing und Lichtenhahn, 1946), 194-98.

[11] *LW*, vol. 45, pp. 199-229. *WA* 11 (307), 314-36.

the Jews, while in his maturer years he was given to the most violent outbreaks. A review of the history of the origin and intention of this treatise leads to a more discerning picture.[12]

The occasion for the treatise was a report made to Luther early in January 1523, that Archduke Ferdinand, brother of the emperor, had accused him of a new error, alleging that he taught that Christ was Abraham's seed. Luther first took the charge to be a joke, but then he had to defend himself publicly against it.[13] In itself the charge was senseless; its purport could only be that according to Luther, Christ was begotten solely from Abraham's sperm. It clearly implies the broader charge that Luther denied the virginity of Mary and regarded Joseph as Jesus' physical father. Luther not only wanted to contest this senseless charge but also to write something useful, explaining why he believed that Jesus was born a Jew. His intention was thus "that I might perhaps also win some Jews to the Christian faith."[14] He criticized the manner in which they had been dealt with till now: "Our fools, the popes, bishops, sophists, and monks—the crude asses' heads—have hitherto so treated the Jews that any one who wished to be a good Christian would almost have had to become a Jew. If I had been a Jew and had seen such dolts and blockheads govern and teach the Christian faith, I would sooner have become a hog than a Christian."[15]

The treatise is divided into two parts. In the first Luther rejected the charge against him; in the second he attempted to set the current debate with the Jews on a new and better footing. It is important to note that the treatise was primarily a defense directed at traditionalists. Only secondarily did it represent intra-Christian reflection on dealings with the Jews. By "Judaism" Luther had in mind those Jews inhabiting Christian lands and clearly reckoned with the fact that "some" of them had converted to Christianity.[16]

At the same time, it is significant that for Luther such Jews as have converted are turning "again to the faith of their fathers, of the prophets and patriarchs."[17] Indeed, Luther was always of the opinion that the believers of the old covenant had been Christians. The Jews would thus only be taking up their true faith once more. The new Reformation view of God could help toward this end. "If the apostles, who also were Jews, had dealt with us Gentiles as we Gentiles deal with the Jews, there would never have been a Christian among the Gentiles."[18]

---

[12] See esp. Brosseder, *Luthers Stellung zu den Juden,* 345-55.

[13] *WA Br* 3 Nr. 574, 26-431. The same charge was clearly raised by others then; see ibid., p. 20, n. 18.

[14] *LW,* vol. 45, p. 200. WA 11, 314, 27-28.

[15] *LW,* vol. 45, p. 200. *WA* 11, 314, 28-315, 2.

[16] So Brosseder, *Luthers Stellung zu den Juden,* 350-51.

[17] *LW,* vol. 45, p. 200. *WA* 11, 315, 16-17.

[18] *LW,* vol. 45, p. 200. *WA* 11, 315, 19-21.

Nevertheless, this treatise of Luther was not a missionary tract. It obviously had an apologetic, missionary slant,[19] but served ultimately only to inform Christians about treating Jews in more friendly fashion. Further, Luther did not deal with specific themes with which he always dealt in earlier and later debate with the Jews, such as especially the Jews' legalism, their "works-righteousness," but also their obduracy, for which he drew particular support from Romans 9–11. He did not deal with these questions here, since his aim was not a thorough discussion of Jewish-Christian problems. For methodological reasons, however, Luther's views on these other questions should not be ignored. They are assumptions that Luther constantly held, and must be added to his explicit statements in the 1523 treatise.

The result is that interpretations that regard the treatise of 1523 as opening a totally new view on the relation between Jews and Christians do justice neither to its intention nor to Luther's theological conviction. In 1523 Luther did not hope that the Jews as a whole or even in great part would be open to the gospel as understood in the Reformation. He nevertheless reckoned with the conversion of a "few" of them. Still, the proposal that Jews should be dealt with in more friendly fashion is worth noting.

LUTHER'S LATER ATTITUDE TOWARD THE JEWS

Luther's numerous statements about the Jews from the 1520s and 30s must be passed over here. Instead, we briefly evaluate his later writings where he appeared to speak quite differently of the Jews.

For various reasons, the mature Luther's attitude toward the Jews was no longer merely the same as earlier. Significantly, in August 1536, the elector John Frederick issued an edict by which Jews were forbidden to sojourn and work in Electoral Saxony. Even traveling throughout the country was denied them. It is an open question whether Luther exerted any influence on the composition of this edict; in any event he might have been informed of the reasons for it.[20] In the midst of this crisis one of the towering representatives of Judaism in that period, Josel von Rosheim of Lower Alsace,[21] labored to intervene with the Saxon elector, for which purpose the Strassburg Council handed him a letter of recommendation to the elector. Further, on April 26, 1537, the Strassburg reformer Wolfgang Capito wrote to Luther requesting that he allow Josel opportunity for conversation, or at least read his petition and if possible hand it on to the elector.[22]

---

[19] Thus Wilhelm Maurer, "Die Zeit der Reformation," in *Kirche und Synagoge: Handbuch zur Geschichte von Christen und Juden,* vol. 1, ed. Karl Heinrich Rengstorf and Siegried v. Kortzfleisch (Stuttgart: Klett, 1968), 363-452, here 378-91; further, Brosseder, *Luthers Stellung zu den Juden,* 354.

[20] *WA* 54, 24.

[21] On the person of Josel, see *WA Br* 8 Nr. 3152.

[22] *WA Br* 8 Nr. 3152.

Luther declined. In his June 11, 1537, letter to Josel, he stated in fairly friendly fashion: "My dear Jesel! I would most gladly intercede for you with my most gracious lord, both in word and letter, just as my treatise [*That Jesus Christ Was Born a Jew*, 1523] did great service to all of Judaism." Then the letter reads: "Because your people so shamefully misuse this service and undertake such things as we Christians must not endure from them, they have exempted me from every claim I might otherwise have been able to make with princes and lords."[23] Luther indicated that he always advocated friendly treatment of the Jews, being "of the opinion that God would some day graciously regard them and bring them to their Messiah."[24] He mentioned his own treatise,[25] but in the letter's conclusion one detects a harsher note: "Take this from me in a friendly way, for your admonition. For the sake of the crucified Jew whom none shall take from me, I would gladly do my best for all you Jews, if you did not use my favor for your hardening."[26] According to a statement in his Table Talks, Luther did in fact read Josel's petition, but then replied: "Why should we give permission to these rascals who injure people in body and property and with their superstitions cause many Christians to fall away?" Luther was referring to reports according to which Jews in Moravia circumcised Christians and were now calling them "Sabbatarians."[27]

Of these events it must first be said that Luther was of the opinion that Jews were proselytizing Christians; and second, he feared that they were exploiting the amity he favored, with the result that their "hardening" was worsening.[28] From this perspective he arrived at those harsh utterances in his later treatise *On the Jews and Their Lies* (1543).

In this rather comprehensive piece Luther intended first of all to point to the Jews' "pride and boasting."[29] For this purpose he discussed their lineage from the patriarchs, circumcision, the law of Moses from Sinai, the possession of Canaan, Jerusalem, and the temple. In all this he of course admitted that the Jews were

---

[23] *WA Br* 8 Nr. 3157, 2-8.

[24] *WA Br* 8 Nr. 3157, 10-11.

[25] *LW,* 47, pp. 65-98 (*Against the Sabbatarians,* 1538). *WA* 50, 309, 312-37.

[26] *WA Br* 8 Nr. 3157, 56-59.

[27] *LW,* vol. 54, p. 239. *WA* TR 3, Nr. 3597, p. 442, 4-12.

[28] See *LW,* vol. 47, p. 137. *WA* 53, 417, 2-12.

[29] *LW,* vol. 47, p. 149. *WA* 53, 449, 1. Of late, doubt has been shed on its genuineness. See the report, "Ist Luthers 'Juden'-Schrift eine Fälschung?" by Monika Beck in the New York journal *Aufbau,* for Friday, January 1, 1993, p. 6. The report tells of the researches of the Oxford lecturer Eva Berndt, who for seemingly good reasons argues that this treatise cannot be from Luther. The most important, apparently, is "that as early as 1536 (the onset of the trial against Agricola) this printing . . . is . . . cited . . . word for word as coming from Luther" (ibid., p. 6, col. 3). On the other hand, we must call attention to the fact that witnesses to its publication give no occasion for suspecting the treatise's genuineness; next, that its content corresponds with other statements of the mature Luther. Thus, for the time being, we must as usual assume its genuineness.

chosen by God but also emphasized that they should not boast. As for circumcision, it lost significance once the Jews persecuted the prophets and thus "God himself, whose word they preached."[30]

What applies now is that God truly honored them highly by circumcision, speaking to them above all other nations on earth and entrusting his word to them. And in order to preserve this word among them, he gave them a special country; he performed great wonders through them, ordained kings and government, and lavished prophets upon them who not only apprised them of the best things pertaining to the present but also promised them the future Messiah, the Savior of the world. It was for his sake that God accorded them all of this, bidding them look for his coming, to expect him confidently and without delay. For God did all of this solely for his sake: for his sake Abraham was called, circumcision was instituted, and the people were thus exalted so that all the world might know from which people, from which country, at which time, yes, from which tribe, family, city, and person, he would come, lest he be reproached by devils and by men for coming from a dark corner or from unknown ancestors. No, his ancestors had to be great patriarchs, excellent kings, and outstanding prophets, who bear witness to him.[31]

Next, Luther entered on the "main subject" and disputed the Jews' prayer to God for the Messiah:

Here at last they show themselves as true saints and pious children. At this point they certainly do not want to be accounted liars and blasphemers but reliable prophets, asserting that the Messiah has not yet come but will still appear. Who will take them to task here for their error or mistake? Even if all the angels and God himself publicly declared on Mount Sinai or in the temple in Jerusalem that the Messiah had come long ago and that he was no longer to be expected, God himself and all the angels would have to be considered nothing but devils, so convinced are these most holy and truthful prophets that the Messiah has not yet appeared but will still come. Nor will they listen to us. They turned a deaf ear to us in the past and still do so, although many fine scholarly people, including some from their own race, have refuted them so thoroughly that even stone and wood, if endowed with a particle of reason, would have to yield. Yet they rave consciously against recognized truth. Their accursed rabbis, who indeed know better, wantonly poison the minds of their poor youth and of the common man and divert them from the truth.[32]

---

[30] *WA* 53, 436, 6-7. Cf. *LW*, vol. 47, p. 161.
[31] *LW*, vol. 47, p. 163. *WA* 53, 438, 15-29.
[32] *LW*, vol. 47, p. 176. *WA* 53, 449, 3-18.

What is significant about this text is that Luther is convinced that the rabbis are knowingly and deliberately distorting the truth, and keeping from the Jewish people the knowledge of Jesus as Messiah. His real intention was thus to set forth the objective right of the Christian interpretation of the Old Testament in view of Christ against Jewish exposition of Old Testament messianic prophecies. In their exposition, the Jews approximate the Christian heretics and especially the so-called fanatics, with whom Luther in fact often linked them. According to Luther what is common to all is that they pervert the truth against better knowledge. For fifteen hundred years the Jews have heard the truth but have rejected it. So they are not excused—which involves incurring a "sevenfold guilt."[33]

On the basis of this judgment Luther arrived at his harsh proposals: (1) Jewish synagogues should be set afire, since Moses (Deut. 13:13ff.) wrote that a city which practices idolatry should be destroyed by fire. (2) Houses of the Jews should be razed, since the Jews practice idolatry in them just as in their schools. (3) Their "prayer books and Talmudic writings, in which such idolatry, lies, cursing, and blasphemy are taught," should be confiscated. (4) "On pain of loss of life and limb" their rabbis should be forbidden to teach any longer; they have forfeited their office, due to their false doctrine. (5) Safe conduct should be denied them, "for they have no business in the countryside, since they are not lords, officials, tradesmen, or the like. Let them stay at home." (6) Their usury should be prohibited, all cash and treasure of silver and gold taken from them and "put aside for safe keeping," since they have gained their riches through usury. (7) They should be given tools to become craftsmen and earn their pay in the sweat of their brow.[34] In this way the Jews should lose rights they would previously have had.

What is first to be said of these proposals against their sixteenth-century background is that Luther was taking up suggestions long made from another side.[35] They are neither original nor harsher than those that others at the time had made, and across all ecclesiastical and spiritual persuasions. For the rest, they must be compared with punishments awaiting heretics, as a rule, the punishment of death. Finally, behind these proposals a universally shared conviction must be kept in mind, that is, that in a commonwealth only one religion may be publicly practiced, lest the common peace and blessing of God be imperiled. According to the conviction held then, the juxtaposition of various religions in a city or territory threatened the public peace, indeed, would evoke the wrath of God.

These references are intended neither to relativize nor to excuse Luther's proposals. After the fearful twentieth-century persecutions of the Jews, Christian churches must engage in self-critical inquiry concerning the causes and intellectual

[33] *LW*, vol. 47, p. 287. *WA* 53, 537, 18-28.
[34] *LW*, vol. 47, pp. 268-72. *WA* 53, 523, 1-526, 6.
[35] See, e.g., Brosseder, *Luthers Stellung zu den Juden*, 370-77.

precursors of such horrible anti-Semitism. In doing so, however, understanding must first be summoned for assumptions and limitations existing in earlier times.

In any critical inquiry into Luther's attitude toward the Jews, quite different considerations must prevail that we shall only name here, without weighing any one of them in detail.

First, there is the absolute necessity for religious tolerance, nonexistent in the sixteenth century and recognized in the modern period as an absolute requirement only after a long and extremely painful process, slowly achieved.

Second, place must be given to theological inquiry into Luther's argument. What is absent here in Luther is the self-critical question as to whether the picture that he was drawing of Jewish religion actually applied, or whether he had retained assumptions that an unbiased examination would have had to correct. Since from his own experience as well as from his studies of the history of the church Luther was sufficiently aware of the fateful significance of prejudice, and since he continually complained that on the Roman side none gave him fair hearing, it would not be inappropriate to expect of him greater caution toward entrenched opinions or prejudices. What should also be kept in mind is that the picture he drew of the legalism of Jewish religion so well suited his polemic against works-righteousness that "the Jews" were simply a cipher for one who justifies oneself. Be that as it may, Luther did not subject his judgments to critical examination. In this regard, he was captive to the views of his time. It is also true that he did not exceed the judgments conditioned by the time.

Finally, we lack a dialogue having to do with the content of Jewish faith. Such a dialogue never occurred in the sixteenth century. In newer researches a few noteworthy attempts have been made.[36] To take up and intensively to tend this dialogue is an important task, just as in any case such a dialogue belongs to an independent reading.

---

[36] This is true especially of Brosseder, *Luthers Stellung zu den Juden*.

BIBLIOGRAPHY

Bibliographical references are roughly in chronological order.

CHAPTER I. CRITERIA FOR DESCRIBING LUTHER'S THEOLOGY

Theodosius Harnack, *Luthers Theologie mit besonderer Beziehung auf seine Versöhnungs-und Erlösungslehre.* 2 vols. Erlangen: Theodor Blaesing, 1862-86; reprint Munich: Chr. Kaiser, 1927.

Julius Köstlin, *The Theology of Luther in Its Historical Development and Inner Harmony,* trans. by Charles E. Hay. Philadelphia: Lutheran Pub. Society, 1897.

Reinhold Seeberg, *Text-book of the History of Doctrines,* translated by Charles E. Hay. Grand Rapids: Baker, 1952.

Karl Holl, *Gesammelte Aufsätze zur Kirchengeschichte.* Vol. 1: *Luther.* Tübingen: Mohr, 1921; 7th ed. 1948.

Erich Seeberg, *Luthers Theologie: Motive und Ideen.* Vol. 1: *Die Gottesanschauung.* Göttingen: Vandenhoeck & Ruprecht, 1929. Vol. 2: *Christus: Wirklichkeit und Urbild.* Stuttgart: Kohlhammer, 1937.

———— *Luthers Theologie in ihren Grundzügen.* Stuttgart: Kohlhammer, 1940; reprint 1950.

Philip S. Watson, *Let God Be God: An Interpretation of the Theology of Martin Luther.* Philadelphia: Fortress Press, 1947.

Emanuel Hirsch, *Lutherstudien.* 2 vols. Gütersloh: Bertelsmann, 1954.

Ernst Wolf, *Peregrinatio* [vol. 1]: *Studien zur reformatorischen Theologie und zum Kirchenproblem.* Munich: Chr. Kaiser, 1954; 2d ed. 1962.

Gerhard Ebeling, "Luther, II. Theologie," *RGG* 4 (3d ed. 1960), 495-520.

Paul Althaus, *The Theology of Martin Luther,* translated by Robert C. Schultz. Philadelphia: Fortress Press, 1966.

Gerhard Ebeling, *Luther: An Introduction to His Thought,* translated by R. A. Wilson. Philadelphia: Fortress Press, 1970.

Lennart Pinomaa, *Sieg des Glaubens: Grundlinien der Theologie Luthers,* edited by Horst Beintker. Berlin/Göttingen: Vandenhoeck & Ruprecht, 1964.

Friedrich Gogarten, *Luthers Theologie*. Tübingen: Mohr, 1967.

Rudolf Hermann, *Gesammelte und nachgelassene Werke*. Vol. 1: *Luthers Theologie,* edited by Horst Beintker. Göttingen: Vandenhoeck & Ruprecht, 1967.

Hans Joachim Iwand, *Luthers Theologie,* edited by Johann Haar. Munich: Chr. Kaiser, 1974 (= Hans Joachim Iwand, *Nachgelasssene Werke* 5).

Reinhold Weier, *Das Theologieverständnis Martin Luthers*. KKTS 36. Paderborn: Bonifacius, 1976.

Gerhard Ebeling, *Lutherstudien*. Vol. 2: *Disputatio de Homine,* 3 parts. Tübingen: Mohr, 1977-89.

Jaroslav Pelikan, *The Christian Tradition: A History of the Development of Doctrine*. Vol. 4: *Reformation of Church and Dogma*. Chicago: University of Chicago Press, 1984.

Ulrich Asendorf, *Die Theologie Martin Luthers nach seine Predigten*. Göttingen: Vandenhoeck & Ruprecht, 1988.

Albrecht Peters, *Kommentar zu Luthers Katechismen,* edited by Gottfried Seebass. 3 vols. Göttingen: Vandenhoeck & Ruprecht, 1990-94.

Alister E. McGrath, *Luther's Theology of the Cross: Martin Luther's Theological Breakthrough*. Grand Rapids: Baker, 1990.

Karl-Heinz zur Mühlen, "Martin Luther (1483-1546). II. Theologie," *TRE* 21 (1991), 530-67.

Scott Hendrix, "Luthers Theologie," *EKL* (3d ed. 1992), 3:211-20.

CHAPTER 2. THE SITUATION IN THE CHURCH AROUND 1500

Bernd Moeller, *Spätmittelalter*. KIG 2. Göttingen: Vandenhoeck & Ruprecht, 1966.

Martin Anton Schmidt, "Die Zeit der Scholastik," *HdBDThG,* 1:567-754.

A. W. Weiler, *Heinrich von Gorkum (+1431): Seine Stellung in der Philosophie und der Theologie des Spätmittelalters*. Hilversum/Einsiedeln/Zurich/Cologne: P. Brand, 1962.

Denis R. Janz, *Luther on Thomas Aquinas: The Angelic Doctor in the Thought of the Reformer*. VIEG 140. Stuttgart: Franz Steiner Wiesbaden, 1989.

Erwin Iserloh, *Gnade und Eucharistie in der philosophischen Theologie des Wilhelm von Ockham: Ihre Bedeutung für die Ursachen der Reformation*. VIEG 8. Wiesbaden: Steiner, 1956.

Wilhelm Ernst, *Gott und Mensch am Vorabend der Reformation: Eine Untersuchung zur Moralphilosophie und-theologie bei Gabriel Biel*. EthSt 28. Leipzig: St. Benno, 1972.

Heiko A. Oberman, *Spätscholastik und Reformation*. Vol. 1: *Der Herbst der mittelalterlichen Theologie*. Tübingen: Mohr, 1965.

Erich Kleineidam, *Universitas Studii Erffordensis: Überblick über die Geschichte der Universität Erfurt im Mittelalter 1392-1521*. Vol. 1. EThSt 14. Leipzig: St. Benno, 1964; 2d ed. 1985. Vol. 2. EThSt 22. Leipzig: St. Benno, 1969.

Kenneth Hagen, ed., *Augustine, the Harvest, and Theology (1300-1650): Essays Dedicated to Heiko Augustinus Oberman in Honour of His Sixtieth Birthday*. Leiden: Brill, 1990.

Heiko A. Oberman, ed., *Gregor von Rimini: Werk und Wirkung bis zur Reformation*. Spät-mittelalter und Reformation 20. Berlin/New York: de Gruyter, 1981.

Berndt Hamm, *Frömmigkeitstheologie am Anfang des 16. Jahrhunderts: Studien zu Johannes von Paltz und seinem Umkreis*. BHTh 65. Tübingen: Mohr, 1982.

Markus Wriedt, *Gnade und Erwählung: Eine Untersuchung zu Johann von Staupitz und Martin Luther*. VIEG 141. Mainz: P. von Zabern, 1991.

CHAPTER 3. THE THEOLOGICAL SITUATION AROUND 1500, ESPECIALLY IN ERFURT AND WITTENBERG

On Occamism at Erfurt:

Helmar Junghans, *Ockham im Lichte der neueren Forschung*. AGTL 21. Hamburg: Lutherisches Verlagshaus, 1968.

Wilhelm Ernst, *Gott und Mensch am Vorabend der Reformation: Eine Untersuchung zur Moralphilosophie und -theologie bei Gabriel Biel*. EthSt 28. Leipzig: St. Benno, 1972.

Erich Kleineidam, *Universitas Studii Erffordensis: Überblick über die Geschichte der Universität Erfurt im Mittelalter 1392-1521*. Vol. 1. EThSt 14. Leipzig: St. Benno, 1964; 2d ed. 1985. Vol. 2. EThSt 22. Leipzig: St. Benno, 1969.

Wolfgang Urban, "Die 'via moderna' an der Universität Erfurt am Vorabend der Reformation," in: *Gregor von Rimini, 311-330* (see in addition the review by Leif Grane, *ThLZ* 108 [1983], 276-79).

On Humanism at Wittenberg and in Luther:

Helmar Junghans, "Der Einfluss des Humanismus auf Luthers Entwicklung bis 1518," *LuJ* 37 (1970) 37-101.

Maria Grossmann, "Humanismus in Wittenberg, 1486-1517," *LuJ* 39 (1972), 11-30. Idem, *Humanismus in Wittenberg 1485-1517*. Nieuwkoop: De Graff, 1975.

Helmar Junghans, *Der junge Luther und die Humanisten*. Weimar: Böhlau, 1984; see in addition Berndt Moeller, *ThLZ* 111 (1986), 602-4.

On Traditions of Significance for Luther:

Adolf Hamel, *Der junge Luther und Augustin: Ihre Beziehungen in der Rechtfertigungslehre nach Luthers ersten Vorlesung 1509-1518 untersucht*. 2 vols. 1934-35; reprint, Hildesheim/New York: Georg Olms, 1980.

Bernhard Lohse, "Die Bedeutung Augustins für den jungen Luther (1965)," in *Evangelium in der Geschichte*, Studien zu Luther und der Reformation ed. Leif Grane, Bernd Moeller und Otto Hermann Pesch. Göttingen, 1988, 11-30.

Dorothea Demmer, *Lutherus interpres: Der theologische Neuansatz in seiner Römerbriefexegese unter besonderer Berücksichtigung Augustins*. UKG 4. Witten: Luther Verlag, 1968.

Leif Grane, *Modus loquendi theologicus: Luthers Kampf um die Erneuerung der Theologie (1515-1518)*. AThD 12. Leiden: Brill, 1975.

Bernhard Lohse, "Zum Wittenberger Augustinismus; Augustins Schrift de Spiritu et Littera in der Auslegung bei Staupitz, Luther und Karlstadt," in *Augustine, the Harvest, and Theology (1300-1650): Via Augustini. Augustine in the Later Middle Ages, Renaissance and Reformation. Essays in Honor of Damasus Trapp, OSA,* edited by Heiko A. Oberman and Frank A. James III. Leiden: Brill, 1991.

On Staupitz:

Ernst Wolf, *Staupitz und Luther: Ein Beitrag zur Theologie des Johannes von Staupitz und deren Bedeutung für Luthers theologischen Werdegang.* QFRG 9. Leipzig: M. Heinsius Nachfolger, 1927.

David Steinmetz, *Luther and Staupitz: An Essay in the Intellectual Origins of the Protestant Reformation.* Duke Monographs in Medieval and Renaissance Studies 4. Durham: Duke University Press, 1980.

Lothar Graf zu Dohna, "Staupitz and Luther: Continuity and Breakthrough at the Beginning of the Reformation," in *Via Augustini,* 116-29.

Markus Wriedt, *Gnade und Erwählung.* Mainz: P. von Zabern, 1991.

On Mysticism:

Erich Vogelsang, "Luther und die Mystik," *LuJ* 19 (1937), 32-54.

Arthur Rühl, *Der Einfluss der Mystik auf Denken und Entwicklung des jungen Luther.* Diss., Marburg, 1960.

Heiko A. Oberman, "Simul genitus et raptus. Luther und die Mystik" (1967), in Oberman, *Die Reformation: Von Wittenberg nach Genf,* 45-89. Göttingen: Vandenhoeck & Ruprecht, 1986 (respecting misconceptions occasioned by the title, I need to stress that the formula *simul genitus et raptus* does not appear in the sources but is Oberman's conceptualization, intended to summarize his thesis regarding the influence of mysticism on Luther).

Bengt R. Hoffman, *Luther and the Mystics: A Reexamination of Luther's Spiritual Experience and His Relationship to the Mystics.* Minneapolis: Augsburg Publishing House, 1976.

Reinhard Schwarz, "Martin Luther (1483-1546)," in *Grosse Mystiker: Leben und Wirken,* edited by Gerhard Ruhbach and Josef Sudbrack, 185-202, 375-80. Munich: Beck, 1984.

On Bernard of Clairvaux:

Erich Kleineidam *BHTh*, "Ursprung und Gegenstand der Theologie bei Bernhard von Clairvaux und Martin Luther," in *Dienst der Vermittlung: FS zum 25 jährigen Bestehen des philosophisch-theologischen Studiums im Priesterseminar Erfurt,* 221-47. EThSt 37. Leipzig: St. Benno, 1977.

Theo Bell, *Divus Bernhardus: Bernhard von Clairvaux in Martin Luthers Schriften* (Dutch, 1989). VIEG 148. Mainz: P. von Zabern, 1993.

Franz Posset, "St. Bernard's Influence on Two Reformers: John von Staupitz and Martin Luther," *Cistercian Studies* 25 (1990), 175-87.

————"Bernhard von Clairvauxs Sermone zur Weihnachts-, Fasten- und Osterzeit als Quellen Luthers," *LuJ* 61 (1994), 93-116.

Bernhard Lohse, "Luther und Bernhard von Clairvaux," in *Bernhard von Clairvaux: Rezeption und Wirkung im Mittelalter und in der Neuzeit,* edited by Kaspar Elm, 271-301.

Wolfenbütteler Mittelalter-Studien 6. Wiesbaden: Harrassowitz, 1994.

Chapter 4. Luther's Personal Development

Otto Scheel, *Martin Luther: Vom Katholizismus zur Reformation.* Vol. 1: *Auf der Schule und Universität.* 3d ed. Tübingen: Mohr, 1921. Vol. 2: *Im Kloster.* 3d/4th eds. Tübingen: Mohr, 1930.

Martin Brecht, *Martin Luther: His Road to Reformation, (1483-1521),* translated by James L. Schaaf. Minneapolis: Fortress Press, 1985.

Bernhard Lohse, *Martin Luther: An Introduction to His Life and Work,* translated by Robert Schultz. Philadelphia: Fortress Press, 1986. *Martin Luther und die Reformation in Deutschland: Katalog der Ausstellung zum 500. Geburtstag Martin Luthers, veranstaltet vom Germanischen Nationalmuseum Nürnberg in Zusammenarbeit mit dem Verein für Reformationgeschichte.* Frankfurt am Main: Insel Verlag, 1983.

Martin Brecht, *Martin Luther (1483-1546),* Stuttgart: Colwer, 1981-87, 513-30.

Chapter 5. The Uniqueness of Luther's Theology

Walther von Loewenich, *Luther's Theology of the Cross,* translated by Herbert J. A. Bouman. Minneapolis: Augsburg Publishing House, 1976.

Erich Seeberg, *Luthers Theologie: Motive und Ideen.* Vol. 1: *Die Gottesanschaung.* Göttingen: Vandenhoeck & Ruprecht, 1929. Vol. 2: *Christus: Wirklichkeit und Urbild.* Stuttgart: Kohlhammer, 1937.

Wilhelm Maurer, *Von der Freiheit eines Christenmenschen: Zwei Untersuchungen zu Luthers Reformationsschriften 1520/1521.* Göttingen: Vandenhoeck & Ruprecht, 1949.

Ernst Wolf, "Die Christusverkündigung bei Luther," in *Peregrinatio,* [1:] 30-80.

Gerhard Ebeling, "Cognitio Dei et hominis," in *Lutherstudien,* Vol. 1: *Disputatio de Homine,* 3 parts. Tübingen: Mohr, 1977-89, 1:221-27.

———— *Lehre und Leben in Luthers Theologie,* Opladen: Westdeutscher Verlag, 1984, 3:3-43.

Reinhold Weier, *Das Theologieverständnis Martin Luthers.* KKTS 36. Paderborn: Bonifacius, 1976.

Marc Lienhard, *Luther:Witness to Jesus Christ: Stages and Themes of the Reformer's Christology,* translated by Edwin H. Robertson. Minneapolis: Augsburg Publishing
House, 1982.

———— "Luthers Christuszeugnis," in *Leben und Werk Martin Luthers von 1526 bis
1546: Festgabe zu seinem 500. Geburtstag,* edited by Helmar Junghans, 1:77-92;
2:748-55. Göttingen:Vandenhoeck & Ruprecht, 1983.

Oswald Bayer, "Oratio, Meditatio,Tentatio. Eine Besinnung zu LuthersTheologiever-
ständnis," *LuJ* 55 (1988), 7-59.

CHAPTER 6. BASIC THEOLOGICAL IDEAS IN LUTHER'S MARGINAL NOTES ON AUGUSTINE AND PETER LOMBARD (1509/1510)

Otto Scheel, *Die Entwicklung Luthers bis zum Abschluss derVorlesung über den Römerbrief,*
SVRG 100, 1910), 61-230.

Werner Jetter, *Die Taufe beim jungen Luther,* 109-74. BHTh 18. Tübingen: Mohr,
1954.

Bernhard Lohse, *Ratio und Fides,* Göttingen: Vandenhoeck Ruprecht, 1958, 22-29.

Reinhard Schwarz, *Fides, Spes und Caritas beim jungen Luther unter besonderer Berücksichtigung der mittelalterlichen Tradition,* 5-75. AKG 34. Berlin: de Gruyter, 1962.

Bernhard Lohse, *Mönchtum und Reformation: Luthers Auseinandersetzung mit dem Mönchsideal des Mittelalters,* 213-26. FKDG 12. Göttingen:Vandenhoeck & Ruprecht,
1963.

———— "Dogma und Bekenntnis in der Reformation:Von Luther bis zum Konkordienbuch," in *HdBDTHG.* Vol. 2: *Die Lehrentwicklund im Rahmen der Konfessionalität,* 1-166,
esp. 2-4.

Jared Wicks, *Luther's Reform: Studies on Conversion and the Church*, esp. 118-22. Mainz:
Verlag P. von Zabern, 1992.

CHAPTER 7. EARLY REFORMATION THEOLOGY IN THE FIRST PSALMS LECTURE (1513-1515)

Erich Vogelsang, *Die Anfänge Luthers Christologie nach der ersten Psalmenvorlesung, insbesondere in ihren exegetischen und systematischen Zusammenhägen mit Augustin und
der Scholastik dargestellt.* AKG 15. Berlin/Leipzig: de Gruyter, 1929.

———— *Der angefochtene Christus bei Luther.* AKG 21. Berlin/Leipzig: de Gruyter,
1932.

Gerhard Ebeling, "Die Anfänge von Luthers Hermeneutik" (1951), in *Lutherstudien,*
1:1-68.

———— "Luthers Psalterdruck vom Jahre 1513" (1953), in ibid., 69-131.

———— "Luthers Auslegung des 14. (15.) Psalms in der ersten Psalmenvorlesung im Vergleich mit der exegetischen Tradition" (1953), in ibid., 132-95.

———— "Luthers Auslegung des 44. (45.) Psalms" (1958), in ibid., 196-220.

Werner Jetter, *Die Taufe beim jungen Luther*, 109-74. BHTh 18. Tübingen: Mohr, 1954.

Bernhard Lohse, *Ratio und Fides*, Göttingen: Vandenhoeck Ruprecht, 1958, 30-43.

Albert Brandenburg, *Gericht und Evangelium: Zur Worttheologie in Luthers erster Psalmenvorlesung.* KKTS 4. Paderborn: Bonifacius Druckerei, 1960.

Reinhard Schwarz, *Fides, Spes und Caritas beim jungen Luther under besonderer Berücksichtigung der mittelalterlichen Tradition*, 5-75. AKG 34. Berlin: de Gruyter, 1962, 76-240.

Bernhard Lohse, *Mönchtum und Reformation: Luthers Auseinandersetzung mit dem Mönchsideal des Mittelalters*, 213-26. FKDG 12. Göttingen: Vandenhoeck & Ruprecht, 1963, 227-78.

Reinhard Schwarz, *Vorgeschichte der reformatorischen Busstheologie.* AKG 41. Berlin: de Gruyter, 1968.

Bernhard Lohse, *HdBDThG*, 2:4-10.

Chapter 8. The Structure of Reformation Theology in the Period of Pauline Exegesis (1515-1518)

Ernst Bizer, *Fides ex Auditu: Eine Untersuchung über die Entdeckung der Gerechtigkeit Gottes durch Martin Luther.* 1858. 3d ed. Neukirchen: Kreis Moers Verlag der Buchhandlung des Erziehungsvereins, 1966.

Werner Jetter, *Die Taufe beim jungen Luther,* 109-74. BHTh 18. Tübingen: Mohr, 1954, 255-330.

Bernhard Lohse, *Ratio und Fides*, Göttingen: Vandenhoeck Ruprecht, 1958, 43-54.

Reinhard Schwarz, *Fides, Spes und Caritas beim jungen Luther under besonderer Berücksichtigung der mittelalterlichen Tradition*, 5-75. AKG 34. Berlin: de Gruyter, 1962, 241-413.

Bernhard Lohse, *Mönchtum und Reformation: Luthers Auseinandersetzung mit dem Mönchsideal des Mittelalters*, 213-26. FKDG 12. Göttingen: Vandenhoeck & Ruprecht, 1963, 278-343.

Walter Grundmann, *Der Römerbrief des Apostels Paulus und seine Auslegung durch Martin Luther.* Weimar: Böhlau, 1964.

Dorothea Demmer, *Lutherus interpres: Der theologische Neuansatz in seiner Römerbriefexegese unter besonderer Berücksichtigung Augustins.* UKG 4. Witten: Luther Verlag, 1968.

Matthias Kroeger, *Rechtfertigung und Gesetz: Studien zur Entwicklung der Rechtfertigungslehre beim jungen Luther.* FKDG 20. Göttingen: Vandenhoeck & Ruprecht, 1968.

Oswald Bayer, *Promissio: Geschichte der reformatorischen Wende in Luthers Theologie.*
   FKDG 24. 1971. 2d ed. Darmstadt: Wissenschaftliche Buchgesellschaft, 1989.

Karl-Heinz zur Mühlen, *Nos extra nos: Luthers Theologie zwischen Mystik und Scholastik.*
   BHTh 46. Tübingen: Mohr, 1972.

Leif Grane, *Modus loquendi theologicus: Luthers Kampf um die Erneuerung der Theologie
   (1515-1518).* AThD 12. Leiden: Brill, 1975.

Bernhard Lohse, *HdBDThG,* 2:10-17.

Karl-Heinz zur Mühlen, "Die Erforschung des 'jungen' Luthers seit 1876," *LuJ* 50
   (1983), 48-125.

Gabriele Schmidt-Lauber, *Luthers Vorlesung über den Römerbrief 1515/1516: Ein Vergleich zwischen Luthers Manuskript und den studentischen Nachschriften.* AWA 6.
   Cologne: Böhlau, 1994.

CHAPTER 9. THE REFORMATION DISCOVERY

Luther's Most Important Biographical Statements:

Otto Scheel, *Documente zu Luthers Entwicklung,* Tübingen: Mohr, 1929.

Ernst Stracke, *Luthers Grosses Selbstzeugnis 1545 über seine Entwicklung zum Reformator:
   Historisch-kritisch untersucht.* SVRG 140. Leipzig: M. Heinsius Nachfolger, 1926
   (extract in *Der Durchbruch der reformatorischen Erkenntnis bei Luther,* edited by
   Bernhard Lohse. WdF 123. Darmstadt: Wissenschaftliche Buchhandlung,
   1968—texts chosen for the history of research, 107-14).

Erich Vogelsang, *Die Anfänge Luthers Christologie nach der ersten Psalmenvorlesung, insbesondere in ihren exegetischen und systematischen Zusammenhängen mit Augustin und
   der Scholastik dargestellt.* AKG 15. Berlin/Leipzig: de Gruyter, 1929.

Heinrich Bornkamm, "Luthers Bericht über seine Entdeckung der iustitia Dei," *ARG*
   37 (1940), 117-28.

——— "Iustitia dei in der Scholastik und bei Luther," *ARG* 39 (1942), 1-46.

Ernst Bizer, *Fides ex Auditu: Eine Untersuchung über die Entdeckung der Gerechtigkeit
   Gottes durch Martin Luther.* 1858. 3d ed. Neukirchen: Kreis Moers Verlag der
   Buchhandlung des Erziehungsvereins, 1966, (condensed in *Durchbruch,* 115-
   62).

Gerhard Pfeiffer, "Das Ringen des jungen Luther um die Gerechtigkeit Gottes," *LuJ*
   26 (1959), 25-55 (extract in *Durchbruch,* 163-202).

Albrecht Peters, "Luthers Turmerlebnis," *NZSTh* 3 (1961), 203-36 (extract in *Durchbruch,* 243-88).

Regin Prenter, *Der barmherzige Richter: Iustitia dei passiva in Luthers Dictata super
   Psalterium 1513-1515.* Acta Jutlantica 33/2. Aarhus: Universitetsforlaget, 1961
   (extract in *Durchbruch,* 289-383).

Kurt Aland, *Der Weg zur Reformation: Zeitpunkt und Charakter des reformatorischen Erlebnisses Martin Luthers.* ThEx N.F.123. Munich: Chr. Kaiser, 1965 (extract in *Durchbruch*, 384-412).

Bernhard Lohse, "Die Bedeutung Augustins für den jungen Luther," *KuD* 11 (1965), 116-35.

Otto H. Pesch, "Zur Frage nach Luthers reformatorischer Wende: Ergebnisses und Probleme der Diskussion um Ernst Bizer, *Fides ex auditu*," *Catholica* 20 (1966), 216-43, 264-80 (extract in *Durchbruch*, 445-505).

Bernhard Lohse, "Luthers Auslegung von Ps 71 (72). l. u. 2 in der l. Psalmenvorlesung," in *Vierhundertfünfzig Jahre lutherische Reformation 1517-1967: FS Franz Lau*, edited by Helmar Junghans, Ingetraut Ludolphy, and Kurt Meier, 191-201. Göttingen: Vandenhoeck & Ruprecht, 1967 (extract in *Der Durchbruch: Neuere Untersuchungen*, edited by Bernhard Lohse, 1-13. VIEH Beih. 25. Stuttgart: F. Steiner, 1988).

Matthias Kroeger, *Rechtfertigung und Gesetz: Studien zur Entwicklung der Rechtfertigungslehre beim jungen Luther.* FKDG 20. Göttingen: Vandenhoeck & Ruprecht, 1968, (extract in *Durchbruch: Neuere Untersuchungen*, 14-56).

Ole Modalsli, "Luthers Turmerlebnis 1515," *StTh* 22 (1968), 51-91 (extract in *Durchbruch: Neuere Untersuchungen*, 57-97).

Rolf Schäfer, "Zur Datierung von Luthers reformatorischer Erkenntnis," *ZThK* 66 (1969), 151-70 (extract in *Durchbruch: Neuere Untersuchungen*, 134-53).

Oswald Bayer, *Promissio: Geschichte der reformatorischen Wende in Luthers Theologie.* FKDG 24. 1971. 2d ed. Darmstadt: Wissenschaftliche Buchgesellschaft, 1989, (extract in *Durchbruch: Neuere Untersuchungen*, 154-66).

Reinhard Schinzer, *Die doppelte Verdienstlehre des Spätmittelalters und Luthers reformatorische Entdeckung.* ThEx N.F. 168. Munich: Chr. Kaiser, 1971.

Reinhard Schwarz, "Beschreibung der Dresdner Scholien-Handschrift von Luthers 1. Psalmenvorlesung," *ZKG* 82 (1971), 65-93.

Martin Brecht, "Iustitia Christi; Die Entdeckung Martin Luthers," *ZThK* 74 (1977), 179-223 (extract in *Durchbruch: Neuere Untersuchungen*, 167-211).

Gerhard Müller, *Die Rechtfertigungslehre: Geschichte und Probleme.* Gütersloh: Gütersloher Verlagshaus, 1977.

Wilfried Härle and Eilert Herms, *Rechtfertigung: Das Wirklichkeitsverständnis des christlichen Glaubens. Ein Arbeitsbuch.* Göttingen: Vandenhoeck & Ruprecht, 1980.

Bernhard Lohse, "Dogma und Bekenntnis in der Reformation: Von Luther bis zum Konkordienbuch," *HdBDThG*, 2:17-21.

Otto H. Pesch, "Neuere Beiträge zur Frage nach Luthers 'Reformatorische Wende,'" *Catholica* 37 (1983), 259-87; 38 (1984), 66-133 (extract in *Durchbruch: Neuere Untersuchungen*, 245-341).

Joachim Mehlhausen, "Die reformatorischen Wende in Luthers Theologie," in *Martin Luther im Spiegel heutiger Wissenschaft,* edited by Knut Schäferdiek, 15-32. Bonn: Bouvier, 1985 (extract in *Durchbruch: Neuere Untersuchungen,* 342-59).

Reinhard Staats, "Augustins 'De spiritu et littera' in Luthers reformatorische Erkenntnis," *ZKG* 98 (1987), 28-47 (extract in *Druchbruch: Neuere Untersuchungen,* 365-84).

CHAPTER 10. LUTHER'S ATTACK ON INDULGENCES (1517/1518)

Sources for the Indulgence Controversy:

Luthers 95 Thesen samt seinen Resolutionen sowie den Gegenschriften von Wimpina-Tetzel, Eck und Pierias und den Antworten Luthers darauf, edited by Walther Köhler. Leipzig: Hinrichs, 1903. *Dokumente zum Ablasstreit von 1517.* Edited by Walther Köhler. SQS 2/3. 2d ed. Tübingen: Mohr, 1934.

Dokumente zur Causa Lutheri (1517-1521), edited by Peter Fabisch and Erwin Iserloh. 2 vols. CCath 41-42. Münster: Aschendorffsche Verlagsbuchhandlung, 1988-91.

On the History of Indulgences:

Theodor Brieger, "Indulgenzen," *RE* 9 (1901), 76-94.

Nikolaus Paulus, *Johann Tetzel, der Ablassprediger.* Mainz: Kirchheim, 1899.

————— *Geschichte des Ablasses im Mittelalter vom Ursprung bis zur Mitte des 14. Jahrhunderts.* 3 vols. Paderborn: F. Schöningh, 1922/1923.

Gustav Adolf Benrath, "Ablass," *TRE* 1 (1977), 347-64.

On Luther's Ninety-five Theses and the Early Conflict around Luther:

Ernst Kähler, "Die 95 Thesen: Inhalt und Bedeutung," *Luther* 38 (1967), 114-24.

Erdmann Schott, "Die theologische Bedeutung der 95 Thesen," in *450 Jahre Reformation,* edited by Leo Stern and Max Steinmetz, 70-88. Berlin: Deutscher Verlag der Wissenschaften, 1967.

Heiko A. Oberman, "Wittenbergs Zweifrontenkrief gegen Prierias und Eck: Hintergrund und Entscheidungen des Jahres 1518," *ZKG* 80 (1969), 331-58.

Carter Lindberg, "Prierias and His Significance for Luther's Development," *SCJ* 3/2 (1972), 45-64.

Kurt-Victor Selge, *Normen der Christenheit im Streit um Ablass und Kirchenautorität 1518-1521.* Habilitationsschrift in theology at Heidelberg, 1968/1969 (machine copy).

Wilhelm Borth, *Die Luthersache (Causa Lutheri) 1517-1524: Die Anfänge der Reformation als Frage von Politik und Recht.* Historische Studien 414. Lübeck: Matthiesen, 1970.

Daniel Olivier, *The Trial of Luther,* translated by John Tonkin. London: Mowbrays, 1978.

Friedhelm Jürgensmeier, ed., *Erzbischof Albrecht von Brandenburg 1490-1545: Ein Kirchen und Reichsfürst der Frühen Neuzeit*. Beiträge zur Mainzer Kirchengeschichte 3. Frankfurt am Main: J. Knecht, 1991.

On the links between the University of Wittenberg reform and church conflict:
Walter Friedensburg, *Geschichte der Universität Wittenberg*. Halle: Max Niemeyer, 1917.

Kurt Aland, "Die Theologische Fakultät Wittenberg und ihre Stellung im Gesamtzusammenhang der Leucorea während des 16. Jahrhunderts," in Aland, *Kirchengeschichtliche Entwürfe: Alte Kirche, Reformation und Luthertum. Pietismus und Erweckungsbewegung*, 283-394. Gütersloh: Mohn, 1960.

Martin Brecht, *Martin Luther: His Road to Reformation, (1483-1521)*, translated by James L. Schaaf. Minneapolis: Fortress Press, 1985.

On the **Heidelberg Disputation:**
The Text:
Martin Luther Studienausgabe, edited by Helmar Junghans, 1:186-218. Berlin: Evangelische Verlagsanstalt, 1979 (a better text than *WA* 1, 353-74).

The Philosophical Theses of the *Heidelberg Disputation*
   with Its Probationes:
WA 59, 405-26 (ed. Helmar Junghans).
Edmund Schlink, "Weisheit und Torheit," *KuD* 1 (1955), 1-22.
J. E. Vercruysse, "Gesetz und Liebe: Die Struktur der 'Heidelberger Disputation' Luthers (1518)," *LuJ* 48 (1981), 7-43.
——— "Luther's Theology of the Cross at the Time of the Heidelberg Disputation," *Gr.* 57 (1976), 523-48.
Karl-Heinz zur Mühlen, "Die Heidelberger Disputation Martin Luthers vom 26. April 1518: Programm und Wirkung," in *Semper Apertus: Sechshundert Jahre Ruprecht-Karls-Universität Heidelberg 1386-1986. FS in sechs Bänden*. Vol. 1, revised by Wilhelm Dörr, 188-212. Berlin: Springer, 1985.

Chapter 11. Luther's Dispute with Cajetan over Justification, Faith, and Church Authority

On Cajetan:
Erwin Iserloh/Barbara Hallensleben, "Cajetan," *TRE* 7 (1981), 538- 46.
Barbara Hallensleben, *Communicatio: Anthropologie und Gnadenlehre bei Thomas de Vio Cajetan*. RGST 123. Münster: Aschendorffsche Verlagsbuchhandlung, 1985 (in addition B. Lohse, *ThRv* 83 [1987], 286-89).

Ulrich Horst, "Thomas de Vio Cajetan (1469-1534)," in *Klassiker der Theologie*. Vol. 1: *Von Irenäus bis Martin Luther,* edited by Heinrich Fries and Georg Kretschmar, 269-82, 415-16, 430-32. Munich: Beck, 1981.

On the Encounter between Cajetan and Luther:
Gerhard Hennig, *Cajetan und Luther: Ein historischer Beitrag zur Begegnung von Thomismus und Reformation.* AzTh 2/7. Stuttgart: Calwer, 1966.
Irmgard Höss, *Georg Spalatin 1484-1545: Ein Leben in der Zeit des Humanismus und der Reformation,* 127-43. 1956. 2d ed. Weimar: H. Böhlaus Nachfolger, 1989.
Kurt-Victor Selge, "Die Augsburger Begegnung von Luther und Kardinal Cajetan im Oktober 1518," *JHKGV* 20(1969), 37-54.
Otto Hermann Pesch, "'Das heisst eine neue Kirche bauen.' Luther und Cajetan in Augsburg," in *Begegnung: Beiträge zu einer Hermeneutik des theologischen Gesprächs,* edited by Max Seckler, Otto Hermann Pesch, Johannes Brosseder and Wolfhart Pannenberg, 645-61. Graz/Vienna/Cologne: Styria, 1972.
Jared Wicks, "Thomism between Renaissance and Reformation: The Case of Cajetan," *ARG* 68 (1977), 9-32.
———— *Cajetan Responds: A Reader in Reformation Controversy.* Washington, D.C.: Catholic University of America Press, 1978. Idem, *Cajetan und die Anfänge der Reformation.* KLK 43. Münster: Aschendorff, 1983.
Bernhard Lohse, "Cajetan und Luther," in idem, *Evangelium in der Geschichte,* 44-63. Göttingen: Vandenhoeck & Ruprecht, 1968, 44-63.
Jared Wicks, *Luther's Reform: Studies on Conversion and the Church*, esp. 118-22. Mainz: Verlag P. von Zabern, 1992.

CHAPTER 12. LUTHER'S DEBATE WITH ECK ON THE AUTHORITY OF POPE AND COUNCIL (1519)

Sources:
WA 59, 427-605 (text of the Leipzig Disputation).

Literature:
Joseph Lortz, "Die Leipziger Disputation," *BZThS* 3 (1926), 12-37.
Ernst Kähler, "Beobachtungen zum Problem von Schrift und Tradition in der Leipziger Disputation von 1512," in *Hören und Handeln: FS Ernst Wolf,* edited by Helmut Gollwitzer and Hellmut Traub, 214-29. Munich: Chr. Kaiser, 1962.
Folkert Rickers, *Das Petrusbild Luthers: Ein Beitrag zu seiner Auseinandersetzung mit dem Papsttum.* Diss., Heidelberg, 1967 (machine copy).
Remigius Bäumer, *Martin Luther und der Papst,* Münster: Verlag Aschendorff, 1970, 49-53.

Kurt-Victor Selge, "Der Weg zur Leipziger Disputation zwischen Luther und Eck im Jahr 1519," in *Bleibendes im Wandel der Kirchengeschichte: Kirchengeschichtliche Studien,* edited by Bernd Moeller and Gerhard Ruhbach, 169-210. Tübingen: Mohr, 1973.

———"Die Leipziger Disputation zwischen Luther und Eck," *ZKG* 86 (1975), 26-40.

Martin Brecht, *Martin Luther: His Road to Reformation, (1483-1521),* translated by James L. Schaaf. Minneapolis: Fortress Press, 1985, 299-348.

Kurt Aland, "Luther und die römische Kirche" (1984), in Aland, *Supplementa zu den Neutestamentlichen und den Kirchengeschichtlichen Entwürfen: FS zum 75. Geburtstag,* edited by Beate Köster, Hans-Udo Rosenbaum, and Michael Welte, 26-73. Berlin/New York: de Gruyter, 1990.

CHAPTER 13. LUTHER'S DISPUTE WITH THE SACRAMENTAL TEACHING OF HIS TIME (1519/1520)

Erich Roth, *Sakrament nach Luther.* Berlin: Töpelmann, 1952.

Erwin Iserloh, *Der Kampf um die Messe in den ersten Jahren der Auseinandersetzung mit Luther.* KLK 10. Münster: Aschendorff, 1952.

Hans Grass, *Die Abendmahlslehre bei Luther und Calvin.* BFChrTh 2/47. 2d ed. Gütersloh: Bertelsmann, 1954.

Ernst Bizer, "Die Entdeckung des Sakraments durch Luther," *EvTH* 17 (1957), 64-90.

Hans Bernhard Meyer, *Luther und die Messe: Eine liturgiewissenschaftliche Untersuchung über das Verhältnis Luthers zum Messwesen des späten Mittelalters.* Paderborn: Verlag Bonifacius-Drockerei, 1965.

Carl Fr. Wislöff, *The Gift of Communion: Luther's Controversy with Rome on Eucharistic Sacrifice,* translated by Joseph M. Shaw. Minneapolis: Augsburg Publishing House, 1964.

Ferdinand Pratzner, *Messe und Kreuzopfer: Die Krise der sakramentalen Idee bei Luther und in der mittelalterlichen Scholastik.* Vienna: Herder, 1970.

Hartmut Hilgenfeld, *Mittelalterlich-traditionelle Elemente in Luthers Abendmahlsschriften.* SDHSTh 29. Zurich: Theologischer Verlag, 1971.

Frido Mann, *Das Abendmahl bei jungen Luther.* BÖT 5. Munich: Hueber, 1971.

Martin Brecht, "Herkunft und Eigenart der Taufanschauung der Züricher Täufer," *ARG* 64 (1973), 147-65.

Wolfgang Schwab, *Entwicklung und Gestalt der Sakramententheologie bei Martin Luther.* EHS.T 79. Frankfurt am Main/Bern: P. Lang, 1977.

Joachim Staedtke, "Abendmahl III/3. Reformationszeit," *TRE* 1 (1997), 106-22.

Eberhard Grötzinger, *Luther und Zwingli: Die Kritik an der mittelalterlichen Lehre von der Messe als Wurzel des Abendmahlsstreites.* Zurich/Cologne/Gütersloh: Gerd Mohn, 1980.

Ursula Stock, *Die Bedeutung der Sakramente in Luthers Sermonen von 1519*. SHCT 27. Leiden: Brill, 1982.

Gunther Wenz, *Einführung in die evangelische Sakramenten Lehre*. Darmstadt: Wissenschaftliche Buchgesellschaft, 1988.

———— "Für uns gegeben: Grundzüge lutherischer Abendmahlslehre im Zusammenhang des gegenwärtigen ökumenischen Dialogs," in *Mahl des Herrn: Ökumenischen Studien*, edited by Miguel M. Garijo-Guembe, Jan Rohls, and Gunther Wenz, 223-338. Frankfurt am Main/Paderborn: Bonifacius Druckerei, 1988.

CHAPTER 14. LUTHER'S DISPUTE WITH THE MONASTIC IDEAL (1520/1521)

Rene-H. Esnault, "Le 'De votis monasticis' de Martin Luther," *ETR* 31 (1956), no. 1, 19-56; no. 3, 58-91.

Bernhard Lohse, "Luthers Kritik am Mönchtum," *EvTh* 20 (1960), 413-32.

———— *Mönchtum und Reformation*. Göttingen: Vandenhoeck & Ruprecht, 1963.

Rene-H. Esnault, *Luther et le Monachisme aujourd'hui: Lecture actuelle du De votis monasticis judicium*. Geneva: Labor et fides, 1964.

Heinz-Meinolf Stamm, *Luthers Stellung zum Ordensleben*. VIEG 101. Wiesbaden: Steiner, 1980.

Klaus Reblin, *Freund und Feind: Franziskus im Spegel der protestantischen Theologiegeschichte*. KiKonf 27. Göttingen: Vandenhoeck & Ruprecht, 1988.

CHAPTER 15. LUTHER'S DISPUTE WITH THE WITTENBERG REFORMERS

Hermann Barge, *Andreas Bodenstein von Karlstadt*. 2 vols. Nieuwkoop: B. de Graaf, 1968.

Karl Holl, "Luther und die Schwärmer," in Holl, *Gesammelte Aufsätze zur Kirchengeschichte*, 1:420-67.

Nikolaus Müller, *Die Wittenberger Bewegung 1521 und 1522*. 2d ed. Leipzig: Heinsius, 1911.

Friedel Kriechbaum, *Grundzüge der Theologie Karlstadts,* ThF 43. Hamburg/Bergstedt: H. Reich, 1967.

Helmar Junghans, "Freiheit und Ordnung bei Luther während der Wittenberger Bewegung und der Visitation," *ThLZ* 97 (1972), 95-104.

Ronald J. Sider, *Andreas Bodenstein von Karlstadt: The Development of His Thought 1517-1525*. SMRT 11. Leiden: Brill, 1974.

Ulrich Bubenheimer, *Consonantiae Theologiae et iurisprudentiae: Andreas Bodenstein von Karlstadt als Theologe und Jurist zwischen Scholastik und Reformation.* JusEcc 24. Tübingen: Mohr, 1977.

Bernhard Lohse, "Luther und der Radikalismus," *LuJ* 44 (1977), 7-27. *Andreas Bodenstein von Karlstadt 1480-1541: FS der Stadt Karlstadt zum Jubiläumsjahr 1980.* Karlstadt: Arbeitsgruppe Bodenstein, Michel-Druck, 1980.

Ulrich Bubenheimer, "Luthers Stellung zum Aufruhr in Wittenberg 1520-1521 und die frühreformatorischen Wurzeln des landesherrlichen Kirtchenregiments," *ZSRG.K* 71 (1985), 147-214.

Martin Brecht, *Martin Luther: Shaping and Defining the Reformation, 1521-1532,* translated by James L. Schaaf. Minneapolis: Fortress Press, 1990.

——— "Luther und die Wittenberger Reformation während der Wartburgzeit," in *Martin Luther, Leben, Werk, Wirkung,* edited by Günter Vogler, 73-90. Berlin: Akademie Verlag, 1986.

Ulrich Bubenheimer, "Karlstadt," *TRE* 17 (1988), 649-57.

Bernhard Lohse, "Zum Wittenberger Augustinismus: Augustins Schrift De Spiritu et Littera in der Auslegung bei Staupitz, Luther und Karlstadt," in *Augustine, the Harvest, and Theology,* 89-109.

CHAPTER 16. LUTHER'S DISPUTE WITH RADICAL TENDENCIES TO "RIGHT" AND "LEFT": THE DISTINCTION BETWEEN THE TWO KINGDOMS AND THE TWO GOVERNMENTS

On Luther's Concept of the Temporal Authority in General:

Ernst Kinder, "Gottesreich und Weltreich bei Augustin und bei Luther: Erwägungen zu einer Vergleichung der 'Zwei-Reiche'-Lehre Augustins und Luthers," in *Gedenkschrift für D. Werner Elert: Beiträge zur historischen und systematischen Theologie,* edited by Friedrich Hübner, 24-42. Berlin: Lutherisches Verlagshaus, 1955.

Gustaf Törnvall, *Geistliches und weltliches Regiment bei Luther: Studien zu Luthers Weltbild und Gesellschaftsverständnis.* FGLP 10/2. Munich: Chr. Kaiser, 1947.

Heinrich Bornkamm, *Luther's Doctrine of the Two Kingdoms in the Context of His Theology,* translated by Karl H. Hertz. Philadelphia: Fortress Press, 1966.

Gottfried Forck, *Die Königsherrschaft Jesu Christi bei Luther (1959): Mit einem Beitrag von Bernhard Lohse.* 2d ed. Berlin: Evangelisches Verlagsanstalt, 1988.

Gerta Scharffenorth, *Römer 13 in der Geschichte des politischen Denkens: Ein Beitrag zur Klärung der politischen Tradition in Deutschland seit dem 15. Jahrhundert.* Diss., Heidelberg, 1962.

Johannes Heckel, *Lex charitatis: Eine juristische Untersuchung über das Recht in der Theologie Martin Luthers.* ABAW. PH 36. 1953. Reprint, Munich: Bayerischen Akademie der Wissenschaften, 1963. 2d ed., edited by Martin Heckel. Cologne/Vienna: Böhlau, 1973.

Paul Althaus, *The Ethics of Martin Luther*, translated by Robert C. Schultz. Philadelphia: Fortress Press, 1972.

Gunther Wolf, ed., *Luther und die Obrigkeit*. WdF 85. Darmstadt: E. Klett, 1972.

Ulrich Duchrow, *Christenheit und Weltverantwortung: Traditionsgeschichte und systematische Struktur der Zweireichelehre*. 1970. 2d ed. Stuttgart: Klett-Cotta, 1983.

Karl Trüdinger, *Luthers Brief und Gutachten an weltliche Obrigkeiten zur Durchführung der Reformation*. RGST 111. Münster: Aschendorff, 1975.

Eike Wolgast, *Die Wittenberger Theologie und die Politik der evangelischen Stände: Studien zu Luthers Gutachten in politischen Fragen*. QFRG 47. Gütersloh: Gerd Mohn, 1977.

Hans-Joachim Gänssler, *Evangelium und weltliches Schwert: Hintergrund, Entstehungsgeschichte und Anlass von Luthers Scheidung zweier Reiche oder Regimente*. VIEG 109. Wiesbaden: Steiner, 1983.

On Luther's Attitude toward the Peasants' War:

Paul Althaus, *Luthers Haltung im Bauernkrieg*. 1925. Reprint, Basel: B. Schwaber, 1952.

Martin Greschat, "Luthers Haltung im Bauernkrieg," *ARG* 56 (1965), 31-47.

Eric W. Gritsch, "Martin Luther and Violence: A Reappraisal of a Neuralgic Theme," *SCJ* 3/1 (1972), 37-55.

Johannes Wallmann, "Ein Friedensappell—Luthers letztes Wort im Bauernkrieg," in *Der Wirklichkeitsanspruch von Theologie und Religion: FS Ernst Steinbach*, edited by Dieter Henke, Günter Kehrer, and Gunda Schneider-Fiume, 57-75. Tübingen: Mohr, 1976.

Hermann Dörries, "Luther nach dem Bauernkrieg," in *Ecclesia und Res Publica: FS Kurt Dietrich Schmidt*, edited by Georg Kretschmar and Bernhard Lohse, 113-24. Göttingen: Vandenhoeck & Ruprecht, 1961.

CHAPTER 17. LUTHER'S DISPUTE WITH ERASMUS

On Erasmus:

Erasmus, *De libero arbitrio Diatribe sive Collatio*. Erasmus von Rotterdam: Ausgewählte Schriften, edited by Winfried Lesowsky. Vol. 4. Darmstadt: Wissenschaftliche Buchgesellschaft, 1969.

Roland H. Bainton, *Erasmus of Christendom*. New York: Scribner, 1969.

Robert Stupperich, *Erasmus von Rotterdam und seine Welt*. Berlin/New York: de Gruyter, 1977.

Cornelis Augustijn, *Erasmus: His Life, Works, and Influence*, translated by J. C. Grayson. Toronto: University of Toronto Press, 1991.

Oskar Johannes Mehl, "Erasmus contra Luther," *LuJ* 29 (1962), 52-64.

Ernst-Wilhelm Kohls, *Die Theologie des Erasmus.* 2 vols. Basel: Friedrich Reinhardt, 1966.

————— "Die theologische Position und der Traditionszusammenhang des Erasmus mit dem Mittelalter in 'De libero arbitrio,'" in *Humanitas-Christianitas: FS Walther v. Loewenich,* edited by Karlmann Beyschlag, Gottfried Maron, and Eberhard Wölfel, 32-46. Witten: Luther Verlag, 1968.

Manfred Hoffmann, *Erkenntnis und Verwirklichung der wahren Theologie nach Erasmus von Rotterdam.* BHTh 44. Tübingen: Mohr, 1972.

Heinz Holeczek, "Die Haltung des Erasmus zu Luther nach dem Scheitern seiner Vermittlungspolitik 1520/1521," *ARG* 64 (1973), 85-112.

On Luther's treatise De servo arbitrio:

Karl Zickendraht, *Der Streit zwischen Luther und Erasmus über die Willensfreiheit.* Leipzig: J. C. Hinrichs, 1909.

Martin Doerne, "Gottes Ehre am gebundenen Willen: Evangelische Grundlagen und theologische Spitzensätze in De servo arbitrio," *LuJ* 20 (1983), 45-92.

Gerhard Rost, *Der Prädestinationsgedanke in der Theologie Martin Luthers.* Berlin: Evangelische Verlagsanstalt, 1966.

Harry J. McSorley, *Luther: Right or Wrong? An Ecumenical-Theological Study of Luther's Major Work, The Bondage of the Will.* New York: Newman Press, 1968.

Bernhard Lohse, "Luther und Erasmus," in Lohse, *Lutherdeutung heute.* VR 276. Göttingen: Vandenhoeck & Ruprecht, 1968. Pp. 47-60.

Klaus Schwarzwäller, *Sibboleth: Die Interpretation von Luthers Schrift De servo arbitrio seit Theodosius Harnack. Ein systematisch-kritischer Überblick.* ThEx 153. Munich: Chr. Kaiser, 1969.

————— *Theologia crucis: Luthers Lehre von Prädestination nach De servo arbitrio, 1525.* FGLP 10/39. Munich: Chr. Kaiser, 1970.

Bernhard Lohse, "Marginalien zum Streit zwischen Erasmus und Luther" (1975), in *Evangelium in der Geschichte,* 118-37.

Fredrik Brosche, *Luther on Predestination: The Antinomy and the Unity between Love and Wrath in Luther's Concept of God.* AUU SDCU 18. Uppsala: University of Stockholm, 1978.

Wolfgang Behnk, *Contra Liberum Arbitrium pro Gratia Dei: Willenslehre und Christuszeugnis bei Luther und ihre Interpretation durch die neuere Lutherforschung. Eine systematisch-theologiegeschichtliche Untersuchung.* EHS.T 188. Frankfurt am Main: Long, 1982.

CHAPTER 18. LUTHER'S DISPUTE WITH ZWINGLI: THE LORD'S SUPPER CONTROVERSY

Walther Köhler, *Zwingli und Luther: Ihr Streit über das Abendmahl nach seinen politischen und religiösen Beziehungen.* Vol. 1: *Die religiöse und politische Entwicklung bis zum Marburger Religionsgespräch.* QFRG 6. Leipzig: Verein für Reformationsgeschichte, 1924. Vol. 2: *Vom Beginn der Marburger Verhandlungen 1529 bis zum Abschluss der Wittenberger Konkordie von 1536.* QFRG 7. Gütersloh: Gerd Mohn, 1953.

Paul W. Gennrich, *Die Christologie Luthers im Abendmahlsstreit 1524-1529.* Königsberg: Buch und Steindruckerei von O. Kümmel, 1929.

Walther Köhler, ed., *Das Marburger Religionsgespräch 1529: Versuch einer Rekonstruktion.* SVRG 148. Leipzig: Heinsius Nachfolger, 1929.

Ernst Sommerlath, *Der Sinn des Abendmahls nach Luthers Gedanken über das Abendmahl 1527/1529.* Leipzig: Dörffling und Franke, 1931.

Franz Hildebrandt, *Est: Das lutherische Prinzip.* Göttingen: Vandenhoeck & Ruprecht, 1931.

Hans Grass, *Die Abendmahlslehre bei Luther und Calvin.* Gütersloh: Bertelsmann, 1954.

Ernst Kinder, "'Realpräsenz' und 'Representation.' Feststellungen zu Luthers Abendmahlslehre," *ThLZ* 84 (1959), 881-94.

Hermann Sasse, *This Is My Body: Luther's Contention for the Real Presence in the Sacrament of the Altar.* Minneapolis: Augsburg Publishing House, 1959.

Albrecht Peters, *Realpräsenz: Luthers Zeugnis von Christi Gegenwart im Abendmahl.* AGTL 5. 1960. 2d ed. Berlin: Lutherisches Verlagshaus, 1966.

Susi Hausammann, "Die Marburger Artikel-eine echte Konkordie?" *ZKG* 77 (1966), 288-321.

————— "Realpräsenz in Luthers Abendmahlslehre," in *Studien zur Geschichte und Theologie der Reformation: FS Ernst Bizer,* edited by Luise Abramowski and J. F. Gerhard Goeters, 157-73. Neukirchen-Vluyn: Neukirchener Verlag, 1969.

Gerhard May, ed., *Das Marburger Religionsgespräch 1529.* TLTG 13. Gütersloh: Gerd Mohn, 1970.

Marc Lienhard, *Luther: Witness to Jesus Christ: Stages and Themes of the Reformer's Christology,* translated by Edwin H. Robertson. Minneapolis: Augsburg Publishing House, 1982, 146-84.

Bernhard Lohse, *HdBDThG,* 2:46-64.

CHAPTER 19. LUTHER'S DISPUTE WITH THE ANTINOMIANS

Gustav Kawerau, "Briefe und Urkunden zur Geschichte des antinomistischen Streites," *ZKG* 4 (1881), 299-324.

WA Br 12 Nr. 4269a (Agricola's 17 theses with Luther's glosses).

Gustav Kawerau, *Johann Agricola von Eisleben: Ein Beitrag zur Reformationsgeschichte.* Berlin: Olms, 1881.

————— "Agricola, Johann," *RE* 1 (1896), 249-53.

Ragnar Bring, *Gesetz und Evangelium und der dritte Gebrauch des Gesetzes in der lutherischen Theologie,* 43-97. SLAG 4. Helsinki: 1943.

————— *Das Verhältnis von Glauben und Werken in der lutherischen Theologie.* FGLP 10/7. Munich: Chr. Kaiser, 1955.

Werner Elert, *Zwischen Gnade und Ungnade. Abwandlungen des Themas: Gesetz und Evangelium.* Munich: Evangelischer Verlag, 1948.

Wilfried Joest, *Gesetz und Freiheit: Das Problem des tertius usus legis bei Luther und die neutestamentliche Parainese.* 1951. 4th ed. Göttingen: Vandenhoeck & Ruprecht, 1968.

Hay Gerdes, *Luthers Streit mit den Schwärmern um das rechte Verständnis des Gesetzes Mose.* Göttingen: Göttinger Verlagsanstalt, 1955.

Rudolf Hermann, *Zum Streit um die Überwindung des Gesetzes: Erörterungen zu Luthers Antinomerthesen.* Weimar: H. Böhlaus Nachfolger, 1958.

Jochim Rogge, *Johann Agricolas Lutherverständnis unter besonderer Berücksichtigung des Antinomismus.* ThA 14. Berlin: Evangelische Verlagsanstalt, 1960 (basic for Agricola).

Martin Schloemann, *Natürliches und gepredigtes Gesetz bei Luther: Eine Studie zur Frage nach der Einheit der Auseinandersetzung mit den Antinomern.* TBT 4. Berlin: Töpelmann, 1961.

Wilhelm H. Neuser, *Luther und Melanchthon: Einheit im Gegensatz,* ThEx N.F. 91. Munich: Chr. Kaiser, 1961.

Robert Stupperich, "Die Rechtfertigungslehre bei Luther und Melanchthon 1530-1536," in *Luther und Melanchthon: Referate und Berichte des 2. Internationalen Kongresses für Lutherforschung Münster 8.-13.8. 1960,* edited by Vilmos Vajta, 73-88. Göttingen: Chr. Kaiser, 1961.

Martin Greshat, *Melanchthon neben Luther: Studien zur Gestalt der Rechtfertigungslehre zwischen 1528 und 1537.* UKG 1. Witten: Luther, 1965.

Joachim Rogge, "Agricola, Johann," *TRE* 2 (1978), 110-18.

Bengt Hägglund, "Gesetz und Evangelium im Antinomerstreit," in *Luther und die Theologie der Gegenwart: Referate und Berichte des 5. Internationalen Kongresses für Lutherforschung Lund, Sweden, 14-20. 8. 1977,* edited by Leif Grane and Bernhard Lohse, 156-64. Göttingen: Vandenhoeck & Ruprecht, 1980 (seminar report).

Bernhard Lohse, *HdBDThG,* 2:39-45. Steffen Kjeldgaard-Pedersen, *Gesetz, Evangelium und Busse: Theologiegeschichtliche Studien zum Verhältnis zwischen dem jungen Johann Agricola (Eisleben) und Martin Luther.* AthD 16. Leiden: Brill, 1983.

Ernst Koch, *Johann Agricola neben Luther: Schülerschaft und theologische Eigenart,* 131-50. AWA 5. Cologne/Vienna: Böhlau, 1984.

Chapter 20. Sola Scriptura

Wilhelm Walther, *Luthers Deutsche Bibel: FS zur Jahrhundertfeier der Reformation.* Berlin: E. S. Mittler & Sohn, 1917.

Paul Althaus, "Der Geist der Lutherbibel," *LuJ* 16 (1934), 1-26.

Walther von Loewenich, *Luther und das Johanneische Christentum.* Munich: Chr. Kaiser, 1935.

Gerhard Ebeling, *Evangelische Evangelienauslegung.* Darmstadt: wissenschaftiche Bochcesellschaft, 1962.

Heinrich Bornkamm, *Luther and the Old Testament.* Translated by Eric W. Gritsch and Ruth C. Gritsch. Edited by Victor I. Gruhn. Philadelphia: Fortress Press, 1969.

Ragnar Bring, *Luthers Anschauung von der Bibel.* Luthertum 3. Berlin: Lutherisches Verlagshaus, 1951.

Walther von Loewenich, *Luther als Ausleger der Synoptiker.* FGLP 10/5. Munich: Chr. Kaiser, 1954.

Harald Östergaard-Nielsen, *Scriptura sacra et viva vox: Eine Lutherstudie.* FGLP 10, X. Munich: Chr. Kaiser, 1957.

Rudolf Hermann, *Von der Klarheit der Heiligen Schrift: Untersuchungen und Erörterungen über Luthers Lehre von der Schrift in De servo arbitrio.* Berlin: Evangelische Verlagsanstalt, 1958.

Peter Meinhold, *Luthers Sprachphilosophie.* Berlin: Lutherisches Verlagshaus, 1958.

Jaroslav Pelikan, *Luther the Expositor.* St. Louis: Concordia, 1959.

Heinz Bluhm, "Bedeutung und Eigenart der Lutherbibel," *CTM* 33 (1962), 587-94.

———— *Martin Luther—Creative Translator.* St. Louis: Concordia, 1965.

Friedrich Beisser, *Claritas scripturae bei Martin Luther.* Göttingen: Vandenhoeck Reprecht, 1966.

Bengt Hägglund, "Evidentia sacrae scripturae: Bemerkungen zum 'Schriftprinzip' bei Luther," in *Vierhundertfünfzig Jahre lutherische Reformation 1517-1967: FS Lau,* 116-25.

Ernst Wolf, *Über "Klarheit der Hl. Schrift" nach Luthers "De servo arbitrio,"* in: THL2 92 (1967, 721-30.

Walter Mostert, "Scriptura sacra sui ipsius interpres: Bemerkungen zum Verständnis der Heiligen Schrift durch Luther," *LuJ* 46 (1979), 60-96.

Bernhard Lohse, "Die Aktualisierung der christlichen Botschaft in Luthers Bibelübersetzung" (1980), in *Evangelium in der Geschichte,* 177-93.

Siegfried Raeder, "Luther als Ausleger und Übersetzer der H. Schrift," in *Leben und Werk Martin Luthers von 1526 bis 1546,* edited by Helmar Junghans, 1:153-278; 2:800-805. Göttingen: Vandenhoeck & Ruprecht, 1983.

Werner Führer, *Das Wort Gottes in Luthers Theologie,* Göttinger theologische Arbeiten 30. Göttingen: Vandenhoeck & Ruprecht, 1984.

Bernhard Rothen, *Die Klarheit der Schrift*. 2 vols. Göttingen: Vandenhoeck & Ruprecht, 1990-92 (on vol. 1 see the review by Helmar Junghans, *LuJ* 58 [1991], 132-33).

Albrecht Beutel, *In dem Anfang war das Wort: Studien zu Luthers Sprachverständnis.* HUTh 27. Tübingen: Mohr, 1991.

Kenneth Hagen, *Luther's Approach to Scripture as Seen in His 'Commentaries' on Galatians 1519-1538.* Tübingen: Mohr, 1993.

CHAPTER 21. REASON AND FAITH

Bengt Hägglund, *Theologie und Philosophie bei Luther and in der occamistischen Tradition.* Lund: C.W.K. Gleerup, 1955.

Edmund Schlink, "Weisheit und Torheit," *KuD* 1 (1955), 1-22.

Bernhard Lohse, *Ratio und Fides*, Göttingen: Vandenhoeck Ruprecht, 1958, 22-29.

———— "Reason and Revelation in Luther," *SJTh* 13 (1960), 337-65.

Brian A. Gerrish, *Grace and Reason: A Study in the Theology of Luther.* Oxford: Clarendon, 1962; see in addition B. Lohse, *ThLZ* 88 (1963), 682-84.

Gerhard Ebeling, *Lutherstudien*. Vol. 2: *Disputatio de homine*, part 2, esp. 184-332.

———— "Fides occidit rationem: Ein Aspekt der theologia crucis in Luthers Auslegung von Gal 3,6" (1979), in Ebeling, *Lutherstudien*. Vol. 3: *Begriffsuntersuchungen—Textinterpretationen—Wirkungsgeschichtliches.* Tübingen: Mohr, 1985. Pp. 181-222.

Rudolf Malter, *Das reformatorische Denken und die Philosophie: Luthers Entwurf einer tranzendental-praktischen Metaphysik.* Conscientia: Studien zur Bewusstseinsphilosophie 9. Bonn: Bouvier Verlag Herbert Grundmann, 1980.

Karl-Heinz zur Mühlen, *Reformatorische Vernunftkritik und neuzeitliches Denken: Dargestellt am Werk M. Luthers und Fr. Gogartens.* BHTh 59. Tübingen: Mohr, 1980.

On Luther's Answer at Worms, 1521:

Bernhard Lohse, "Luthers Antwort in Worms," *Luther* 29 (1958), 124-34.

Kurt-Victor Selge, "Capta conscientia in verbis Dei: Luthers Widerrufsverweigerung in Worms," in *Der Reichstag zu Worms von 1521: Reichspolitik und Luthersache,* edited by Fritz Reuter, 180-207. Worms: Stadtarchiv, 1971.

CHAPTER 22. THE VIEW OF GOD

Emanuel Hirsch, *Luthers Gottesanschauung.* Leipzig: Dörffling und Franke, 1930.

Jan Koopmans, *Das altkirchliche Dogma in der Reformation.* BevTh 22. Munich: Chr. Kaiser, 1955.

Helmut Bandt, *Luthers Lehre vom verborgenen Gott.* ThA 8. Berlin: Evangelische Verlagsanstalt, 1958.

Reinhard Schwarz, "Gott ist Mensch: Zur Lehre von der Person Christi bei den Ockhamisten und bei Luther," *ZThK* 63 (1966), 289-351.

Albrecht Peters, "Die Trinitätslehre in der reformatorischen Christenheit," *ThLZ* 94 (1969), 561-70.

Dorothea Vorländer, *Deus Incarnatus: Die Zweinaturenchristologie Luthers bis 1521.* UKG 9. Witten: Luther Verlag, 1974.

Marc Lienhard, *Luther: Witness to Jesus Christ: Stages and Themes of the Reformer's Christology,* translated by Edwin H. Robertson. Minneapolis: Augsburg Publishing House, 1982.

Reiner Jansen, *Studien zu Luthers Trinitätslehre.* Basler und Berner Studien zur historischen und systematischen Theologie 26. Bern: Herbert Lang, 1976.

Horst Beintker, "Luthers Gotteserfahrung und Gottesanschauung," in *Leben und Werk Martin Luthers von 1526 bis 1546,* 1:39-62; 2:732-46.

Bernhard Lohse, "Zur Struktur von Luthers Theologie: Kriterien einer Darstellung der Theologie Luthers," in *Evangelium in der Geschichte,* 237-49.

CHAPTER 23. CHRISTOLOGY

Erich Vogelsang, *Die Anfänge Luthers Christologie nach der ersten Psalmenvorlesung, insbesondere in ihren exegetischen und systematischen Zusammenhägen mit Augustin und der Scholastik dargestellt.* AKG 15. Berlin/Leipzig: de Gruyter, 1929.

———— *Der angefochtene Christus bei Luther.* Berlin: W. de Gruyter, 1932.

Paul W. Gennrich, *Die Christologie Luthers im Abendmahlsstreit 1524-1529.* Königsberg: Buch und Steindruckerei von O. Kümmel, 1929.

Ernst Wolf, "Die Christusverkündigung bei Luther" (1936), in *Peregrinatio,* [1:] 30-80.

Erich Seeberg, *Luthers Theologie: Motive und Ideen.* Vol. 2: *Christus: Wirklichkeit und Urbild.* Stuttgart: Kohlhammer, 1937.

Hans Grass, *Die Abendmahlslehre bei Luther und Calvin.* BFChrTh 2/47. 2d ed. Gütersloh: Bertelsmann, 1954.

Bernhard Lohse, "Luthers Christologie im Ablasstreit," in *Evangelium in der Geschichte: Studien zu Luther und der Reformation.* (Göttingen: Vandenhoeck & Ruprecht, 1988), 287-99.

Albrecht Peters, *Realpräsenz: Luthers Zeugnis von Christi Gegenwart im Abendmahl.* AGTL 5. 1960. 2d ed. Berlin: Lutherisches Verlagshaus, 1966.

Kjell Ove Nilsson, *Simul: Das Miteinander von Göttlichem und Menschlichem in Luthers Theologie.* FKDG 17. Göttingen: Vandenhoeck & Ruprecht, 1966.

Ian D. Kingston Siggins, *Martin Luther's Doctrine of Christ.* YPR 14. New Haven: Yale University Press, 1970.

Ulrich Asendorf, *Gekreuzigt und Auferstanden: Luthers Herausforderung an die moderne Christologie.* AGTL 25. Berlin: Lutherisches Verlagshaus, 1971.

Marc Lienhard, *Luther:Witness to Jesus Christ: Stages and Themes of the Reformer's Christology,* translated by Edwin H. Robertson. Minneapolis: Augsburg Publishing House, 1982.

Dorothea Vorländer, *Deus Incarnatus: Die Zweinaturenchristologie Luthers bis 1521.* UKG 9. Witten: Luther Verlag, 1974.

Marc Lienhard, "Luthers Christuszeugnis," in *Leben und Werk Martin Luthers von 1526 bis 1546,* 1:77-92; 2:748-55.

Karl-Heinz zur Mühlen, "Jesus Christus IV: Reformationszeit," *TRE* 26 (1987), 759-72.

Franz Posset, *Luther's Catholic Christology according to His Johannine Lectures of 1527.* Ann Arbor: University Microfilms International, 1984.

Marc Lienhard, *Au coeur de la foi de Luther: Jesus-Christ.* Paris: Desclée: Proost France, 1991.

Stefan Streiff, *"Novis Linguis Loqui." Martin Luthers Disputation über Joh. 1,14 "verbum caro factum est" aus dem Jahre 1539.* FSÖTh 70. Göttingen: Vandenhoeck & Ruprecht, 1993.

CHAPTER 24. *SPIRITUS CREATOR*

Rudolf Otto, *Die Anschauung vom Hl. Geiste bei Luther: Eine systematisch-dogmatische Untersuchung.* Diss., Göttingen, 1898.

Erich Seeberg, "Der Gegensatz zwischen Zwingli, Schwenckfeld und Luther," in *FS Reinhold Seeberg.* Vol. 1: *Zur Theorie des Christentums,* 43-80. Leipzig: Scholl, 1929.

Regin Prenter, *Spiritus Creator,* trans. John M. Jensen, Philadelphia: Muhlenberg Press, 1953.

Kurt Dietrich Schmidt, "Luthers Lehre vom Heiligen Geist" (1950), in *Gesammelte Aufsätze,* edited by Manfred Jacobs, 111-27. Göttingen: Vandenhoeck & Ruprecht, 1967.

Hayo Gerdes, "Zu Luthers Lehre vom Wirken des Geistes," *LuJ* 25 (1958), 42-60.

Marc Lienhard, "La Doctrine du Saint-Esprit chez Luther," *VC* 76 (1965), 11-38.

Gerhard Heintze, "Luthers Pfingstpredigten," *LuJ* 34 (1967), 117-40.

Klaus Schwarzwäller, "Delectari assertionibus: Zur Struktur von Luthers Pneumatologie," *LuJ* 38 (1971), 26-58.

Gerhard Ebeling, "Luthers Ortsbestimmung der Lehre vom heiligen Geist," in *Wort und Glaube.* 3:316-48.

Eilert Herms, *Luthers Auslegung des Dritten Artikels.* Tübingen: Mohr, 1987.

Ulrich Asendorf, *Die Theologie Martin Luthers nach seinen Predigten,* 203-304. Göttingen: Vandenhoeck & Ruprecht, 1988.

Joachim Heubach, ed., *Der Heilige Geist im Verständnis Luthers und der lutherischen Theologie.* Veröffentlichungen der Luther-Akademie Ratzeberg 17. Erlangen: Martin Luther Verlag, 1990.

Rolf Schäfer, "Der Heilige Geist: Eine Betrachtung zu Luthers Erklärung des Dritten Artikels," *Luther* 61 (1990), 135-48.

Albrecht Peters, *Kommentar zu Luthers Katechismen,* edited by Gottfried Seebass. 3 vols. Göttingen: Vandenhoeck & Ruprecht, 1990-94, Vol. 2: *Der Glaube,* 175-250.

Ulrich Asendorf, "Luthers Theologie nach seinen Katechismenpredigten," *KuD* 38 (1992), 2-19.

Michael Plathow, "Der Geist hilft unsere Schwachheit: Ein actualisierender Forschungsbericht zu M. Luthers Rede vom heiligen Geist," *KuD* 40 (1994), 143-69.

Chapter 25. Humanity as Creature of God

David Löfgren, *Die Theologie der Schöpfung bei Luther.* FKDG 10. Göttingen: Vandenhoeck & Ruprecht, 1960. In addition see the review of Bernhard Lohse, *ThLZ* 86 (1961), 928-31; and of Franz Lau, *LuJ* 29 (1962), 44-51.

Paul Althaus, *Der Schöpfungsgedanke bei Luther.* SBAW.PPH 7. Munich: Bayerischen Akademie der Wissenschaften, 1959.

———— *The Theology of Martin Luther,* translated by Robert C. Schultz. Philadelphia: Fortress Press, 1966.

———— *The Ethics of Martin Luther,* translated by Robert C. Schultz. Philadelphia: Fortress Press, 1972.

Bengt Hägglund, "Luthers Anthropologie," in *Leben und Werk Martin Luthers von 1526 bis 1546,* 1:63-76; 2:747-48.

Gerhard Ebeling, "Der Mensch nach seiner geschöpflichen Bestimmung," in *Lutherstudien.* Vol. 2, part 3, 92-108.

Albrecht Peters, *Kommentar zu Luthers Katechismen,* edited by Gottfried Seebass. 3 vols. Göttingen: Vandenhoeck & Ruprecht, 1990-94, 2:56-91.

Chapter 26. Sin

Rudolf Hermann, *Luthers These "Gerecht und Sünder zugleich."* 1930. 2d ed. Gütersloh: Gütersloher Verlagshaus, 1960.

Erich Seeberg, *Luthers Theologie in ihren Grundzügen.* Stuttgart: Kohlhammer, 1940; reprint 1950, 103-13.

Bernhard Lohse, *Ratio und Fides,* Göttingen: Vandenhoeck Ruprecht, 1958, 59-82.

David Löfgren, *Die Theologie der Schöpfung bei Luther.* FKDG 10. Göttingen: Vandenhoeck & Ruprecht, 1960, esp. 96-116.

Paul Althaus, *The Theology of Martin Luther,* translated by Robert C. Schultz. Philadelphia: Fortress Press, 1966, 141-60.

Hans-Martin Barth, *Der Teufel und Jesus in der Theologie Martin Luthers*, esp. 188-293. FKDG 1. Göttingen: Vandenhoeck & Ruprecht, 1967.

Wilfried Joest, *Ontologie der Person bei Luther*, Göttingen: Vandenhoeck and Ruprecht, 1967, passim.

Gerhard Ebeling, "Der Mensch als Sünder," in *Lutherstudien*. 3:64-107.

CHAPTER 27. JUSTIFICATION

On development in the history of dogma:

Gerhard Müller, *Die Rechtfertigungslehre: Geschichte und Probleme*. Gütersloh: Gütersloher Verlagshaus, 1977.

Otto Hermann Pesch and Albrecht Peters, *Einführung in die Lehre von Gnade und Rechtfertigung*. Die Theologie: Einführung in die Gegenstand, Methoden und Ergebnisse ihrer Diszplinen und Nachbarwissenschaften. Darmstadt: Wissenschaftliche Buchgesellschaft, 1981.

On Luther in particular:

Rudolf Hermann, *Luthers These "Gerecht und Sünder zugleich."* 1930. 2d ed. Gütersloh: Gütersloher Verlagshaus, 1960.

Hans Joachim Iwand, *Rechtfertigungslehre und Christusglaube: Eine Untersuchung zur Systematik der Rechtfertigungslehre Luthers in ihren Anfängen*. 1930. 2d ed. Munich: Chr. Kaiser, 1961.

———— *Glaubensgerechtigkeit nach Luthers Lehre*. 1941. 3d ed. Munich: Chr. Kaiser, 1959.

Werner Elert, *The Structure of Lutheranism*, translated by Walter A. Hansen. St. Louis: Concordia, 1962.

Ernst Wolf, "Die Christusverkündigung bei Luther," in *Peregrinatio*, [1:] 30-80.

———— "Die Rechtfertigungslehre als Mitte und Grenze reformatorischer Theologie," in *Peregrinatio*, 2:11-12.

Albrecht Peters, *Glaube und Werk: Luthers Rechtfertigungslehre im Lichte der Heiligen Schrift*. Berlin: Luthersches Verlagshaus, 1962.

Ole Modalsli, *Das Gericht nach den Werken*. Göttingen: Vandenhoeck and Ruprecht, 1963.

Otto Hermann Pesch, *Theologie der Rechtfertigung bei Martin Luther und Thomas von Aquin*. Mainz: Matthias-Grünewald-Verlag, 1967.

———— *Gerechtfertigt aus Glauben: Luthers Frage an die Kirche*. QD 9. Freiburg/Basel/Vienna: Herder, 1982.

CHAPTER 28. LAW AND GOSPEL

Werner Elert, *The Structure of Lutheranism,* translated by Walter A. Hansen. St. Louis: Concordia, 1962.

Wilfried Joest, *Gesetz und Freiheit: Das Problem des tertius usus legis bei Luther und die neutestamentliche Parainese.* 1951. 4th ed. Göttingen: Vandenhoeck & Ruprecht, 1968.

Johannes Heckel, *Lex charitatis: Eine juristische Untersuchung über das Recht in der Theologie Martin Luthers.* ABAW. PH 36. 1953. Reprint, Munich: Bayerischen Akademie der Wissenschaften, 1963. 2d ed., edited by Martin Heckel. Cologne/Vienna: Böhlau, 1973.

Hayo Gerdes, *Luthers Streit mit den Schwärmern um das rechte Verständnis des Gesetzes Mose.* Göttingen: Göttinger Verlagsanstalt, 1955.

Gerhard Heintze, *Luthers Predigt von Gesetz und Evangelium.* FGLP 10/11. Munich: Chr. Kaiser, 1958.

Ernst Wolf, "Habere Christum omnia Mosi: Bemerkungen zum Problem 'Gesetz und Evangelium,'" in *Peregrinatio,* 2:22-37.

Martin Schloemann, *Natürliches und gepredigtes Gesetz bei Luther: Eine Studie zur Frage nach der Einheit der Auseinandersetzung mit den Antinomern.* TBT 4. Berlin: Töpelmann, 1961.

Gerhard Ebeling, "On the Doctrine of the *Triplex Usus Legis* in the Theology of the Reformation," in *Word and Faith,* translated by James W. Leitch, 62-78. Philadelphia: Fortress Press, 1963.

——— *Luther: An Introduction to His Thought,* translated by R. A. Wilson. Philadelphia: Fortress Press, 1970, 110-24.

——— "Lex est lux—evangelium est Lux," in *Lutherstudien.* Vol. 2, part 3, 545-622.

Paul Althaus, *The Theology of Martin Luther,* translated by Robert C. Schultz. Philadelphia: Fortress Press, 1966, 251-73.

Otto Hermann Pesch, *Theologie der Rechtfertigung bei Martin Luther und Thomas von Aquin,* esp. 66-76. Mainz: Matthias-Grünewald-Verlag, 1967.

CHAPTER 29. THE CHURCH

Ferdinand Kattenbusch, *Die Doppelschichtigkeit in Luthers Kirchenbegriff.* ThStKr 100 (1927/28), 197-347 (also printed separately).

Werner Elert, *The Structure of Lutheranism,* translated by Walter A. Hansen. St. Louis: Concordia, 1962, 255-74.

Ernst Wolf, "Sanctorum Communio: Erwägungen zum Problem der Romantisierung des Kirchenbegriffs" (1942), in *Peregrinatio,* [1:] 279-301.

Johannes Heckel, "Die zwo Kirchen: Eine juristische Betrachtung über Luthers Schrift von dem Papsttum zu Rom" (1956), in Heckel, *Das blinde, undeutliche Wort "Kirche." Gesammelte Aufsätze,* edited by Siegfried Grundmann, 111-31. Cologne/Graz: H. Böhlau, 1964.

Paul Althaus, *The Theology of Martin Luther,* translated by Robert C. Schultz. Philadelphia: Fortress Press, 1966, 287-323.

Wolfgang Höhne, *Luthers Anschauungen über die Kontinuität der Kirche. Eine Studie zu ihrer Einheit, Heiligkeit, Katholizität und Apostolizität.* TBT 38. Berlin: Lutherisches Verlagshaus, 1982.

Carl Axel Aurelius, *Verborgene Kirche: Luthers Kirchenverständnis auf grund seiner Streitschriften und Exegese 1519-1521.* AGTL N.F. 4 Hannover: Lutherisches Verlagshaus, 1983.

Michael Beyer, "Luthers Ekklesiologie," in *Leben und Werk Martin Luthers von 1526 bis 1546,* 1:93-118; 2:755-65.

Vilmos Vajta, "Die Kirche als geistlich-sakramentale communio mit Christus und seine Heiligen bei Luther," *LuJ* 51 (1984), 10-62.

Inge Lönning, "Luther und die Kirche: Das blinde Wort und die verborgene Wirklichkeit," *LuJ* 52 (1985), 94-112; see the additional contributions in the same volume by Otto Hermann Pesch, Scott H. Hendrix, Bernhard Lohse, and Daniel Olivier.

Konrad Hammann, *Ekklesia Spiritualis: Luthers Kirchenverständnis in den Kontroversen mit Augustin von Alveldt und Ambrosius Catharinus.* FKDG 44. Göttingen: Vandenhoeck & Ruprecht, 1989; see the review by Michael Beyer, *LuJ* 58 (1991), 113-16.

Marc Lienhard, *L'Evangile et L'Eglise chez Luther.* Paris: Cerf, 1989.

Hans Theodor Goebel, "Notae Ecclesiae: zum Problem der Unterscheidung der wahren Kirche von der falschen," *EvTh* 50 (1990), 222-41.

Jürgen Lutz, *Unio und Communio: Zum Verhältnis von Rechtfertigungslehre und Kirchenverständnis bei Martin Luther.* KKTS 55. Paderborn: Bonifatius, 1990; see the review by Bernhard Lohse, *ThRv* 87 (1991), 400-402.

CHAPTER 30. OFFICE AND ORDINATION

Hans Grass, *Die Abendmahlslehre bei Luther und Calvin.* BFChrTh 2/47. 2d ed. Gütersloh: Bertelsmann, 1954.

Klaus Tuchel, "Luthers Auffassung vom geistlichen Amt," *LuJ* 25 (1958), 61-98.

Wilhelm Brunotte, *Das geistliche Amt bei Luther.* Berlin: Lutherisches Verlagshaus, 1959.

Regin Prenter, "Die göttliche Einsetzung des Predigtamtes und das allgemeine Priestertum bei Luther," *ThLZ* 86 (1961), 321-32.

Paul Althaus, *The Theology of Martin Luther,* translated by Robert C. Schultz. Philadelphia: Fortress Press, 1966, 323-32.

Heinz Brunotte, *Das Amt der Verkündigung und das Priestertum aller Gläubigen*. Luthertum 26. Berlin: Lutherisches Verlagshaus, 1962.

Hellmut Lieberg, *Amt und Ordination bei Luther und Melanchthon*. KKDG 11. Göttingen: Vandenhoeck & Ruprecht, 1962.

Bernhard Lohse, "Das Verständnis des leitenden Amtes in lutherischen Kirchen in Deutschland von 1517 bis 1918," in *Evangelium in der Geschichte*, 337-56.

Jan Aarts, *Die Lehre Martin Luthers über das Amt in der Kirche: Eine genetisch-systematische Untersuchung seiner Schriften von 1512 bis 1525*. SLAG, A 15. Helsinki: Hameenlinna, 1972.

Peter Manns, "Amt und Eucharistie in der Theologie Martin Luthers" (1973), in Manns, *Vater im Glauben: Studien zur Theologie Martin Luthers: Festgabe zum 65. Geburtstag,* edited by Rolf Decot, 111-216. VIEG 131. Stuttgart: Steiner Verlag Wiesbaden, 1988.

Wolfgang Stein, *Das kirchliche Amt bei Luther*. VIEG 73. Wiesbaden: Steiner, 1974.

Bernhard Lohse, "Zur Ordination in der Reformation," in *Ordination und kirchliches Amt,* 11-18.

Hans-Martin Barth, *Einander Priester sein: Allgemeines Priestertum in ökumenischer Perspective,* esp. 27-53. KiKonf 29. Göttingen: Vandenhoeck & Ruprecht, 1990.

Martin Brecht, ed., *Martin Luther und das Bischofsamt*. Stuttgart: Calwer, 1990 (esp. the following: Markus Wriedt, "Luthers Gebrauch der Bischofstitulatur in seinen Briefen," 73-100; Rolf Decot, "Luthers Kompromissvorschlag an die Bischöfe auf dem Augsburger Reichstag 1530," 109-19; Irmgard Höss, "Luther und die Bischofseinsetzungen in Merseburg und Kammin," 123-30).

Hans-Ulrich Delius, "Das kirchliche Amt in der Sicht der lutherischen Lehre," in *Lehrverurteilungen—kirchentrennend?* Vol. 3: *Materialen zur Lehre von den Sakramenten und vom kirchlichen Amt,* 286-305. Dialog der Kirchen 6. Freiburg/Göttingen: Vandenhoeck & Ruprecht, 1990.

Gerhard Ebeling, "Luthers Gebrauch der Wortfamilie 'Seelssorge,'" *LuJ* 61 (1994), 7-44.

CHAPTER 31. BAPTISM

Reinhold Seeberg, *Lehrbuch der Dogmengeschichte,* 4/1:377-96. Graz: Akademische Druck u. Verlagsanstalt, 1953-54.

Werner Jetter, *Die Taufe beim jungen Luther,* 109-74. BHTh 18. Tübingen: Mohr, 1954.

Karl Brinkel, *Die Lehre Luthers von der fides infantium bei der Kindertaufe*. ThA 7. Berlin: Evangelische Verlagsanstalt, 1958; in addition, Paul Althaus, *ThLZ* 84 (1959), 866-69.

Paul Althaus, *The Theology of Martin Luther,* translated by Robert C. Schultz. Philadelphia: Fortress Press, 1966.

John S. Oyer, *Lutheran Reformers against Anabaptists: Luther, Melanchthon, Menius and the Anabaptists of Central Germany.* The Hague: M. Nijhoff, 1964.

Eberhard Jüngel, "Das Sakrament—was ist das?" *EvTh* 26 (1966), 320-36.

Lorenz Grönvik, *Die Taufe in der Theologie Martin Luther.* AAAbo, A 36/1. Abo/Göttingen/Zurich: Abo Akademi, 1968.

Franz Lau, "Luther und Balthasar Hubmaier," in *Humanitas-Christianitas,* 63-73.

Martin Ferel, *Gepredigte Taufe: Eine homiletische Untersuchung zur Taufpredigt bei Luther.* HUTh 10. Tübingen: Mohr, 1969.

Horst Kasten, *Taufe und Rechtfertigung bei Thomas von Aquin und Martin Luther.* FGLP 10/41. Munich: Chr. Kaiser, 1970.

Gottfried Seebass, "Die Vorgeschichte von Luthers Verwerfung der Konditionaltaufe nach einem bisher unbekannten Schreiben Andreas Osianders an Georg Spalatin vom 26. Juni 1531," *RG* 62 (1971), 193-206.

Karl-Heinz zur Mühlen, "Zur Rezeption der Augustinischen Sakramentsformel 'Accedit verbum ad elementum et fit sacramentum' in der Theologie Luthers," *ZThK* 70 (1973), 50-76.

Christof Windhorst, *Täuferisches Taufverständnis: Balthasar Hubmaiers Lehre zwischen traditioneller und reformatorischer Theologie.* SMRT 16. Leiden: Brill, 1976.

Wolfgang Schwab, *Entwicklung und Gestalt der Sakramententheologie bei Martin Luther,* 303-64. EHS.T 79. Frankfurt am Main/Bern: P. Lang, 1977.

Ursula Stock, *Die Bedeutung der Sakramente in Luthers Sermone von 1519.* SHCT 27. Leiden, 1982.

Karl-Heinz zur Mühlen, "Luthers Tauflehre und seine Stellung zu den Täufern," in *Leben und Werk Martin Luthers von 1426 bis 1546,* 1:119-38; 2:765-70. Göttingen: Vandenhoeck & Ruprecht, 1983.

Albrecht Peters, *Kommentar zu Luthers Katechismen,* edited by Gottfried Seebass. Göttingen: Vandenhoeck & Ruprecht, 1990-94. Vol. 4: *Die Taufe. Das Abendmahl.*

CHAPTER 32. THE LORD'S SUPPER

Walther Köhler, *Zwingli und Luther: Ihr Streit über das Abendmahl nach seinen politischen und religiösen Beziehungen.* Vol. 1: *Die religiöse und politische Entwicklung bis zum Marburger Religionsgespräch.* QFRG 6. Leipzig: Verein für Reformationsgeschichte, 1924. Vol. 2: *Vom Beginn der Marburger Verhandlungen 1529 bis zum Abschluss der Wittenberger Konkordie von 1536.* QFRG 7. Gütersloh: Gerd Mohn, 1953.

Hans Grass, *Die Abendmahlslehre bei Luther und Calvin.* BFChrTh 2/47. 2d ed. Gütersloh: Bertelsmann, 1954.

Hans Grass, *Die Abendmahlslehre bei Luther und Calvin.* BFChrTh 2/47. 2d ed. Gütersloh: Bertelsmann, 1954.

Hermann Sasse, *This Is My Body: Luther's Contention for the Real Presence in the Sacrament of the Altar*. Minneapolis: Augsburg Publishing House, 1959.

Albrecht Peters, *Realpräsenz: Luthers Zeugnis von Christi Gegenwart im Abendmahl*. AGTL 5. 1960. 2d ed. Berlin: Lutherisches Verlagshaus, 1966.

Paul Althaus, *The Theology of Martin Luther*, translated by Robert C. Schultz. Philadelphia: Fortress Press, 1966.

Susi Hausammann, "Realpräsenz in Luthers Abendmahlslehre," in *Studien zur Geschichte und Theologie der Reformation*, 157-73.

Carl Fr. Wislöff, *The Gift of Communion: Luther's Controversy with Rome on Eucharistic Sacrifice*, translated by Joseph M. Shaw. Minneapolis: Augsburg Publishing House, 1964.

Hartmut Hilgenfeld, *Mittelalterlich-traditionelle Elemente in Luthers Abendmahlsschriften*. SDHSTh 29. Zurich: Theologischer Verlag, 1971.

Frido Mann, *Das Abendmahl bei jungen Luther*. BÖT 5. Munich: Hueber, 1971.

Gottfried Hoffmann, *Sententiae Patrum: Das patristische Argument in der Abendmahlskontroverse zwischen Oekolampad, Zwingli, Luther und Melanchthon*. Diss., Heidelberg, 1972.

Wolfgang Schwab, *Entwicklung und Gestalt der Sakramententheologie bei Martin Luther*. EHS.T 79. Frankfurt am Main/Bern: P. Lang, 1977.

Eberhard Grötzinger, *Luther und Zwingli: Die Kritik an der mittelalterlichen Lehre von der Messe als Wurzel des Abendmahlsstreites*. Zurich/Cologne/Gütersloh: Gerd Mohn, 1980.

Bernhard Lohse, "Dogma und Bekenntnis in der Reformation: Von Luther bis zum Konkordienbuch," *HdBDThG*, 2:46-64.

Ulrich Kühn, "Luthers Zeugnis vom Abendmahl in Unterweisung, Vermahnung und Beratung," in *Leben und Werk Martin Luthers von 1526 bis 1546*, 1:139-52; 2:771-75.

Tom G. A. Hardt, *Venerabilis et Adorabilis Eucharistia: Eine Studie über die Lutherische Abendmahlslehre*. FKDG 42. Göttingen: Vandenhoeck & Ruprecht, 1988.

Albrecht Peters, *Kommentar zu Luthers Katechismen*, edited by Gottfried Seebass. Göttingen: Vandenhoeck & Ruprecht, 1990-94. Vol. 4: *Die Taufe. Das Abendmahl*.

CHAPTER 33. THE DOCTRINE OF THE TWO KINGDOMS

Franz Lau, *"Äusserliche Ordnung" und "weltlich Ding" in Luthers Theologie*. Göttingen: Vandenhoeck & Ruprecht, 1933.

Harald Diem, *Luthers Lehre von den zwei Reichen, untersucht von seinem Verständnis der Bergpredigt aus*. BevTh 5. Munich: Chr. Kaiser, 1938.

Ernst Kinder, *Geistliches und weltliches Regiment nach Luther*. SLG 12. Weimar: Hermann Bohlhaus, 1940.

Gustaf Törnvall, *Geistliches und weltliches Regiment bei Luther: Studien zu Luthers Weltbild und Gesellschaftsverständnis*. FGLP 10/2. Munich: Chr. Kaiser, 1947.

Hermann Diem, *Luthers Predigt in den zwei Reichen.* ThEx N.F. 6. Munich: Chr. Kaiser, 1947.

Johannes Heckel, *Lex charitatis: Eine juristische Untersuchung über das Recht in der Theologie Martin Luthers.* ABAW. PH 36. 1953. Reprint, Munich: Bayerischen Akademie der Wissenschaften, 1963. 2d ed., edited by Martin Heckel. Cologne/Vienna: Böhlau, 1973.

Franz Lau, *Luthers Lehre von den beiden Reichen.* Berlin: Lutherisches Verlagshaus, 1953.

Gunnar Hillerdal, *Gehorsam gegen Gott und Menschen: Luthers Lehre von der Obrigkeit und die moderne evangelische Staatsethik.* Göttingen: Vandenhoeck & Ruprecht, 1955.

Paul Althaus, "Luthers Lehre von den beiden Reichen im Feuer der Kritik," *LuJ* 24 (1957), 40-68.

Johannes Heckel, *Im Irrgarten der Zwei-Reiche Lehre.* München: Chr. Kaiser Verlag, 1957.

Heinrich Bornkamm, *Luther's Doctrine of the Two Kingdoms in the Context of His Theology,* translated by Karl H. Hertz. Philadelphia: Fortress Press, 1966.

Gottfried Forck, *Die Königsherrschaft Jesu Christi bei Luther (1959): Mit einem Beitrag von Bernhard Lohse.* 2d ed. Berlin: Evangelisches Verlagsanstalt, 1988.

Gerhard Ebeling, "The Necessity of the Doctrine of the Two Kingdoms," in *Word and Faith,* 386-406.

Ernst Wolf, "Königsherrschaft Christi und lutherische Zwei-Reiche-Lehre," in *Peregrinatio,* 2:207-29.

Paul Althaus, *The Ethics of Martin Luther,* translated by Robert C. Schultz. Philadelphia: Fortress Press, 1972.

Hermann Dörries, "Luther und das Widerstandsrecht," in Dörries, *Wort und Stunde,* Göttingen: Vandenhueck and Ruprecht, 1966-70, 3:195-270.

Ulrich Duchrow, *Christenheit und Weltverantwortung: Traditionsgeschichte und systematische Struktur der Zweireichelehre.* 1970. 2d ed. Stuttgart: Klett-Cotta, 1983.

Hermann Kunst, *Evangelischer Glaube und politischer Verantwortung: Martin Luther als politischer Berater seiner Landesherrn und seine Teilnahme an den Fragen des öffentlichen Lebens.* Stuttgart: Evangelisches Verlagswerk, 1976.

Eike Wolgast, *Die Wittenberger Theologie und die Politik der evangelischen Stände: Studien zu Luthers Gutachten in politischen Fragen.* QFRG 47. Gütersloh: Gerd Mohn, 1977.

Martin Honecker, "Zur gegenwärtigen Interpretation der Zweireichelehre," *ZKG* 89 (1978), 150-62.

Reinhard Schwarz, "Luthers Lehre von den drei Ständen und die drei Dimensionen der Ethik," *LwJ* 45 (1978), 15-34.

Niels Hasselmann, ed., *Gottes Wirken in seiner Welt: Zur Diskussion um die Zweireichelehre.* 2 vols. Zur Sache 19-20. Hamburg: Lutherisches Verlagshaus, 1980.

Karl Dietrich Erdmann, "Luther über Obrigkeit, Gehorsam und Widerstand," in *Luther und die Folgen,* edited by Hartmut Löwe and Hans-Jürgen Roepke, 28-59. Munich: Chr. Kaiser, 1983.

Hans-Joachim Gänssler, *Evangelium und weltliches Schwert: Hintergrund, Entstehungs-geschichte und Anlass von Luthers Scheidung zweier Reiche oder Regimente.* VIEG 109. Wiesbaden: Steiner, 1983.

Gerhard Müller, "Luthers Beziehung zu Reich und Rom," in *Leben und Werk Martin Luthers von 1526 bis 1546,* 1:369-402; 2:849-60.

Erwin Iserloh and Gerhard Müller, eds., *Luther und die politische Welt: Wissenschaftliches Symposium in Worms vom 27-29. X. 1980,* revised by Johannes Koch. Historische Forschungen 9. Stuttgart: F. Steiner Wiesbaden, 1984 (with various contributions).

CHAPTER 34. ESCHATOLOGY

On eschatology:

Paul Althaus, *Die letzten Dinge: Lehrbuch der Eschatologie.* 1922. 5th ed. Gütersloh: Bertelsmann, 1949.

———— *The Theology of Martin Luther,* translated by Robert C. Schultz. Philadelphia: Fortress Press, 1966.

Ole Modalsli, *Das Gericht nach den Werken.* Göttingen: Vandenhoeck and Ruprecht, 1963.

Ulrich Asendorf, *Eschatologie bei Luther.* Göttingen: Vandenhoeck & Ruprecht, 1967.

George W. Forell, "Rechtfertigung und Eschatologie bei Luther," in *Reformation 1517-1967,* edited by Ernst Kähler, 145-5. Berlin: Evangelische Verlagsanstalt, 1968.

Fritz Heidler, *Die biblische Lehre von der Unsterblichkeit der Seele: Sterben, Tod, ewiges Leben im Aspekt lutherischer Anthropologie.* FSÖT 45. Göttingen: Vandenhoeck & Ruprecht, 1983.

———— *Luthers Lehre von der Unsterblichkeit der Seele.* Ratzeburger 1. Erlangen: Martin Luther Verlag, 1983.

Ole Modalsli, "Luther über die Letzten Dinge," in *Leben und Werk Martin Luthers von 1526 bis 1546,* 1:331-45; 2:834-39.

Werner Thiede, *Auferstehung der Toten—Hoffnung ohne Attraktivität?* FSÖT 65. Göttingen: Vandenhoeck & Ruprecht, 1991.

———— "Nur ein ewiger Augenblick: Luthers Lehre vom Seelenschlaf zwischen Tod und Auferweckung," *Luther* 64 (1993), 112-25.

On the concept of history:

Ernst Schäfer, *Luther als Kirchenhistoriker.* Gütersloh: Bertelsmann, 1897.

Walther Köhler, *Luther und die Kirchengeschichte nach seinen Schriften zunächst bis 1521.* Vol. 1/1. Hildesheim/New York: Georg Olms, 1900 (further sections did not appear).

Hanns Lilje, *Luthers Geschichtsanschauung,* FurSt 2. Berlin: Furche Verlag, 1932.

Hermann Wolfgang Beyer, "Gott und die Geschichte nach Luthers Auslegung des Magnificat," *LuJ* 12 (1939), 110-34.

Heinrich Bornkamm, "God and History," in *Luther's World of Thought,* translated by Martin H. Bertram, 206-17. St. Louis: Concordia Publishing House, 1958.

Hans-Walter Krumwiede, *Glaube und Geschichte in der Theologie Luthers: Zur Entstehung des geschichtlichen Denkens in Deutschland.* FKDG 2. Berlin: Evangelische Verlagsanstalt, 1952.

Heinz Zahrnt, *Luther deutet Geschichte.* Munich: P. Müller, 1952.

John M. Headley, *Luther's View of Church History.* New Haven: Yale University Press, 1963.

Martin Schmidt, "Luthers Schau der Geschichte," *LuJ* 30 (1963), 17-63.

Hermann Dörries, "Luthers Verständnis der Geschichte," in Dörries, *Wort und Stunde,* 3:1-83.

Gottfried Seebass, "Antichrist," IV: Reforations uno Neuzeit, in TRE 3 (1978), 28-43.

Reinhard Schwarz, "Die Wahrheit der Geschichte im Verständnis der Wittenberger Reformation," *ZThK* 76 (1979), 159-90.

Gustav Adolf Benrath, "Geschichte/Geschichtsschreibung/Geschichtephilosophie," *TRE* 12 (1984), 630-43.

Gerhard May, "'Je länger, je ärger'? Das Ziel der Geschichte im Denken Martin Luthers," *ZW* 60 (1989), 208-18.

CHAPTER 35. EXCURSUS: LUTHER'S ATTITUDE TOWARD THE JEWS

Reinhold Lewin, *Luthers Stellung zu den Juden: Ein Beitrag zur Geschichte der Juden in Deutschland während des Reformationszeitalters.* NSGTK 10. 1911. Reprint, Aalen: Scientia Verlag, 1973.

Kurt Meier, "Zur Interpretation von Luthers Judenschriften," in Meier, *Kirche und Judentum: Die Haltung der evangelischen Kirche zur Judenpolitik des Dritten Reiches,* 127-53. AKG.E 7. Halle [Salle]: M. Niemeyer, 1968.

Joachim Rogge, "Luthers Stellung zu den Juden," *Luther* 40 (1969), 13-24.

Johannes Brosseder, *Luthers Stellung zu den Juden im Spiegel seiner Interpreten: Interpretation und Rezeption von Luthers Schriften und Äusserungen zum Judentum im 19. und 20. Jahrhundert vor allem im deutschsprachigen Raum.* BÖT 8. Munich: M. Hueber, 1972 (basic).

Ernest Gordon Rupp, *Martin Luther and the Jews.* London: Council of Christians and Jews, 1972.

——— "Martin Luther and the Jews," *NedThT* 31 (1977), 121-35.

Johannes Peter Boendermaker, "Der Graben war noch sehr tief: Martin Luthers zwiespältiges Verhältnis zum Judentum," *LM* 18 (1979), 585-89.

Heiko A. Oberman, *The Roots of Anti-Semitism in the Age of Renaissance and Reformation,* translated by James I. Porter. Philadelphia: Fortress Press, 1984.

————— "Luthers Beziehungen zu den Juden: Ahnen und Geahndete," in *Leben und Werk Martin Luthers von 1526 bis 1546*, 1:519-30; 2:894-904.

Peter von der Osten-Sacken, *Katechismus und Siddur: Aufbrüche mit Martin Luther und den Lehrern Israels*. Veröffentlichungen aus dem Institut Kirche und Judentum 15. Berlin/Munich: Chr. Kaiser, 1984.

Johannes Brosseder, "Lutherbilder in der neuesten Literatur zum Thema: Martin Luther und die Juden," in *Europa in der Krise der Neuzeit. Martin Luther: Wandel und Wirkung seines Bildes*, edited by Susanne Heine, 89-111. Vienna/Cologne/Graz: H. Böhlaus Nachfolger, 1986.

Johannes Wallmann, "Luthers Stellung zu Judentum und Islam," *Luther* 57 (1986), 49-60.

INDEX OF NAMES

INDEX OF SUBJECTS